Managing Dynamic Technology-Oriented Businesses:

High Tech Organizations and Workplaces

Dariusz Jemielniak
Kozminski University, Poland

Abigail Marks
Heriot-Watt University, UK

Managing Director:	Lindsay Johnston
Senior Editorial Director:	Heather A. Probst
Book Production Manager:	Sean Woznicki
Development Manager:	Joel Gamon
Development Editor:	Myla Merkel
Assistant Acquisitions Editor:	Kayla Wolfe
Typesetter:	Nicole Sparano
Cover Design:	Nick Newcomer

Published in the United States of America by
Business Science Reference (an imprint of IGI Global)
701 E. Chocolate Avenue
Hershey PA 17033
Tel: 717-533-8845
Fax: 717-533-8661
E-mail: cust@igi-global.com
Web site: http://www.igi-global.com

Library of Congress Cataloging-in-Publication Data

Managing dynamic technology-oriented businesses: high tech organizations and workplaces / Dariusz Jemielniak and Abigail Marks, editors.
     p. cm.
  Includes bibliographical references and index.
  Summary: "This book explores the culture of modern high-tech workplaces and the different challenges and opportunities that new technologies present for modern workers and employers, reviewing various management practices throughout the world"--Provided by publisher.
  ISBN 978-1-4666-1836-7 (hbk.: alk. paper) -- ISBN 978-1-4666-1837-4 (ebook: alk. paper) -- ISBN 978-1-4666-1838-1 (print & perpetual access: alk. paper) 1. High technology industries--Management. 2. High technology industries--Employees. 3. Information technology--Management. 4. Knowledge workers. I. Jemielniak, Dariusz. II. Marks, Abigail, 1971-
  HD62.37.M356 2012
  658--dc23
                            2012015429

British Cataloguing in Publication Data
A Cataloguing in Publication record for this book is available from the British Library.

All work contributed to this book is new, previously-unpublished material. The views expressed in this book are those of the authors, but not necessarily of the publisher.

Editorial Advisory Board

Table of Contents

Detailed Table of Contents

Alexandra Gerbasi, Grenoble Ecole de Management, France & California State
University Northridge, USA
Dominika Latusek, Kozminski Business School, Poland

This chapter presents results from the qualitative field study conducted in a Silicon Valley-based American-Polish start-up joint venture. It investigates the issues of collaboration within one firm that is made up of individuals from two countries that differ dramatically in generalized trust: Poland and the United States. The authors explore differences between thick, knowledge-based forms of trust and thin, more social capital-oriented forms of trust, and they discuss how these affect collaboration between representatives of both cultures. Finally, the authors address how these differences in trust can both benefit an organization and also cause it difficulties in managing its employees.

Malgorzata Ciesielska, Teesside University, UK
Zilia Iskoujina, Newcastle University, UK

This chapter analyzes trust, open innovation, and software development modes. Basing on the case of GNOME – Nokia collaboration, it shows how trust can be perceived as a strategic resource, which is actually the crucial ingredient of successful collaboration. The dichotomy of the professional (expert) trust and the political trust is proposed as an interpretive key to understanding trust enactment in open source communities.

A.T. Juntunen, University of Helsinki, Finland

This chapter investigates and analyzes the management of capabilities in virtual teams in a business network context. This is a qualitative case study in the ICT-sector in Finland. This chapter will demonstrate that the organizations have a good chance to succeed if they can harness the external and internal knowledge and utilize the capabilities and knowledge in virtual teams to support organizational goals and strategies. It also illustrates the importance of trust in building and maintaining relationships. This chapter aims to contribute to the prior strategic management and business networks research.

Chapter 4

Andrea Roofe Sattlethight, Innovative Strategies, LLC., Miami, USA
Sungu Armagan, Florida International University, USA

This chapter explores an alternative approach to group processes in the virtual environment as a system of alliances, encompassing leader, member, and group. The purpose of this research is to determine if a system of alliances encompassing leader, member, and team exists in the virtual environment. The authors explore the applicability of alliances to a 21st century management environment by testing a conceptual model using 20,000 bootstrapped samples of 96 employed professionals and students studying in an online environment. They find evidence that group processes in a technology-mediated environment can be defined by a three-way-system of alliances in which the leader plays a less dominant role than in traditional groups. The authors find that the individual's relationship with the group may be built through a trust relationship with other members rather than a direct relationship with the leader. Directions for future research and implications for management practice are also discussed.

Chapter 5

Irene Lorentzen Hepsø, Sør-Trøndelag University College/Trondheim Business School, Norway
Vidar Hepsø, Norwegian University of Science and Technology, Norway

The authors address how performance indicators are configured and engineered in ERP-systems to follow up the activities of the knowledge workers in an oil and gas company. ERP-systems enable the development of new performance indicator systems, and give management simple dashboard tools to follow up and compare the performance of the organizational members across time and space. Decisions in organizations are increasingly taken on the basis of these abstract indicators that work as signs and inscriptions. This makes the development of such accounting indicators an interesting area of research because the representation of such indicators will to a large extent govern the decision making and practices of the organization. Who inscribes and controls the indicators controls the business. The authors discuss the development of such indicators as an inscription and translation process and how the indicators develop as a consequence of negotiations between influential actors. Finally, they address the consequences of these indicators and argue that they are dependent upon three key issues: the validity of the indicators, their reliability, and how indicators are negotiated. The authors' research question is how do disparate organizational groups interplay with physical and technical elements to create indicators determining the work of high-tech business practitioners?

Chapter 6

Marie-Josée Legault, Téluq-UQAM, Canada
Kathleen Ouellet, Université de Montréal, Canada

This chapter draws on 53 interviews from a case study led in Montreal in 2008 to demonstrate the existence of Unlimited and Unpaid Overtime (UUO) among video game developers and illustrate an emerging workplace regulation model of working time in the videogame industry. It brings to light a sophisticated and efficient system of rewards and sanctions, both material and symbolic, that drives professional workers in these trades to adopt a "free unlimited overtime" behavior despite the Act Respecting Labour Standards. Efficiency of this system is rooted in combined Project Management (PM) as an organisation mode and high international mobility of the workforce that both makes portfolio and reputation utterly important. This chapter focuses on (de)regulation of working time only, but it opens a path to theoretically account for (de)regulation of work among an expanding workforce: the "new professionals" in knowledge work.

This chapter identifies a new pattern of bargaining for technology, based upon nine months' ethnographic fieldwork amongst the engineers of a Telco's research and development department. Bargains for smartphones were initiated by the employee and negotiated with the employer by reference to the productivity discourse of the vendor. After a honeymoon phase of exploration, the reality of operation was markedly different, resulting, in several cases, in the disposition of the smartphone or, in one case, the disposition of the employee to leave. Such bargains were driven by conceptions of the personal and organisational use value of the artefact, and this finding reveals shortcomings in the drivers, influences, and stages of adoption found in existing models. A new conceptual framework is presented that facilitates exploration of the contribution of personal and organisational use value to technology adoption.

This chapter takes you to a data security workplace in Finland. It presents reflections on the tensions of managing selves and others, as experienced by the employees and the managers. It argues that a generally critical approach to normative management may overlook the actual complexity and ambiguous nature of the late modern cultural environment. Both self-authoring and manipulative moves are made difficult by the amalgamating hegemonic and countercultural currents. The author points at chances for resistance through new forms of literacy. Instead of dropping "culture" as a conservative or managerial pursuit, we must learn to navigate successfully in the broken cultural landscape of today's workplaces. The very same images that can be used for manipulation are open to more solidary configurations by the cultural and social imagination of organizational members.

Interactions between professionals and managers are vital to medical and commercialization outcomes. This chapter considers how boundaries between professionals and managers are expressed through language in two contexts: between researchers and managers in temporary Australian hybrid industry-research organizations and within the same individual performing a hybrid clinician-manager role in

Australian health care organizations. Semi-structured interviews of twenty scientists, engineers, and managers, focusing on their experiences, and perceptions of occupational culture, revealed that language norms contributed to knowledge creation, and played a role in maintaining a hierarchy among research institutions. Semi-structured interviews of twenty doctors and managers, focusing on their perception and experience of the hybrid clinician manager's role within health care organizations, revealed that professional identity influenced language norms used by doctors and managers and contributed to the tensions experienced in their interactions. Distinctive patterns of argumentation and language were identified as typical of commercial and research occupations and were also distinctive in doctors working in hybrid clinician manager's roles. The scientists, engineers, and managers working in hybrid industry-research organizations and the doctors and managers working in health care organizations reported frustration and reduced effectiveness of argumentation due to different norms for dissent.

Chapter 10

Engineers most often organise their work in projects and consequently project management becomes an essential part of an engineer's work and working life in general. Even if most engineers are trained in project management, it seems that this is a challenge to most engineers. It also seems that the traditional project management tools are not always sufficient when it comes to managing engineering projects. In this chapter, an engineering project is examined, and it turns out that the language, the stories, and the narratives connected to the project is of greater importance to the engineers than the formal project management tools that were offered to the engineers. It also turns out that the term "project" could itself be a problem when it comes to fulfilling the project goals. Therefore, it is concluded that when working on engineering projects, language, stories, and narratives are just as important to the engineers as any other element in the project.

Chapter 11

Material storytelling is used here to denote a material-discursive understanding of technology, and how technology works in organizations in terms of story performance. The idea is that technology configures organizations in spatial, temporal and material terms. We are inspired by Karen Barad's work in quantum physics in developing the term material storytelling, which relies on a material-discursive understanding of storytelling. By introducing material storytelling we resituate the hegemonic relationship of discourse and language over matter. As such technology regains a central space in both understanding and managing organizations. It implies that attention is relocated to the petty and lowly everyday routines, techniques and material artifacts, which are implicit in what we do in everyday life but govern the agential possibilities for acting in this world. We frame the chapter as a story of material storytelling of a change project in a bank. We experiment with the writing style by going back and forth between two different layers of text. The first layer tells the stories of material storytelling, while the other draws out the theoretical/methodological implications of this approach in terms understanding and managing technology.

Chapter 12

This chapter demonstrates how contemporary imaginary structures, which urge us to move up in life by making the most of the possibilities we are faced with, may operate in an industrial setting where users are involved in the production of heavy duty vehicles. Opening up new domains for value creation, devoid of established norms and regulations, this appeal to elevate ourselves arguably provides little guidance for how to do so. Demanding ever more from those subjected to its call, this appealing power, the chapter suggests, follows the logic of the Lacanian superego, which according to Salecl (2004, p. 51) "commands the subject to enjoy yet at the same time mockingly predicts that he or she will fail in this pursuit of enjoyment." As such, it makes out a central component in a creative force that feeds excessive outgrowths, which perpetually contribute to pervert, displace, and fragment established grounds for value creating activities within this industrial domain.

This chapter explores the mechanism of how structural and behavioral organizational characteristics lead to organizational deterioration as a source of organizational decline. First, using an original construct of organizational deterioration named "organizational deadweight" that is defined as ineffectual managerial load at the middle management level, the authors explore the relationships between the organizational characteristics and organizational deadweight. Data was collected through a questionnaire survey in 2006 involving more than 942 respondents from 128 business units of 16 large Japanese firms. The results suggest that reference to formal strategic planning, participation in the planning process, and vertical communication improve deterioration, whereas organizational size and layered hierarchical structure aggravate it. Finally, the authors discuss the roles of vertical communication and formal planning to safeguard against deterioration.

This chapter analyses the influence of organizational culture components, defined in Hofstede's (1991, 2001) cultural framework (i.e., power distance, individualism/collectivism, assertiveness focus, and uncertainty avoidance), and empowerment on innovation capability, and examines the differentiations in their influence. The hypotheses are tested by applying Structural Equations Modeling (SEM) methodology to data collected from Information Technology professionals from high-tech companies. Results of the analyses have yielded that power distance is found to be negatively associated with both empowerment and innovation capability, whereas uncertainty avoidance is negatively related to innovation capability, but positively related to empowerment. Collectivism is found to be positively related only to empowerment; yet no significant relationship was revealed between collectivism and innovation capability. In addition, no significant relationship was found between assertiveness focus and empowerment or innovation capability. Empowerment is also found to be significantly and positively related to innovation capability. In terms of managerial practice, the study helps clarify the key role played by cultural dimensions in the process of shaping an empowering and innovative work environment. Findings also reveal that managers should focus on participative managerial practices (e.g. empowerment) to promote innovation capability of high-tech companies by considering the cultural tendencies of employees in the organization.

Chapter 15

Ben Tran, Alliant International University, USA

The "glass cliff" is a term coined by Professor Michelle Ryan and Professor Alex Haslam in 2004. Their research demonstrates that once women (or other minority groups) break through the glass ceiling and take on positions of leadership, they often have different experiences from their male counterparts. Specifically, women are more likely to occupy positions that can be described as precarious and thus have a higher risk of failure, either because they are in organizational units that are in crisis, or because they are not given the resources and support needed to thrive. The success of the glass cliff, as a phenomenon, rests on three factors. First, it relies heavily on the quality and quantity of data available, as well as the reliability of the data. Second, it relies heavily on the acceptance, utilization, and application of its existence, for a lack of acknowledgment, acceptance, utilization, and application of any phenomenon, concept, and theory will result in extinction. Third, this phenomenon, in reality, is quite taboo in a male dominated society, regardless of culture. Nevertheless, the glass cliff, as a phenomenon, is quite neoteric, and is typically not spoken of, nor referred to when men communicate, in the same way that men do not usually refer to the glass ceiling, or the glass escalator. The purpose of this chapter is to delve into and explore the concept of the glass cliff faced by women in high-tech corporations, and how the glass cliff affects their career advancement and identity growth through empirical data. The chapter then provides three recommendations on resolving the glass cliff phenomenon, and concludes with whether the glass cliff as a phenomenon is convertible to become a theory.

Preface

HIGH-TECH ENVIRONMENTS: TO BOLDLY GO

The high-tech work environments of work, and of the new knowledge workers (Alvesson, 2004; Jemielniak, 2012; Marks & Baldry, 2009), have been a topic of growing interest from researchers in management and organization science. These environments are in many ways different from the traditional organizational settings.

For example, software engineers and other professionals in high-tech industries seem to enact their identities differently from their counterparts in the traditional professions (English-Lueck, Darrah, & Saveri, 2002; Jemielniak, 2008; Marks & Scholarios, 2007; Marks & Thompson, 2010; Westenholz, 2006). High tech environments and career perceptions are also strongly gendered (Bourne & Özbilgin, 2008; English-Lueck, 2011).

High-tech professionals' work-life balance is seriously affected by the organizational pressure and normative control, and knowledge workers are often in strong opposition to management (Jemielniak, 2007; Kunda, 1992; Scholarios & Marks, 2004). In addition, time spent at work plays a symbolic, ritualistic role in negotiating social position and status in knowledge-intensive organizations (Jemielniak, 2009; Perlow, 1997; Sharone, 2004). Workers in high-tech environments are often subject to burnout and excessive managerial pressure. The high-tech environment is also unpredictable, and is often a venue of distrust among key actors (Baba, 1999; English-Lueck, et al., 2002; Latusek & Jemielniak, 2007).

At the same time, high tech professionals often perceive work as a "serious game" (Strannegård & Friberg, 2001), and not drudgery: they involve in playful behaviors at work (Hunter, Jemielniak, & Postuła, 2010). Software engineers often participate in non-paid, open collaboration production (Lakhani & Von Hippel, 2003).

Modes of collaboration established in virtual and high-tech communities are similarly transforming workplace relations in the brick-and-mortar organizations (Benkler, 2006). They precede and foreshadow more general trends in organizational designs (Argyris, 1973; Beck, 2000; Castells, 2004). Understanding the high-tech workplace, and learning about the management practices and routines in knowledge intensive companies is, thus, of utmost importance for contemporary management scholars and practitioners. This volume addresses all of these urgent issues and more.

Gerbasi and Latusek present results of a qualitative study on a high-tech start-up from Silicon Valley. The chapter explores the problem of trust in joint ventures, between Polish and American partners. Cultural differences, determining varied reliance on knowledge-based and social capital-based kinds of trust are explored. The advantages and disadvantages of building trust in relation to teams, peers, and organizations are considered.

Ciesielska and Iskoujina analyze trust, open innovation, and software development modes. The study of the GNOME and Nokia collaboration shows how trust can be perceived as a strategic resource, which is actually the crucial ingredient of successful collaboration. In particular, they distinguish the professional (expert) trust and the political trust. This dichotomy is proposed as an interpretive key to understanding trust enactment in open source communities.

Juntunen brings the focus to management of virtual teams. Through a qualitative analysis of virtual teams in a commercial ICT environment in Finland, he describes their success factors, balancing internal and external knowledge. Like Ciesielska, he emphasizes the importance of trust in the IT environment, and especially in fostering long-term strategic relationships.

Roofe-Sattlethight and Armagan's chapter continues the explorations of virtual work processes. It analyzes the relations and alliances among leaders, members, and teams in a virtual environment. Their quantitative study indicates that such a three-way alliance indeed emerges, but the role of the leader is smaller than in non-virtual settings. Members tend to develop their relationship with the group by building rapport with other members, rather than through the leader.

Lorentzen Hepsø and Hepsø's study offers insight into ERP systems, on the example of performance indicators used in an oil and gas company. The aggregated performance measurement algorithms are often used in knowledge-intensive companies, and yet their development, as well as actual implementation, is rarely studied from within the organization, in particular with the use of actor-network theory.

Legault and Ouellet have a look at the video game industry. They focus on the issue of time management and long hours spent at work, in the accounts of 53 game designers from Canada. The system of normative control, as well as work evaluation and reputation building, enforced through organizational expectations of "professionalism" are described and offered as a possible explanation of overtime unpaid work that is regularly expected, even when it is prohibited under the law.

Russell's contribution, relying on a long-term, ethnographic study, describes a case of high tech gadgets negotiated by employees. Through an analysis of engineers bargaining for smartphones, he shows how organizations can increase their control over the employees through new technologies, and how the employees make a rod for their own backs.

Trux's piece, similarly to Russell's, pertains to the topic of normative control. She describes the new forms of organizational resistance, emerging in knowledge-intensive organizations. She recognizes the contemporary methods of managerial propaganda and coercion, yet suggests that the new organizational configurations and bifurcation of identities also benefit the counter-managerial employee movement.

Kippist, Hayes, and Fitzgerald delve into the topic of language used between managers and professionals. They research it by comparing two contexts: researchers discussing with managers in Australian hybrid industry-research and health care organizations. Interestingly, several modes of dissent and distinctive patterns of communication were noted. This study indicates that successful management in knowledge-intensive organizations depends on proper argumentative strategies.

Henriksen's chapter departs from the traditional academic discourse by introducing a narrative approach to technology studies. By introducing storytelling, as well as antenarrative analysis, he offers an alternative perspective on software project development. He brings interesting insights into a story of a failed project, which is particularly interesting given that success stories are much more likely to be shared.

Jørgensen and Strand follow the narrative analysis, and propose a new material-discursive understanding of technology in a form of "material storytelling." They show the usage of technology in organizations in terms of story performance. Consequently, they resituate the relationship of discourse and technology, and shift the focus of organization studies from human agents to everyday routines, and human-nonhuman actants.

Sköld and Olaison's piece delves into Lacanian and Deleuzian interpretations of late capitalism's dynamics. In an unusual analysis of a heavy-duty industry (trucks), incorporating storytelling, they describe different stakeholders and narratives at play, negotiating perceptions of the product, imaginary scenarios, and desires. They show the marketing background and enacted fantasies, linking customers and suppliers.

Karube, Kato, and Numagami's chapter presents the results of a project on relations between an organization's features and its likelihood of deteriorating. Their study relies on a large sample of questionnaires from 16 Japanese corporations. It shows that both an organization's size and its hierarchical structure contribute to its deterioration; participative planning, vertical communication channels, and strict and precise strategy building process prevent it.

Ertürk's study is a timely application of Hofstede's organizational culture framework. His findings indicate that power distance is negatively associated with both empowerment and with innovation capability. Uncertainty avoidance, however, is also negatively related to innovation capability, but positively related to empowerment. Collectivism is positively related only to empowerment. These results support the thesis that knowledge work is particularly compatible with participative management techniques.

Finally, Tran explores the "glass cliff" in high tech environments. He studies women in positions of leadership, who are put on the glass cliff of more precarious and riskier posts than their male counterparts. Following an analysis of empirical data, Tran proposes the possible paradigm shift needed to recognize the glass cliff, and why it is still taboo.

Dariusz Jemielniak
Kozminski University, Poland

Abigail Marks
Heriot-Watt University, UK

REFERENCES

Alvesson, M. (2004). *Knowledge work and knowledge-intensive firms*. Oxford, UK: Oxford University Press.

Argyris, C. (1973). *On organizations of the future*. Beverly Hills, CA: Sage Publications.

Baba, M. (1999). Dangerous liaisons: Trust, distrust, and information technology in american work organizations. *Human Organization, 58*(3), 331–346.

Beck, U. (2000). *The brave new world of work*. Cambridge, MA: Polity Press.

Benkler, Y. (2006). *The wealth of networks: How social production transforms markets and freedom*. New Haven, CT: Yale University Press.

Bourne, D., & Özbilgin, M. F. (2008). Strategies for combating gendered perceptions of careers. *Career Development International, 13*(4), 320–332. doi:10.1108/13620430810880817

Castells, M. (Ed.). (2004). *The network society: a cross-cultural perspective*. Cheltenham, UK: Edward Elgar Pub.

English-Lueck, J. (2011). Prototyping self in Silicon Valley: Deep diversity as a framework for anthropological inquiry. *Anthropological Theory, 11*(1), 89–106. doi:10.1177/1463499610397115

English-Lueck, J. A., Darrah, C. N., & Saveri, A. (2002). Trusting strangers: Work relationships in four high-tech communities. *Information Communication and Society, 5*(1), 90–108. doi:10.1080/13691180110117677

Hunter, C., Jemielniak, D., & Postuła, A. (2010). Temporal and spatial shifts within playful work. *Journal of Organizational Change Management, 23*(1), 87–102. doi:10.1108/09534811011017225

Jemielniak, D. (2007). Managers as lazy, stupid careerists? Contestation and stereotypes among software engineers. *Journal of Organizational Change Management, 20*(4), 491–508. doi:10.1108/09534810710760045

Jemielniak, D. (2008). Software engineers or artists – Programmers' identity choices. *Tamara Journal for Critical Organization Inquiry, 7*(1), 20–36.

Jemielniak, D. (2009). Time as symbolic currency in knowledge work. *Information and Organization, 19*, 277–293. doi:10.1016/j.infoandorg.2009.08.002

Jemielniak, D. (2012). *The new knowledge workers*. Cheltenham, UK: Edward Elgar.

Kunda, G. (1992). *Engineering culture: Control and commitment in a high-tech corporation* (Rev. ed.). Philadelphia, PA: Temple University Press.

Lakhani, K. R., & Von Hippel, E. (2003). How open source software works. *Research Policy, 32*(6), 923–943. doi:10.1016/S0048-7333(02)00095-1

Latusek, D., & Jemielniak, D. (2007). Trust in software projects: Thrice told tale. *The International Journal of Technology . Knowledge in Society, 3*(10), 117–125.

Marks, A., & Baldry, C. (2009). Stuck in the middle with who? The class identity of knowledge workers. *Work, Employment and Society, 23*(1), 49–65. doi:10.1177/0950017008099777

Marks, A., & Scholarios, D. (2007). Revisiting technical workers: professional and organisational identities in the software industry. *New Technology, Work and Employment, 22*(2), 98–117. doi:10.1111/j.1468-005X.2007.00193.x

Marks, A., & Thompson, P. (2010). Beyond the blank slate: Identities and interests at work . In Thompson, P., & Smith, C. (Eds.), *Working Life: Renewing Labour Process Analysis*. London, UK: Palgrave Press.

Perlow, L. A. (1997). *Finding time: How corporations, individuals, and families can benefit from new work practices*. Ithaca, NY: ILR Press.

Scholarios, D., & Marks, A. (2004). Work-life balance and the software worker. *Human Resource Management Journal, 14*(2), 54–74. doi:10.1111/j.1748-8583.2004.tb00119.x

Sharone, O. (2004). Engineering overwork: Bell-curve management at a high-tech firm . In Epstein, C. F., & Kalleberg, A. L. (Eds.), *Fighting for Time: Shifting Boundaries of Work and Social Life* (pp. 191–218). New York, NY: Russell Sage Foundation.

Strannegård, L., & Friberg, M. (2001). *Already elsewhere: Play, identity and speed in the business world*. Stockholm, Sweden: Raster Förlag.

Westenholz, A. (2006). Identity work and meaning arena: Beyond actor/structure and micro/macro distinctions in an empirical analysis of IT workers. *The American Behavioral Scientist, 49*(7), 1015–1029. doi:10.1177/0002764205285183

Chapter 1

Cultural Differences in Trust in High-Tech International Business Ventures:
The Case of a US-Poland Cooperation

Alexandra Gerbasi
Grenoble Ecole de Management, France & California State University Northridge, USA

Dominika Latusek
Kozminski Business School, Poland

ABSTRACT

This chapter presents results from the qualitative field study conducted in a Silicon Valley-based American-Polish start-up joint venture. It investigates the issues of collaboration within one firm that is made up of individuals from two countries that differ dramatically in generalized trust: Poland and the United States. The authors explore differences between thick, knowledge-based forms of trust and thin, more social capital-oriented forms of trust, and they discuss how these affect collaboration between representatives of both cultures. Finally, the authors address how these differences in trust can both benefit an organization and also cause it difficulties in managing its employees.

INTRODUCTION

In high-tech work environments, the problem of boundaries can be particularly challenging for both managers and workers (Jemielniak, 2012). Increasingly, work happens across boundaries of many types: time (e.g. in IT-service companies that have branches all around the world and are in operation 24 hours a day), space (virtual teams when people from all over the world work together on the same projects [Bosch-Sijtsema, et al., 2011; Fruchter, et al., 2010]), and culture in its many forms (professional cultures, national cultures). In this chapter, we explore this issue in one particular context, namely in the case of IT business ventures that require cooperation of IT professional from two cultural contexts: Poland and the United States. Existing research indicates that these two countries should differ greatly in

DOI: 10.4018/978-1-4666-1836-7.ch001

terms of trust (cites), but as we will show later in this chapter, these countries are very similar in regard to interpersonal form of trust, while differ dramatically as far as generalized trust is concerned. We contend that both forms of trust are complementary as far as success of business cooperation is concerned and different levels of trust across societies may have an impact on interorganizational collaborations (e.g., Ariño, de la Torre, & Ring, 2001; Madhok, 1995). This is especially true in business relations that are rarely characterized by individual level trust developed on the basis of interaction between people (Lane & Bachmann, 1997; Zucker, 1986). Moreover, as Zaheer and Zaheer (2006) point out, collaboration partners from different countries may not only be characterized by differing levels of general trust, but they are also likely to bring different conception of trust to the business relationship. But, as they noted (Zaheer & Zaheer, 2006, p. 22): "While strategic and structural bases of asymmetry among JV [Joint Ventures] or alliance partners, such as equity ownership and the possession of resources, capabilities, or knowledge, have been explicitly examined (e.g., Hamel, et al., 1989; Khanna, et al., 1998), the *social bases of asymmetry*, such as imbalance in trust, especially arising from national cultural origins, have received little if any attention, although researchers have noted the existence of the problem." This chapter seeks to address this gap by exploring first the differences in trust between the U.S. and Poland and then how these differences play out in a joint venture between individuals of both cultures.

This research also touches on two topics that have been understudied phenomena in management research. First, the outflow of young IT professionals from transitional economies to the U.S. has received limited attention, primarily due to difficulties in access to data. Traditionally, Poland has been known for high quality education in the sciences, especially mathematics and computer science. Young, Polish programmers have

consistently won prestigious world competitions. However, this has not translated into growth of IT businesses in Poland, as most of the most talented young engineers choose careers abroad. In addition, outsourcing IT services to Poland and setting up development centers in Poland has become a popular form of doing business for international companies seeking access to talent pools and streamlining their cost structure.

Second, software development, typical of knowledge-intensive field, constitutes a serious challenge for contemporary management theorists and practitioners (Nonaka, 1994; Nonaka, Toyama, & Nagata, 2000; Nurmi, 1999). This is largely because the main activities in knowledge-intensive work are difficult to control and evaluate, as they are oriented toward innovation and problem solving, and constitute a "black box" for bystanders (Austin & Larkey, 2002; Ditillo, 2004; Winch & Schneider, 1993). Moreover, the organization of work in software development projects produces pronounced asymmetries between actors, for example in terms of knowledge (Alvesson, 2004; Cross & Cummings, 2004), which are reinforced by problems with observational control, due to immaterial nature of activities of knowledge workers (Austin & Larkey, 2002). Therefore, high-tech environment is quite often regarded as very stressful and riddled with uncertainty (Goodwin, 2002; Humphrey, 1997; Kesteloot, 2003). Therefore, one would expect that in such environments the need for governance mechanisms based on trust would be particularly high, and that this can become problematic in cross-cultural situations when the two parties differ in terms of generalized trust.

In order to address these issues we first review the results of World Value Survey to illustrate the cultural differences between Poland and United States in respect to trust. Then, we review the existing literature to explain the emergence of these differences. Next, we provide some excerpts from our empirical study of a US-Poland business cooperative that highlight how the differences in generalized trust can have positive and negative impacts on the organization. Finally, in the concluding remarks we develop a framework for interpreting these results in the light of trust theories.

NATIONAL DIFFERENCES IN TRUST: RESULTS OF THE WORLD VALUES SURVEY

In order to examine the predicted differences between the US and Poland, we compare data from the 2005 World Values Survey (World Values Survey, 2005). In both countries, respondents were asked several questions regarding the degree to which they trust specific others. The questions inquire about trust in close relationships such as family that we term "thick" trust, and move to more distant relationships (people you know personally, people in your neighborhood, people you meet for the first time) to strangers (people of a different nationality) that characterize "thin" trust. In order to examine the differences between the US and Poland we compare the mean scores on those measures for individuals from both countries (see Table 1).

First, we investigate a measure of "thick" trust: trust in members of your family. There is not a significant difference between the US and Poland?" $t_{(2162)} = .53$, p = n.s. This indicates there is no difference in "thick" trust between the US (3.71) and Poland (3.70).

As the object of trust becomes more distant or "thin," the predicted differences between the two countries emerge. When asked "how much do you trust the people in your neighborhood?" significant differences emerge $t_{(2162)} = 3.73$, p < .05. Individuals in the US (2.9) trust people in their neighborhood significantly more than do Poles (2.8). Americans (3.26) also trust the people they personally know significantly more than Poles (2.96) $t_{(2162)} = 12.90$, p < .05. The findings suggest even when the object of trust is someone individuals interact with

Table 1. Means and standard deviations of trust measures in the US and Poland

	USA	Poland
How much do you trust your family	3.71	3.70
	(0.50)	(0.52)
How much do you trust the people in your neighborhood*	2.90	2.80
	(0.60)	(0.66)
How much do you trust people you know personally?*	3.26	2.96
	(0.56)	(0.54)
How much do you trust people you meet for the first time?*	2.30	2.06
	(0.70)	(0.66)
How much do you trust people of another nationality?*	2.78	2.37
	(0.62)	(0.70)
N	1205	959

Notes: Standard deviations are in parenthesis

All variables are coded so that a higher score indicates more trust (1= no trust at all, 4=trust completely)

* p < .05, two-tailed test

on a regular basis knowledge-based trust is less likely to develop in Poland than the US. When the object of trust becomes even more distant or abstract, the differences between Americans and Poles become even more apparent. When asked "how much they trust people they have met for the first time," Americans (2.30) are significantly more likely to trust people they meet for the first time than are Poles (2.06), $t_{(2162)} = 8.52$, p <.05. Americans (2.78) also expressed significantly more trust in people of a different nationality than did Poles (2.37), $t_{(2162)} = 14.24$, p < .05. This finding suggests that developing and maintaining relationships may be more difficult in Poland than in the US.

The results suggest a qualitative difference between trust in family relationships and trust in all other types of social relations. As mentioned above, the types of trust examined above encompass two distinct forms of trust: knowledge-based trust or thick trust, and thin trust (Baier, 1986;

Cook, et al., 2005; Hardin, 2002; Meyerson, et al., 1996; Williamson, 1993). Trust in family members is directly cognitive and is built through repeated interactions with family members. There is much less uncertainty in interacting with family members, not only does the individual have a history of interaction with the family member, but the family itself serves as a closed network that prevents malfeasance. However, "thick" trust cannot carry the burden of making all of our relationships work, as well as making the social life in the macro-scale function properly (Cook, 2008). The type of trust that enhances broader social relationships is "thin" trust. This encompasses trust outside of close relationships such as trust in acquaintances, neighbors, strangers, foreigners, etc. The absence of "thin" trust makes relationships (even trivial ones) outside of close relationships difficult and can hinder many arenas of life: social, economic, political, etc.

WHERE DO DIFFERENCES COME FROM? CULTURAL/ HISTORIC BACKGROUND OF THE DIFFERENCES ON TRUST

Generalized trust is a product of culture and history (Sztompka, 1996, 1999), as it emerges from an accumulation of collective experiences shared by groups of people. This type of trust constitutes a cultural rule that can govern behavior, as it constitutes a part of collective framework of perception and interpretation. During the last decades, Poland and the United States were the arenas of two radically different cultural developments: while Poland has been an autocratic regime for almost 50 years and then experienced the 'shock therapy'—rapid transition of the 90s—the United States during this period were considered an almost ideal type of democracy. As Sztompka (1999) argues, "all other things being equal, the culture of trust is most likely to appear in a democracy than in any other type of political system" (p.

139). Therefore, the low levels of generalized trust in Poland reflect the historical experience of totalitarianism and subsequent transformation. The socialist state fostered suspicion and hostility and it promoted wide-spread erosion of trust. There are several aspects of socialist culture that contributed to the erosion of trust. Mainly, it was the long-lasting opposition between private and official sphere of life—with strong association of the private sphere with 'good' and 'truth' and the public sphere with 'bad,' 'fake,' and 'lies.' People were trying to outsmart the authorities in many ways and there was no sense of 'ownership' in respect to the State that was considered as imposed by the Soviets, and thus illegitimate. Distrust towards everything that was linked to the state and its institutions was coupled with faith (sometimes even blind) into everything that was coming from private sources or foreign (Western) media. All authorities, both local and central were perceived as hostile and alien. Even the little amount of social capital that remained after decades of life under Soviet domination was subsequently destroyed by transformation of the early 1990s. In an instant, the uncertainty became further exacerbated as the old order fell apart and new rules had not yet emerged. Corruption due to lack of transparency in the transition was wide-spread, often going undetected and unpunished.

Under the socialist state, there was a strong reliance on closed networks of trust. Individuals accomplished many everyday tasks and engaged in barter outside of the state system though networks of trusted associates (Marin, 2002). The uncertainty that accompanied the transition away from socialist rule reinforced this reliance on interpersonal bonds that provided security and continuity. While closed networks (such as family members) provided a safety net during times of change, the reliance on these networks instead of building formal institutional had negative consequences, including creating a base for corruption and cronyism (Peev, 2002; Rose-Ackerman, 2001a, 2001b). The patterns of social life formed under Soviet domination turned out to be a double-edged sword, because, on one hand, distrust towards the state and reliance on personal connections was a useful pattern of defense against oppression and provided shelter from indoctrination and totalitarian control. On the other hand, this did not contribute to building a more democratic open society. The closed networks that evolved in Poland constitute what Cook and Gerbasi (2009) call "thick" trust. This type of trust arises in social relations that are close and familiar such as family ties and long-term friendships. These ties were important to survival under the socialist regime, whereas "thin" trust (i.e. generalized trust) was less important and perhaps even detrimental to survival.

With this distinction between the two cultures as a background, we now turn to an examination of how the differences impact a high-tech joint-venture between a US firm and a Polish firm.

METHOD

The empirical data that we draw on were collected in the course of a research project on Polish and American work culture in high-tech environments conducted in Silicon Valley in 2007 and 2008. The research was qualitative and ethnographical (Kostera, 2007; Rosen, 1991), and also inspired by grounded theory principles (Glaser & Strauss, 1967). Since its aim was exploratory, we chose qualitative methods in order to provide most insight into the field (cf. Edelman, et al., 2004). We used the following techniques of data collection: observations, studies of professional publications and open-ended interviews.

The company reported in this study is a joint venture between Poles and Americans. The firm offers outsourcing of IT functions to a development center located in Wroclaw, Poland. The operations were run from the office in San Francisco. Although the American part of the joint-venture was significantly smaller in numbers (only four employees, in comparison to around 70 engineers

in the Development Center in Wroclaw), it was responsible for management and sales within the enterprise, while the Polish partner performed development tasks (technology development center) and was subordinate to the U.S. office. All of the individuals involved in projects on the American side were interviewed for this research project.

Following guidelines for inductive research (Glaser & Strauss, 1967) as well as some previous ethnographies conducted in high-tech context (Hargadon & Sutton, 1997) at the beginning the aim of the project was mainly descriptive. According to methodological recommendations (Jankowicz, 2000; Kostera, 2007) the researcher's intervention into the narratives of people in the field was as limited as it was possible. Then, it was an iterative process of academic dialogue engaging both of us that brought us to the point when our model arrived at the final version presented in this chapter. (Alvesson & Skoldberg, 2000; Tillmar & Lindkvist, 2007).

THE STUDY (EXCERPTS)

The company, MOUSE[1], at the time of the research was a start-up based in San Francisco that offered IT outsourcing services to companies in Silicon Valley. It was established in 2006/2007 by Greg, an American of Polish origin, now CEO of MOUSE. Greg's idea behind funding MOUSE was to utilize the knowledge base that exists in Poland for the benefit of Silicon Valley companies. During interviews he frequently highlighted that while Poland has great potential in IT, in particular well-educated engineers, it still lacks a lot of experience and expertise as far as sales and marketing of this knowledge is concerned.

With the sales force based in San Francisco and the development center in Wroclaw, MOUSE was offering IT solutions for US-based companies, mainly companies from Silicon Valley. The business model of the company included outsourcing of IT services, mainly the development of applications. While the US-based unit was responsible for sales and initial contact with the customer, all the engineering work was being done in the development center located in Wroclaw, Poland. This, Greg said gave the company its competitive edge: low-cost and high-quality engineering on the Polish side and access to best customers/developed market in the United States.

Several other recurring topics emerge from the field material regarding doing business with Poland. In addition to the cost advantage and relatively well-developed IT infrastructure, two characteristics of the Polish workforce seem to play particularly important role: high level of education engineering and strong loyalty of the Polish employees towards their employer.

As far as the differences between the Poles and American are concerned, one of our interviewees, Evan, suggested that there does not seem to be a gap in terms of knowledge or engineering skills. What they need to work on, however, is mutual understanding within the triangle: the U.S. part of the firm, the development center in Poland, and the US-based customer. As Evan further points out, the general approach towards customers in IT projects is significantly different among Americans and Poles. In the area of customer service there has not been a real attempt to build understanding between partners, rather it is clearly stated that the Poles should "learn," "be educated," or "adopt" Silicon Valley style of approaching customers.

EVAN: Poland has a big learning curve ahead of them in terms how to deal with American clients. (...) In the U.S. the concept of the customer is number one. And... sometimes...they [Poles] want us to take an approach with the customer that we can't take.

The Poles find it difficult to accept customer's suggestions of changes in their projects, because the Poles tend to exhibit strong sense of authorship in their work. It appears that, according to American interviewees, the Polish engineers focus

much more on defending their ideas and through that their professional reputation rather than on fulfilling the actual needs of the customer. This is line with previous research on Polish software engineers which reported that developers in Poland often treat customers as "inferior," "laymen," and "naïve" (Jemielniak, 2007).

EVAN: Poles take great pride in their work and are less willing to even construct the criticism and they start defending their work vs. actually listen to the customer. And the customer is not interested in defending your work. And when you are in a mode of defending your work, you are not in the mode of listening to what the customer wants. It is a huge difference.

Apart from technological expertise, as one of our interviewees said, one characteristic of employees in Poland makes them very valuable assets for the company. Polish engineers tend to be very loyal to their companies. Compared to the U.S., and especially to Silicon Valley standards, Poles change jobs very infrequently (Jackson & Mach, 2009).

EVAN: The other [strength] is the retention. People have a very low attrition rate. There is an option of keeping these developers for longer periods.

The habit of staying with one employer over longer periods of time constitutes an element of what our interviewees termed "strong work ethic." This ethic is mentioned as one of the arguments behind the decision to do business in Poland. According to an American participant in our study, it reinforces the Poles' willingness to learn.

EVAN: [When they don't know something] I see enough openness in different people to [admit it and] say "yeah"... that coupled with very strong work ethic is a very strong combination. I see a lot of potential in working with development center in Poland versus some other places.

Furthermore, loyalty is emphasized as a major difference in attitudes between the Poles and the Americans. In Poland loyalty towards the employer is significantly higher than in the Silicon Valley, therefore it acts as a force that pushes organizational networks towards closure. On the one hand, it is considered valuable as it increases internal cohesion of organization and makes managing of the organization easier (thanks to lower turnover), but on the other hand people used to Silicon Valleys' openness and flexibility find it unusual.

Evan: [Poles] have a strong sense of loyalty... they find it hard to understand why we change [jobs](...) We don't see it as disloyal when you leave.... (...) In other words... you are not just loyal to the company, you also have to be loyal to the customer. [In Poland] the loyalty is more to the company than to the customer.

Other differences concern relations inside the organization, in particular between the U.S. and Polish parts of the firm. The communication styles of Poles and American are very different; in fact it was mentioned by all our interviewees. They highlight the fact that the Poles tend to be rather wary about expressing emotional reactions in work-related situations, which the Americans find as an obstacle in effective and quick problem solving.

Evan: In general, Americans are a lot more outspoken about emotions. If they are frustrated with the process they will tell you. And it is not a bad thing because they will tell you want to do about it. I think Poles are a bit more reserved about negative emotions, or just emotions in general... maybe it is considered a little impolite..... but if you don't [agree on certain things] early then it just grows...

Moreover, as our US-based interviewees say, they see an expectation in their Polish partners of relationships to be "less superficial" (Evan). It seems that what is considered casual or professional standard in business relations in the US is perceived by the Poles as not sufficient in terms of interpersonal relationships. This corresponds with the concepts of "thin" and "thick" trust. In this context, Silicon Valley seems to represent a culture glued together by "thin trust" and open networks, whereas Poland, where strong interpersonal relationships appear to be more valued, resembles the culture of "thick trust" and closed networks

In summary, the characteristics of relationship between the Polish and American units of MOUSE seem to be in line with the distinction between "thick" (interpersonal) and "thin" (generalized) trust that we set out in the introductory parts of this chapter. The loyalty towards the employer displayed by the Polish developers is a reflection of a tendency to build trust based on close relationships and limited openness to the world outside of the organization (including careful/watchful attitude towards the customer). Similarly, the high value attached to delivering even casual promises, indicates that the Poles are more concerned about building up relationships based on "thick" form of trust in the workplace.

DISCUSSION

In the light of our empirical study, it seems that the impact of generalized trust on collaboration within multicultural environments in knowledge-intensive work may be more complicated that we were led to believe. What we find particularly interesting, is that trust in its both forms that usually is seen as a positive, in the context of cross-cultural high-tech work seems to be a double-edged sword. To shed some light on this phenomenon, the distinction between generalized and interpersonal form of trust is particularly instrumental.

Strong trust ties that are characteristic for Polish employees of MOUSE constitute a solid foundation for building commitment and distinct organizational culture of the company. Polish employees are not likely to change jobs easily which makes turnover rate in the company lower than among engineers in the United States. In this sense the cultural attitude and reliance of strong ties that developed under the socialist system, now in the free-market reality seems to be an ally in building commitment that is a necessary part of strong organizational culture.

This result is also interesting when we consider that the dominant form of work organization in high-tech is project team-based work. Most of technology products are developed within project teams and smooth team functioning as well as agile project team management is crucial for its success. Trust is key component of it. Thus, cultural inclination of Poles to identify with their teams and build strong commitments provides a supportive environment for teamwork.

On the other hand, however, the deficiency in respect to more abstract relationships ("thin" form of trust) makes Polish employees of MOUSE wary of outsiders. This may have negative impact on relations with parties that are considered "external" to the company. As the excerpts of our study indicate, this may concern, for example, interaction with clients, which may pose potential threats for operations of the company.

The findings of this study require further analysis and related research. First, it suffers obvious limitations resulting from the method adopted. As we aimed mainly at exploration, it can rather serve as a resource of well-grounded hypotheses and predictions that need to be further studied and confirmed in more rigorous analysis. Second, as we focused on only one part of relationship (Americans) it would be crucial to

gather information from Poles in similar type of study. Third, our analysis was restricted to knowledge-intensive type of work. It would be interesting to see how Poles and Americans act in collaborative contexts in other types of work. From a more practical perspective, it would be interesting to see practical implications of this analysis that would serve as guide for managers running cross-cultural projects in cultures that differ in the level of thin forms of trust.

REFERENCES

Alvesson, M. (2004). *Knowledge work and knowledge-intensive firms*. Oxford, UK: Oxford University Press.

Alvesson, M., & Skoldberg, K. (2000). *Towards a reflexive methodology*. London, UK: Sage.

Ariño, A., de la Torre, J., & Ring, P. S. (2001). Relational quality: Managing trust in corporate alliances. *California Management Review, 44*, 109–131.

Austin, R., & Larkey, P. (2002). The future of performance measurement: Measuring knowledge work. In Neely, A. (Ed.), *Business Performance Measurement—Theory and Practice*. Cambridge, UK: Cambridge University Press. doi:10.1017/CBO9780511753695.021

Baier, A. (1986). Trust and antitrust. *Ethics, 96*, 231–260. doi:10.1086/292745

Bosch-Sijtsema, P. M., Fruchter, R., Vartiainen, M., & Ruohomäki, V. (2011). A framework to analyze knowledge work in distributed teams. *Group & Organization Management Journal, 36*(3), 275–307. doi:10.1177/1059601111403625

Cook, K., Hardin, R., & Levi, M. (2005). *Cooperation without trust?* New York, NY: Russell Sage Foundation.

Cook, K. S. (2008). The limits of trust: How institutions take up where trust leaves off. *Focus (San Francisco, Calif.)*, *12*, 49–51.

Cook, K. S., & Gerbasi, A. (2009). Trust: Explanations of social action and implications for social structure. In Bearman, P., & Hedstrom, P. (Eds.), *The Oxford Handbook of Analytical Sociology*. Oxford, UK: Oxford University Press.

Cross, R., & Cummings, J. N. (2004). Tie and network correlates of individual performance in knowledge-intensive work. *Academy of Management Journal*, *47*, 928–937. doi:10.2307/20159632

Ditillo, A. (2004). Dealing with uncertainty in knowledge-intensive firms: The role of management control systems as knowledge integration mechanisms. *Accounting, Organizations and Society*, *29*, 401–421. doi:10.1016/j.aos.2003.12.001

Edelman, L. F., Bresnen, M., Newell, S., Scarbrough, H., & Swan, J. (2004). The benefits and pitfalls of social capital: Empirical evidence from two organizations in the United Kingdom. *British Journal of Management*, *15*, 59–S69. doi:10.1111/j.1467-8551.2004.00406.x

Fruchter, R., Bosch-Sijtsema, P. M., & Ruohomaki, V. (2010). Tension between perceived collocation and actual geographical distribution in project teams. *International Journal of AI & Society*, *25*(2), 183–192. doi:10.1007/s00146-009-0254-x

Glaser, B. G., & Strauss, A. L. (1967). *The discovery of grounded theory: Strategies for qualitative research*. Chicago, IL: Aldine Pub. Co.

Goodwin, J. (2002). *Is software always late?* Retrieved from http://www.joelgoodwin.com/wander/Articles/mad/IsSoftwareAlwaysLate.html

Hamel, G., Doz, Y. L., & Prahalad, C. K. (1989). Collaborate with your competitors - And win. *Harvard Business Review*, *67*(1), 113–139.

Hardin, R. (2002). *Trust and trustworthiness*. New York, NY: Russell Sage Foundation.

Hargadon, A., & Sutton, R. (1997). Technology brokering and innovation in a product development firm. *Administrative Science Quarterly*, *42*, 716–749. doi:10.2307/2393655

Humphrey, W. S. (1997). *Managing technical people: Innovation, teamwork, and the software process*. Reading, MA: Addison-Wesley.

Jackson, J. E., & Mach, B. W. (2009). Job creation, job destruction, labour mobility and wages in Poland, 1988-1998. *Economics of Transition*, *17*, 503–530. doi:10.1111/j.1468-0351.2009.00358.x

Jankowicz, A. D. (2000). *Business research projects*. New York, NY: Thomson Learning.

Jemielniak, D. (2007). Managers as lazy, stupid careerists? *Journal of Organizational Change Management*, *20*, 491–508. doi:10.1108/09534810710760045

Jemielniak, D. (2012). *The new knowledge workers*. New York, NY: Edward Elgar Publishing.

Kesteloot, L. (2003). *Why software is late*. Retrieved from http://www.teamten.com/lawrence/writings/late_software.html

Khanna, T., Gulati, R., & Nohria, N. (1998). The dynamics of learning alliances: Competition, cooperation, and relative scope. *Strategic Management Journal*, *19*, 193–210. doi:10.1002/(SICI)1097-0266(199803)19:3<193::AID-SMJ949>3.0.CO;2-C

Kostera, M. (2007). *Organizational ethnography: Methods and inspirations*. Lund, Sweden: Studentliteratur.

Lane, C., & Bachmann, R. (1997). Co-operation in inter-firm relations in Britain and Germany: The role of social institutions. *The British Journal of Sociology, 48*, 226–254. doi:10.2307/591750

Madhok, A. (1995). Revisiting multinational firms' tolerance for joint ventures: A trust-based approach. *Journal of International Business Studies, 26*, 117–137. doi:10.1057/palgrave. jibs.8490168

Marin, D. (2002). Trust versus illusion: What is driving demonetization in the former Soviet Union? *Economics of Transition, 10*, 173–200. doi:10.1111/1468-0351.00107

Meyerson, D., Weick, K. E., & Kramer, R. M. (1996). Swift trust in temporary groups. In Kramer, R. M., & Tyler, T. R. (Eds.), *Trust in Organizations: Frontiers of Theory and Research*. Thousand Oaks, CA: Sage.

Nonaka, I. (1994). A dynamic theory of organizational knowledge creation. *Organization Science, 5*, 15–37. doi:10.1287/orsc.5.1.14

Nonaka, I., Toyama, R., & Nagata, A. (2000). A firm as a knowledge-creating entity: A new perspective on the theory of the firm. *Industrial and Corporate Change, 9*, 1–20. doi:10.1093/icc/9.1.1

Nurmi, R. (1999). Knowledge-intensive firms. In *The Knowledge Management Yearbook 1999-2000*. London, UK: Butterworth-Heinemann.

Peev, E. (2002). Ownership and control structures in transition to 'crony' capitalism: The case of Bulgaria. *Eastern European Economics, 40*, 73–91.

Rose-Ackerman, S. (2001a). Trust and honesty in post-socialist societies. *Kyklos, 54*, 415–443.

Rose-Ackerman, S. (2001b). Trust, honesty and corruption: Reflection on the state-building process. *European Journal of Sociology, 42*, 526–570. doi:10.1017/S0003975601001084

Rosen, M. (1991). Coming to terms with the field: Understanding and doing organizational ethnography. *Journal of Management Studies, 28*, 1–23. doi:10.1111/j.1467-6486.1991.tb00268.x

Sztompka, P. (1996). Trust and emerging democracy: Lessons from Poland. *International Sociology, 11*, 37. doi:10.1177/026858096011001004

Sztompka, P. (1999). *Trust: A sociological theory*. Cambridge, UK: Cambridge University Press.

Tillmar, M., & Lindkvist, L. (2007). Cooperation against all odds: Finding reasons for trust where formal institutions fail. *International Sociology, 22*, 343–366. doi:10.1177/0268580907076575

Williamson, O. E. (1993). Calculativeness, trust, and economic organization. *The Journal of Law & Economics, 36*, 453–486. doi:10.1086/467284

Winch, G., & Schneider, E. (1993). Managing the knowledge-based organization: The case of architectural practice. *Journal of Management Studies, 30*, 923–937. doi:10.1111/j.1467-6486.1993.tb00472.x

World Values Survey. (2005). *Download data files of the values studies*. Retrieved March 15, 2010 from http://www.worldvaluessurvey.org/

Zaheer, S., & Zaheer, A. (2006). Trust across borders. *Journal of International Business Studies, 37*, 21–29. doi:10.1057/palgrave.jibs.8400180

Zucker, L. G. (1986). Production of trust: Institutional sources of economic structure. In Barry, S., & Cummings, L. (Eds.), *Research in Organizational Behavior*. Greenwich, CT: JAI Press.

ENDNOTE

[1] Names of companies and people in the text are changed.

Chapter 2
Trust as a Success Factor in Open Innovation:
The Case of Nokia and GNOME

Malgorzata Ciesielska
Teesside University, UK

Zilia Iskoujina
Newcastle University, UK

ABSTRACT

This chapter analyzes trust, open innovation, and software development modes. Basing on the case of GNOME – Nokia collaboration, it shows how trust can be perceived as a strategic resource, which is actually the crucial ingredient of successful collaboration. The dichotomy of the professional (expert) trust and the political trust is proposed as an interpretive key to understanding trust enactment in open source communities.

INTRODUCTION

Historically, the software development sector has been ruled by two alternative logics of action: close and open coding (Weber, 2004). On the one hand, the classic business approach benefits from the intellectual property rights concept. This institution of law secures profits from the produced in-house innovations. Internally developed source code is converted into binary version and offered on the market with particular licenses to use it as well as restrictions about copying, modifying, and distributing. The alternative perspective for developing software solutions is an open source process, which is based on free access to the source code and permission to make changes and introduce innovations by the broad community of developers. Open licenses are often characterised by the "viral rule," which says that the modified

DOI: 10.4018/978-1-4666-1836-7.ch002

code or software containing and Open Source code has to be distributed as the same type of license as the original piece of code. This means that any company using Open Source code in its software development must release the altered code on the Open Source Software (OSS) license. Here, the institution of law is used for a contrary purpose than in the case of intellectual property rights.

Nowadays, OSS can be neither underestimated nor ignored by business players, and many companies aim to take advantage of the Open Source movement by either passively using OSS (one-way benefit) or more actively participating in OSS projects, submitting patches and developing external collaboration networks. Nokia (Jaaksi, 2006, 2007), IBM, Intel, and even Procter and Gamble (Chesbrough, 2006) have incorporated open innovation models to expand their R&D. Customers and users can easily contribute their explicit and tacit knowledge to a company's R&D processes as technology development and internet availability make the distinction between work and hobby more difficult (Westenholz, 2003). The organisational consequences of OSS strategies are significant:

The open source process undercuts conventional business logics. The GPL[1] does more than just release control of the source code; it explicitly establishes a situation in which no one can control the source code. This forces a dramatic shift in the underlying structure of the software business (Weber, 2004, p. 192).

The Open Source-business collaboration is especially interesting in the setting in which contributors-coders participate both as private persons and as contractual partners or employees. Moreover, the boundaries of known identities, such as a software developer and a software user and entities like a company and a community, are transgressing as a result of interactions between the two worlds (Westenholz, 2009). While in the organisational or intra-organisational context trust

is considered as a means of facilitating exchange of resources and information (Uzzi, 1996, Tsai & Ghoshal, 1998), the specific setting of the competing logics (closed-proprietary products vs. quasi-public goods) possesses questions about the common grounds of the Open Source-business collaboration. By analysing an empirical case, we argue that trust is a crucial strategic resource that makes this cooperation fruitful. We start with the theoretical framework based on trust literature, where we discuss its importance in off- and online relations. We also introduce the concepts of, political trust and trust in expertise, which we argue are of key importance in open innovation networks. Then after we discuss data collection methods via case studies, in data analysis part of the chapter, the case studies on Nokia and Open Source, GNOME, Nokia's politics of involvement in GNOME, and trust in expertise of GNOME community members will be discussed. The case studies will be followed by the discussion on the two-dimensional taxonomy of trust.

OUR FRAMEWORK

The studies in origins and nature of different concepts of trust, including in particular institutional and personal relations, structural, cognitive, and affective sources of trust as well as various targets provide a framework for our study. This section looks at the current state of literature on trust showing gaps in our understanding of development trust in the setting of Open Source-business collaboration. It also unfolds the concepts of political trust and trust in expertise, which we found particularly important in the studied setting.

Unfolding the Trust as a Strategic Resource

Trust as one of the preconditions of co-operation (Gambetta, 1988; Hardin, 2002, 2006; Lane & Bachmann, 1998, 2000). Trust theories have been used to understand B2C or C2C e-commerce phenomena (Xiong & Liu, 2003; Hardin, 2006; Jones & Leonard, 2008), development of dedicated commercial IT/software solutions (study of distrust by Latusek, 2007), the existence of online communities (Wiertz & Ruyer, 2007), online collaboration in global virtual teams (Jarvenpaa, Knoll, & Leinder, 1998; Jarvenpaa & Leidner, 1999), and attributes for knowledge sharing (Faraj & Wasko, 2001; Bauer & Koeszegi, 2003; Roberts, 2006).

Trust is also considered as a facilitator of knowledge sharing (Ishaya & Macaulay, 1999; Jarvenpaa & Leidner, 1999; Faraj & Wasko, 2001; Bauer & Koeszegi, 2003; Jarvenpaa, Shaw, & Staples, 2004; Roberts, 2003, 2006; Collins & Smith, 2006). For instance, Steil, Barcia, and Pacheco (1999) discuss that in online communities it is particularly important to promote intensive socialisation activities to enable knowledge sharing. Amin and Roberts (2008) add that online communities work well if there is a high level of interpersonal trust. Similarly argues that Trust, familiarity and mutual understanding in social and cultural contexts are fundamentals for the successful sharing of tacit knowledge (Roberts, 2000a, 2006) and may become a key factor for successful virtual organisations (Ishaya & Macaulay, 1999).

In this chapter, trust is conceptualised according to as "communicative, sense-making process that bridges disparate groups" (Hardy, Phillips, & Lawrence, 1998, 2000, p. 69) and as "an efficient mechanism to coordinate exchange relationships characterised by high uncertainty, high interdependence between transaction partners, or when both process and output control are not possible" (Bauer & Koeszegi, 2003, pp. 28-29). Similarly, following the work of Mayer, Davis, and Schoorman (1995, p. 712), we argue that bridging between people and groups requires some level of "the willingness of a party to be vulnerable to the actions of another party based on the expectation that the other will perform a particular action important to the trustor, irrespective of the ability to monitor or control that other party." Within organisational and interpersonal settings, the discussion applies Hardin's (2006) approach to trust as a cognitive, calculative phenomenon. Moreover, as Lewis and Weigert (1985, p. 456) claim, "trust is a necessary condition of social existence, but its enactment is also a matter of individual decision and interpretation." As such, it is important to be able to acknowledge that trust has been often substituted with the power relation, even if such a substitution was not initially evident. Hardy, Phillips, and Lawrence (1998, 2000) further noted that—in addition to the different forms of trust—trust can be also be limited to its façades. Meanwhile, in symmetrical power structures, trust can be either spontaneous or generated; the concept of the façade of trust describes the situation of a power-based relationship in which the stronger party creates an illusion of trust. Finally, Sztompka (1999) indicates that—to understand trust-building processes in any given setting—one needs to be able to recognise and differentiate among various targets of trust that are often mutually interdependent. This particular sensitivity of targets of trust is applied in the current case study analysis.

Trust in the Internet-Mediated Environment

Creating trust within an Internet-mediated environment is an emerging research topic in business and organisation studies and has become one of the key problems for companies engaging in online activities. In particular, two contexts of Internet (trust) relations are discussed in the literature. First, trust concerns the possibilities of online commerce (Xiong & Liu, 2003; Hardin, 2006). Second, although much less was done to understand trust in online co-operation, its importance in the virtual form of organisations was widely (Ishaya & Macaulay, 1999; Jarvenpaa & Leidner,

1999; Faraj & Wasko, 2001; Bauer & Koeszegi, 2003; Jarvenpaa, Shaw, & Staples, 2004; Roberts, 2003, 2006; Collins & Smith, 2006).

In the particular area of OSS projects, two trust-related issues have been raised. From the perspective of business organisations, the key question is whether companies should get involved in any Open Source activities. Articles in professional journals focus primarily on potential problems with the security of Open Source programs. Although some very enthusiastic descriptions exist of successful usage of OSS in private companies (Balog, 2007; Harrison, 1989), many concerns are still communicated (Greene, 2007). For instance, Hissam, Plakosh, and Weinstock (2002) believe that OSS is more vulnerable to attack than commercially developed programs, arguing that open code helps cyber criminals gather data and facilitates their attack. Although this way of thinking is very much in line with the property rights logics, the authors point out an important aspect of online community life: the problem of distinguishing 'good' members from 'bad' ones.

Second, the discussions regarding the existence of trust built through online communication have become important. For instance, Russell Hardin (2006) argues that Internet relationships are typically one-shot transactions in which the use of common norms, beliefs, and sanctions does not work due to the nature of the Internet as a vast, decentralised system. It this sense, the Internet's characteristics, and dynamics make contexts for social activity peculiarly extreme; indeed, in most cases the creation of online (social) communities is not possible. However, the results of Osterloh and Rota's (2004), Roberts's (2006), Ciesielska's (2010), and Iskoujina's (2010) empirical studies seem to contradict some of Hardin's conclusions. Similarly, Matzat (2004) argues that Internet usage in fact has social consequences, including the creation of online groups (communities). In addition, Jarvenpaa, Knoll, and Leinder (1998) claim that co-ordination in virtual teams can be achieved primarily by building trust relationships and shared

communication systems; therefore, they suggest that trust is an important issue for enhancing online collaboration (Handy, 1995), and success of the virtual organisation (Bauer & Koeszegi, 2003) found that trust between the members is fundamental for the success of McKnight et al. (1998) developed the initial trust model to clarify high initial trustworthiness and trust in newly formed relationships or in temporary virtual teams. The model by Dirks and Ferrin (2001) builds upon the assumption that trust reduces uncertainty in social perceptions where cooperative or productive activity takes place. Jarvenpaa, Shaw, and Staples (2004) find that when there is less uncertainty, the interpretation process becomes unnecessary, reducing the role of trust. Trust effects may not be necessarily direct and linear. Trust provides important benefits for IT-enabled relationships, such as in OSS communities. Ishaya and Macaulay (1999) argues that trust is a key factor for successful virtual organisations, where social control is based on self-direction and self-control. Given that trust is an important factor in any team, it plays even more critical role in a virtual team. That is because of their nature face-to-face interactions may happen less than in traditional organisations, or sometimes even never happen. Following this line of thought, it seems that most studies that primarily emphasise the role of swift trust in online collaboration deal with virtual teams, which are established to finalise a particular task known from the beginning (Jarvenpaa, Knoll, & Leidner 1998). Yet they are temporary in terms of their existence, and collaboration is the focus in accomplishing the given target.

What differentiates OSS projects is that they have a rather continuous task: the never-ending struggle to upgrade the software code, either by fixing the bugs or by developing new functionalities. The continuity of the task is derived from the character of the work itself. New functions create new bugs; new upgrades fix one bug, but introduce others. In this sense, OSS communities will always have work to do until participants are interested in the emerging product (software). At the same time, OSS communities are temporal groups—not in the sense of the time span and defined task, but in terms of structures and participants. Their membership is in flux.

Dual Taxonomy of Trust in Open Innovation

Based on the previous discussions, the concepts of trust and trust emergence still require further—especially empirical—examination. In particular, further explanation of the trust issues within Open Source–business collaboration is needed. To address this gap, this chapter presents an empirically driven description of the trust relations between Nokia corporation and a mainstream OSS project - GNOME. Basing on the material gathered about the sources and forms of trust in this setting, two cognitive elements became especially important: political trust and trust in expertise:

- We use the concept of political trust in a different way than in most trust-related literature, where it is often related to trust in democracy and the political system as part of more impersonal trust relations (for instance see Mishler & Rose, 2001). Here, political trust is a trust towards the organisation that its declarations and presentations will be followed by coherent actions.
- Trust in expertise is the trust given to a person that this person is professionally capable of providing quality solutions for given or taken tasks. In both cases, the trust is granted without certainty or control over the situation.

The next sections are structured to present the political (dis)trust as well as trust in the expertise. The material is divided into two parts: the Nokia's approach to involve-

ment in OSS and Nokia- GNOME relations within the independent OSS community. First we will introduce our research design.

RESEARCH DESIGN

The data collected for this study was primarily qualitative in nature and concerned software development processes incorporated into a single R&D project: the Nokia Internet tablet series. Within the general case study-approach, there were two main sources of data: the secondary sources, including website repositories, and face-to-face interviews.

Case Studies

Case studies of Nokia and GNOME were chosen as an example of a change of a big organisation originally working on a close-code basis, into an Open Source movement participant and beneficiary. The special interest was given to the Internet tablet development—a product fully commercialised in 2009 and that for years has served more as an experimentation site for R&D and collecting feedback from the market rather than a source of profit. Empirical work was regularly conducted from July 2007 until November 2009.

Secondary Data

Secondary sources included written online materials from Nokia and co-operating projects (e.g., statements, presentations, discussions, blog posts) combined in a form of a nethnographic study (Kozinets, 1997, 1998, 2002) as well as previous studies on Nokia (Ghosh, 2006; Dittrich, 2007). Due to the interests of the various involved parties, identities and names of the informants referred to are fictive. Only some publicly accessible opinions and statements are quoted using real names and positions.

Interviews

Semi-structured and unstructured anthropological interviews (Spradley, 1979; Kostera, 2003, 2005) were conducted in the Nokia Research Centre in Helsinki (June 2008) as well as during international conferences and projects gatherings—namely, the OSS Conference (July 2007), Linux Tag (May 2008), GUADECs (July 2008 and 2009), and Maemo Summits (September 2008 and October 2009). Some interviews were recorded and transcribed, but many took the form of a private talk. The notes from private talks were taken ex post.

During the interviews, the word *trust* was rarely used if not directly asked about. When the researcher openly asked about trust, interviewees understood trust to be a good quality of OSS. However, some of the observations and indirect questions about trust relations within projects indicated that it was a present issue in the field (although not named). For instance, one person refused to give an interview because of a contract they signed with Nokia. They apologised profusely, but they also admitted that even in the middle of the night they would remember the fine for revealing any details about projects on which they were working. Surprisingly, contrary to the interviews, trust appeared to be an issue, but depending on the case, its focus differed. However, this provided only a perspective of how the trust concept is communicated by the project participants, while the offline data were used as interpretative lenses for what we can read in on- and off-line materials.

Analysis of Data

The analysis of the material was twofold. In the first step, the project's websites were examined for trust-related discussions, and then coded accordingly to the sources of trust. Gnome.org was thoroughly searched to identify all instances containing the words *trust* and *trustworthy*. This exercise was followed by a detailed analysis of all identified examples, choosing trust-related topics, which were searched through again.

The second step involved searching through interview transcripts and field notes for the indication of political trust/distrust and trust/distrust in expertise. During this second stage, quotes and stories related to the institutional forms of trust were identified for inclusion in this chapter.

OPEN INNOVATION SETTING

Nokia and Open Source

Nokia is primarily associated with cellular phone manufacturing, but its broader strategy is mobile connectivity. For the last several years, the company has been working on a new embedded system for its devices. This was a reactive response to the actions of other important players in the market, who were already working on the idea of smart phones packed with Internet browsing and multimedia utilities, especially Apple iPhone, and later Google's Android. The release of the first iPhone in mid 2007 and then the first Android phone in October 2008 had tremendous consequences for Nokia's incomes, as the company had problems with meeting the new demand (Figure 1). At that time, Nokia's hopes were in the series of the Internet tablets, which could replace Symbian phones in the future.

Although the Internet tablet R&D project was initiated in 2002 with the Nokia 7700 media device, the first N770 model was announced 3 years later. The second generation of tablet N880 was rolled out at the beginning of 2007. In December that same year, the third generation N810 became widely available in stores. Until that time tablets were kept as a separate range from the phones. Finally, in November 2009, the N900 was launched—the first tablet device with a SIM card dedicated for the mass market.

Nokia's Internet tablets were supposed to be different from the existing Nokia phone range,

Figure 1. Comparison of Nokia, Apple, and Google annual total revenues and operating incomes[2] (2007-2010); source: finapps.forbes.com

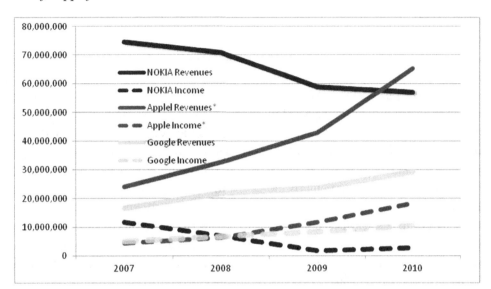

not only in terms of their functionality, but also because there was a whole new operating system developed to run on them. The Nokia project was an initial step to create "an open-source product for broadband and Internet services"; Nokia declared that it would be regularly co-ordinating and launching new versions of the software (Janne Jormalainen, vice president of Nokia, quoted in Sharma, 2005). Maemo operating system, similarly to Android, was composed mostly of Free/ Libre Open Source Software (F/LOSS). For the most part, the Maemo operating system was built from Open Source components, although it also incorporates third-party proprietary modules and patches provided by Nokia. The operating system is internally developed and managed by Nokia, which has absolute power over releases. External contributions to the Maemo operating system are possible through mainstream projects, such as by participating in GNOME or Linux kernel projects. This means that no external developers have a direct influence on the operating system development or release.

On the contrary, GNOME is a fully external Open Source Software project that was already well established when Nokia decided to join it. Nokia's interest was mostly concentrated on using and developing GNOME/GTK+ Application Framework, GNOME VFS File Access, a structural file library, and a configuration management. Some are still components of the Maemo operating system. Up to 2010, Maemo operating system's core comprised the Linux operating system kernel, the GCC compiler, the GNOME UI framework (Hildon UI provides components over GNOME), GNU C libraries, and Debian Packet Management.

In 2010, there was a sudden shift in NOKIA's strategy, which resulted first in handing the Maemo project to Intel. Although the new project MeeGo is a continuation of Maemo platform, it is mostly Intel's responsibility, and Nokia announced in 2011 that they are preparing handsets running Windows Mobile. This strategical regress from open source to closed-mode strategies may have been shocking for most of subcontractors, but at the same it was a result of a very difficult open source-business setting, in which Nokia had problems building trust among collaborators. This trust building issues will be analysed further in the case studies.

GNOME

Nokia's Politics of Involvement in GNOME

GNOME—the GNU Network Object Model Environment—is a free software desktop project that provides both an *intuitive and attractive* desktop environment as well as the GNOME development platform for building applications (http://www.gnome.org/about/). Nokia is one of the many companies interested in GNOME, particularly the usage of some components for embedded devices. Today Nokia is part of the GNOME foundation, but it can still only try to affect the work done via its programmers. Nokia as a single company does not formally have the power to make decisions on behalf of the project.

Nokia first demonstrated at the GUADEC, the annual GNOME Users' And Developers' European Conference, in summer 2005 in Stuttgart. As a cornerstone sponsor, Nokia made a presentation on its work done with GNOME and GStreamer-related technologies (http://2005.guadec.org). This presentation correlated with the launch of Nokia's first Internet tablet device. The executive director of the GNOME Foundation, Timothy Ney (2005), said at that time that, "We're very excited about the release of the Nokia 770 Internet Tablet," and he expressed his gratitude to Nokia for donating the proceeds from the sales of 500 Nokia 770 devices to the GNOME Foundation (http://2005.guadec.org/press/releases/nokia_donation.html). During GUADEC 2006, four different sessions related to the Nokia 770 (http://live.gnome.org/GUADEC2006). Nokia continued to contribute to Open Source and GNOME in subsequent years as well as financially sponsoring GUADEC at the gold level in 2006, 2007, and 2008. In 2009, the Nokia group Qt Software and Maemo.org became a platinum sponsor of GUADEC.

Trust relations with any of the companies involved in GNOME are rarely discussed on public Internet fora. Although this is considered a sensitive issue, the topic is present in more personal communications. Nokia is posed in contrary to companies like Red Hat, which is considered as a truly Open Source company that is very much immersed in the ideology as well. In addition, one of the GNOME founders originated from this organisation. The GNOME developer (2009) explained the researcher the difference between Nokia and Red Hat: "Red Hat runs this community disinterestedly," which is evident in the way it hosts community servers and participates in the project. Nokia, on the other hand, is purposeful; nobody exactly knows what the company is up to for several months. However, things are not just back and white in this field; lines are blurred. Yet ultimately, doubts exist about Nokia's open strategy:

I think Nokia is one of the examples off the far wrong side of how things should be done. Red Hat is on the other side. But Novell is not so clearly on the side, which does it right, but they are traditionally an open-source company. While Red Hat always was an open-source company and always make everything [open] out, Novell didn't. So inside Novell there is still this fight going on. So the line is blurry (GNOME developer, 2008).

Nokia's political decision about the acquisition of the Trolltech ASA in June 2008, later renamed Qt Development Frameworks (http://qt.nokia.com), was crucial for its involvement in the GNOME project. Qt is a cross-platform application development framework, a well-known widget library widely used for the development of graphical user interface programs. It is free and Open Source software distributed under the terms of the GNU Lesser General Public License.

Along with Qt, one of the most popular toolkits for the X Window System—GTK+—was developed within the GNOME project. As advertised on the official website http://www.gtk.org: "GTK+ is a highly usable, feature rich toolkit for creating graphical user interfaces which boasts cross platform compatibility and an easy to use API." Here emerges the basic conflict of interests. During GUADEC 2009, Nokia was openly advertising the usage of Qt and offering jobs for developers, which was not appreciated by GTK+ developers. Even more ironic for the GNOME community, the non-GPL Qt library used by the KDE project[3] became one of the reasons for GNOME's creation. In 1997, the GNOME project was started to develop a fully open platform.

"We don't like them anymore" one of the GNOME developers (2009) stated, expressing dissatisfaction about Nokia's actions. It was considered rather offensive to the GTK+ developers that Nokia came to their conference promoting a competitive toolkit. It was perceived as showing a lack of respect for their work. As a sponsor, Nokia had requested to put a Qt logo on the name badges, which was widely protested by covering the Qt logo with various stickers. GNOME community members showed solidarity in this protest, which surprisingly also concerned most of the Nokia-employed developers who originated from GNOME. In addition to the purely emotional reactions, Nokia involvement in Qt development means no further contribution to GTK+ and probably also much less participation in the GNOME project in subsequent years. This has happened despite previous assurances from the Nokia PR that the acquisition of Qt would not change the company's relations with GNOME. Clearly, it has.

Trust in Expertise of GNOME Community Members

Cognitive trust building is supported by GNOME is several ways. The emphasis is on transparency and individual performance. "Can I have my pseudonym, "billsmith," as my gnome.org account name? I use it everywhere online and want to protect my real identity?" is marked as a Frequently Asked Question. The answer to this query is a simple "no":

There must be an immediately obvious connection to your full, real name. The community is based on transparency and trust. Pseudonyms and hidden identities do not play well with that (http://live. gnome.org/AccountNameFAQ).

GNOME is also known as an originator of a special type of avatars called *hackergotchis*. These are usually real photos head cutouts with a shadow drop that first appeared on art.gnome.org and were subsequently used on a blog aggregator of GNOME programmers and contributors called Planet GNOME. The examples could be found on http://planet.gnome.org. By using *hackergotchis* as avatars, people recognise each other more easily. They also help other people recognise contributors from around the planet and create the impression that—despite the distance—people actually get to know each other over time. More importantly, the system tracks reputation scores and badges so people can easily recognise the authors of submitted patches and expressed opinions (http://live.gnome.org/ClausSchwarm/HowtoGetMore-Contributors). Somebody with several hundred posts becomes more reliable as people feel more confident about his/her professional advice and contributions. Finally, all these actions are purposeful as trust is recognised as an element of project life and a condition for its development:

Not stated among the arguments for and against wiki is the obvious: that you can easily secure wiki behind an intranet, and that is where wiki excels, among a contained, gated community, where trust is implicit and granted on the basis of all individuals being known to the community (http://live.gnome.org/WhyWikiWorks).

Being trusted or a trustworthy person is a requirement often expressed while talking about any contribution to the GNOME project. "It's easy to build up trust over time" (http://live.gnome.org/Sysadmin/AdvisoryMeeting/FormalTeam). If one wants to become a GTG developer, "we have to know you and trust you for your contribution." In practice, this means that:

If you contribute code, we should have confidence that you are now a gtg master and that you've fully understood our coding rules. It usually means that your latest patches were all merged without any need to resubmit them (http://live.gnome.org/gtg/becoming%20a%20gtg%20developer).

Several levels of functions and trust-related positions exist in the projects; parallel to sysadmins, account team members, trusted translators, trusted editors, etc., there are also "superusers"— "trusted user names with wiki system administration super powers (not to be confused with ACL admin rights!)"[4] GNOME project participants are supposed to trust the trusted. This saves time and assures the quality of work:

If you want to translate the documentation shipped with your application, please contact your own language team. You can find a complete list of all the team here: http://l10n.gnome.org/teams/.

Each team is very dedicated to their work and have high translation standards: all maintainers should trust the translation team and can only accept translations coming from members of a translation team (http://live.gnome.org/DocumentationProject/Translations).

GNOME makes sure that translators are assessed both on their motives and drives as well as their expertise in the subject. The Team Coordinator within translation projects is responsible for approving individuals' translator accounts. This process is not taken lightly, as with such accounts comes much power:

Approving means testifying the trust to this applicant and that he or she will follow the rules and not misbehave, and testifying that the applicant is

a real existing contributor to this language team and really in need of an account. The co-ordinator should not approve of applicants for which any of this is not true (http://live.gnome.org/TranslationProject/TeamCoordinatorResponsibilities).

Similarly, it is not a thread to anonymous voting in foundation elections if the Election Committee can link ballots to members (as they are responsible for the voting process and are able to issue new ballots if a member loses the original one):

I don't think this can be fixed without lowering the security of the system. The committee is already trusted not to rig the election, so I don't think this is too big of a deal (http://live.gnome.org/AnonymousVoting).

For those interested in working as an account team member, "we need to know a little bit about you." The most preferred candidates are the existing foundation members with a history of involvement in the project. If that is not the case, the "references to any previous work you have done in the open source community, or the names a couple of Foundation Members that can vouch that you are responsible, trustworthy and of good character, etc." are needed (http://live.gnome.org/AccountsTeam).

Moreover, the need for trust is indicated as the biggest problem of maintaining an active sysadmin team. Many people want to help, but this requires giving them a "dangerous level of access to the GNOME systems" (http://live.gnome.org/Sysadmin/AdvisoryMeeting/FormalTeam). Gaining trust is primarily based on cognitive, personal aspects: quality involvement and willingness to help out with the GNOME project. If patches through a review process are perceived as beneficial, people are eventually given direct commit access. Unfortunately, people who are given a high level of trust in expertise are very often occupied with other tasks and generally are not particularly sysadmin experts. Therefore, a

Table 1. Linux screen reader - how to contribute

1. Check the project ideas page. Let us know if you want to help implement any of the short term features by emailing the LSR mailing list (lsr-list@gnome.org).
2. Let us hear your novel ideas. Most new features only require that you write a script or device extension to LSR rather than modify the deep internals. Discussing your ideas on the LSR mailing list (lsr-list@gnome.org) will ensure you're not headed for more work than is necessary.
3. Understand the concepts in the LSR workbook and the structure of the code in the LSR epydoc. Working on the core will be difficult if you don't have a working knowledge of the architecture and codebase.
4. Create a development sandbox so you can hack without having to reinstall after each change.
5. Become versed in the LSR code style guidelines. We like to run a tight ship.
6. Implement your idea.
7. Submit patches. We will review your initial contributions to the core to establish trust and pedigree.
8. Become privileged. We may grant commit permissions after one or more successful contributions to the core.

Source: http://live.gnome.org/LSR/CoreDevelopers

trust issue remains in regard to filling vacancies on the team:

I think you'd basically have to have an application process. Candidates would need to give information about their experience with sysadmin, have a demonstrated commitment to GNOME by work on bug-triaging/translations/coding/whatever and be people known to the community (maybe just by hanging out on #sysadmin for a few months). The team leader, in consultation with the rest of the team, would have the responsibility for encouraging people to apply and collecting data about applicants (http://live.gnome.org/Sysadmin/AdvisoryMeeting/FormalTeam).

Applicants need to meet two main requirements before they are admitted to the core sysadmin team:

At least a few years of practical hands-on experience working in a Linux-based systems administration environment. A certain level of competence is required. We do not have any apprenticeship or training positions open at this time.

A history of practical contributions to the GNOME project. This demonstrates that you are capable of sparing time to help, are genuinely enthusiastic about GNOME and have demonstrated a certain level of trustworthiness and responsibility (http://live.gnome.org/Sysadmin/AdvisoryMeeting/FormalTeam).

To prove their trustworthiness and expertise, candidates are strongly advised to start at least hanging out on the sysadmin discussion forum, be acquainted with day-to-day problems, and eventually join in and offer real-time advice. "[W]e would not accept anyone into the sysadmin group until we are familiar with them and know that they are capable and trustworthy enough to start dealing with any issues themselves" is clearly stated on the "Helping Sysadmin" guide (http://live.gnome.org/HelpingSysadmin). Similar points are made in relation to other subprojects and groups, as in the Linux Screen Reader (Table 1) or Subversion:

With an increased amount of trust and responsibility, you may even be asked to start maintaining a module within GNOME Subversion—or indeed, one of your own that you may have imported [Getting the most out of Subversion in GNOME].

Meanwhile, developers working for Nokia are highly evaluated as experts and many trust their expertise. Many originate from the project and collaborate on it even after their contract with Nokia ends. GNOME developers work with people; people are respected and their professionalism noticed. It does not matter which company they subcontract to or are employed by at the moment; it is still the personal, cognitive judgement of their expertise and professionalism that counts:

I guess for the community most of the time it's more about the name, I mean the person who is sending the patch and not the corporation. If they know you by name and they know that their work is good then it doesn't matter because you are working for Nokia today but you can be working for Intel or whoever else tomorrow. [...] You have people that are moving, so at the end of the day they are just these people. And they might have those moments but it does not really matter because they are not really tied to those corporations (Nokia developer, 2008).

Trust is also expressed toward Nokia managers: "Trust Quim Gil to promote it [=Hildon]" (http://live.gnome.org/Hildon/MigrationToGnome). However, it was obvious at that time it was actually in managers' and Nokia's best interest to promote Hildon. Thus, this situation highlights corporate politics and Quim's expertise based on expectations about acting according to his job description and the corporate policy. Yet in most other cases, discrepancies at the political level have resulted in the company being distrusted in a community, despite Nokia's people knowledge and expertise. This distrust stems from unpredictability at the political level. One cannot be closed while preaching openness:

Nokia have a lot of very good people and those people are respected from the software community, but everyone makes fun of the way that Nokia handles things [...] I mean everyone acknowledges that they do good stuff, or at least some good stuff, but on the other hand people also make fun of them due to their closeness. I mean, it is not even the people are pissed, people just think, thank God I am not a Nokia employee (GNOME developer, 2008).

For many Open Source developers at Nokia, the corporation is a strange environment with which to deal. Partly by ignoring it, they help progress their project:

That was one of the things that surprised me this kind of 'we have these Nokia values and we have this kind of brainwashing stuff.' But from the beginning it was like 'who believes this?' Maybe it sounds nice, I just didn't understand it. Coming from outside all this stuff seems pointless, it doesn't make sense. But they are still trying to go around—but this, it is ignored as part of the Nokia world. Most of us, we just ignore it. It is probably something that managers believe in. But maybe a few developers believe in this stuff also. But most of the people just don't care (Nokia developer, 2008).

In addition, people's trust is easy to lose in the end. Sometimes intrinsic trust put in a person's quality of work and reputation is removed if that person does not perform well. One of the mentors in Summer of Code 2007 was "hard to contact and get feedback about students' progress" and consequently was described during debriefing as an "untrusted mentor" (http://live.gnome.org/SummerOfCode2007/Debrief), which probably meant the individual had no chance of working in this function again. Similarly, sometimes wiki discussion pages do not work as well as people expect because they can be easily sabotaged, either by hostile comments and ranting:

Look for opinions. Oppose them. Generate controversy, especially heated debate over ambiguous subjects. This will raise the level of noise and frustration, driving people away.

Or by purposeful information distortion:

Look for facts. Distort them. Replacing complicated data with slight changes can be detected, but only if a person is willing to pour over it and validate it. A difference engine and source control help when source material is changed in a complex, subtle ways. But enough accumulated errors cause a failure of trust (http://live.gnome.org/WhyWikiWorks).

Information on the official project pages is not always updated and valid. This is a classic problem facing software development projects when documentation is the least wanted task and literally unnecessary for the software to work. However, well-documented software is more likely to be further developed.

One should really be very careful about trusting anything on developer.gnome.org other than API documentation—lots of it is so out-of-date as to be more harmful than helpful. I haven't read through everything there thoroughly (though I have at least skimmed it at some point in the past), so I can't comment on all of the links below but this general warning should be noted (http://developer. gnome.org).

Summary of Findings

The GNOME community has worked out a system that supports building cognitive trust. They have focused on securing transparency in the project, making sure that people and their contributions are easy to track. Using real names and real photos as well as linking patches and opinions to particular developers makes this collaboration more personal. Reputation ranks and badges instantly indicate an individual's level of involvement and expertise. *Trusted* (i.e. important) positions are given to developers who have proven their expertise and political coherence. Trust in an individual's professionalism and expertise is easy to lose if one is not acting accordingly to the expectations.

On the other hand, the participants of GNOME are also corporations like Nokia. On several occasions Nokia showed that its declarations and plans might have little to do with subsequent actions. The company simply did not realise that Open Source is not about promises, but about outcomes. Talks and public relations have no importance if they are not followed by genuine involvement. This

strategy made GNOME developers distrustful of Nokia's political decisions. Programmers can make fun of Nokia's closeness, but when Nokia unexpectedly withdrew from a large portion of the community project, it caused a serious threat for the whole project.

DISCUSSION: THE TWO-DIMENSIONAL TAXONOMY OF TRUST

Trust is not a straightforward clear phenomenon. In the case of the Open Source-business hybrid co-operation, it is especially evident how not only expertise and professionalism count as a positive clue of trustworthiness, but the concept of political (dis)trust also comes into play. Consequently, trust should be analysed as a two-dimensional phenomenon of political trust and trust in expertise; acting toward just one side is not enough to be considered as a "trusted" partner. Trust in the Open Source setting is a mix of professionalism and motivations, expertise and politics. Although the political aspect of trust seems to have more organisational-level significance, trust in expertise and professionalism is the basis for the whole Open Source process and cannot be achieved without it. Trust in expertise is always personal, regardless of organisational or corporation affiliations. In both cases, this trust is a cognitive construct. It is given and withdrawn during interactions as a calculative outcome of the evaluation of other people and organisations' behaviours. Institutionalised solutions are only used to secure the co-operation in situations of distrust between parties. Institutional trust refers to the higher order and is detached from the interorganisational and interpersonal relation and the Open Source-business setting.

Political Trust

As described, Nokia's involvement in OSS is twofold. First, the company participates, uses, and develops upstream projects like GNOME. Second, Nokia created its own product-related Maemo. org website, which is aimed at encouraging the independent development of practical applications for Nokia's devices on the open basis. Since the Open Source movement is considered to be meritocratic and professionally oriented, the primary concerns and Nokia's actions were directed at gaining the necessary expertise. Meanwhile, acting according to traditional business public relations, Nokia started to advertise itself as a corporation seriously engaged in open co-operation. However, the political and expertise dimensions were in a way treated separately, although they both constitute necessary conditions for the trust-building relationship (see Figure 2).

It is important for people to trust in the company's motives and declarations. Here, the political trust issue reveals its importance. Nokia entered the Open Source world with a clear account. The gain of political trust was mostly a matter of keeping promises and maintaining coherent behaviour. Yet this was not always the case. The extensive public relations and workload efforts put into GNOME were to a large extent lost because of the top corporate decisions. Some were difficult to make not only for the external OSS projects, but also for the Nokia Open Source operations. In the political sense, the discrepancy between words and actions led to a loss of political trust and less and less positive feedback for any new corporate declarations of support.

Trust in Expertise

In order to be able to deal with the Open Source style of work, Nokia successfully recruited, employed, or subcontracted good developers—mostly those already working on the chosen projects. The company used their skills and reputations to gain expertise and trust in this expertise. Simply using this hiring strategy enabled Nokia to move

Figure 2. Two-dimensional taxonomy of trust in the open source-business setting

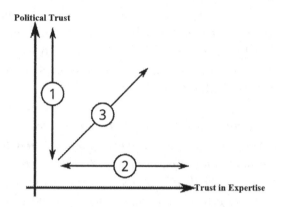

along the horizontal axis and gain—interpersonal in its character—trust in expertise (2) (see Figure 2). After all, OSS communities—particularly GNOME in this case—are focused on transparency and evaluation of individuals.

Combination of Political Trust and Trust in Expertise in the Ideal World

Trust in the Open Source setting is gained through long-term involvement, building both political trust and trust in one's expertise along arrow (3) on the graph (see Figure 2). Due to the common lack of political trust, the institutions of contracts and licences are used to ensure appropriate behaviour. They are detached from the personal or intra- and inter-organisational relations and relate to the higher social order and punishment mechanisms. Companies make sure that the responsibilities and consequences of not delivering the service are in place by introducing contracts. Similarly, Open Source developers are free to choose the license type for their code and by the law enforce the correct behaviour.

Both political trusts and trust in expertise have played important roles in GNOME. Nokia developers working on the Internet tablet project have mostly come from the upstream OSS communities; they have already gained trust and are respected in GNOME and Maemo.org. The trust in Nokia's people expertise is high in both cases, but there are differences in the political dimension. To a certain extent, in Maemo.org Nokia could ignore the political issues because it maintains almost total control over the projects. The trust discourse presented on Maemo.org and during summits and other meetings is a form of management of meaning. Nokia's public relations created a façade of trust despite having no real participation or inclusion of the community; meanwhile, Nokia's genuine opposition is hardly present or taken seriously.

CONCLUSION: TRUST AS A SUCCESS FACTOR IN OPEN INNOVATION

The empirical study of cognitive aspects of trust led to the formation of a two-dimensional taxonomy of trust. This model indicates the trust-related problems that business organisations face when switching from closed to open or hybrid innovation mode. It is not only important to show expertise and gain trust as professional contributors; it is equally important to be open and truthful in its declarations. When the political element is not fulfilled, the higher-level solutions are applied—here, in the form of trust in the legal system and/ or the exercise of power relations. This model leads to two conclusions. On the one hand, while Sztompka's (1999) argument was that in many cases the targets of trust are often combined and mutually dependant, trust relations at different levels can significantly differ and be quasi-independent. Meanwhile, several targets of trust must be conferred to enable the successful and satisfactory completion of all parties' collaboration. On the other hand, this study develops a discussion about the "trust on the Internet," going beyond

transaction-oriented concepts of trust, which deal with depersonalised and occasional contacts of unknown individuals or companies. Contrary to Hardin's (2006) conclusion that Internet relationships are typically narrowly focused and reflect commercial transactions, this chapter has shown that among online communities of collaborators valuable and long-term interactions can occur in which political and expertise targets of trust play a critical role. Furthermore, this study demonstrated that—in addition to institutional and social trust previously noted in online collaborations (Jarvenpaa, Knoll, & Leinder, 1998; Matzat, 2004)—the cognitive aspects of trust play an important role.

This research is highly relevant for practitioners, especially in business organisations that want to pursue Open Source but have no Open Source background. The discussion has outlined the potential dangers of talks / action decoupling strategies. The study is also informative for academics, showing that empirical investigations of trust need to be conducted at different levels of analysis and that those levels (sometimes) constitute different solutions to the same trust-related problem. Finally, it shows that the organisation's power position does not necessarily eliminate the possibility of building interpersonal trust.

On the other hand, this study has several limitations. First, it is based on a longitude study of only one company and two OSS projects. Therefore, without additional studies, the findings may be difficult to translate into more general conclusions. Second, the analysis concentrates primarily on written materials and interview transcripts and less on long-term observations and—because of the company's policy—totally lacks the researcher's participation in the internal Nokia-Open Source subcontractors work. The data contain a local understanding of trust. As this chapter aimed to provide insights into localised understanding of trust, without imposing theoretical concepts on the field of study, the interviewees were not directly asked about the trust relationship. However, it would be relevant to continue this research and explore other cases, comparing their results in order to identify similarities and differences. Finally, using different methodology that focused either on quantitative queries or on localised storytelling, would allow for new perspectives on the findings.

ACKNOWLEDGMENT

This research was conducted at the Copenhagen Business School and was partly funded by the Velux Fond, Denmark.

REFERENCES

Amin, A., & Roberts, J. (2008). *Community, economic creativity, and organization.* Oxford, UK: Oxford University Press. doi:10.1093/acpr of:oso/9780199545490.001.0001

Arrighetti, A., Bachmann, R., & Deakin, S. (1997). Contract law, social norms and inter-firm cooperation. *Cambridge Journal of Economics, 21*(2), 171–195. doi:10.1093/oxfordjournals.cje. a013665

Balog, T. (2007, March 5). Face-off: Should you trust your network to open source? Yes. *Network World.* Retrieved 11 October 2008 from http://www.networkworld.com

Bauer, R., & Koeszegi, S. T. (2003). Measuring the degree of virtualization. *The Electronic Journal for Virtual Organizations and Networks, 5.*

Calhoun, C. (1992). The infrastructure of modernity: Indirect social relationships, information technology, and social integration. In Haferkamp, H., & Smelser, N. (Eds.), *Social Change and Modernity* (pp. 205–236). Berkeley, CA: University of California Press.

Chesbrough, H. (2006). *Open innovation: The new imperative for creating and profiting from technology.* Boston, MA: Harvard Business School Press.

Ciesielska, M. (2010). *Hybrid organizations: A case of the open source-business setting.* Frederiksberg, Denmark: Copenhagen Business School Press.

Collins, C., & Smith, K. (2006). Knowledge exchange and combination: The role of human resource practices in the performance of high-technology firms. *Academy of Management Journal, 49*(3), 544–560. doi:10.5465/AMJ.2006.21794671

Dittrich, K. (2007). Nokia's strategic change by means of alliance networks: A case of adopting the open innovation paradigm? In Sangeetha, K., & Sivarajadhanavel, P. (Eds.), *Nokia Inc: A Global Mobile Leader.* Chennai, India: Icfai University Press.

Drazin, R., Glynn, M. A., & Kazanjian, R. K. (1999). Multilevel theorizing about creativity in Organizations: A sensemaking perspective. *Academy of Management Review, 24*(2), 286–307.

Faraj, S., & Wasko, M. M. (2001). *The web of knowledge: An investigation of knowledge exchange in networks of practice.* Retrieved from http://citeseerx.ist.psu.edu/viewdoc/summary?doi=10.1.1.12.4559

Gambetta, D. (1988). Can we trust trust? In Gambetta, D. (Ed.), *Making and Breaking Cooperative Relations* (pp. 213–237). Oxford, UK: Basil Blackwell Ltd.

Ghosh, R. A. (Ed.). (2006). *Study on the economic impact of open source software on innovation and the competitiveness of the information and communication technologies (ICT) sector in the EU: Final report.* Retrieved from http://ec.europa.eu/enterprise/ict/policy/doc/2006-11-20-flossimpact.pdf

Greenberg, P. S., Greendberg, R. H., & Antonucci, Y. L. (2007). Creating and sustaining trust in virtual teams. *Business Horizons, 50*, 325–333. doi:10.1016/j.bushor.2007.02.005

Greene, R. (2007, March 5). Face-off: Should you trust your network to open source? No. *Network World.* Retrieved 11 October 2008 from http://www.networkworld.com

Handy, C. (1995). Trust and the virtual organization. *Harvard Business Review, 73*, 44–50.

Hardin, R. (2002). *Trust and trustworthiness.* New York, NY: Russell Sage Foundation.

Hardin, R. (2006). *Trust.* Cambridge, UK: Polity Press.

Hardy, C., Phillips, N., & Lawrence, T. B. (2000). Distinguishing trust and power in interorganizational relations: forms and façades of trust. In Lane, C., & Bachmann, R. (Eds.), *Trust Within and Between Organizations* (pp. 64–87). Oxford, UK: Oxford University Press.

Harrison, A. (1998). In Linux we…trust? *Software Magazine, 18*(12), 32-42.

Hissam, S. A., Plakosh, D., & Weinstock, C. (2002). Trust and vulnerability in open source software. *IEE Proceedings. Software, 149*(1), 47–51. doi:10.1049/ip-sen:20020208

Ishaya, T., & Macaulay, L. (1999). The role of trust in virtual teams. *The Electronic Journal for Virtual Organizations and Networks, 1*, 140–157.

Iskoujina, Z. (2010). *Knowledge sharing in virtual organisations: The case of open source software communities.* PhD Dissertation. Durham, UK: Durham University.

Jaaksi, A. (2006). *Building consumer products with open source.* Retrieved from http://www.linuxdevices.com/articles/AT7621761066.html

Jaaksi, A. (2007). Experiences on product development with open source software. In J. Feller, B. Fitzgerald, W. Scacchi, & A. Sillitti (Eds.), *Open Source Development, Adoption and Innovation,* (pp. 85-96). Springer/IFIP.

Jarvenpaa, S. L., Knoll, K., & Leinder, D. E. (1998). Is anybody out there? Antecedents if trust in global virtual teams. *Journal of Management Information Systems, 14*(4), 29–64.

Jarvenpaa, S. L., & Leidner, D. E. (1999). Communication and trust in global virtual teams. *Organization Science, 10*, 791–815. doi:10.1287/orsc.10.6.791

Jarvenpaa, S. L., Shaw, T. R., & Staples, D. S. (2004). Toward contextualized theories of trust: The role of trust in global virtual teams. *Information Systems Research, 15*, 250–267. doi:10.1287/isre.1040.0028

Johnson, D., & Grayson, K. (2005). Cognitive and affective trust in service relationships. *Journal of Business Research, 58*(4), 500–507. doi:10.1016/S0148-2963(03)00140-1

Jones, K., & Leonard, L. N. K. (2008). Trust in consumer-to-consumer electronic commerce. *Information & Management, 45*, 88–95. doi:10.1016/j.im.2007.12.002

Kostera, M. (2005). *Antropologia organizacji: Metodologia badan terenowych* [Anthropology of organization: Methodology of field research]. Warsaw, Poland: PWN.

Kozinets, R. V. (1998). On netnography: Initial reflections on consumer investigations of cyberculture. In Alba, J., & Hutchinson, W. (Eds.), *Advances in Consumer Research* (*Vol. 25,* pp. 366–371). Provo, UT: Association for Consumer Research.

Kozinets, R. V. (2002). The field behind the screen: Using netnography for marketing research. *JMR, Journal of Marketing Research, 39*(1), 61–72. doi:10.1509/jmkr.39.1.61.18935

Kozinetz, R. V. (1997). I want to believe: 'A netnography of the x-files' subculture of consumption. *Advances in Consumer Research. Association for Consumer Research (U. S.), 24*, 470–475.

Kroeger, F. (2009). *The institutionalization of trust: Understanding the creation and collapse of escalating trust spirals in economic life.* Paper presented at the Annual Meeting of the SASE Annual Conference. Paris, France. Retrieved from http://www.allacademic.com/meta/p314382_index.html

Lane, C., & Bachmann, R. (2000). *Trust within and between organizations.* Oxford, UK: Oxford University Press.

Latusek, D. (2007). *Zaufanie i nieufnosc w relacji sprzedawca-nabywca w polskim sektorze IT.* [The trust and distrust in seller-buyer relation in the Polish IT sector]. Ph.D. Thesis. Warsaw, Poland: Wyzsza Szkola Przedsiebiorczosci i Zarzadzania im.

Lewis, J. D., & Weigert, A. (1985). Social atomism, holism, and trust. *The Sociological Quarterly, 26*(4), 455–471. doi:10.1111/j.1533-8525.1985.tb00238.x

Lewis, J. D., & Weigert, A. (1985). Trust as a social reality. *Social Forces, 63*, 967–985.

Lindström, M., & Janzon, E. (2007). Social capital, institutional (vertical) trust and smoking: A study of daily smoking and smoking cessation among ever smokers. *Scandinavian Journal of Public Health, 35*, 460. doi:10.1080/14034940701246090

Luhmann, N. (1979). *Trust and power: Two works.* New York, NY: Wiley.

Matzat, U. (2004). Cooperation and community on the internet: Past issues and present perspectives for theoretical-empirical internet research. *Analyse & Kritik, 26*, 63–90.

Mayer, R. C., Davis, J. H., & Schoorman, F. D. (1995). An inte- grative model of organizational trust. *Academy of Management Review, 20*, 709–734.

McAllister, D. J. (1995). Affect- and cognition-based trust as foundations for interpersonal cooperation in organizations. *Academy of Management Journal, 38*(1), 24–59. doi:10.2307/256727

Meyerson, D., Weick, K. E., & Kramer, R. M. (1996). Swift trust and temporary groups. In Kramer, R. M., & Tyler, T. R. (Eds.), *Trust in Organizations: Frontiers of Theory and Research* (pp. 166–195). Thousand Oaks, CA: Sage Publications.

Mishler, I. W., & Rose, R. (2001). What are the origins of political trust? Testing institutional and cultural theories in post-communist societies. *Comparative Political Studies, 34*(1), 30–62. doi:10.1177/0010414001034001002

Osterloh, M., & Rota, S. (2004). Trust and community in open source software production. *Analyse & Kritik, 26*, 279–301.

Pixley, J. (1999). Impersonal trust in global mediating organizations. *Sociological Perspectives, 42*(4), 647–671.

Roberts, J. (2000). From know-how to show-how? Questioning the role of information and communication technologies in knowledge transfer. *Technology Analysis and Strategic Management, 12*, 429–443. doi:10.1080/713698499

Roberts, J. (2003). Trust and electronic knowledge transfer. *International Journal of Electronic Business, 1*, 168–186. doi:10.1504/IJEB.2003.002172

Roberts, J. (2006). Limits to communities of practice. *Journal of Management Studies, 43*, 623–639. doi:10.1111/j.1467-6486.2006.00618.x

Shapiro, S. (1987). The social control of impersonal trust. *American Journal of Sociology*, *93*(3), 623–658. doi:10.1086/228791

Sharma, D. C. (2005, May 25). Nokia debuts Linux-based web device. *CNET News*. Retrieved from http://news.cnet.com/Nokia-debuts-Linux-based-Web-device/2100-1041_3-5720066.html

Spradley, J. P. (1979). *The ethnographic interview*. New York, NY: Holt, Rinehart and Winston.

Steil, A. V., Barcia, R. M., & Pacheco, R. C. S. (1999). An approach to learning in virtual organizations. *The Electronic Journal for Virtual Organizations and Networks*, *1*, 69–88.

Sydow, J. (2002). Understanding the constitution of interorganizational trust. In Lane, C., & Bachmann, R. (Eds.), *Trust Within and Between Organizations* (pp. 31–63). Oxford, UK: Oxford University Press.

Sztompka, P. (1999). *Trust: A sociological theory*. Cambridge, UK: Cambridge University Press.

Tsai, W., & Ghoshal, S. (1998). Social capital and value creation: The role of intrafirm networks. *Academy of Management Journal*, *41*, 12–20. doi:10.2307/257085

Uzzi, B. (1996). The sources and consequences of embeddedness for the economic performance of organizations: The network effect. *American Sociological Review*, *61*, 674–698. doi:10.2307/2096399

Weber, S. (2004). *The success of open source*. Boston, MA: Harvard University Press.

Westenholtz, A. (2009). Institutional entrepreneurs performing on meaning arenas: Transgressing institutional logics in two organizational fields. *Research in the Sociology of Organizations*, *27*, 283–311. doi:10.1108/S0733-558X(2009)0000027011

Westenholz, A. (2003). *Identity work in the fractures between open source communities and the economic world*. Working Paper No. 2003.16. Washington, DC: IOA/CBS.

Wiertz, C., & Ruyter, K. (2007). Online communities: Beyond the call of duty: Why customers contribute to firm-hosted commercial. *Organization Studies*, *28*, 347–376. doi:10.1177/0170840607076003

Xiong, L., & Liu, L. (2003). A reputation-based trust model for peer-to-peer ecommerce communities. In *Proceedings of the IEEE International Conference on E-Comerce (CEC 2003)*. IEEE Press.

Zaheer, A., McEvily, B., & Perrone, V. (1998). Does trust matter? Exploring the effects of interogranizational and interpersonal trust on performance. *Organization Science*, *9*(2), 141–159. doi:10.1287/orsc.9.2.141

ENDNOTES

[1] General Public Licence, one of the most common licences among Open Source Software developers.

[2] Data as of end of September each year, others as of end of December. All numbers in thousands USD.

[3] Similar to GNOME, an OSS project offering a user interface for Linux.

[4] See HelpOnSuperUser. Used for making full backups, software installation, language installation via SystemPagesSetup, etc; source: http://live.gnome.org/HelpOnConfiguration.

Chapter 3
Management of Virtual Teams and Capabilities in Business Networks

A.T. Juntunen
University of Helsinki, Finland

ABSTRACT

This chapter investigates and analyzes the management of capabilities in virtual teams in a business network context. This is a qualitative case study in the ICT-sector in Finland. This chapter will demonstrate that the organizations have a good chance to succeed if they can harness the external and internal knowledge and utilize the capabilities and knowledge in virtual teams to support organizational goals and strategies. It also illustrates the importance of trust in building and maintaining relationships. This chapter aims to contribute to the prior strategic management and business networks research.

INTRODUCTION

The relational and dynamic aspects of virtual teams in business networks and interdependence of network actors produce crucial, but insufficiently addressed, challenge for management. This chapter describes a new business development based on multiple business models and networks. In addition, a pioneering actor as the case organiza- tion in this study was, it had to develop specific managerial capabilities in order to be able to fine-tune the existing processes to adjust to new demands and market changes, to launch new services, and to advance from the development of basic technologies to the commercialization and marketing of ICT products and home commerce services. Its services included new technologies, like broadband, Internet, and mobile in Finland.

DOI: 10.4018/978-1-4666-1836-7.ch003

According to Henry Chesbrough (2006, pp. 45-52), firms need to leverage the abundance of knowledge outside their own companies to be successful. Furthermore, recent years have shown an exceptional growth in demand for inter-organizational collaboration (Achrol & Kotler, 1999; Brandenburger & Nalebuff, 1996; Gulati, 1998; Hagedoorn, 1990, 1995; Powell, et al., 1996; Spekman, et al., 2000) resulting from the rapid pace of technology development along with the dispersion of knowledge and technological resources. To be competitive and survive in a network economy, companies need technological knowledge and resources to develop products and processes. Specifically, they need to connect their organization through vertical and horizontal networking strategies to other market players in order to gain new knowledge and innovations beyond their immediate organizational boundaries (Håkansson & Snehota, 1995; Kogut & Zander, 1997; Powell, et al., 1996; Teece, et al., 1997; Teece, 2000). These different forms of interorganizational collaborations consist of supplier and marketing or distribution networks, technological-innovation and product-development networks, and various competitive alliances used, for example, to establish industry standards (Ford, et al., 2002; Frels, et al., 2003; Möller & Halinen, 1999).

New business creation is not an independent, isolated process but a collective process that requires interaction and cooperation with other actors. It involves the establishment and maintenance of a network of relationships with other organizations including suppliers, competitors, and customers (cf. Håkansson & Snehota, 1995). It also involves creation and maintenance of capabilities needed in management and production of services. Over and above the managerial challenges inherent in a business creation, high-tech firms, like in this case study, face unique challenges due to technology-driven services and markets. These firms need to cope with exceptionally short product life cycles in the face of fast changing technology

and R&D-partnerships are often used for creating new technological platforms and dominant solutions (Blomqvist, 2002; Möller & Rajala, 1999). Therefore, an understanding the management of resultant business relationships and capabilities needed has become a critical factor determining success in contemporary business. This study will demonstrate that the business development and success in this case study was based on adaptive and adjusting virtual teams and management of different business networks. It also discusses of what kind of network management capabilities were needed in virtual team management. This is a qualitative, longitudinal, single case study in the ICT-sector in Finland. This chapter aims to contribute to the prior strategic management and business networks research.

BACKGROUND AND KEY TERMS

The research builds on the prior strategic management literature, Resource-Based View of the firm (RBV), economic sociology and social networks research, and industrial network approach by examining the previous research of strategic management and business networks. This section will also present the concept definitions used in this chapter.

There is a vast amount of previous research of business networks, and therefore, this chapter presents only the most relevant ones in this chapter. The amount of literature also results in multiple concept definitions, like the researchers in strategic management and Resource-Based View (RBV) (See e.g. Brandenburger & Nalebuff, 1996; Jarillo, 1993; Parolini, 1999) consider networks strategic networks and value nets, whereas economic sociology and social networks research (Powell, et al., 1996) and industrial network approach (e.g. Håkansson & Ford, 2002; Håkansson & Snehota, 1995) argue the character and evolution of business networks.

In the recent research, business networks are defined as a set of relationships between companies where they engage in multiple two-way relationships to bring products and services to the market (e.g. Aldrich, 1998; Parolini, 1999).

Moreover, during the last decade, we have seen an enormous growth in organizational collaboration and creation of business networks with multiple goals like, for example, R&D, competitive alliances, distribution channel networks, and buyer-supplier configurations (see e.g. Achrol & Kotler, 1999; Amit & Zott, 2001; Cartwright & Oliver, 2000; de Man, 2004; Frels, Shervani, & Srivastava, 2003; Gulati, 1998; Powell, Koput, & Smith-Doerr, 1996; Spekman, Isabella, & MacAvoy, 2000; Srinivasan, Lilien, & Rangaswamy, 2006).

Achrol (1997) argued that one of the critical changes in the 21st century is from dyadic business relationships towards multi-actor value-creating business networks. The network perspective implies that the actors in business networks are interconnected and interacting with each other in value creation (Ford, Gadde, Håkansson, & Snehota, 2003; Brass, Galaskiewicz, Greve, & Tsai, 2004).

Virtual organizations are an example of short-term networks. Usually these virtual organizations are combined for certain activities or projects, like product development. The reliance on virtual interaction increases the availability of combined new knowledge for the members of inter-organizational R&D projects located physically apart, like in virtual teams of this case study. In knowledge management, the concept of combination is a process of merging diverse explicit knowledge items into more complex and systemic sets of explicit knowledge. It involves gathering, combining, disseminating, editing, and storing of explicit knowledge. It is often characterized by virtual interaction (Mohrman, et al., 2003; Nonaka & Konno, 1998; Nonaka & Takeuchi, 1995), like in the virtual teams of this case study.

A hub company in this study depicts an organization that gives direction and goals for the business network, negotiates roles in the network, and decides of the structure of the network. Ritter, Wilkinson, and Johnston (2004) argued that no single hub could provide direction or control to any network. However, many studies consider that it is possible for a single firm to manage networks (see e.g. Dyer, 1996; Dyer & Nobeoka, 2000; Dyer & Singh, 1998, 2000; Lorenzoni & Lipparini, 1999).

The previous research on business models rests in many respects on strategy discussion and draws on strategic concepts and issues (see e.g. Osterwalder, 2004; Tikkanen, et al., 2005). The business model defines the portion of the value that the business creates internally (Chesbrough, 2006b, p. 177), and what part of the business is either outsourced, or created and delivered by the other network partners. According to Chesborough (2006a, 2006b), the firm's R&D projects can be launched internally or externally, and new knowledge and information can enter the project in its various stages. He labeled this model as an open innovation because there are many ways how the new ideas and knowledge can flow into the process and many ways of how it can flow out into the market. Open innovation concept includes the transition from traditional closed, internal innovation process towards open innovation using external partners and exploiting external knowledge in creating new business or products and services. These external partners and knowledge sources can be constant partners in a jointly agreed business network or they can be temporary sources of information and knowledge for the companies. In addition, to be competitive and survive in a network economy, companies need diversified knowledge and resources to develop new and innovative products and processes. Specifically, they need to connect their organization through vertical and horizontal networking strategies to other market players in order to gain new knowledge beyond their immediate organizational boundaries (Håkansson & Snehota, 1995; Kogut & Zander, 1997; Powell, et al., 1996; Teece, et al., 1997). In Teece's (1986) view, the firm must bear the responsibility for how best to harness innovation opportunities and be profitable.

Trust and dependence are elementary qualities in relationships in business networks. Some level of trust is a necessary condition for all repeated interorganizational transactions (Ring & Van de Ven, 1992; Das & Teng, 1998), and as a relationship develops further, the interdependence between the partners is likely to increase (Pfeffer & Salancik, 1978). However, the growing dependence can lead to partner's opportunistic behavior, the magnitude of expected coordination costs, and the challenges of the relationship coordination (Gulati & Singh, 1998; Krishnan, et. al., 2006).

A business model is defined here as a system for products, services or their portfolio, including a description of business actors and their roles, relationships, resources and activities in a value network, with the aim of creating maximum value throughout the network. The business model ties together the elements of business strategy and business processes (see Osterwalder, 2004; Rajala, Rossi, & Tuunainen, 2003). In addition, the business model is said to be a concept of business, defining business-specific characteristics and sources of revenue. It specifies where the company is positioned within a specific business in its configured value-creating network (see e.g. Rajala, Tuunainen, & Korri, 2001). It also consists of an organization's own dynamic, interrelated capabilities as well as other external resources. In addition, the business model contains control and governance enabling capabilities to constantly maintain and reinvent itself in order to meet the objectives of network members and stakeholders and to satisfy customers. Interaction between actors in a business network generates an integrated value creation expressed as a business model. Besides creating benefits, interaction between actors can also be demanding and nonprofitable, and therefore sometimes hinder access to other business opportunities.

RESEARCH STRATEGY AND METHODOLOGY

The following sections will describe the case organization, the organization, and management of virtual teams in multiple business models and networks.

In order to capture the creation dynamics of a new business and processual changes, a longitudinal study was required in a field that is characterized by technological and commercial change and uncertainty. The ICT sector and the multimedia and Internet-driven business were seen to match well the requirements of both technological and commercial turbulence. Part of this study is based on a longitudinal study in 1990-2003 made in Elisa (see Juntunen, 2005). However, an additional study was made for this chapter to update the facts. The timeframe of this study is 1990-2007. A longitudinal, single case study method was chosen because examination of the case over very long periods, assisted in identifying patterns of change that otherwise might have been missed. This method also helped to capture the complexity of the structural dynamics within a network context, particularly in a field that is characterized by technological and commercial change and uncertainty (Huber & Van de Ven, 1995).

The focal business (HCB) and managers were studied for a period of 19 years. This time span helped to capture the evolutional and intentional development of managerial capabilities in collaborative networks and virtual team management leading to new business development.

Research documentation in this case study consists of both information about the telecommunication industry and HCB's development during the period under study. About twenty persons representing various business units and Elisa's subsidiaries of and cooperating partners were interviewed during the period of 1999-2007. Data gathered consists of articles, project documents, e-mails between members of the projects, memorandums concerning strategy and business plans and annual reports from the years 1990-2007. Even if majority of the material came from HCB- and Elisa-based sources, this does not diminish the value of the conceptualized findings, however. It can be claimed that the conceptualized findings have more general relevance, particularly for firms operating in dynamic, rapidly changing fields characterized by several interlinked technologies. It is also claimed that this relevance reaches beyond the limited historical period. Of the research method and research design (see e.g. Miles & Huberman, 1994; Yin, 1994).

Description of the Case Organization

Based on the brief literature review and the author's experience of the ICT-sector, this section first describes the case organization. The case organization is the business group called the Home Commerce Business Group (HCB), and it is a business group within Elisa Corporation. HCB launched several industry projects with its network partners to develop user interface technologies, modular technology platforms, design platforms for wireless products, service platforms for broadband technologies, 4G systems and system concepts, hardware for wireless data gathering, as well as software for managing digital content. HCB started in 1995 with multiple R&D projects and developed to a unit with multiple business models and different technology platforms and solutions that were used in different business units in Elisa. HCB's business networks and process development changed over the years due to technologies, like broadband, Internet and mobile. It also describes how HCB developed their managerial practices in their different networks. HCB is part of Elisa.

Elisa is a leading Finnish communications and ICT solutions company offering a comprehensive range of communications services, including voice and data services, connections to the Internet, customized ICT solutions and network operator services. Elisa started in 1882 in Helsinki, Finland.

It has the longest telecommunication history in Finland. Elisa is a forerunner of new mobile and content services (Elisa's annual report 2006). Its core business areas are the fixed network and the mobile network including Internet-based services (Juntunen, 2005). Elisa operates in Finland and in carefully selected international market areas, and provides international services in association with its partners, Vodafone and Telenor (Elisa's annual report 2006).

By the end of 2007, Elisa's 3G network covered 75 percent of Finland's population and was the best network in terms of coverage and reception. Elisa has an approximate market share of 50 per cent of 3G users. The fact that Elisa exceeded the limit of one million 3G customers proved that allowing bundling had a positive effect on Elisa's overall market development. The basic figures, i.e. turnover and the number of employees, of the case corporation changed during the timeframe of 1990-2007. The amount of personnel was 3,000 in 2007 as it was also in 1990 (Elisa's annual report 2007). However, in 1990, the turnover was roughly 800 M€[1] when in 2007 the turnover was about 1.57 billion. The highest amount of employees were in the year 2000 about 8000 employees and the turnover in 2000 was about 1,500 M€. This shows the hype of ICT-sector in the middle and late 1990s and the burst of the "IT-bubble" in early 2000s with the decrease in the number of employees.

Management and Organization

HCB had a leading edge in home networking in 1990s but it was facing growing competition by the start of 2000. The case organization had known when to pursue small markets aggressively, such as the future home in the mid 1990s, rather than substantial markets, and when to allocate capital to projects that did not promise the best returns at first. Indeed, this pioneer spirit differentiated Elisa and HCB from the main competitors who either missed the opportunity or entered the business late. HCB engaged in strategic conduct that was more typical to pure Internet startups: the rise of dominant design, a focus on specific products and services, and an acceleration of R&D-process innovation, with costs of process changes remaining modest. To maintain its position as the pre-eminent provider of the new technology-based home commerce services and security services in Finland, HCB had to continue to enhance both content and site services and further diversify revenues, achieving cost savings through process redesign in order to remain dynamically efficient in the future and excel in attracting and keeping capable employees in its virtual teams.

The strategic management of HCB was in the hands of the same person who had started this business in the early R&D-projects in 1990s, Timo Simula. He had also led the development process of HCB since it started in 1995. He controlled and coordinated the direction of the business and was responsible for the strategy and profitability of business as a whole.

The operational management was in the hands of Sami Masala, who was manager of the whole Mega-concept and responsible for long-term technological and business assessments. HCB's management also regularly reviewed their operating plans, in particular the phases of ongoing projects and proposals. They also made recommendations for procedural and organizational changes where they considered it necessary or essential for the business. They had quarterly reviews of their business plans with Elisa's senior management.

The personal relationships of HCB's management were based on trust, an important factor in the formation of the networks. It was also a basis in the commencement of cooperation between network actors. Besides an economic or technological connection to the network, good social connections between the network actors as well as within HCB and its external and internal contacts were also considered essential.

The outsourcing of certain activities required managerial contracting capabilities to control the outsourced activities, to manage processes to gain the full value of specialization for the network, to gain flexibility and more strategic value. It also required a managerial capability not only to make operational changes quickly but also to sculpt customer offerings via a network of actors involved in service-production and delivery.

The different project teams within HCB became the organizational repository of knowledge of integrated technologies and systems, providing continuity in corporate business development. Superior technology integration was seen to be a critical element for future success. The technology-related information and knowledge base expanded within Elisa Corporation and HCB as a direct consequence of the R&D-networking. Intensified collaboration strengthened knowledge of markets and competitors and made it easier to assess one's own capabilities and knowledge in comparison to existent market and product scenarios.

The following sections describe how the coordination and governance was executed. It also exemplifies the managerial capabilities needed and created in the virtual teams serving the different business networks.

Business Models

This section will describe the business models managed by HCB during the years of this study.

Dynamically changing competitive environments such as the ICT-sector require and provide opportunities for more than one business model. As the environment changes, different models offering diverse customer value propositions are more compatible to changing situations. By continually changing their business models, thereby challenging organizational rules and creating new industry standards, HCB managed to keep ahead of the competition. In this way, they tried to proactively shape and build the future to which they aspired. They attempted to avoid the traditional planning method they had seen in Elisa Corporation and its main competitors because they considered

Table 1. HCB's business models

The description cooperative business network	The business models
A-net: a virtual city of Helsinki	An information service -portal, a virtual community -portal service
Nettiplus: the customer self-service platform for certain specific products	A self-service portal
Mega-concept's business nets: smart home services, intelligent home network solutions, billing and service platform, customer access platform to different networks, including fixed-line, mobile, broadband, multimedia and Internet networks	A home networking and service portal, A virtual community, A collaboration platform, A third party marketplace (meaning a common marketing front end and the provision of transaction support to multiple businesses), A value chain integrator
Efodi: an e-learning portal, a virtual community for teachers, students, publishers and schools	An e-learning portal, A virtual community, A value chain integrator
Emma: an online music portal; Emma integrated value chains of music producers to related music materials and online banking services in e-business.	An online music portal, A value chain integrator
Chinchilla	An e-payment portal, An e-business transaction rating platform
Mobile Payment: an e/m-payment portal. It also integrated the value chains of different parties and industries including telecommunication companies, IT-companies and finance sector's actors.	An e-/m-.payment portal, mobile-Internet service delivery, A value chain integrator

that it hindered organizational development by promoting strategies that repeated past strategies undertaken by others. Adopting and conforming to existing internal boundaries might have caused HCB to overlook both business opportunities and threats arising in a knowledge-intensive, interconnected competitive environment. Moreover, HCB was able to detect and develop elementary technological and business enabling capabilities that could be used to develop, create, provide, and coordinate a changing array of products and product-platforms.

To create and develop new business models required visioning and managerial capabilities. HCB's different business models are described in Table 1. All these business models included both internal and external partners. Internal partners were from different subsidiaries or corporate units. The external partners were from different industries or public sector agencies. These different business models were based on collaborative business networks.

Coordination and Governance through Different Meetings

The coordination and governance of technology and service architecture as well as the related contracts was complex because there were many internal and external parties involved. In addition, coordination across organizational boundaries and the integration of different business processes was challenging. The coordination of a technical architectural platform required managerial capabilities that could divide the activities needed to be performed into defined processes and into appropriate, that is, case-by-case judged written contracts.

The governance and communication channels needed could be broken down into the following elements described in the next sections.

HCB's Management team was responsible for service acquisition and integration, coordination and evaluation. They were responsible for ensuring that the contracts signed were followed and that outsourced activities were done according to agreements. In addition, they were responsible for seeing that HCB fulfilled its own part of the contract according to agreements made. The corporate senior management was responsible for corporate level changes and decisions. The Information Management was accountable for corporate level changes and decisions regarding IT/IS and data security issues. The corporate legal team was responsible for producing initial drafts of contracts, assessing, reviewing, commenting, and/or approving business contracts made. The Human Resources Department was responsible of creating and maintaining the internal Knowledge Management (KM)-network. The KM-network was responsible of efficient knowledge sharing and transfer within the corporation between different departments and subsidiaries. The Product Management was responsible for the commercialization of products and services. In addition, the customer service team was responsible for customer service and billing issues. The customers included the pilot, potential, and existing (old) customers. The customers were either individuals or organizations. The partner organizations in business and R&D networks were responsible for the delivery and maintenance of commonly agreed activities in their contracts.

HCB's management created own coordination style and processes. Some formal meetings were held with the senior management of the case corporation and the corporate Research Center as well as with the corporate-level R&D networks. In addition, there were also theme-based meetings with the KM-network's members. Examples included information regarding the managerial practices of a new business, new technologies and their possibilities within a learning context or recruitment because HCB was seen as the most attractive new, growing business and R&D sector within the case corporation.

Besides, the formal and theme based meetings there were also regular, weekly meetings with Product Management (PM) in order to find out customers' needs, complaints or new development suggestions, meetings relating to ongoing projects, meetings with current and potential partners and also monthly meetings with the middle managers of different departments and units. There were also product/service related meetings with potential, piloting, and existing customers to boost the selling of new services.

Virtual Teams

HCB's partnering teams did not form fixed, hierarchical organizational structures. The teams were virtual, changeable, and flexible according to business needs. They were formed so that there was always a development manager for a certain area of the business, with expertise in a certain industry, who gathered his own resources from the available project managers, marketing assistants, and technology experts. The partnering team then contacted the appropriate sections of the other organization to initiate cooperation and to fulfill the activities needed.

The business manager controlled the whole business chain and processes. The business manager coordinated and controlled the cross-functional activities between the partnering teams and industries involved. He also created future business scenarios together with the case corporation Research Center and with the Head of Development (manager of HCB).

After product development was terminated, the switch between R&D and Product Management (PM) teams was planned according to the R&D process. Some activities of the R&D process would be performed in-house and some outsourced to external partners with specific capabilities and resources. The division of what to perform in-house and what were given to the partners depended on the service and product in question. If the activity or knowledge was considered important for retaining or creating the competitive advantage then it was performed in-house.

Product Management was responsible for the product and service maintenance, the recording, and correction of the errors found in existing products, making new versions of products and packaging products with other products. Product Management also assessed new products and tested them before launching them on to the market. The Product Management was continuously in contact with customer service networks and with HCB's product development. It also planned and followed marketing campaigns together with the corporate marketing unit.

The products and platforms developed in HCB were used as platform products or as part of services in many different business units within the corporation.

Many times the same persons were critical having crucial knowledge of specific technology or service, and therefore, the teams swapped the key members between the teams. This also assisted in knowledge transfer, mentoring of junior members of the teams and creating a larger knowledge base of the services and technologies. In addition, this study concludes that teams with extensive prior collaboration experience with their partner were able to upgrade and develop deeper collaboration-relationship than unfamiliar partners. The swapping of senior team members between teams assisted in the upgrading of the collaboration process.

Capability Development

The capabilities developed and needed in this business network development in 1990-2007 related to the business, technology, organization, actors, and the business network as an entity.

Technology-related capabilities and knowledge gained included the integration of technologies and e-business–facilities. Project-related capabilities and knowledge consisted of the management of multiple projects, the necessity for the provision of different contracts according to partner or project and project planning within the business context.

Business-related capabilities and knowledge incorporated negotiation capabilities, competencies related to e-business and associated processes, business strategy and planning, business modeling including the creation of a business concept, Human Resources Management (HRM) and leadership skills.

Network-related capabilities and knowledge included how to coordinate the network's activities and how to orchestrate the actors towards common goals.

Actor-related capabilities and knowledge consisted of industry-related knowledge, knowledge of different actors' organizations and skills and resources related knowledge.

Moreover, HCB had to be capable of developing strong communication channels with all levels in the case corporation because they had to motivate acceptance of their R&D-projects and business concepts. They did this by regular and theme-based meetings with different levels of internal partners, mangers and external partners and customers. Besides developing the communication channels, HCB's personnel and particularly managers needed good communication skills. Their strong vision involved also sidestepping the usual organization channels and working directly with partners and with whomever was a suitable partner from their point of view. HCB's managers were also capable of creating an atmosphere that encouraged creativity, independency, and experimentation.

Managerial capabilities were needed to organize relationships and orchestrate-actors. The more traditional managerial capabilities included personnel management (HRM), business process planning, budgeting, and strategy development.

In summary, managerial capabilities needed and developed can be divided into two groups: The network level managerial capabilities included the mobilization of network actors, the control of information flow between actors, the contract management of actors in varied roles and of difference importance within a network, collective strategy planning, and the coordination of internal and external resources. The business level managerial capabilities included personnel management (HRM), internal resource management, internal cooperation, business strategy planning, and product strategy planning and budgeting. In addition, dynamic organizational capabilities created involved both new learning and the renewal of existing capabilities.

Challenges

Different alliances, business nets, R&D forums, and large-scale project networks provided different types of learning experiences. This, on the other hand, lead to variations in the contracting used for coordinating and managing relationships in the emerging business nets. In brief, they provided broad knowledge of the collaboration and partnering-related demands in HCB's network environment.

HCB realized that they should be careful especially with relationships characterized by low interfirm trust and deep dependence between partners due to possible opportunistic behavior. They observed opportunistic behavior in their first business networks until they learned how to manage the business networks and their partners. The increase of mutual trust building within the network and decrease the interdependence between the network-members were the main solutions discovered. Mutual trust building required the following: information sharing, long-term commitment, and repeated interaction between the hub and the other actors in the business network.

The Innovative Services and Technology Adaptation

Several of the business networks outlined in Table 1 were based around innovative services, enabled by the very high rates of technology adoption in Finland. The basis for the high technology development and technology innovations in Finland was laid down over decades, and Finnish public and private R&D organizations have invested heavily in ICT and the concept of information society (See Castells & Himanen, 2002). Even if the ICT industry's productivity and innovation capability is good, the service productivity, especially in public services, is not that high, because the low use of high-tech in for example, in the health care area. The Finnish ICT companies, such as Nokia and the case company, are more capable of adapting new ideas and to commercialize new technologies to new, innovative services by using the resources of their business networks and efficient in orchestrating their networks. Some of the business networks outlined in Table 1 included public sector actors like for example, A-net. The public-private partnerships enhance the technology adaptation and inventing new innovative services in public sector.

In addition, this chapter concluded that HCB acquired knowledge in the formation of new business and product ideas by gathering information from various internal and external sources by using virtual teams and dynamic networking and maximizing the usage of internal and the external resources in creating new products and services. This supports previous studies in open innovation (Chesbrough, 2006a, 2006b; Laursen & Salter, 2006) and organizational learning (Cyert & March, 1963; Nonaka & Konno, 1998; Nonaka & Takeutchi, 1995). Orchestrating the virtual teams can lead to the renewal of organization and its processes (cf. Lambert & Cooper, 2000, p. 75). The business renewal can happen in multiparty projects, like in this case study, through new knowledge and incremental innovations in the existing value system (See Möller, 2011; Möller & Rajala, 2007)

SUMMARY

This chapter set out to explore the management and organization of virtual teams in a business network context by creating and maintaining certain network capabilities. The results of this study suggest that various technologies and partner-specific capabilities are necessary. However, the network-management capabilities may play key role in determining the degree to which it is possible for a company to learn to improve their managerial skills, and how they can manage their inter-organizational business models and networks better than before.

This study contributes to the emerging body of literature on managing business networks and strategic management as well as RBV research (see, for instance, Achrol & Kotler, 1999; Amit & Zott, 2001; Cartwright & Oliver, 2000; de Man, 2004; Frels, Shervani, & Srivastava, 2003; Gulati, 1998; Powell, Koput, & Smith-Doerr, 1996; Spekman, Isabella, & MacAvoy, 2000; Srinivasan, Lilien, & Rangaswamy, 2006) by emphasizing the importance of the virtual team management in the management practices of alliances developing new businesses.

When considering the development of HCB and its business networks, which managed to create some of the top-selling products and service platforms of today, then perhaps the first successful strategic action of the senior management in the 1990s, was to set up this HCB. This separate group was compact enough to be driven by small gains and was not constrained by the parent's organizational norms and rigid hierarchical rules. During the years from 1998 to 2000, Elisa's senior management firmly believed in the commercial success of these new technologies and the new services based on them. This confidence assisted HCB in the achievement of its goals. The experience gained in many projects assisted in the creation of the successful business models. The senior management kept allocating resources to HCB through the late 1990s. HCB did not have major difficulties in finding financing for its projects from either inside the corporation or from the national or European level technology funds. The numerous R&D projects and different collabora-

tive forms completed from 1990 to 2003 provided insight and direction, suggesting the types of new knowledge, resources, and capabilities required when constructing architecture based on new enabling technologies such as multimedia, Internet, and broadband.

The most important success factor contributing to HCB's success in a new business development in a networked environment was the efficient management and operation of the business processes, organization of virtual teams in business service development. In addition, to survive in the fast-changing environment the HCB as "an adaptive organization" (Radjou, et al., 2006) were more like a shifting "constellation" (Mintzberg, 1979; Toffler, 1985) that had linkages (Pinfield, et al., 1974) with its decentralized organizational units. These linkages were for example linked organizational groups like functional teams, cross-functional teams, special task forces or project teams. The adaptive organization in this chapter is a networked organization with internal and external partners and flexible decision processes (cf. Möller, et al., 2005; Juntunen, 2010).

The governance and coordination of resources required both formal managerial processes and flexibility in executing business operations. The coordination of activities necessary to forbear or transfer skills and the establishment of the prerequisite communication channels is a dynamic capability that varies across organizations (cf. Vonortas, 2000). Technology within the HCB business should be seen as an enabler that influenced strategies, business models, processes and activities (cf. Sawhney, Gulati, Paoni, & Kellog Tech Venture Team, 2001). The more complicated the business environment became and the more complex the technology architecture was, the greater the need was for effective managerial processes. The various business and R&D -networks, contacts, products and services of the various actors from different industries created requirements for divergent knowledge and capabilities. An effective coordination structure was needed in order to manage all the internal and external resources.

As a summary, the development of mutual trust in business networks supported the previous studies (see e.g. Jarimo, et. al., 2005; Pajunen, 2006). Consistent with the findings of Doz (1996) and also Doz and Hamel (1998) this study reveals that the learning and the transfer of knowledge are seen necessary for a successful development of network relationships through evolutionary cycles over time. Moreover, according to Mintzberg, Ahlstrand, and Lampel (1998, pp. 175-231) in professional organizations that operate in highly complex environments, collective learning is necessary as the knowledge required to create strategy is widely dispersed, and further, organizations facing new situations usually have to engage in a process of learning in order to understand emerging change as exemplified by the introduction of technological breakthroughs like the Internet and mobile-technologies.

This study provided new insights regarding practical business management within a network context. As this study was conducted from the focal actor's (the hub organization's) perspective, the most important area of practical business management that this study has contributed to is the development and maintenance of knowledge base and capability pool within the HCB.

FUTURE RESEARCH DIRECTIONS

The objectives of this study provide interesting objectives that permits more exploration. This study is subject to a number of limitations. First, it has been argued that knowledge creation processes are highly sensitive to the pervasive effect of culture (see, for instance, Glisby & Holden, 2003). Therefore, the future studies should also consider the importance of organizational culture as well as the impact of international teams and different nationalities with their own cultural

impact. Moreover, the empirical part of the study covered only on single longitudinal case study in the Finnish ICT sector. The empirical data was limited, and therefore, the further research should include a development of a managerial tool to assist the creation of the interfirm relationship and capability management in complex business networks. In addition, the operationalization of technological and business specific knowledge conversion processes are complex and therefore require more attention in future studies.

REFERENCES

Achrol, R. S. (1997). Changes in the theory of interorganizational relations in marketing: Toward a network paradigm. *Journal of the Academy of Marketing Science*, *25*(1), 56–71. doi:10.1007/BF02894509

Achrol, R. S., & Kotler, P. (1999). Marketing in the network economy. *Journal of Marketing*, *63*, 146–163. doi:10.2307/1252108

Aldrich, D. (1998). The new value chain. *Informationweek*, *700*, 278–281.

Blomqvist, K. (2002). *Partnering in the dynamic environment: The role of trust in asymmetric technology partnership formation*. Lappeenranta, Sweden: Lappeenranta University of Technology.

Brandenburger, A. M., & Nalebuff, B. J. (1996). *Co-opetition*. New York, NY: Doubleday.

Brass, D. J., Galaskiewicz, J., Greve, H. R., & Tsai, W. (2004). Taking stock of networks and organizations: A multilevel perspective. *Academy of Management Journal*, *47*(6), 795–817. doi:10.2307/20159624

Cartwright, S. D., & Oliver, R. W. (2000). Untangling the value web. *The Journal of Business Strategy*, *21*(1), 22–27. doi:10.1108/eb040055

Castells, M., & Himanen, P. (2002). *The information society and the welfare state: The Finnish model.* Oxford, UK: Oxford University Press. doi:10.1093/acprof:oso/9780199256990.001.0001

Chesborough, H. (2006a). *Open innovation: A new paradigm for understanding industrial innovation.* Paper presented at IMIO. New York, NY.

Chesborough, H. (2006b). *Open innovation: Researching a new paradigm.* Oxford, UK: Oxford University Press.

Chesborough, H. (2006c). *Open business models: How to thrive in the new innovation landscape.* Oxford, UK: Oxford University Press.

Cyert, R., & March, J. (1963). *A behavioral theory of the firm.* Englewood Cliffs, NJ: Prentice Hall.

de Man, A.-P. (2004). *The network economy: Strategy, structure and management.* Cheltenham, UK: Edward Elgar.

Eisenhardt, K. (1989). Building theories from case study research. *Academy of Management Review, 14*(4), 532–550.

Ford, D., Gadde, L.-E., Håkansson, H., & Snehota, I. (2003). *Managing business relationships.* Chichester, UK: John Wiley & Sons Ltd.

Frels, J. K., Shervani, T., & Srivastava, R. K. (2003). The integrated networks model: Explaining resource allocations in network markets. *Journal of Marketing, 67,* 29–45. doi:10.1509/jmkg.67.1.29.18586

Glisby, M., & Holden, N. (2003). Contextual constraints in knowledge management theory: The cultural embeddedness of Nonaka's knowledge creating company. *Knowledge and Process Management, 10*(1), 29–36. doi:10.1002/kpm.158

Gulati, R. (1998). Alliances and networks. *Strategic Management Journal, 19*(4), 293–317. doi:10.1002/(SICI)1097-0266(199804)19:4<293::AID-SMJ982>3.0.CO;2-M

Gulati, R., & Singh, H. (1998). The architecture of cooperation: Managing coordination costs and appropriation concerns in strategic alliances. *Administrative Science Quarterly, 43*(4), 781–814. doi:10.2307/2393616

Hagedoorn, J. (1990). Organizational modes of inter-firm co-operation and technology transfer. *Technovation, 10*(1), 17–30. doi:10.1016/0166-4972(90)90039-M

Hagedoorn, J. (1995). Strategic technology partnering during the 1980s: Trends, networks and corporate patterns in non-core technologies. *Research Policy, 24*(2), 207–231. doi:10.1016/0048-7333(94)00763-W

Håkansson, H., & Ford, D. (2002). How should companies interact in business environments. *Journal of Business Research, 55,* 133–139. doi:10.1016/S0148-2963(00)00148-X

Håkansson, H., & Snehota, I. (Eds.). (1995). *Developing relationships in business networks.* London, UK: Routledge.

Hooley, G., Broderick, A., & Möller, K. (1998). Competitive positioning and the resource-based view of the firm. *Journal of Strategic Marketing, 6*(2), 97–116. doi:10.1080/09652549800000003

Huber, G. P., & Van de Ven, A. H. (Eds.). (1995). *Longitudinal field research methods: Studying processes of organizational change.* Thousand Oaks, CA: SAGE Publications Inc.

Jarillo, J. C. (1993). *Strategic networks: Creating the borderless organization.* Oxford, UK: Butterworth-Heinemann.

Jarimo, T., Pulkkinen, U., & Salo, A. (2005). Encouraging suppliers to process innovations: A game theory approach. *International Journal of Technology Intelligence and Planning, 1*(4), 403–423. doi:10.1504/IJTIP.2005.008590

Juntunen, A. (2005). *The emergence of a new business through collaborative networks: A longitudinal study in the ICT sector*. Hershey, PA: IGI Global.

Juntunen, A. (2010). Developing efficient processes and network management in new business creation in the ICT-sector. In Wang, M., & Sun, Z. (Eds.), *Handbook of Research on Complex Dynamic Process Management: Techniques for Adaptability in Turbulent Environments*. Hershey, PA: IGI Global.

Kogut, B., & Zander, U. (1997). Knowledge of the firm, combinative capabilities, and the replication of technology. In Foss, N. J. (Ed.), *Resources, Fims and Strategies – A Reader in the Resource-Based Perspective*. Oxford, UK: Oxford University Press. doi:10.1287/orsc.3.3.383

Krishnan, R., Martin, X., & Noorderhaven, N. (2006). When does trust matter to alliance performance? *Academy of Management Journal, 49*(5), 894–917. doi:10.5465/AMJ.2006.22798171

Lambert, D., & Cooper, M. (2000). Issues in supply chain management. *Industrial Marketing Management, 29*(1), 65–83. doi:10.1016/S0019-8501(99)00113-3

Laursen, K., & Salter, A. (2006). Open for innovation: The role of openness in explaining innovation performance among UK manufacturing firms. *Strategic Management Journal, 27*(2), 131–150. doi:10.1002/smj.507

Leblebici, H., Salancik, G. R., Copay, A., & King, T. (1991). Institutional change and the transformation of interorganizational fields: An organizational history of the US radio broadcasting industry. *Administrative Science Quarterly, 36*(3), 333–363. doi:10.2307/2393200

Mintzberg, H. (1979). *The structuring of organizations*. Englewood Cliffs, NJ: Prentice-Hall.

Mintzberg, H., Ahlstrand, B., & Lampe, J. (1998). *Strategy safari: The complete guide through the wilds of strategic management*. London, UK: Prentice Hall Financial Times.

Mohrman, S. A., Finegold, D., & Mohrman, A. M. (2003). An empirical model of the organization knowledge system in new product development firms. *Journal of Engineering and Technology Management, 20*(1-2), 7–38. doi:10.1016/S0923-4748(03)00003-1

Möller, K. (2010). *Value networks and innovation*. Berkeley, CA: University of California.

Möller, K., & Halinen, A. (1999). Business relationships and networks: Managerial challenge of network era. *Industrial Marketing Management, 28*, 413–427.

Möller, K., & Rajala, A. (1999). Organizing marketing in industrial high-tech firms: The role of internal marketing relationships. *Industrial Marketing Management, 28*(5), 521–535.

Möller, K., & Rajala, A. (2007). Rise of strategic nets – New modes of value creation. *Industrial Marketing Management, 36*, 895–908. doi:10.1016/j.indmarman.2007.05.016

Möller, K., Rajala, A., & Svahn, S. (2005). Strategic business nets – Their types and management. *Journal of Business Research*. Retrieved from http://impgroup.org/uploads/papers/4462.pdf

Nonaka, I., & Konno, N. (1998). The concept of ba: Building a foundation for knowledge creation. *California Management Review, 40*(3), 40–47.

Nonaka, I., & Takeuchi, H. (1995). *The knowledge-creating company*. Oxford, UK: Oxford University Press.

Osterwalder, A. (2004). *The business-model ontology – A proposition in design science approach*. Academic Dissertation. Lausanne, France: Université de Lausanne.

Pajunen, K. (2006). Living in agreement with a contract: The management of moral and viable firm stakeholder relationships. *Journal of Business Ethics, 68*(3), 243–258. doi:10.1007/s10551-006-9013-9

Pfeffer, J., & Salancik, G. R. (1978). *The external control of organizations: A resource dependence perspective*. New York, NY: Harper and Row.

Pinfield, L. T., Watzke, G. E., & Webb, E. J. (1974). Confederacies and brokers: Mediators between organizations and their environments. In Leavitt, H., Pinfield, L., & Webb, E. (Eds.), *Organizations of the Future: Interaction with the External Environment* (pp. 83–110). New York, NY: Praeger.

Powell, W. W., Koput, K. W., & Smith-Doerr, L. (1996). Interorganizational collaboration and the locus of innovation: Networks of learning in biotechnology. *Administrative Science Quarterly, 41*, 116–145. doi:10.2307/2393988

Radjou, N., Daley, E., Rasmussen, M., & Lo, H. (2006). *The rise of globally adaptive organizations: The world isn't flat till global firms are networked, risk-agile, and socially adept*. New York, NY: Forrester.

Rajala, R., Rossi, M., & Tuunainen, V. K. (2003). *A framework for analyzing software business models*. Paper presented at ECIS 2003. Naples, Italy.

Rajala, R., Rossi, M., Tuunainen, V. K., & Korri, S. (2001). *Software business models - A framework for analyzing software industry. Technology Review*. New York, NY: TEKES.

Ring, P., & Van de Ven, A. (1992). Structuring cooperative relationships between organizations. *Strategic Management Journal, 13*(7), 483–498. doi:10.1002/smj.4250130702

Rosenbröijer, C.-J. (1998). *Capability development in business networks*. Doctoral Dissertation. Helsinki, Finland: Swedish School of Economics and Business Administration.

Sawhney, M., Gulati, R., Paoni, A., & Kellog Tech Venture Team. (2001). *Tech venture: New rules on value and profit from Silicon Valley*. New York, NY: Wiley and Sons, Inc.

Spekman, R. E., Isabella, L. A., & MacAvoy, T. C. (2000). *Alliance competence: Maximizing the value of your partnerships*. New York, NY: John Wiley & Sons.

Srinivasan, R., Lilien, G. L., & Rangaswamy, A. (2006). The emergence of dominant designs. *Journal of Marketing, 70*(2), 1–17. doi:10.1509/jmkg.70.2.1

Teece, D. J. (1986). Profiting from technological innovation: Implications for integration, collaboration, licensing and public policy. *Research Policy, 15*, 285–305. doi:10.1016/0048-7333(86)90027-2

Teece, D. J., Pisano, G., & Shuen, A. (1997). Dynamic capabilities and strategic management. *Strategic Management Journal, 18*(7), 509–533. doi:10.1002/(SICI)1097-0266(199708)18:7<509::AID-SMJ882>3.0.CO;2-Z

Tikkanen, H. (1996). Pohjoismaisen verkostolähestymistavan tieteenfilosofiset perusteet. *The Finnish Journal of Business Economics, 45*(4), 384–403.

Tikkanen, H., Lamberg, J. A., Parvinen, P., & Kallunki, J. P. (2005). Managerial cognition, action and the business model of the firm. *Management Decision, 43*(6), 789–809. doi:10.1108/00251740510603565

Toffler, A. (1985). *The adaptive corporation*. New York, NY: McGraw Hill.

Vonortas, N. S. (2000). Multimarket contact and inter-firm cooperation in R&D. *Journal of Evolutionary Economics*, *10*, 243–271. doi:10.1007/s001910050014

ADDITIONAL READING

Adler, P. S. (2001). Market, hierarchy, and trust: The knowledge economy and the future of capitalism. *Organization Science*, *12*(2), 215–234. doi:10.1287/orsc.12.2.215.10117

Adler, P. S., Goldoftas, B., & Levine, D. I. (1999). Flexibility versus efficiency? A case study of model changeovers in the Toyota production system. *Organization Science*, *10*(1), 43–68. doi:10.1287/orsc.10.1.43

Alajoutsijärvi, K., Möller, K., & Rosenbröijer, C.-J. (1999). Relevance of focal nets in understanding the dynamics of business relationships. *Journal of Business-To-Business Marketing*, *6*(3), 3–35. doi:10.1300/J033v06n03_02

Amit, R., & Zott, Ch. (2001). Value creation in e-business. *Strategic Management Journal*, *22*, 493–520. doi:10.1002/smj.187

Anderson, J. C., & Narus, J. A. (1999). *Business market management: Understanding, creating and delivering value*. Upper Saddle River, NJ: Prentice Hall.

Anderson, P., & Tushman, M. L. (1990). Technological discontinuities and dominant designs: A cyclical model of technological change. *Administrative Science Quarterly*, *35*(4), 604–633. doi:10.2307/2393511

Araujo, L. (1998). Knowing and learning as networking. *Management Learning*, *29*(3), 317–336. doi:10.1177/1350507698293004

Araujo, L., Dubois, A., & Gadde, L.-E. (2003). The multiple boundaries of the firm. *Journal of Management Studies*, *50*(5), 1255–1277. doi:10.1111/1467-6486.00379

Birkinshaw, J., Nobel, R., & Ridderstråle, J. (2002). Knowledge as a contingency variable: Do the characteristics of knowledge predict organization structure? *Organization Science*, *13*(3), 274–289. doi:10.1287/orsc.13.3.274.2778

Bradach, J., & Eccles, R. (1989). Price, authority, and trust: From ideal types to plural forms. *Annual Review of Sociology*, *15*, 97–118. doi:10.1146/annurev.so.15.080189.000525

Brown, J. S., & Duguid, P. (2001). Knowledge and organization: A social practice perspective. *Organization Science*, *12*(2), 198–213. doi:10.1287/orsc.12.2.198.10116

Cartwright, S. D., & Oliver, R. W. (2000). Untangling the value web. *The Journal of Business Strategy*, *21*(1), 22–27. doi:10.1108/eb040055

Castells, M. (1996). *The rise of the network society*. Cambridge, MA: Blackwell.

Chesborough, H., Hansen, M., Nohria, N., & Sull, D. (2000). Networked incubators: Hothouses of the new economy. *Harvard Business Review*, *78*(5), 74–84.

Chesborough, H., & Teece, D. (1996, January-February). When is virtual virtuous: Organizing for innovation. *Harvard Business Review*, ▪▪▪, 65–73.

Cravens, D. W., Shipp, S. H., & Crawens, K. S. (1994). Reforming the traditional organization: The mandate for developing networks. *Business Horizons*, *37*(4), 19–28. doi:10.1016/0007-6813(94)90043-4

Crowston, K., & Scozzi, B. (2002). Open source software projects as virtual organisations: Competency rallying for software development. *IEE Proceedings, 149*(1).

Das, T., & Teng, B. S. (1998). Between trust and control: Developing confidence in partner cooperation in alliances. *Academy of Management Review*, *23*(3), 491–512.

Dougherty, D. (1992). Interpretative barriers to successful product innovation in large firms. *Organization Science, 3*(2), 179–202. doi:10.1287/orsc.3.2.179

Doz, Y. (1996). The evolution of cooperation in strategic alliances: Initial conditions or learning processes? *Strategic Management Journal, 17,* 55–83. doi:10.1002/smj.4250171006

Doz, Y., Santos, J., & Williamson, P. (2001). *From global to metanational.* Boston, MA: Harvard Business School Press.

Doz, Y. L., & Hamel, G. (1998). *Alliance advantage: The art of creating value through partnering.* Boston, MA: Harvard Business School Press.

Dyer, J. H. (1996). Specialized supplier networks as a source of competitive advantage: Evidence from the auto industry. *Strategic Management Journal, 17*(4), 271–292. doi:10.1002/(SICI)1097-0266(199604)17:4<271::AID-SMJ807>3.0.CO;2-Y

Dyer, J. H., & Nobeoka, K. (2000). Creating and managing a high-performance knowledge-sharing network: The Toyota case. *Strategic Management Journal, 21,* 345–367. doi:10.1002/(SICI)1097-0266(200003)21:3<345::AID-SMJ96>3.0.CO;2-N

Dyer, J. H., & Singh, H. (1998). The relational view: Cooperative strategy and sources of inter-organizational competitive advantage. *Academy of Management Review, 23*(4), 660–679.

Dyer, J. H., & Singh, H. (2000). Using alliance to build competitive advantage in emerging technologies. In Day, G. S., Schoemaker, P. J. H., & Gunther, R. E. (Eds.), *Wharton on Managing Emerging Technologies.* New York, NY: John Wiley & Sons, Inc.

Granovetter, M. (1973). The strength of weak ties. *American Journal of Sociology, 78,* 1360–1380. doi:10.1086/225469

Grant, R. M. (2007). *Contemporary strategy analysis concepts, techniques, applications* (6th ed.). Oxford, UK: Blackwell Publishing.

Håkansson, H., & Persson, G. (2004). Supply chain management: the logic of supply chains and networks. *International Journal of Logistics Management, 15*(1), 11–26. doi:10.1108/09574090410700202

Hinterhuber, A. (2002). Value chain orchestration in action and the case of the global agrochemical industry. *Long Range Planning, 35*(6), 615–635. doi:10.1016/S0024-6301(02)00160-7

Husler, C., & Ronde, P. (2007). The impact of cognitive communities on the diffusion of academic knowledge: Evidence from the networks of inventors of a French university. *Research Policy, 36,* 288–302. doi:10.1016/j.respol.2006.11.006

Jarillo, J. C. (1993). *Strategic networks: Creating the borderless organization.* Oxford, UK: Butterworth-Heinemann.

Lambe, C. J., Spekman, R. E., & Hunt, S. D. (2002). Alliance competence, resources, and alliance success: Conceptualization, measurement, and initial test. *Journal of the Academy of Marketing Science, 30*(2), 141–158. doi:10.1177/03079459994399

Lipparini, A., & Fratocchi, L. (1999). The capabilities of the transnational firm: Accessing knowledge and leveraging inter-firm relationships. *European Management Journal, 17*(6), 655–667. doi:10.1016/S0263-2373(99)00056-0

Normann, R., & Ramirez, R. (1993). From value chain to value constellation: Designing interactive strategy. *Harvard Business Review, 71*(4), 65–77.

Parolini, C. (1999). *The value net: A tool for competitive strategy.* Chichester, UK: John Wiley & Sons Ltd.

Porter, M. E. (1985). *Competitive advantage: Creating and sustaining superior performance.* New York, NY: Free Press.

Rindfleisch, A. (2000). Organizational trust and interfirm cooperation: An examination of horizontal versus vertical alliances. *Marketing Letters*, *11*, 81–95. doi:10.1023/A:1008107011529

Sivadas, E., & Dwyer, F. R. (2000). An examination of organizational factors influencing new product success in internal and alliance-based processes. *Journal of Marketing*, *64*(1), 31–49. doi:10.1509/jmkg.64.1.31.17985

Weick, K. (1995). *Sensemaking in organizations*. Thousand Oaks, CA: SAGE Publications, Inc.

Yin, R. K. (1994). *Case study research - Design and methods*. Beverly Hills, CA: Sage Publication.

Zollo, M., Reuer, J. J., & Singh, H. (2002). Interorganizational routines and performance in strategic alliances. *Organization Science*, *13*(6), 701–713. doi:10.1287/orsc.13.6.701.503

KEY TERMS AND DEFINITIONS

Activities: Activities seem to appear in sequences or in chains (Porter, 1985). In this view, company is seen as a set of activities that are performed to design, produce, market, deliver, and support its product.

Actor: Actor is an organization or an individual that perform activities, control resources, and create value via transformation of resources.

Business Model: A business model is defined here as a system for products, services or their portfolio, including a description of business actors and their roles, relationships, resources and activities in a value network, with the aim of creating maximum value throughout the value network.

Business Network: Business network refers to any intentional collaborative form of a clearly defined group of actors having observable connections, processes, and rules of conduct with each other. Participants of a business net are aware of their connections and they have chosen to participate based on perceived value, benefits, and/or strategic advantages.

Hub: A hub company is an organization that gives direction and goals for the business network, negotiates roles in the network, and decides of the structure of the network.

Network Position: The position in a network is defined by the characteristics of the company's relationships and the benefits and commitments that arise from them.

Networking: This term encompasses all of the interactions of a company or individual in the network.

ENDNOTE

[1]   Finland used Finnish marks in 1990-2000.

Chapter 4
Group Processes in the Virtual Work Environment:
Evidence for an Alliance-Building Dimensionality

Andrea Roofe Sattlethight
Innovative Strategies, LLC., Miami, USA

Sungu Armagan
Florida International University, USA

ABSTRACT

This chapter explores an alternative approach to group processes in the virtual environment as a system of alliances, encompassing leader, member, and group. The purpose of this research is to determine if a system of alliances encompassing leader, member, and team exists in the virtual environment. The authors explore the applicability of alliances to a 21st century management environment by testing a conceptual model using 20,000 bootstrapped samples of 96 employed professionals and students studying in an online environment. They find evidence that group processes in a technology-mediated environment can be defined by a three-way-system of alliances in which the leader plays a less dominant role than in traditional groups. The authors find that the individual's relationship with the group may be built through a trust relationship with other members rather than a direct relationship with the leader. Directions for future research and implications for management practice are also discussed.

DOI: 10.4018/978-1-4666-1836-7.ch004

INTRODUCTION

The tools [technology] were important, but they clearly weren't enough to create an effective connection between people when they were distant (Kostner, 1996, p. 54).

Cyberspace, also known as the virtual environment, is a critical component of the 21st century business environment. The virtual organization may consist of people, application and other service providers, and software and equipment-heterogeneous modules (Bauer & Köszegi, 2003; Mowshowitz, 1997). Bauer and Köszegi argue that the final output of the virtual organization is the result of a trust relationship among the providers. That is, trust is a social 'coordination mechanism' of which technology is the physical agent. A major challenge for virtual team leaders is the development of a cohesive unit of members 'building mutual trust and cooperation' (Araujo, 2004; Cohen & Gibson, 2003; DeRosa, Hantula, Kock, & D'Arcy, 2004; Kasper-Fuehrer & Ashkanasy, 2001; Malhotra, Majchrzak, & Rosen, 2007; Mitchell & Zigurs, 2009) to accomplish the mandate of the team. As distance among members hinders the establishment of interpersonal relationships and communication modes that promote trust, the leader in the virtual environment, also referred to as the *e-leader*, is challenged to facilitate team building for successful task accomplishment (Kostner, 1996; Malhotra, et al., 2007; Scales, 1998). Trust is the foundation of alliances and team building (Scales, 1998).

Alliance building is a means by which a group achieves cohesiveness. Burlingame, Fuhriman, and Johnson (2002) define cohesion as a system of alliances spanning leader-group, member-group, member-leader, and member-member alliances. In this chapter, we apply the alliance-building paradigm identified by Burlingame et al. to an examination of team processes in the virtual or technology-mediated environment. Leadership roles are devolved to team members in the form

of shared leadership in the virtual environment. As the distinction between leader and virtual team members become blurred, the four-way system of alliances may be translated into the team action, transition and interpersonal processes defined by Marks, Mathieu, and Zaccaro (2001), and the e-leader's team building and task accomplishment roles identified by Hertel (2004). Team action processes as defined by Marks et al. consist of planning and evaluation, while transition processes consist of coordinating, monitoring, and support. Interpersonal processes consist of conflict management, motivation, and confidence building and affect management.

The purpose of the current study is to determine if the four-way system of alliances identified by Burlingame, Fuhriman, and Johnson (2002) is applicable in the virtual environment. In this study, we translate conventional elements of group processes to the virtual environment in the form of a system of alliances, spanning leader, member, and virtual team members. The virtual team is a flexible organizational form arising from the use of technology-mediated processes (Piccoli, Powell, & Blake, 2004; Powell, Piccoli, & Ives, 2004). The theoretical relevance of the present study lies in its extension of current management literature on cohesiveness to the virtual environment. Its practical relevance is highlighted by the need for managers to improve their understanding of the characteristics of group processes in the virtual environment. Managers will need to adapt to an environment of reduced face-to-face interaction while retaining motivation at the team and individual levels, and taking advantage of the synergies created by task interdependence (Hertel, et al., 2004). According to Powell et al. and Piccoli et al., the virtual team offers the opportunity for companies to operate with greater flexibility by harnessing resources regardless of time and spatial distance. This chapter contributes to practice by helping virtual team managers identify areas of focus for team building and task accomplishment.

Conventional management theory defines action and transition phases of team processes (Marks, et al., 2001; Marks, DeChurch, Mathieu, Panzer, & Alonso, 2005), leadership task accomplishment, and team building and mentoring actions (Dionne, Yammarino, Atwater, & Spangler, 2004). In the virtual environment, there is much interdependency among goals, task, and outcomes (Hertel, et al., 2004; Malhotra, et al., 2007). The task and interpersonal dimensions of today's complex work environment are consistent with the definition of the virtual environment as a socio-technical system. Herein, interpersonal relationships and human intelligence allow the group to carry out its task, while technology and artificial intelligence facilitate effective task completion. We suggest that effective team building stimulates trust among members, which aids the growth of positive alliances among members (i.e., member-member alliances), between each member and the group (i.e., member-group alliances), and between e-leader and each member (i.e., e-leader-member alliance). Our findings support the presence of a system of alliances that include member-member, member-group, and e-leader-group. We find that a positive relationship exists among each component of this system of alliances. Furthermore, we find that e-leader-member alliances are only associated with e-leader-group alliances.

The current study contributes to the literature in a number of different ways. First, our conceptual framework extends the definition of cohesion to include the alliance construct used in the psychotherapy literature (Burlingame, et al., 2002) and applies this extension to a technology-mediated environment. Our conceptual model extends the discussion of relationships identified in the management literature on teams and leadership to reflect alliances. Second, we evaluate the associations among the system of alliances to determine the configuration of the system of alliances and the significance of each component. We begin the chapter with an overview of the role of technology in the work environment and

cohesiveness in groups. We then discuss the nature of alliances among leader, member, and group. We review relevant literature in support of alliances spanning leader-member, leader-group, member-group, and member-member, followed by a theoretical framework including the hypotheses. After presenting the methodology, we provide the results of a correlation analysis based on a system of latent and manifest variables to demonstrate whether these alliances are present. We end the chapter with a discussion including implications for management practice as well as avenues for future research.

BACKGROUND

Technology in the Work Environment

The technology-mediated work environment of the 21st century influences the nature of group processes (Chudoba, Wynn, Lu, & Watson-Manheim, 2005; Kirkman & Mathieu, 2004; Kirkman & Mathieu, 2005; Malhotra, et al., 2007) by virtue of its socio-technical nature. Artificial intelligence and automated processes aid task accomplishment, which results in efficiency (Hiltz & Turoff, 1981; Hiltz, 1988; Turoff, 1985). However, the technology-mediated environment consists of discontinuities, which hinder interpersonal relationships. For example, spatial distance influences the quality of the alliance-building process (Golden & Veiga, 2008) and its outcomes by establishing discontinuities of location and technology (Chudoba, et al., 2005; Maznevski & Chudoba, 2000). High spatial distance and time differences among employees presents challenges for alliance building where members experience feelings of alienation (Golden, Veiga, & Dino, 2008). Trust is a fundamental requirement for team success in a technology-mediated environment in that it assumes greater importance when members are separated by time and space, and use different technologies (Sarker, Valacich, & Sarker, 2003).

Spatial distance between members and the e-leader neutralize task and relationship dimensions of focused leadership (Hertel, et al., 2004; Kerr & Jermier, 1978; Orlikowski, 2002). Differences in technology among locations pose challenges for coordination efforts (Chudoba, et al., 2005; Malhotra, et al., 2007). The richness of the technology medium has the potential to disrupt harmony through miscommunication. On the other hand, technology, if well implemented and seamlessly integrated, can facilitate improved coordination, communication, information sharing, and accountability (Griffith, 1999). In addition, technology may improve cohesiveness (Gibson & Gibbs, 2006; Kahai, Fjermestad, Zhang, & Avolio, 2007; MacDuffie, 2007; Maznevski & Chudoba, 2000), for example, through usage of a social networking component. Therefore, the outcome of alliances among group members may depend on the elements of the technology infrastructure and the commitment of stakeholders to its use in accomplishing the team's charter (Igbaria, 1998; Remidez, Stam, & Laffey, 2007).

Cohesiveness

Cohesiveness is defined in the management literature as "the resultant forces which are acting on the members to stay in a group" (Festinger, 1950). Cohesiveness consists of interpersonal attraction, group pride, and commitment to task (Back, 1951; Festinger, 1950; Festinger, Schachter, & Back, 1950; Festinger & Thibaut, 1951; Mullen & Copper, 1994; Zaccaro & Lowe, 1986). Cohesion causes members to want to remain in the group (Burlingame, et al., 2002; Hill, Koocher, & Norcross, 2005). Cohesion or cohesiveness is the result of multiple alliances among the individuals comprising the team (Burlingame, et al., 2002). This view takes into account the interrelationships between outcomes at different levels of the organization (Hox, 2002; Rousseau, 1985; Tse, Dasborough, & Ashkanasy, 2008) and offers a multi-level rather than a uni-level perspective on the nature of group processes.

Cohesiveness, as defined in the management literature, reflects the relationships among members (Back, 1951; Back, 1951; Festinger, 1950; Festinger & Thibaut, 1951; Zaccaro & Lowe, 1986). Other definitions of cohesiveness have focused on the individual's feeling of belonging to the group and morale (Bollen & Hoyle, 1990). As such, cohesiveness is related to many group processes (Burlingame, et al., 2002; MacKenzie & Tschuschke, 1993). The relationship between member and group provides one of two initial stimuli for the member to remain in the group (Burlingame, et al., 2002; Hofmann, Morgeson, & Gerras, 2003).

The virtual team consists of e-leader and followers. The current research suggests that relationship with the e-leader provides the other stimulus for the member to remain part of the group where the e-leader may be the initial contact for the member's relationship with the group. This relationship may serve as the member's initiation into the group and provide the building block for a positive relationship among members. E-leader team building actions facilitate group cohesiveness by 'building mutual trust and cooperation' (Hertel, Niedner, & Herrmann, 2003; Hertel, et al., 2004). Mentoring actions enhance and reinforce the relationship between member and leader (Hofmann, et al., 2003; Ilies, Nahrgang, & Morgeson, 2007). Interpersonal relationships exhibited by the e-leader in the course of task coordination reinforce e-leader-group alliances, eliciting the loyalty of the group. Therefore, each alliance (e.g., member-member, member-group) contributes to improving group cohesiveness. We suggest that group processes reflect a four-way system of alliances in a technology-mediated environment (See Figure 1). Table 1 highlights the framework for the analysis of the group processes discussed in the current study.

Figure 1. Team processes: a four way system of alliances in a technology-mediated environment

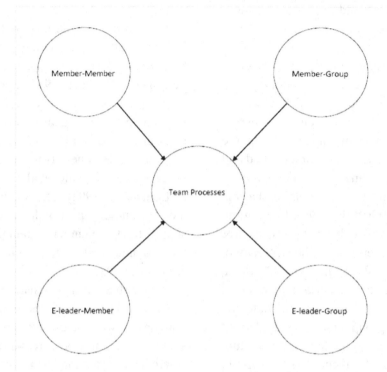

Table 1. Framework for the analysis of group processes and leadership

Member-member alliance (Back, 1951; Festinger, 1950; Hertel, Geister, & Konradt, 2005; Marks, et al., 2001; Zaccaro & Lowe, 1986)	Cohesiveness: • Task related • Interpersonal relationships	Team Processes: Transition: • Planning • Evaluation Action: • Coordinating • Monitoring • Support Interpersonal: • Conflict and affect management • Motivation/Confidence building
Member-group alliance	Trust, based on member reputation and performance	
Leader-member alliance (Graen & Uhl-Bien, 1995)	Leader-Member-Exchange (LMX)	
E-Leader–group alliance (e-leadership measure	Leader team building and task accomplishment behaviors	

THEORY AND HYPOTHESES

Member-Member Alliance

The cohesiveness construct applied in this study encompasses interpersonal and task based dimensions described by Zaccaro and Lowe (1986). Interpersonal dimension (i.e., interpersonal attraction) is the extent of social interaction among team members or their attraction to the group as a prestigious entity. The group develops its cohesive character depending on the strength of members' liking for each other or to the extent that group membership is considered to be desirable (Back, 1951; Festinger, 1950; Zaccaro & Lowe, 1986). The commitment to the task refers to the strength of the desire of members to complete the task successfully. Teams that are more committed to the task tend to be more efficient than those that are less committed to the task (Back, 1951; Zaccaro & Lowe, 1986). In the work environment, the task-based dimension of cohesiveness may be translated into the four phases of the virtual team life cycle described by Hertel et al. (2005). The four phases are preparation, launch, performance management, and team development. Interpersonal attraction underlies all phases of the virtual team life cycle.

Member-Group Alliance

Cohesiveness is characterized by 'belongingness and morale' (Bollen & Hoyle, 1990). At the individual level, cohesiveness is an internal state and is defined based on subjective criteria (Jewell & Reitz, 1981). Belongingness and morale have their counterparts in the member-group alliance building process and are the result of a trust relationship between the member and group (Burlingame, et al., 2002). We define the state of trust as being perceptual in nature and a result of a member-group alliance building process. During task accomplishment, the development of trust may overlap with elements of the taxonomy of

team processes (Marks, et al., 2001), where each is dependent on the other to deliver according to plan. Trust is the ultimate outcome of a successful member-group alliance (Wech, 2001) and is a critical factor underlying the success of teams in a technology-mediated environment (Araujo, 2004; Jarvenpaa, Knoll, & Leidner, 1998; Jarvenpaa & Leidner, 1999; Sarker, et al., 2003; Scales & Rubenfeld, 2005; Scales, 1998). The professional isolation caused by telecommuting may have an adverse impact on individual feelings of belongingness and work outcomes (Golden & Veiga, 2008). In the virtual environment, the individual's relationship with the team benefits from an appreciation of the diversity of its membership (Malhotra, et al., 2007). If the individual has positive experiences with the group, the individual develops the confidence to forge closer ties with individual members. In other words, the member-member alliance is enhanced by a positive member-group alliance (MacKenzie & Tschuschke, 1993). In hypothesis form:

Hypothesis 1. In a technology-mediated environment, positive member-group alliance is associated with positive member-member alliance.

E-Leader-Member Alliance

A positive relationship between the e-leader and member engenders the beginnings of the trust relationship between member and group (Whitener, Brodt, Korsgaard, & Werner, 1998). As the member interacts with fellow team members and task accomplishment progresses under positive e-leadership, there is a growing feeling of belongingness and morale. Cohesiveness is reinforced when leader team building behaviors are successful. The current research is based on the premise that the member's experience with the leader builds confidence in fellow team members (Hoyt & Blascovich, 2003). The relationship between the individual and leader, also known as the leader-member exchange, plays a major role in determining outcomes at the individual level (Graen & Uhl-Bien, 1995; Ilies, et al., 2007). We suggest that the e-leader-member alliance mirrors aspects of the performance management phase of the life cycle model (Hertel, et al., 2005) and the underlying interpersonal relationships. The individual compares the quality of the relationship with the e-leader with that of other team members. The leader-member exchange is also influenced by the actual or perceived quality of the relationship experienced by the individual team member during the planning, evaluation, and coordination and monitoring processes (Hofmann, et al., 2003; Ilies, et al., 2007). Employees who perceive their relationship with the e-leader to be of a lesser quality than that of co-workers attribute a lower value to their leader-member exchange and develop negative perceptions of their value in that environment (Mayer, Keller, Leslie, & Hanges, 2008). This negative outcome affects the quality of member-group alliance and leader-member exchange (MacKenzie & Tschuschke, 1993). Therefore, in hypothesis form:

Hypothesis 2a. In a technology-mediated environment, a positive e-leader-member alliance is associated with a positive member-group alliance.

Hypothesis 2b. In a technology-mediated environment, a positive e-leader-member alliance is associated with a positive member-member alliance.

E-leader-Group Alliance

The leader-member alliance is established through the fulfillment of roles that encourage unity and harmonious relationships in the group while providing conditions conducive to fulfilling the mandate of the group (Burlingame, et al., 2002; McGrath, 1964). The current study proposes that e-leader roles in the leader-member exchange reflect the team development and performance management phases of the virtual team lifecycle

(Hertel, et al., 2005). During task accomplishment, the development of a positive e-leader-group relationship reinforces the member-group, member-member and leader-member alliances. We suggest that the positive e-leader-member alliance facilitates a positive member-group alliance. To the extent that each individual experiences the same outcome from the e-leader, the group as an entity also experiences increased levels of cohesiveness (Harris, 2004; Mayer, et al., 2008; Mayfield & Mayfield, 2007; Mayfield & Mayfield, 2007; Tse, et al., 2008; Wech, 2001). E-leader team building actions instill confidence in team members. Overall, e-leader task accomplishment behaviors directed at the team have an impact on the members, which influences the member-group alliance, the member-member alliance, and the e-leader-member alliance. The foregoing arguments result in the following hypotheses:

Hypothesis 3a. In a technology-mediated environment, a positive e-leader-group alliance is associated with a positive member-member alliance.

Hypothesis 3b. In a technology-mediated environment, a positive e-leader-group alliance is associated with a positive member-group alliance.

Hypothesis 3c. In a technology-mediated environment, a positive e-leader-group alliance is associated with a positive e-leader-member alliance.

METHODS

The current research inquires into the nature of relationships among the four-way system of alliances identified in the previous discussion. Specifically, we assessed the magnitude and significance of pair-wise correlations among the dimensions representing the four alliances (i.e., member-member, member-group, e-leader-member, and e-leader-group) to ascertain that these alliances are important elements of team processes in a technology-mediated environment (See Figure 2).

Figure 2. Preliminary model of a system of alliances in a technology-mediated environment

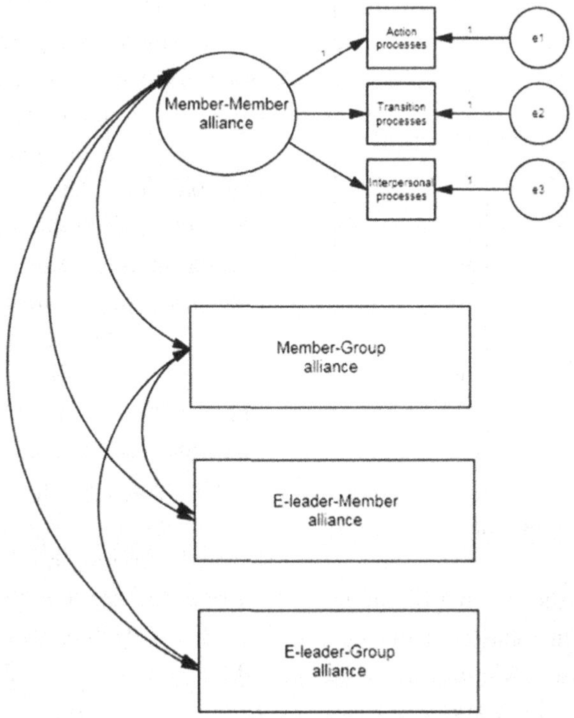

Data

The participants consisted of 125 employed professionals from the East Coast of the U.S.A. and undergraduate students enrolled in online classes in the College of Business of a research university in the South East U.S.A. Of these, 96 provided adequate data. The data was found to be missing at random with Little's MCAR test statistic of 19.484 (df=13, p=0.109). The sample distribution among the demographic variables is presented in Table 2. Most individuals worked in relatively small teams (i.e., 10 individuals or less), and are located within the same time zone as the rest of the team. The professionals were more likely to report a history of previous work experience with team members than students were. Table 2 summarizes the sample demographics.

Measures

We collected data using the SurveyConsole online survey application. We used an instrument, which is based on the action, transition, and interpersonal processes among members (Marks, et al., 2001), as a proxy to measure the alliance among members. This instrument by Marks et al. is part of a taxonomy used to describe team processes. According to Marks et al, three types of transition processes reflect mission analysis, goal specification, and strategy formulation and planning. Action processes reflect monitoring progress toward goals, resource and systems monitoring, team monitoring and backup, and coordination. Transition processes reflect mission analysis, goal specification, and strategy formulation and planning. Interpersonal processes reflect

Table 2. Sample demographics

Variables	% of sample
Gender Male Female	53 47
Type of Team Student Professionals	60 40
Worked together in the past No Yes	28 72
Team size 5 persons or less 6–10 persons more than 10 persons	26 51 23
# of time zones spanned by the team One More than one	76 24

conflict and affect management, and motivating and confidence building.

The current study defines the member-member alliance using the three-dimensional team process construct defined by Marks and Mathieu (2001). The action processes defined by Marks and Mathieu map onto the launch and performance management phases described by Hertel et al. (2005). We suggest that transition processes map onto the preparation and team development phases of the virtual team life cycle described by Hertel et al. In addition, the interpersonal processes, defined by Marks and Mathieu, underlie all phases of the virtual team life cycle, described by Hertel et al. Similarly, we suggest that leader team building actions are closely associated with planning and evaluation team transition processes defined by Marks and Mathieu, while leader task accomplishment actions are associated with coordination and monitoring team action processes described by Marks and Mathieu.

We used Sarker's (2003) trust instrument as a proxy to measure member-group alliance. This measure of the alliance between the member and group was based on the member's perception of the personality, behavior, and reputation of fellow team members. The 35-item instrument consisted of three sub-scales, representing trust based on personality, institutional, and cognitive factors. The cognitive factor consisted of five sub-scales-stereotyping based on message, technology, physical appearance/behavior, reputation categorization, and unit grouping. In the interest of brevity, we selected the sub-scales measuring trust based on personality, physical appearance/behavior and reputation categorization, as they seemed to capture the alliance between member and group in the most effective way. The sub-scales consisted of 12 items. We measured the leader-member alliance using the member-based items of the Leader-Member Exchange (LMX) instrument (Graen & Uhl-Bien, 1995).

The leader-group alliance was measured by an instrument designed for this study to identify leader behaviors in a virtual environment based on both the academic and practitioner literature (Avolio & Kahai, 2003; Cascio & Shurygailo, 2003; Dionne, et al., 2004; Kahai, et al., 2007; Keller, 1986; Keller, 1992; Kostner, 1996). All 11 items were included. A single factor solution yielded the highest loadings and best fit (chi-square=506, df=119; p<0.001). Factor loadings ranged from 0.92 to 0.97. Table 3 contains selected items from the e-leader-group measure.

We assessed the magnitude and significance of pairwise correlations among indicators of the four alliances. A structural model generated estimates of the hypothesized relationships among the variables. The Bollen-Stine bootstrap pro-

Table 3. Selected items of the e-leader-group measure

Item	Factor Loading
The leader identifies critical pieces of information necessary for the team to do the job	0.977
The leader is supportive of my desire to improve	0.970
The leader encourages team members to listen to each other	0.948

vided confidence intervals of the parameters (Enders, 2005; Henderson, 1989; Muthén & Muthén, 2002). Mono method bias was reduced using procedural and statistical techniques as recommended by Podsakoff, Mackenzie, Lee, and Podsakoff (2003). Mono-method bias is a potential threat to the validity of the study. Procedural techniques used to reduce the mono method bias were the online delivery of the survey and the absence of the investigator from the administration process. In addition, the survey was administered to different types of audiences including students and professionals. Furthermore, the survey was conducted on students from different classes and professionals from different organizations. The Harman one-factor test was used to identify the presence of mono-method bias.

RESULTS

Factor Loadings and Reliability

The three dimensions of the measure of member-member alliance loaded in the manner anticipated by previous research (Marks, et al., 2001). We removed two of the 12 items of the member-group alliance (trust) scale to resolve a negative eigenvalue. The reliability of the sub-scales exceeded 0.9 on each dimension. The reliability of the member-group alliance (trust) measure proved to be 0.89 based on the six items. Of the remaining ten items, six loaded onto a single factor. The items were developed under different technological conditions, and for use in an online classroom environment, seven years ago (Sarker, et al., 2003). It is typical for item loadings to differ greatly when applied to a different sample under different conditions. The reliability of the e-leader-group alliance measure proved to be 0.867 based on 11 items. The exploratory factor analysis of the Leader-Member Exchange revealed the presence of a single underlying dimension, which parallels

Table 4. Tests of reliability

Scale	Number of items	Cronbach's alpha
Member-member alliance: • Action processes • Transition processes • Interpersonal processes	9 12 9	0.918 0.951 0.935
Trust	6	0.891
LMX	7	0.832
E-Leadership	11	0.867

extant literature. Its reliability was 0.832 based on seven items. Table 4 provides details of the reliability tests.

Mono-Method Bias

There is no evidence of mono-method bias as the Harman one factor test indicated the presence of more than one factor in the un-rotated solution. The un-rotated factor solution yielded 2 factors, which, together, accounted for 68% of the variance. The ratio of the factor loadings was 2:1, or 47% and 21% for the first and second factors respectively.

Findings

The Bollen-Stine bootstrapped version of the chi square statistic takes into account the unknown nature of the underlying distribution and missing values. The bootstrapped results, based on 20,000 samples of 96, indicates a good model fit (χ^2 (df = 29) = 10.071, p=0.806). The Root Mean Square Error of Approximation (RMSEA) was 0.009 (p=0.622). The Comparative Fit index was 1.000. The fit indices and the standardized residuals point to good model fit. The modification indices did not offer theoretically meaningful recommendations for improvement of the model. Table 5 presents relevant fit indices.

None of the demographic variables was significant in the model. The three dimensions of

Table 5. Tests of model fit

Number of successful computations	20,000
Degrees of freedom	10
Chi-Square Test of Model Fit	10.071
P-Value	0.4343
Bootstrap P-Value	0.8061
CFI	1.000
RMSEA	0.009
Probability RMSEA <= .05	0.622

(Bootstrapped samples)

member-member alliances were statistically significant ($p<0.001$) with the highest loading attributable to interpersonal processes among the members. Three of the four alliances were statistically significant; however, the relationships among them assumed varying forms (See Figure 3). The strongest relationship was observed between member-member and member-group alliance ($r=0.448$, $p<0.001$), which supports Hypothesis 1. There was no association between e-leader-member alliance and member-group alliance. Therefore, the findings did not support Hypothesis 2a. There was no relationship between e-leader-member alliance and member-member alliance. The findings, therefore, did not support Hypothesis 2b. The member-member alliance, defined as the individual's perception of the nature of action, transition, and interpersonal processes among members, was positively related to the e-leader's team building and task related behaviors ($r=0.155$, $p=0.017$), which is in support of Hypothesis 3a. The member-group alliance, defined as being based on perceptions of the reputation and actions of the other members, was positively related to the e-leader's team building and task related behaviors ($r=0.12$, $p=0.006$), which supports Hypothesis 3b. The e-leader-member alliance, defined as being based on the member's perceptions of quality of the professional and interpersonal relationship with the leader, was

positively related to the e-leader's team building and task related behaviors, that is, the e-leader-e-group alliance ($r=0.131$, $p<0.001$). This supports Hypothesis 3c. Table 6 highlights the estimates for the structural coefficients. Standardized coefficients are presented and un-standardized coefficients appear in parentheses.

The coefficient of determination associated with each indicator measures the percentage of its variation, which is explained by the constructs with which it is associated (Kline, 1998). The relationships between member-group alliance and e-leader-group alliance proved to be significant influences on the nature of the alliance among members of the group. Together, they accounted for 88% of the variation in action processes, 67% of the variation in interpersonal processes, and 40% of the variation in transition processes. The influences on other alliances were of lesser magnitude. The relationship between member-member alliance and e-leader-group alliance accounted for approximately 6% of the variation in member-member and e-leader-group alliances. The e-leader-group alliance accounted for 10% of the variation in e-leader-member alliance. The e-leader-member and member-group alliances accounted for 2% of the variability in the e-leader-group alliance. Table 7 lists the coefficient of determination for each indicator.

Our analysis identified three manifest variables that explained the member-member alliance. Together they accounted for 64% of the variation in the relationship among members (member-member alliance). Interpersonal processes such as conflict and affect management, accounted for 48% (i.e., 75% of the explained variation). Transition processes such as goal setting and resource allocation accounted for 11%, and action processes accounted for 6% of the variation in the member-member alliance. Table 8 lists the percentage contribution of the variation of each manifest variable.

Figure 3. Revised model of a system of alliances in a technology-mediated environment

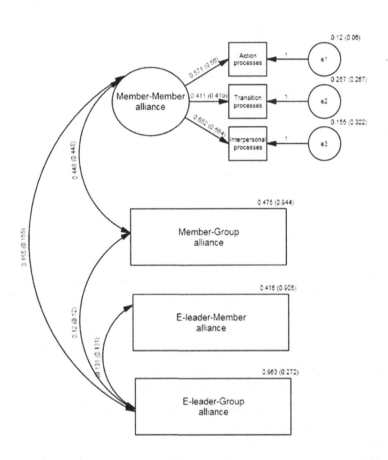

DISCUSSION

The findings suggest that in a technology-mediated environment group processes can be defined by a three-way system of alliances, encompassing leader-group, member-member, and member-group. Our final model differs from that of Burlingame et al. (2002) by the exclusion of the leader-member alliance. The findings are consistent with previous research based on an international sample of over 200 students and academic researchers (Roofe, 2009). Our results reveal that member-member alliance indeed reflects the action, transition, and interpersonal processes as suggested by Marks et al. (2001). In addition, according to our results,

the e-leader-member alliance bears no relevance to the system of alliances except for its association with the leader-group alliance. Furthermore, the member-group alliance based on trust aids the growth of a positive member-member alliance. Finally, a positive member-group alliance is related to a positive e-leader-group alliance.

The uni-dimensional nature of the e-leadership construct suggests that, in the technology-mediated environment, there is a synergy between the task accomplishment and team building roles of the e-leader. The team-building role of the e-leader in the technology-mediated environment (Kostner, 1996) is accentuated by the importance of the member-member alliance and member-group alliance

Table 6. Structural coefficients

	Estimate*	Standard Error (S.E.)	Estimate/S.E.	Two-Tailed P-Value

Member-Member Alliance by
  Group transition processes
  Group interpersonal processes
  Group action processes
	0.411 (0.419)
	0.560 (0.571)
	0.652 (0.664)
		0.060
		0.069
		0.060
			6.864
			8.155 10.893
				0.000
				0.000
				0.000

Member-Member Alliance with
  Member-Group Alliance (Trust)
  E-Leader-Group Alliance
  (E-Leadership team building and task accomplish-
ment behaviors)
	0.448 (0.448)
	0.155 (0.155)
		0.079
		0.065
			5.677
			2.395
				0.000
				0.017

Member-Group Alliance (Trust) with
  E-Leader-Group Alliance
  (E-Leadership team building and task accomplish-
ment behaviors)
	0.120 (0.12)	0.044	2.738	0.006

E-Leader-Group Alliance
  (E-Leadership team building and task accomplish-
ment behaviors) with
  E-Leader-Member Alliance
	0.131 (0.131)	0.035	3.770	0.000

*Standardized coefficients are in parentheses.

Table 7. Coefficients of determination

Group transition processes	0.396
Group action processes	0.880
Group interpersonal processes	0.678
Member-Group Alliance (Trust)	0.056
E-Leader-Member Alliance	0.095
E-Leader-Group Alliance (E-Leadership team building and task accomplishment behaviors)	0.020

Table 8. Variance explained by manifest variables

Component	Initial Eigenvalues			Extraction Sums of Squared Loadings		
	Total	% of Variance	Cumulative %	Total	% of Variance	Cumulative %
1	14.312	47.708	47.708	14.312	47.708	47.708
2	3.211	10.705	58.412	3.211	10.705	58.412
3	1.735	5.784	64.196	1.735	5.784	64.196

within our analysis. The member-member alliance and member-group alliance appears to be more important than the leadership role. The absence of a significant relationship between e-leader-member alliance and member-group alliance suggests that the effect of leader behaviors on the individual is channeled through the group. The individual's relationship with the group is enhanced by the e-leader's team building behaviors toward the group rather than by a direct relationship between the individual and the leader. The contribution of interpersonal processes among members, over and above the task related dimensions, is consistent with the alliance-building dimensionality of the research. This study confirms the importance of interpersonal processes and alliance building in the virtual environment.

Implications for Management Practice

Our analysis indicates that focused leadership gives way to a participative leadership role in the technology-mediated environment. Leadership assumes a less dominant role in a virtual team because of the inherent spatial discontinuity of a technology-mediated environment. The leadership role may even be shared among team members because of discontinuities of time, space, and processes (Jermier & Kerr, 1997). Leadership functions and reporting relationships must be adapted to this new environment (Malhotra, et al., 2007). There will be challenges to such a model where lines of authority and reporting traditionally follow a hierarchical structure. Technology may be adapted to build trust among members over time (Araujo, 2004), such as through social media, as well as for mentoring and team building (Avolio, 2005).

In accordance with our finding on the high contribution of interpersonal processes to the relationship among members, we suggest that technology should be adapted to enhance task accomplishment by enhancing interpersonal

processes such as through video-conferencing. We further suggest that team-building activities should focus on reducing feelings of isolation and alienation among members so that members integrate with the group. An example is embedding social networking facilities within the technology infrastructure. While we have not explored these particular causal relationships, it is possible that the e-leader's efforts at team building could stimulate positive member-member alliances. As the alliances among members develop, a cohesive unit may form and the member-group alliance may strengthen. The member-group and the member-member alliances may form a self-reinforcing cycle. Therefore, we suggest that organizations foster e-leader-group alliances given their positive effects on team cohesiveness. Furthermore, the e-leader-member alliance is built through task accomplishment and mentoring activities. In the technology-mediated environment, with its discontinuities of time, space, and technology, the role of the e-leader in directing the activities of the team may be perceived as separate from the leader's role as a fellow team member. This is consistent with the shared nature of leadership in the virtual environment; a concept alluded to in the work of Kerr and Jermier (1978).

Limitations and Directions for Future Research

We acknowledge the limited scope of this study. In particular, this study is limited to a relatively small sample size. While we used bootstrapping to minimize the limitation of using a small sample, future research may benefit from evaluating the hypotheses using a larger sample. We also encourage future researchers to compare the cohesiveness of teams with varying degrees of virtuality to shed light into the specific relationship between virtuality and team cohesiveness. Furthermore, there may be a conflict between the flat organizational structure of a virtual team and the hierarchical nature of a bureaucratic environment, and between the organic nature of a virtual team and the less flexible approach of a bureaucratic environment in an organization. Given that our sample is limited to corporate professionals and students, it may be beneficial for future researchers to evaluate our model in different environments, especially where a less flexible hierarchical structure exists such as in the military or government.

ACKNOWLEDGMENT

The current study is part of a larger study on leadership and team processes in a technology-mediated environment. The conceptual model was presented at the Annual Meeting of the Eastern Academy of Management, 2010. The current study benefitted from the comments of three anonymous reviewers of the Eastern Academy of Management. The chapter also benefitted from the comments of Dr. Kimberly Coffman, formerly of Florida International University's Writing Center, and Dr. Srini Ramaswamy, member of the Association of Computing Machinery (ACM).

REFERENCES

Araujo, A. L. (2004). *Trust in virtual teams: The role of task, technology and time*. Ph.D. Dissertation. Oklahoma City, OK: The University of Oklahoma.

Avolio, B. J. (2005). *Leadership development in balance: Made/born*. Englewood Hills, NJ: Lawrence Erlbaum and Associates.

Avolio, B. J., & Kahai, S. (2003). Adding the "e" to e-leadership: How it may impact your leadership. *Organizational Dynamics, 31*(4), 325–338. doi:10.1016/S0090-2616(02)00133-X

Back, K. W. (1951). Influence through social communication. *Journal of Abnormal and Social Psychology, 46*(1), 9–23. doi:10.1037/h0058629

Bauer, R., & Köszegi, S. T. (2003). Measuring the degree of virtualization. *Electronic Journal of Organizational Virtualness, 5*(2), 25.

Bollen, K. A., & Hoyle, R. H. (1990). Perceived cohesion: A conceptual and empirical examination. *Social Forces, 69*(2), 479–504.

Burlingame, G. M., Fuhriman, A., & Johnson, J. E. (2002). Cohesion in group psychotherapy. In Norcross, J. C. (Ed.), *Psychotherapy Relationships that Work: Therapist Contributions and Responsiveness to Patients* (p. 452). Oxford, UK: Oxford University Press.

Cascio, W., & Shurygailo, S. (2003). E-leadership and virtual teams. *Organizational Dynamics, 31*(4), 362. doi:10.1016/S0090-2616(02)00130-4

Chudoba, K. M., Wynn, E., Lu, M., & Watson-Manheim, M. B. (2005). How virtual are we? Measuring virtuality and understanding its impact in a global organization. *Information Systems Journal, 15*(4), 279. doi:10.1111/j.1365-2575.2005.00200.x

Cohen, S. G., & Gibson, C. B. (2003). *Virtual teams that work: Creating conditions for virtual team effectiveness*. San Francisco, CA: Jossey-Bass.

DeRosa, D. M., Hantula, D. A., Kock, N., & D'Arcy, J. (2004). Trust and leadership in virtual teamwork: A media naturalness perspective. *Human Resource Management, 43*(2-3), 219. doi:10.1002/hrm.20016

Dionne, S. D., Yammarino, F. J., Atwater, L. E., & Spangler, W. D. (2004). Transformational leadership and team performance. *Journal of Organizational Change Management, 17*(2). doi:10.1108/09534810410530601

Enders, C. (2005). An SAS macro for implementing the modified bollen-stine bootstrap for missing data: Implementing the bootstrap using existing structural equation modeling software. *Structural Equation Modeling, 12*(4), 620–641. doi:10.1207/s15328007sem1204_6

Festinger, L. (1950). Informal social communication. *Psychological Review, 57*(5), 271–282. doi:10.1037/h0056932

Festinger, L., Schachter, S., & Back, K. W. (1950). *Social pressures in informal groups: A study of a housing project*. New York, NY: Harper & Bros.

Festinger, L., & Thibaut, J. (1951). Interpersonal communication in small groups. *Journal of Abnormal and Social Psychology, 46*(1), 92–99. doi:10.1037/h0054899

Gibson, C. B., & Gibbs, J. L. (2006). Unpacking the concept of virtuality: The effects of geographic dispersion, electronic dependence, dynamic structure, and national diversity on team innovation. *Administrative Science Quarterly, 51*(3), 451.

Golden, T. D., & Veiga, J. F. (2008). The impact of superior–subordinate relationships on the commitment, job satisfaction, and performance of virtual workers. *The Leadership Quarterly, 19*(1), 77–88. doi:10.1016/j.leaqua.2007.12.009

Golden, T. D., Veiga, J. F., & Dino, R. N. (2008). The impact of professional isolation on teleworker job performance and turnover intentions: Does time spent teleworking, interacting face-to-face, or having access to communication-enhancing technology matter? *The Journal of Applied Psychology, 93*(6), 1412–1421. doi:10.1037/a0012722

Graen, G. B., & Uhl-Bien, M. (1995). Relationship-based approach to leadership: Development of leader-member exchange (LMX) theory of leadership over 25 years: Applying a multi-level multi-domain perspective. *The Leadership Quarterly, 6*(2), 219–247. doi:10.1016/1048-9843(95)90036-5

Griffith, T. L. (1999). Technology features as triggers for sensemaking. *Academy of Management Review, 24*(3), 472.

Harris, J. K. (2004). What you don't know can't hurt you: The interactive relationship between leader-member exchange and perceptions of politics on job satisfaction. *Journal of Behavioral and Applied Management, 5*(3), 188–203.

Henderson, C. R. (1989). Taxes, market structure and international price discrimination. *Journal of World Trade, 23*(6), 147.

Hertel, G., Geister, S., & Konradt, U. (2005). Managing virtual teams: A review of current empirical research. *Human Resource Management Review, 15*(1), 69–95. doi:10.1016/j.hrmr.2005.01.002

Hertel, G., Konradt, U., & Orlikowski, B. (2004). Managing distance by interdependence: Goal setting, task interdependence, and team-based rewards in virtual teams. *European Journal of Work and Organizational Psychology, 13*(1), 1. doi:10.1080/13594320344000228

Hertel, G., Niedner, S., & Herrmann, S. (2003). Motivation of software developers in open source projects: An internet-based survey of contributors to the Linux kernel. *Research Policy, 32*(7), 1159–1177. doi:10.1016/S0048-7333(03)00047-7

Hill, S. S., Koocher, G. P., & Norcross, J. C. (2005). *Psychologists' desk reference* (2nd ed.). Oxford, UK: Oxford University Press.

Hiltz, S. R. (1988). Productivity enhancement from computer-mediated communication: A systems contingency approach. *Communications of the ACM, 31*(12), 1438–1454. doi:10.1145/53580.53583

Hiltz, S. R., & Turoff, M. (1981). The evolution of user behavior in a computerized conferencing system. *Communications of the ACM, 24*(11), 739–751. doi:10.1145/358790.358794

Hofmann, D. A., Morgeson, F. P., & Gerras, S. J. (2003). Climate as a moderator of the relationship between leader-member exchange and content specific citizenship: Safety climate as an exemplar. *The Journal of Applied Psychology, 88*(1), 170–178. doi:10.1037/0021-9010.88.1.170

Hox, J. (2002). *Multilevel analysis: Techniques and applications*. New York, NY: Routledge.

Hoyt, C. L., & Blascovich, J. (2003). Transformational and transactional leadership in virtual and physical environments. *Small Group Research, 34*(6), 678–715. doi:10.1177/1046496403257527

Igbaria, M. (1998). Special section: Managing virtual workplaces and teleworking with information technology. *Journal of Management Information Systems, 14*(4), 5.

Ilies, R., Nahrgang, J. D., & Morgeson, F. P. (2007). Leader-member exchange and citizenship behaviors: A meta-analysis. *The Journal of Applied Psychology, 92*(1), 269–277. doi:10.1037/0021-9010.92.1.269

Jarvenpaa, S., Knoll, K., & Leidner, D. E. (1998). Is anybody out there? Antecedents of trust in global virtual teams. *Journal of Management Information Systems, 14*(4), 29.

Jarvenpaa, S., & Leidner, D. (1999). Communication and trust in global virtual teams. *Organization Science, 10*(6), 791–815. doi:10.1287/orsc.10.6.791

Jermier, J., & Kerr, S. (1997). Substitutes for leadership: Their meaning and measurement—Contextual recollections and current observations. *The Leadership Quarterly, 8*(2), 95–101. doi:10.1016/S1048-9843(97)90008-4

Jewell, L. N., & Reitz, H. J. (1981). *Group effectiveness in organizations*. Glenview, IL: Scott, Foresman and Company.

Kahai, S., Fjermestad, J., Zhang, S., & Avolio, B. J. (2007). Leadership in virtual teams: Past, present, and future. *International Journal of e-Collaboration, 3*(1), 1.

Kasper-Fuehrer, E. C., & Ashkanasy, N. M. (2001). Communicating trustworthiness and building trust in interorganizational virtual organizations. *Journal of Management, 27*(3), 235–254.

Keller, R. T. (1986). Predictors of the performance of project groups in R & D organizations. *Academy of Management Journal, 29*(4), 715–726. doi:10.2307/255941

Keller, R. T. (1992). Transformational leadership and the performance of research and development project groups. *The Journal of Applied Psychology, 91*(1), 202–210. doi:10.1037/0021-9010.91.1.202

Kerr, S., & Jermier, J. (1978). Substitutes for leadership: Their meaning and measurement. *Organizational Behavior and Human Performance, 22*, 375. doi:10.1016/0030-5073(78)90023-5

Kirkman, B. L., & Mathieu, J. E. (2004). *The role of virtuality in work team effectiveness*. New York, NY: Academy of Management.

Kirkman, B. L., & Mathieu, J. E. (2005). The dimensions and antecedents of team virtuality. *Journal of Management, 31*(5), 700. doi:10.1177/0149206305279113

Kline, R. B. (1998). *Principles and practice of structural equation modeling*. New York, NY: The Guilford Press.

Kostner, J. (1996). *Virtual leadership*. New York, NY: Warner Books.

MacDuffie, J. P. (2007). HRM and distributed work: Managing people across distances. *Academy of Management Annals, 1*, 549–615. doi:10.1080/078559817

MacKenzie, K. R., & Tschuschke, V. (1993). Relatedness, group work, and outcome in long-term inpatient psychotherapy groups. *The Journal of Psychotherapy Practice and Research, 2*(2), 147–156.

Malhotra, A., Majchrzak, A., & Rosen, B. (2007). Leading virtual teams. *The Academy of Management Perspectives, 21*(1), 60–70. doi:10.5465/AMP.2007.24286164

Marks, M. A., DeChurch, L. A., Mathieu, J. E., Panzer, F. J., & Alonso, A. (2005). Teamwork in multiteam systems. *The Journal of Applied Psychology, 90*(5), 964–971. doi:10.1037/0021-9010.90.5.964

Marks, M. A., Mathieu, J. E., & Zaccaro, S. J. (2001). A temporally based framework and taxonomy of team processes. *Academy of Management Review, 26*(3), 356–376.

Mayer, D. M., Keller, K. M., Leslie, L. M., & Hanges, P. J. (2008). When does my relationship with my manager matter most? The moderating role of coworkers' LMX. *Academy of Management Proceedings,* 1-6.

Mayfield, M. R., & Mayfield, J. R. (2007). *The role of group atmosphere and LMX relationships on worker performance and job satisfaction: Positive findings and recommendations for team enhancement.* Unpublished Manuscript. Retrieved October 31, 2008, from http://comm.research.arizona.edu/ingroup/docs/GroupAtmosphereandLMX-PaperwithReferences.pdf

Maznevski, M. L., & Chudoba, K. M. (2000). Bridging space over time: Global virtual team dynamics and effectiveness. *Organization Science, 11*(5), 473–492. doi:10.1287/orsc.11.5.473.15200

McGrath, J. (1964). *Leadership behavior: Some requirements for leadership training.* Washington, DC: Office of Career Development.

Mitchell, A., & Zigurs, I. (2009). Trust in virtual teams: Solved or still a mystery? *SIGMIS Database, 40*(3), 61–83. doi:10.1145/1592401.1592407

Mowshowitz, A. (1997). On the theory of virtual organization. *Systems Research and Behavioral Science, 14*(4), 373–384. doi:10.1002/(SICI)1099-1743(199711/12)14:6<373::AID-SRES131>3.0.CO;2-R

Mullen, B., & Copper, C. (1994). The relation between group cohesiveness and performance: An integration. *Psychological Bulletin, 115*(2), 210–227. doi:10.1037/0033-2909.115.2.210

Muthén, L. K., & Muthén, B. O. (2002). How to use a monte carlo study to decide on sample size and determine power. *Structural Equation Modeling, 9*(4), 599–620. doi:10.1207/S15328007SEM0904_8

Orlikowski, W. J. (2002). Knowing in practice: Enacting a collective capability in distributed organizing. *Organization Science, 13*(3), 249–273. doi:10.1287/orsc.13.3.249.2776

Piccoli, G., Powell, A., & Blake, I. (2004). Virtual teams: Team control structure, work processes, and team effectiveness. *Information Technology & People, 17*(4), 359. doi:10.1108/09593840410570258

Podsakoff, P. M., MacKenzie, S. B., Lee, J., & Podsakoff, N. P. (2003). Common method biases in behavioral research: A critical review of the literature and recommended remedies. *The Journal of Applied Psychology, 88*(5), 879–903. doi:10.1037/0021-9010.88.5.879

Powell, A., Piccoli, G., & Ives, B. (2004). Virtual teams: A review of current literature and directions for future research. *The Data Base for Advances in Information Systems, 35*(1), 6. doi:10.1145/968464.968467

Remidez, H. Jr, Stam, A., & Laffey, J. M. (2007). Web-based template-driven communication support systems: Using shadow netWorkspace to support trust development in virtual teams. *International Journal of e-Collaboration, 3*(1), 65. doi:10.4018/jec.2007010104

Roofe, A. (2009). *A model of e-leadership and team processes: A multivariate application.* Paper presented at the 2009 Joint Statistical Meetings. Washington, DC.

Rousseau, D. M. (1985). Issues of level in organizational research: Multi-level and cross-level perspectives. *Research in Organizational Behavior, 7*, 1–37.

Sarker, S., Valacich, J., & Sarker, S. (2003). Virtual team trust: Instrument development and validation in an IS educational environment. *Information Resources Management Journal, 16*(2), 35. doi:10.4018/irmj.2003040103

Scales, D. C., & Rubenfeld, G. D. (2005). Estimating sample size in critical care clinical trials. *Journal of Critical Care, 20*(1), 6–11. doi:10.1016/j.jcrc.2005.02.002

Scales, R. (1998). Trust, not technology, sustains coalitions. *Parameters: US Army War College Quarterly, 28*(4), 4.

Tse, H. H. M., Dasborough, M. T., & Ashkanasy, N. M. (2008). A multi-level analysis of team climate and interpersonal exchange relationships at work. *The Leadership Quarterly, 19*(2), 195–211. doi:10.1016/j.leaqua.2008.01.005

Turoff, M. (1985). Information, value, and the internal marketplace. *Technological Forecasting and Social Change, 27*, 357–373. doi:10.1016/0040-1625(85)90017-4

Wech, B. A. (2001). *Team-member exchange and trust contexts: Effects on individual level outcome variables beyond the influence of leader-member exchange.* Ph.D. Dissertation. Baton Rouge, LA: Louisiana State University.

Whitener, E. M., Brodt, S. E., Korsgaard, M. A., & Werner, J. M. (1998). Managers as initiators of trust: An exchange relationship framework for understanding managerial trustworthy behavior. *Academy of Management Review, 23*(3), 513–530.

Zaccaro, S. J., & Lowe, C. A. (1986). Cohesiveness and performance on an additive task: Evidence for multidimensionality. *The Journal of Social Psychology, 128*, 547. doi:10.1080/00224545.1988.9713774

Chapter 5
Creation of Indicators Determining the Work of High-Tech Business Practitioners:
Validity, Reliability, and Negotiation Revisited

Irene Lorentzen Hepsø
Sør-Trøndelag University College/Trondheim Business School, Norway

Vidar Hepsø
Norwegian University of Science and Technology, Norway

ABSTRACT

The authors address how performance indicators are configured and engineered in ERP-systems to follow up the activities of the knowledge workers in an oil and gas company. ERP-systems enable the development of new performance indicator systems, and give management simple dashboard tools to follow up and compare the performance of the organizational members across time and space. Decisions in organizations are increasingly taken on the basis of these abstract indicators that work as signs and inscriptions. This makes the development of such accounting indicators an interesting area of research because the representation of such indicators will to a large extent govern the decision making and practices of the organization. Who inscribes and controls the indicators controls the business. The authors discuss the development of such indicators as an inscription and translation process and how the indicators develop as a consequence of negotiations between influential actors. Finally, they address the consequences of these indicators and argue that they are dependent upon three key issues: the validity of the indicators, their reliability, and how indicators are negotiated. The authors' research question is how do disparate organizational groups interplay with physical and technical elements to create indicators determining the work of high-tech business practitioners?

DOI: 10.4018/978-1-4666-1836-7.ch005

INTRODUCTION

Knowledge intensive work is increasingly sought controlled directly or discretely by Information and Communication Technology (ICT), putting the knowledge worker increasingly under corporate control. From a strategic and coordination perspective, it makes sense that management should be able to follow up the activities sufficiently to develop appropriate work design and work processes, and as a consequence be able to put forward strategies for prioritized areas and cooperative relations. Such a management mindset has worked in the past and is providing a strong motivation to continue a command and control approach of the business. This chapter is intended for those interested in the dynamics between accounting practices and organizational control with ICT whether from an engineering, accounting or organization science perspective. We address ERP-systems, short for enterprise resource planning, a special type of ICT that integrate data from all facets of the business, including planning, manufacturing, sales, and marketing modules. SAP, one of these ERP-systems, is not standard off-the-shelf software; it is a meta-software within a workflow architecture that connects a database to the above modules. Without data specifications (how and what data will be stored) and business processes (how business transactions are sequenced and draw upon or modify this data), the ERP-system will not fulfill its purpose (Quattrone & Hopper, 2006, p. 225).

ERP-systems also differ from other information systems in their complexity, scale and organizational impact (Kallinikos, 2004), and deserve greater attention with regard to their impact on organizational control (Ignatiadis & Nandhakumar, 2009). Some of the embedded features of the ERP-system and its system of control will have consequences for the work of knowledge workers (Kallinikos, 2004). Even though direct automation of knowledge workers expertise in ERP-systems is not likely, a more moderate consequence for knowledge work is the change of the social structures of the organization. New experts are created and previous expertise is made redundant. An ERP system also measures individual performance in new ways. A higher degree of standardization and codification of work is necessary. There are increasing demands to data management and discipline. Data must be entered "correctly" the first time, if not the integrated features of the ERP-system will have unforeseen consequences (Hanseth, et al., 2001). ERP improves accounting control by increasing visibility in two ways; both the amount of information and the speed at which it becomes available. Such systems change the focus of management accounting from financial to physical (Dechow & Mouritsen, 2005, p. 691). An ERP system shrinks distances, particularly in making centralized or shared services possible (Quattrone & Hopper, 2005, p. 737).

However, it is not our intention to address ERP-systems in general in this Chapter. We are more concerned with the *indicators* that are configured and engineered to follow up the activities of the knowledge workers *based on the input from ERP-systems.* An *indicator* is defined as a sign that tries to present vital features of given parts of an organizational reality aggregated and detached from its local contexts of time and space.

The multi-disciplinary activities of today's knowledge intensive businesses are complex. Managers located far away from the operational activities must follow up work and take decisions in areas where they have little expertise. As a response to the increasingly complexity of knowledge intensive businesses software companies have developed tools to systematize and simplify this complexity through models and indicators. ERP-systems with real-time data enable the development of performance indicators based on this information, and give management simple dashboard tools to follow up the performance of the knowledge workers. As such, accounting systems like SAP are able to compress time and space (Robson, 1992). In essence, the integrated approach to control and automation in an ERP-system makes a traditional form of hierarchical supervision less important and decisions are increasingly taken on the basis of these indicators (Quattrone & Hopper, 2005, 2006).

Actor network theory has over the years earned a central place in the mobilization processes around the development and inscriptions of new accounting systems and indicators (i.e. Robson, 1992; Chua, 1995; Baxter & Chua, 2003; Mouritsen, et al., 2009). An *inscription* here is any item or a configuration of such items that can transform a material substance into a figure or diagram. Chua (1995, p. 115) draws the parallel between the development of new accounting indicators and the scientific controversies in the world of Latour (1999). We continue in this tradition and address the consequences of these indicators. Here we argue that they are dependent upon three key issues. First the validity or relevance of the indicators, and second their reliability. Finally, how indicators emerge as a consequence of negotiations between influential actors. Our research question is: "How do disparate organizational groups interplay with physical and technical elements to create indicators determining the work of high-tech business practitioners?"

The structure of the Chapter is as follows. We start with the case, method and present our theoretical perspective. This is followed up with a presentation of the case, the development of new accounting practices and indicators that accompany the implementation of an ERP-system. We analyze the case in relation to our theoretical perspective and provide a conclusion.

CASE AND METHOD

The case from a multi-national oil and gas company presented is probably the biggest ERP-deployment in Norway ever. The primary activities of the company are exploration of new oil and gas fields, operation and maintenance of a number of offshore oil and gas production installations, operation and maintenance of refineries, transportation, marketing, and distribution of intermediate and end products. The operational community addressed in our cases is organized in the Exploration and Production unit, in this paper named EPN. It consists of the people that work on the 15 oil and gas producing assets that the company operates, and the land organization that supports these offshore environments. The ERP-programme reported directly to top management, counted 300 people at the most and lasted for five years. Their mandate was to develop and facilitate implementation of the ERP-system and its accompanying organizational solutions.

The work presented in this Chapter is an interpretative, longitudinal case study (1996-2001). The first author has followed the design and implementation of the ERP-system, the accompanying work processes, and organizational change closely for four years. She followed the programme from the start through the implementation as part of her PhD-work (Hepsø, 2005). The second author had a role in the ERP feasibility-study and followed the interaction between the consultancy team and participating assets during the development of work processes and business cases leading up to the ERP-deployment decision in 1996. Empirically, this study draws upon several sources: participant observations, semi- and unstructured interviews and paper-based as well as electronic documentation (Hepsø & Hepsø, 2007). A total of 120 different meetings have been observed over the period. These meetings include central project meetings, local project meetings at the different sites as well as management meetings and divisional meetings. A total of 40 semi- and unstructured interviews have been conducted. Interviews typically lasted 1–5 hours. The search for data has resulted in about 1000 pages of hand-written notes, including reflections and comments added immediately after the interviews. The oil company, operating within a sector with a strong tradition for highly codified quality regimes, keeps an extensive record of paper-based and electronic information. We have had access to: reports, memos, slide presentations, and email discussions.

PANOPTIC CONTROL: VALIDITY, RELIABILITY, AND NEGOTIATIONS

Not surprisingly, the metaphor of the Panopticon has been used to denote the characteristics of ERP-systems and how such systems control the behavior of knowledge workers. Sia et al. (2002) were among the first to study ERP-systems with a panoptic lens and show that ERP-systems can entail both tighter management control and empowerment of employees. However, ERP deployments tend to be biased towards increased panoptic control unless there is clear Management intent to do otherwise (Sia, et al., 2002, pp. 33-35). Taking Sia et al.'s work further Elmes et al. (2005) addressed two contradictory features in ERP-systems; reflective conformity and panoptic empowerment. Reflective conformity denotes the integrated nature of the ERP-systems and how it leads to increased discipline by users. At the same time they must be reflective in order to harvest the organizational benefits from the ERP-systems. Panoptic empowerment grows out of the greater visibility of information provided by the integrated database of the ERP-system. The paradox is that this visibility can empower the employees to do their work more efficiently. However, the cost is that their contribution to the ERP-system is more visible both to managers and peers, which also makes it easier to exercise control. Both reflective conformity and panoptic empowerment is strongly linked to indicator development. We will now address three main features validity, reliability, and negotiations to address indicator development.

By *validity of indicators* we mean to what degree the sign depicts what is relevant or represent a proper resemblance with the real phenomenon. However, our criteria of relevance are related to

the long-term operative challenges and development of the company's activities. Management accounting signs allow the health of a company to be "imaged and counted indirectly" (Chua, 1995, p. 2005). We examine how indicators are translated into practice and argue that what makes an indicator actionable is not a property of its definition. Accounting indicators in an ERP-system represent in many respects Jean Baudrillard's semiotic hyper-reality (Baudrillard, 1995). This is a world that is both a representation and reality, where accounting and indicators are accepted as approximations of the real thing. "Reality" is recognized only when re-produced in simulation or mediated via the ERP-system. Quantitative accounting inscriptions in an ERP system makes it easier to exercise a comparative, normative judgment, which also creates the foundation for action from a distance. Indicator development can be seen as a continuing refinement of mobile, stable and combinable inscriptions that expedite long distance control (Robson, 1992).

A heterogeneous actor network must be mobilised and sustained for the accounting practice to move from claims to facts (Latour, 1999). A lack of alignment between inscriptions and the objects to which they refer to in the world is a problem for those that wish to act at a distance (Robson, 1992, p. 691). The practice of action at a distance means to align calculations developed in one setting to action performed in another setting. The indicators configured in the ERP-system can enable real time data flow seamlessly from a local to a central location. At this *centre of calculation* (Latour, 1999, p. 304) the output from indicators can be interpreted, integrated and re-combined in numerous configurations. Such a centre evolves via its ability to compare and combine, to dominate inscriptions through processes of aggregation, equation buildings, graphs, charts and accounts across stretches of space and time (Dambrin & Robson, 2009, p. 46). Action at a distance now becomes possible. Real-time and global visibility collapse traditional notions of time and space making integrated, centralized management achievable (Dechow & Mouritsen, 2005).

You can have weak or strong inscriptions for action. Economic indicators are strong inscriptions and they are part of a larger program. Inscriptions link practices and makes mobilization possible. Indicators as inscriptions do their best when they can be moved, recombined in new patterns, and superimposed into new inscriptions (Dambrin & Robson, 2009, p. 12). Simple indicators can be aggregated into financial figures. As Ahrens and Chapman (2007) argue the extent to which indicators are perceived as functional and useful, or as dysfunctional and problematic, is situational contingent.

Accountants and SAP designers may rarely physically see the products or locations or people they represent. Their tools make abstract references to objects using entries originated by transactions denoting the existence of say products 'in stock' (another abstraction) in the guise of a number. Accounting describes costs, revenues, and so forth in their absence even when references like 'inventory' refer to concrete objects in the warehouse... (Quattrone & Hopper, 2006, p. 229).

By the *reliability of indicators we mean to what extent the output provided by indicators can be trusted.* Spraakman (2008) addresses the relationship between accounting signs and their underlying realities. He evaluates the consequences of using bar codes and ERP systems to track products in real terms in a company that changed the inventory classification system as a part of the ERP-implementation. Instead of recording an inventory item as $10 for an unspecified shirt, the company also recorded, i.e., a men's Arrow shirt, blue, 16.5 inch neck, and 32 inch sleeve. Spraakman shows how ERP systems with barcodes influence management accounting use of signs. The number of unspecified objects decreased dramatically to be followed by a large increase in the specification and codification of the inventory objects. He argues that accounting

signs reflect exchange value rather than use value. In this sense, a dollar transaction like the $10 shirt is a market transaction. However, use value is concerned with physical properties or qualitative attributes such as the men's Arrow shirt above. Although products or services have different qualities as use values, as exchange values they differ only by quantity. This difference between use and exchange value has also been discussed by Quattrone and Hopper (2006):

For example, a spare part purchase may be classified as maintenance and repairs and charged against a production department's operating costs, or it can be attributed to a design error, charged to an engineering department, and classified as a capital cost. How this transaction is represented influences performance measures and accountability within the firm. Moreover, who can post, classify, access information, and when, has management control consequences. Computer technologies such as ERPs may be replacing hand-written ledgers but seeing things through double-entry book- keeping remains an issue (Quattrone & Hopper, 2006, p. 235).

Reflective conformity (Elmes, 2005) already presented becomes important here. The integrated nature of the ERP-systems must be accompanied by increased user discipline. At the same time use of the accounting system must be reflective and attentive to maintain the reliability of the data and minimize the challenge with double entry book-keeping.

EMPIRICAL DATA: ACCOUNTING AND INDICATOR DEVELOPMENT

Process and Context

We now present examples from indicator development. Standardisation was one of the crucial ideas of the ERP-programme and one of the main slogans for the programme was:

Similar activities should be organized similarly.

This slogan fitted the "best practice"-regime of the 90s. It also meant that activities should be measured the same way using the same indicators across the company. The ERP and workflow solutions developed the first year should be implemented without local adjustments throughout the entire organization during the next three years by local implementation projects. To develop solutions appropriate for all business assets the ERP-project wanted the business assets to take part in the development process with their best people. The ERP-programme manager told us:

If the operative units expect us to listen to their voices they must approach us now, the battle is going on in this very minute. It is now that it is possible to take their needs and expectations into consideration. When the solutions are developed and we start the implementation process, it will be too late. We cannot change the practices at this stage. Deviations to our standard practices will not be tolerated. If someone gets their change requirements through not only their own solutions will be changed, even the standard solution has to be changed. The solutions shall be identical all over.

The business assets had several prioritized activities; to keep up the production and HSE targets were more important indicators. The competence profile of the ERP-development team thus became very different from what the ERP-project foresaw. Operative personnel with local knowledge from the business units were poorly represented. The development team was better characterized as generalists. This made the business assets sceptical to the ERP-solutions and their appropriateness for company operations. Just before the ERP-implementation one of the assets established a committee to recommend the best way to organize the operative work in the assets. This committee consisted of offshore personnel only, and 50% of them represented the trade-unions. In a meeting in this committee one of asset representatives said:

Our asset asks EPN-management to come up with a document that states clearly how stringent each asset must follow the 'best practices.' It is difficult to have new organizational solutions dumped on our heads by people that do not know our organization.

The worries about the solutions being too general, and not made to fit the needs of local operations, were a real concern. One of the consultants that represented the development team told us:

I'm not in this house every day, I work with different companies at the same time. There are many companies working with the same solutions now. Working on several projects at the same time is OK. In the end it is the same solutions we deliver to all companies

The "best practices" existed in the SAP software workflow library. The development process was to choose between these alternatives, build work processes to fit the chosen IT-standard, and adjust the IT-solution and the work processes. SAP competence turned out to be a critical factor that made it necessary to engage more consultants than planned.

The implementation project was a typical BPR (Business Process Reengineering) project. The representations articulating and spreading the best practices were heavily influenced by the BPR-literature. Even examples and jokes (!) presented by the ERP-project members came from the BPR-literature. The large amount of consultants, combined with the location of the programme organization outside the rest of the company, made them develop their special language. Employees elsewhere in the organization noticed this, and a key company member of the ERP-organization said:

We have developed our special language in the office settings where we work here in Stavanger. It is a mix of oil-company, Gemini London and BPR-literature.

As presented in the introduction of this case, the EPN looked upon themselves as the dominant contributor and 'money machine' both vis-a-vis the company and in relation to the Norwegian state. They wanted to set the standards for the new indicators themselves. To illustrate their priority of Health, Safety, and Environment (HSE) the offshore personnel talked about their situation as "working and living on a bomb." The ERP-members told they acted on a CEO-management mandate. They should in their point of view be in position to define corporate and EPN work practices and indicators. The ERP-programme and EPN did not establish common arenas. EPN did not involve themselves in the arenas the ERP-programme invited them. The ERP-programme avoided at least some of the EPN arenas in which they were invited. A vague understanding of each other roles and hardly any common arenas made them develop different perspectives of the implementation in EPN, both of the 'best practices' and indicators developed in the ERP-system. These two quotes from one business asset in their preparation for implementation illustrate the atmosphere: The first is a report from the change committee (offshore personnel) to the management:

Technicians feel that they have succeeded in running operations efficiently according to the organizational concepts in place and that this concept can be further developed to give even more improvements. They believe they can develop world class standards through this concept. The main problem is that nobody is able to explain how the new practices will be more efficient. We have talked with the best ERP-people, but they cannot tell us.

The second quote is from offshore personnel involved in the asset implementation of the ERP-project. Andrew, Bill, and Charles stated after having a meeting on the new practices and discuss this in relation to the existing ways of measuring performance:

Andrew: I have had information meetings with 3-4 assets, nobody understands the logic behind the reorganization. Are we not running our facilities good enough today?

Bill: I have met people offshore and mailed everybody. The feedback was crystal-clear. Everybody wanted to further develop our existing concept. They don't see how they can make more money by changing their work practices. The work environment in general, HSE and keeping up the production are what matters. The last McKinsey benchmarking shows that we are 'world-class.' I do not understand why we should implement practices that will reduce the revenue of our facilities.

Charles: We have no advantages to present, and I can see the potential in developing our own concept further. This is the first step, what will be the next? Is this honesty? Why do they want us to participate in this? Why don't they just implement it and take the beating afterwards? The strategic agenda is set no matter how!

These EPN-employees found it difficult to understand the logic of the ERP-programme, the new indicators and the implementation of the 'best practices.' We now present two examples of the negotiation processes from the implementation of the ERP-system and the accompanying indicators.

The Integrated Team Concept

The overall objective was to move the hierarchical and function based organization to a process oriented organization. One of the concepts developed was "an integrated team" as the smallest building block of a production asset. Integrated team was intended to be an important indicator since the company wanted to compare the performance of the various integrated teams in and across the assets: "Similar activities should be organized similarly." We describe what happens when this sign is tried inscribed across time and space to fuel the development of a centre of calculation. When EPN ignored and did not prioritize giving resources to the ERP-programme, the ERP-programme management had to take new steps to align their agenda with that of EPN. The integrated team concept was seen as something that could bridge and align the agenda. This concept is inspired by Herbst's (1976) work on autonomous work teams and alternatives to hierarchies. In the ERP-programme the integrated team was responsible for operation and maintenance of the technical systems, including all activities and costs related to these systems. "Integrated" meant that several functions and disciplines were present in the team doing various parts of the work. This form of organization is in many ways a contrast to the functional and domain oriented organization.

The ERP-programme inscribed functionality in the new company SAP-solution. Integrated teams were to become the primary organizational practice via inscribing it as an indicator. The prevailing practice in most assets was that work was centered around hierarchical and domain specific groups like mechanics and electricians. Middle management coordinated the necessary work across the domains. Some of the oldest assets had employed senior operators as a kind of foreman that did considerable middle management jobs like planning and reporting routines. Since this role led to an extra-level in the hierarchy and was tricky vis-à-vis the idea of an integrated team, it could not be accepted in the quest for a process-oriented organization. The role of the senior operator had caused lot of discussion between the ERP-project and the assets. The assets wanted to maintain the senior position for several reasons.

First, because they argued the senior operators performed an important quality control of health, environment and safety issues, and second because in addition to middle management the position of senior operators represented a career opportunity for the operators.

The next move to enforce integrated team, as an indicator through the ERP-system was to make specifications in the "work-center" that required integrated teams. The essence was to combine the principles of reflexive conformity and panoptic empowerment (Elmes, 2005). A work-center is a work organization unit in the ERP-system that defines where and when an activity must be performed. They can be machines, people or production lines or in this case integrated teams. Work centers also provide access to role-specific functions in SAP. As such the structure of a work center depends on the user organization roles and this predefines the access to relevant messages, alerts, reports, and documents. In order to do work and maintenance out in the production facility, a work-order has to be written and approved in the ERP-system. The ERP-system had inscribed a particular procedure for work-orders. For each work-order, the necessary types of personnel resources had to be selected by the "work-center"; i.e. mechanics and electricians in order to plan the work in a proper way. The problem was that the ERP- programme had configured the IT system in such a way that "integrated team" was the only selected category of personnel resources. This was done because it was inscribed as a key indicator. It was not possible to specify disciplinary skills needed for a particular work task; for instance a particular certificate of apprenticeship. At first, it seemed that the enforcement of the integrated team indicator should become an accepted organizational standard. The first asset in EPN to implement the ERP-standard accepted this inscription reluctantly after a quarrel. During the second implementation, in the next production asset, the collaboration between the various implementation leaders became of larger importance. Each of the 15 business/production assets had chosen an implementation leader responsible for the local implementation project. Headed by EPN's ERP-coordinator these 15 implementation leaders met every second week to get news and discuss the ERP-programme. Starting to understand the ERP-system, the nature of new indicators and translating their interests around the ERP-system, they disagreed with the work-center inscription. The strength these implementation leaders mobilized left the ERP-programme with no option but to change the work-center inscription for the second implementation. In the new configuration of the ERP-system specified functions like electrician and mechanic and not only integrated team were made available as available resources. To maintain a core concept of an integrated standard, the first asset also had to change their version of the work center standard. The consequence was that the indicator integrated team became tiresome to follow up but the ERP-programme still wanted to pursue this possibility.

When the ERP-programme was unable to enroll the inscription of both the work centers and the process oriented organization another strategy emerged. A detour was needed to enroll new alliance partners. With top management commitment, the new element tried enrolled to support the indicator was an offer of a new wage category. The assets that chose integrated teams as the organizational model would automatically receive compensation in the form of a new wage category. This was a considerably increase in salary for the offshore workers and should make them more positive to the concept of integrated teams. Another consequence of this new wage category was that the operators reached the salary level of senior operators that had been an established working practice in some assets.

The ERP-programme succeeded in removing the senior operator function, but the integrated team model became mainly an espoused idea in most assets. It never became an indicator that was used to follow up the work of offshore workers.

The assets kept their old organizational structure but adjusted the existing functions and gave them new names more in line with the concepts of the time. As reported by one of the implementation leaders in one of the assets:

Yes, we have integrated teams. To support the SAP-idea of integrated teams we have developed two teams. Most of the operations offshore were included in one huge integrated team.

EPN business assets interpreted the new indicators based on their interests, programs, agendas and existing practices. When they tried to align the 'best practices' and new indicators developed by the ERP-project with their existing practices, they found that some matched satisfactory and became enrolled. Other 'best practices' and indicators were accepted through small modifications. A number of indicators did not fit the EPN-identity and were not accepted. The ERP-project had envisioned and developed a complete system of 'best practices' and IT-applications that included a number of new indicators. This holistic system of ERP business processes should provide the added value through its unity. However, EPN split the various elements up into different standards, enabling the EPN business assets to pick those elements and indicators they found most appropriate based on their program and their agendas. The holistic ideas and their effects were not harvested.

The Integrated Supply Chain

Over a number of years, the company had been developing frame contracts with major suppliers. Lack of coordination vis-à-vis suppliers was perceived as a general challenge and existing contracts were not sufficiently used by the local purchasers. The ERP-project saw the potential in improving the logistics and purchasing process since it matched the ideas and standards of the ERP-system. Since BPR process thinking and logistics have been closely connected, there was no surprise that the business cases showing the largest saving potentials were within the supply chain. Embedded in the ERP-system was the inscription of an integrated supply chain where the ordering of new items was handled according to a standard supply chain workflow with accompanying indicators. A number of new indicators were set up to control the purchasing process and follow up the inventory of the assets. When changes in the work-flow were executed this would have immediate consequences in the other modules of the ERP-system. The request for a particular item was initiated in the plant maintenance module reported in a cost structure in the economy module. The time used for the work by each employee doing the work was registered in the HR module. All activities associated with the movement of the item was within the logistics module (picking the item from the storage and activating an order to the supplier). This integration enabled automation of several functions. Automation requires a set up of predefined inventory codifications of items. This codification in conjunction with the frame contracts facilitated the development of a standardized system in which the suppliers could codify their items according to this standard. The company therefore had a codified purchasing standard that could be enrolled in an ERP-system. The consequence of the inscription of the integrated value chain was that it facilitated the removal of the purchasers as gatekeepers in the logistic chain. Control via indicators should replace their role. Since the inscribed workflow was automated and pretty standardized the people offshore could order the items themselves through the ERP-system. This idea was an empowerment of the offshore operators. At the same time it enabled the potential removal of the intermediate purchaser function. As in the previous example the principles of reflexive conformity and panoptic empowerment were sought combined. Even though the standards and the ERP system facilitated the decreasing role of the purchaser function this function was still needed to create economy-of-scale effects both

within and across assets. Since not all purchased items could be handled with the emerging codification system the purchasers competence were needed. Asset management also regarded the radical empowerment of the operators too risky and wanted to manage the supply chain of their organization, control operational costs and coordinate the overall activities of the asset.

In our first encounters with the external consultants working with the development of key procurement and supply chain principles, they presented the expected gain from this domain. A considerable amount of this revenue came from the 'virtual storehouse' concept.' Each asset had its own storage for critical replacement items. Some assets shared the same storehouse, but kept the inventory strictly separate. The type and number of indicators to follow up the inventory and logistics process differed among the assets. The ERP-consultants had figured out that by keeping just one storage with a common set of indicators for all assets would save considerable inventory and costs along the supply chain. However, as EPN became aware of this concept it was soon abandoned. Each asset is a juridical unit, a joint venture consisting of several oil-company partners. The ownership of the storage had to be aligned with the existing judicial and accounting structure, where the indicators in use in the assets supported the existing judicial accounting principles. The inventory articles were also poorly standardized across the assets. Thus, the economy-of-scale did not meet the expected gains.

ANALYSIS

We have followed the ERP-project of an oil company and looked in particular on the development of indicators that accompanies the development process. These indicators are configured and engineered to follow up the activities of the knowledge workers based on the input from ERP-systems. ERP systems change the focus on management accounting from financial to physical, enabled a shrinking of distances and making centralized or shared services possible. There were many strong and independent assets with unique local practices. Since the ERP-projects ambition was to develop best practices, compare across functions, and centralise, it is relevant to see the development of new indicators as something that goes on within a framework of a centre of calculation. The ERP-project is about developing a centre of calculation to ease control at a distance with new indicators. In this work, both with the integrated team and the supply chain examples the project tried to make action at a distance possible by aligning or linking calculations and existing practices in one asset to calculations and action performed in another asset. It was the indicators configured in the ERP-system through the integrated team and the integrated supply chain that should enable real-time data-flow seamlessly from a local to a central location. The local output from the indicators we presented could be interpreted and integrated, recombined in numerous configurations with the help of SAP and increase management control. Throughout the ERP-deployment this centre of calculation (manifested as the ERP-project) evolved by trying to (not always successfully) compare and combine, to dominate inscriptions through processes of aggregation, equation buildings, graphs, charts and accounts. Much of the strategies and communication with EPN was of this character. Even though many of the initial ambitions were never harvested some of these inscriptions survived and formed a program that made action at a distance easier to accomplish after the ERP-implementation. The issue of organizational control was also important since the ERP-deployment changed accounting control by increasing visibility, both the amount of information and the speed at which it became available.

To understand some of the basic principles behind the ERP-deployment strategy we have to revisit the concepts of reflective conformity and panoptic empowerment. Without the successful deployment of these principles the ERP-system would not work. Reflective conformity presupposes increased user discipline, reflective and attentive users. Panoptic empowerment grows out of the greater visibility of information, which empowers the employees to do their work more efficiently, thereby making their work more visible and also making it easier to exercise control. We now analyse the case in relation to first, the validity and relevance of the indicators and second, their reliability vis-à-vis the business. Stability of the indicators relies upon the building and maintaining the relationship between the inscription as a 'sign' and the object, it signifies.

Validity and relevance. Did the company develop sufficient relevant solutions and indicators for the local practice during this year of adjustments? The ERP-programme was generously sponsored, and selected those consultants in Europe supposed to be most competent for the task. The "best practice" they developed was expected to be best, and that no one would argue against. The ERP-programme management was eager to have experienced and highly respected practitioners from the different assets on the developing team. For several reasons EPN-management did not prioritize the ERP-programme, mainly due to more urgent increased production initiatives. Increased revenue and produced oil were more important than administrative improvements. It follows from this that indicators supporting increased revenue and produced oil were more important than administrative indicators that supported more narrow admin processes.

External consultants developing equal solutions for all their customers coupled with the lack of operative resources in the developing team made it difficult to build solutions (indicators) fitting local practice. The most extreme indicators suggested were related to the virtual inventory, presented as a considerable part of the estimated cost reduction. It did not last long before the ERP-programme was told it was not viable because of both juridical and practical reasons. Solutions this inappropriate were easily detected. Looking for relevance, the first question is how relevant the standard indicators of the ERP-systems are to the local practice? As companies invest in these systems to benefit from the high level of standardization that reduce operational costs of the IT-system, they prefer to use the standards as far as possible. The next question is if it is possible to change local practice to fit the standard ERP-solutions? This question involves the physical and technical systems of the work place, if the practice supported by the ERP-standards fits the existing architectural structure. If not, the technical and physical structure might be rebuilt without too much additional costs. In our case, this was not feasible. The question of changing practice might also be juridical, as in the virtual storage example. When each asset is a juridical unit with a board and owners, it is not proper to build a virtual storage with shared ownership among the assets. It is also a question of competence, understanding, and motivation. Do the employees have the proper competence? Do they lack an understanding of the ideas behind the indicators, or are they unwilling to change practice? The company in this case chose to adjust the standard solutions to their organization. The problems of relevance then should not be as much of a problem for this company than for those selecting the standards without adjustments. Even though there were some problems of relevance in this case as well.

A multi-sited implementation brings difficulties of relevance, as indicators relevant for one asset might be of less relevance for another asset. Oil and gas production assets are developed and built on specifications delivered by a project defining the technical, physical and organizational solutions as an integrated whole based on the last technical and organizational competence. This is why these assets are unique and there are considerably differences between them, physical as well as technical and organizational. The new field developments (new assets) of the company were developed in parallel with the ERP-programme. We could easily see the similarity in the organizational ideas of the ERP-programme and the practice developing in these assets. They were physically and technically built to support the organizational practice of integrated teams. The oldest assets were built for a traditional functional organization. Considerably changes of the physical structure on an offshore installation are not realistic. Integrated team was therefore not considered as suitable for the older installations. These functionally organized installations had an extra hierarchical level, the senior operator. The organizational solutions developed by the ERP-programme meant huge differences for some assets, when other assets felt quite comfortable, as the solutions seemed to be quite similar to the existing practice. Lack of relevance of the ERP-solutions for some assets created a huge difference between the ERP-programme and the EPN-implementation leaders. The implementation leaders claimed the ERP-project was too theoretical and far away from a practical reality. When it came to the details, the new assets felt more or less the same. Even though the big picture was comparable, the concrete procedures felt problematic for them as well. For instance the "work-center" as designed by the ERP-programme suited neither the old nor the new assets. The design was understood as an attempt to inscribe integrated team to enforce this organizational structure. But all assets wanted flexibility to specify the accurate competence needed for a task, and urged the ERP-programme to redesign the work-center even though this meant lots of work for both the ERP-programme and the assets already implemented the first version. EPN had a dominating role, was the company's breadwinner and the ERP-programme had to listen to their demands. We could see that the first version had plenty of indicators that were not relevant or valid for the operational activities, but through tough negotiations the implemented version were relevant and accepted.

Reliability. When it comes to reliability, the consequences are not as detectable as those of validity. The intricate level of integration of ERP-systems means the demands for consistency are strong. The work order registered by an operator generates data for four modules; Plant maintenance, Purchase, Human Resource and Economy. If the operator enters wrong numbers, this failure escalates through the automatic processes across the modules. The reliability of the data and all indicators building on these data are then reduced. The discipline needed is significant. Every day every employee in the company enters crucial data feeding the algorithms generating indicators for decision-making. To make failures are human, and we need to suppose some failures are made in this process of providing input through workflows. The question is how reliable the input to the indicators is as we know there are poor data input moving through the automatic generated processes characterizing the ERP-systems? Let us go back to the supply chain. When the ERP-system is this closely connected to all the nitty-gritty details of practice, every item needs to be identified in the system. Our company had a lot of material items in use that were not codified, and started a huge process of codification to make all items uniquely identified. If all operators are permitted to order items and frame contracts decide to which supplier the order are delivered, there cannot be any un-codified items. However in practice, technology and systems are not stable, there will always be situations where new items not codified are needed. This issue is just one facet of reliability, the degree of un-codified material and how this 'disorder' is treated.

Coordinators such as senior operators and purchasers were removed to reduce hierarchy and make the organization more process oriented. They had hands on competence and understanding difficult to automate. Middle managers also had a crucial task in coordination. The practice where middle managers approved all travel documents and work orders was important for information management. Through this practice, middle managers always knew what was going on, an ideal situation for them to coordinate people and

activities. The ERP-project handled this by letting all employees provide the input directly, without middle management approval. An important part of the information management practice was reduced through automation. Many of the existing practices to check reliability of data had to be re-constructed with the deployment of, and it took considerable time before these quality assurance processes where up and running again.

CONCLUSION

Four main phases constitute ERP-projects: ideas and intentions, development, implementation, and new practice. In our case, different actors were involved and had a dominating role in different phases. The ERP-programme was established with a top management mandate. The programme was the dominant actor regarding ideas of why and how the project would be planned and executed. Since top management regarded the intended consequences of the ERP-deployment as very important, the needed resources were mobilised and a programme project manager hired. Translation of the top management ideas to accounting indicators and work processes became the main task for the ERP-programme. Since operational competence was hard to enlist, the ERP-programme recruited external consultants, administrative staff, and young ambitious employees with little operational experience. In the development phase, the external consultants were the dominant actor in the translation of ideas to indicators. Version one of indicators were mainly identical to standards developed by consultants for several enterprises across branches, the down side too little relevance vis-à-vis operational practice. Local business assets were responsible for the implementation. Operational experts became aware of the ERP-programme, they had discussed it for a while, but the negotiations between the local assets and the ERP-programme turned serious when the implementation was coming up. As responsible for the implementation and given its strong position in the company, the local assets managed to re-negotiate several indicators. New versions were developed based on indicators more valid and relevant in relation to the operational practice. The indicators were implemented and new practice established. The practitioners had the dominant role in this phase. A combination of the inscriptions of negotiated and implemented indicators and the practitioner's translations of these indicators led to new operational practices. Management accounting was changed in accordance with most top management intentions. However, promised cost benefits did not meet the business case presented by the ERP-programme, due to the negotiated structure of implemented work process and accounting indicators. Still, the infrastructure and accounting system made possible further development of process orientation, cost control, standardization across assets, and an integrated centre of calculation. Both empowerment and panoptic control were increased.

REFERENCES

Ahrens, T., & Chapman, C. (2006). Doing qualitative research in management accounting: Positioning data to contribute to theory. *Accounting, Organizations and Society, 31*(8), 819–841. doi:10.1016/j.aos.2006.03.007

Ahrens, T., & Chapman, C. (2007). Management accounting as practice. *Accounting, Organizations and Society, 32*(1-2), 1–27. doi:10.1016/j.aos.2006.09.013

Baudrillard, J. (1995). *Simulacra and simulation*. Ann Arbor, MI: University of Michigan Press.

Baxter, J., & Chua, W. F. (2003). Alternative management accounting research -Whence and whither. *Accounting, Organizations and Society, 28*(2-3), 97–126. doi:10.1016/S0361-3682(02)00022-3

Chua, W. F. (1995). Experts, networks and inscriptions in the fabrication of accounting images: A story of the representations of three public hospitals. *Accounting, Organizations and Society, 20,* 111–145. doi:10.1016/0361-3682(95)95744-H

Dambrin, C., & Robson, K. (2009). *Multiple measures, inscription instability and action at a distance: Performance measurement practices in the pharmaceutical industry*. Retrieved from http://econpapers.repec.org/paper/ebgheccah/0928.htm

Dechow, N., & Mouritsen, J. (2005). Enterprise resource planning systems, management control and the quest for integration. *Accounting, Organizations and Society, 30,* 691–733. doi:10.1016/j.aos.2004.11.004

Elmes, M. B., Strong, D. M., & Volkoff, O. (2005). Panoptic empowerment and reflective conformity in enterprise systems-enabled organizations. *Information and Organization, 15*(1), 1–37. doi:10.1016/j.infoandorg.2004.12.001

Hanseth, O., Ciborra, C., & Braa, K. (2001). The control devolution: ERP and the side effects of globalization. *The Data Base for Advances in Information Systems, 32*(4), 34–46. doi:10.1145/506139.506144

Hepsø, I. L. (2005). *Fra ide til praksis: En studie av endringsprosessen BRA i Alpha Oil*. [From idea to practice: A study of the BRA-change process in Alpha Oil]. PhD Dissertation. Trondheim, Norway: Norwegian University of Science and Technology.

Hepsø, I. L., & Hepsø, V. (2007). Conceptions of us-and-them in organizational reification, translation and legitimation processes: Two best practice and business process initiatives in Alpha Oil oil and gas operations. *Systems, Signs & Action, 3*(1), 134-161. Retrieved from http://www.sysiac.org/

Herbst, P. G. (1976). *Alternatives to hierarchies*. Leiden, Norway: M. Nijhoff Social Sciences Division. doi:10.1007/978-1-4684-6945-5

Ignatidas, I., & Nandhakumar, J. (2009). The effect of ERP system workaround on organizational control: An interpretivist study. *Scandinavian Journal of Information Systems, 21*(2), 59–90.

Kallinikos, J. (2004). Deconstructing information packages organizational and behavioural implications of ERP-systems. *Information Technology & People, 17*(1), 8–30. doi:10.1108/09593840410522152

Latour, B. (1999). *Pandora's hope: Essays on the reality of science studies.* Boston, MA: Harvard University Press.

Mouritsen, J., Hansen, A., & Hansen, C. Ø. (2009). Short and long translations: Management accounting calculations and innovation management. *Accounting, Organizations and Society, 34*(6-7), 738–754. doi:10.1016/j.aos.2009.01.006

Ouchi, W. G. (1977). The relationship between organizational structure and control. *Administrative Science Quarterly, 22*(1), 95–113. doi:10.2307/2391748

Quattrone, P., & Hopper, T. (2005). A 'time-space odyssey': Management control systems in two multinational organizations. *Accounting, Organizations and Society, 30*, 735–764. doi:10.1016/j.aos.2003.10.006

Quattrone, P., & Hopper, T. (2006). What is IT? SAP, accounting and visibility in a multinational organization. *Information and Organization, 16*, 212–250. doi:10.1016/j.infoandorg.2006.06.001

Robson, K. (1992). Accounting numbers as 'inscription': Action at a distance and the development of accounting. *Accounting, Organizations and Society, 17*(7), 685–708. doi:10.1016/0361-3682(92)90019-O

Sia, S. K., Tang, M., Soh, C., & Boh, W. F. (2002). Enterprise resource planning (ERP) systems as a technology of power: Empowerment or panoptic control. *The Data Base for Advances in Information Systems, 33*(1), 23–37. doi:10.1145/504350.504356

Spraakman, G. (2008). *A reality check for management accounting.* Retrieved from http://ssrn.com/abstract=1080433

KEY TERMS AND DEFINITIONS

BPR: Business Process Re-Engineering.
ERP: Enterprise Resource Planning.
EPN: Exploration and Production Norway.
HSE: Health, Safety, and Environment.
SAP: German vendor of ERP-software.

Chapter 6

So Into It They Forget What Time It Is?
Video Game Designers and Unpaid Overtime

Marie-Josée Legault
Téluq-UQAM, Canada

Kathleen Ouellet
Université de Montréal, Canada

ABSTRACT

This chapter draws on 53 interviews from a case study led in Montreal in 2008 to demonstrate the existence of Unlimited and Unpaid Overtime (UUO) among video game developers and illustrate an emerging workplace regulation model of working time in the videogame industry. It brings to light a sophisticated and efficient system of rewards and sanctions, both material and symbolic, that drives professional workers in these trades to adopt a "free unlimited overtime" behavior despite the Act Respecting Labour Standards. Efficiency of this system is rooted in combined Project Management (PM) as an organisation mode and high international mobility of the workforce that both makes portfolio and reputation utterly important. This chapter focuses on (de)regulation of working time only, but it opens a path to theoretically account for (de)regulation of work among an expanding workforce: the "new professionals" in knowledge work.

DOI: 10.4018/978-1-4666-1836-7.ch006

INTRODUCTION

The video game industry is a booming, prosperous multinational business dominated by a few big console manufacturers (Microsoft, Sony, Nintendo) and a handful of large video game publishers (Electronic Arts, Activision, Konami, Ubisoft, THQ) that exert significant control over downstream companies, particularly game design studios. Some of the industry giants have their own game design studios and/or buy games developed by smaller studios (Dyer-Witheford & de Peuter, 2009). Private research consultants are all forecasting strong growth for the industry in the West (Androvich, 2008), despite latent threats of outsourcing to countries with lower labour costs (Dyer-Witheford & de Peuter, 2009; Dyer-Witheford, 2005). It is even thought that the video game industry will soon dwarf all other entertainment sectors in terms of revenue (Fahey, 2005).

The situation is the same in Canada[1], where game studio revenue is exceeded only by that of the film and television industry and book publishing (Dyer-Witheford, 2005). Canada ranks sixth internationally in the video game industry, and its two main production hubs are Montreal and Vancouver. In Quebec, 25 of 39 studios are in Montreal and account for 81% of the jobs, which makes the city the main game development centre, with a total of 8,000 jobs forecast for 2011 (Dumais, 2009, p. 10). The Government of Canada is very generous in its support for the industry, and the Government of Quebec even more so, primarily through tax breaks for Montreal's Cité du multimédia, where up to a quarter of game production costs are said to be funded by government. Elsewhere in Canada, studios can also take advantage of federal tax exemptions for research and development (Alliance Numerique, 2003, 2008).

For many years, the problem of the long working hours that are typical of the industry has been played down in favour of an idealized image of a work-as-play ethos (Deuze, Bowen, & Allen, 2007; Dyer-Witheford, 2002, 2005) or 'playbour' (Kuchlich, 2005). Overwork is far from a rare phenomenon, however (De Peuter & Dyer-Witheford, 2005; Dyer-Witheford & Sharman, 2005, p. 203-204; Dyer-Witheford & De Peuter, 2006, p. 607-612). Overtime hours, meaning those that exceed the number specified in the employment contract, are referred to as 'crunch time.' In theory, designers are asked to work on evenings and weekends only during the days or weeks leading up to the shipping date for the game or a production milestone (IGDA, 2004, p. 13). In practice, however, overtime is more often the rule than the exception, according to the results of an on-line survey of 994 members of the International Game Developers Association (IGDA, 2004), amounting to 10% of its members in 2005 (IGDA, 2005).

Unpaid overtime is widespread in this industry. In the United States and elsewhere, video game designers are exempted from the legislative provisions governing payment for overtime hours:

Non-compensation of overtime hours. Nearly all game developers in the US are under "exempt" status, meaning that their overtime is uncompensated. Developers elsewhere must often work under similar conditions (IGDA, 2004, p. 49).

In Quebec, this noteworthy devastating trend is a significant drag on the industry: 70% of studios encounter recruitment problems (Dumais, 2009, p. 4) and retaining creative staff is a real issue (IGDA, 2004, p. 21; Chung, 2005).

In this chapter, we report on the working hours in the Quebec industry as reflected in the comments of 53 designers working in major on-line and console video game studios in Montreal, and on compensation for those hours. We then describe the legal framework that applies in Quebec, and how Quebec studios manage overtime within this framework. Afterwards, we compare the local industry with the industry as a whole in the West and report on our respondents' dissatisfaction with the local situation, which is comparable to that of the industry as a whole. The resulting portrait immediately raises the question: When overtime is not paid, in violation of the applicable statutory framework, how do companies get these in some respects unhappy developers to work so many hours of unpaid overtime? We put forward an explanation that is based on the existence of an informal, albeit highly effective system of rewards and punishments that relies primarily on the importance attached to reputation in an industry resolutely focused on creation and innovation.

Professional Group Studied

The qualifications of the people who work in this sector vary widely. The core of the industry consists of highly skilled game designers who have postsecondary training in computer science or the arts. They are on the young side (age 18–35; only 18% are over 35), childless (77%), have partners (66% as opposed to 57% in the general population), and are generally well paid ($60,000 on average in 2006); the vast majority (90%) are men. They are just beginning their careers (74.4% have been in the industry for 8 years or less) and therefore have little experience (56% say that their peers have been in the industry for 2 to 5 years). Even among the development team 'leads', fewer than 10% have more than 10 years' experience (De Peuter & Dyer-Witheford, 2005; IGDA, 2004, p. 15).

Both upstream and downstream, a host of contractual workers are employed in quality control and electronic materials manufacturing. Among them are testers, who have a precarious status and are paid minimum wage (Dyer-Witheford & de Peuter, 2009). Game development industry jobs break down as follows:

- 32% in programming
- 24% in quality control (testers, quality assurance technicians, software, support services, etc.)

- 23% in artistic production (3D artists, illustrators, 3D animators, interface designers, etc.)
- 10% in game design (scriptwriters, game designers, level designers)
- 10% in production management (production managers, producers, project managers, creative directors, artistic directors, technical directors) (Dumais, 2009, p. 4).

In this chapter, we will be dealing solely with game designers, a skilled industry segment that accounts for 76% of the workforce. Game design work is often described as the embodiment of the post-Fordist mode of production: a place of autonomy, innovation and self-realization virtually free of the contradictions inherent in capitalism (De Peuter & Dyer-Witheford, 2005)—and where it is totally 'cool' to work:

For millions of young men (and many aging ones, and some women) from Shanghai to Montreal, a job making virtual games seems employment nirvana—a promise of being paid to play. And it is true that for designers, programmers, and producers the industry offers creative, well paid work involving the most positive possibilities of "immaterial labour": Scientific know-how, hi-tech proficiency, cultural creativity, and workplace cooperation (Dyer-Witheford & de Peuter, 2009).

Game design jobs are full-time (96%) and permanent (93%), while part-time or contract positions are more common in testing and software (Dumais, 2009, p. 7). Game designers recognize the creative, gratifying dimension of their work, which stems from the undeniable level of complexity and stimulation (IGDA, 2004, p. 12). Flexible working hours, casual dress code, free meals, physical fitness facilities, funky interior design, a relaxed atmosphere that accommodates people with attitude or an offbeat sense of humour (De Peuter & Dyer-Witheford, 2005) are indeed part of the package, but don't tell the whole story. The industry also has a dark side.

Our Study

To draw up a profile of the situation in Quebec, in the summer of 2008 we surveyed 53 designers working in major Montreal on-line or console game studios (few work in the wireless or pocket video game segments)—Ubisoft (28), A2M (Artificial Mind & Movement) (15), Electronic Arts (EA) (3), Gameloft (3)—and a few who are independent or work in microstudios employing just a handful of designers (4). In view of our small sample size, our study deals solely with the salaried designers of major studios. Each of the big studios has between 300 and 2,000 employees.

We recruited our respondents by word of mouth, to begin with, and then by using the snowball method (asking respondents to refer other potential respondents to us), as well as by posting notices on the *International Game Developers Association* (IGDA) website and by soliciting respondents during IGDA social activities.

Our sample consists of equal numbers of men and women, despite the low proportion of female workers in the industry. We make no claims about statistical representativity, as our aim in establishing the sample was to help us understand the low numbers of women in the sector.

The designers are well educated: 98% of them have completed some form of post-secondary education, whether a diploma from a junior college or specialized private institute, a university certificate, or a bachelor's degree or master's degree. The breakdown of respondents by level of education (highest level attained) is shown in Table 1.

Their income level is also high when compared with the Quebec population in general: 62% of the respondents have an annual salary of over $50,000, even though over half of them (53%) have a level of education below a university bachelor's degree.

They are a distinctly young group, with an average age of 31.5 and 73% of them aged between 24 and 35. (Among IGDA members, the proportion of designers in the same age bracket is estimated to be 81.6% (IGDA, 2004, p. 15). They are generally much better paid than the average worker in their age group with their level of education, as Table 2 shows.

Our respondents are producers (project managers) or associate producers, game or level designers, programmers, sound designers, 2D or 3D artists, modellers or animators; some were 'leads' (team leaders) or support employees for designers in each of these areas. We excluded senior managers and managerial staff who are not subject to the provisions regarding payment of overtime hours (Quebec Act respecting labour standards, sec. 54[3]).

Table 1. Breakdown of respondents by level of education

Level of education	Number of respondents	%
Secondary	1	1.9%
Junior college, specialized private institutes of equivalent level or university certificate	27	51.0%
Bachelor's degree	21	39.6%
Master's degree	4	7.5%
Total	**53**	**100%**

Table 2. Average employment income of respondents with mean age of 31.5 and of Canadian population age 25 to 34, by highest level of education attained

	Junior college diploma	University degree
Average employment income – respondents	$54,583	$64,483
Average employment income – overall Canadian population age 25-34*	$29,627	$42,882

* Source: Statistics Canada, 2006 Census, Statistics Canada Catalogue No. 97-563-XCB2006054.

With the exception of contract employees, designers are not in principle excluded from the right to collective labour relations and have a right to unionize. However, they are neither unionized nor organized in any way in an advocacy group at any of the industry's studios, although they can join an association, such as the IGDA, which in the last few years has begun to play an advocacy role.

WORKING HOURS IN THE VIDEO GAME INDUSTRY

For 60% of designers, a typical work week amounts to over 46 hours, with 40% working between 46 and 55 hours, and the other 20% putting in over 55 hours. Most studios regularly go through crunch time in the lead up to milestones (according to 57% of respondents) or shipping (20% of respondents). These periods can last two weeks or more than two months (IGDA, 2004, p. 18).

During crunch time, 30.4% of respondents put in 55 to 65 hours a week, 35.2% 65 to 80 hours and 13% over 80 hours. Only 2.5% of them said they never do overtime. Half of respondents (51.7%) felt that management sees crunch time as being a normal part of the industry. For approximately the same proportion of respondents (46.8%), overtime is unpaid (IGDA, 2004, p. 19), but in the video game industry, this kind of statement is too vague to be taken at face value, as there is some confusion between partial compensation and pay, as we will see later.

The designers who answered the IGDA survey enjoy working in the industry (62% giving a rating of over 7 out of 10), but 35% are planning to leave the industry in the next five years and the majority (51.2%) plan to leave within the next 10 years. The long working hours are a factor in this anticipated exodus, with 23.7% of respondents saying they would like to see something done about this aspect of their jobs. As we have seen, most designers are young and have no children; a majority of them (61.5%) say they cannot see

themselves continuing to work at the same rate, as the long hours may have a negative impact on their lives outside of work, especially with family and friends (IGDA, 2004, p. 16-18).

The IGDA survey draws attention to the fact that long working hours can have adverse consequences for both the designers and the industry, with accumulated fatigue reducing employee performance at work (IGDA, 2004, pp. 10-11, 33-34; Dyer-Witheford, 2005). The industry's idealized image was shattered in 2004 when the human toll was revealed in a post to *LiveJournal* by a woman who felt like a widow because her husband, a designer at Electronic Arts in Los Angeles, spent so much time at work; at the time, 90-hour weeks were the norm (Dyer-Witheford & de Peuter, 2009; Hoffman, 2004). This first post did not make any threat, did not suggest taking any action; it simply expressed the woman's weariness and indignation. What it did do was trigger an avalanche of posts echoing what she had said, which led to the filing of three class action suits at Electronic Arts and two other studios, Vivendi Universal Games and Sony Computer Entertainment. The suits were certainly successful in terms of compensation for the designers (Handman, 2005). And studio managers also changed their practices—though not in any fundamental way, as we shall see in the case of the industry in Montreal.

INTERPRETATIVE FRAMEWORK: IMPORTANCE OF THE PORTFOLIO AND REPUTATION IN GETTING HIGHLY SKILLED, HIGHLY MOBILE WORKERS ON BOARD

In studying the video game industry, we have intentionally disregarded individual factors associated with long working hours (factors relating to personality type, need for money, age, ambition), not because they are irrelevant, but simply because the practice is so widespread in the industry. Individuals obviously agree to go along with it, but we are interested in the organizational and economic factors that push so many game designers to accept the practice.

A number of factors can be cited to explain the trend toward increasing unpaid overtime among workers who are in fact legally entitled to be compensated for it; this phenomenon is often associated with the intensification of work (Green, 2001). In the general economy, high unemployment rates stoke competition among those offering their services, and those who remain employed experience this competition in the form of pressure to perform; employees who can continue to work beyond the regular paid hours, either at home or at the office, do so in order to earn a good performance appraisal, or even out of a fear they might otherwise be laid off; but high unemployment is not a feature of the video game industry, which in fact suffers from a shortage of skilled labour.

Nevertheless, the industry does share other factors with the general economy that are noted in these studies: flattened hierarchical structures offering fewer possibilities for promotion to a larger pool of candidates; and increasing internal competition. On the product market, organizations face growing competition in several sectors and react by cutting production costs; this intensification is promoted and presented as a condition for survival of the domestic industry. Management often does not need to mention it or to ask for overtime in order to get it (Aronsson, 1999; Burke, 2009; Campbell, 2002b). Similarly, in the video game industry, nothing guarantees a developer that its product will be a big hit with consumers; flops are more common than winners:

Game budgets skyrocket, but fewer than 5% of development projects actually break even once they reach the marketplace. [...] If the game fails to sell at a healthy pace during the 4-6 weeks following its release, retailers will quickly pull it from the shelves and replace it with something new (IGDA, 2004, p. 22).

It is a well-known fact that a very small proportion of games published become successful in the marketplace. In 1999, fewer than 3% of PC games available on the market, and about 12% of console titles, sold more than 100,000 copies—a figure that is itself often far below the breakeven point (IGDA, 2004, p. 42).

In skilled positions, there is no clear finish line to indicate that the product or service has been completed, as it can always be improved. Among white-collar workers paid by the hour, who are often competing in a hyperactive job market, persistent confusion clouds the boundary separating them from employees on fixed-rate contracts, based on the delivery of results. Indeed, while they are evaluated on the basis of results, they are paid by the hour ... for the fixed, artificial duration of a regular work week:

The study raises the question of whether the amount of unpaid overtime worked also indicated deeper changes in the nature of work. An increasing group of white-collar workers are working as if they were on result-based contracts, while in fact there are both employed and remunerated on the basis of time worked (Aronsson, 1999, p. 1).

Fixed-rate contracts, in which pay is based on results, without regard for the number of hours worked, are on the rise (Campbell, 2002b, p. 133). Yet even when employees are not on fixed-rate contracts, both managers and the employees themselves behave as if they were.

We have learned from earlier studies on IT workers in B2B technology services that in the context of project-based work organization[2], the loyalty to the employer that was highly valued in the Fordist period of rapid industrial growth has been replaced by labour mobility that is valued equally by workers and their employers (Alvesson, 2000; Barley & Kunda, 2004; Baruch, 2001, 1998; Cappelli, 1999; DeFillippi, 2003; Chasserio & Legault, 2009). This has been made clear by the study of nomadic or portfolio careers in the knowledge economy (Arthur & Rousseau, 1996; DeFillippi & Arthur, 2006; Panasuraman, Greenhaus, & Linnehan, 2000). In these contexts, commitment is defined as a willingness to do whatever it takes in the short term; it is an employee's personal investment in the success of the project (Anderson-Gough, Grey, & Robson, 2000; Courpasson, 2000, pp. 187-232; Singh & Vinnicombe, 2000). Many of the manifestations of commitment to work remain the same in short-term commitment: give all one's time and energy to one's work, always be available and flexible, on one's own initiative and without waiting to be told, go beyond one's basic job description. Time spent at work is one of the first signs of commitment and is often the most important thing in a performance appraisal (Chasserio & Legault, 2009).

The degree of independence that knowledge workers enjoy when working on a project is granted to them in exchange for their commitment to meet objectives, for which they assume responsibility and on which their performance appraisal depends (Gadrey, 2000, p. 203; Legault & Chasserio, 2010). In return, they work unlimited hours because the overriding objective is to satisfy the customer, and the employee's appraisal and reputation depend on the customer's satisfaction. The importance attached to reputation and a competitive portfolio ensures employees' dedication to their responsibilities and proves to be a far more effective instrument of control than any form of authority. Even if they are paid by the hour, professionals who care about their portfolio must commit themselves to results and give top priority to the quality of the product. Given this context, overtime can be seen as a personal choice based on a professional attitude (Legault & Chasserio, 2012; Perlow, 1999, Teuchmann, Totterdell, & Parker, 1999). True professionals, it is argued, will invest their leisure time in the hopes of payback in the long term, in the form of more rapid advancement (Campbell, 2002b, p. 131; Song, 2009).

We shall see that the video game industry, which is closely related to the movie industry and to which it is often compared, is an environment conducive to the development of nomadic careers, where labour mobility is high and the portfolio is a key factor. Game designers negotiate their working conditions individually, and their individual negotiating power is based on their reputation. Even though workers in the industry are often salaried employees paid by the hour, rather than on fixed-rate contracts, their careers are based on their reputations, results and individual merits. This kind of system creates confusion between the fixed-length lump-sum contract and the open-ended hourly-wage contract.

OVERTIME HOURS OF OUR RESPONDENTS

Frequent

Our survey respondents normally put in long hours, from 35 to 50 hours per regular workweek. A third of them (18) normally work over 40 hours a week: 8 normally do from 40 to 50 hours a week and the other 10 over 50 hours.

During crunch time, an average of 14 hours needs to be added *to the weekly working hours stated by the respondents* and the workweek can range between 45 and 90 hours. Half of the designers increase their hours per week by fewer than 10 during crunch time. Crunch time can last from a few weeks to a few months, and 45 (85%) of our respondents said that during this time the length of their workweek varies and is hard to be precise about. In our view, the only way to accurately gauge the phenomenon of overtime in the industry would be through time-budget studies in which hours worked are actually recorded rather than estimated a posteriori.

Some respondents do not do overtime (15%) or do little overtime (11%), and we will see further on why and how they manage it. For over half of respondents (52%), overtime occurs in the lead up to milestones or shipping, and for 22% of the designers surveyed, it is standard practice, rather than the exception.

Unlimited and Unpaid

Unlimited, unpaid overtime is by far the biggest problem mentioned by the video game designers we surveyed. 'Unlimited' refers to the fact that there are no guidelines limiting the number of overtime hours a designer can be expected to put in; it is the designer's responsibility to work as much as necessary. 'Unpaid' means that the employee receives no payment, whether at the regular rate or at a premium rate, for the overtime hours worked; it does not mean there will be no form of compensation:

Unpaid overtime is a heterogeneous category, which can take varied forms. The fact that these varied forms are all categorised as 'unpaid' does not mean that there is no compensation. As I argue at length elsewhere (Campbell, 2003), unpaid overtime can be associated with different types of compensation, ranging from retention of the goodwill of the employer (and therefore retention of the job) to more elaborate benefits such as a higher base salary and access to accelerated promotion and performance bonuses (Campbell, 2002b, p. 146).

There may be some sort of compensation, but it is not guaranteed, and there is no assurance that it will be proportional to the number of hours worked:

- At the end of the year, an amount is allocated to the project designers on the basis of the money made on the game, which is then divided up between the designers, based on their contribution, as estimated by the leads and the producers, and paid out in the form of bonuses. How are contributions estimated? The criteria are wholly

at the discretion of the superiors, and the time spent on a project is only one criterion; ideas and their significance in the completion of the final product, to take just one example, may be given more weight.

- Leads promise time off as compensation, and grant it, at the end of the project, based on discretionary criteria and without any constraint about time off being proportional to the number of overtime hours actually worked. Managers are free to decide the amount of time off and when designers will be permitted to take it; it is not the designers' choice to make.

From a human resources management point of view, a reward distribution system linked to performance is one of the keys to understanding the industry (Gaume, 2006). Performance pay is a widespread practice in mass production and in management positions, generally based on precise measurements of performance and the awarding of corresponding remuneration. In the video game industry, the commercial success of a game is easier to measure than performance at work. Yet designers can put hours and hours of work into a high quality game that turns out to be a commercial flop. Their performance may have nothing to do with the failure, but they still will not be paid for the overtime hours they put in:

For a game company, compensation heavily biased towards bonuses and royalty sharing can be tempting. For one thing, it helps keep base salaries low, thus allowing the company to complete projects on smaller budgets and therefore increasing the odds of obtaining contracts from publishers. For another, in the event of a hit, everyone involved can expect a handsome payoff. However, given the fact that only a small fraction of games ever recoup their advances, much less generate significant royalties, this is usually a fool's bargain (IGDA, 2004, p. 49).

Some small studios limit, keep track of and pay for overtime, but they pay for overtime hours at the regular rate rather than at a premium rate. Designers get paid for every hour they work, but not at the legal rate. Furthermore, only 4.3% of IGDA survey respondents said they are paid for overtime (IGDA, 2004, p. 19), which makes it a marginal phenomenon in an industry where the standard practice is not to pay for overtime:

(How is overtime paid?) It isn't. Not at any video game company. It's systematically not paid and not banked. My company—and this is rare—lets us bank them and take time off later, but it's strictly one hour off for one hour worked. That's why I don't do overtime. I don't see why I should come in to work a half-day on Sunday if all I'm going to get is a half-day off [during the week]. It would be a half-day out of my family time and I can't add it to my family time during the week. My daughter's in daycare and my wife works at the same company I work at (H-10-19-04-A-25-06-08-13-19).

A quarter of our respondents explicitly refuse to do overtime, and here a distinction must be made between 'star' designers and the common or garden-variety designer. When designers explicitly refuse to work overtime, in general, their refusal has the effect of shutting them out of higher-profile projects (and studios). As a result, they are forced to lower their sights to work on projects where the producers will accept this refusal, or to take a project support position, in which duties are spread out more uniformly throughout the year. Parenthood and health problems are two grounds for refusing to do overtime that are generally accepted by employers.

Some designers explicitly refuse to do overtime, but still manage to get assigned to high-profile projects. These stars have rare, indispensable skills, are very much in demand, and have acquired considerable individual bargaining power. Star status is granted only to a distinguished minority, however, and as we have seen, three quarters of our

respondents put in overtime and are not paid for it, although they may receive partial compensation.

What statutory provisions apply to these workers? Montreal's video game design studios come under Quebec jurisdiction within the Canadian confederation.

Quebec Legal Framework

Under Quebec labour law, an employee may be obliged to work overtime, and be paid for it at the regular rate plus at least 50%, *if asked by the employer* (Act respecting labour standards, RSQ, chapter N-1.1, sec. 52-55). In addition, June 24 is an official holiday that is normally not worked, and the rare permitted exceptions do not include video game production (National Holiday Act, RSQ, chapter F-1.1).

In principle, an employee may not refuse to do overtime. However, the Act respecting Labour Standards (ALS) sets limits:

- An employee may refuse to work more than 4 hours over his or her normal hours, or, if the regular work day is 10 hours or longer, more than 14 hours in the same day.
- An employee who does not have a set daily work schedule may refuse to work more than 12 hours per 24-hour period.
- An employee may also refuse to work after doing more than 50 hours in the same week (ALS, sec. 59.0.1).
- An employee whose presence is required to fulfil obligations relating to the care, health, or education of the employee's child or the child of the employee's spouse, or because of the state of health of the employee's spouse, father, mother, brother, sister, or one of the employee's grandparents, even though he or she has taken the reasonable steps within his or her power to assume those obligations otherwise, such as by trying to find a babysitter, may refuse to work overtime (ALS, sec. 122[6])[3].

The ALS excludes certain employees from its benefits, including senior managers (ALS, sec. 3[6]) and other managers who are not subject to the provisions regarding payment of overtime (ALS, sec. 54[3]). In this study, we have excluded video game designers who have this status; most workers, including game designers, could be included in the definition of employees covered by the Act.

There is a tendency to forget the legal foundation of a premium pay rate for overtime hours, but it is worth recalling that the lawmakers' intention was not only to oblige employers to compensate employees for the inconvenience, but also to discourage employers from using this measure instead of creating new jobs. An additional general public health objective of the provisions is to protect workers from the increased risk of accident and illness stemming from fatigue (Amar, 2007; Burke, 2009; Campbell, 2002b, p. 111; Pereira, 2009, p. 6; Sunter & Morrissette, 1994).

Employers Can't Ask for or Require It, Much Less Keep Track of It

The legislative provisions clearly state that an employer who explicitly asks an employee to work overtime must pay for the overtime hours; conversely, if the employer does not want to pay for the overtime, he cannot ask, much less require, an employee to work it.

As a result, the existence of overtime is more or less covered up by the industry; indeed, the cover-up starts with the use of the term 'crunch time' rather than 'overtime'. It continues with the fact that designers are never actually forced to put in overtime. Project managers explain what needs to be done for the project, raise the possibility or suggest to employees that overtime might be a good idea, and the team designers decide to stay at work, *on their own initiative*, mentioning two possible forms of compensation, bonuses and time off in lieu.

Any accounting of overtime hours would be equivalent to admitting that overtime exists, which is a violation of the Act respecting Labour Standards (ALS) if it is not paid at a premium rate. Therefore, in the studios where our respondents work, no records are ever kept of overtime hours.

This prompts the following question: If they do not pay overtime, how do employers foster a great willingness among designers to do overtime?

One current explanation in the video game community is that designers are driven by their passion for gaming, as many of them are big gaming fans, association members, ex-testers or 'modders'. Here it is important to distinguish between passion and addiction to work, which would require more subtle measures than those cited in support of passion as the motivator for putting in unpaid overtime hours (Burke & Fiskenbaum, 2009). While designers may well have a passion for gaming, that alone cannot explain all the unpaid overtime hours in the industry and worked by our respondents, since many of them are harshly critical of the practice (IGDA, 2004, pp. 16-18). On the other hand, the passion for gaming is undoubtedly a powerful mobilizing force that employers can use as part of a more complex system of punishments and rewards aimed at fostering a willingness to do unpaid overtime.

HOW IS SUCH WILLINGNESS TO WORK UNPAID OVERTIME FOSTERED?

The great willingness of video game designers to do overtime seems paradoxical, so how is it fostered? Below we propose an explanation based on the existence of an informal, yet extremely effective system of incentives and punishments. This extraordinarily coherent system is particularly effective because of the enormous importance attached to reputation in the world of innovation and creation.

Compensated, but Not Paid

In video game design studios, overtime is not paid. In some cases, however, overtime hours are 'compensated' in the form of a bonus or time off in lieu (compensatory leave) when a project is over, but these two forms of compensation are doled out at the discretion of the producer and the leads, and are therefore in no way comparable with pay.

While actually putting in the overtime hours, all a designer gets is a free meal:

(How is overtime paid? normal wage or extra?) By food, they give you a meal every night that you stay overnight during crunch time and I think the amount is 15 $ and you have to stay 3 hours minimum to get that meal (F-03-14-U-26-05-08-01-07).

The only way they can be said to be indirectly paid is through the meals they eat during the overtime, which are paid for by the employer (H-13-07-E-17-06-08-01-07).

The system of bonuses awarded on a discretionary basis to the designers of games that turn a profit is the official concrete reward for the overtime hours worked. Since the bonuses are conditional on the game making money, however, there is no guarantee that they will ever be paid:

You can get a bonus when the game is sold, but you never know, in the meantime, whether you'll still be at the same company, or whether the game will get bad reviews and no one will buy it, or whether there'll be an economic recession or whatever. You may never actually get your bonus (F-03-18-U-13-06-08-01-07).

The producer has no assurance that the game will be a hit with consumers; flops are much more common than commercial successes.

Nevertheless, this conditional, even improbable recognition motivates employees to work extra hard on the design of the game, in the hopes that it will be a hit, no matter how unpredictable success may be. In other words, while part of an employee's pay is guaranteed (for regular working hours), the other part depends on how the game goes over with consumers:

So, often [the overtime] isn't paid directly. It's more ... that people will get bonuses at the end of the project based on what they invested in it, including overtime. And based on the money the game makes, which is another reason why people stay at work longer, to make a better game that they think is bound to pay out more once the project is finished (H-15-13-U-09-06-08-01-07).

Designers must therefore rely on a promise of deferred compensation conditional on the commercial success of the game, which leads them to put in more overtime hours in the hopes of increasing their bonus. As they obviously want to earn as much as possible for their overtime hours, it is in their best interests to seek out game projects that have a better chance of making more money. Since commercial success is hard to predict, being dependent on so many factors, compensation for working overtime is partly a matter of luck:

So it's definitely not a reward for effort. It's not a reward for doing good work in general [...] which is terribly insulting [...] because I've spoken to a lot of my friends and they all say the same thing. That's, we're working on projects x, y, z, which look interesting or fun ... But no, you have to look at the project's potential. What bothers me is that professionally, technically and administratively, the whole idea of bonuses is a failure. It's not a bonus for effort or perseverance, it's a bonus for luck in choosing the right project and a bonus for turning a profit (H-06-13-U-19-06-08-01-07).

On top of this element of luck comes the arbitrary aspect involved in the immediate superiors' assessment of each designer's contribution to the project as a whole. Without considering the number of overtime hours worked, the lead estimates the contribution each person has made to the final product:

Obviously there has to be some sort of reward if you're asking for an extra effort, but you also have to look at what the person has delivered: What has the person accomplished? How did it relate to the project? What was their contribution? Not just the number of hours they spent at the office (F-18-02-U-22-07-08-01-07).

Bonuses are in no way proportional to the hours worked, and the lack of correlation between the estimated contribution and the allocated reward inevitably generates dissatisfaction:

Afterwards, the pay is at the discretion of the project producer. Sometimes agreements are struck on the basis of one for one, or sometimes four for one [...] But it's always intentionally left very vague ... what they call 'at the producer's discretion'. But nothing's written down. I know it's a big taboo topic and has been for like ... years (F-09-02-U-31-07-08-01-07).

Producers' discretionary leeway when it comes to handing out bonuses is broad enough to raise doubts about the equity of the process. This is where the first form of punishment can come into play, with the possibility that a designer may be deprived of compensation:

There are no penalties [for refusing to do overtime] ... Though, maybe ... While there aren't any direct penalties, there are performance bonuses which can be affected. And I've known people who've had their bonuses cut completely [...] It's all very hush-hush ... It depends on whether you're friends

with the boss [...] It's a pretty unfair system (F-22-02-A-17-07-08-13-19).

In contrast, designers who are flexible and willing to work overtime are rewarded when bonuses are paid out.

Exclusion from Peer Network

There is a generation gap when it comes to willingness to do overtime. While experienced designers have acquired a critical take on how studios manage overtime, novice designers are just starting to build their portfolios and reputations (keep in mind that most designers in the industry are too young to have much experience) and so are willing to work long hours. Their willingness puts a great deal of pressure on other employees who would like to refuse to do overtime:

The juniors who work alongside me are all there Saturday and they really put their heart and soul into it. They put in lots of hours because they want to produce a great game. [...] Sometimes I can see just how easy it is, especially with young people just out of school. All they want is to establish themselves, to learn and to be appreciated, so they don't hesitate to do whatever hours are necessary (F-03-18-U-13-06-08-01-07).

There is also peer pressure stemming from solidarity and team spirit, which is a major element in a designer's reputation:

Periodically, yes, I would say that the social pressure is on much more than legal pressure. [...] It's a hard thing to say, [...] I've never had a place that could physically chain me in the building, but the influence of the social and sort of [...] peer pressure, it's like also you know that you have your career in their hands and if you... As a team player that's gonna affect your progress within the company (F-08-11-I-01-08-08-01-07).

We're never forced to do overtime, it's never an obligation. But still, there's always pressure ... How can I put it? Social pressure ... from the other members of the team. So that's an important point. In fact, it happens all the time in video games, that people work overtime ... unpaid, and the managers of the video game companies pretty well take it for granted (H-15-13-U-09-06-08-01-07).

Peer relations are a key link in the job-finding network that is essential to a designer's internal and external mobility, no less important than the portfolio and the employer performance appraisal. Designers are extremely dependent on one another, because of the importance of information on available jobs and recommendations for hiring.

Any designers who get shut out of the informal peer network often find that they aren't recommended for future projects and are forced to go through the formal process to get another assignment (or another job) when a project ends. Decisions about reassignment may then be made by a company's human resources department, for instance, and a designer's preferences will then count for far less:

Or you can wait until human resources, the project reassignment advisor comes to see you, gives you an appointment and offers you a choice of projects, but though they give you the impression you can choose a project, in actual fact they've already decided where they want to put you. So it's always far better if you can make your own arrangements on the QT, so that the person can say: 'I want so-and-so on my project. I've already worked with her'. It's a much easier way to get where you want to go (F-03-18-U-13-06-08-01-07).

The advantage of being referred by peers is that a recommendation facilitates the project hiring process. But the only ones who get recommended are those who are known for being flexible and good team players, especially in the weeks leading

up to milestones and shipping, when the number of hours that have to be put in goes up.

Training and Updating of Knowledge

The vast majority of respondents said that it was absolutely necessary for them to keep updating their knowledge, which is a characteristic that the video game sector shares with all production activities in innovative industries. Continuous updating of knowledge is essential for employees who want to maintain their employability, develop a broad range of skills and ensure the originality of what they contribute as individuals and produce as part of a team. Competition between workers in the industry is fierce, and up-to-date knowledge is a key factor in determining where a person ranks in the hierarchy of designers. As video game design is a non-unionized sector, pay varies significantly, on the basis of unofficial criteria, which management is not bound to systematize or reveal. Informally, however, respondents often say that a designer's portfolio is a major criterion in decisions about hiring and pay, as well as being a trump card in salary negotiations. Knowledge also has an influence on hiring, and since mobility is so highly valued, designers have an interest in maintaining their employability and, therefore, the quality of their portfolio. Willingness to do overtime is the key to the higher-profile projects, and working on those projects provides designers with an informal opportunity to gain valuable knowledge and training.

Performance Appraisal

Yearly or twice-yearly performance appraisals play a fundamental role in the careers of video game industry workers, as they can lead to promotions, involvement in the best projects and pay increases. Immediate superiors assess a designer's performance in conjunction with human resources staff. Willingness to work overtime is one of the appraisal criteria; it is viewed as an indicator of employee commitment, both to the customer and to the success of the project. A committed employee is 'someone who'll deliver':

I didn't consider refusing, because you always want to show how competent you are, how good you are, that you're someone they can rely on, someone who'll deliver. 'Someone who'll deliver' is a phrase you often hear. So I didn't even think of refusing, because I still wanted to do the job I'd been assigned to do (F-18-02-U-22-07-08-01-07).

When you go out sometime for 5 à 7, people will joke with me that I'm the girl that never does overtime. And I'm like: "ha! ha!"... (So it's not so funny for you to hear that?) No, because I know I get evaluated every six months and I know it will affect evaluation if people perceive me as being the girl that doesn't go for the extra mile (F-10-16-G-26-06-08-01-07).

While there is no obligation to do overtime, designers think long and hard before refusing, especially in the early years of their careers:

Yes [you can refuse to work overtime], but it's discouraged ... it doesn't make a good impression on the employer (H-06-16-G-23-07-08-01-07).

I mean technically you could [refuse overtime work], but if the project's got to get done it's got to get done and if you don't get it done in time... I don't know if anybody ever tested that (F-18-01-G-29-05-08-01-07).

A refusal to do overtime, say the respondents, can lead to dismissal, whether directly or in some disguised form:

I don't really know people who won't work the overtime. Because if you're on a team, let's say if the programmer refuses to work overtime, the game doesn't get finished for that day and

doesn't get sent to the people at headquarters who have to review it every couple of days and he gets blamed. No I don't think you really can. You can but you'd probably be fired quickly (F-10-16-G-26-06-08-01-07).

If you constantly refuse to do overtime, especially if you don't have a good reason, they might give you a pain-in-the-ass job or projects for a year, things you really don't want to do, in the hopes that you'll just leave. [...] So sometimes they'll just make life difficult for you if you don't have a good reason why you can't do OT (H-05-02-U-27-06-08-13-19).

Designers who 'really excel', not people who just do their job, earn good performance appraisals. The influence of the appraisal on other aspects of work makes it of major strategic importance in a world where reputation and the portfolio count above all else (De Peuter & Dyer-Witheford, 2005).

Annual Remuneration

Since designers have no collective bargaining unit, they negotiate their pay individually. This can mean huge disparities between workers in the same job. There are two major factors that can lend weight to an employee's negotiating position when asking for a raise: a threat to quit and join a competitor and a good performance appraisal, which itself is often based on a willingness to put in overtime:

I don't think you can [refuse to do overtime]. At least, it's as if you can't. They don't say anything, but ultimately, when it's appraisal time at the end of the project, they don't forget that on that particular day you weren't there. [...] And it's based on those times that they judge how you've worked, how you've done throughout the year, whether you've kept to your work schedule, whether you've exceeded your expectations, whether you've produced quality work, whether you've got along with people, things like that. That's when you hope you'll get a raise. So, generally speaking, you have to be nice, because even if you've worked hard, they'll often dredge up some detail about what you did 10 months earlier [laughs] (H-23-02-U-04-06-08-01-07).

Reputation

In the video game industry, horizontal mobility not only enables workers to negotiate significant pay raises, but also to apply for higher positions, provided they have a solid reputation. Similarly, getting a salary increase by threatening to jump ship is also dependent on having a good reputation:

You really have to be careful about your reputation in this job. We animators move around a lot from one company to another, so we all know each other. I know the animators in virtually all the companies in greater Montreal. That's how we find jobs, it's really through contacts, so you have to be careful (F-03-18-U-13-06-08-01-07).

In the project management structure that characterizes the industry, the producer is responsible for recruiting the members of the team that will be needed for a project. Employees' reputations are thus their main references. Of course, reputations are based on professional success, on scarce, valuable skills, on innovative ideas and on technical achievements. But that is only part of the story. Reputations are also based—if we go by what our respondents have to say—just as much on having a team mindset and being willing to do overtime, on account of the constraints specific to project management. The expertise required to bring a group project of this kind to completion on schedule and within budget is highly valued in the industry. While some of our respondents were

critical of the process, they were all extremely aware of the impact that a refusal to do overtime would have on an employee's reputation:

Legally, for instance, the employer does not have the right to force me to work overtime, let's say. On the other hand, however, I know that the industry has to work that way to a certain extent because even if you always intend to be on schedule, there are always problems that crop up, so you're always behind schedule. And personally, I want the game to be good. I want it to be good because it adds to our reputation as a company and as individuals, too ... which helps if I'm looking for another job. So, even if my employer doesn't force me to, in a sense I sort of have to anyway. I think it's good that they don't tell me I have to work overtime, but it's sort of insinuated anyway ... you know, it's just unspoken (H-05-16-W-09-06-01-07).

At the same time, everyone is well aware of the risks associated with anything that can tarnish one's reputation in the industry, especially opting to take legal action for payment of unpaid hours:

So you're always thinking: if it's the company against me, then I can go ahead and file a claim, but on the other hand, you won't be doing your reputation any good because it's certainly going to become public or ... It's such a small industry, everyone knows each other, so such and such a company is going to know that I took legal action against another company, that I stirred up trouble, so there's a good chance they won't want to hire me if they know that. If I ever file a claim, I might have to look for my next job outside the country, or at least outside Montreal (F-10-12-U-12-05-08-01-07).

Promotion and Assignment to High-Profile Projects

In the video game industry, reputation is a worker's greatest asset at hiring time, a passport to both upwards and horizontal mobility. Workers who want to be on the design team for a high-profile game will not only have their portfolios evaluated, but also their history of buckling down to meet the requirements for project success. Higher-profile projects generally involve more overtime hours:

Certainly [I can refuse to do overtime]. It's definitely frowned upon and, like I said, there are lots of projects going on in the company and it probably wouldn't be long before I'd be working on a dog game or something like that. Everyone knows each other and for their project, they try to get people they know are hard-working and so on (H-06-13-U-19-06-08-01-07).

Whether you like it or not, for projects ... there are in-house interviews. From one project to the next, there's your reputation, there's tracking follow-up and there are references: 'I'd like to have him on my project ...' I myself have been through lots of interviews, on both sides of the table, so I've seen how it works (H-06-13-U-19-06-08-01-07).

Given that high-profile projects very often require employees to do overtime, an employer can know from experience, which designers are willing and give preference to those that have a reputation for being dedicated to the cause. Consideration for coveted positions that involve decision making (such as lead designer, artistic director and producer) and assignment to high-profile projects are directly tied to reputation, which itself is often associated with a willingness to do overtime, albeit not exclusively, of course.

Mobility and the System of Rewards and Punishments

We have seen that employees who work overtime are compensated in the form of bonuses or time off in lieu. Since designers want to be paid for the overtime hours they work, they put even greater efforts into production of the game to ensure it will be a success.

Doing overtime helps a worker's chances of being included in the informal peer network, which is very important for job mobility; it also increases the chances of a good performance appraisal, which improves one's chances of a pay raise and enhances one's reputation; in turn, reputation improves one's chances of promotion, assignment to higher-profile projects and increases mobility, which is highly valued in the industry because it not only provides opportunities for learning and travel, but is also a key asset when it comes time to negotiate a raise in pay, and mobility, in turn, is a factor in a good reputation. That is how the system works, with its own implacable internal logic.

The same system is just as effective at punishing designers who are not particularly interested in doing overtime: they won't be compensated, even if the game is a commercial success and they have contributed to it; they will be more or less excluded and their peers will not recommend them for high-profile projects; they will not be exposed to the most advanced technology; they won't get as good a performance appraisal or be as well paid as their peers; their portfolio will suffer as a result because they won't have the kind of reputation that aids mobility. As time goes by, they will be more or less condemned to stay put.

The desire for mobility plays a fundamental role in designers' willingness to do overtime, as the more they want to rise up the ladder (hierarchical management positions, high-profile projects) or move horizontally (other studios, other countries), the more vulnerable they become to the system of rewards and punishments. Conversely, designers who attach more importance to family life, or who have already been ill, often decide to rethink their priorities and consider taking less strategic positions in the industry, less at the forefront, but more amenable to the achievement of a work-life balance.

CONCLUSION

Overtime hours in the video game industry are not only normal and long, but also unpaid. Even though the Quebec industry is subject to the provisions of the Act respecting labour standards, its practices are legally ambiguous, because managers and supervisors do not actually ask designers to work overtime and claim that overtime is never compulsory, but that designers do it on their own initiative. Some of our respondents did indeed say they refused to work overtime. However, they usually end up having to limit their career ambitions as a result.

While some designers are compensated for these 'willingly worked' overtime hours, compensation is not guaranteed. Moreover, when they are compensated, it is only in part, and the amount of compensation is uncertain and entirely at the discretion of management. The way overtime is managed is a source of significant dissatisfaction. Nonetheless, the system of rewards and punishments would appear to be a very effective means of getting employees to put in a lot of overtime, given that most designers go along with it, despite the criticisms and dissatisfaction revealed by our survey respondents. The system is founded on the importance attached to reputation in a creative, innovative environment where there is strong competition between designers to be chosen for high-profile projects.

While a passion for video games certainly exists and may well explain why designers continue to put in unpaid overtime, it does not mean that they agree with the principle of it; many of them are critical of the practice. As we have seen, 61.5% of respondents to the IGDA survey said they could not see themselves keeping up the same pace, because the long hours could have an adverse impact on their lives outside of work, especially on family and friends (IGDA, 2004, p. 18). In the United States, some designers have opted for the class action route. The information that appears on the *Gamewatch* website is updated by video game designers who monitor and report on studio management practices, including working hours.

At the same time, the passion for gaming is a powerful mobilizing force that producers' representatives can use to their advantage as part of a more complex system of rewards and punishments.

Neither purely voluntary and freely agreed to (rare), nor required and forced (likewise rare), video game industry overtime comes under the broad category of "voluntary but expected" working hours (Campbell, 2002b, p. 141). Alternatives to overtime are not on the agenda, and a number of circumstances set limits on the options open to designers who want to increase or maintain their mobility in the industry and aspire to work on high-profile games. Employees still feel a need to have their own personal lives and their own free time, but it is a need that is very hard to reconcile with these constraints.

The more widespread the practice of unlimited, unpaid overtime becomes, the more institutionalized it becomes and the harder it is to contest:

When unpaid overtime becomes widespread in individual workplaces, occupations or industries, another layer of difficulty is laid down. Unpaid overtime can easily appear as just a condition or aspect of the job, as part of an implicit contract of employment that employees accept when they enter the job. It can be a condition that is simply tolerated or perhaps even welcomed as a sign of the high status of the job. In such cases, unpaid overtime appears institutionalised, as part of a new definition of what is normal or expected in the job. Reluctance to undertake unpaid overtime can appear as a reprehensible personal fault – as a breach of a contract with supervisors and colleagues (Campbell, 2002b, p. 128).

Our findings are limited in scope, being valid only for salaried designers employed by large studios in the greater Montreal area. To gain a better understanding of overtime in the industry, more studies will be needed, including case studies of small studios, comparative interregional and international studies, and quantitative surveys of large aggregate groupings.

As we have seen, video game production is a major industry, and the generous government support it enjoys sends a paradoxical message about the statutory provisions respecting overtime (Pereira, 2009, p. 4). The long working hours raise ethical issues that need to be addressed, as they have an impact on worker health, quality of family life, productivity (mistakes resulting from fatigue), income and equity (when the hours are unpaid yet necessary and, in a way, requested), the impact on the unemployment rate, employment equity for workers who are unavailable for such flexible hours (including parents and women), and the transfer of the cost of the health risks to these workers (Burke, 2009; Burke & Fiskenbaum, 2009; Campbell, 2002a, 2002b; Dembe, 2009; Jacobs & Gerson, 2001; Kanai, 2009). At a time when sustainable development has become a watchword, organizations must assume their corporate ethical responsibility for the sustainable development of the individuals they employ and their families.

REFERENCES

Alliance Numerique. (2003). *Analyse de positionnement de l'industrie du jeu interactif au Québec*. Montreal, Canada: SECOR Consulting.

Alliance Numerique. (2008). *Étude de positionnement de l'industrie du jeu interactif au Québec*. Montreal, Canada: SECOR Consulting.

Alvesson, M. (2000). Social identity and the problem of loyalty in knowledge-intensive companies. *Journal of Management Studies*, *37*(8), 1101–1124. doi:10.1111/1467-6486.00218

Amar, J. (2007). Travailler plus pour gagner… quoi au juste? *Controverses*, *6*, 180–182.

Anderson-Gough, F., Grey, C., & Robson, K. (2000). In the name of the client: The service ethic in two professional services firms. *Human Relations*, *53*(9), 1151–1174. doi:10.1177/0018726700539003

Androvich, M. (2008). Industry revenue $57 billion in 2009, says DFC. *Game Industry Biz*. Retrieved from http://www.gamesindustry.biz/articles/industry-revenue-57-billion-in-2009-says-dfc

Aronsson, G. (1999). Paid by time but judged by results: An empirical study of unpaid overtime. *International Journal of Employment Studies*, *17*(1), 1–15.

Arthur, M. B., & Rousseau, D. M. (1996). *The boundaryless career: A new employment principle for a new organizational era*. Oxford, UK: Oxford University Press.

Barley, S. R., & Kunda, G. (2004). *Gurus, hired guns, and warm bodies: Itinerant experts in a knowledge economy*. Princeton, NJ: Princeton University Press.

Baruch, Y. (1998). The rise and fall of organizational commitment. *Human Systems Management, 17*(2), 135–143.

Baruch, Y. (2001). Employability – A substitute to loyalty? *Human Resource Development International, 4*(4), 543–566. doi:10.1080/13678860010024518

Burke, R. J. (2009). Working to live or living to work: Should individuals and organizations care? *Journal of Business Ethics, 84,* 167–172. doi:10.1007/s10551-008-9703-6

Burke, R. J., & Fiskenbaum, L. (2009). Work motivations, work outcomes, and health: Passion versus addiction. *Journal of Business Ethics, 84,* 257–263. doi:10.1007/s10551-008-9697-0

Campbell, I. (2002a). Extended working hours in Australia. *Labour & Industry, 13*(1), 91–110.

Campbell, I. (2002b). Snatching at the wind? Unpaid overtime and trade unions in Australia. *International Journal of Employment Studies, 10*(2), 109–156.

Campbell, I. (2003). Puzzles of unpaid overtime. In Zeytinoglu, I. (Ed.), *Flexible Work Arrangements: Conceptualizations and International Experiences* (pp. 25–43). The Hague, The Netherlands: Kluwer Law International.

Cappelli, P. (1999). *The new deal at work.* Boston, MA: Harvard Business School Press.

Chasserio, S., & Legault, M.-J. (2009). Strategic human resources management is irrelevant when it comes to highly skilled professionals in the Canadian new economy! *International Journal of Human Resource Management, 20*(5), 1113–1131. Retrieved from http://www.informaworld.com/smpp/title~db=all~content=g911806569 doi:10.1080/09585190902850307

Chung, E. (2005, August 15). Dream jobs in hell. *Toronto Star,* p. C6.

Courpasson, D. (2000). *L'action contrainte: Organisations libérales et domination.* Paris, France: PUF.

De Peuter, G., & Dyer-Witheford, N. (2005). A playful multitude? Mobilising and counter-mobilising immaterial game labour. *FibreCulture Journal, 5.* Retrieved from http://journal.fibreculture.org/issue5/depeuter_dyerwitheford.html

DeFillippi, R. J. (2003). Organizational models for collaboration in the new economy. *Human Resource Planning, 25*(4), 7–18.

DeFillippi, R. J., & Arthur, M. B. (2006). The boundaryless career: A competency-based perspective. *Journal of Organizational Behavior, 15*(4), 307–324. doi:10.1002/job.4030150403

Dembe, A. E. (2009). Ethical issues relating to the health effects of long working hours. *Journal of Business Ethics, 84,* 195–208. doi:10.1007/s10551-008-9700-9

Deuze, M., Bowen, M. C., & Allen, C. (2007). The professional identity of gameworkers. *International Journal of Research into New Media Technologies, 13*(4), 335–353. doi:10.1177/1354856507081947

Dumais, J.-F. (2009). *L'emploi dans l'industrie du jeu électronique au Québec en 2009: Un portrait sommaire de la situation.* Retrieved from http://www.technocompetences.qc.ca/apropostic/etudes

Dyer-Witheford, N. (2002). Cognitive capital contested. *Multitudes, 10.* Retrieved from http://multitudes.samizdat.net/Cognitive-Capital-Contested.html

Dyer-Witheford, N. (2005). Digital poetics in the vernacular: The political economy of Canada's videogame industry. *Digipopo/Public, 31.* Retrieved from http://www.digipopo.org/content/digital-poetics-in-the-vernacular-the-political-economy-of-canadas-videogame-industry?pg=4

Dyer-Witheford, N., & De Peuter, G. (2006). EA Spouse and the crisis of video game labour: Enjoyment, exclusion, exploitation, exodus. *Canadian Journal of Communication, 31*, 599–617.

Dyer-Witheford, N., & de Peuter, G. (2009). Empire@play: Virtual games and global capitalism. *CT Theory Multimedia Journal*. Retrieved from http://www.ctheory.net/articles.aspx?id=608

Dyer-Witheford, N., & Sharman, Z. (2005). The political economy of Canada's video and computer game industry. *Canadian Journal of Communication, 30*, 187–210.

Fahey, R. (2005, October 10). Videogames to lead entertainment sector boom through 2009, says PWC. *Games Industry*. Retrieved from http://www.gamesindustry.biz/content_page. php?aid=12135

Gadrey, J. (2000). *Nouvelle économie, nouveau mythe?* Paris, France: Flammarion.

Gaume, N. (2006). Nicolas Gaume's views on the video games sector. *European Management Journal, 24*(4), 299–309. doi:10.1016/j. emj.2006.05.005

Green, F. (2001). It's been a hard day's night: The concentration and intensification of work in late twentieth-century Britain. *British Journal of Industrial Relations, 39*(1), 53–80. doi:10.1111/1467-8543.00189

Handman, D. H. (2005). Electronic Arts settles a class action overtime lawsuit for $15.6 million: Red flags and practical lessons for the entertainment software industry. *Entertainment Law Reporter, 27*(6). Retrieved from http:// www.entertainmentlawreporter.com/archive/ v27n06/270601.htm

Hoffman, E. (2004). *EA: The human story*. [blog post]. Retrieved from http://ea-spouse.livejournal. com/274.html

IGDA. (2004). *Quality of life in the game industry: Challenges and best practices*. Retrieved from http://www.igda.org

IGDA. (2005). *IGDA 2005 annual report*. Retrieved from http://archives.igda.org/about/annual_report_05.php

Jacobs, J. A., & Gerson, K. (2001). Overworked individuals or overworked families? Explaining trends in work, leisure and family time. *Work and Occupations, 28*(1), 40–63. doi:10.1177/0730888401028001004

Kanai, A. (2009). Karoshi (work to death) in Japan. *Journal of Business Ethics, 84*, 209–216. doi:10.1007/s10551-008-9701-8

Kuchlich, J. (2005). Precarious playbour: Modders and the digital games industry. *Fiberculture, 3*(5). Retrieved from http://journal.fibreculture. org/issue5/depeuter_dyerwitheford.html

Legault, M.-J., & Chasserio, S. (2010). La domination dans le modèle de production de haute performance dans la gestion de projets. In Malenfant, R., & Bellemare, G. (Eds.), *La Domination au Travail: Des Conceptions Totalisantes à la Diversification des Formes de Domination* (pp. 99–124). Québec, Canada: PUQ.

Legault, M.-J., & Chasserio, S. (2012). *Professionalization, risk transfer, and the gender gap in IT firms. International Journal of Project Management, 30*(6).

Panasuraman, S., Greenhaus, J. H., & Linnehan, F. (2000). Time, person-career fit and the bundaryless career. In Cooper, G. L., & Rousseau, D. M. (Eds.), *Time in Organizational Behaviour*. New York, NY: Wiley.

Pereira, R. (2009). *The costs of unpaid overtime work in Canada: Dimensions and comparative analysis*. Masters Thesis. Athabasca, Canada: University of Athabasca.

Perlow, L. A. (1999). The time famine: Toward a sociology of work time. *Administrative Science Quarterly, 44*, 57–81. doi:10.2307/2667031

Rubery, J. (1998). Working time in the UK. *Transfer, 4*(4), 657–677.

Singh, V., & Vinnicombe, S. (2000). What does "commitment" really mean? Views of UK and Swedish engineering managers. *Personnel Review, 29*(2), 228–258. doi:10.1108/00483480010296014

Song, Y. (2009). Unpaid work at home. *Industrial Relations: A Journal of Economy and Society, 48*(4), 578-588.

Sunter, D., & Morrissette, R. (1994). Les heures consacrées au travail. *L'emploi et le Travail en Perspective, 6*(3), 1–8.

Teuchmann, K., Totterdell, P., & Parker, S. K. (1999). Rushed, unhappy and drained: An experience sampling study of relations between time pressure, perceived control, mood and emotional exhaustion in a group of accountants. *Journal of Occupational Health Psychology, 4*(1), 37–54. doi:10.1037/1076-8998.4.1.37

ENDNOTES

[1] In keeping with Dyer-Witheford (2005), cited here, we have defined the Canadian video game industry as all the studios in the sector that operate in Canada, rather than as only studios that are Canadian-owned.

[2] The huge importance attached to project-based work organization and to the rhetoric around professionalization needs to be examined separately and studied in Legault & Chasserio, 2012.

[3] This right to refuse to work overtime does not, however, apply in the event of danger to the life or safety of the population, in case of disaster or if it is inconsistent with a code of ethics that applies to the employee. Employers in the video game industry are subject to provincial legislation, but employers that come under Canadian federal jurisdiction are also subject to similar standards respecting pay at an increased rate for overtime (Canada Labour Code, SC, c. L-2, sec. 174) and a maximum work week of 48 hours (Canada Labour Code, sec. 171).

Chapter 7

Making a Rod for One's Own Back:
Employee Bargaining for Smartphones in a Telco's R&D Department

Christopher Russell
Cardiff Metropolitan University, UK

ABSTRACT

This chapter identifies a new pattern of bargaining for technology, based upon nine months' ethnographic fieldwork amongst the engineers of a Telco's research and development department. Bargains for smartphones were initiated by the employee and negotiated with the employer by reference to the productivity discourse of the vendor. After a honeymoon phase of exploration, the reality of operation was markedly different, resulting, in several cases, in the disposition of the smartphone or, in one case, the disposition of the employee to leave. Such bargains were driven by conceptions of the personal and organisational use value of the artefact, and this finding reveals shortcomings in the drivers, influences, and stages of adoption found in existing models. A new conceptual framework is presented that facilitates exploration of the contribution of personal and organisational use value to technology adoption.

INTRODUCTION

Smartphones are an increasing presence in the pockets and palms of professionals. Blending the information power of a small personal computer and the telecommunication power of a mobile phone, they accompany the person from home to the office and back. By their disregard for any work-life boundary, they become artefacts of potential personal benefit and thus disrupt our understanding of technology adoption in organisations. For such understanding is shaped by, or at least captured in, models developed for older technological artefacts and other organisational forms. Models which take the perspective of the manager and imply the stages of technology adoption are unproblematic, rational and planned. This chapter presents an empirical enquiry into

DOI: 10.4018/978-1-4666-1836-7.ch007

how smartphones are being bargained for in the Research and Development (R&D) department of a telecommunications company (Telco). The chapter is structured as follows. The Background section identifies personal costs and benefits of smartphone use in organisations, as found in the extant literature. It notes that these studies do not identify which, if any, participants had initiated the bargaining for a smartphone. A method for exploring the bargains struck by employees is then outlined. The section R&D Engineers and their Smartphones describes episodes and presents interview fragments showing examples of bargaining for smartphones found in the telco. The following section Implications for Existing Models of Technology Adoption reveals, on the basis of this case, shortcomings in the extant models, both in terms of the stages used to understand such adoption and the drivers and influences thought to determine such adoption. On the basis of this analysis, the section Future Research Directions outlines a conceptual framework which could be used, cognisant of the identified potential pitfalls, in future studies. The chapter then draws conclusions from the bargains found in the Telco.

BACKGROUND

Through their mobility and functionality smartphones, even organisation-provided ones, have become technological artefacts of personal significance. Research to date has identified benefits and costs for individuals of organisational smartphone adoption. For instance, in terms of benefits, smartphones may liberate an employee from their desk (Ling, Julsrud, & Krogh, 1997), help them maintain connection with family and friends (Wajcman, Bittman, & Brown, 2008) and reduce their short-term stress by enabling them to keep up with their emails (Mazmanian, Orlikowski, & Yates, 2005) whilst waiting for an egg to boil (Towers, Duxbury, Higgins, & Thomas, 2006). In terms of costs, smartphones

may increase the employee's long-term stress as their ability to keep up with emails actually generates more emails (Mazmanian, et al., 2005), help create new family conflicts (Fenner & Renn, 2010) as family members resent the intrusion of smartphones into shared time and space (Middleton, 2007) and limit the employee's rest and recuperation as others expect them to read and act upon messages at whatever the time of day or even night (Middleton, 2007). In some of these studies smartphones were dished-out across an organisation, division or role as part of a management-led technological change project (e.g. Mazmanian, Yates, & Orlikowski, 2006; Mazmanian, et al., 2005; Orlikowski, 2007). In others it is not clear whether, or which, employees may have initiated the adoption of the smartphone itself (e.g. Ling, et al., 1997; Middleton, 2007; Middleton & Cukier, 2006; Towers, et al., 2006; Wajcman, et al., 2008). As a result, it is not possible to discern how employees who have exercised agency in the procurement of the smartphone have subsequently experienced it in use. Such non-mandated adoption and use would be expected based upon the benefits for individuals of the use of smartphones in organisations outlined above. Based upon the Scandinavian literature of employee initiated adoption or development of other technologies and systems (Bødker, et al., 1987; Ehn, 1988; Ehn, Kyng, & Sundblad, 1983) one could assume that having exercised agency in the procurement of the smartphone, the employee is more inclined to experience, and report, the benefits as opposed to the costs of their use. A recent study of smartphone experiences also suggests that it makes sense that voluntary users 'would more likely frame their experience in a positive light, focusing on the benefits' (Matusik & Mickel, 2011, p. 23) and suggests the need for future research to examine this. Further, one might expect that whilst such employees exercise agency in the adoption of the smartphone, over time the smartphone itself may exercise agency over the employee (Latour, 1987; Orlikowski & Iacono, 2001).

To explore the bargains struck by employees for smartphones an ethnographic study was conducted amongst engineers in the R&D department of a telco for nine months. Ethnography was chosen as a method, which would enable both employees' interpretations and enactments to be recorded. This combination—suggested for future research on the influence of non-mandated adoption (Matusik & Mickel, 2011)—is important for the limitation of self-reported data and smartphone use has been identified (Mazmanian, et al., 2006): there appears to be a discrepancy between the interpretation of smartphone-using employees themselves and those around them (Mazmanian, et al., 2005; Middleton & Cukier, 2006). Ethnography enabled employees' interpretations to be captured via in-depth interviews and their enactments to be captured via participant observation. All (22) engineers were interviewed at least once, most in multiple interview-fragments as work permitted. The engineers were not observed equally for as a participant I also had tasks to perform which required more interaction with some engineers and less with others. The situation of the entire R&D department in one open plan office mitigated this limitation. Longitudinal fieldwork is the best approach for analysing the complexities of technological innovation (Newman & Robey, 1992) for it addresses the limitation of static data, collected at one point in time, which does not enable differences between pre-adoption and post-adoption beliefs and attitudes to be identified (Karahanna, Straub, & Chervany, 1999; Matusik & Mickel, 2011; Mazmanian, et al., 2006). Conducting a longitudinal ethnography thus enabled evolution in smartphone-using employees' interpretations and enactments to be captured.

Engineers in the R&D department of a telco could be considered something on extreme case of ethnographic site (Oates, 2006), chosen because of their likely propensity to initiate the adoption of smartphones themselves. Gender, age, and experience have been identified as influencing usage intention and behaviour (Venkatesh, Morris, Davis, & Davis, 2003): being male, being younger, and being experienced with the given technology are considered to have a positive influence on usage intention and behaviour. The department consisted of variously skilled engineers: software, electronic, electrical and network specialisms were represented. All were employed to research and develop the smartphones themselves or the infrastructure around them or the app(lication)s on them and thus they were intimately familiar with their features. The engineers were solely male: although women did work in the R&D department they did so in roles relating to administration, finance, human resources and liaison with internal 'customers.' The average age of the engineers was 36 years. In terms of academic capital (Bourdieu, 1984) it can be said that those engineers who had joined the department in the previous five years (13 out of 22) were all graduates. Prior to this the department had not recruited recent graduates, rather had recruited experienced engineers, both from within and without the organisation, some of whom had further education and/or professional qualifications rather than higher education. Taken together, these characteristics of the sample would suggest a population highly likely to initiate smartphone adoption. The next section presents data collected from this population.

R&D ENGINEERS AND THEIR SMARTPHONES

Engineers were tempted by the perceived novelty and status of the smartphone and by its features. By virtue of being an engineer in R&D they expected to have the latest smartphone. This expectation of an engineer in R&D was also held by others, both within and without the organisation: 'One of the first things my friend Dave, from uni, asks me is: "What've you got in your pocket now then?"

…as we only speak every few months I'm sure he expects my answer to be different each time' (First Engineer). Most of the engineers (15 of 22) were of a grade that had recently been divested of their company cars, so smartphones were now one of the few perks of the job; all worked in an environment where corporate-branded casual clothes were the norm so smartphones were one of the few signs of status to those beyond the department. Within the department engineers would seek to out-do each other's acquisition, whether through the acquisition of a new smartphone or via defence of their current squeeze: 'It's a form of "top trumps"' (Second Engineer). In this game, it was not just the technical specification that mattered, but also the perceived usefulness of the smartphone's features: such information was obtained by the engineers from vendor advertising and trade press.

Vendor discourse, whether direct through advertising or mediated through media such as trade press, helped create engineers' consideration of the smartphone's worth for their employer and for themselves, whether in their work or non-work life. The fusion of work and non-work capabilities in smartphones has formed the basis of much of their advertising, for instance: 'Work smarter and play harder with the Omnia Pro.' (Samsung, 2010). Similar adverts, observed in the R&D department, proceeded to identify various functions e.g. store music, play games, review a presentation, open a spreadsheet. For the conscientious Third Engineer the appeal of the smartphone was the potential of these functions to enable him to transcend his human limitations: 'There are only so many hours in the day, and minutes in the hour, and this will help me confine admin to those otherwise wasted moments, like whilst waiting for the server to reboot.' Fourth Engineer simply cut and pasted text concerning the more work-related functions from a vendor's website into the business justification box on the asset request form used to initiate the purchase of a smartphone. He confided, as he gestured first at the picture of the requested

smartphone and then at his form: 'Actually, what I really want it for is instant messaging but this sounds better…it's a steal' (Fourth Engineer). It seemed like a bargain, in the sense of 'a steal,' to Fourth Engineer; the realisation that he would at some point be expected to utilise the smartphone for these work capabilities, to fulfill the bargain in the sense of an exchange, had not yet dawned.

Once in an engineer's palm a game was typically the first app to be used. 'Look at this,' said Fifth Engineer pointing at a screen containing player statistics for a Tetris-style game, 'I've played it 67 times, and I only got it yesterday.' Other non-work activities quickly followed: downloading music, following football scores, checking bank accounts. These were particularly observed whilst engineers travelled between meetings on company-provided transport, where conventional Internet access was not possible. However, they also enabled non-work activity in the office, even when conventional Internet access was possible. In contrast to laptops or desktops, smartphones were never inspected or serviced by Telco's technicians and the data traffic across the mobile phone network, in contrast to the office network, was beyond their surveillance. Together with the small screen of the smartphone this meant that they could be used away from the gaze of managers. Indeed, on a couple of occasions an engineer was observed using a smartphone to view pornographic pictures and videos. As time passed, Fourth Engineer was made more aware of the bargain, as in an exchange, which he had struck, for the smartphone's small screen and use of the mobile phone network brought limitations as well as opportunities. He asked, with reference to a clip of a goal in football: 'It's a glimpse of the action, granted, but can you appreciate the skill?' As the benefits dulled, the costs brightened.

The phase of play and exploration, having established familiarity with the smartphone and accessibility via the smartphone, was the prelude to use as suggested by the business justification. Towards the beginning of this longitudinal study, there was little expectation that an engineer would use the smartphone for work purposes. Essentially, it was used as a conventional mobile phone and as an automated filofax: notes were made, appointments recorded and contact details stored. An engineer was even free to dispose of the smartphone if he wished: one was observed being put on sale in an online marketplace, a second was put at the back of a drawer, a third was apparently passed on to a son. However, during the course of this longitudinal study expectations seemed to change. Initially it was expected that an engineer would respond to email within a day if he happened to be in the office. It was accepted that he might legitimately be elsewhere: visiting partner research organisations such as universities; attending meetings of standards groups such as the International Telecommunications Union; going to trade fairs and conferences; working at the test laboratory or liaising with marketing and other divisions of the organisation. Towards the end an engineer was expected to use his smartphone to check his email. As Sixth Engineer said: 'I don't feel like I can go down to the test lab anymore and just "experiment." I've got to be available to respond to messages, and even if I don't actually get one, I don't feel I can really commit to my project, as in my research and development project, not the project in terms of the bureaucracy of it. I'd rather have a chance to actually work on it rather than have to say when I'll have finished it.' There was a feeling that as highly skilled innovative engineers, used to autonomous working, email, in this manner, did not serve the needs of their work, it had become an impediment to it. An engineer was also expected to use his smartphone to update his calendar throughout the day. As a consequence, he also routinely checked the calendars of those not in the office to ascertain the validity of their absence. Invalid or insufficient explanations would result in—at best—subtle or—at worst—sly remarks to the person concerned, their peers or more senior managers in the department.

R&D and the monitoring of the whereabouts of engineers came to a head when a new service was developed. The service ran on a smartphone and enabled one to see the location of fellow subscribers to that network. The innovation lay not so much in the technology, but in the fusion of data: the information of a subscriber's strength of signal vis-à-vis three or more masts, used by any network to determine which mast your call will be directed through, and a standard digital mapping service. The phone numbers used in the trial were those of recent recruits. During a demonstration of the service to a senior figure the unexpected location of Sixth Engineer was exposed: instead of being in a neighbouring town—for a medical appointment—he was several hundred miles away. Fifth Engineer, the trial lead, considered this 'unfortunate.' However, ultimately for him this was proof that 'it could be a useful service, for parents to track their children, for instance, not just, or specifically, for employers to track employees.' Sixth Engineer, meanwhile, had definite cause to regret having his smartphone: 'I thought this would set me free to work whenever, wherever but instead it's just another shackle.' Exposed by his smartphone, Sixth Engineer was disposed to leave the Telco shortly afterwards.

More regular and mundane smartphone uses also prompted regret and guilt. Third Engineer reflected: 'I had hoped it would help me to achieve more in terms of R&D, but it seems I'm only achieving more in terms of admin, and not just at the expense of R&D.' He went on to recount the tale of his wife giving birth to their child: 'Having the [smartphone] meant that I could be there in the hospital without feeling guilty about what might be happening at work but I now feel guilty that I had it with me at all, for I was there but not really there: I feel I missed out on what is such a rare and important moment.' Despite misgivings, which nearly prompted him to 'dump it,' he felt the impossibility of return: 'Once you've had a smartphone, there's no going back; if I'm on a journey and the battery dies I get so fretful not being able, for instance, to find out whether my connection is on time, or what the test match score is.' Fourth Engineer spoke of regrets, as if of a relationship post-honeymoon and pre-breakup: 'We had a lot of fun to begin with but now it's getting serious I'm not so sure.' He went on to explain: 'When I filled out the asset request form, I hadn't actually expected that I would end up having to use it for responding to work emails and reviewing reports.' The calling-in of the promised productivity seemed to coincide with the onset of post-consumption blues. The solution to this, for Fourth Engineer, was not to abandon smartphones but simply to replace his current squeeze: 'As long as I'm playing and exploring I can deal with the rest...and the newer model has a much higher-resolution screen.'

Summarising his experience, and what he had observed of others,' Seventh Engineer remarked, whilst gesticulating to the smartphones in front of us: 'It's hard to tell the impact without the benefit of hindsight; maybe in five years you or I could look back and see what great products or services were developed here.' He continued: 'My guess now, for what it's worth, is there won't be any: we've become too focused on the trivial and day-to-day instead of the long-term and complex.' Of course, there was one service which has proved significant: that of displaying the location of subscribers; a service now commercialised and packaged in various forms, for example Facebook places. However, this was contemporaneously in more advanced stages of development elsewhere and was also not without its costs, as explored above. More generally, smartphones could be said to have been used far more for the trivial than for the original.

IMPLICATIONS FOR EXISTING MODELS OF TECHNOLOGY ADOPTION

This section explores the bargains for smartphones found in the Telco with reference to existing models of technology adoption, and, in so doing, considers both the stages of bargaining and what drove and influenced these stages. Most researchers investigating the adoption of new technologies select a model from the various available 'off-the-shelf': the theory of reasoned action, the Technology Acceptance Model (TAM), the motivational model, the theory of planned behaviour, the model of personal computer utilization, the innovation diffusion theory, the social cognitive theory and the Unified Theory of Acceptance and Use of Technology (UTAUT). Some of these build upon others: TAM (Davis, 1989) draws upon the theory of reasoned action; UTAUT (Venkatesh, et al., 2003) draws upon both TAM and the theory of planned behaviour. TAM is the 'dominant theoretical model' (McMaster & Wastell, 2005, p. 386), indeed, it is 'one of the most influential theories in Information Systems' (Benbasat & Barki, 2007, p. 211). It forms the basis of several studies of mobile technology adoption (Koivu-maki, Ristola, & Kesti, 2008; Yu, Yu, Liu, & Yao, 2003), however its dominance 'has caused a high degree of enforcement, conformity, and lack of innovation'; 'it provides a potentially useful bridge to antecedents and consequences of adoption, but the bridge seems to have become an end in itself' (Benbasat & Barki, 2007, p. 216). UTAUT, seeks to supersede TAM and other models. It forms the basis of several other studies of mobile technology adoption (Garfield, 2005; Lu, Yu, & Liu, 2009).

From Ease-of-Use and Usefulness to Personal and Organisational Use Value

TAM consists of 'a small set of key attributes of technology...bearing deterministically on the decision to adopt, or to reject' (McMaster & Wastell, 2005, p. 386). These key attributes are the perceived usefulness defined as 'the degree to which a person believes that using a particular system would enhance his or her job performance' (Davis, 1989, p. 320) and the perceived ease-of-use defined as 'the degree to which a person believes that using a particular system would be free from effort' (Davis, 1989, p. 320). In UTAUT these are retained although renamed as performance expectancy and effort expectancy, and supplemented by two other key determinants (social influence and facilitating conditions). Performance expectancy and perceived usefulness essentially mean the potential positives for the organisation whereas effort expectancy and perceived ease-of-use mean the potential negatives for the individual employee. Personal usefulness would appear to be irrelevant or assumed to be congruent with organisational usefulness.

This ethnographic study in a Telco's R&D department has revealed that potential personal positives are significant in influencing adoption. Although it might be possible to define these personal positives as personal usefulness such a term implies judgment. Use value is broader than usefulness as a concept for it does not suggest an employer focus and nor does it imply judgment, thus it can provide better for play. Use value can be divided into organisational and personal use value. The former would be the consideration—or prediction—of what is best for the employer; the latter what is best for the employee whether in their work or non-work life. These two drivers of smartphone adoption are both influenced by vendor discourse. For instance, in the Telco, Fourth Engineer was observed cutting and pasting text from a vendor's website onto the form used to request the purchase of a smartphone. The copied text presented the smartphone as a productivity tool for the employer. Instant messaging with friends, the real reason for his request, was a function featured in the discarded text, which presented the smartphone as a consumer good.

Exchange value, traditionally conceived as the product of such manipulation of use value, seemed insignificant for him, or indeed for the other engineers. As with a child (Adorno & Jephcott, 2010), exchange value was deferred as a concern to the person who pays. This might not always be so. An 'empowered' employee might wish to minimise the exchange value as there may be a trade-off, for instance, a laptop might come out of the same training/resources budget as conference attendance. A dissatisfied employee might be motivated to maximise the exchange value so as to have the most—detrimental—impact upon the organisation's success.

The appropriation of a work-provided artefact for communicating with friends and family and for the consumption of pornography, as observed in the Telco, can constitute employees consuming use values for themselves rather than producing them for their employer. This can be a form of resistance or misbehaviour as it is an example of appropriating 'materials for some other purpose than the productive process' (Thompson & Ackroyd, 1995, p. 616). As such, it can circumscribe the totalising rationalisation of the labour process. There has been 'the virtual removal of labour as an active agency of resistance in a considerable portion of theory and research' (Thompson & Ackroyd, 1995, p. 615), both critical and mainstream, because the intent of managerial practice—as embodied in discourse or texts—is conflated with its outcome. The case of the Telco, in contrast, shows that management need not be the prime mover in bargaining. As such this constitutes a return to post-war research which revealed how employees were 'active and innovative in attempts to survive in employment, recurrently breaking rules and actively re-negotiating them on a continuous basis, with a management frequently tolerant of, accommodating to, or conniving in, such practices' (Thompson & Ackroyd, 1995, p. 616). In terms of the development of a new location-based service using smartphones, it could even be stated the company was dependent upon such misbehaviour.

Exploring Between and Beyond Intention and Use

Perceptions of personal and organisational use value are not just shaping intention and use but also informing negotiation and even initiating adoption. In TAM the afore-mentioned drivers of perceived usefulness and perceived ease-of-use determine behavioural intention to use and actual system use. In UTAUT these are retained although slightly renamed as behavioural intention and use behaviour. Such a division makes sense, for intentions are rarely fully reflected by practice, but this longitudinal study reveals the need for a more nuanced conception, entailing initiation, negotiation, exploration, operation, and disposition.

The authors of UTAUT declare that it 'provides a useful tool for managers to assess the likelihood of success for new technology introductions and helps them understand the drivers of acceptance in order to proactively design interventions (including training, marketing, etc.) targeted at populations of users that may be less inclined to adopt and use new systems' (Venkatesh, et al., 2003, p. 425). In TAM, likewise, managerialism is explicit in its intention to be used by—and serve the purposes of—management. Implicit in both is also the assumption that the manager will be initiating the adoption of a new technology by others. This does not permit the possibility of employee-initiated adoption, a possibility realised by engineers in the Telco. It may well be that elsewhere the employees who have the power to initiate the adoption of smartphones are managers, but that it is their own adoption that they are concerned with. This may be considered a form of managerial misbehaviour, something that 'few researchers have concerned themselves with' (Collinson & Ackroyd, 2005, p. 306).

In bargains of old, the employer's proposal of a new technological artefact would prompt a period of employer-led negotiation. This stage could embrace negotiation of specification but also negotiation between employer and employee and between different levels of management. In terms of employer-employee negotiation it has been found that it is at this stage that trade unions are most likely to be involved (Williams & Steward, 1985); in terms of negotiation between different levels of management it has been found that at this stage budgetary constraints and considerations play an important role in determining which system is selected (Noon, 1989). Typically, employees would oppose the artefact but after a period of negotiation would be appeased by a concession such as 'technology pay' (Noon, 1989). Facilitating conditions, a driver in UTAUT, does not capture the potential two-way nature of such negotiation, or the fact that negotiation itself is determined by perceptions of personal and organisational use value. In the Telco, organisational use value, as encapsulated in the employee's completed asset request form, was the starting point for such negotiation. This was not what really motivated Fourth Engineer but was permitted by the fact that smartphones, to a greater extent than the new technologies of old, permit a variety of uses of varying benefit for employer and employee. Third Engineer had seemingly internalised his employer's objectives and sought 'biographic solutions of systemic contradictions' (Beck, 1992, p. 137). In most cases, the employee's completed asset request form was the end point of negotiation too, for the head of R&D perceived the organisational use value of such smartphones whether in improving co-ordination or prompting new service development. Such negotiated bargains for smartphones were initially individual and idiosyncratic: 'i-deals' (Rousseau, 2005). However, they became collective through emulation.

At the time, TAM was conceived there was limited difference between the intended use of a technology at the time of its purchase and that to which it would be put in practice. The magnitude of difference between these uses has increased, especially since the advent of networked computers in the 1990s (Greenbaum, 2004). A computer purchased for maintaining accounts could then be used to send emails, not just to colleagues, but also friends and family. Later on, such an artefact could be used to shop online or download music and videos. Smartphones extend this potential difference, for with their mobile phone and network connection, they can be used outside—and even surreptitiously within—the office, away from the gaze of colleagues and managers, for personal purposes. In the Telco, engineers used their devices to: follow football scores; check their bank accounts; download music; view (sometimes pornographic) pictures and videos. Employers in general may have little control, for the artefacts—where traces of such activities may be left—are rarely, if ever, inspected or serviced by their technicians and the data traffic across a mobile phone network—in contrast to the office network—is beyond their surveillance. Some foresee or have experienced problems (Sørensen & Pica, 2004); others see that such personal use may not preclude—and may be the prelude to—use as management intended. In the Telco, this was the position of the head of R&D. It would have been possible to monitor data traffic across the mobile phone network as all Telco-provided smartphones were subscribed to its own network. Where employees were monitored via their smartphone, in the case of the location-based services trial, this was at the effort of other employees, although, of course, such effort may have been the result of management pressure to deliver new services with minimal resources and may have been expended with management's implicit consent.

The assumption of mainstream knowledge-worker management literature—and practice—that 'complementary personal and organizational transformation is...achievable' (Bell & Taylor, 2003, p. 345) has enabled a supposed change in the approach of management from 'imposing control' to 'eliciting commitment' (Walton, 1985). Engineers in the Telco, as with knowledge-workers in general, were granted supposed privileges, such as the right to work flexibly or to dress casually. However, such privileged flexibility was only for 'as long as they [fulfilled] commitments and [did] not arouse attention' (Kunda, 1992, p. 48). 'Some of the more overt trappings of bureaucratic control systems and managerial power [were] relaxed, disguised, or reinterpreted' but 'the enhanced flexibility, structural ambiguity, looser behavioural controls, and less rigid supervision of work behaviour' was balanced by 'an additional overlay of control' (Kunda, 1992, p. 220): peer-management. This overlay was provided for, whether intended or not, by smartphones and was 'manifested in very subtle forms of group pressure' (Kunda, 1992, p. 219) such as the emerging expectations of regular checking of emails and updating of calendars, and in a far less subtle form by the service developed in the R&D department. The case study supports the assertion that a team-oriented, flat hierarchy 'covertly revives interpersonal suspicion, sibling-like rivalry...at the same time as it overtly, officially, promotes egalitarian team mate cooperation, familial warmth, and over-riding commitment to the product' (Casey, 1999, p. 172). The high-tech employees of the Telco had 'been "empowered"...which boils down to bearing responsibility for making themselves relevant to the company' (Bauman, 2002, p. 34). In trying to exercise this responsibility by developing a new service by their own volition, they did, however, act irresponsibly, doing one of their own a disservice. The engagement phase of anticipation and the honeymoon phase of play and exploration was thus the prelude to resentment and/or guilt, when the mention of fruits such as blackberries, oranges and apples brought pain rather than pleasure.

Engineers and managers frequently enquiring via email about one another's progress did not solely impact negatively on the individual employee for 'such disruptions can impede attainment of the organization's goals' (Perlow, 1997, p. 84). This was certainly the case in the telco, for employees complained of not having the space to think, even if their smartphone did not ring, buzz, or beep. As Perlow states, because engineers 'do not know when they will be interrupted, even long periods without interruption are not recognized as opportunities for deep concentration' (Perlow, 1997, p. 78); this may be done only in retrospect. Creativity was thus 'undermined unintentionally every day...for entirely good reasons—to maximize business imperatives such as coordination, productivity, and control' (Amabile, 1998, p. 77). The personal and organisational experiences of smartphone use in the telco suggest two stages of use: exploration when the possibilities are experimented with, and operation when routine use becomes the norm. Such routine use eventually comes to an end such as when, as in the Telco, a smartphone is sold through an online marketplace or put at the back of a drawer.

FUTURE RESEARCH DIRECTIONS

One weakness of TAM and UTAUT is that they primarily rely upon quantitative data. When they have been appropriated for qualitative research (e.g. UTAUT in Garfield, 2005) their findings have been prematurely prescribed. 'Neat geometric models such a[s] TAM are like pastry cutters that produce nice regular shapes, but only at the expense of editing out everything else not contained in the model' (McMaster & Wastell, 2005, p. 396). UTAUT is still a pastry cutter, even though it is a much fancier one. Personal use value-driven, employee-led, bargaining is, at least to an extent, 'covert and subterranean' (Collinson & Ackroyd, 2005, p. 306). As such it is 'inevitably...difficult to identify and research' (Collinson & Ackroyd, 2005, p. 306), even more so when depending upon 'large data sets and increasingly available quantitative survey materials, rather than in-depth or longitudinal fieldwork' (Thompson & Ackroyd, 1995, p. 619). So that it is possible to 'see' personal use value-driven, employee-led, bargaining a broader, qualitative, frame needs to be developed. Moving beyond simple variables such as age, Bourdieu's capitals have been adopted as

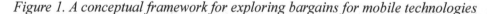

Figure 1. A conceptual framework for exploring bargains for mobile technologies

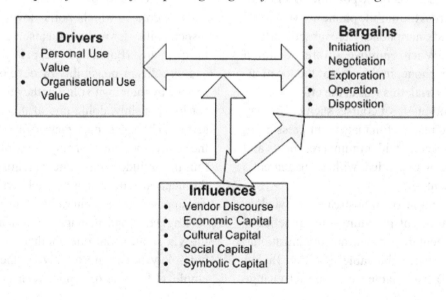

broad categories to encompass what actors bring from their habitus into the field of play, such as in a study of the digital divide (Kvasny & Keil, 2006) where it was found that these capitals influence adoption, even of 'free' services. To explore the key set of economic capital, cultural capital, social capital, and symbolic capital (Bourdieu, 1984) with reference to this population would be a chapter in its own right, however, it is considered that these, together with vendor discourse, influence the drivers of perceived personal and organisational use value. A conceptual framework is presented in Figure 1, which integrates findings from such broader literature with those from this ethnographic study.

The use of a qualitative method in this study has produced knowledge that has more depth than it has breadth. The specific organisational context of the R&D department of the Telco could be considered relatively unique in a couple of key aspects. First, engineers in the R&D department of a telco could be considered something of an extreme case of ethnographic site (Oates, 2006), because of their likely propensity to initiate the adoption of smartphones themselves. Second, the department was subject to a number of other changes concurrent with the identified bargains for smartphones: the roll out of a company-wide innovation inducement scheme; the global integration—i.e. reduction—of research and development resources; the re-layering of the management hierarchy; the recruitment of cheap labour—i.e. centrally-funded graduate trainees on placement—and the abolition of 'seed money' to develop concept demonstrators. It is considered that the above conceptual framework could be used in future qualitative research on exploring patterns of adoption and their driving or influencing factors within other organisational contexts. Recognising that the particular arrangement of patterns and factors will differ between spatio-temporal contexts, it may well need revision as a result of such research, but it is hoped that this conceptual framework is transferable, at least in part, to other contexts. Ultimately, the only way to establish the resulting conceptual framework's generalisability to a new setting is to test it in that setting (Lee & Baskerville, 2003).

Utilising this conceptual framework in critical fieldwork is not without potential pitfalls. Two aims of critical research are emancipation and non-performative intent (Howcroft & Trauth, 2008). If research results in employers or vendors restricting or exploiting the personal use value of smartphones then these will not be fulfilled. Due to the lack of central control over smartphone adoption (Sørensen & Pica, 2004)—whether by the technology, human resource or finance functions—access would need to be of sufficient breadth, depth and duration. With regard to personal use value-driven, employee-led, bargaining, which might be considered a form of misbehaviour, employees may be more forthcoming in an anonymous survey rather than an interview. However, it would be difficult to construct a survey that might penetrate through the possible false or faulty consciousness of employees on issues such as the impact of vendor discourse on their actions. Longitudinal ethnography, as employed in this case, would avoid such limitations. Further, when exploring the role of vendor discourse it may be challenging to reconcile the possible false consciousness of the employee with the possible false presumption of the researcher regarding the effect of such discourse, the latter a leap of which Adorno has been accused (Crook, 1994). Whilst this research has been concerned with work-provided smartphones and their possible use for play, research is also required on self-provided smartphones and their possible use for work. Likewise, research is required on how the commercial location-based services now available, such as Facebook places, impact beyond play in the workplace.

CONCLUSION

This research identified—and provides for the possibility of identifying further—new technology bargains, bargains driven by personal as well as organisational use value and shaped by vendor discourse. The enhanced employee agency implied by this might suggest that the bargain favours the employee, enabling them to consume use value for themselves as opposed to producing exchange value for their employer. However, the interplay of the personal with the organisational in this context was more complex. As a particular form of the engineer's work life—administration—encroached further upon their non-work life and their research and development work they became no more productive, although certainly more controlled. The empowerment of self- and peer-management meant little in practice for the engineer: the structural pressures and demands made it impossible not to let administrative work permeate into their other work and non-work life; as a consequence, neither personal nor organisational use value were ultimately maximised. Thus, in initiating the adoption of smartphones—and, indeed, in creating new services for them—these high-tech employees could be said to have made a rod for their own back.

REFERENCES

Adorno, T. W., & Jephcott, E. F. N. (2010). *Minima moralia: Reflections from damaged life*. London, UK: Verso.

Amabile, T. M. (1998, September-October). How to kill creativity. *Harvard Business Review*.

Bauman, Z. (2002). *Society under siege*. Cambridge, UK: Polity Press.

Beck, U. (1992). *Risk society: Towards a new modernity*. London, UK: Sage.

Bell, E., & Taylor, S. (2003). The elevation of work: Pastoral power and the new age work ethic. *Organization*, *10*(2), 329–349. doi:10.1177/1350508403010002009

Benbasat, I., & Barki, H. (2007). Quo vadis, tam? *Journal of the Association for Information Systems*, *8*(4), 212–218.

Bødker, S. (1987). A utopian experience: On design of powerful computer-based tools for skilled graphic workers. In Bjerknes, G. (Eds.), *Computers and Democracy* (pp. 251–278). Aldershot, UK: Avebury.

Bourdieu, P. (1984). *Distinction: A social critique of the judgement of taste*. London, UK: Routledge.

Casey, C. (1999). Come, join our family: Discipline and integration in corporate organizational culture. *Human Relations*, *52*(2), 155–178. doi:10.1023/A:1016980602039

Collinson, D., & Ackroyd, S. (2005). Resistance, misbehavior, dissent. In Ackroyd, S., Batt, R., Thompson, P., & Tolbert, P. S. (Eds.), *The Oxford Handbook of Work and Organization*. Oxfor, UK: Oxford University Press.

Crook, S. (1994). Introduction: Adorno and authoritarian irrationalism. In *Adorno: The Stars Down to Earth and Other Essays on the Irrational in Culture* (pp. 1–33). London, UK: Routledge.

Davis, F. D. (1989). Perceived usefulness, perceived ease of use, and user acceptance of information technology. *Management Information Systems Quarterly*, *13*(3), 319–340. doi:10.2307/249008

Ehn, P. (1988). *Work-oriented design of computer artefacts*. Stockholm, Sweden: Arbetslivscentrum.

Ehn, P., Kyng, M., & Sundblad, Y. (1983). The utopia project: On training, technology and products viewed from the quality of work perspective. In Briefs, U., Ciborra, C. U., & Schneider, L. (Eds.), *Systems Design for, with, and by the Users* (pp. 427–438). Amsterdam, The Netherlands: North-Holland.

Fenner, G. H., & Renn, R. W. (2010). Technology-assisted supplemental work and work-to-family conflict: The role of instrumentality beliefs, organizational expectations and time management. *Human Relations*, *63*(1), 63–82. doi:10.1177/0018726709351064

Garfield, M. J. (2005, Fall). Acceptance of ubiquitous computing. *Information Systems Management*, (n.d), 24–31. doi:10.1201/1078.10580530/45520.22.4.20050901/90027.3

Greenbaum, J. (2004). *Windows on the workplace*. New York, NY: Monthly Review Press.

Howcroft, D., & Trauth, E. M. (2008). The implications of a critical agenda in gender and IS research. *Information Systems Journal*, *18*(2), 185–202. doi:10.1111/j.1365-2575.2008.00294.x

Karahanna, E., Straub, D. W., & Chervany, N. L. (1999). Information technology adoption across time: A cross-sectional comparison of pre-adoption and post-adoption beliefs. *Management Information Systems Quarterly*, *23*(2), 183–213. doi:10.2307/249751

Koivumaki, T., Ristola, A., & Kesti, M. (2008). The effects of information quality of mobile information services on user satisfaction and service acceptance-empirical evidence from Finland. *Behaviour & Information Technology*, *27*(5), 375–385. doi:10.1080/01449290601177003

Kunda, G. (1992). *Engineering culture: Control and commitment in a high-tech corporation*. Philadelphia, PA: Temple University Press.

Kvasny, L., & Keil, M. (2006). The challenges of redressing the digital divide: A tale of two US cities. *Information Systems Journal*, *16*(1), 23–53. doi:10.1111/j.1365-2575.2006.00207.x

Latour, B. (1987). *Science in action: How to follow scientists and engineers through society*. Milton Keynes, UK: Open University Press.

Lee, A. S., & Baskerville, R. L. (2003). Generalizing generalizability in information systems research. *Information Systems Research*, *14*(3), 221–243. doi:10.1287/isre.14.3.221.16560

Ling, R., Julsrud, T., & Krogh, E. (1997). The goretex principle: The hytte and mobile telephones in Norway. In Haddon, L. (Ed.), *Communications on the Move: The Experience of Mobile Telephony in the 1990s*. Farsta, Sweden: Telia.

Lu, J., Yu, C.-S., & Liu, C. (2009). Mobile data service demographics in urban China. *Journal of Computer Information Systems*, *50*(2), 117–126.

Matusik, S. F., & Mickel, A. E. (2011). Embracing or embattled by converged mobile devices? Users' experiences with a contemporary connectivity technology. *Human Relations*, *64*(8), 1001–1030. doi:10.1177/0018726711405552

Mazmanian, M., Yates, J., & Orlikowski, W. (2006). Ubiquitous email: Individual experiences and organizational consequences of blackberry use. *Academy of Management Annual Meeting Proceedings, 66*.

Mazmanian, M. A., Orlikowski, W. J., & Yates, J. (2005). Crackberries: The social implicaitons of ubiquitous wireless e-mail devices. In C. Sørensen, Y. Yoo, K. Lyytinen, & J. I. DeGross (Eds.), *Designing Ubiquitous Information Environments: Socio-Technical Issues and Challenges,* (pp. pp. 337-344). New York, NY: Springer.

McMaster, T., & Wastell, D. (2005). Diffusion – Or delusion? Challenging an IS research tradition. *Information Technology & People, 18*(4), 383–404. doi:10.1108/09593840510633851

Middleton, C. A. (2007). Illusions of balance and control in an always-on environment: A case study of blackberry users. *Continuum: Journal of Media & Cultural Studies, 21,* 165–178. doi:10.1080/10304310701268695

Middleton, C. A., & Cukier, W. (2006). Is mobile email functional or dysfunctional? Two perspectives on mobile email usage. *European Journal of Information Systems, 15*(3), 252–260. doi:10.1057/palgrave.ejis.3000614

Newman, M., & Robey, D. (1992). A social process model of user-analyst relationships. *Management Information Systems Quarterly, 16*(2), 249–266. doi:10.2307/249578

Noon, M. A. (1989). *New technology and industrial relations in provincial newspapers: Computerisation and bargaining power of journalists.* Unpublished Doctoral Dissertation. London, UK: Imperial College.

Oates, B. J. (2006). *Researching information systems and computing.* London, UK: SAGE.

Orlikowski, W. J. (2007). Sociomaterial practices: Exploring technology at work. *Organization Studies, 28*(9), 1435–1448. doi:10.1177/0170840607081138

Orlikowski, W. J., & Iacono, C. S. (2001). Research commentary: Desperately seeking the 'it' in IT research - A call to theorizing the IT artifact. *Information Systems Research, 12*(2), 121–134. doi:10.1287/isre.12.2.121.9700

Perlow, L. A. (1997). *Finding time: How corporations, individuals, and families can benefit from new work practices.* Ithaca, NY: Cornell University Press.

Rousseau, D. M. (2005). *I-deals: Idiosyncratic deals employees bargain for themselves.* London, UK: M.E. Sharpe.

Samsung. (2010). *Work Smarter and Play Harder with the Omnia Pro.* Retrieved 25 October, 2010, from http://www.samsung.com/uk/consumer/mobile-phones/mobile-phones/qwerty/GT-B7330QKAXEU/index.idx?pagetype=prd_detail

Sørensen, C., & Pica, D. (2004). *Out-of-sight shouldn't mean out-of-mind: Why corporates need to get control of their wireless assets.* London, UK: London School of Economics and Political Science.

Thompson, P., & Ackroyd, S. (1995). All quiet on the workplace front? A critique of recent trends in British industrial sociology. *Sociology, 29*(4), 615–633. doi:10.1177/0038038595029004004

Towers, I., Duxbury, L., Higgins, C., & Thomas, J. (2006). Time thieves and space invaders: Technology, work and the organization. *Journal of Organizational Change Management, 19*(5), 593–618. doi:10.1108/09534810610686076

Venkatesh, V., Morris, M. G., Davis, G. B., & Davis, F. D. (2003). User acceptance of information technology: Toward a unified view. *Management Information Systems Quarterly, 27*(3), 425–478.

Wajcman, J., Bittman, M., & Brown, J. E. (2008). Families without borders: Mobile phones, connectedness and work-home divisions. *Sociology, 42*(4), 635–652. doi:10.1177/0038038508091620

Walton, R. E. (1985, March-April). From control to commitment in the workplace. *Harvard Business Review.*

Williams, R., & Steward, F. (1985). Technology agreements in Great Britain: A survey 1977-83. *Industrial Relations Journal, 16*(3), 58–73. doi:10.1111/j.1468-2338.1985.tb00526.x

Yu, J., Yu, C.-S., Liu, C., & Yao, J. E. (2003). Technology acceptance model for wireless internet. *Internet Research, 13*(3), 206–222. doi:10.1108/10662240310478222

ADDITIONAL READING

Adorno, T. W. (1991). *The culture industry*. London, UK: Routledge.

Avgerou, C. (2002). *Information systems and global diversity*. Oxford, UK: Oxford University Press.

Avgerou, C., & McGrath, K. (2005). Rationalities and emotions in IS innovation. In Howcroft, D., & Trauth, E. M. (Eds.), *Handbook of Critical Information Systems Research* (pp. 299–324). Cheltenham, UK: Edward Elgar.

Avgerou, C., & McGrath, K. (2007). Power, rationality, and the art of living through socio-technical change. *Management Information Systems Quarterly, 31*(2), 295–315.

Beath, C., & Orlikowski, W. J. (1994). The contradictory structure of systems development methodologies. *Information Systems Research, 5*(4), 350–377. doi:10.1287/isre.5.4.350

Braverman, H. (1998). *Labor and monopoly capital* (25th Anniversary ed.). New York, NY: Monthly Review Press.

Brooke, C. (2002a). Critical perspectives on information systems. *Journal of Information Technology, 17*, 271–283. doi:10.1080/0268396022000017789

Brooke, C. (2002b). Editorial: Critical research in information systems. *Journal of Information Technology, 17*, 25–47. doi:10.1080/02683960210154139

Brooke, C. (2002c). What does it mean to be "critical" in IS research? *Journal of Information Technology, 17*, 49–57. doi:10.1080/02683960210164336

Bunting, M. (2004). *Willing slaves: How the overwork culture is ruling our lives*. London, UK: HarperCollins.

Campbell-Kelly, M. (2003). *From airline reservations to sonic the hedgehog: A history of the software industry*. Cambridge, MA: MIT Press.

Duane, A., & Finnegan, P. (2007). Dissent, protest and transformative action: An exploratory study of staff reactions to electronic monitoring and control of e-mail systems in one company based in Ireland. *Information Resources Management Journal, 20*(1), 1–13. doi:10.4018/irmj.2007010101

Hakken, D., & Andrews, B. (1993). *Computing myths, class realities*. Boulder, CO: Westview.

Hirschheim, R., & Klein, H. K. (1994). Realizing emancipatory principles in information systems development. *Management Information Systems Quarterly, 18*(1), 83–109. doi:10.2307/249611

Howcroft, D., & Wilson, M. (2003a). Paradoxes of participatory practices: The janus role of the systems developer. *Information and Organization, 13*, 1–24. doi:10.1016/S1471-7727(02)00023-4

Howcroft, D., & Wilson, M. (2003b). Participation: 'Bounded freedom' or hidden constraints on user involvement. *New Technology, Work and Employment, 18*(1). doi:10.1111/1468-005X.00107

Jaros, S. J. (2005). Marxian critiques of Thompson's (1990) 'core' labour process theory: An evaluation and extension. *Ephemera, 5*(1), 5–25.

Jay, M. (1973). *The dialectical imagination*. Berkeley, CA: University of California.

Kaarst-Brown, M. L., & Robey, D. (1999). More on myth, metaphor and magic. *Information Technology & People, 12*(2), 192–217. doi:10.1108/09593849910267251

Miller, D. (1995). Consumption as the vanguard of history: A polemic by way of introduction. In Miller, D. (Ed.), *Acknowledging Consumption: A Review of New Studies* (pp. 1–57). London, UK: Routledge.

Myers, M. D., & Young, L. W. (1997). Hidden agendas, power and managerial assumptions in information systems development. *Information Technology & People*, *10*(3), 224–240. doi:10.1108/09593849710178225

Postrel, V. (2003). *The substance of style: How the rise of aesthetic value is remaking commerce, Culture, and consciousness*. New York, NY: HarperCollins.

Robey, D., & Boudreau, M.-C. (1999). Accounting for the contradictory organizational consequences of information technology: Theoretical directions and methodological implications. *Information Systems Research*, *10*(2), 167–197. doi:10.1287/isre.10.2.167

Rose, H., McLoughlin, I., King, R., & Clark, J. (1986). Opening the black box: The relation between technology and work. *New Technology, Work and Employment*, *1*(1), 18–26. doi:10.1111/j.1468-005X.1986.tb00077.x

Wilson, M. (2002). Making nursing visible? Gender, technology and the care plan as script. *Information Technology & People*, *15*(2), 139–158. doi:10.1108/09593840210430570

KEY TERMS AND DEFINITIONS

Bargain: An agreement between two parties and, more broadly as here, the resulting goods or services received or rendered as a result.

Exchange Value: The quantity of other commodities an artefact could be traded for.

Misbehaviour: An active set of practices to appropriate time, work, product or identity within the workplace.

Resistance: A negative reaction to power (whether embodied in a role, institution, or artefact).

Smartphone: A technological artefact that blends the information power of a small personal computer and the telecommunication power of a mobile phone.

Use Value: The power of an artefact to satisfy a want (whether necessary, useful, or simply pleasant).

Vendor Discourse: Communication from sellers of artefacts, whether mediated or direct in written, oral, or multimodal form.

Chapter 8

In the Name of Flexibility:
Three Hidden Meanings of "The Real Work" in a Finnish Software Company

Marja-Liisa Trux
Aalto University School of Economics, Finland

ABSTRACT

This chapter takes you to a data security workplace in Finland. It presents reflections on the tensions of managing selves and others, as experienced by the employees and the managers. It argues that a generally critical approach to normative management may overlook the actual complexity and ambiguous nature of the late modern cultural environment. Both self-authoring and manipulative moves are made difficult by the amalgamating hegemonic and countercultural currents. The author points at chances for resistance through new forms of literacy. Instead of dropping "culture" as a conservative or managerial pursuit, we must learn to navigate successfully in the broken cultural landscape of today's workplaces. The very same images that can be used for manipulation are open to more solidary configurations by the cultural and social imagination of organizational members.

INTRODUCTION

Knowledge economy is the dominant call today, as much in official national and multinational strategies as in the rhetoric of corporations. Organizations must meet demands for innovativeness and quick learning. As the human imagination is a hard thing to control, the managerial elites have tended to turn from Taylor-like physical control to more psychological forms that lead discreetly to the desired outcomes. No direct monitoring is needed to guarantee maximal input from the workforce. Manipulated workers themselves define high objectives and devote themselves to their tasks,

DOI: 10.4018/978-1-4666-1836-7.ch008

sometimes at the risk of their health. The limits of this approach are attained in cases where increased pressure to produce ever new innovative solutions on time and respecting consumer demands has led *de facto* to decreased creativity and burnout symptoms. To the frustration of the fashionable faith in managerial omnipotence, it seems that the sought-after revolutionary innovation just cannot be merely called into being, but may instead appear as a byproduct of leisurely playful activity. Indeed, market pressures and innovations seem to mix like oil and water. How can any realist management strike a balance between these two?

Alongside rather primitive retreats to tight control, the past decade has also witnessed fairly 'democratic' and participatory moves, partly as an inheritance from the high-tech industry's most typical professional culture, referred to alternatively as 'nerd culture,' 'hacker ethics,' or 'techies culture.' The field of high-tech management is by no means dominated by manipulative forms. Very different approaches coexist, and managers as much as workers rely upon one or another of them in the underdefined cultural conditions of late capitalism. Local societal and institutional conditions bring further variation to the arenas of industrial relations, regulatory practices, and work cultures.

This chapter is based on ethnography in a middle-sized Finnish software company F-Secure[1], mainly in its Helsinki headquarters and by comparison in a Silicon Valley subsidiary[2]. I went to the organization originally to inquire into ethnicity and its management, since the company had a relatively high proportion of foreign workers. I soon learned that there was no management related to ethnicity. The first round of my inquiry in 2000 suggested that foreigners in Helsinki were nevertheless exceedingly happy about what they called "Finnish management." Why? Could it be explained in terms of the workers being so lucky— middle-class with stable incomes, during a boom and with a common professional identity? Largely, of course. They were, however, happiest about

the more sustainable traits in management style, such as investment in education and respect for personal autonomy. The foreigners summarized it as "air of democracy."

After the downturn, F-Secure's "democracy" came under attack, but survived and was even institutionalized in some organizational practices. Yet its acting out in the social exchange of daily work is continuously contested and defended in the face of the postmodern pressures of investor relations, financial insecurity, consumer demands, market strategies, and technological development—all of which may and do cause sudden turbulence that needs to be checked, often curtailing the freedom of the workers. In this day-to-day balancing action, cultural forms like the discourses around 'flexibility' take the role of tools for self-management and managing others. Both workers and managers attempt to construct situated identity and agency, but their attempts are confused by the ambiguity of connotative links and the absence of clear addresses in dialog with the world.

"FLEXIBLE" WORK AND ITS CULTURAL CONTEXT

Many writers have drawn attention in the last two decades to the widespread use of the image of 'flexibility' in dominant postmodern discourse, especially concerning work and production. For Richard Sennett, this is one of the cornerstones in the talk of the managerial elites or "Davos men" (Sennett, 1998). Liberated from the iron cage of rigid organizations, workers must now survive the fierce competition of postmodern, unpredictable markets, selling their capabilities anew each day and renewing their skills as best they can (Sennett, 2006). I have myself listened to a representative of the Confederation of Finnish Industries reciting the necessary qualities of today's workers as "creativity, curiosity, interaction, development, renewal, faith in one's own opportunities, target setting, interest in the customer, skill to tackle in the network of ever more differences, social skills, learning from other cultures and transformability." He also quoted Charles Darwin as having said that "only the most transformable [sic] survive"[3] (Pokela, 2005).

As the American anthropologist Emily Martin has shown, the image of the flexible citizen is not confined to the realm of work alone. She has followed its occurrences in U.S. society from discourses concerning immunology to health and fitness and then to workplaces. Borrowed from medical jargon, the public discourse started during the 1960s and 1970s to apply the idea of resistance to various microbes as a key element in the popular image of the good citizen, who took care of her organism (by means of a healthy diet, exercise, and a regular life style) so that it could react to each illness attack fittingly, nimbly, and intelligently—beating off the intruding germs. This soon led to the corresponding image of the citizen as a flexible, trained body, adapting quickly to each new environmental challenge, and then to the present image of the ideal postmodern worker, seizing each new opportunity as it comes (See Martin, 1994). Like individuals, organizations must also be elastic. Even dinosaurs must dance[4]. The latest episode can be discerned in repetitive accounts of the competitiveness of national economies against each other. Which country is going to get this year's flexibility prize?

Manipulative Hooks

Manipulative control in IT has played upon several hooks, caching the computer experts by elements in their heterogeneous cultural heritage. Since the beginnings of this professional subculture, mutual solidarity among fellow programmers was sustained through help and sharing of information. Reputations among colleagues were achieved by (sometimes extreme) devotion of time and energy. Countercultural elements nurtured suspicion towards authorities and underlined individuality in the professional identity. 'Hackers' were the cowboys of the digital frontiers in a genuinely American way.[5] Liberation from the 'iron cage' of hierarchical organizations was their watchword and they committed themselves and many of their organizations to this goal of turning a new page in the history of work. This call for flexible, engineer-centred organization was answered at least in some of the trend setting organizations of northern America, as witnessed by Gideon Kunda (1992), but the devil was already in the paradise. Serving the die-hard value of instrumental rationality, manipulative employers found it easy to make engineers 'devote' themselves to the company vision, 'help' the employer and feel free to work day and night like the good entrepreneurs they all were.

When the IT bubble burst, soon after the turn of millennium, things got complicated. During the downturn of the years 2001-2003, in the disillusionment that ended or at least problematized the flirtation between countercultural and neo-liberal elements, some employees at F-Secure seemed to take sides with the employer, tightening their belt in the hope of a reward for their loyalty. Others seemed to be questioning the motives of the employer more deeply. Judging by its decisions, the management oscillated between radical democratic experiments as one option, cost cutting in panic as another one and neo-liberal faith in flexible, globally distributed production as a third option.

I must remind you that I do not refer to 'management' as a term of firmly organized action following a script or manipulative plot, and backed by massive power—as in business school accounts of strategic management. Instead, I look at it sideways, as a more threatened form of activity, managing (or not managing) to do something: to steer the boat, to prevent it from sinking, to negotiate with the crew, to guess where one might be amid the turbulent waters, and to choose among plausible options for the next move. No more does individual workers' 'self-management' refer to means of self-control for someone else, or making more money to their employer, but more generally—much more generally—doing their work, living among each other and pursuing personal and professional growth. In my case company, the managers, on the whole, share the professional subculture of their workers. The cognitive and moral confusion that followed the downturn concerned them as well as the workers, though of course with different positioning. Members of the managerial class have significantly more power than their subordinates, but they may have no better understanding of what to do with that power; how should they understand the present situation, what does it mean—and, thus, who they are themselves. Despite the fact that these uncertainties may be poorly recognized and reflected upon by the people themselves, they point at the need to tackle the question of *agency* in a heterogeneous cultural environment under strong pressure to change.

Uncertain Agency

The American anthropologist Sherry Ortner has argued since the 1980s for taking up agency as the pivotal point between cultural (semiotic) and social (power relations) forces or structures (Ortner, 1984, 2005). Building on the works of Bourdieu, Giddens, Sahlins, Geertz, and Sewell, who each in their distinct ways have tried to reintroduce agency into the heart of social theory, Ortner offers a picture of the individual's (or a group's) unique, historical existence, struggle for survival and a meaningful life. Her aim is to avoid both the danger of conceiving human subjects as blind carriers of tradition, and the opposite danger of seeing them as nameless marionettes of power structures. In her approach, they have partial freedom, limited by fears, passions, hopes, restrictions, and bonds of all kinds. Ortner is seeking a way to look at life from the subordinates' position: as a struggle for a foothold, however small. Thus her ideas lend theoretical support to many current ethnographies describing the problematic or narrow, even mar-

Table 1. Comparison of Jameson's and Sennett's analysis of postmodernism according to Ortner

Jameson:	Sennett:
waning of affect, depthlessness	indifferent work ("just a job"), masks of cooperativeness by the bosses
spatial disorientation	temporal disorientation ("no long term")

ginal life-spaces of various powerless groups in late modern societies—including immigrants and other inhabitants of transnational social places. As an extension, it may be adapted to accounts of the stratified and unstable life-spaces of employees in the high tech companies. Substantially wealthier than marginal immigrants as they are, their lives are still profoundly marked by the power differentials present in their own organizations and the encompassing business ecology.

Ortner presents two readings of *postmodern consciousness*: Fredric Jameson (Ortner, 2005, pp. 41-42) and Richard Sennett (Ortner, 2005, pp. 43-44). Jameson was much criticized in the 1980s. His account appeared then as somewhat fancy, over dramatized and socially ungrounded, but the third millennium has shown us how postmodernism can strike. In Sennett's description of work under the 'new capitalism', futurological visions have become a reality, albeit a rather ugly one. According to Ortner, the two are talking about same things (see Table 1).

Both are pointing to the need to restore meaning and orientation in the postmodern world, which has become uninterpretable and illegible. We must learn to read our world and show others how to read it, says Ortner (2005, pp. 44–46). Countercurrents of subjectivity exist just as countercurrents of culture do. According to Ortner, subjectivities are complex and reflexive: while few people fully embody the dominant culture, and some are totally subjected by it, most are, nevertheless, partial misfits. They partially internalize, partially reflect upon and react against it (Ortner, 2005, p. 45).

In Ortner's account, the multi-layered and reflexive cultural consciousness provides the grounds for questioning the dominant culture. I would compare this to the historian William Sewell's theorizing on misfits between cultural model and reality that provide the grounds for cultural change and transformative/alternative movements. (See Sewell, 1999.) Both are dynamic, non-totalizing accounts of culture.

However, how exactly is culture woven into social life? According to Dorothy Holland et al. (1998), cultural forms are the tools of self-management (or self-authoring) as much as managing others. They are the currency of all social fields, including workplaces. These authors have combined the ideas of Bakhtin and Vygotsky; and rewritten the borders of that combination to the theory of *fields* by Bourdieu. The result is a theoretical edifice that takes on the duty of explaining the intricacies of learning to live one's identity—or identities. Their attempt can be seen as an answer to the call made by Sherry Ortner for bridging the cleft between semiotic structures and power structures. Their account of *heteroglossia* is useful for understanding the present conditions where people attempt to form their 'voice' out of a multitude of different and differently positioned 'voices' of others (Holland, et al., 1998, pp. 181-183). As *spaces of authoring,* workplaces like the one I describe are difficult to outline, marked by uneven power positions, insecure and changing, but they are not beyond human bricolage and not immune to countercultural offensives and dialogization. Accounting for the process of authoring enables us to understand the struggle involved and the time and effort it takes.

F-SECURE CORPORATION

How might people fare in a Finnish high-tech company? Would they show signs of struggle at-tempting to cope with the uncertain postmodern organizational environment and its manipulative hooks? First, let's have a look at what kind of a workplace is in question.

F-Secure Corporation is a data security company. It protects individuals and businesses against computer viruses and other threats spreading through the Internet and mobile networks. Its products include antivirus, network encryption, desktop firewall with intrusion prevention, anti-spam and parental control. A constant vigil is kept at the company headquarters in Helsinki against any new malware. Founded in 1988, F-Secure was listed on the (then) Helsinki Exchanges in 1999. In addition to Finland, the company has offices in the USA, Sweden, Norway, France, Belgium, Denmark, the Netherlands, Germany, Italy, Poland, the United Kingdom, India, Malaysia, Australia, Hong Kong, and Japan.

F-Secure's retailers and distributors have expanded to about 100 countries. As its products are to an important degree distributed through Internet service providers and mobile operators, direct marketing to individual consumers is less important. In the Finnish context, F-Secure is a middle-sized organization. Its personnel doubled from 200 to 400 during the boom (1999-2000), and toward the end of my research (2004) had come down to an intermediate level of approximately 300[6]. In Finland, it is well known as one of the flagships of turn-of-millennia technology. Its enlistment created long lines of popular investors on the streets of Helsinki. Today it has a more consolidated reputation, at times a quasi-official position as the favorite source for journalists wanting to ask anything related to Internet threats. According to the management, F-Secure is well known in the Nordic countries, somewhat in Europe, but scarcely at all in the United States. Indeed, as I talked to the American employees, many of them started with reflections on working for a *small* company, overshadowed by large competitors.

At my first visit to F-Secure, I was given a list of the company's values. The HR manager took

Table 2. F-Secure's company values, as given in 1999

Value	Explanation
1. People	Both 'fellows' (refers to all organizational members) and customers are important.
2. Innovation	Mistakes are allowed. "There can be no learning if we fear mistakes."
3. Integrity	Legality, justice, openness. "We go beyond that stipulated by law in order to treat people well, and to protect the environment."
4. Building clocks	"When somebody makes an innovation at work, it must be put on the wall like a clock, so that others can use it too."
5. Fun and joy	"Working must also be fun."

care to explain them to me, as they were—according to him—the basis of the attractiveness of F-Secure as an employer, both nationally and internationally (see Table 2).

While interviewing the workers, I asked their opinion of the values. Most agreed that they were both the right values for the business and principles that were observed in the everyday life. Some had reservations concerning the best ways to realize the values, and their relative weight. One employee (from the U.S.) said that "integrity" was a very Nordic value, a "social-democratic" feature of the organizational life.

F-Secure was no longer a start up when the bubble burst and the IT-sector began its downturn. Crisis management apparently took over, and management of creativity was set aside. In addition to cutting all extravagant benefits (and some rather modest ones), people were laid off. Those with temporary contracts were the first to go in Helsinki. The remaining employees were still recovering from this experience when I returned in 2002.

I found no widespread use of temps as a regular means of 'enhancing' productivity. It seems that people were first taken on as temps. Later on, their contracts were made permanent. At the downturn, those who "had not regularized their contracts" faced the greatest risk of being laid off. It remains unclear whether this tendency to avoid hosts of half-outsiders within the company is related to a communitarian management style or to the demands of risk management in

the digital security industry (many workers told me that their backgrounds had been studied by the Finnish Security Police at the request of the company). Risk management has in any case not precluded the growing use of subcontractors, for instance the (cheaper) programming workforce in St. Petersburg.

According to the Americas manager, the company had intended to enlist on NASDAQ, but this was dropped when the downturn hit.[7] Its founder and long-term CEO is still the principal owner.

"FINNISH MANAGEMENT IS WONDERFUL"

How were the workers faring before the downturn struck, when the newly turned page of the history of work was still pure and stainless? Since the company had no experience in diversity management, but an ethnically mixed workforce[8], I was curious to see how they were doing. The first round of my inquiry suggested they were doing fine in Helsinki. To my unbelieving ears, the foreign interviewees *all* insisted that they were exceedingly happy about what they called "Finnish management." In spite of differences in job titles, gender and country of origin, all related spontaneously that they greatly appreciated the company culture and operating methods.

"Management is really good here. Thwarting innovation wouldn't work in this business anyway.

Table 3. Foreign employees' perception of management methods at boom time

Flow of information	Openness, no secrets (but one has to ask for information)
Operations	Efficiency; the organization is able to react quickly, action is taken following a decision The culture is sensible and looks for practical solutions The culture is flexible, not bound by formalities Oral agreements
Treatment of employees	Individual employees and their time are respected, and employees are listened to and trusted Mutual support among colleagues, supervisors offer help
Organization	Organization is flat and feels democratic

This is a good model, no matter where you are from. It is wonderful to see that you are getting respect."[9]

If there was any difference, westerners in particular admired the flexibility and efficiency of "Finnish management methods." People from Russia and Asia emphasized freedom and respect for individuals, but even these differences were slight. The foreigners gave a consistent picture of what the company was like. Table 3 presents the recurrent topics in this talk, as much in their words as possible.

Could the foreign employees' happiness be explained in terms of the workers being so lucky at the height of boom, soon after arrival in a new country? No doubt, that is a major reason. It does, however, merit attention that what they were happiest about were not the stock options or the company sponsored holiday trips abroad, but the more sustainable traits in management style: investment in education, respect for personal and professional autonomy, listening to the workers etc.

Finns were somewhat less excited, mostly noting that the workplace had "filled expectations." Some even criticized the company for overdoing it:

"Sometimes informality and spoken agreements lead to ambiguity about who is going to do what."[10]

PROFESSIONAL AND MORAL DIMENSIONS OF WORK

What kind of work is being done at F-Secure and who are the people who do it? As far as I tell from the glimpses offered in the interviews, work at F-Secure presents a fairly typical array of duties in the product-centered IT-sector. The pivotal function seems to be the anti-virus laboratory with its researchers, and the large number of people in "development teams" producing the programs destined to customers. Other works consist of supporting scientific expertise (a mathematician), localizing, pre- and post sales support, sales, marketing, managerial work, secretarial work, legal assistance, HR, communications etc. According to the HR manager, the requirements for recruiting anti-virus analysts include for instance familiarity with "old fashioned" programming languages, nowadays less common amongst western IT-professionals. Recruitment is extremely focused, sometimes causing long delays in filling vacant positions, as fitting applicants are rare even among the global workforce. Michael, a Spanish expert, had been recruited in 2002 in the midst of the toughest downturn when unemployment offices received a wave of IT-professionals as client. There had been a search of six months for a fitting applicant.

Despite his young age and only two years at F-Secure, Michael gives a typical expert professional's account of his work. To him, the work essence is the centre of identity and what most matters to him. He divides the tasks into two categories as "interesting cases," when there are some particularly evil viruses or something new technically, such as:

"...cases where you really need to put a lot of time but that are interesting. And I even continue doing it at home, because it's like I have to find out what this does."[11]

"...there is a lot of very simple viruses like created by the teenager that need réclame from the Internet, that put it together and put some insulting stuff inside it. ... That is never going to make it anywhere, maybe to something like a hundred computers and that's all. ... So here I see a lot of those. Sometimes I spend like four weeks analyzing these like shit. And some of these are not even proper viruses, some of them don't even work well. ... We still have to check what they do, because we do good work. And we don't if we don't check them. ... So it's kind of a monotonous kind of work sometimes, looking at another one and another one, and another one."[12]

I have heard a popular opinion about anti-virus researchers, asserting their proximity to the 'hackers' disseminating the viruses. While this can be understood from the perspective of the security industry (policemen and criminals; inspectors and stock speculators), as a wry sort of appreciation for the virtuoso criminal, I would not forget the more general tendency of any expert professionals to identify with their work, require a level of challenge matching or extending their capacities, to learn new things and to expect due appreciation. Michael also likes the media appearance, being interviewed by newspapers for instance, concerning special cases that attract public attention. Is he any different from the university researcher dreaming of public attention and a solid reputation among fellow scientists?

The anti-virus research is also based on constant vigil, and workers like Michael are bound during their free time to come to work within two hours in case of need. This is a feature he has come to "hate," something that casts a stressful shadow over all free time activities.

"I never got woken up actually in the middle of the night. I've had to stay up to three or four at night, and I have woken up at seven. But nothing like four o'clock at night I haven't had to come to work at that time. ... But still having to stay in the office and work... Once it was my birthday and a Sunday, and I stayed the whole day in the office. There are those kinds of things."

Michael does not have children, but some colleagues do, and their tightrope walk between the urgencies of home and work make Michael think twice about having children.

Most of the employees are middle-class people, sons and daughters of 'good families' and between their twenties and forties. Hence, I felt deceivingly at home with them, as they talked about their studies and travels and experiences at settling and forming a family. Among the foreigners interviewed were people from Australia, the United States, India, Switzerland, Norway, France, Portugal, Spain, Denmark, and Russia. Most of them could not be described as *visible minorities*. The Russians, however, do suffer a collective stigma in Finland, related to national history. There is a special derogatory reference to Russians, one that Wierzbowsky—one of the virus researchers—said was used on him by a customer, but never by a fellow colleague. It was as if they had invented a firewall to keep out all the discrimination, competition, neo-nationalism and ethnicising evils of our time.

They were also pretty well off financially. The first round took place at the height of the hype. The young men (there were some women, but the male 'voice' dominated, which is hardly a surprise) not only had stable incomes, but they all benefitted from stock options, a new phenomenon invested with many personal life prospects and hopes of a bright future. Perhaps even more importantly, the boom time atmosphere seemed to offer boundless opportunities for personal development, social and geographical mobility, and even social heroism for the avant-garde of high technology. At that time most were adherents of the 'fresh page' doctrine (in Richard Sennett's terms) stating that human creativity would be liberated from the 'iron cage' of military-like bureaucracies, work would become play, and new inventions, such as the Internet, would liberate the rest of human kind to a new dawn. I welcome any doubtful readers to review some of the boom time books and financial magazines for a reminder of the social context of my informants' comments that may look naive in retrospect[13].

One more factor overcoming socio-demographic differences is professional identity. Most of the employees are IT-professionals, but many of them vigorously reject the term 'nerd,' since it has indeed been used as a stereotypic and degrading label. In my reading, 'nerds' are not those clinically introvert Aspergerians the general prejudice would imagine, spending days literally glued to their keyboards with their fingers sticky from the grease of chips and the sugar of soft drinks. The offices of these professionals are not littered with scattered papers, pizza boxes, and empty bottles. In my limited knowledge, they are decent, if somewhat arid offices where variably social persons work alone, in pairs and in teams. Teamwork, sequentially organized into projects, is their bread and butter, and social skills a topic frequently coming up in their talk. Some have a room of their own, others share rooms. To my knowledge there are no open-plan offices, but there are lobbies for coffee breaks. According to Michael, "we hang around in the lobby and talk and brain-storm, and things like that." Others, like Mark, the scientific advisor, have a lonelier sort of position. Some of the foreigners suggest that they may at times refrain from joining a social gather-

ing because, as Bharat, the Indian localizer said, "just because of me they have to talk in English."

Some of them are close friends, and they participate in outdoor days and company parties like any Finnish workers. The most striking thing I observed happened in the first of the two Christmas parties that I attended. Contrary to the custom in Finland, where Christmas parties are a routine organizational event, spouses were invited. This had almost the same effect as bringing parents to an adolescents' party; there were no drunkards under the tables. The party was lively; people danced, but remained almost sober. In the other party, I found myself in the midst of a yelling and singing audience to a rap group, formed among the employees and cutting some dash even beyond the organization, I was told. In both cases, foreigners were present and mixing with Finns.

While the general prejudice has concentrated on personality issues, I find the moral dimensions of professional identity more interesting. It is difficult to find a reference word fitting and acceptable to all professionals in the digital sector. Some prefer this and others that, and any inquiry is likely to lead to lengthy discussions with multiple and controversial recommendations. Perhaps I developed a slight preference to 'nerd' over 'hacker' because the later uncomfortably seemed also to refer to my informants' professional antagonists in this particular sub-industry: the producers and disseminators of computer viruses. I understand a different preference, and apologize for possibly hurting somebody's professional or subcultural identity.

Computer experts are to a varying degree participants in a truly global network of fellow professionals. They have their own role models and their own Mecca, Silicon Valley. While most programmers never make a pilgrimage to California, and not everybody shares the ideas of the most radical bearded gurus, their existence lends to the whole professional current some aura of expertise, innovativeness, and potential for social consequences—hence, moral importance. In addition, the most obvious quality of this identity is its transnational nature. Through the 1960s on to the very recent past, the 'nerds' formed one of the natural audiences, and gave birth for their part, to the still innocent and emancipatory 'fresh page' discourse, in the variation that has been called "hacker ethics" (Gere, 2006; Himanen, 2001; see also Kaplan, 1999). *They* had broken the power of central computers and distributed computing to each one's desk, *they* were teaching IT-skills to all, *they* were providing everyman with CIA-proof encrypting programs, *they* had stunned the business elites with open source code—the fruit of *their* transnational communities[14]. Asking about the role of ethnicity at work, I heard a dozen variations on the idea: borders are absurd, distances can be overcome[15]. If these people would lower themselves to the petty game of ethnic distinctions, would they not betray, among other things, their professional identity?

MANAGEMENT PRACTICES AT HYPE AND DOWNTURN

Returning to the workplace in 2002 after the downturn in IT, I found that the work ethos had suffered a blow. Disillusionment and fear for jobs were not given an ethnic attribution, however. Rather, the whole issue of ethnicity and cultural differences was wiped away, neutralized. The dominant culture among most Finnish workers strongly advocated for "practical solutions" against "multicultural bureaucracy." Apart from the passing comments of the foreigners, according to which F-Secure was "a Finnish-like company," nobody gave me even half a reason to suspect that they might be discriminated against on the basis of ethnicity. Suddenly expelled from their formerly sheltered position, the workers had to face the same economic insecurities and corrosive pressures against their professional morale as any other group of workers under the postmodern conditions. Yet these tensions were not ethnicized.

This is remarkable in the context of the steep economic cycle they had gone through, and the fact that no special attention had been directed to diversity by the management. Instead of looking for scapegoats from among their colleagues, many of the workers openly and passionately criticized the management in terms of market and technology choices, enlistment and other financial decisions, and the way costs were cut.

The workers' perception of "democracy" does not seem ungrounded in the light of the fact that like many high tech companies, F-Secure is a young organization founded by a handful of friends. The founder-CEO used to sit on the floor when they ran out of chairs at monthly meetings. That no longer happens, but more established forms of "democracy" flourish; in addition to the monthly meetings, an advisory workers' council with elected representatives to meet top management offers a regular forum for a two-way flow of information. This is in fact a mandatory body in all Finnish organizations of a certain size. The general opinion has recently much regretted the fact that these "cooperative councils" (*yt-neuvottelukunta*) only meet to handle the strictly stipulated matters involved in layoffs. The letter of law is thus observed, while its spirit is neglected. In this matter F-Secure follows its own path.

Burnout counter-offensives were taken already at boom time to discredit the self-imposed image of the tireless programmer. At the downturn, the bulk of the workforce attained a family founding age, and family-values now rule, making it legitimate to avoid traveling, for instance. Extra hours are counted. In spite of this, the distance between the workers and the management has grown most noticeably since the layoffs, and more subtly by the growth of the personnel, and by postmodern demands for consumer service and stakeholder impression management. This is not an exceptional course of development among Finnish IT-companies. According to a review of management practices (Ruohonen, 2004, p. 22), business has come to dominate technology, product-focused organizations have turned to service, and all employees must now learn to deal with customers.

Layoffs, mergers, and re-engineering have created insecurity, which in turn has led the workers to unionize and join unemployment funds. Unionization is at a high level in Finland, like in the other Nordic countries, and extensive (post WW2) legislation and political culture has tied the triangle of unions, employers, and state authorities together, though not without tension. The IT-sector however, has been a notable exception, for reasons probably linked to its short and wealthy history and its (American) ideational roots in extreme individuality—including neo-liberal tenets of economic individuality (Gere, 2006, p. 138). The downturn profoundly shook this constellation, causing a rush to more Nordic forms of industrial relations. At F-Secure, unionization also reached a level that, according to Finnish legislation, required appointment of a company-level representative of the technology employees' union from among the workers.

In Finnish ICT-companies, work pace and quality demands have increased (Ruohonen, 2004). Global outsourcing means that software development is no longer the best source of income[16]; companies earn better by continuous service contracts. Big software development projects are risky because margins have narrowed, and only a few Finnish companies have succeeded in them. Most companies look forward to the roles of service provider and partner in a knowledge network, though not all. Because of its products, F-Secure for instance is continuously oriented towards program development, and its service provision is tied to its products.

Business development has had its counterpart in management culture. The unofficial, spoken agreement type of management "by the kitchen table" with generous economic benefits was commonly used at the hype time to attract skilled workforce—a rather mobile workforce (Ruohonen, 2004, p. 27). Now the companies appreciate

somewhat more formal methods such as hierarchy, departments, guidelines, and job descriptions. Workers pay attention to 'sensible' things like attractive and meaningful jobs, a healthy workplace atmosphere, organizational culture, management methods, and an interesting substance (Ruohonen, 2004, p. 28). In sum, fancy has turned into the normal, solid and sensible. This picture applies fairly well to managerial culture at F-Secure, with the exception that solid and sensible things were always at the top of the list, even at hype.

As an organization, F-Secure seems to be relying on what the Finnish sociologists Juha Antila and Pekka Ylöstalo (2002) have termed the *proactive mode*, allowing the workers to influence both the products and the working conditions in exchange for the expectation that they bear responsibility and take initiative in the flow of events. Product design and marketing are coupled, and the mode also includes cooperation with various stakeholders. In the case of F-Secure, sustainability as a related idea is visible in efforts to shrink the 'ecological foot print' by using green energy and by joining a corporate responsibility network.

"Democratic" management in a "sustainable" organization? I admit that the description may seem naive. Have I simply overlooked the clever workings of managerial exploitation? To the extent that the workers themselves may be doing so, this may be true. However, the workers were not uncritical; they openly criticized the industry, the customers, and the management. It was a very different discourse from those outlined by Kunda in "Engineering Culture" (1992). One of my informants with experience of organizations in Russia and the U.S. highly appreciated the fact that problems can be acknowledged and conflicting interests negotiated instead of pretending that there is always a win-win situation. Of course, the management is not bound to its subordinates' views; there is only a kind of enlightened autocracy, not real democracy. Does the management after all hear the bottom-up flow of wisdom? The company does not escape the basic tension of any centrally led organization, and it is part of late modern capitalism. Something still seems to alleviate the worst pain that might be caused by these pressures. I have, however, only the workers' understandings of what that something might be. My material points at what they consider the sources of their feeling of an "air of democracy" and the varying ways in which they engage themselves in its defence.

I have myself worked in many Finnish organizations, and some have been almost like this case, but most have been much more authoritarian and controlling. It seems to me now that the firm is really exceptional, but in *general management culture*, and not in the absence of diversity management. DM practices are only now beginning to take foot in Finnish organizations, and mostly through the initiative of public authorities. At the turn of the millennium, they were virtually non-existent in all Finland. In this desert of ethnicity-celebration, I had found an oasis full of content foreigners. So I started wondering: does generally "democratic" and participatory management take the place of diversity management—is it perhaps even better, considering all the criticism regarding hidden control and 'divide-and-conquer' management that the later has received?[17] The other way round, discrimination is often just another name for exploitation, junk-job reality being the true source of culture-attributed or ethnicized problems (Trux, 2000). Does this mean that when there is no exploitation there are no problems?

Not all is well at F-Secure, however. In my present understanding, they simply do not cope with diversity. They do not understand what is going on in the existing transcultural reality (not that many of us would). The HR manager was afraid that open discussion of the issue would spark conflict, and the Finns unfortunately believed that they can go on working in the "normal" way without bothering themselves about whatever understandings of normality other people might have. They want no self-reflection, and are not

well prepared for it either. Between indolence and discrimination, there seems to be only a thin line.

THREATENED PROFESSIONAL IDENTITY

If 'nerds' were culturally dominant during the boom, now the pace is set by economists. Research programs with a large investment of work and human commitment are abandoned because of managerial strategies based on the market situation. "The boys must stop polishing their products for ever and adding extra features," the HR manager said, "because consumers just want the basic, inexpensive, and easy-to-use." It is difficult to imagine a worse blow to the professional heirs of the Promised Land once called the *knowledge society*. Wierzbowsky, as one of the employees who must keep watch over the Internet, described his job after the downfall: "Something between janitor and medical." His irony hardly covered the disillusionment.

From labor market perspective, the employees have come down from expectations of social mobility. Instead of making the companies compete for their workforce, they must now be content if they even have work with some continuity. Below the higher ranks of management, the value of stock options has melted away. Fearing loss of economic control over the company, management cut off all boom era luxury benefits and some more common ones as well. Some workers strongly criticized this, as further proof of the management's inaccurate understanding of the situation, exaggeration of danger and undervaluation of the comfortable conditions necessary for innovative work. One of them was Noam. I met Noam in the autumn of 2003. When I had asked about "democracy" and the bottom-up flow of information in the company, the HR manager had mentioned him. According to the manager, the employees do use the chance to debate in the monthly meetings. "When Noam brings out his checked notebook, we can be sure that tough questions will follow."

Noam is an engineer, calling himself "a nerd," and a project manager. Though he is himself officially part of management, he works directly with products and near his team members when the teams are small and at F-Secure they often are. For him, the project manager is "the guy that does everything that the others don't do" and "the 911." He reflected on his stressful position and my comment on his light tone by stressing commitment to quality, learning, and respect for deadlines. He took a retrospective look at his company to tell me how he has come to where he is now, professionally.

"So, last project for instance we had a 12 per cent delay, in a project which was the biggest so far in this company. So, things are going more or less ok. ... I think one of the things that is important for this... Not just for me but the whole R&D organization where I work, was we had a manager that had a vision ... for the department, and he was able to implement that. So we were able to improve all the time and become I would say much more professional now than we were last time when you were here in 2000. "[18]

Among all the casual, easy-to-talk-to F-Securians, Noam was one of the most open. Alternatively, did I simply feel that we had a common moral stand, which made me sympathize with him? I only know that we ended our conversation in 'joint imagination' on the future of capitalism and on Brazilian culture.

Aside from passionate ideas about his profession and the organization in which he works, Noam also showed a markedly balanced approach, bringing up various perspectives and considering the limitations of his own information. He had come to F-Secure in typical boom-era fashion, by publishing one of his university projects on the Internet while he was finishing his studies in his native country in southern Europe. Somebody at

F-Secure saw it and he soon had an invitation to a job interview.

"And so basically I finished the project that I published on the Internet. Then I was contacted to come here. Then I came here and talked to the people and what convinced me was talking to the actual people who were doing the actual work, not really the management ... But it was really seeing the people and how happy they were and the relationship they had with each other which was very close and friendly. And so that convinced me basically to try it, try it out. I always wanted to work abroad anyway, so it was a good first step. "

Noam lamented the disappearance of "vision" from the company. He felt himself very much at odds with the downturn atmosphere of disillusionment. In his view, the 'nerds' do not live by salary alone. In addition, they want to change the world and serve the larger society.

"So my point or my... The perfect workplace is where there is always this vision. Of course for that you have a how should I say, a non-materialistic approach, or not just a materialistic approach. ... To the work. ... So you have to have a notion of what are then things that keep the people together. ... This was one of the things that I said once to [the CEO's first name] when we had this... Had this traditional talking to people as they came into the company, when the company was still small enough. It was in –98. ... And I told him that why are we going public, because there is more important things to do. A company has its responsibility towards its environment and especially to its people, because the company only exists... the capitalist way of looking at this is that companies exist to make profit... My way of looking at this is that the company exists to make profit so that it can invest in the society where it is. So that the society can grow and it can grow with the society. And I think that when we get to the point where the company is to make

profit, that's where the pleasure ends. ... Because [then] profit is what drives you. And profit is not a vision. It's a number."

Noam draws a line from this thought to the way the workers are treated. According to him, investing in people is no longer important for the company. Everything is being sacrificed to economize, which is also ridiculous, since the resulting cost cuts are small, while the entire productivity of the company rests on human input. The latest on the list for cuts was removing all plants from the offices, a decision that very much unnerved him.

While many of his colleagues had left the organization, Noam was still there. The reason he gives was not solidarity towards the company, but solidarity towards old friendships. He would not like to leave his colleagues.

Describing an ideal job or ideal work he would like to do, Noam vigorously defends his view of professional pride and craftsmanship against what he perceives as a financial shift in values.

"So obviously knowledge was more important than money there. And the fact that I was finding a company in the capitalist world that was trying to do the things that I thought were important was something special. And I said ok that it's clear that I want to be in this company. I don't want to be in an open office where everybody wears a suit and everything we do is to work the day for making the money day after day and that's it ... Then the work is over. That's not what I was looking for. That's one of the reasons why I liked F-Secure, at that time: Data Fellows. Maybe the name change is also something telling about the company, because we changed the name because of the marketing value of 'F-Secure'. ... So the perfect work, again to go back to the initial question is where you can fulfill yourself, not by feeling happy for being at work but being proud of what you do. ... And not necessarily being proud, you know, you're doing a big piece of money, nobody loves that. You don't need to do that to be proud.

You can do a chair and be proud. ... Because you can see that you have done it perfectly. ... And it works and it fulfils its cause. ... And you feel that you have done it better than the previous chair."

The situation might be described from Richard Sennett's point of view as a workforce struggling beneath an imposed order of "new capitalism" and that would not be far from truth. The recent changes had indeed hollowed out the self-confidence of the people I had met three years earlier, and their efforts to explain and get a hold on the situation ran in many directions, incoherent. That is only one part of the story. In 2000, many praised flexibility, innovativeness, risk, and irreversible change. At that time these values were still framed within the "hacker ethics" and the workers believing in them were supported by a sense of economic security and social status. Work was "exciting." It was the ethos Sennett calls *fresh page thesis*, the predecessor of neo-liberal thought, as we would now call it. Those who do not admit that these values can do harm still tend to perceive them in that innocent light (including both managers and workers). Following Sherry Ortner, I distinguish between varying degrees of reflexivity toward the dominant forms, from total incorporation to becoming aware and turning against them. This process may be especially difficult for high-tech professionals because they had previously anchored their professional identity in good part in the same values now imposed upon them in a new merciless tone[19]. Flexibility is not what it used to be. In Bourdieusian terms, the violence made here is of the symbolic type.

Concerning flexibility, a further irony can be observed; anti-virus work is yet another *mise en scène* of the flexible citizen, pointing to the older image of the human body equipped with an intelligent, adaptable defence system. Anti-virus products for the pc can thus be compared with anti-germ (typically lactobacillus, vitamins or vaccinations) products destined to the consumer as a biological organism. In this setting, the virus researchers are given the role of 'flexibility champions' to help us all improve our flexibility.

PRAGMATISM

Despite the fact that it is real and disturbing, the tension between utopian and postmodern images does not in itself adequately describe the situation at F-Secure. For the Finnish members of the organization (and possibly some others as well), there is a third way to understand flexibility. In all my attempts to inspire reflection upon culturally constituted practices at work—and indeed anything to do with culture or ethnicity—I was discouraged by their firm belief in the primacy of practical and material matters over the cultural[20].

Niilo, a Finnish worker, made a very interesting observation; he said that the 'company way' arises from avoiding "multicultural bureaucracy"—by simply doing the job and keeping the customer happy. His organizational ideal concentrates on the main goal and how to achieve it by concrete action. On the one hand, it coincides with the observation that joint action brings people together despite all divisions. On the other hand, it speaks for a pragmatic approach elevated to the degree of a value in itself. *Away with all bureaucracy, the main thing is that ordinary work gets done.* This is a tradition that has greatly shaped work and administration in Finland. Ethnology has drawn attention to it as both a peasant tradition with a history of self-reliant, marginal subsistence agriculture (Apo, 1996a, 1996b)—peasant pragmatism—and as a part of national self-understanding, an ideal image of 'the pragmatic Finn' as a naive but faithful underclass (Lehtonen, et al., 2004).

At F-Secure, pragmatist reasoning was a ubiquitous, unquestioned value that people like Niilo fully embodied without any awareness or reflection on its peculiarity or national symbolism. Other material also supports the view that pragmatist values prevail in the workplace. "Bureaucracy" was the belittling term applied to anything

that would come between the people and their practical tasks. This is what the foreign workers praised as "Finnish management" or an "efficient way to work": cutting out ceremonies and time-consuming formalities, being brief, taking the initiative. This is also a common self-complacent discourse among Finnish business elites. Nevertheless, it has some truth in it. It can be a way to a very flexible order, giving priority to 'the real work'. Its downside is that it sometimes becomes a straightforwardly advancing bulldozer, ignoring and pushing aside all questions and alternatives.

There is great power in pragmatism; it doubtless supports organizational cohesion. Although I present it here as a local culture, variations of pragmatism are numerous elsewhere as well. The protestant work culture described by Max Weber is the classic: *virtue is in 'the real work'* (compare with Prasad 1997)[21], but the "fresh page" endorsed by the boom-era utopians was another (*finally we are free to do 'the real work'*), and so is the present postmodern ethos of flexibility (*you shall be paid only for 'the real work'*). These forms are not completely reducible to each other. They lead instead in different directions and imply varying frames.

The peasant work ethic used to impose extreme persistence—to a degree of work cult, with delayed gratification. Unlike in most forms of capitalism, the delay is not understood to be life-long, however. Instead, a proper rhythm of work and leisure is expected. Neither is compensation expected to reach beyond the median level of one's reference group, but continuity and respect at work are crucial. The logic is of a bonding type, very different from the promiscuous indifference characteristic of the "new capitalism" (cf. Sennett, 2006). What may remain unclear to the workers, and indeed to their managers as well, is that while according to the peasant pragmatism belt tightening promises a better fate in the next phase of the productive cycle, or by the next harvest, the same abstinent behavior under the efficiency demands of late capitalism will not bring a reward, only greater demands, based on the logic of constantly intensifying competition. In the workplace context, this is both convenient and confusing. For instance, the workers may come to take sides with the management, in the way Niilo was suggesting, as far as peasant pragmatism is glossed over with capitalist ideas of efficiency, and this would be consistent with a more entrepreneurial strand of the professional culture. On the other hand, they may also come to question the company's goals (what is it that it is practical for), like Noam. This approach would find support in the professional culture's countercultural strands.

Why would any workers take Niilo's stand? In contrast to the recent demands for continuously growing productivity, the description by Antila and Ylöstalo (2002) of the *proactive mode* of business organization can be read as a description of an ideal form of management under Finnish-like pragmatism (the peasant form or some derivative of it). The idea that the workers are allowed to influence products and working conditions in exchange for the expectation that they bear responsibility and take initiative is proof of the assumptions that 1) they are believed to have the capacity to do so and 2) that the employer is compelled or propelled to surrender her power to some extend. The first assumption obviously connotes the view that all wisdom is not located in the boardroom, but workers are an intellectual resource concerning business organization. The second assumption has often been linked to the moderative tension introduced by the former socialist bloc as a potential threat to Western market economy. I would suggest that a longer perspective be used here.

While some companies today certainly dispose of their workers easily and relocate production to sites where the workforce is replaceable, faceless and docile, others like F-Secure employ 'empowering' measures to keep the people they need. Employees have not always been plentiful and exchangeable, and rarely were at Finnish latitudes during pre-industrial times. Whenever people have been exploited (and indeed they have been) and disposed of readily, the consequences have been hard for the rulers, who themselves could not escape the physical environment. Going through the annual cycles in the world's northernmost agricultural regions for centuries introduced an imperative as great or greater than the two generations of socialist neighbors. Workers were simply too scarce and precious to waste—and they knew how to survive better than their elite rulers. Taking into consideration that the present rulers—business managers—are in large part from modest, often rural families with their history galvanized by only two or three generations age, even a simple carrying over of the peasant current would not be surprising, but we need not assume it. Things can also be reinvented. Moreover, in the face of growing ecological and other global imperatives for drastic changes in the industrial-capitalist process, is a preoccupation with survival a matter of the past or of the future?

Pragmatism need not remain linked to rural forms. Urban forms of pragmatism embrace cultural items from impermeable use-and-rinse children's trousers for playing outdoors and economical combined generation of heat and electricity, to handy Nordic kitchens with hang-up-to-dry cupboards liberating spouses from drying the dishes, not to mention electronic equipment destined for modern consumers. In effect, it says: *Save time and energy, find new intriguing technologies to liberate yourself!* In the proactive mode, the tension between employers and employees does not disappear, but is joined by the powerful quest to survive. This quest is seldom presented as such, but cut down to countless local innovations, nice and handy ways to cope with all the (working) life's small to middle-sized puzzles. There is a latent, tacit expectation of a certain kind of ideal attitude by the managers from the workers, and vice versa. Pleasurable work "proceeds smoothly," as the Finnish engineer Matti put it[22].

There have been some inquiries into the way pragmatist attitudes mark the professional subculture of economists in Finland (the second important professional group at F-Secure). According to Leppälä and Päiviö (2001), mainstream business students believe in the primacy of the working life and do not involve themselves too deeply in theoretical elaborations. They prepare themselves for business activity in which one must advance continuously and keep ahead of competitors, without hesitation or reflection. The relative roles of variations of pragmatism in this discourse fall beyond the scope of the present study. If its development has been anything akin to the vicissitudes of other professional cultures in Finland, however, it seems likely that at least peasant pragmatism alongside more generally Western (American?) capitalistic pragmatisms would be amalgamating in such attitudes; once again, the consequences are both convenient and confusing.

HETEROGLOSSIA

Three different approaches to flexibility (and related values) clash at F-Secure: the dominant postmodern form, the professional idealistic form, and the mostly unreflected, constitutive form of peasant pragmatism. My aim is not to confirm that the number of noticeable cultural forms at F-Secure is three. Instead, I use this limited example to draw attention to the multitudinous and contested nature of cultural environment and the chances for counterculture and alternative reactions offered by it.

In the present situation, while the late capitalist economy (perhaps in its agony) is demolishing pre-existing economic and social structures, insecurity and underdefined conditions has become every-day reality even at F-Secure. People struggle to gain a foothold by drawing from available cultural forms, but this has proved to be difficult. Surface similarity and deep differences in culturally constituted models make navigation a confusing experience. Description of the cultural forms—or

currents—present at work is also a challenge for research. The challenge is worth meeting, however, since a light scratch in this direction reveals that—contrary to the claims of many speakers in hegemonic positions—even the management in all organizations is not totally converted to the new dominant forms; the same confusion is present in many organizational members' understanding. The degree of reflexivity varies, as do the particular forms applied.

A cultural critique can clarify underlying assumptions of older or 'traditional' structures—we can expect several partially overlapping layers of them. In the same way, a cultural critique must shed light on underlying assumptions of the new cultural forms introduced by hegemonic distributors. Critiques of this kind would not be written for academic audiences only, but also for the people themselves, to meet their needs for meaning and orientation. It is their agency that research would, in the final analysis, try to serve.

Only after we see what is on the table, can we start to craft our answer. There is always more to be put on the table than the latest fashions of late capitalist 'world culture'. Locality is not dead. Even in organizations erasing all spontaneous production of it, in the centers and halls of the global economy, people still carry shreds of localities with them, under the skin so to say, in their minds, in the form of structures of feeling. 'People' includes here all humans present, from customers and partners, secretaries, legal assistants, engineering and marketing professionals to all kinds of managers. Knowing that the struggle is not over—that whatever the hegemonic forms presently introduced, alternatives and ingredients for potential future alternatives are at hand—is vital.

Equally important is the observation made above, that not even the management totally incorporates the new hegemonic forms, but rather hovers much like the workers (and the researcher), between different forms. As noted above, the Finnish managers share (at least) with their

Finnish workers the tendency to confuse peasant pragmatism with late capitalist endeavors. This may occur without any reflection, or it may cause varying degrees of mixed feelings. Some of the managers (including the founders of the organization) also share the professional subculture with their engineering workforce, again with strong urges for solidary conduct and countercultural forms blended with the entrepreneurial spirit and individualism that can in turn be combined with neo-liberal forms. The steps taken are therefore hesitant and controversial. Management tries to protect the social capital of the organization from the most predatory effects of the late capitalist environment, while still accepting (or half-accepting) its dominant neo-liberal ideology. We all engage in fostering or resisting images like 'flexibility' without the full awareness of their resonances, contradictions and entanglements with various discourses. The identity of the ultimate speaker in any given utterance remains ambiguous.

Since identification of 'voices' in the heteroglossia is difficult and time-consuming, so is the crafting of one's own identity. To what address should one direct a response to claims of flexibility, for instance? Is it your fellow 'nerd,' a pragmatic Finnish manager appealing to you for doing a project flexibly, or is it a voice of the "Davos men" speaking with his mouth[23]? Managers have it no easier: how to dissipate lingering suspicions that the latter is the case at moments when it is not? Are they sure they know themselves with whose words they are speaking at any given moment? Where the immigrant employees and managers lucidly praising Finnish type pragmatism in F-Secure's practices or were they rather charmed by a reflection of some well-internalized form of capitalist flexibility they had imported in their own pockets? Who are the persons, social forces, and power positions in this kind of field that has become ghost wrestling? We need maps, no matter how broken and changing the cultural landscape is. Perhaps in that case even more desperately.

ACKNOWLEDGMENT

This is a new edited version of a chapter published previously as (2008) "Identifying Flexibilities" in Dariusz Jemielniak & Jerzy Kociatkiewicz (Eds.), *Management Practices in High-Tech Environments*, (pp. 330-350). Hershey, PA: IGI Global.

REFERENCES

Apo, S. (1996a). Agraarinen suomalaisuus – Rasite vai resurssi? [The agrarian Finnishness – Burden or resource?] In Laaksonen, P., & Mettomäki, S.-L. (Eds.), *Olkaamme siis Suomalaisia: Kalevalaseuran Vuosikirja* (pp. 75–76). Helsinki, Finland: SKS.

Apo, S. (1996b). Itserasismista positiivisiin suomalaisuuksiin. [From self-imposed racism to positive Finnishnesses] In Apo, S., & Ehrnrooth, J. (Eds.), *Millaisia Olemme: Puheenvuoroja Suomalaisista Mentaliteeteista*. Helsinki, Finland: Kunnallisalan Kehittämissäätiö.

Gere, C. (2006). *Digitaalinen kulttuuri*. Turku, Finalnd: Faros.

Grey, C. (2009). *A very short, fairly interesting and reasonably cheap book about studying organizations* (2nd ed.). London, UK: Sage.

Himanen, P. (2001). *The hacker ethic. A radical approach to the philosophy of business*. New York, NY: Random House.

Holland, D., Lachicotte, W. Jr, Skinner, D., & Cain, C. (1998). *Identity and agency in cultural worlds*. Boston, MA: Harvard University Press.

Kaplan, D. A. (2000). *The silicon boys and their valley of dreams*. New York, NY: Harper Collins.

Kunda, G. (1992). *Engineering culture: Control and commitment in a high-tech corporation*. Philadelphia, PA: Temple University Press.

Lehtonen, M., Löytty, O., & Ruuska, P. (2004). *Suomi toisin sanoen* [Finland in other words]. Tampere, Finland: Vastapaino.

Leppälä, K., & Päiviö, H. (2001). *Kauppatieteiden opiskelijoiden moraalijärjestys: Narratiivinen tutkimus kolmen eri pääaineen opiskelusta Helsingin kauppakorkeakoulussa.* [Moral order among students of economics: A narrative inquiry into studying three major subjects at Helsinki School of Economics]. Helsinki, Finland: Publications of the Helsinki School of Economics and Business Administration.

Litvin, D. R. (1997). The discourse of diversity: From biology to management. *Organization, 4*(2), 187–209. doi:10.1177/135050849742003

Lorbiecki, A., & Jack, G. (2000). Critical turns in the evolution of diversity management. *British Journal of Management, 11*(3).

Martin, E. (1994). *Flexible bodies: The role of immunity in American culture from the days of polio to the age of AIDS.* Boston, MA: Beacon Press.

Ortner, S. B. (1984). Theory in anthropology since the sixties. *Comparative Studies in Society and History, 126*(1), 126–166. doi:10.1017/S0010417500010811

Ortner, S. B. (2005). Subjectivity and cultural critique. *Anthropological Theory, 5*(1), 31–52. doi:10.1177/1463499605050867

Pokela, P. (2005). *Paper.* Paper presented at a Conference on Diversity. Helsinki, Finland. Antila, J., & Ylöstalo, P. (2002). *Proaktiivinen toimintatapa: Yritysten ja palkansaajien yhteinen etu?* [Proactive mode: Common asset for companies and employees?]. Helsinki, Finland: Työministeriö.

Prasad, P. (1997). The protestant ethic and the myths of the frontier: Cultural imprints, organizational structuring and workplace diversity. In Prasad, P. (Eds.), *Managing the Organizational Melting Pot: Dilemmas of Workplace Diversity.* Thousand Oaks, CA: Sage.

Roberts, F. M. (1989). The Finnish coffee ceremony and notions of self. *Arctic Anthropology, 26*, 20–33.

Ruohonen, M. (2004). Johtamiskulttuurien muutos ICT-yrityksessä – Hypestä todellisuuteen. [Changing management culture in an ICT-company – From hype to reality] In Ruohonen, M. (Eds.), *Tietoyritysten Muuttuvat Työkulttuurit.* Tampere, Finland: Tampere University Press.

Sennett, R. (1998). *The corrosion of character: The personal consequences of work under the new capitalism.* New York, NY: Norton.

Sennett, R. (2006). *The culture of the new capitalism.* New Haven, CT: Yale Univ. Press.

Sewell, W. (1999). Geertz, cultural systems and history: From synchrony to transformation. In Ortner, S. (Ed.), *The Fate of "Culture": Geertz and Beyond.* Berkeley, CA: University of California Press.

Trux, M. (2000). Monimuotoinen työyhteisö. In M. Trux (Ed.), *Aukeavat ovet: Kulttuurien Moninaisuus Suomen elinkeinoelämässä.* Helsinki, Finalnd: WSOY.

Trux, M. (2005). Ei sitä meillä kukaan kato – Kansainvälisyys ja monietnisyys helsinkiläisellä IT-työpaikalla. ["Nobody looks at that here" – Internationality and multiethnicity at an IT-workplace in Helsinki]. *Työpoliittinen aikakauskirja, 2*, 49–69.

Trux, M. (2010). *No zoo – Ethnic civility and its cultural regulation among the staff of a Finnish high-tech company. Acta Universitatis Oeconomicae Helsingiensis.* Helsinki, Finland: Aalto University School of Economics.

ENDNOTES

[1] According to a mutual agreement with the company, I use its true name in this text. All arguments and conclusions are my own, however, and the picture I give refers to my experiences and material from the period of 1999 to 2004. The research on which this chapter is based was supported in part by grants from the The Finnish Work Environment Fund, The Foundation for Economic Education, and the Finnish Ministry of Labor. Sections of this chapter have appeared earlier in Trux (2000, 2005, and 2010).

[2] The fieldwork had three 'episodes': first I made a round of interviews and some participant observation at the headquarters in 1999-2000 as part of a larger project, reported in Trux (2000). I returned to the 'site' (though they had moved within the Helsinki region) and conducted more interviews with some more participant observation during 2002-2004, the present tense referring to 2004. Although I had the opportunity to follow the organisation and the workers through the ups and downs of those years, the central weakness of the ethnography is that I had no access to the actual working offices, beyond a few times I managed to slip in at the responsibility of individual informants, and there were a few parties and meetings I attended. In the manner of high-tech companies, F-Secure frustratingly limited my presence at their premises to the visitors' zone. Taking into consideration that the company is engaged in the security business, this was perhaps to be expected. As a pay-off, at the independence-access -dimension I ended up near the independent end. Still, one has to read my account against the fact that it is heavily biased towards the discursive level. Of course no ethnography has anything like a direct access to reality. Moreover, the process is completed only when the report is written and read. I have attempted to compose my account so that the 'voice' of each informant appears like it was, a fully political doorkeeper to his or her experience, with a due reaction to my presence and many references to absent others. Within this longer period in and about the Helsinki headquarters, I made a two week trip to a Silicon Valley unit. The findings of that brief but intense visit are discussed in Trux (2010).

[3] Here's a pretty example of the present flair in what we might call *la pensée économique*. In correct biological terms, the phrase would of course rather refer to Lamarck than Darwin, but the spirit of social Darwinism is more important to the speaker, apparently, than any scientific content. The survival of the fittest translates with no difficulty at all into survival of the nimblest.

[4] See for instance Grey's (2009) description of change management.

[5] See Gere (2006) for the history of the multiple roots of this hybrid form, ranging from engineers' and radio-amateurs' ideals, to Californian entrepreneurship, to the hippy movement, anti-government dispositions, and all kinds of liberalisms. Utopian and dystopian visions have gone hand in hand through this story that is revealingly compatible with the story of the digitalizing (Western) society.

[6] Since then, the number of employees has continued to grow, reaching 700 in 2008.

[7] Successive acquisitions have since brought the former Helsinki Exchange under the same ownership as NASDAQ.

[8] At the beginning of my inquiry, the proportion of foreigners was estimated to be 13% of the workforce. When I last asked about this, the HR secretary estimated that people who had come as immigrants accounted for as much as 20% of the personnel in Helsinki. All these figures are unofficial since the law

in Finland, as in many other continental European countries, bans records based on ethnic identity.

9   Wierzbowsky, a virus researcher, interviewed on 29.2.2000. All names of informants appearing in this text are pseudonyms that they invented for themselves.

10   Matti, software engineer, interviewed on 19.5.2000. Translated from Finnish by the author.

11   Michael, virus researcher, interviewed on 16.3.2004.

12   Since the completion of the fieldwork, I have learned that new trends in Internet crime are replacing the individual hacker with more organised structures capable of gaining a good income and of investing in professionalised R&D activity. As a result, malware spreading through the Internet and mobile networks is of an increasingly high quality, thus presenting greater challenges for the anti-virus companies. See for instance F-Secure's chief research officer Mikko Hyppönen's presentation at Youtube: http://www.youtube.com/watch?v=zyJ4KM_bv84

13   The following is another example of the atmosphere of avant-gardism: The HR manager was visibly pleased with himself, as he explained to me how the company's new logo was reminiscent of Superman's badge. It was only half a joke, since in fact their job is to protect not only businesses, but also public organisations such as hospitals, municipalities and schools—and in the end individual consumers—against various digital threats.

14   See Gere (2006) for an account of the role of countercultural movements in democratizing and demilitarizing the digital technologies after the Second World War.

15   These were in fact words of Maria Cecilia Duffau Echevarren, an Uruguayan ex-prisoner of conscience, in her letter of thanks to Amnesty International: "The most important

thing is that … between us, human beings, it has been proved that borders are absurd, languages are surmountable, that distances can be overcome, because the heart is big… and people like you keep the hope of a new dawn alight."

16   Nokia was not among the surveyed companies. The conclusions are based on findings in small and middle-sized IT-service providers and multimedia companies.

17   See Litvin (1997) and Lorbiecki and Jack (2000).

18   Noam, software engineer, interviewed on 23.9.2003.

19   Although I concentrate here on the image of 'flexibility,' individualism is another hook between the 'hacker ethic' and neoliberalism, as described before.

20   Here, for simplicity's sake, I comply with the informants' dualism. As a scholar of culture, I do not, however, believe in it. For me, the practical, the material, and the cultural are not mutually excluding categories, but rather ideas on different levels, or different points of view upon the same reality. Culture, as a cultural anthropological concept, also includes material culture and all the myriads of practices that people create.

21   Following Weber, the religious roots of capitalism are most often located somewhere among the 'Protestants,' though more specifically among Calvinists. Finns made no protests, but became Protestants by their Swedish king's decision, and the form to which they were converted was Lutheran. Being no historian of religions, I content myself with noting that the idea of 'providence' as legitimating overt celebration of one's riches in front of others is still fundamentally against the grain here; witness the regrets of high ranking business observers that "it is very difficult to instill on entrepreneurial spirit in Finland, because people are envious of each other's success."

The reference in such comments is usually North American. Whether the egalitarian strands were introduced by Lutheran ethics and/or had some older source, ultimately in pre-Christian values, is beyond the topic here. See, however, Roberts (1989) for the delicate balancing of egalitarian and individualist values in Finnish rural life of the 1970s.

[22] This is not to say that this kind of pragmatism is a cultural phenomenon found only in Finland. The precise combination of present-day features and frames is probably unique, but similar strands are most certainly to be found elsewhere, with a historical connection to this form or without. Neither is the description an argument for the absolute prevalence of the form within the territory of the Finnish nation-state (there are competing ideals) or of the certainty of its being carried over to the future. Judging by its wide circulation in present-day society, and its speedy conver-sion into ever new interpretations in new fields of activity, I am tempted to predict that it will not slow down very soon or in the face of only moderate contesting forms. The fact that the idea of survival has also repeatedly offered an easy 'hook' by which to rally all social classes to the rescue of the nation-state—including the elites' privileges—is no disproof of its existence or a warrant for any simple reduction to *upper structure ideology*.

[23] As a matter of fact, there was a woman at the head of the anti-virus team at F-Secure. The Bulgarian immigrant expert was unfortunately too busy to participate in my study. In spite of the recent appearance of women in technical professions, however, the technical-managerial positions in the Finnish IT-sector are still overwhelmingly male dominated. Therefore, in waiting for the day to say, factually, "with her mouth," we must be content with the masculine pronoun.

Chapter 9
Professional and Managerial Language in Hybrid Industry–Research Organizations and within the Hybrid Clinician Manager Role

Louise Kippist
University of Western Sydney, Australia

Kathryn J. Hayes
University of Western Sydney, Australia

Janna-Anneke Fitzgerald
University of Western Sydney, Australia

ABSTRACT

Interactions between professionals and managers are vital to medical and commercialization outcomes. This chapter considers how boundaries between professionals and managers are expressed through language in two contexts: between researchers and managers in temporary Australian hybrid industry-research organizations and within the same individual performing a hybrid clinician-manager role in Australian health care organizations. Semi-structured interviews of twenty scientists, engineers, and managers, focusing on their experiences, and perceptions of occupational culture, revealed that language norms contributed to knowledge creation, and played a role in maintaining a hierarchy among research institutions. Semi-structured interviews of twenty doctors and managers, focusing on their perception and experience of the hybrid clinician manager's role within health care organizations, revealed that professional identity influenced language norms used by doctors and managers and contributed to the tensions experienced in their interactions. Distinctive patterns of argumentation and language were identified as typical of commercial and research occupations and were also distinctive in doctors working in hybrid clinician manager's roles. The scientists, engineers, and managers working in hybrid industry-research organizations and the doctors and managers working in health care organizations reported frustration and reduced effectiveness of argumentation due to different norms for dissent.

DOI: 10.4018/978-1-4666-1836-7.ch009

INTRODUCTION

This chapter discusses the results and implications of a two-part research study and considers how boundaries between professionals and managers can be expressed through differences in language in two Australian contexts: between researchers and managers in temporary hybrid industry-research organizations and within the same individual performing a hybrid clinician-manager role in hospital settings. The results of these two studies add to the professional identity and culture literature and may benefit organizations experiencing communication challenges between professionals and managers. An overview of the two contexts is provided, first the Australian Cooperative Research Centre (CRC) context is introduced, followed by the creation of the hybrid clinician manager in Australian health care organizations. This is followed by examples of how professional identity influences communication between professionals and managers.

Corporate Research Centre's as Hybrid Industry-Research Organizations

From the 1980s, governments of industrialized economies have looked to innovations involving the generation and reconfiguration of knowledge as a path to achieving a competitive advantage (Gibbons, et al., 1994; Lehrer & Asakawa, 2004; Nowotny, Scott, & Gibbons, 2001; Premus, 2002). From a commercial perspective, the attractions of entering collaborative research partnerships include access to complementary physical and intellectual assets, reductions in product development time, cost, and risk, and increased organizational and financial flexibility (Senker & Sharpe, 1997). The creation of hybrid research organizations, that use resources and/or governance structures from more than one existing organization (Borys & Jemison, 1989), has been a feature of the response to government

and business pressures for increased innovation. The evolution of "Triple Helix" organizations, in which private firms and publicly funded research groups collaborate with the support of government funding, has been traced across Europe, the USA, Latin America and Asia (Etkowitz & Leydesdorff, 2000). In addition to a rapid geographical spread, the number of hybrid industry-research centers in operation has also quickly increased (Gray, Lindblad, & Rudolph, 2001; Premus, 2002) as has the percentage of industry and government funding they attract (Gray, et al., 2001). Clearly, the operation of hybrid organizations composed of government, business, and research groups within national systems of innovation is a subject worthy of attention.

Hybrid industry-research organizations share some of the management challenges encountered by joint-venture partners from the same industry. Boundary issues between the partner organizations, threats to the hybrid organizations stability from the sovereignty of member organizations, and the challenge of reconciling disparate goals, technologies and organizational cultures can occur even when commercial organizations, in the same industry combine (Borys & Jemison, 1989). The merger of HP and Compaq (Burgelman & McKinney, 2006) provides a recent and instructive example of the difficulties that can be encountered even between commercial organizations from the same industry segment. Temporary collaborations between industry and research partners present even more complicated structural, managerial, and organizational cultural challenges than those that have made mergers and acquisitions between comparable commercial organizations into acknowledged high-risk endeavors (Barringer & Harrison, 2000).

The context for the first part of this study is four hybrid industry-research organizations in the Australian Cooperative Research Centre (CRC) program. The Australian CRC program provides an example of government intervention to stimulate innovation through encouraging collaborative arrangements. Australian government funding policies changed in 1990 to encourage research institutions, commercial organizations, and government bodies to work closely together to commercialize promising ideas and technologies. CRCs are composed of research, government and industry members working together to bring an invention to market and operate as trans-disciplinary, temporary organizations intended to link discovery, application and use.

Innovation generally involves the practical application of new knowledge. This requires at least two types of occupational cultures; the exploratory roles performed by "pure" researchers, and pragmatic, systematic roles filled by a variety of commercial occupations. Commercialization activities combine the discoveries of one occupational group, such as scientists, with the commercial skills of engineers and managers (Steiner, 2000). Therefore, bringing innovative ideas to markets involves interactions across occupational cultures and inter-occupational tension may be implicit in innovation. In CRCs different occupational groups display preferences for knowledge-creation or money-making (Hayes & Fitzgerald, 2007).

Australian Health Care Organizations

The context of the second part of the study is Australian health care organizations, specifically public hospitals in New South Wales. Changes similar to those impacting research organizations occur in health care organizations throughout the world. Changing economic ideology in Western liberal democracies is driving health care policy and the organization of health care services toward free market economics (Mickan & Boyce, 2006). Free market economics favour the introduction of economic rationalist and competitive reforms that challenge the traditional managerial and professional cultures on which health services have been founded (Mickan & Boyce, 2005). Health care organizations originated in humanistic beliefs

around social responsibility and good patient care. With economic rationalist reform comes an inherent tension between economic efficiency and what is seen as good patient care. In other words, there is a tension between what is best for the health care organization, as a business, and what is best for the patient.

Health care organizations in Australia have experienced ongoing change as they respond to governmental, societal, and technological forces (Duckett, 2008). As health care organizations adapt to changes in governments, budgets and organizational structure, the roles of individuals working in them have also changed. One specific group of health care professionals that combine clinical and managerial roles are what we call "hybrid clinician managers." Hybrid clinician managers are doctors who take on a dual clinical and managerial role within the health care organization (Fitzgerald & Ferlie, 2000). Hybrid clinician managers are at the intersection of the clinical and managerial domain within the health care reform agenda (Braithwaite & Hindle, 2001). As such, from an organizational point of view, hybrid clinician managers are an important conduit at the intersection of the business of health and the practice of health, and literally embody tensions between professional medicine and economic management.

Hybrid clinician managers span two professional boundaries that have different language norms and opposing views of managing health care organizations. Their hybrid roles are strongly influenced by their medical professional identity (Hotho, 2008) developed through their medical training and work experience. In their managerial role they see themselves as doctors first which influences how they make their managerial decisions (Kippist & Fitzgerald, 2006). Their medical professional identity appears to present barriers to managerial problem solving, particularly when dealing with health service managers.

Health service managers are professional managers within health care organizations who have formal management qualifications and experience in managing health services. Health service managers broadly emphasise populations, public accountability, systems and resource allocations, where as clinicians see their role as individually providing a professional service to patients (Abbott, 1988). Each of these roles brings with them different professional values and language norms.

We argue, based on interviews with scientists, engineers, doctors and managers that the styles of argument used in occupational groups within hybrid industry-research organizations and health care organizations may act as a barrier to communication and hence a barrier to organizational functioning and problem solving. This is significant, given the increasing number of professionals, with little or no management education, moving into management positions in hybrid industry-research and health care organizations in Australia. Analyzing different argumentation styles extends existing research into occupational norms for debate to include innovation, commercialization processes, and the context of triple helix organizations and health care organizations.

Argumentation in Triple Helix Organizations

In triple helix organizations, argumentation, which we define as the action or process of reasoning systematically in support of an idea, commonly occurs in groups composed of more than one occupation. For an extensive review of argumentation theory, see Sillince (2002). Rational or scientific argumentation uses logical reasoning about competing ideas, for an extended period, until the topic has been exhaustively analyzed. Far from being an outmoded form of rhetoric at risk of extinction, scientific argumentation plays a vital role in the creation of knowledge. Programs to measure and increase the teaching of argumentation in school science are being implemented in the UK (Erduran, Simon, & Osbourne, 2004). Although scientific and academic groups are skilled in and accustomed to using constructive dispute to produce creative

ideas and outcomes, occupational norms that proscribe dissent may restrict their effectiveness in cross functional groups. In addition, the value of minority opinions and constructive dissent in increasing group creativity while guarding against "groupthink" is well documented (Nemeth, 1997). However, members of business cultures, which in the main value cohesion and conformity (Pech, 2001), may view signs of disagreement between researchers as alarming and predictive of failure.

Scientific forms of argumentation have been identified as poorly adapted to public debate of trans-scientific social issues such as global warming (Ziman, 2000). The challenges of engaging in argumentation across the boundaries of national cultures (Liu, 1999), and rhetorical traditions (Dolinina & Cecchetto, 1998) have also been acknowledged. The use of language, dialogue, and argumentation is an occupational culture construct, policing acceptable communication within the group. As McKerrow (1980, p. 31) noted:

...communities are typified by the specific rules which govern argumentative behavior, by social practices which determine who may speak and with what authority, and by their own "display" of these rules and social practices in response to challenges from within and outside the community.

Furthermore, McKerrow asserted that when individuals from two communities with different standards for judging the strength and appropriateness of arguments argue, the choice is to select one set of argumentation standards or "face a contradiction that cannot be easily resolved." However, little attention has been directed to the potential impact of conflicting norms for argumentation upon the commercialization phase of innovation in either traditionally structured or triple helix industry-research organizations.

In health care organizations, discussions between hybrid clinician managers and health service managers are centred on the need for greater efficiency and effectiveness of service delivery. These discussions are influenced by differing values and language norms of each and therefore can be seen to cause confusion and conflict between the two groups.

Hybrid Clinician Managers and Professional Identity

Professions have control over specialised scientific or expert knowledge (Abbott, 1988; Hotho, 2008; McDonald, 1999). Holding specialised knowledge allows the profession to define jurisdiction over competing occupational groups, autonomy and supports a professional identity (Abbott, 1988). Professions need to maintain their jurisdiction, in order to remain successful. To do this they control access to education, training, professional labour markets (McDonald, 1995) and professional accreditation and prescription of career paths (Daniels & Johansen, 1985).

Professions develop dialogue and practices that gain, legitimise, and maintain control over their professional work, enable political and economic autonomy and demonstrate dominance over other professional groups this is seen to give professions privileged status in society (Freidson, 1994; Larson, 1977) .

Professional identity is developed through a variety of avenues, in the course of socialisation into ones profession (Apker & Eggly, 2004) by role models (Hotho, 2008) and through one's career progression (Hall, 1995). Professionals become part of a specific group holding specialised knowledge and skills. Through increasing competence in their profession they progress or move into new and different roles. They may seek others within their profession whom they regard with high esteem, as role models as they mature into their professional position.

Professional identity could, therefore, be described as an organic process that changes as an individual is socialised, trained and inducted into their professional role. It is a process that requires observation; observation of oneself and others, as well as being observed by others. We describe professional identity as how professionals see themselves, how they see others, and how others see them (Fitzgerald, 2002).

It is well established that doctors are part of an old profession whose values are steeped in tradition, authority, autonomy, and self regulation (Abbott, 1988; Freidson, 1984; Illich, 1987). Through socialisation in their medical training doctors, see themselves as the dominant occupation within health care organizations. The language norms of medicine and other clinical occupations working in health care organizations have developed from the medical model and dominate health care practice.

However, it appears when doctors progress into a hybrid role within health care organizations their medical professional identity remains dominant (Kippist & Fitzgerald, 2008). Many doctors come to this role with little management education or skill; it appears that they do not see their management role as requiring any extra knowledge or skill to that obtained in their medical training (Kippist & Fitzgerald, 2008). Some doctors acknowledge lack of management education or skills can be a disadvantage, however they claim lack of time as a reason for not pursuing such skills (Kippist & Fitzgerald, 2009). We presume from this that clinicians see themselves, and their profession, as being superior to that of management. However, their lack of management education or knowledge brings the disadvantage of not understanding the language norms of business and this has been shown to contribute to conflict between hybrid clinician managers and the health services managers in health care service delivery.

Culture and Innovation

When organizational culture is considered in studies of innovation, integrationist assumptions of consistent values and beliefs are often made (Martin, 2002). For example, entire organizations are identified as exemplars of innovation culture, despite known subcultural differences amongst its members. Moreover, systems of innovation are compared and contrasted across nations and continents (Lehrer & Asakawa, 2004), assuming organizational cultural homogeneity exists within the boundaries of nations or even economic communities.

In contrast to mono-cultural representations of organizations, the three-perspective view of organizational culture (Martin, 2002; Meyerson & Martin, 1987) identifies three cultural patterns co-existing in an organization's culture at any one time. These are the integration, differentiation, and fragmentation perspectives. At any time, one pattern may be dominant and more easily detected than the other two. However, over time or due to environmental changes, the organization's culture will be dynamic; the currently dominant perspective will recede and other frames will become more visible.

An *integration* perspective focuses on cultural manifestations that have consistent interpretations, and regard organizational culture as a clear consensus without ambiguity. The *fragmentation* perspective claims relations between cultural manifestations are neither clearly consistent nor inconsistent and views ambiguity, not clarity, as the core of culture. Viewed through the frame of fragmentation, consensus is transient and issue specific.

The *differentiation* perspective focuses on cultural manifestations that have inconsistent interpretations, and result in organizational groupings. The differentiation perspective considers consensus to exist only in subcultures. Subcultures may exist in harmony, independently, or in conflict; however, within a subculture there is clarity. Recent research has pointed to the existence of subcultures within hybrid industry-research organizations (Hayes & Fitzgerald, 2005; Siegel, Waldman, Atwater, & Link, 2004).

Subcultures and Innovation

Subcultures are defined as groups that have unique patterns of values and behaviors, providing a distinctive identity. Subcultures can be consistent or inconsistent with the dominant culture of the organization (Trice, 1993). Every large organization consists of potential subcultures. For example, subcultures may exist based on characteristics of gender, ethnicity, profession, age, functional division or geographic location, wage levels, and employment status (Kunda, 1992). Hybrid industry-research organizations are likely to import occupational subcultures along with the individuals recruited from research, commercial and government institutions. In addition to other group behavior, professional and occupational affiliations influence argumentation styles (Sillince, 2002).

Subcultures in Health Care Organizations

For example, when observing cultural domains in a hospital, we are able to confidently predict occupational membership (medical manager, medical clinician, nurse manager, nurse clinician, other manager, other), professional membership (doctor, nurse or other) and functional membership (manager or clinician) of sub-groups. The success of argumentation between the sub-groups (e.g. doctors and managers) is closely related to the thickness of boundaries between them, and the permeability of these boundaries. Organizational uniqueness lies in the adaptation of professions to shift paradigms towards confluence.

Hence, while existing literature acknowledges the functions of argumentation in knowledge creation, it does not necessarily address the difficulties of occupational cultural differentiation within hybrid organizations. This research explores business and research modes of argumentation and gives insight into their potential to act as a barrier to commercialization. It also examines paradoxes in the language and experience of the hybrid clinician manager.

METHODOLOGY

The research adopted a qualitative methodology to explore the roles of the research participants in both CRC and hospital settings. Both organizational contexts typically consist of individuals from a variety of professions aligned with a particular industry, located within a broad context of Australian society. Therefore, a qualitative methodology was chosen as the most appropriate approach for this research, as it allows the researcher to develop patterns or themes from multiple means of individual's experiences (Creswell, 2003). As social activities occurring within organizational and national cultures, commercialization processes in a complex social system suit holistic investigation using qualitative methods.

Due to the qualitative nature of the research, purposive sampling was used to recruit research participants. A total of twenty scientists, engineers, and business managers were recruited from four CRCs. Two of these CRCs were from the Information and Communications Technology sector and two were from the Biomedical sector. The organizations' maturity ranged from newly formed with only a few years of operation to twenty years of operation for a publicly listed company that developed out of the CRC program. Twenty doctors and health service managers were recruited from four Australian public hospitals. The doctors who participated in the research were hybrid clinician managers currently working in combined managerial and clinical roles. The health service managers were senior managers working in executive positions within the hospitals.

Semi structured interviews were used to collect the data. The interview questions were broadly framed around the research participants' experiences and perceptions of differing sub cultural norms, including styles of debate. The interviews were conversational and new questions were based upon themes revealed by previously completed interviews, this allowed a systematic approach to collecting the data. The interviews were recorded and transcribed verbatim. QSR N-Vivo® software was used to aid detailed coding and analysis of the collected research material, facilitating the interpretation process. Member checks, in which the data and interpretations were provided to participants for correction, verification, and challenge, were used to increase the credibility of the research. Through the analytic phase of the project, a number of core themes emerged from the data that will be discussed in the results and analysis section. Through a reflective, iterative process, we interrogated theme content to explore relationships between and within the themes.

Despite the suitability of the selected methodology, the research findings depend upon the memory, insightfulness, and honesty of the interviewees. The findings are also constrained by time, place, and the changeable nature of individual perspectives. Although the findings cannot be readily extrapolated into other contexts, they may be helpful to provide an understanding of some communication challenges encountered in inter occupational collaboration.

However, as the following section illustrates, the insights provided by the interviewees extends existing theory to consider the potential impact of inter-occupational argumentation on the functioning of hybrid industry-research centers and health care organizations. Therefore, further research into professional and occupational subcultures, professional identity, and commercialization processes in the context of CRCs and health care organizations in Australia is appropriate.

RESULTS AND ANALYSIS

First interviews in CRCs are analysed and the results reported. This is followed by the outcomes of the interviews with hybrid clinician managers in Australian health care organizations.

Argumentation as an Occupational Norm in CRCs

In the CRCs, scientists, engineers, and managers from government and private sectors described distinctive patterns of argumentation as typical of research and commercial occupations. Descriptions of scientific and research group debates were consistent with earlier reports (Nemeth, 1997; Ziman, 2000). Specifically, restrictions on the amount of time allocated for discussion, the likelihood of reaching a clear conclusion and expectations of action resulting from debate were very different for commercial and research communities. Both commercial and academic groups agreed that researchers enjoyed debate and viewed it as an important part of their identity. As stated by a scientist, who moved to a management position:

The important aspect is inquiry into "What's the best focus?" It's not inquiry for the sake of "Let's muck around." And that's often the criticism of science going into commercialization. Inquiry is a necessary process before you arrive at an agreed way forward. That's very stimulating and something I really, really miss in shifting from that culture ... difference of opinion is part of the creative process.

The importance of dissent as a tool to hone solutions through a verbal contest of ideas and as a symbol of scientific identity was evident. When asked if the academic and research members of the CRC enjoyed debating amongst themselves, a public sector manager responded that it was a core part of their professional identity, stating:

They'll [researchers] consider [debate] very much part of their reason for existence and if they didn't have that debate I think they would see themselves as not representing their profession. .... The debate may well air a range of options and different opinions and approaches and thoughts and so forth but it doesn't crystallize an outcome. And for the private sector all that debate's good, but if it doesn't bring you closer to an absolute outcome, an absolute decision, well then all it is, is debate. It may be very worthwhile from the academic point of view but time is money when it comes to the private sector.

Sharing the view that business communication should be action-oriented and produce a clear conclusion a product development engineer remarked:

There were meetings that only scientists used. They had a university common room meeting culture. They would sit and talk about the latest discoveries in the field; it was just a big chinwag. And that was work. Because they were scientists... they'd talk about the latest things in the field and if it didn't relate to the thing I was trying to make I couldn't care less. I used to get dragged along to them occasionally but, operations point of view, meetings to me were a waste of time. I do the communication I need to do as I need to do it.

Similar comments by other participants indicated a clear understanding and acknowledgement of differences, both in the acceptability of dissent and the desirability of reaching a clear conclusion in a specified time. Researchers appeared comfortable with, and even proud of their ability to use "talking as thinking" in a mono-cultural group, in contrast to commercial interviewees who preferred talking to be preparation for action. Comments made regarding time limits for debate link argumentation norms to different temporal orientations towards pace and punctuality held by the two broad occupational groups (Hayes, 2007).

Participation in Argumentation and Occupational Subcultural Boundaries

Participation in extended bouts of rational argumentation was reported to be restricted to members of groups involved in knowledge creation, whether located in academic, public, or private sector organizations. Interviewees spoke of extended and heated, but congenial debates occurring between researchers while commercial representatives present did not participate. Individuals from non-research groups only became involved to stop the debate if they thought it had gone on for too long. A public sector manager described the motivations of business and government representatives present during the debates as follows:

Private sector, their role tends to be very vested interests, hence narrow focus and short and sharp, not bringing in a whole range of otherworldly thoughts into the process but short, sharp and focused. From the government perspective, the government input is more generalized than the private sector, whether it's going to be useful from a government perspective. Not as focused and as to the point as the private sector but still somewhat focused relative to what the academic debate might be.

There was general agreement that research debates were closed to non-members, indicating that styles of argumentation may help to create and reinforce occupational boundaries. Tolerance of discussions without time limits and with ambiguous outcomes was identified as an important difference. As a manager commented when asked if rational arguments reached final and lasting conclusions:

Well sometimes they do. Sometimes they just peter out in the context of "Yes, there's differing opinion on the subject" and if there's no categorical resolve well then everyone can go back to their

corners agreeing that there's differing opinions which could be revisited at a later date.

The argument repertoires reported are consistent with the norms of scientific argument, which include a preference for a written format, a well-informed audience, no imposed time limits and little expectation that a "Yes" or "No" conclusion will be reached to support a particular course of action (Ziman, 2000). On the other hand, business decisions have been reported to be based upon patterns of preparation that do not conform to the typical pattern of argumentation used in research communities (Werder, 1999).

Occupation Specific Argumentation as a Barrier to Commercialization

In addition to functioning as an occupational identity construct, rational argumentation may constitute a barrier to commercialization. As a scientist explained:

The clash occurred where ...the mode of working within the culture of science is one that's driven by inquiry, which is driven by brainstorming. The commercial product managers wanted to focus on one approach only and pin it down, no divergence whatsoever. Even the mode of discussion, conversation, engagement, was so different and the commercial guys found it quite threatening and kept saying, "Stop arguing!" ... But it's viewed as the dysfunctionality of the [scientific] group, and sort of a threatening aspect. And a couple of times where I've sort of gone into "science mode" of really wanting to understand "Why and how," has been seen as threatening. Here as well [referring to new employer].

A manager from the same CRC offered the following rejoinder when asked about the need for scientists to engage in rational argumentation to identify the best possible solution:

I generally think that there is a, sensible way forward with a number of options that you can discuss but you should be aware of the options beforehand. And the thing is scientists always say, "You don't know," and therefore just stop planning for it, which does drive me nuts. ... And that's not really thinking far enough ahead. And that I've seen many, many times, that scientists focus on the next few experiments, and being completely unable to handle uncertainty and complexity which is odd given that's what they should be doing, and I think that is what business does all the time. If you haven't told somebody something might go wrong and it does, it might be blindingly obvious to a scientist but if you haven't told your supporters and investors of the possibility then they are certainly going to see vigorous debate as a failure.

Researchers recognized the value and complementary potential of contributions from both research and business cultures, but saw managerial language norms intruding on their professional judgments of the "correct" way to conduct research, and degrading the quality of work produced. For example:

And that difference in culture, the way a scientist will approach a problem is to look at all the possibilities and then choose, and pursue a particular path. The way these guys were doing it was choosing the path and not deviating from it and just going down further and further into that. Now both of them absolutely constructive because you have that broader engagement to come up with a better solution that you then feed into the very necessarily so, straight-jacket type focus. ... What that did then, by quelling that inquiry, it actually reduced the standards. The sort of consensus approach reduced the standards of work created. There was a mediocrity that came into the work. It was very interesting, an absolute culture change that occurred.

From the perspective of the researchers, attempts by business people to limit debate were dismissed as "micro-management" and indicative of a desire to "dictate" technical solutions to problems they were not qualified to address. Researchers reported dismay and distrust upon hearing business people publicly announce project timeframes based upon what they viewed as a naively optimistic view when dealing with non-routine discovery work; that everything would run to schedule. Both commercial and research informants reported business people viewing rational argumentation as a sign of occupational dysfunction, indicating inadequate forward planning, or suggestive that the proposed solution will fail.

At least three points emerge from the previous discussion. First, argumentation styles can act as occupational and subcultural norms. Second, the use of distinctive occupational argumentation repertoires may not facilitate communication in cross-functional meetings and thirdly, argumentation style may influence perceptions about project statuses and likely outcomes. Undoubtedly, the diverse forms of argumentation favored by research and commercial occupations provide a sense of group identity and are suited to their differing tasks and organizational environments. However, different argumentation styles may reduce the ability of inter-occupational contributions to commercialization to be accepted and recognized as constructive.

Argumentation and the Hybrid Clinician Manager's Role

Professional identity can be seen to influence the norms and language of argumentation. The results indicate part of a clinician's professional identity is that of a sense of superiority over other clinical and non-clinical members of the health care organization. It appears that they only take debates seriously when engaged with a member of their own medical specialty as described here by a non-clinical senior manager:

What I have found is that you have two medical clinicians talking to each other they are more inclined to be seriously challenging. Where, if you have a clinician who is not of the same speciality or profession, they don't have the same clinical understanding and through that challenging process the response will be, "Do you have expertise in this field?

When doctors undertake hybrid clinician management roles their clinical professional identity dominates, this can be seen in the lack of acknowledgement or understanding of the language of management. The domination of their clinical professional identity may be due to lack of skill or confidence in their management role and hence they use their medical dominance in discussions with management as a guard. As one clinician manager stated when asked about his knowledge of management language:

I picked it up and I am still learning. I still get confused. Ever since the Area has restructured and decisions were put back to the facility rather than go through a network. It's slowly happening and I am still learning the language. I have got to sit down at some stage and go through the budget and work out where we are spending the money.

In health care organizations, it is regarded as the manager's role to engage with their subordinates to implement strategies that increase efficiency and effectiveness. Effective change requires managers to understand why and how these strategies will drive change. The professional identity of the hybrid clinician manager appears to be dominated by trying to maintain the status of the medical profession and its identity through organizational decision-making. Differences in how managers and doctors view organizational responsibilities within the health care organization can block communication, as described by a non-clinical manager:

There are a lot of senior clinicians who are in those roles and they have a whole lot of clinicians behind them. It still has not reached the level where clinician managers are saying, 'Yes I know where you are coming from, I know we have this capacity problem, yes I know we have this problem so we need to work together to fix it.' It is clinicians have this problem and that problem and we have to do something about it.

Both the hybrid clinician managers and the non-clinical managers recognised the lack of management knowledge as a challenge when discussing management issues in health care organizations. It was predominantly the non-clinical managers that spoke of the hybrid clinician manager's professional dominance as an area of ongoing frustration when discussing managerial problems and potential solutions with hybrid clinician managers.

Clinical Professional Identity as a Barrier to Solving Problems

Professional identity was also a barrier to engaging hybrid clinician managers as managers who are part of the larger health care organization. Some hybrid clinician managers showed lack of commitment to their managerial role. A health service manager (non-clinical manager) sees their role as their profession. Those interviewed had all completed some form of management training either through the university or through the hospital. Hybrid clinician managers see their management role as added onto their "professional role." They see themselves as doctors first, hence when organizational pressure becomes too great they respond by threatening to drop their management role and retreat to their clinical role as described by this hybrid manager:

There is a whole game which you need to explore about managing up and the impact of managing up being a doctor as opposed to being an administra-

tor. They can't tell me in the final analysis what to do. Because I can walk out of the administrative job and they can't sack me. I would just go back to being a doctor. I could make that amount of many in private practice in an eighth of the time that I do the administration. Money is irrelevant.

Doctors separate themselves from the health care organization's policies and processes. A doctor's professional identity provides them autonomy within the health care organization. This health service manager was clearly frustrated when asked a question regarding how doctors are recruited into hybrid roles:

The guy who subsequently became the Department Head had been effectively acting in the role in a kind of informal way for a long time, they (clinicians) were concerned about the delay and wanted to know why he wasn't already in the position. They had already voted him into the role. I said I appreciate democracy as much as anybody else does but it doesn't work that way. It is not a democracy we have a process and the process is by expression of interest and we arranged to call one soon.

Professions provide individual professionals with scripts to draw on for their daily practice. These scripts inform their practical knowledge as well as being the basis of evaluation (Hotho, 2008). When doctors expand the boundary of their profession and undertake management roles they are influenced by their medical identity when dealing with their clinical colleagues.

Getting their team to understand (management issues) and be able to take it back to their clinical colleagues. Now lots of clinician managers probably understand it (management issues), they know its importance, but they understand it and they are happy to support it, they do all of that when they are in this room. But once they go out there (to their clinical colleagues) it is a very

different story. That's the difficulty. I don't know whether there is a solution to it. Even though the clinician managers who are very good they understand it and say they agree, they still find it hard to sell it back to their colleagues or find the words around it to sell.

Doctors will also use the power in their professional group to delay or slow down the implementation of a policy they do not professionally believe is in the interest of their patients. When asked what are the benefits of being a doctor in the hybrid role this hybrid clinician-manager stated:

My role sometimes gets a bit awkward because sometimes I can see where the clinicians are coming from but have the pressure from administration because we need to cut cost. Well it comes of costs and it will affect patient safety and that is where clinicians come from because at the end of the day we are advocates for patient's safety. It works both ways, as the more there is an objection (from the clinicians) the longer it takes (the policy) to implement.

CONCLUSION

How Can Communication between Different Occupational Groups be Improved?

Argumentation patterns typical of commercial and research groups reveal their occupational values and assumptions. In commercial settings, action and results are valued, particularly as focus upon speed as a competitive strategy has increased over the past fifteen years (Vinton, 1992). This leads to argumentation patterns favoring quick decisions oriented towards taking action to achieve short-term organizational goals. This commercial argumentation is not easily reconciled with scientific values of accuracy and thorough understanding.

Furthermore, popular management texts praising "strong" business cultures that display consensus and conformity (Pech, 2001) may have exacerbated perceived differences between the two groups' use of argumentation, contributing to commercial perceptions of scientific argumentation as an occupational and organizational problem.

Research or academic styles of argumentation are characterized by vigorous dissent to create and continuously improve ideas and are not timed while business debates are reported to be action oriented, timed, and managed to a definite conclusion. In commercial groups, dissent may be perceived as a threat to group cohesion, group hierarchies and the efficient execution of business plans. Members of research groups report enjoying intellectual dissent, consider it to be constructive and value it as a key part of their professional identity. When the groups are separate, they can follow their own norms in parallel. When combined in cross-functional teams, encountering seemingly foreign standards for debate can create frustration and may jeopardize commercialization outcomes. Members of each community generally regard the debating norms of the other group as unusual and an obstruction to equal participation (even to the extent of applying labels such as "dysfunctional"), creating barriers to communication and commercialization. At the same time, members of both groups maintain their occupational subcultural boundaries and identity by continuing their distinct argumentation style in a combined forum, even when doing so impedes communication.

The argumentation rituals used by research and commercial groups may reflect their underlying reward systems and motivation towards producing knowledge or making money. Mutual conflict exists between business pressures for speed and punctuality and research emphasis on thorough understanding to protect and enhance scholastic reputations. Moreover, the different forms and norms of debate and rhetoric fit two key roles in innovation: imagining the as yet non-existent product or service and making it concrete. Scientific or rational argumentation plays a complementary role to business modes of debate through the creation and testing of ideas vital in the early stages of the commercialization process. Focusing on a specific form of a new product or service, and organizing the team to fund, test, and manufacture in volume to meet set deadlines provides the corresponding applied role.

In contrast to Levine's (2006) assertion that conflict is detrimental to an organization's culture, Roberto (2005) champions the benefits of conflict in improving the quality of decisions, provided that it is paired with a consensus to execute decisions once they are made. In one CRC signs existed for a cross-pollination of researcher culture, with its willingness to question and debate, with a commercial focus on planning and execution essential for the survival of the participating Small and Medium Enterprises (SMEs). This did not occur serendipitously, but only by the conscious design and action of the CEO, working through the CRC's Communications Manager. The CEO commented on the issue of using "creative dissent" in meetings of commercial and research members, and the fact that some of the industry partners had adopted rational argumentation as a technique for use inside their own organizations:

I found it productive then [in a public sector organization] and still do, when used sparingly. So it has wider application than just in the academic domain. Yes, I think some SME's do use it, especially in their innovation activities, because this where the employees are given a little more latitude to question and explore.

Nevertheless, it is unlikely that there will be wide-spread adoption of research forms of argumentation by industrial participants in triple helix organizations, or that research participants will willingly accept arguments based on consensus or formal organizational authority. The debating norms of each occupational culture govern that community, are acquired through training or socialization, and their display indicates that an individual chooses to remain a member of that group (McKerrow, 1980). Hence, the differing argumentation styles of research and commercial groups will be resistant to change. Nevertheless, if members of triple helix organizations understand and are aware of the norms and debating rituals of business and research occupational subcultures it may be possible to reduce misunderstandings and support successful commercialization. To obtain the benefits promised from the formation of hybrid industry-research groups, it is important that each occupational subculture be free to employ its own subculturally appropriate rhetorical forms in homogenous, single occupation meetings. However, a consciousness of differences in styles of debate and modified use of research and business argumentation when occupational subcultures meet, are likely to be advantageous.

Within the health care context argumentation patterns between clinical professionals and managers also reveal their occupational values and assumptions. However, these differences are displayed somewhat differently to the commercial and research groups in the hybrid industry research organizations.

Changes in health care organizations have seen some doctors increase their organizational responsibilities through combining management and clinical roles as hybrid clinician managers (Fitzgerald & Ferlie, 2000). In the current economic environment of health service delivery hybrid clinician-managers are required to understand the business of health. Health care organizations have limited resources to support new and expanding technology, pharmaceuticals, and human resources. Furthermore, pressure for organizational efficiency has seen the introduction of a range of performance indicators in clinical settings. Therefore, the business of health is now the driver for the practice of health. Hence, the business of health requires managers to have management knowledge and skills to drive organizational efficiency and cost reduction.

The role of the hybrid clinician manager is seen as an important role within the health care organization as it appears to be the bridge between the practice of health and the business of health (Iedema, Degeling, Braithwaite, & White, 2003). In medicine, the dominant ideology values reasoning and articulation of medical colleagues and effectively silences alterative worldviews (Apker & Eggly, 2004). Therefore, organizational decisions that affect the clinical work practice of clinicians need the backing of the hybrid clinician-manager before they can be implemented. Their view of their profession and their professional domain can effect organizational functioning and obstruct implementation of organizational policies.

When hybrid clinician managers come to the role lacking management skills and knowledge they do not have sufficient understanding of management language needed to communicate effectively with health service managers (Edwards, 2003). Although hybrid clinician managers and health service managers see quality and patient safety as important each value different aspects, clinicians are responsible for their patient's quality of care and safety. Health service managers have direct responsibility for ensuring the health care organization keeps within its allocated budget. Both professions have the same overall goal, although different views for accomplishing them. Therefore, hybrid clinician managers and health service managers not only have differences in the professional language they use and understand they also have different professional values that influence how they approach organizational problem solving.

When viewed from the traditional, integrationist perspective of organizational cultural research, both hybrid industry-research organizations and health care organizations face the challenge of operating within an organizational cultural paradox; the beliefs, values and assumptions held by groups within the organization are seemingly contradictory and yet valid. The divergent bodies of knowledge and skills that make the parties attractive to each other, and provide reason to collaborate, simultaneously create difficulties in communication and cooperation.

However, recognition of the dominance of the differentiation view of organizational culture in these organizations may allow professionals to resolve the apparent paradox through acknowledging, respecting and facilitating productive interactions between dissimilar, but ultimately complementary occupational cultures. Clear agreement and enthusiasm for high-level goals can co-exist with fundamental assumptions and values that are in conflict.

In organizations where professional and managerial occupational subcultures have worked separately and are required to work together to reach a common organizational goal, there needs to be recognition that they have occupied separate thought worlds, used different norms and have disparate assumptions about goals and methods of working. The distance between the assumptions, beliefs, values and norms of the subcultures necessitates acknowledgement, and conscious effort to accommodate their differences. Both are efficient and effective in their own contexts, but thought, effort and action are needed to improve inter-occupational working patterns, communication and outcomes. Whether or not a hybrid industry-research organization thrives and becomes productive, or health care organizations improve organizational functioning and problem solving, will depend to some extent on the management of occupational cultural differences between its professional and managerial members.

ACKNOWLEDGMENT

The researchers would like to thank the participants for their generosity in allowing us to benefit from their time and experience.

REFERENCES

Abbott, A. (1988). *The system of professions: An essay on the divisions of expert labour*. Chicago, IL: University of Chicago Press.

Apker, J., & Eggly, S. (2004). Communicating professional identity in medical socialization: Considering the ideological discourse of morning report. *Qualitative Health Research, 14*(3), 411–429. doi:10.1177/1049732303260577

Barringer, B. R., & Harrison, J., S. (2000). Walking a tightrope: Creating value through interorganizational relationships. *Journal of Management, 26*(3), 367–403. doi:10.1177/014920630002600302

Borys, B., & Jemison, D. B. (1989). Hybrid arrangements as strategic alliances: Theoretical issues in organizational combinations. *Academy of Management Review, 14*(2), 234–248.

Braithwaite, J., & Hindle, D. (2001). Acute health sector reform: An analysis of the Australian senate's proposals. *Australian Health Review, 24*(1). doi:10.1071/AH010003

Burgelman, R. A., & McKinney, W. (2006). Managing the strategic dynamics of acquisition integration: Lessons from HP and Compaq. *California Management Review, 48*(3), 5–27.

Creswell, J. W. (2003). *Research design: Qualitative, quantitative and mix methods approaches* (2nd ed.). Thousand Oaks, CA: Sage Publications.

Daniels, M. R., & Johansen, E. (1985). The role of accreditation in the development of public administration as a profession: A theoretical and empirical assessment. *Public Administration Quarterly, 8*(4), 419–441.

Dolinina, I. B., & Cecchetto, V. (1998). Facework and rhetorical strategies in intercultural argumentative discourse. *Argumentation, 12*, 167–181. doi:10.1023/A:1007739713653

Duckett, S. J. (2008). The Australian health care system: Reform, repair or replace? *Australian Health Review*, *32*(2), 322–329. doi:10.1071/AH080322

Edwards, N., Martin, McLellan, Alastair, Abbasi, & Kamran. (2003). Doctors and managers: A problem without a solution? *British Medical Journal, 326*, 609. doi:10.1136/bmj.326.7390.609

Erduran, S., Simon, S., & Osbourne, J. (2004). TAPing into argumentation: Developments in the application of Toulmin's argument pattern for studying science discourse. *Science Education*, *88*(6), 915–933. doi:10.1002/sce.20012

Etkowitz, H., & Leydesdorff, L. (2000). The dynamics of innovation: From national systems and "mode 2" to a triple helix of university-industry-government relations. *Research Policy*, *29*, 109–123. doi:10.1016/S0048-7333(99)00055-4

Fitzgerald, J. A. (2002). *Doctors and nurses working together: A mixed method study into the construction and changing of professional identities.* Western Sydney, Australia: Sydney.

Fitzgerald, L., & Ferlie, E. (2000). Professionals: Back to the future? *Human Relations*, *53*(5), 713–740. doi:10.1177/0018726700535005

Freidson, E. (1984). The changing nature of professional control. *Annual Review of Sociology, 10*, 1–20. doi:10.1146/annurev.so.10.080184.000245

Freidson, E. (1994). *Professionalism reborn.* Oxford, UK: Polity Press.

Gibbons, M., Limoges, C., Nowotny, H., Schwartzman, S., Scott, P., & Trow, M. (1994). *The new production of knowledge: The dynamics of science in contemporary societies.* London, UK: Sage Publications.

Gray, D. O., Lindblad, M., & Rudolph, J. (2001). Industry-university research centers: A multivariate analysis of member retention. *The Journal of Technology Transfer*, *26*, 247–254. doi:10.1023/A:1011158123815

Hayes, K. (2007). *Triple helix organisations, knowledge-stewarding communities of practice and perceptions of time: The hunters and gatherers of commercialisation.* Paper presented at the 8th European Conference on Knowledge Management. Barcelona, Spain.

Hayes, K., & Fitzgerald, A. (2005). *Preliminary findings of an investigation into interactions between commercial and scientific occupational cultures in hybrid research organisations.* Paper presented at the Proceedings of the 6th International CINet Conference. Brighton, UK.

Hayes, K. J., & Fitzgerald, J. A. (2007). Business and research forms of debate: Argumentation and dissent as barriers to the commercialisation of innovations in hybrid industry-research organisations. *International Journal of Technology. Policy and Management*, *7*(3), 280–291.

Hotho, S. (2008). Professional identity - Product of structure, product of choice. *Journal of Organizational Change Management, 21*(6), 721–742. doi:10.1108/09534810810915745

Iedema, R., Degeling, P., Braithwaite, J., & White, L. (2003). It's an interesting conversation i'm hearing: The doctor as manager. *Organization Studies*, *25*(1), 15–33. doi:10.1177/0170840604038174

Illich, I. (1987). *Disabling professions.* New York, NY: Marion Boyers.

Kippist, L., & Fitzgerald, J. A. (2006). *The value of management education for hybrid clinician managers.* Paper presented at the ANZAM. Rockhampton, Australia.

Kippist, L., & Fitzgerald, J. A. (2008). *Managers are from Mars and doctors are from Venus.* Paper presented at the ANZAM. Aukland, New Zealand.

Kippist, L., & Fitzgerald, J. A. (2009). Organisational professional conflict and hybrid clinician managers. *Journal of Health Organization and Management, 23*(6), 642–655. doi:10.1108/14777260911001653

Kunda, G. (1992). *Engineering culture: Control and commitment in a high-tech corporation.* Philadelphia, PA: Temple University Press.

Larson, M. S. (1977). *The rise of professionalism.* Berkeley, CA: University of California Press.

Lehrer, M., & Asakawa, K. (2004). Pushing scientists into the marketplace: Promoting science entrepreneurship. *California Management Review, 46*(3), 55–76.

Levine, S. (2006). *High performance organizations: Creating a culture of agreement. Handbook of Business Strategy* (pp. 375–380). London, UK: Emerald.

Liu, Y. (1999). Justifying my position in your terms: Cross-cultural argumentation in a globalized world. *Argumentation, 13*, 297–315. doi:10.1023/A:1007866519621

Martin, J. (2002). *Organizational culture: Mapping the terrain.* Thousand Oaks, CA: Sage Publications Inc.

McDonald, C. (1999). Human service professionals in the community services industry. *Australian Social Work, 52*(1), 17–25. doi:10.1080/03124079908414105

McDonald, K. M. (1995). *The sociology of the professions.* London, UK: Sage Publications.

McKerrow, R. E. (1980). *Argument communities.* Paper presented at the First Summer Conference on Argumentation. Annandale, VA.

Meyerson, D., & Martin, J. (1987). Cultural change: An integration of three different views. *Journal of Management Studies, 24*(6), 623–647. doi:10.1111/j.1467-6486.1987.tb00466.x

Mickan, S. M., & Boyce, R. A. (2006). Organisational change and adaptation in health care. In *Managing Health Services: Concepts and Practice* (2nd ed., pp. 59–83). Sydney, Australia: Mosby Elsevier.

Nemeth, C. J. (1997). Managing innovation: When less is more. *California Management Review, 40*(1), 59–74.

Nowotny, H., Scott, P., & Gibbons, M. (2001). *Re-thinking science: Knowledge and the public in an age of uncertainty.* Malden, MA: Blackwell Publishers Inc.

Pech, R. J. (2001). Termites, group behaviour, and the loss of innovation: Conformity rules! *Journal of Managerial Psychology, 16*(7), 559–574. doi:10.1108/EUM0000000006168

Premus, R. (2002). Moving technology from labs to market: A policy perspective. *International Journal of Technoloy Transfer and Commercialisation, 1*(1/2), 22–39. doi:10.1504/IJTTC.2002.001775

Roberto, M. A. (2005). *Why great leaders don't take yes for an answer: Managing for conflict and consensus.* Upper Saddle River, NJ: Wharton School Publishing.

Senker, J., & Sharpe, M. (1997). Organizational learning in cooperative alliances: Some case studies in biotechnology. *Technology Analysis and Strategic Management, 9*(1), 35–51. doi:10.1080/09537329708524268

Siegel, D. S., Waldman, D. A., Atwater, L. E., & Link, A. N. (2004). Toward a model of the effective transfer of scientific knowledge from academicians to practitioners: Qualitative evidence from the commercialization of university technologies. *Journal of Engineering and Technology Management, 21,* 115–142. doi:10.1016/j.jengtecman.2003.12.006

Sillince, J. A. A. (2002). A model of the strength and appropriateness of argumentation in organizational contexts. *Journal of Management Studies, 39*(5), 585–618. doi:10.1111/1467-6486.00001

Steiner, C. (2000). Teaching scientists to be incompetent: Educating for industry work. *Bulletin of Science, Technology & Society, 20*(2), 123–132. doi:10.1177/027046760002000206

Trice, H. M. (1993). *Occupational subcultures in the workplace.* Ithaca, NY: ILR Press.

Vinton, D. E. (1992). A new look at time, speed and the manager. *The Academy of Management Executive, 6*(4), 7–16.

Werder, A. (1999). Argumentation rationality of management decisions. *Organization Science, 10*(5), 672–690. doi:10.1287/orsc.10.5.672

Ziman, J. (2000). Are debatable scientific questions debatable? *Social Epistemology, 14*(2/3), 187–199. doi:10.1080/02691720050199225

Chapter 10
The Engineering Project as Story and Narrative

Lars Bo Henriksen
Aalborg University, Denmark

ABSTRACT

Engineers most often organise their work in projects and consequently project management becomes an essential part of an engineer's work and working life in general. Even if most engineers are trained in project management, it seems that this is a challenge to most engineers. It also seems that the traditional project management tools are not always sufficient when it comes to managing engineering projects. In this chapter, an engineering project is examined, and it turns out that the language, the stories, and the narratives connected to the project is of greater importance to the engineers than the formal project management tools that were offered to the engineers. It also turns out that the term "project" could itself be a problem when it comes to fulfilling the project goals. Therefore, it is concluded that when working on engineering projects, language, stories, and narratives are just as important to the engineers as any other element in the project.

INTRODUCTION

Engineers, such as Niels, work on projects; and Niels was struggling with "PRO2," a project in production management. He liked his work, even if it was challenging and sometimes frustrating. The PRO2 project was about developing the manufacturing system of "The Company." This was a rather intriguing task as the engineers in The Company had previously successfully completed

the PRO1 project. The PRO1 project was about the manufacturing process itself, but PRO2 was even larger as it concerned the entire supply chain that The Company was part of. Therefore, projects were nothing new to Niels and his colleagues; they knew how to work on a project and they knew how to successfully complete projects and even if the PRO2 project was larger than anything they hitherto had embarked on, they were quite confident that this new challenge was a possible future success.

DOI: 10.4018/978-1-4666-1836-7.ch010

Engineers have always worked on projects. Famous engineers of yesteryear like Isambard Kingdom Brunel and George Stevenson are largely described by, and best know because of, their projects. Reading through a biography of Brunel (Rolt, 1957; Buchanan, 2006; Vaughan 2003), for example, is to read through his various projects. Brunel took on his first project at the age of nineteen when he replaced his father as manager of the Thames tunnel project; he died at the age of fifty-three when he was just about to finish what proved to be his last project—the great steam ship "Great Eastern." In the intervening period of a most productive life, he built railroads, tunnels, bridges, ships, and others of great importance to the industrial revolution. Brunel was an engineer; he was also a project manager not only concerned with the technical side of project management, but also concerned with the economics and organisation of his projects. According to several of his biographers, Brunel lived to pursue the technical challenges of his projects and viewed the economic side as an, at times, cumbersome necessity. Maybe that was why most of his projects were technically groundbreaking, yet more often than not also economic/financial disasters. The technical side was Brunel's real labour of love. From his life story, we can see that projects are nothing out of the ordinary to engineers; project management was part of engineering right from the start of the modern profession. When engineering established itself as a profession during the nineteenth century, what we today term project management was an integrated part of the profession. Brunel would have got nowhere with his various projects that we still rightfully admire today, such as the Clifton Suspension Bridge in Bristol over the river Avon, to give an example, without the basic tools of project management.

For today's engineer, no matter which branch of engineering an eager young person enters, one of the first steps on the career ladder is usually termed "project manager." This was also the case for Niels; he started out as a project manager.

Now, Niels holds the title of vice-president of the Manufacturing Development Department (MDD) where he is responsible for several projects, including parts of the PRO2 project. The PRO2 project is part of a larger change process in The Company. Global sales and production and a very rapid growth in turnover and number of employees placed stronger demands on the management of the production process. In this sense, the PRO2 project aims at reaching a classic goal within production management; namely, rationalisation of the production process in order to meet new marketplace demands and to possibly do it faster than the competitors.

This change process, however, changed the company from one-of-a-kind or 'batch' production process based mainly on craft principles to an industrial enterprise with mass production and mass production principles. Before PRO2, PRO1 was a traditional production process optimisation project; lean principles, streamlining, etc. PRO2 takes this much further and is aimed at the entire supply chain. PRO2 consists of five sub projects. The first of these sub-projects is called Common IT Platform, aimed at developing a common IT platform for all production units. The second is called First Factory, aimed at developing a structure for deciding the division of work between the different production units and MDD, especially concerning documentation of changes. The third is called Knowledge Teams and is concerned with developing a system for knowledge sharing between production units, so that good ideas from one production unit could be of use in other units. The fourth is called Continuous Improvement, a classic principle within production management, aimed at optimising production and the supply chain. The fifth, and final, sub-project is concerned with Material Flow. These all had ambitious problem statements; some of them were successful and some were not.

This chapter reports on a study of project management in relation to the First Factory project, and its "narrative" and "story" within The Company.

First factory is really a change project, that is, a project of organisational change. More specifically, we are interested in using the study findings in understanding how the engineers engaged in the project conceptualised project management. We distinguish between two terms in that process; narrative and story. The project was from the beginning guided by a so-called project charter, which outlined the intentions of the project, and we will treat this here as a narrative. A narrative is conceived of here as a finished and fixed story with a certain structure and with well-defined logics and values. The engineers then have to turn the intentions of the project charter into reality. They do that by telling stories in their everyday working lives. These stories are very different from the fixed narrative of the charter and the intention of this chapter is to investigate the role of both narrative and story in the management of the project. It turns out, in the course of the project, that the charter and its narrative fixes the project and thereby, in itself, becomes a problem for the realisation of the intentions of the charter. Instead, the stories of the engineers everyday work seems to be much more important for the realisation of the project; consequently, the implications for project management are that the project managers should consider the importance of these everyday working-life stories and be more cautious when it comes to the narratives of the project charter.

The chapter is structured as follows; firstly, we introduce the First Factory project and the work of the project manager Niels. Then we consider the relationship between the story, narrative, and project management facilitated by a short introduction to what is known as rational project management and its shortcomings. The First Factory project was officially closed down; yet it lived on and became successful and how this became somewhat surprisingly possible is described in the following section. Finally, we draw on some conclusions and implications of this seemingly paradoxical outcome.

THE PROJECT: FIRST FACTORY

While the projects concerned with material flow, IT-systems etc. were classic production engineering optimisation exercises, the First Factory project represented a different kind of challenge. Niels liked the ideas behind the project. In the process towards mass production, the documentation procedures had gradually become centralised; this meant that any changes made in existing production should be documented at the MDD. This had the consequence that any change, even minor ones, had to be approved by Niels and his team in his department. This was done in order to ensure that the production process was similar in all factories. However, it also meant that the MDD was disturbed time and time again; sometimes with questions of little major relevance and this took a lot of time and resources. If successful, the First Factory project would relieve the MDD department of some work, and grant more independence to the factories; and establish a system that ensured uniformity within the various production processes. As Niels put it: "Some of the things they [the factory managers] want to make decisions on make perfect sense—so, there were a lot of good things in it. So, I support this in many ways—and there is a lot that I want to get rid of. It makes things easier for me and it makes things easier for them."

The project charter is a piece of paper describing content, aims, and goals of any project. The charter also describes the resources and the manpower necessary for reaching the prescribed goals. However, the project charter for the First Factory project was not as precise in its formulations and statements as the engineers in the MDD would have wished. The vision of First Factory states "The vision is to ensure clear roles and identity for each factory within The Company, production factories. Successfully collect, evaluate and share product specific production knowledge within The Company's production units and act as a bridge to MDD, executing Mark upgrades and NPI." It is not exactly clear what is meant by this—successfully execute, etc. and the rest of the charter was just as vague in its formulations. The milestones, the roles, the deliverables—everything was only mentioned and it is obvious from the document that it is not a finished document to the same degree as the project charters of the other PRO2 projects. One member of the project group had read it through and sent a copy, with annotated comments, to Niels—it was full of question marks and questions such as "Are we ready for this?" "What does this involve?" or "Is the knowledge base sufficient to anchor lessons learned?"

At a meeting in late December between the presidents of the factories and MDD, the charter was approved and the project was ready to launch in the following new year, but it never happened. The project was put 'on hold,' in effect terminated. At the meeting in December, the president of the MDD had approved the charter, but the rest of the management group in the MDD did not like the charter—they perceived it to be much too loose and far too vaguely formulated. They feared that the charter left room for too many conflicts, especially concerning what they called the interface between the different factories and the MDD; that is, the precise division of work or labour between the different departments. This interface was crucial, because it decided who was doing what, and a constant battle between the factories and the MDD would not be beneficial to anyone in the opinion of these pragmatic engineers. The problem with the charter was that it was made by a group of managers from the factories—MDD people had not been involved at all in its design and formulation. The charter was approved by the MDD, but when the people from MDD saw the final document they did not like it—worse, they were suspicious of it. They were, however, much in favour of the idea of negotiating a new interface between MDD and the factories, the present system was too bureaucratic and too heavy to handle. For example, when the factories got new ideas and implemented changes in the

production processes they should also document these changes—but, as noted above, this documentation had to be carried out by MDD. MDD is a development department and they were not very, or overly, interested in existing production processes; they wanted to give the factories the freedom to do the documentation. This, however, was not the problem. The problem was that when the final charter reached MDD the people there viewed the charter as a kind of coup by the factory managers, as an attempt to remove tasks and assignments that were normally the preserve and responsibility of MDD, and transfer them to the factories instead. Even if those in MDD wanted to see some of these documentation tasks disappear from their remit, there were certainly some who would not simply let go of any decision-making powers. They informed the president of MDD that this project was impossible and that it could only result in conflict between MDD and the factories, constant negotiations, or even a continuous power game about who would have the right to do what. The First Factory sub-project of PRO2 was consequently put "on hold."

PROJECT, STORY, AND NARRATIVE

With a point of departure in Niels' story about his projects, the intention here is to conceptualise the phenomenon of the project (Henriksen, et al., 2004). Project management is part of the curriculum in most forms of engineering education. A standard course in project management would most often present what is known as a "rational approach." This approach is concerned with planning, setting goals, finding resources, finding manpower or personnel, etc. The library is replete with books on project management and most of them present a rational planning approach, where project management is reduced to a mere technical planning exercise, like the activities going on when producing the project charter introduced above. That is one of the main ideas within the early industrial management vocabulary. Some of this is very good as it provides advice on how to plan, structure and budget a project; and some of it provides the reader with some very good examples and case studies of good and bad project management. However, it still rests on a rational paradigm of goal setting, planning, implementation, control, and evaluation. The problem is the naivety of such writings; the naïve realist epistemology, the neglect of the political power struggles, and the inability to conceptualise important aspects of the project, most notably the project itself. Davidson Frame's (2003) work is a good example of such writings. His book is very good, make no mistake—there are far worse books on project management out there. It provides clever advice on how to plan, schedule, budget, etc. a project. It gives advice on how to understand the role of projects in present day organisations, on how to set goals, and finally how to plan and control projects.

The problems of the rational paradigm have, of course, been the target of severe criticism (see e.g. Cicmil & Hodgson, 2006, 2007; Maylor, 2006; Winter, 2006). One notable critique is found in Maylor et al. (2006). According to this research the problem with the rational model is first and foremost that it treats project management as if it were rational, universal, and deterministic; a kind of one size fits all of the project management discipline, neglecting the fact that projects are full of uncertainty, ambiguity, and doubt, and that projects are much more complex phenomena than anticipated in so-called rational models of project management. As an alternative, Winter (2006) propose that the perspective on project management changes from the rational paradigm to a much more complex and dynamic perspective. This means that the linear conception should be replaced by complex understandings; that the instrumental models should be replaced by conceptions emphasising the social interactions among people, the narrow single discipline approach should be replaced by a broader multidisciplinary approach; and finally, that the focus on achieving

a single goal or product should be replaced by an idea of value creation (Maylor, et al., 2006).

Yes, that is correct, the change from project to projection, from noun to verb, from thing to action is absolutely necessary for any substantive understanding of the project phenomenon. This critique is very similar to other critiques of management in particular and social science in general for forgetting the lived real lives of people involved in the process of creating, organising, and managing the lifeworld (Alvesson & Wilmott, 1992; Parker, 2002; Henriksen, et al., 2004; Jørgensen, 2007).

If we ask the question "What is a project?" we run the risk of asking for the essence of the project; this would be unfortunate as we noted in the critique above, a project is a complex and diverse beast, and due to its complexity it is doubtful if we could ever find that essence. Rather, we could try to conceptualise the process of projecting (from noun to verb) and through the stories of Niels and his project possibly gain some insight and get closer to the actions that make a project.

Despite its inherent essentialism the question "What is a project?" could be a reasonable point of departure when we want to know what Niels and his colleagues are doing. Davidson Frame tries to define the project: they are "goal oriented, they involve coordinated undertaking of interrelated activities, and they are of finite duration, with beginnings and ends. They are all, to a degree unique" (Davidson Frame, 2003, p. 2). Well without our everyday understanding of projects we would not stand a chance if we had to rely on Davidson Frame's description. As a conceptualisation of the project, it would not do very much for those of us who see beyond narrow simplistic rational confines.

The word *project* comes from the Latin word *projectum* from the Latin verb *proicere*, "to throw something forwards" which in turn comes from *pro-*, which denotes something that precedes the action of the next part of the word in time, and *iacere*, "to throw." The word "project" thus actually originally meant "something that comes before anything else happens." Today to project something means in our everyday language to plan something, to want something to happen in the future and because of this—the orientation towards a future—projecting also becomes synonymous with ambiguity and uncertainty. In the German language it is possible to make a similar analysis of the word "entwerfen"—to throw—which had taken the meaning of "to sketch, design, draft, draw up, depict, outline" or as a noun, "Entwurf," is a "sketch, outline, design, blueprint, draft" (Inwood, 1999, p. 176). With this we see that project and projecting is about the future and future possibilities and therefore also about uncertainty, unexpected outcomes, and possibly failure. It is about actions we want to or promise to take, goals we want to reach, and how we want to reach them. With this, the project becomes a promise for the future and in more sinister interpretations and more fanciful endeavors they become wishful thinking. Based on the aforementioned critical understandings of the project it would now be possible to state the following about projects and thereby avoid the rational simplistic models, and also come closer to a conceptualization of the project: projects are complex, projects have a lot of stakeholders, and these stakeholders have their own agendas and their own reasons for joining the project. Consequently, there are many narratives and discourses involved. Projects are an ever-changing flux of events. Projects are social interactions. Projects are power games. They are changeable in the sense that the purpose of the project is negotiated and can change during the lifespan of the project. All projects are socially constructed (Henriksen, et al., 2004).

Davidson Frame (2003, p. 7) very rightly points to the narrative structure of projects. Projects have a beginning, middle and end, at least when the project is formulated as a promise, similar to the project charter we met above. Boje (2001, 2008) wants us to distinguish between story and narrative. Narrative is then a structured story with a beginning middle and end, with a plot and

which portrays a fixed reality (see also Mølbjerg Jørgensen & Boje 2010). The narrated story has a specific idea of what kind of logics operate in the world, with a fixed idea of what would count as facts, and with a set of values that determines right and wrong (Henriksen, et al., 2004). The narrated story is then a very strong claim about the world and the realities. According to Boje, the story, or as he calls it the ante-narrative, is open, not fixed. Boje calls the story a bet, in the sense that it does not have a fixed logic, and facts and values are open for debate in the story, and therefore changeable.

Narrative is characterised by its structured nature. A story on the other hand is characterised by its openness, but what really makes that difference between story and narrative is the language in use. If we look at the language of story and narrative we could say that while narrative is characterised by its statements, story is characterised by it speculative character. This needs an explanation as speculation holds a somewhat dubious status in our everyday language. Speculation normally signals something that is not trustworthy, something that is without relation to any circumstances in the real world, or to risky investments made for the sake of profit alone, but speculation could also mean that we think very hard on something and try to find new ways in the world. Following Gadamer (1992, p. 465) speculative or speculation should have a different status, as speculation originally means to mirror something.

The word speculative here refers to the mirror relation. Being reflected involves a constant substitution of one thing for another. When something is reflected in something else, say, the castle in the lake, it means that the lake throws back the image. If we now use the word 'speculative' as it was coined by philosophers around 1800 and say, for example, that someone has a speculative mind or that a thought is rather speculative, behind this usage lies the notion of reflection in a mirror. Speculative means the opposite of the dogmatism of everyday experience. A speculative person is someone who does not abandon himself directly to the tangibility of appearances or to the fixed determinateness of the meant, but who is able to reflect or—to put it in Heglian terms—who sees that the 'in-itself' is a "for-me" (Gadamer, 1992, p. 466).

Speculation then becomes part of a question and answer dialectic where we speculate, that is asking questions about the state of the world and its realities. This is the hermeneutic experience with its question and answer logic. In this way, speculation is very similar to the concepts of thinking, philosophizing, etc. The methods we use when we want to know more about unknown worlds and realities. Contrary to the idea of speculation stands the "statement." A statement is telling us what the world and the realities "is" like. Period. No questioning, no doubt, no paradoxes, no openness. The world is like this or like that. The statement is often preferred in scientific discourses, e.g. in the form of the definition, but such a one-sided addiction to statements would severely restrict our thinking and interesting questions and thereby important understandings would never appear.

If we confer this distinction between speculation and statement to the idea of story and narrative, we see that in story speculation dominates statement. The openness, the questioning, the search for new knowledge. Likewise, the dominant feature of narrative is the statement. In the structured narrative, we are told what the world would look like. Narrative is not very good at including speculation. If we think of a special kind of narrative like the parable where the whole idea of the narrative is to tell and from that telling or relating conclude some kind of general lesson (Boucher, 1981). With this, we are also told what kinds of logics, facts, and values operate in the world. This is not to say that we could do without narratives. In the case of the parable a good parable can make us speculate, make us think differently. Therefore, both story and narrative are

important parts of the project. It is obvious that the project charter is a narrative. The project charter tells a story about what is going to happen in the future—the promise, but also how that is going to happen. The project charter was definitely a narrative pointing at something to be achieved in the future. It has a certain distinct logic that tells the reader that if we do this, then that will happen. It tells what is granted the status of facts, and in terms of values, it tells what is right and wrong. The project charter is a narrative; it informs the reader about visions, objectives, and scope of the project (plot). It informs us about the actors, it informs us about the time involved (beginning, middle, end) as it has an implementation plan, and there is a certain tension and uncertainty inherent in the charter as it informs us about the risks, assumptions and constraints. All elements of a good narrative are in place. In this sense, the project charter is a statement.

However, the project charter is also only a narrative—it tells what might happen, if... but in order to realise the goals formulated in the charter we need more. We need actors, actions, and we need those everyday stories where the visions of the project are interpreted and made sense of—speculation—so the members of the teams realising the visions can understand what it is all about. Story is a bet, says Boje (2001, p. 2), and so is the project. The story, in contrast to the narrative, includes all those utterances we relate to each other in our everyday conversations. They are not plotted, they do not necessarily have a beginning, middle, and end structure and the realities of the story are not fixed, but are constantly up for speculation and negotiation. Boje calls this the ante-narrative, as it exists before the story is narrated and fixed. The purpose of the story is sense making, we speculate and try to find a useful logic, some useful facts and the values that can make sense of the matter, e.g. the project. We try to answer the question, "what is going on here?" Latour (1991) argues that modern technological systems are simultaneously social, discursive, and real. That is, if we want to understand modern technologies—such as the PRO2 project—we should consider them as social systems, as systems of language and as systems of real existing objects. The point is that our understanding should encompass all three elements in a unified narrative and in cohesive stories such as the history of the project outlined here, and not as separated narratives of language, cooperation, and technologies. The stories we tell are the media for our collective speculation and act as a collective memory in the project and are therefore essential for the success of the project.

There are several stories, and several types of stories, at stake when researching stories in the project (Czarniawska, 1998, p. 65). There are the stories that the actors involved tell each other while working on the project; these are "the preferred sense-making currency of human relationships among internal and external stakeholders" (Boje, 1991, p. 106). These stories are the stories that the actors tell one another during the course of the project; when they meet each other at official project meetings, when they meet in the corridors, when they talk on the phone, when they talk to each other during a lunch- or coffee break, via email, etc. These stories hold the everyday life of the project together. They are used as sense making and they are used as political tools as well. Therefore, they also change over time and the stories are not necessarily told in the same way to all actors involved; and not all stories are told to everybody. Gossip, smear campaigns, cliques etc. exist and consequently there is an element of ethics is this kind of storytelling (Jørgensen & Boje, 2010).

The project is consequently both narrative and story and the project is to translate the multiple stories into a narrative. Not as Boje says, "to impose counterfeit coherence and order on otherwise fragmented and multi-layered experiences of desire" (Boje, 2001, p. 2), but to take the fragmented stories and through the process of speculation, projecting and conceptualisation to bring order and coherence to the fragmented.

Sometimes this process is successful and the project vision is realised; Brunel's bridges and railroads worked as intended in most cases—in some cases they didn't.

Besides these stories that the actors tell each other, there are the stories the actors tell me in their conversations with me. They sometimes have the structure of a narrative, but as I intend to engage in a dialogue with its mutual question and answer logic (Henriksen, et al., 2004, p. 152) the narrative is sometimes toned down and speculation can take place. Finally, there is the story I tell about the project, as in this chapter. This story should have a strictly narrative structure; else, the reader might end up confused, which would be quite unfortunate for this type of text.

THE FAILED PROJECT THAT LIVED ON

The process of speculation and projecting, of ordering and creating coherence is by no means a neat and ordered process. It involves politics, power games, and the creation of new, alternative, and subversive stories and narratives. Niels could only confirm all of this. The First Factory project was terminated even if there were some very good ideas behind it. The faith of the project is definitely a result of politics, different agendas, different discourses, and different stories and narratives. Even if Niels liked the intentions of the project, he and his colleagues said they saw the project charter as an attempted coup and they did not at all like the reality laid out in the narrative of the project charter.

The charter was not a joint effort (Between the factories and the MDD). It was written by the factory managers. They live in an operations world; we in MDD live in a ... more in a development world. Our primary interface is the development department and we constantly hear 'there are new products coming, new products, new products. ...

The operations departments (the factories) see the products they have today, and they want to optimize them. They do not know that new things will arrive tomorrow and the day after tomorrow and the day after.' So, there is no reason to start to optimize. But this also means that when there is a question to us 'would you like to help us with this or that' and we say 'there is no reason to do that' (because you will get a new product very soon) and then they get angry and say 'why do you not help us? Then we might as well do it ourselves.' 'But they cannot' because of the present procedures and business processes.

What is at stake here is a political game, a conflict of the distribution of resources but also a clash of realities and worldviews; as pointed out by Niels, there is a development reality in MDD and an operations reality in the factories. These realties have very different values and logics and it is obvious from Niels' story that this is so (Henriksen, et al., 2004). While the MDD holds a kind of development logic emphasizing future products and espousing values that inform the MDD people that developing manufacturing processes of new products is much better than optimizing the processes of existing products. On the contrary, the factory people find optimization of existing production processes much more important than products they have not yet seen yet. These different realities and logics are reproduced and strengthened by the existing systems and procedures. While working for the development department the MDD is granted man-hours for their work, this is not the case when working for the factories. For the factories, the situation is somewhat different. Their systems target better production—as do almost all other manufacturing entities—so, optimization of existing products is at the forefront; participating in projects and concerns for future products are deemed less important as the operations logic dominates.

With this enhanced understanding, one can see that there is every reason for the First Factory

project to fail. Nevertheless, even if there were these differences in the way that people in the different departments looked at things, there seemed to be much more at stake here. The project charter was made by the factory managers and the MDD people had not been involved at all. Niels sees this as the main problem. "But I would say that the people that made that charter think they had found the best technical solution that is workable. That was why they are so angry. They have not, they think, put in all these hidden agendas that we … as we read between the lines in the MDD. … It is us who see them—we see ghosts. And, and it is then [that] dialogue becomes difficult. They think that they have come up with a rational technical solution, I do not think they attempted any coup—well one or two of them maybe, they are also very different." So, because they were excluded from the process that produced the charter, created the narrative, the MDD people were very suspicious. Niels again emphasized this as the main problem. "I think that everybody misunderstood what this project was all about—the project was about making the charter. When the charter was finished the project was finished, because then we did agree. It is quite obvious that both parties think that the others are stupid right now." To Niels, the First Factory project was about negotiating the so-called interface between the factories and the MDD. This was important but it failed because of the suspicion and the misunderstandings. The project failed because only one party made the narrative that was supposed to guide the project. They, and they alone, narrated the story of First Factory and by fixing a certain logic and fixing what would count as facts and values in the project, they were seen as similar to those attempting a coup. The "rational technical solution" was seen as a political instrument even if it was not intended to be. The project charter narrative was read with a lot of suspicion in the MDD—they saw ghosts—and the project was consequently terminated.

Niels is certain it would have been possible for the parties to sit down and produce a charter that everybody could find satisfactory. They could have produced a joint narrative, which could have guided the project. Instead, Niels had to do something else. He still finds parts of the First Factory project relevant and necessary and therefore he wants to continue with the project, just in another context. "I will have to do this myself without making it into a project. Because when it is a project then it gets some kind of status, but if I say 'do you know what, this and that you are allowed to do from tomorrow and I will make a business process and send it out for some kind of consultation.' It will take two days' work. It is not a project; it is just an assignment. And it will slip through. Strange—if it is a project, then it can put things 'on hold.'"

The project failed, because it was never launched as a project. Due to different realities, different systems and processes, different aims and goals, the project was terminated—a promising project negotiating the interface or the borders between the departments which was needed. One side made the charter and the other side misread it. One side was perceived to be attempting a coup and the other side moved to prevent it. One side presented a rational, technical solution, and the other side saw … ghosts!

This story confirms the view that projects are complex endeavors full of politics, conflict, and constant negotiations on what is the project. Even if the First Factory project was not launched as a project, it lived on and it definitely had its 'history of effect' (Gadamer, 1992, p. 300). It lived on because its viable goals and aims are still present on the agendas of the parties involved. Niels would like to see a solution to the problems of the interface between the departments. It also had the consequence that the lines drawn between the department in terms of attempted coups, ghosts, and misreadings are not the most fruitful background for future cooperation between them.

CONCLUSION

It is striking that all the way through this narrative, and the stories of the failed project technology has hardly played any role—neither in the project charter itself, nor in Niels' stories about the project. It was an engineering project supposed to solve engineering problems in a manufacturing context, but the two parties involved never got to that. Niels mentioned that he was sure that the factory managers thought that they had provided a rational, technical solution and had made everybody aware of that through the project charter. However, reading through the project charter today it is hard to see any rational technical solutions; rather, one can see a narrative, stating what the world should be like and ought to look like. The classic conflict in production management between development and operations became very obvious and was played out once again in the project; and the problems that the project should have solved, lived on, yet Niels proposes a more modest solution to these.

One of the more paradoxical conclusions of this is that the project stands a far better chance of reaching its goals when it is not 'projected' as a project anymore. As long as the project was a project it was locked up in a narrative, the realities were fixed, and not everyone participating in the project could accept this. The problems that the project was supposed to solve still exist, but when the project was put on hold or terminated, problems were once again open for debate and new stories and narratives could be told about them. Thereby the project would stand a far better chance of solving the problems. This also shows the importance of story and narrative in the project and the danger of fixing the realities in a narrative. By cancelling the project and thereby opening the discussion once again, the realities of the project could be negotiated and the parties involved could all have their say in the project. This, in turn, shows the complexity of projects.

The rational planning paradigm of project management, as represented by Davidson Frame and others, will eventually fall short if we try to understand the events in the First Factory project through such a narrow paradigm. The important events after the termination of the project, the events that possibly will give the project a second life and second chance of success, would not be included in such simplistic understandings. It is argued here that the critical paradigms emphasising complexity and ambiguity stand a far better chance of conceptualising "the project."

The project is simultaneously social, discursive and real (Latour, 1991) and the implication of the PRO2 story for project management is consequently that even if the project charter is an important and indispensable element of the project, the charter and the rational project management paradigm cannot stand alone. The project is social, discursive, and real and in order to make the project a success, that is to reach the goals of the charter, the actors involved need to work on the social aspects and the languages as well. Therefore, project management is just as much about the everyday stories that hold the project together, and any project manager should be aware of the types of logics, facts, and values that are communicated in these everyday stories (Henriksen, et al., 2004, p. 145). Most project managers would like to avoid misunderstandings and conflicts in their projects, and the way to accomplish this, or at least to minimise this, is to become more concerned with the stories told.

REFERENCES

Alvesson, M., & Wilmott, H. (1992). *Critical management studies*. Thousand Oaks, CA: Sage.

Bauman, Z. (2000). *Liquid modernity*. Oxford, UK: Polity Press.

Boje, D. (1991). The storytelling organisation: A study of story performance in an office-supply firm. *Administrative Science Quarterly*, *36*(1), 106–126. doi:10.2307/2393432

Boje, D. (2001). *Narrative methods for organisation and communication research*. Thousand Oaks, CA: Sage.

Boje, D. (2008). *Storytelling organization*. Thousand Oaks, CA: Sage.

Boucher, M. I. (1981). *The parables*. Wilmington, NC: Michael Glazier Inc.

Buchanan, A. (2006). *Brunel – The life and times of Isambard Kingdom Brunel*. London, UK: Hambledon Continuum.

Cicmil, S., & Hodgeson, D. (2007). The politics of standards in modern management: Making "the project" a reality. *Journal of Management Studies*, *44*(3).

Cicmil, S., & Hodgson, D. (2006). New possibilities for project management theory: A critical engagement. *Project Management Journal*, *37*(3), 111–122.

Czarniawska, B. (1998). *A narrative approach to organisation studies*. London, UK: Sage.

Davidson, F. J. (2003). *Managing projects in organizations – How to make the best use of time, techniques and people*. San Francisco, CA: Jossey-Bass.

Gadamer, H.-G. (1992). *Truth and method*. New York, NY: Crossroads.

Henriksen, L. B. (2004). *Dimensions of change*. Copenhagen, Denmark: CBS Press.

Latour, B. (1993). *We have never been modern*. Hemel Hempstead, UK: Harvester Wheatsheaf.

Maylor, H. (2006). Special issue on rethinking project management. *International Journal of Project Management, 24*(8). doi:10.1016/j.ijproman.2006.09.013

Mølbjerg Jørgensen, K. (2007). *Power without glory.* Copenhagen, Denmark: CBS Press.

Mølbjerg Jørgensen, K., & Boje, D. (2010). Resituating narrative and story in business ethics. *Business Ethics (Oxford, England), 19*(3), 253–264. doi:10.1111/j.1467-8608.2010.01593.x

Parker, M. (2002). *Against management.* Oxford, UK: Polity Press.

Rolt, L. T. C. (1957). *Isambard Kingdom Brunel.* New York, NY: Penguin.

Vaughan, A. (2003). *Isambard Kingdom Brunel – Engineering knight errant.* London, UK: John Murray Publishers.

Winter, M. (2006). Directions for future research in project management: The main findings of a UK government-funded research network. *International Journal of Project Management, 24*(8). doi:10.1016/j.ijproman.2006.08.009

Chapter 11
Stories of Material Storytelling[1]

Kenneth Mølbjerg Jørgensen
Aalborg University, Denmark

Anete M. Camille Strand
Aalborg University, Denmark

ABSTRACT

Material storytelling is used here to denote a material-discursive understanding of technology, and how technology works in organizations in terms of story performance. The idea is that technology configures organizations in spatial, temporal and material terms. We are inspired by Karen Barad's work in quantum physics in developing the term material storytelling, which relies on a material-discursive understanding of storytelling. By introducing material storytelling we resituate the hegemonic relationship of discourse and language over matter. As such technology regains a central space in both understanding and managing organizations. It implies that attention is relocated to the petty and lowly everyday routines, techniques and material artifacts, which are implicit in what we do in everyday life but govern the agential possibilities for acting in this world. We frame the chapter as a story of material storytelling of a change project in a bank. We experiment with the writing style by going back and forth between two different layers of text. The first layer tells the stories of material storytelling, while the other draws out the theoretical/methodological implications of this approach in terms understanding and managing technology.

INTRODUCTION

Material storytelling (Strand, 2010) denotes a material-discursive understanding of technology and how technology works in organizations in terms of story performance. The idea implied here is that technology configures organizations in spatial, temporal, and material terms. As such, no distinction exists between organization and technology in the sense that organizations

DOI: 10.4018/978-1-4666-1836-7.ch011

are technologies that configure the world. As a material-discursive configuration, organizations are apparatuses of storytelling; apparatus is a term used by Karen Barad (2007), a theorist inspired by quantum physics. Material storytelling, viewed as a material-discursive understanding of storytelling, is developed here from Barad's work.

Material storytelling implies a fundamentally different understanding of technology to what has been prevalent in the literature to date. Dominant understandings of technology place humans in the center of organizations and as having the upper hand in terms of controlling technology. This is the case for traditional, modern, and humanist conceptions of technology where this is presumed to be 'in the hands' of humans. Such humans are equipped with universal qualities like rationality and are, therefore, able to both design and use technology progressively for the common good of the people concerned (e.g. Wolfe, 2010, p. 45).

Social constructionist understandings of technology located within post-humanism also place humans in control of technology. These approaches assume that "…the decentering of the human by its imbrication in technical, medical, informatics and economic networks is increasingly impossible to ignore" (Wolfe, 2010, p. 99). They, however, still view technology as a humanist social construct in the sense that technology is viewed as a discursive construction where discourse, language and culture are presumed to have the upper hand in constructing technology with the importance of matter and materiality simply left unattended or ignored.

By introducing the term 'material storytelling' in this chapter, we aim to re-situate this hegemonic relationship of discourse and language over matter. This demands that technology regains a central space in both understanding and managing organizations. Instead of granting too much perceived power to human agents, power is relocated to the seemingly insignificant, petty and lowly everyday routines, techniques and material artifacts which are implicit in what we do in everyday life but

none-the-less govern the agential possibilities for acting in this world. It follows, from this perspective, that technologies and their effects are deemed to be the results of the entanglement of human and non-human agencies.

We can now state that we understand technology as iterative material-discursive intra-action through which space, time, and matter are continuously reconfigured. The term intra-action is also appropriated from Karen Barad's work; it denotes that phenomena never exist in themselves but are always relationally entangled and constituted. Entanglement does not refer to being intertwined with one another but "… to lack an independent, self-contained existence" (Barad, 2007, p. ix).

Intra-action is used instead of terms like interconnection or interaction because they presume the existence of separate entities. Material storytelling denotes the central role of materiality as well as discourse in constructing organizational life. More specifically, material storytelling denotes "… the iterative (re)materialization of the relations of production; and the agential possibilities and responsibilities for reconfiguring the material relations of the world" (Barad, 2007, p. 224).

In this chapter, we also draw on Benjamin's (1999) and Derrida's (2004) works on storytelling and story as something very different from narrative. We twist it into material storytelling by combining it with Karen Barad's work on agential realism. Barad elaborates on Bohr's work on apparatuses into a conception of practice as material-discursive, where apparatuses are seen as active constituents of the world. They are part of the intra-activity of the world, are open-ended practices and are material configurations and (re) configurings of the world, and they produce and reconfigure spatiality and temporality (Barad, 2007, p. 146).

Our thesis is that resituating the relationship between language and materiality opens new spaces for marginalized other(s) voices, and creates a different kind of awareness of how power relations work in the workplace; hence providing us with a different awareness of how to work with organizational change. We frame the chapter as a story of material storytelling of a change project in a bank, which we simply refer to as The Bank in the chapter. We experiment with the writing style by going back and forth between two different layers of text. The first layer tells the stories of material storytelling from The Bank, while the other draws out the theoretical/methodological implications of this approach. We hope that what we mean by 'material storytelling' and possible implications for managing technology become clearer and clearer as the stories unfold.

Thus, the first layer tells material stories from The Bank. The second layer includes intersections of breathing spaces that answer the following questions: (1) what does a material storyteller do? (2) what are the implications in terms of understanding the relationship between technology and organizations? and (3) what implications can be inferred in relation to the management of technology? The following section introduces the case study.

INTRODUCTION TO THE CASE STUDY

The story of material storytelling is centered around a significant event in The Bank that was a result of a change project which we refer to here as 'the technology project.' This management decision has been analyzed more thoroughly in an earlier work through genealogical analysis by a co-author (Jørgensen, 2007) of this particular chapter. In this chapter, we explore further, and highlight and reconfigure those aspects of the case study that have the most immediate relevance for the study of the relations between technology, work and management.

We enter into the stories in November 1997, which is when the decision is made as a result of a change project that had the following characteristics:

1. The change project was initiated in the context of the implementation of a new basic IT-system in The Bank. The development and maintenance of such systems had historically been organized with an external IT-supplier and it is also this supplier that develops the new system. Parallel to the development of the new system, a set of recommendations for the future organization of bank work is also prepared.

2. The change project aims at rationalizing work routines in The Bank's local departments. These rationalizations include sales and administration of financial services like loans, deposits, pension, real estate, and so on. They also include sales and administration of financial services to business companies such as cash flow, payment service, business loans, and others.

3. The change project introduces a new functional division of labor in that the technology project divides work into three new functions and categories: consultant, back-office, and service.

4. The change project also implies a new geographical division of labor. Linked to the idea of a new functional triadic division of labor is the idea that back-office tasks are to be centralized in some of the big departments. Thus, documents are increasingly to be sent back and forth between departments.

This represents quite a substantive set of organizational changes. We focus on the decision to implement this new functional and geographical division of labor. At the outset, the decision is surprising as it runs counter to the recommended division of labor proposed by the external IT-supplier. This organization argues that work processes are considerably facilitated for loan case processing and authorization since registration agreements and customer information are noted and entered only once and then recycled for documents, credit recommendations etc. For that reason the IT-supplier argues against a sharp division of labor since this is not considered efficient because of the requirement of very precise information in the communication between consultants and back-office workers.

The IT-supplier recommends an organization of work consistent with how work was organized prior to the technology project since the system, in their opinion, will facilitate extant case procedures; therefore, it speaks against the new functional and geographical division of labor. Instead The Bank, in its November 1997 decision, decides on the reverse of what is recommended. This decision is, however, carefully planned and is focused explicitly on the technologies of bank work. The story shows how relations of power were embedded in the old bank-work technologies, which implied a serious conflict among The Bank's strategic storytelling, and the material storytelling of traditional bank work. Further, the story shows that it was through an explicit focus on technology that a more balanced and harmonious relationship between language and matter was eventually accomplished.

We thus highlight the role of intra-active material storytelling in relation to working life in organizations; a material storytelling that at one stage impeded organizational and professional development in The Bank but on the other hand also governed the possibilities and responsibilities for (re)configuring work in this bank.

WHAT DOES A MATERIAL STORYTELLER DO?

In this first breathing space, we will attempt to answer the question of what a material storyteller does. We do this through examples that come from the material that was collected during the case study. Through this section, we gradually make the transformation from storytelling to material storytelling.

The first example is from an interview with an employee in The Bank's internal IT-department. The specific role that the department played in The Bank was to tailor IT-systems to The Bank's market. Given this specific role, the collaboration with the external IT-supplier was crucial for their performance in The Bank.

Interviewer: How is the relationship with the IT-Company?

Interviewee: This a major issue. It is clearly an important cooperative partner for us... (but)... this cooperation is replete with problems. You may have to talk to some of the politicians about this. In my view, the problems are that the IT-Company - the union we have - designs standard solutions, which fit the average bank. Then there are some banks that require greater functionality because they are bigger. They have more products. During the times that I can remember, we tried to reach an agreement that the IT-Company designs the basic part. In return they work with an open structure, which allows us - by means of different tools, for example our data-warehouse tools - to ensure that the latter become an integrated part of the basic system. I don't know what goes wrong. Maybe I do know - now you tape it and that doesn't matter. In reality, it is probably about political power. Can you stay in business longer if you use the IT-Company? Can you get agreement that the IT-Company provides standard solutions all the way through? Maybe the smaller and medium sized companies can see an advantage here ... I don't know. But politically the IT-Company has had an advantage in maintaining total control of all IT. I think we can feel that in our daily work. We are being harassed ... and it is daily stuff. Suddenly we are cut off from using these tools and these development facilities ... So, politically we need an agenda that states that the IT-Company designs standard systems and works, in return, with an open interface where we can work with the tai-

lored part. Sometimes this is more characteristic of politics than it is of cooperation.

Walter Benjamin (1999, p. 86) has argued that an orientation towards practical interests is characteristic of many born storytellers. Storytelling, in other words, finds its source of inspiration in the practices of everyday life. We are, in other words, interested in the seemingly lowly, pitiful, dull and grey everyday life. In this way, we link people's stories to what they do. Story is a performance and it has both substance in the form of actions and materialization and significance in the sense that what they do is enmeshed with meaning. In this case, his story is linked to his everyday performance using tools, development facilities, and the practical circumstances of coordination and collaboration with the external IT-company, and all the complexities that follow.

This is living storytelling at work (e.g. Jørgensen & Boje, 2010), and we just have to learn to see the 'life' in it. Great storytelling is always rooted in the people and the practical interests of the people, primarily in a milieu of craftsmen as noted by Benjamin (1999, p. 100); in this case, craftsmen such as IT-professionals and bankers. Derrida (2004, p. 82) argues that a story has no borderlines; it is at once larger and smaller than itself. It is entangled in a play with other stories, is part of the other, makes the other part of itself etc. and it remains utterly different from its homonym, narrative. We believe that this is exactly what is described in the small story noted above. It does not last for more than a minute; yet what the interviewee addresses is extremely complex.

He tells a story of his experiences with the external IT-company and he tells it as entangled in a play with other stories. "His" practice is not his own alone; it emerges through a complex intra-play of many different stories. There are multiple stories simultaneously present in the story: there is the story of the external IT-company; the story of the raison d'être of the external IT-company—for instance, "…the union, we have—designs standard

solutions, which fits the average bank"; and there are stories of bigger banks versus smaller ones. There are many stories and many people.

There are the "politicians," who are the managers in The Bank; and the researcher asking questions that are interesting in relation to research and who, in a sense, guides the story. In addition, "the tape-recorder," which represents a threat yet becomes an active participant in the telling. We meet the story of the internal IT-department that is supposed to tailor IT to The Bank's local needs. One cannot forget his professional background, and the professional values that he brings with him, and which emerge as frustrated descriptions of what dominates his work in The Bank.

It follows that we can deduce some important points about stories and storytelling from this one simple fragment of less than sixty seconds in time. First of all, storytelling draws its inspiration from the practical matters of the world as noted above. Second, storytelling has great sensitivity towards the multiple voices that are present in any social situation. Being is not a sealed-off entity; conversely, being emerges through the 'intra-action' and 'entanglement' of multiple living stories. From these points, we can deduce the third. The storyteller is not interested in reducing these stories to a narrative or an essence because this would violate the principle of multiplicity.

As noted by Benjamin, a storyteller does "… not aim to convey the pure essence of the thing, like information or a report" (Benjamin, 1999, p. 91). Storytelling is unlike modernity's mode of communication which, according to Benjamin, was characterized by information and which made Benjamin foresee the end of storytelling (1999, p. 83); he further argued that in modernity, "… no event any longer comes to us without being shot through with explanation" and that "... half the art of storytelling is to keep a story free from explanation as one reproduces it" (1999, p. 89).

It now follows, and becomes somewhat clearer, that a storyteller is not interested in deducing the plot from such a transcript or wringing out the essence of the text to use Derrida's phrase (2004, p. 72). Nothing could be less interesting. Rather, the storyteller is much more interested in contextualizing the transcript. This implies giving such a transcript, for example, a before and after, locating it in a particular space, and describing what matters and why it matters, but without wringing out an essence or describing the linear cause-effect logic between events; because that would imply that the story would become lifeless and petrified, which it isn't.

A storyteller tries to clarify the socio-political circumstances in which the story was produced and thereby try to gain an understanding—but not explanation—of why the story was framed like this in the first place. This is the fourth characteristic of storytelling. It is interested in mapping out the political circumstances in which the story was produced instead of figuring out the linear logic in it. It follows that a storyteller recognizes what Derrida has referred to as the violence of the text (2002, p. 296), and thus that a story represents and reproduces hegemonic relationships. In this case, the story is told from a particular position in The Bank and with particular intentions in mind, and these conditions frame how other people, groups, and institutions are positioned in the telling.

To be as concise as possible, stories are produced in complex political circumstances where a multiplicity of voices is present. The storyteller takes an interest in clarifying these circumstances in seeking why the text was framed like this in the first place. She is not looking for any essential truth. In research terms, this means relating story fragments to other story fragments in order to piece the puzzle together and gain a deeper and deeper understanding of the complexities and entanglements involved. The fragment from before could for instance be related to a story like the one below, which is a fragment from an interview with a sales consultant from one of The Bank's local departments.

Interviewer: Why are there so many documents?

Interviewee: I don't know... That's because our system is so bad. Now I mentioned car loans before OK. Technically, it is like that I have to go into one system to enter a loan. I have to enter the persons' social security number. Afterwards the customer pops us, provided that he is in there (in the system) in advance. OK. Then I enter all the information – that is everything that will happen with this loan. There will be security and things like that. Then I have to write a security?? Then I need to enter his name again. Then I have to write a declaration of pledge. Once more I need to enter his name. Then I have to make the property mortgage deed on this car. And believe me I need to enter his name again. And on the three documents that I mentioned before, I need to enter the type of car. At the end I need to go into our security registration system and enter the same car and the same information that was just entered three times already. That's when I think the system is so bad. It should be like ... when I have entered the man, he is in there - he appears on all five documents. When I have entered the car, it will be on all four documents where it is needed. That's really heavy today. But I think that probably none of the documents can be spared. They go to different institutions within The Bank - right. But it is sick to enter the same data in so many different places ... and to have to spend an hour ... instead of entering it once, then I push a button - then of course it takes some time to print it. That's what it is. Then you at least ... then it doesn't matter that you are disrupted. Then the data are in there. I think that's the biggest problem.

Interestingly, she is talking here about some of the consequences of the IT-division of labor in The Bank. She does so from a different perspective, which involves her professional voice (the inherent sarcasm and frustration in her description), the voices of the whole legal apparatus around bank work, the voices of different institutions within The Bank etc. In this sense, these different institutions and organizations talk through all the documents and the paperwork involved in bank business and the important role of IT in handling all these documents. Note for instance that the question was about documents; she answers as if the question concerned the system. The point is that the paperwork and IT were, and continue to be, closely entangled.

We can now infer two more implications from this. First, by carefully arranging and rearranging different story fragments in relation to each other, we gain a thicker (Geertz, 1973) and more comprehensive understanding of what is at stake in bank work, what the different voices are, and why people talk and act the way they talk and act. These are stories that emerge from the practicalities of bank work. In other words, stories are seen as embedded in concrete spatial and material circumstances that give the stories material substance; and the now, hopefully for the reader, unavoidable observation that material conditions themselves are implicated in storytelling.

This is the second implication, which takes the point of materiality even further, and where we may now begin to elaborate on the notion of material storytelling. The point is not only that different voices materialize themselves in paperwork, IT, and systems. The point is that materiality has agency in constituting bank work and in constituting the 'good bank worker.' Barad notes that matter matters and she resituates the hegemonic relationship of language over matter that she claims has dominated science studies since the linguistic turn (Barad, 2007, pp. 132-133). She argues that matter should not be subordinated to language but rather, that we need to create a more balanced understanding of practice as being material-discursive instead of being mainly discursive.

Barad's work is thus important because it twists our notion of story towards a material-discursive onto-epistemology where a more balanced understanding is achieved of what constitutes story. Story should be viewed as a multimodal configuration of the world, which emerges from

diffractive interferences of different material, natural, linguistic, or bodily forces that combine in a mutual constituent relationship whereby the world and its boundaries are enacted through what Barad terms 'agential cuts.' Through these agential cuts the world is configured in spatial, temporal and material terms. These agential cuts emerge themselves from complex intra-actions of spatial, temporal, and material forces. Due to these intimate entangled mutual constitutive relationships she prefers to use the term 'spacetimemater' instead of space, time, and matter.

In other words, the entangled state of the figuration of bodies and the configurations of artifacts and spaces "tell" stories in organizations and play significant roles in organizational performance. Consequences are dramatic since terms such as intentionality, identity, memory etc. are reconsidered as phenomena that do not belong to individuals; neither are these phenomena solely discursive constructs. Karen Barad notes that when we attend to the complex material conditions that are needed to specify intentions, we are prevented from assuming that intentions are pre-existing states of mind, and that they can be meaningfully assigned to individuals. Instead, intentions are attributable to a complex network of human and non-human agents.

Stories emerge not only from discourse but also from the material conditions. To understand what configures stories, we need to address Barad's notion of mattering. Matter is not a fixed substance, rather "… matter is substance in its intra-active becoming—not a thing but a doing, a congealing of agency. Matter is a stabilizing and destabilizing process of iterative intra-activity" (Barad, 2007, p. 151). It follows from the notion of intra-activity that matter is not a fixed property of independently existing objects; rather, "… matter refers to phenomena in their ongoing materialization" (Barad, 2007, p. 151).

Consequently, matter is a discursive production in the important sense that discursive practices are themselves material reconfigurations of the world

(Barad, 2007, p. 151). Discursive practices are thus themselves fully implicated in the dynamics of intra-activity through which phenomena come to matter, and therefore mattering "… is a dynamic articulation/configuration of the world (Barad, 2007, p. 151). Materiality and discourse are mutually implicated in the dynamics of intra-activity. Materiality is discursive since material phenomena are inseparable from apparatuses of bodily production and discursive practices are always already material; materiality and discourse do not stand in a relationship of exteriority to each other (Barad, 2007, pp. 151-152).

Applied to technology, this means that technology is not a social construction. It needs to be reconsidered from a material-discursive point of view and to be understood as specific, dynamic, contingent and iterative material storytelling whereby space, time and matter are dynamically and contingently (re)configured. Material objects and spaces have agency and co-govern talk and action in the same vein as discourse. With respect to the case study described in this chapter, relations of power are also embedded in systems, techniques, IT, case procedures, documents, spaces, all of which play an active role in constituting organizational performances.

The dull, lowly, and grey everyday routines and materiality that are part of everyday life in The Bank plays a very active role. Humans do not control technology. We might as well say that people are being controlled by technology. Instead of granting too much power to human agents, power is relocated to the seemingly insignificant, petty and lowly everyday routines, techniques and material artifacts that are implicit in what we do in everyday life but none-the-less govern the agential possibilities and responsibilities for configuring this world, or our world, or The Bank's world.

To provide a further illustrative example, we can address another story fragment from The Bank. More precisely, we are speaking of a memo called "Memo 15," which described the results of an organizational analysis in some of The Bank's local departments, which had been selected as test departments in a major organizational change program.

Hurdles for Using Time More Efficiently

Heavy Administration (especially in business)

- Internal papers, reports, for example - security cards, ordinary cards, engagement cards, customer data cards, main cards, observation and appropriation lists, account analysis.
- Internal procedures, for example - in relation to credit authority (linked to bank workers, not customers), credit authorizing afterwards (same as credit authority), losses/provisions (differences between individual criteria and annual budget criteria), treatment of crisis engagements, too many levels in the decision making process, sales (are given low priority in relation to solving internal tasks).
- Too many meetings about questions, which have been solved.
- Bad indoor climate (business)
- Lack of data discipline (private) Lack of planning and follow-up
- Lack of top management-information to the local departments and too many uncoordinated initiatives/campaigns "from the top" that are not followed up. Initiation of campaigns before the material is present, sudden solutions, top management reaction too slow on local problems, need for annual planning, unclear boundaries on the responsibilities of higher management levels.
- No/inadequate individual job-descriptions
- No clear boundaries of own tasks/responsibilities/decision authority, no clear management priority of tasks, no recognition

of efforts; nobody is responsible for the archive.

- Inadequate IT-education, 'heavy' technique.
- The techniques are too slow, without integration and with too many different user-guides."

What we can observe described here are very concrete material substances in the form of a heavy bureaucratic system. Does it remind us of something? We think it does, and it was actually a very significant piece of text in the analysis. It underlines the importance of materiality in storytelling. More specifically, it has similarities to the heavy system described by the sales consultant and the problematic relationship between the external IT-supplier and the The Bank's internal IT-department.

A small piece of information underlines the point of the power of materiality in organizational life. Memo 15 was produced in August 1994. The two interviews, from which we saw samples above, were conducted in March 1998. We will return to the case study in the next section, which is the first layer of material storytelling. For now, we summarize the answers to the question: What does a material storyteller do? Thus far, we have deduced the following six characteristics.

- A material storyteller is concerned with the concrete practicalities of life.
- She assumes that organizational life evolves through material-discursive intra-action. A material storyteller assumes that a story emerges through iterative material-discursive intra-activity. Technology is understood as specific, dynamic, contingent, and iterative material storytelling whereby space, time, and matter (spacetimematter) are dynamically and contingently (re)configured.
- She assumes that these material stories are plural. In any given story performance a

plurality of voices always speak; that is, of entangled material-discursive stories that come together in the story.

- She assumes that material stories are non-linear, unfinished, and open. Material stories do not follow a logical path. They are dynamic, contingent, and iterative reconfigurations of spacetimematter.
- She assumes that material stories privilege particular voices instead of others. Relations of power are always embedded in dynamic, contingent (re)materialization of organizational life and from where particular truths and moralities are framed instead of others and thus give privilege to particular voices instead of others.
- She never seeks to wring out the essence of a story; she is interested in understanding why the story was framed like this in the first place. She tries to gain an understanding by mapping the political circumstances in which the story was framed.

Now that the substance of this chapter has, hopefully, become somewhat clearer, we enter into another layer of material storytelling from The Bank.

MATERIAL STORYTELLING: THE STORY OF THE VALUE PROJECT

We now return to The Bank, and the events that lead to the production of the central document, Memo 15, mentioned above. It was produced as part of a change project that lasted for two years, and which we call the value project. It looks, at first glance, like a seemingly boring document telling a story of little interest. Where is all the nice talk about visions, values, identity, culture, and learning that dominates much of humanistic management?

This is perhaps how mainstream management would judge it, because it is incapable of seeing the stories in documents like these. We find it interesting here because it somehow describes how powerful the lowly, insignificant routines and procedures are in constituting work. In this case, it describes some technological hurdles or constraints for change in The Bank, and in fact was produced as a result of a hurdle race seminar—an organizational analysis with the aim of removing hurdles for change

In this way, it provided a counter story to the wonderful stories that had come to dominate in The Bank's headquarters in the early nineties, and which was manifest in the language of the value project. The value project was an example of an unbalanced way of thinking, where language was considered to be superior to matter. In fact, matter in the form of IT, programs, and systems was considered to be "neutral in regard to the organization," and "... independent of competition" as noted by some of the interviewees. The key point that we wish to emphasize here is that they were not granted, nor ever recognized as having, any important kind of agency.

When the value project emerges in 1993, it subsequently becomes a kind of storytelling, which had a focus on new concepts and new values but granting very little, if any, agency to the materiality of bank work. It begins in the headquarters in a staff function concerned with organizational development. The language of the value project is symbolic of the strategy of value management, which is the established top management language at this point in time. In a statement, it is noted that The Bank has the right values but these values have not yet had the appropriate effect on employees' actions. By the spring of 1993, the project had gathered support among the top managers in The Bank. We can introduce one more actor, who is important in this process – an external consultant, who along with an internal project secretary, become the central actors in organizing and managing the value project.

The main ideas of the project are presented at a seminar in May 1993 and contain a differentia-tion of customers, who are storied as belonging to three different groups, 1st, 2nd, and 3rd division customers. Subsequently, the intention is to differentiate products and services according to these three groups. It implies that the 1st and 2nd division customers are storied as The Bank's core customers. For these goals to come true a series of new types of agreements and information systems are needed to support the values of a more sales-oriented organization. Further, there are thoughts of changing personnel policy towards job development and decentralization of competence and some decision making to the employees.

During 1993, the value project had been marketed and sold in the headquarters. Apparently, this is legitimate storytelling. Consensus exists at this point in the headquarters and nobody has contradicted it. The project is formally approved in October 1993. New concepts have entered The Bank at this point. One is the 'value contract,' which is introduced by the external consultant. This contract is an agreement between an employee and a manager so that the employee can take over certain assignments based on such contracts. A 'value agreement' is an agreement between The Bank and its customers, which helps clarify if the customers have the same values as The Bank. Engagements with customers, who are storied as not having the same values as The Bank and deemed have the status as 3rd division customers, are to be liquidated or removed as gently as possible. The Bank will attempt to develop some other 3rd division customers to 1st or 2nd division customers. Yet another concept is called 'life-long economic security' which is to guarantee credit worthiness and economic security for The Bank's best customers.

We can observe at this point that the value project uses fancy and abstract language, which is far away from the actual materialization of the project, which is the differentiation of customers into three different groups. In the project work, subgroups are also taught to use scientific principles such as reliability, validity, and relevance.

It is a new language, a form of storytelling, which we note once again, seems far away from the materiality of bank work. Therefore, the project's legitimacy is only superficial and it never becomes really anchored in The Bank.

The value project enters into some of its decisive phases in July-August 1994 where the new sales products, services, organizational concepts, and IT-systems have been developed. These were to be tested in some of the local departments in the period from November 1994 to May 1995. The project is beginning to become deadly serious for The Bank. The context, however, changes for the project just before the test begins.

The Bank's managing director resigns in 1994. At this point the top management structure changes and two different camps with different ideas of running a bank become much more visible. The top management responsibilities are divided between two executives in The Bank. One is generally in favor of the strategies of value management; the other is described as a more traditional bank manager. Secondly, it is decided to establish a group to provide an independent evaluation of the project. This means that two groups will evaluate the project after the test of the products and tools. The first group consists of the steering committee of the project. The second is Group 2, which consists of two members, who have high positions in headquarters and are managers in two of the staff functions.

It is within these socio-political conditions that the hurdle race seminar is conducted in July and August 1994. Between the lines, one notes a clash of different voices speaking through memo 15. We may imagine how the project is perceived at the test departments. While people are struggling with daily problems, and complain about top heavy administration and internal procedures, to slow IT-techniques, etc., some people pop up and begin to tell stories containing value contracts, lifelong economic security, reliability, validity and relevance and speak of new scoring systems, and

new techniques, so that they can better clarify the values of the customers; a cacophony of voices.

The impact, unsurprisingly, is not positive as this interview excerpt with one of the top managers of the bank reveals.

Interviewer: If you go in and read the report, then it sounds like the first years it runs nice and quietly. It runs like an internal project in the headquarters. Then it is going to be implemented or tested, then I don't know, then something happens with the managers in the local departments (the test places) and you know. How did they perceive the project?

Interviewee: Well, they thought it was a completely stupid project, because I can remember one of the headlines. Why do people come to The Bank, because when they come to The Bank and when they go out again, we should have made some money - otherwise, there is no purpose of having a bank. If the customers cost us money, every time they come in here, then of course it doesn't work. We began to talk about lifetime guarantees and different things right - value contracts - and we spoke of a value agreement, and it's a way of thinking which is somewhat different from the traditional credit thinking, which dominates this organization, and what happens is simply that the people, who are involved in this project, they are mentally two-three steps ahead and ehh ... they tend to be perceived as a little bit self-righteous compared to the ordinary bank people, who say that we are going to lose a lot of money. Why are we going to give people guarantees for the next 20 years, when we can't even keep it up in two? So the mental distance on what is this really all about, we had a lot of trouble with that ... (Interview with a manager from headquarters).

In the autumn of 1994, the project disintegrates. It occurs because of a clash of strategic storytelling and the opposing agencies materialized in procedures, paperwork, systems, and information technology. This is like two different worlds, where the very abstract words of the value project clashes with very concrete practices in the test departments. This is not because the people in the test departments resist change. It is rather that the value project overlooks material agencies and bypasses the real problems instead of offering an answer to them.

On a meeting in August 1995, the project is stopped, closed down, buried, terminated. The background to this decision stems from two opposing recommendations. The steering committee recommends full implementation; conversely, the independent group argues strongly for a termination of the project. The final decision is to terminate the project. This is the end of value management in The Bank. It is followed by a different composition of the top management group, a new strategy, and a new change project called 'the technology project.'

TECHNOLOGY AND ORGANIZATIONS

Matter matters. This is the central point of material storytelling. The intra-play of materiality and discourse, as argued above, was a central problem throughout the history of the value project, where we witnessed a struggle of abstract language against concrete bank practices. When technology is conceptualized as intra-active material storytelling, we emphasize the agencies of the different voices and conditions of spaces, systems, procedures, governance structures, and information technologies. In The Bank, these agencies maintained an old bookkeeping culture in spite of a general recognition among its human agents of the necessity of creating a more sales-oriented culture.

What was very clear from the value project was that the people who designed it misunderstood the material storytelling taking place in The Bank's local departments and thereby the apparatus (dis-

cussed below) linked to the complexity of doing bank work and its concrete materialization in routines, procedures, career ladders, techniques, systems, and information technologies. These are the fundamentals of bank work. If these apparatuses do not work, banking itself does not work.

The power of these material-discursive practices is visible from the fact that the interviews that described the heavy system and the problematic organization of IT in The Bank were conducted in 1998. However, in 1994, we found descriptions that had remarkable similarities to what the interviewees said four years later. In our view, this conveys both the power of technology in constituting bank work and the power of matter in technology in constituting, in this case, bank work, or banking as broadly defined.

Bank work was here conveyed as a complex, entangled, intra-active network of material-discursive practices that framed living storytelling; for example, the alienation of IT-workers and sales consultants, which was very difficult to overcome. Technology, according to material storytelling, is not separated into separate entities like knowledge, skills, systems, and techniques. Technology is an intra-active entanglement of materiality and discourse, where technology becomes equal to the notion of apparatus; a concept that Barad elaborates from Bohr's notion of apparatus.

According to Barad, apparatuses are particular physical arrangements and conditions than enable and constrain knowledge practices (Barad, 2007, p. 147). Barad argues that this account is different from Foucault's notion of discursive practice, which she describes as the local socio-historical material conditions that enable and constrain disciplinary knowledge practices (Barad, 2007, p. 147). Materiality is important for Foucault, but according to Barad, it remains subordinate to discourse, which is considered to enable and constrain materialization and not the other way around.

As an alternative to Foucault's understanding, Barad describes apparatuses as particular material-discursive practices. They do not simply embody human concepts and take measurements but are active constituents of the world. Apparatuses produce differences that matter. They are not neutral instruments or techniques in the hands of speaking actors—they are boundary-making practices that are formative of both matter and meaning, productive of, and part of, the phenomena produced.

Further, apparatuses are of the world. They are material configurations/dynamic reconfigurations of the world and they are dynamically reconstituted as part of the ongoing intra-activity of the world. Apparatuses are open-ended practices that are active constituents of the world; they also participate in reconfiguring temporality and spatiality. Subsequently stories emerge from the material-discursive conditions where some stories become more possible and likely than others.

In the apparatuses of bank work encountered in this case study, book-keeping and administrative skills were central. They had been installed through a complex mixture of disciplinary procedures and traditions, and through the materialization of strategic decisions concerning the organization of information technology in The Bank. These disciplinary practices included:

- **Education and Training**: Traditionally education was initiated through a trainee position, where the employees were hired when they were very young. The education was a combination of theoretical training and practical training on a wide variety of the basic procedures related to bookkeeping and administration.
- **Career**: The hierarchy in The Bank was created as a career ladder. Employees started at the bottom of the system as trainees, and worked themselves up. All managers in headquarters had been brought up and socialized in this traditional manner.
- **The Institutional Set-Up**: Law related to car loans, real estate loans, the tax law, financial regulation, etc.

- **Control**: The structure in the local departments, which traditionally were very hierarchical.
- **Division of Labor**: Before the technology project, The Bank was organized around a principle of totality, which meant that an employee was responsible for all procedures in a case.

To these forces, we need to add the technologies in which these different voices were materialized: the basic information technology systems and thus the relationship between The Bank and the external IT-supplier. In The Bank, a story existed that competitiveness was independent of IT. But employees in The Bank found themselves surrounded by computers. At that point in time, it had already become impossible to carry out any routine procedure without the interference or involvement of some IT-system.

All procedures in regard to basic bank case processing were IT-based. These included payments, accounts, interest rate deductions, foreign transactions, deposits, conversion of foreign currency, registration of securities, ATMs, etc. At this stage, we remind the reader of the descriptions from the interviews concerning paperwork and IT-systems and we remind you about memo 15 from the value project. Other significant stories from these interviews and memo 15 relate to the problematic division of labor between the external IT-supplier and The Bank's local IT-department.

The external IT-supplier designed and controlled the systems that were used to run basic bank business while the local IT-department designed and tailored systems to The Bank's own market. The stories revealed how important the relationship was in relation to the constitution of bank work, where we observed a tension between sales orientation and the old book keeping culture in the very design of the IT-systems as noted by this former employee in the local IT-department.

Interviewee: The border was always bookkeeping because our IT-supplier ... they don't take anything in that they haven't made themselves. You are not allowed to make a system that communicates the other way, so we have always lived in two worlds, and it has always been a world where technology development was controlled by the IT-supplier, because the hardware, which is there, it must be used to run the basic business and everything else has to adapt to it, and the limitations that ensue.

The voice of the external IT-supplier was always present in the value project through its materialization in IT-systems, and through its co-constitution of bank work. The material storytelling that took place in the local departments thus became a problem for the strategic storytelling that dominated The Bank's headquarters at this point in time. We may draw some implications in regard to understanding organizations, and the role of technology within them. Organization and technology are not two different entities but are mutually constitutive.

Arendt contends that the ability to speak a language is what makes an actor an actor. It is through the spoken word that the actor identifies what he does, has done and intends to do (Arendt, 1998, pp. 178-179). What we learn from this case, however, is that language should not be granted too much power. This has been the problem in most social science theory since the linguistic turn (Barad, 2007, p. 132).

Further, Arendt proposes that language is multiple and that meaning is co-constructed through storytelling and that this storytelling is always concerned with the matters of the world. She however maintains the term interaction and thus the idea of separate entities where language is dominant over matter. This is where material storytelling significantly differs; it is inspired by Barad's term intra-action, which implies the entanglement of both language and matter, and where the relationship of the discursive and the

material is resituated and democratized such that both are presumed to have agency.

There is little doubt that matter had a dominant role in the case story of The Bank presented here. Technology as intra-active material storytelling implies a democratization of material and human voices where materiality is granted a far more powerful voice in understanding actions. Techniques, systems, skills, procedures, and spaces do not participate as neutral servants of language and actors in configuring organizational actions. They are much more active constituents of reality in the sense that they co-create The Bank's world.

Technology may now be viewed as a complex intertwining and entanglement of different forces where the material and the discursive, the subject and the object, the I and the other, are relationally and mutually constituted. Technologies shape bank work; and bank work, or banking, shape technologies. Apparatuses shape actors, beliefs, strategies and stories; and vice versa. It follows that it does not make sense to speak of separate entities or dualisms such as those noted above. Human action now needs to be understood as the intra-action of the material and discursive—a term that signals the intimate relationship of matter and discourse.

In this connection, it is perhaps not surprising that it is a new basic system, which triggers the next major change project in The Bank, namely a project, which we call 'the technology project.'

MATERIAL STORYTELLING: THE TECHNOLOGY PROJECT

We may now address an example of change management where materiality was taken seriously, namely 'the technology project' in The Bank. It is communicated as a simple rationalization project in preparing for the implementation of a new basic system; but, as will see, it seems to be much more than that. At this point The Bank's organization threatens to fall apart. Confidence between headquarters and the local departments is low. In the headquarters alone, a lot of people have witnessed how two years of work has been wasted. The account numbers are discouraging with great deficits. Essentially, this is a bank in serious crisis.

A new management group is constituted in this situation. An IT-department is established and The Bank hires an IT-manager. This signals a stronger focus on IT. In addition, the new management group is just waiting for a proper occasion—and it has been under way for some time; at a relatively early stage before 1995, the IT-supplier had worked on developing a new basic system. As the year 2000 comes closer, this need becomes even more pressing, because the old basic system is deemed unsafe from Y2K problems. The Bank expects a new basic system and it triggers a debate about how this new system will affect work.

These debates become the occasion for initiating yet another organizational change project, the technology project. It is formulated towards the end of 1996. The goal is to rationalize work processes by 5-10% and to prepare the organization for the new basic system. These rationalizations also include employee dismissals. After the experiences with the value project, the top management group has considered things very carefully. The result is a gray, boring and Taylorist project. It seems to be without any grain of vision at all; its rhetoric is not designed to make headlines, unlike the aesthetic tones of previous more abstract projects.

This project is different and has the characteristics of taking into account the practical and concrete materiality and circumstances of work. There are no fancy words, no large symbols, and no big promises in the technology project. The contrast from the storytelling of the value project is almost complete. It is material storytelling that drives the project forward in the sense that it is technology itself that has pushed forward some very detailed and concrete considerations about The Bank's routine procedures. The technology

project is totally different from the value project. While the latter was abstract and dominated by words and without little recognition of material agency, the technology project is very concrete—almost to the extreme—and focused on small routine procedures and activities that are unquestionably at the heart of bank work.

The long-term goal remains the same, namely to create a more sales-oriented organization. But instead of focusing on values, the technology project focuses directly on technology—how to do bank work—and in which the material conditions play a decisive part. Even if it sounds simple, it is a major turnaround from previous efforts because its purpose is to break up a very strong material-discursive power that is communicated in IT-systems, the work procedures, the career patterns, and the education and training of the employees. It is radical.

The technology project focuses on rationalizing the administrative procedures and takes its point of departure in the work of the sales consultants in the local departments. Sample criteria include as little paperwork as possible, pre- and self-control to the highest possible extent, reduction of delivery time and administration, as few organizational levels as possible, avoidance of double entry, and a maximum of electronic control.

In this way, it is very concrete and down-to-earth. In June 1997, the project's main proposals are discussed at a seminar where it begins to take a concrete shape and the major decisions of the project are sketched out. Nine points concerning the organization of The Bank are discussed as follows:

- Interfaces between customers and employees, private
- Interfaces between customers and employees, business
- Credit procedures, private
- Credit procedures, business
- Fee, interest rates and products
- Organization private

- Organization business
- Organization/management
- Others.

These issues have been put on the agenda by the new basic system in the sense that these issues are described in the handbook of the new basic system. The handbook has been worked out by a group of people representing the users of the systems; a recognition that IT-systems are very influential in governing work conditions. This is also the case with the most important points in the whole project, which concern the organization of the private and business segments. The three categories consultant, back up, and service employee are defined and discussed in the handbook of the new basic system and they become the main categories of reference in the technology project.

This division of labor is the most controversial as it comprises the heart of the whole organization and influences almost all departments and every employee in the local departments. The term "consultant" is the category, which covers the sales functions, the "back-up" covers the administrative tasks, and the term "service" covers the tasks at the cash desk (payments out of accounts, small loans, small paperwork tasks, etc.).

Materiality is a main concern in the technology project, and the overall emphasis on technology is underlined by the project organization. There are three levels in this organization. The top management group has overall responsibility for the project, and it must approve all decisions. The top management group also participates in the steering committee, which is the main group in the project and where proposals and problems are discussed and negotiated. It consists of 15 people at a top management or middle management level. Both headquarters and the local departments are represented in the steering committee. The third level consists of people participating in the sub-projects. Finally, there is a project group that takes care of all practical matters in running the project.

The project organization highlights the strategic emphasis on creating a broad alliance with most of the most influential management represented. It also underlines the concern for, and focus on, the material conditions in The Bank in the sense that all project participants, at all levels, are deeply immersed in very concrete practical problems. This may be further empirically observed through the establishment of a number of sub-projects, which are run from August to November 1997. These projects are described below. The people mentioned in italics are the project owners, who are responsible for the subproject.

Projects

Private

- Future departmental structure: *Top management group*
- Future structure within the strategic areas: *Manager in Innovation*
- Job and function descriptions: *Manager in Personnel*
- Definition of consulting, back-up and expedition tasks: *Manager in Personnel*
- Work organization: *Manager of a local department*
- Credit procedures: *Manager in the credit office*

Business

- Future Departmental Structure: *Top management group*
- Choice of strategic areas and future structure within it: *Vice manager*
- Job and function descriptions: *Manager in Personnel*
- Definition of consulting, back-up and service tasks: *Manager in Personnel*
- Work organization: *Manager of a local department*

- Credit procedures: *Manager in the credit office*

General Issues

- Fee, interest rate, and product-structure in the basic system: *Manager in Marketing*

Note that almost all sub-project owners are members of the steering committee and some are even members of the top management group. This is an important part of the strategy as noted by this manager from The Bank's headquarters.

Interviewee: ...in opposition to this project (The value project), where you took the project out of the organization, and when you were going to implement it, then all of these people could say, who is that and who is that, because you were given an assignment, where you had been told in the Planning Committee and the management group, that in this assignment you had to be successful in Well man. It runs across all of those things here. You were mentally behind, because you hadn't participated in all these processes. Our projects today don't necessarily have a better quality, but more people have been involved in the processes. Then you're also mentally prepared to say that if this situation occurs, then we do like this, because we have discussed it. Up here (in the value project) you're outside these discussions, so you're not mentally prepared to say what we will do, because you haven't been part of these discussions. It gives another kind of mental basis for handling different situations. So the difference is that up here it is the value project and here is the technology project. The difference is that this one (the technology project) is made by the organization in the organization.

The point is that this structure provides the whole process with a form of legitimacy and flexibility in regard to unforeseen events—events that will always occur in the complex intra-relationships of materiality and discourse. The point is not that this leads to agreement and consensus on all points but its opposite. Despite the lack of agreement and consensus, there is still broad support for the project. There is for example a strong counter-argument in regard to the division of labor, which is the most important part of the project. The argument is for a team-based cross functional organization, where a group of people divides the responsibilities among them in relation to consulting tasks, back-up tasks, and service tasks. Consensus is never reached on this important point, but this does not affect the broad support for the overall technology project.

The final decision is made at a management meeting in November 1997. The result is a sharp functional as well as a geographical division of labor. It is a complete separation of people in different categories. The back-ups for example are to be located in a separate room and are not visible to the customers; further, many departments do not have any back-ups but will have their paperwork done elsewhere. It thus requires new job descriptions and a standardization of procedures in regard to handling and coordinating tasks. It also implies a more clear-cut hierarchy among The Bank's employees.

Two things are surprising in relation to this decision. The first is the decision to reintroduce a sharp division of labor, which seems like a return to Taylor's principles. The second surprise is that it is the reverse of what was recommended in the handbook of the basic system, but it makes sense by relating this decision once again to the technology and how it influences and governs organizational action, work, and banking in general. Because one of the top managers argues strongly that it is an element in creating flexibility and changing practices in the local department by separating organizational development from technological development.

Interviewer: No, but I thought a little bit more about the new basic system and the technology project - they are in any case related?

Interviewee: Only from the presumption that when you are going to make something in the basic system, you are going to make an organization, products and everything right, Then you're going to turn over every stone. When we believe that there is a need to make some efficiency improvements, then it's efficient that we go out and turn that stone, then we look at two things at the same time. The basic system did not pull any of this through. The technology project is totally independent of the system.

KMJ: Yes, I am aware of that.

HQ: The basic system was delayed right. Person A tried to convince us that we were going to couple the two projects together because then we could have a greater effect faster. I was happy that it didn't happen, because I was afraid that the project would be delayed, that is, if we felt that our organization was dependent on our technology development, then we would stand still and thereby create a lot of disappointments, because when you initiate such an analysis, then people count on that it becomes something. You can run the new work processes without the new basic system.

He insisted on looking at the technology project and the new basic system separately, and not together, and it was quite strange because he had not even been asked a question about it! He was very determined on keeping the two projects apart because he did not want organizational development to be conditional on technological development. When The Bank, in February 1998, carries through a test of the new division of labor, the goal of this test states explicitly that the results were independent of the basic system. This is yet more evidence that an important goal

is that the division of labor should be able to run independently of the new basic system. In other words, The Bank's information technology is one of the primary drivers of the technology project. The IT-systems once again make their impact in strategic decisions and changes in The Bank, but this time, materiality has been taken seriously. The whole technology project works on the condition that information technology actually speaks and conditions the stories in The Bank.

In other words, The Bank tries to create more space for developing the organization by sharply separating functions. This indicates a possible lack of faith that the new basic system will fulfill the promises made by the IT-supplier. In May 1998, the decision turns out to be very wise, since the new basic system is delayed by one year. The sharp division of labor is then a way of trying to create flexibility and thus breaking through the power relations in the local departments, hence creating the conditions for future changes. These power relations are characterized as intra-active material-discursive practices that constitute the technology of bank work.

With the new division of labor, problems related to the organization of information technology in The Bank are concentrated within one group, namely the people who become administrative workers. The highest-ranking group is the sales consultants. In other words, the new division of labor implies the definition of a more clear-cut hierarchy in the local departments. Even if the people behind technology project try to hide this fact behind a myth that the three categories are equal, it is the strongest, the most experienced, those who are willing to educate themselves, or the young career-minded who become the consultants.

These comprise the key employees. Their positions are strengthened. Among these strong employees, there is also a silent support for the project since they dislike the old system and all its administrative work, and are glad to be rid of such work. The categorization is then carried through without major problems. The back-ups and service employees are of course not pleased with the situation. These are stories from the old administration-people, who have not changed very much for years, those who have not been willing to educate themselves, the inexperienced, those who have been on leave, etc. These are the losers in the game. The big losers are those employees who are left go, who lose their jobs during the rationalization and the implementation of the project.

In reality however, the categorization is an adaptation to an informal hierarchy, which was already there in the first place, but perhaps had its weaknesses because it was informal and not official policy. In regard to the implementation of the new routines for coordinating and carrying through tasks, these also slowly fall in place. It takes a little while longer and there are conflicts in many of the departments but at the beginning of 1999, nine months after implementation had begun, the new division of labor had been carried through.

Other stories then become more likely. From then on, new words and concepts enter The Bank. Words like sales culture and the learning organization begin to pop up. The technology project was in other words only a frontrunner for a series of other changes in The Bank. With the new division of labor, headquarters has gained something they can work with. It has partially unlocked the situation in the local departments and partially liberated key employees from the basic system. But it is also clear that The Bank has defined the group, which will be the center of future activities, namely the sales consultants.

The groups of back-ups and service employees have been placed in a waiting or holding position. Further, the problems with the IT-systems have not been resolved. When the basic system is implemented in 1999, it is an example that The Bank has not yet liberated themselves from the effects of the basic system. In this situation, there are breakdowns, screens that go blank, and serious disruptions of ordinary routines so that pen and paper sometimes have to be reintroduced.

These "child diseases," to use the managing director's expression, last for almost six months. Likewise, the integration problems between the basic system and the internally developed sales oriented systems have not been solved and for that reason alone, The Bank uses a lot of extra resources on bank work.

MANAGING TECHNOLOGY: SOME IMPLICATIONS

What have we learned from these material stories? As noted, we are not looking to wring out the essence of this story. In such a case, we would do violence and create a narrative removed from the realm of everyday speech (e.g. Benjamin, 1999, p. 86). This will not do for a real story, which in Benjamin's words is useful in containing a moral or practical advice. A storyteller is a man, who has counsel for his readers (p. 86) and this also holds for a material storyteller.

Counsel woven into the fabric of real life is wisdom (Benjamin, 1999, p. 86). We hope to have made the case that real life in organization is inevitably shaped as material storytelling; as the intra-action of materiality and discourse. Language is not superior to technology, nor is language superior to matter within technology. Rather, these categories do not exist as separately divided entities. There is a close intimate relationship between them, which means that materiality is inherent in living storytelling. It follows that stories are, in fact, material stories.

As the case study in The Bank, hopefully, illustrates, material storytelling is also complexity storytelling. This is the first practical advice from the case study, which conveyed the complexity of bank work and how materiality governed actions and competence to the extent that it caused the termination of one change program, and one strategy, and also caused changes in the top management group. It is also conveyed by the fact that the changes were underway for almost six years in order to get the basic bank business to run in what was deemed to be an appropriate manner for running a bank.

The first implication for change management is that the complex intra-actions of the material and discursive cannot be ignored in change management. Instead, these intra-actions often have to take center stage. The key point is that managing technology is central to change management. Change management is not a question of playing with language or organizing dialogues but instead a question of multiple, complex, petty and lowly intra-actions that are played out in, govern, and actually constitute the fabric of real organizational life.

This leads to the second implication, namely that the language of change management has to be concerned with the practicalities of work but of course still maintain the broader sense of direction. The concrete advice from the case study would be to stay within the everyday language of the organization when one wishes to change it. This includes being concerned with the lowly dull routines—in fact, those routines that have become so routine that we hardly notice them anymore; that are practically tacit. We think that this is a key challenge in change management. It implies an ability to understand these routines from within but also to see the big picture in the small details.

This presents a formidable task for leaders, consultants, and other change management professionals, who are often separate and distant from the matters they are supposed to change and, therefore, are not part of the everyday material-discursive intra-actions that constitute the organization; hence they are not gifted the legitimacy to change the material-discursive relations from within.

We can draw out some further advice for change management. Firstly, we had the value project, which used abstract words, and which ignored the material substance of bank work. We noticed how the project was not properly anchored in The Bank and we noticed how organizational circumstances slowly got the better of the project. Secondly, we had the technology project where we saw a top management group working with the basic routines of bank work. It was a top managed bottom-up process in the sense of creating the conditions for broad participation; in reality, the top management group was all over the place in the technology project. There were no fancy words, no academic terms, not even simple management concepts. In addition, if there were management concepts these were not communicated but went through a process of translation into everyday practice.

There was no glory and we should not glorify the process either, because many people paid the price for the technology project, and they did it on questionable grounds. Still it worked in the sense that people knew what it was all about and generally could identify their own practices within the new framework.

REFERENCES

Arendt, H. (1998). *The human condition*. Chicago, IL: The University of Chicago Press.

Barad, K. (2007). *Meeting the universe halfway – Quantum physics and the entanglement of matter and meaning*. Durham, NC: Duke University Press.

Benjamin, W. (1999). The storyteller - Reflections on the work of Nikolai Leskov. In Arendt, H. (Ed.), *Illuminations* (pp. 83–107). London, UK: Pimlico.

Boje, D. M. (2008). *Storytelling organizations*. London, UK: Sage.

Derrida, J. (2002). The theater of cruelty and the closure of representation. In Derrida, J. (Ed.), *Writing and difference* (pp. 292–316). London, UK: Routledge. doi:10.1215/00440167-9-3-6

Derrida, J. (2004). Living on. In Bloom, H., Man, D., Derrida, J., Hartman, G., & Miller, J. H. (Eds.), *Deconstruction and criticism* (pp. 62–142). London, UK: Continuum.

Jørgensen, K. M. (2007). *Power without glory – A genealogy of a management decision*. Copenhagen, Denmark: CBS Press.

Jørgensen, K. M., & Boje, D. M. (2010). Resituating narrative and story in business ethics. *Business Ethics: A European Perspective, 19*(3), 251-262.

Strand, A. M. C. (2010). *Material storytelling as identity re-work*. Paper presented at the Sc'Moi Conference. Alexandria VA.

Wolfe, C. (2010). *What is posthumanism*. Minneapolis, MN: University of Minnesota Press.

ENDNOTE

[1] The authors acknowledge valuable comments made by the editors of the book, two anonymous reviewers, and David O'Donnell.

Chapter 12
Excessive Value Creation:
Under the Tyranny of a New Imaginary

David Sköld
Uppsala University, Sweden

Lena Olaison
Copenhagen Business School, Denmark

ABSTRACT

This chapter demonstrates how contemporary imaginary structures, which urge us to move up in life by making the most of the possibilities we are faced with, may operate in an industrial setting where users are involved in the production of heavy duty vehicles. Opening up new domains for value creation, devoid of established norms and regulations, this appeal to elevate ourselves arguably provides little guidance for how to do so. Demanding ever more from those subjected to its call, this appealing power, the chapter suggests, follows the logic of the Lacanian superego, which according to Salecl (2004, p. 51) "commands the subject to enjoy yet at the same time mockingly predicts that he or she will fail in this pursuit of enjoyment." As such, it makes out a central component in a creative force that feeds excessive outgrowths, which perpetually contribute to pervert, displace, and fragment established grounds for value creating activities within this industrial domain.

INTRODUCTION: THE TYRANNY OF THE NEW IMAGINARY

In response to Ivan Karamazov's famous contention, that if the human soul is not immortal and if there are no absolute virtues—if God is indeed dead—then everything is permitted, the French psychoanalyst Jacques Lacan willfully maintains the opposite: "if God doesn't exist, then nothing at all is permitted any longer" (Lacan, 1988, p. 128).

At a first glance, this dictate certainly seems quite counter-intuitive. What Lacan appears to be suggesting here, however, is that in a secularized time, when religious beliefs no longer regulate our conduct and the ways in which we may strive to enjoy ourselves, new socio-symbolic orders are soon established in their place. Often, these orders are far more demanding than religious doctrines ever were, calling for significant degrees of subjection, discipline, and self-sacrifice. In addition, to Lacan, their emergence is to be understood as

DOI: 10.4018/978-1-4666-1836-7.ch012

a consequence of our unwillingness to confront the fact that the freedom granted us in a secular age *is in fact it*—that which we always dreamt of. They stem, to put it somewhat differently, from an inextricable incapacity to truly enjoy the freedom entailed by the withdrawal of God's authority. They stem from a structural inability to revel in all the possibilities laid bare in the absence of an afterlife, and in the absence of specific virtues to which we had better devote ourselves to ever get a taste of the pure pleasures of paradise. It is simply easier on us to establish external orders that block our access to immediate pleasures than to confront our inability to fully embrace what they have to offer. It is easier to let ourselves be stolen of the enjoyment that we are striving for, than to confront its unbearable presence. "Neurotics prove that to us every day," declares Lacan (1988, p. 128), as he draws on his experience from psychoanalytic practice to support the claims concerning self-imposed regulations and prohibitions.

The scope of Lacan's observations reaches far beyond neurotic obsessions and the clinical setting, however. As for instance Renata Salecl (2010; see also Salecl, 2004) has pointed out, they have never been more apposite than in today's neoliberal, free-market capitalism—which is characterized by an abundance of choice and a strong emphasis on self-realization. As kids, we are for instance faced with breakfast cereals often outnumbering the accumulated age of our parents. On our way to becoming full-grown citizens we are—provided that we have the grades—supposedly free to choose the education and the career path of our liking. As dating and mating material, and consumers of various romantic utopias, we are confronted with countless matching services, and innumerable potential partners (Illouz, 1997). As socially responsible grown-up residents we may, on a more mundane note, choose the provider of yet another most basic commodity such as electricity, to name but a minuscule of the everyday choices that determine how we realize ourselves.

Taken together, these many possibilities set the stage for a Lacanian analysis of our era.

In Salecl's (2004) analysis, this stage has, moreover, been draped in a "new imaginary" that has come to reign late capitalist dynamics. Shaped by the socio-symbolic order we are embedded in, this new imaginary is one that urges us to elevate ourselves and move up in life: to choose a breakfast cereal like Alpha-Bits, which not only stills our hunger and provides energy, but also makes us spell-bound; to surpass the social standing of our parents; to find a man or woman more well-heeled, good-looking, intelligent, and charming than we ever thought we deserved; and to find a greener and cheaper energy provider. We are, in short, encouraged to make the most of the choices offered to us; use them so as to better tailor our lives and become better versions of ourselves. As part and parcel of this kind of imaginary, past decades have witnessed an excessive procreation of enticing manuals and how-to handbooks in areas ranging from dating advice to energy savings. Typically, such manuals promote a number of prohibitive rules and principles to which we need to subject in order to elevate ourselves and our way of life; rise above quotidian hardships and everyday struggles, to reach a state of harmony and fulfillment. A most notable example is the best-selling *The Rules Series* from the mid 90s—a catchy, but also very strict and indeed quite oppressive disciplinary program that presents itself as dating and mating advice for women in search of Mr. Right (see, e.g., Salecl, 1998, 2004, 2010; Žižek, 1999).

In our undecided times, Salecl suggests that we have become used to getting a bit of support from symbolic rules of this kind—something to refer to, and hold on to, in place of religious dogmas, for instance. However, she observes a change with respect to how the symbolic universe as of late has come to manifest itself—and with it, the new imaginary. The strategies promoted to attain the promises nurtured by this nexus of symbolic structures and imaginary formations have grown ever more open-ended. In the realms of self-help literature this is reflected by books with impressive covers and titles such as *All About Me*, but with the pages mostly left blank, guided only by simple questions, it is now up to the reader to design the formula for success. Operating in a similar fashion within the realm of dating are arguably sophisticated Web templates, provided by various online dating services. In the current times of self-realization, we are now expected to provide the content ourselves—an attitude which soon reveals itself as one skims through a daily newspaper. For although the dating season is closing in, and we are advised to update our online dating profiles to attract the attention of potential partners, or create one if we have not yet done so, we are not provided with any firm guidelines on how this is best achieved. Rather, "for a profile to attract others and sift out those who would never match, you must dare to stand out and bring out who you really are," because "like your job application you should fill your profile with that which makes you unique." And lest you forget, "be as positive as possible, even if life has been treating you hard" (Sigurdh, 2010, *authors' translation*).

According to Salecl, being yourself is far from an easy task, however (see also Fleming, 2009). In fact, the observations outlined above, and especially the open-endedness of contemporary conditions, set the stage for exploring how the constitution of today's consumer society stands in relation to anxiety, stress and mental disorders. A key insight in this regard, is how we subject ourselves to rules, regulations, and prohibitions to ward off the anxiety that stems from our confrontation with all sorts of possibilities, and the enjoyment that offers itself to us as we are turned into the master's of our own destinies. Such an analysis, which indeed is based on Lacan's thinking, thus ties back to the opening quote by illustrating how the withdrawal of authority stands

in relation to prohibition, and also to misgivings that have come to plague contemporary society.

Certainly acknowledging the problematic nature of these conditions, and the hardships they entail, we wish to emphasize that the kind of imaginary outlined by Salecl by no means is operative only within realms of consumption. Rather, the present analysis attempts to demonstrate that in a post-industrial economy, in which consumers and users are involved in the creation and production of goods, services, and experiences, this kind of imaginary also constitutes a significant creative force. One that perverts, displaces, and fragments established orders and values; perpetually gives rise to new unanticipated knowledge; and grows unmanageable, inconvenient off-shoots that turn the ground for economic value creation topsy-turvy. As such, this force operates in a way that also has significant implications for our understanding of how spearheaded knowledge, and socio-symbolic orders that regulate what is deemed valuable in high-tech realms, come into being. In addition, how such value creating practices, along with the knowledge they generate, ultimately escape our attempts to tame or incorporate them into established socio-economic structures—how they resist being managed, as it were. Let us illustrate this dynamic by means of an example taken from traditional realms of knowledge intensive, high-tech industrial production, namely the automotive industry.

ENTER THE CUSTOMIZING SCENE, WHERE EVERYTHING IS POSSIBLE

Within the heavy duty vehicles industry, symbolic structures that feed the kind of imaginary outlined by Salecl is far from a new phenomenon. In 1982, the Italian truck manufacturer Iveco made an attempt to enter the Swedish transportation market. In order to create a buzz around the company's products, Grandiesel Lastbilar AB—Iveco's Swedish general agent—settles an arrangement with Swedish trucking magazine *Trailer* to join forces and launch a contest together. The rules of the game are simple enough: "The challenge is to design an Iveco 190 Turbo truck, just the way you want it" (Iveco, 1982, p. 33, *authors' translation*).

Explaining in somewhat more detail how to partake in the contest, the guidelines tell potential participants that:

You shall put together a proposal for how the truck is to be painted. You shall also propose how it is to be equipped. Do you want US exhaust pipes and air conditioning? Do you want a loud signal horn and a rooftop spoiler? And crushed polyester plush for the interior? Well, it is up to you to decide. (Iveco, 1982, p. 33, authors' translation)

At your disposal is the magazine's centerfold. Containing the empty contours of an Iveco vehicle, it begs you to design and color the exterior, and fit it with the extra equipment of your choice. In addition, you have to complete two outline drawings of the interior. The first prize is a trip to the manufacturing facility in Turin, and "best of all: the vehicle winning the drawing contest will be materialized" (Iveco, 1982, p. 33, *authors' translation*).

Contributions by young pen artists abound. At a yearly trucking festival arranged partly by *Trailer* a few months after the launch of the contest, numerous designs submitted to the magazine are put on display, and the attendants are encouraged to vote for their personal favorite. A year later, at the same yearly festival, Iveco again steals part of the show by finally living up to its promise. One of the main attractions is a materialized version of Per Berner's composition, named "The Cowboy." Per himself is invited up on stage to receive a check the size of a bathing towel for his "neat clean proposal in good taste with simple but elegant design, few add-ons, and sober decorations" (Sjöberg, 1983, p. 38, *authors' translation*). The check is used to cover expenses for his upcoming trip to Italy.

Spectacles of this kind have also been accompanied by marketing messages encouraging customers to stand out and recognize their individuality by getting their truck a bit more customized than their peers'. Over the years, the Swedish truck manufacturer Scania—blessed with the most dedicated customer following within the industry—has placed great emphasis on the virtue of keeping with the most custom-tailored work tool. For more than forty years, the company has persistently worked with a modular construction and production principle. With plentiful configurations within each modular building block and standardized interfaces between the different modules—between chassis, cabin, engine and transmission, for instance—this principle has offered the customer vast amounts of possible product permutations. Some figures assert that the Scania-customer is faced with more than two million different ways of assembling the basic product that leaves any of the company's industrialized production facilities. Consequently, the marketing material that has been issued by the company since the early 1980s has posited the Scania truck as one giant combinatorial puzzle, and never tired of emphasizing the degree of customization immanent to this construction and production principle (see Sköld, 2010, for a more detailed illustration of this).

On the trucking scene—i.e., among enthusiastic users, in trucking media, at festivals, *et cetera*—keeping with a truly customized product has, however, come to mean something quite different than merely making the most of the many possible permutations pertaining to the basic construction. Ordering any kind of heavy duty vehicle requires quite a bit of involvement by the customer also post the industrialized production process—where the basic construction oftentimes is equipped with a bodywork and all sorts of add-on equipment, adapting the vehicle to its specific transportation task. What defines a truly customized truck—one which is also fitted with innumerable extra features to lend it a distinctive appearance—is that the customer puts in a considerable amount of work in this post production process; cares for every last detail, and perhaps even loses him or herself in all the possibilities opening up throughout this process. Due to all the adjustments required after the industrialized production process, putting together a truly customized vehicle is thus a far more open-ended process than is, buying an ordinary car, for instance.

Does this mean that everything is permitted? Consider the following episode.

It is a late morning in mid-February. Lennart, who runs a waste management firm in Stockholm, has had to check into his local Scania unit to have some hydraulic hoses replaced. It so happens that also another of his drivers has headed the same way. Waiting for the maintenance work to be completed, they linger among the many vehicles that sit around the service halls. One of them is a quite ambitious piece of work, with a lot of add-on equipment, customized paint jobs, extra lights and storage boxes in stainless steel. Both Lennart and his fellow co-worker, Matte, are somewhat familiar with the owner of the vehicle, who according to hearsay is very proud of how the project is progressing. But as the two colleagues inspect the work together, discuss it, and notify one another about the different details, hardly any part of it gets their approval: the steel-coated front bumper lends it the look of an off-road vehicle; the refurbished body work, which just recently has been renovated, suffers a terrible groundwork; and the paint job is sloppy all over. Furthermore, storage boxes are not properly aligned, extra lights are mounted asymmetrically. In addition, lying around the maintenance hall is the sunscreen, adjusted so as to hold a pair of extra headlights. Lennart and Matte laugh and ironise about the work, which has only been initiated at this stage. It doesn't look very promising, so carelessly done, with the openings for the extra headlights having been fashioned *after* the sunscreen was painted.

Although the creation, to a layman, certainly seems ambitious enough with its many lavish decorations, Matte and Lennart appear to consider it a failure of sorts. Few are the details that live up to the unarticulated standards governing this practice. Whilst all is indeed possible here, little does seem to be permitted.

WHERE EVERYTHING IS POSSIBLE, NOTHING IS EVER ENOUGH

The incident at the local Scania unit is played out only a couple of weeks after Lennart has himself placed an order for a new, custom-tailored vehicle to his waste management fleet. Supposedly, the prohibitive logic discerned above also regulates his own customizing efforts, and to a certain extent the workings of this entire movement. Let us take a closer look at this proposed dynamics by further acquainting ourselves with this material practice, and by tracing out a few connections that seem central to how it has spread and developed. At this point, in mid-february, the specifications and the plans for the new creation are certainly the most extravagant yet. The idea is to make it fit for distinguished appearances at various exhibitions, and perhaps even win a trophy in some trucking contest—to move up a notch compared to the last vehicle ordered from his cherished manufacturer. This means paying attention to every last detail, even the quality of the chassis paint. Building from the ground up, is the motto that guides Lennart's efforts—just like it did the pioneering deeds of Sven-Erik "Svempa" Bergendahl in the early 1980s.

Elevating the ambitions in this manner also calls for external design expertise. Therefore, free-lance designer and Svempa's key collaborator for the past 25 years, Jan Richter, has been called in to assist with the rather extensive decorative work required post the industrial production of the cabin and chassis: to redesign the bodywork, fit it with all sorts of paraphernalia, work out suitable color schemes and logotypes, envelop the entire vehicle in a decorative paint job, and transform the interior so as to lend it a fancy finish.

Materializing the opulent plans will, however, prove a strenuous and frustrating experience. Lennart's relation to the once so awe-inspiring Svempa has already been marked by grudge and resentment. During the current project relationships to a number of sub-suppliers will soon develop in similar directions and become difficult to handle, since the quality of the work rarely lives up to Lennart's lofty expectations. Richter will make a habit out of having his client wait in despair for design drawings—which are indeed impressive enough when they finally do arrive. However, with a number of disturbances of this kind, the many operations involved in the post-production process will soon transgress all time frames and deadlines, and acclaimed performances will be significantly delayed. Over the course of the lengthy project, new possibilities will also reveal themselves, and thereby expand the imagined potential that resides in this kind of creation. Moreover, new ideals will enter the stage, making some of the major points of reference for the project—such as Carsten Nielsen's Jade Idol—somewhat obsolete. In fact, some ten months into the project, after having spent considerable efforts on trying to materialize the ambitious plans that are still taking shape in mid-February, Lennart will sneer at his own impressive creation. This, while dreaming away about the next one: "if only I push this mess through, I will start it off right away." Next time around, he seems to be reasoning, it might just be possible to realize the full potential of the basic construction, and further explore, if not exhaust, the many possibilities on offer. With respect to present pursuits, however, it seems as if nothing is ever enough.

Judging by the shape and form of Lennart's efforts, it is evident that fancy feature articles, memorable marketing campaigns, and dramatized events have greatly impacted his interests and as-

pirations, as well as the skills and the knowledge that he has acquired over the years. However, the most important component in this web of influences, which seems to regulate the dynamics of the customizing scene, are the pioneering efforts of fellow customers—customers who have gone to great lengths to perfect the products in question; whose endeavors have been narrated, again and again, by trucking media; and whose creations have been displayed center-stage at trucking festivals, transportation exhibitions and various marketing gimmicks. Deemed the King of Customizing in Sweden in the early 80s, the above-mentioned Svempa is one such figure who has relentlessly pushed forward, gotten the possibility to assemble spectacular show-trucks for Scania, and even become part of the marketing efforts springing from the company's headquarters. Having made it as customizing entrepreneur, he and his team have opened their own styling unit, Svempas, and even initiated a number of limited edition series of Scania vehicles.

More than a former idol of Lennart's—and many other customizing fans'—Svempa could possibly also be understood as a material extension of the kind of attitude that seems to be urging Lennart forward towards that next project. To get an idea of what such insistent pursuits may lead to, let us take a closer look at Svempas' professional, limited edition activities. A first line, issued in 2000, was fitted with various add-on equipment in Svempas' own garage: leather-covered seats, hi-fi equipment, chromed side-pipes and wheel hubs, aluminum gangways, striping, and metallic-painted trim. Contracted by Scania, Svempas was in this project in charge of choosing sub-suppliers, handled all the logistics involved in getting extravagant features in place, and carried out much of the groundwork required to trim the vehicles—all of it after the industrialized assembly process. As one could expect, a number of complications arose over the course of the project, and only in Italy was the reception strong enough to motivate a sequel.

Come a second series, and several of Svempas' affiliated sub-suppliers were overruled by those in charge of the collaboration at the Scania headquarters. Kept black, Scania also eliminated the problematic metallic painting procedure—which in the first series had been carried out through several scattered operations post the production line. And so in 2003, when a third limited edition line was to be produced, Svempas was to large extents steered out of the project and the production process as Scania attempted to integrate as much as possible of the more excessive customizing measures into the industrialized production process. Again aiming for metallic paintworks, the cabins were to be finalized in close affinity to one of the company's production plants, so as to shorten lead times and keep the items in the ordinary production flow. This time, Svempas were only engaged as a supplier of certain peripheral details.

As premium product packages have turned into recurring offerings, Scania has in this way attempted to take over much of the initiatives and operations that have grown out of committed customers. However, these efforts to subsume both Svempas' expertise and the work of affiliated sub-suppliers have proven to be very difficult, with customers complaining about the quality of the finished works. In fact, key customers have explicitly requested that Svempas once again be put in charge of the customizing work: developing the concept and supervising the production, to ensure the quality throughout the process. When the Italian Scania distributor, Italscania ordered a series of 32 lavishly decorated trucks in connection with the release of a new Scania tractor in the spring of 2006, this kind of a setup was a principal requirement. Without Svempas' superintendence, there wouldn't have been any order.

With the new form of collaboration, Italscania orders vehicles from Scania and the customizing work directly from Svempas. Undoubtedly, this arrangement has granted Svempas a greater degree of autonomy relative the customer. Moreover, the retained independence is yet another component through which Svempa and his team have demonstrated, for all those whose collective efforts constitute the customizing scene, that persistent efforts may well pay off—that major commitment might in fact attract the interest of marketing officials, and perhaps even the company's top management. Besides Lennart's efforts, which could of course be understood as an imitation of his former idol, a magazine like *Trucking Scandinavia* showcases numerous other young drivers whose creations and aspirations appear to have been heavily influenced by Svempa and his team.[1] Tommy Kurås, aged 30, and living in Oslo, is portrayed as one who does not only keep with a stylish, custom-tailored vehicle, but who also "has an impressive talent for drawing and an eye for good taste" (Molin, 2005, p. 45, *authors' translation*). Having been illustrating trucks for more than 20 years, and with more serious aspirations for the last 13 or 14 years, Tommy reveals that he would not mind helping other drivers to better the design of their vehicles. Having spent a year in a design program, he is even supposed to have some of the credentials.

WITH EVERY SYNTHESIS, A REST

What we have seen in the two previous sections appears to be a number of highly material consequences that have grown out of an open-ended product and procurement process. Propelled by an imaginary that has reveled in the potentialities involved in this realm, these consequences appear to be of a structural or systematic kind: the outcome of a dialectical interplay between material practice and a de-centered imaginary that has come to encircle it. Presumably, this is an interplay that keeps breeding different forms of offshoots from the various gaps and interstices that emerge as customers are drawn into the production processes by captivating customizing and co-creation fantasies—symbolic structures and imaginary scenarios inviting them to co-create and co-produce their work tools. To get somewhat more specific, we have seen how marketing campaigns have emphasized the undecided character of promoted products, and how they, in so doing, have posited the custom-made as a desirable ideal. We have seen how certain pioneers have begun to explore different openings that this implies, and how young audiences have been encouraged to follow in their footsteps. Adopting the ideals promoted by marketing discourse, we have seen how both pioneering customers and dedicated fans and followers appear to have taken it upon themselves to make the marketing promises come true. Incorporated into marketing campaigns, we have even seen how such parties, in their own ways, have come to operate as a kind of supplements that lend support to the promises conveyed. Namely, that the vehicle manufacturers *are in fact capable* of delivering that which their customers most desire.

Furthermore, we have seen how spectacular narrations of enthusiastic and sometimes relentless pursuits to complete the creations in question have given rise to symbolic laws that dictate what may, and what may not be done in this realm, where—as the saying often goes—everything is indeed possible. Supposedly, we have also seen how manufacturers attempt to coin and control the dictates of this symbolic universe, along with the imaginary scenarios they shape—for instance by praising the moderate and the sober. However, the fantasies seem to fall into the hands of the pioneering figures animating them, as these figures are elevated within the socio-symbolic orders that grow in-between customer and manufacturer, and regulate what is really desirable in these realms. Their involvement has demonstrated that the vehicle manufacturers are not in fact capable of truly customizing the end product without the customers' involvement, with icons such as Svempa having emerged as a kind of figures who sustain this entire customizing fantasy.

With these processes repeating themselves, time and again, iconic figures appear, moreover, to fall from sublime positions with others taking their place. Despite Svempas' impact on the customizing scene, and the fact that the Italian customers seem to have been pleased with the latest limited edition series, Lennart is not equally impressed, for instance. Discussing the vehicles some six months after the episode at the service unit, he holds the entire project in contempt. His verdict: the vehicles are way too modest with respect to special features; too many of the principles guiding true customizing work have been compromised. Besides, several of the features that have indeed been included in the package are not to his liking anyway. Consequently, Lennart claims that he cannot understand who would ever buy such a vehicle. Lennart's suspicion towards Svempas' latest limited edition series may well be a manifestation of the traumatic relationship that he has come to develop towards the customizing king in recent years. From Lennart's point of view, this former idol of his appears to have compromised the ideals he once embodied—and hence betrayed the symbolic laws which ever since have been guiding the practice that has emerged in the wake of his pioneering efforts (cf. Sköld, 2009). While suffering such a fall among specific followers on the local scene, Svempa appears, however, only to have begun his ascent to stardom in yet another segment of the market. What we have seen in the sections above, presumably, is how these movements appear to contribute to a fragmentation of the guiding ideals of the customizing scene, generating a variety of imaginary scenarios that each frame aspirations and desires in their own particular way. Whereas the symbolic universe cultivated between customer and manufacturer appears to circulate around an interest in customizing, *how* this interest is particularized for different sets of followers hence seems to vary quite considerably—which also pertains to the orders and hierarchies emerging within this symbolic universe.

In other words does the customizing fantasy conveyed by various marketing campaigns, trucking media, festivals and exhibitions, appear to nurture a range of different customizing interests, each developing along slightly different trajectories—and in directions that might even contradict one another. With respect to the products in question, this fantasy appears, on the one hand, to cultivate a desire for the excessively decorated, completed vehicles bearing Svempas' signature. On the other hand, it appears to cultivate a desire for the utterly undecided creation, the open-ended basic construction that enables the customer to co-create and express his or her distinctive preferences—around the completion of which customers may form a subjectivity as custom builders. With respect to the broader experience of keeping with a customized truck, the customizing interest has supposedly also opened up new imaginary scenarios, which have come to cultivate a desire for establishing oneself as a celebrated post-production entrepreneur, one day equipped with a design house of one's own.

Hence, in this economy of desire it is as if open-ended fantasy formations disclose new possibilites, generate new promises, and feed numerous new imaginary scenarios and interests that are similar in kind, but nevertheless deviate from one another and take off in different and unanticipated directions. In addition, attempts to subsume the knowledge and the values growing along these offshoots, in-between the customer and manufacturer, tend to further fragment and displace these interests. It is as if attempts to take control over the symbolic structures that determine the promises and the imaginary ideals surrounding Scania's product offerings contribute to opening new avenues for the customers' desires. It is as if attempts to bridge the gap between customer and manufacturer rather tear it open, by generating all sorts of perturbations or material outgrowths; and as if every attempt to incorporate and subsume the symbolic structures emerging in-between the two rather fragments them, with the effect of multiply-

ing the coordinates and the future directions of customers' desires on the customizing scene. It is as if every higher synthesis that is supposed to bring customer and manufacturer closer together and add value to the offerings, also adds other kinds of values to the industry. Rather than bringing harmony between the two parties, resolving the tension that separates them, it is as if every higher synthesis—every *Aufhebung*—displaces and perverts the ground for their interplay.

PERVERSION AS PROTECTION AGAINST A LAW RUN AMOK

Let us return to Lacan's thinking. For one could easily imagine a structural rationale for the kind of dialectic movement encountered above—one that goes back to Lacan's understanding of how processes of identification may be conceptualized, and that centers on the workings of the Lacanian superego in subject formation processes. Arguably, such a theoretical move draws attention to how entering the pervert subject position appears to function both as a way of coping with the pressure of the superego, and of subverting—or perverting, as it were—the grounds from which it operates. To clarify this dynamics, let us start by revisiting Lacan's thinking around how processes of identification and subject formation may be constituted.

Central to Lacan is the distinction between imaginary and symbolic identification. Whereas the former pertains to images or ideal models, which we do our best to imitate and take after, the latter is concerned with the position in the socio-symbolic order from which we see ourselves when we strive to emulate our imaginary ideals (cf. Žižek, 1989). To be more precise, imaginary identification could be said to circle around the Ideal Ego—this being, in Lacan's thinking, the ideal that we model our ego towards and against, strive to reach up to, but which remains inaccessible to us. In this way, imaginary identification never quite succeeds, but revolves around the Ideal

Ego, or "the small other," as it is also referred to in Lacan's work.

Symbolic identification, on the other hand, is concerned with "the big Other," or the socio-symbolic order as it is particularized for the subject. It refers to the processes through which we, as subjects, are inscribed into an intricate web of socio-symbolic relations—provided with a name, and different kinds of titles and narratives that determine our social standing. Put somewhat differently, symbolic identification is concerned with the processes through which the big Other intervenes in our existence and grants us a specific socio-symbolic space to occupy or embody. Answering this call of the Other—subjecting to the symbolic mandates cast upon us—forms the basic tenet for the formation of a subjectivity, wherefore symbolic identification in Lacan's thinking makes out the primary form of identification. That which gives, as it were, the coordinates for imaginary identification.

If the Ideal Ego is central for imaginary identification, symbolic identification has its correlate in the Ego-Ideal. This is the authority or ideal that regulates what kind of role we want to assume in the social order. We might think of it as the unconscious ground from which identification processes are enacted; a kind of agency, that watches over us, evaluates our movements within the socio-symbolic realm, and gives the shape of our Ideal Ego. This agency could thus be understood as that which guides the continuous interplay between the symbolic and imaginary identification—which is to say, the processes through which we form a subjectivity. As such, it lends stability to us by specifying what the Other demands of us. In addition, the pressure it exerts makes us channel our drives and desires on the terms given by pre-existing socio-symbolic structures, rather than follow irrational drives and desires. Slavoj Žižek (2007) explains: "For Lacan, the seemingly benevolent agency of the Ego-Ideal that leads us to moral growth and maturity, forces us to betray the 'law of desire' by way of adopting the 'reasonable' demands of the existing socio-symbolic order" (p. 81).

When Salecl draws attention to the abundance of choice, and the open-ended character of the imaginary that has come to reign contemporary society, she also proposes that the Ego-Ideal has lost quite a bit of its guiding power. The demand from the Other has grown increasingly vague now that it is up to ourselves to determine our future by enjoying the possibilities we find most attractive. However, as mentioned initially, this is no easy task. Especially not when we are being overwhelmed with appealing images that we are encouraged to take after. With the withdrawal of the Ego-Ideal, Salecl instead underlines an alternative dynamics that has come into play, and that has come to exert an all but negligible pressure on us in contemporary society. This is one that plays on our guilt. In addition, it does so precisely by bombarding us with Ideal Egos so plush and plenteous that we cannot but fail in our attempts to emulate them. The regulating agency of this dynamics goes, in Lacanian psychoanalysis, by the name of the superego. According to Salecl, "the superego functions as the voice that commands the subject to enjoy yet at the same time mockingly predicts that he or she will fail in this pursuit of enjoyment" (Salecl, 2004, p. 51).

Let us take a closer look at this agency, which Žižek (2007) has described as "the necessary obverse of the Ego-Ideal" (p. 81). Conflating symbolic identity—which traditionally has come with a number of constraints—with excess-enjoyment,[2] the superego could be understood as an agency that posits various forms of obligations associated with our socio-symbolic standing as voluntary, and something that we should engage in only if we find pleasure in doing so. Pointing, moreover, to rewarding or favorable consequences that will stem from our willful engagement, it nevertheless leaves us little choice but to go "all in." Hence, rather than merely operating as an agency that grants us permission to do what we like, it urges us to take pleasure in the most mundane of efforts, and make of our humdrum strivings something so marvelous and magnificent that our efforts cannot be but insufficient. The Lacanian superego could thus be understood as an agency that drives us ever further in our pursuits. But under whose supervision success is kept out of the way, forever located just beyond the horizon. It could be understood as an agency under whose supervision anything and everything is permitted, but nothing is ever enough. As Žižek (2005) puts it, *"the superego is a law 'run amok' in so far as it prohibits what it formally permits"* (p. 66, *original in italics*).

As has already been implied, giving in to this rampaging law is a hazardous move. With respect to the feelings of guilt it imparts to us, Žižek (2005) further elaborates on its brutal mode of operation:

Our sacrificing to the superego, our paying tribute to it, only corroborates our guilt. For that reason our debt to the superego is unredeemable: the more way pay it off, the more we owe. Superego is like the extortioner slowly bleeding us to death—the more he gets, the stronger his hold on us. (p. 67)

This raises the question how someone who is chased around, or hystericized, by the scornful grin of the superego may survive the situation, and find at least temporary shelter from the vicious maelstrom of guilt and anxiety otherwise impending without entirely giving up on the desire for upward movement, standing out from the crowd, and being granted recognition from the socio-symbolic setting.

One such strategy, implicated by both Salecl and Žižek,[3] is to assume what in clinical terms is the pervert subject position. That is, a position through which the subject attempts to take the symbolic law into its own hands; through which it assumes to know for the Other, and to embody what is most dear to the Other—although the Other has withdrawn from its sight and this by no

means is obvious, or, for that matter, undisputed. Rather than being torn asunder by a flickering, wavering desire radiating from a fragmented, de-centered Other, the pervert places himself at the core of the Other's fantasy; shielding himself from the superego injunction to indulge in every enticing imaginary scenario encountered, he places himself at the core of the fundamental fantasy which brings them together in the first place, assuming to embody the Other's most desired object. Salcel (2004) writes: "While the neurotic constantly has questions with regard to desire, the pervert has an answer—he has found satisfaction and has no doubt about what he or the Other wants" (p. 87).

A slightly different way of putting it, would be to say that assuming the position of the pervert implies that one overidentifies with fantasy by striving to *be* the law; to be made part of its operation. Žižek (2004b) explains:

In contrast to the 'normal' subject, for whom the Law functions as the agency of prohibition which regulates (the access to the object of) his desire, for the pervert, the object of his desire is Law itself—the Law is the Ideal he is longing for, he wants to be fully acknowledged by the Law, integrated into its functioning. (p. 820)

What the pervert gains satisfaction out of is thus "the very obscenity of the gesture of installing the rule of Law" (Žižek, 2004b, p. 820).

In the face of the Other's withdrawal, and the dissolution of strong Ego-Ideals that grant us support, the pervert subject is thus one who seizes power, and takes to constituting new symbolic laws and regulations within the interstices of the socio-symbolic fabric. In doing so, the pervert places himself at the heart of a fantasy that makes the Other come into being. To the extent that the pervert's pursuits have any kind of impact and give rise to any kind of following, the fantasy that props up the Other's existence is arguably placed in the hands of passionate and perverted fans and followers. By installing new authorities within the socio-symbolic order, such inverting processes supposedly lead to the formation of new Ego-Ideals, as well as Ideal-Egos, which will guide further action, and contribute to the generation of further material aberrations.

FANTASY FRAGMENTING

As pioneering customers make a career out of conspicuous adaptation of their work tools, the conditions and the business logic of their operations will inevitably change. As they go from excessively decorating their own vehicles, to collaborating with the manufacturing organization over eye-catching creations and one-off projects, which are subjected to tight deadlines and strict cost control, the customizing activity will inevitably be governed by other criteria than it once was. With the move from excessive utility—i.e., utility exploding in a frenzy of excessive measures—to excess becoming the ground and the bare necessity of the business operation, an actor such as Svempa will supposedly find himself in a situation whereby he will have to compromise and negotiate some of the symbolic dictates, norms, and ideals once established in the wake of his efforts. Being dependent on prototypes and residue from various testing labs hardly allows him to keep up with old mottos such as "a true custom-builder specifies and cares for every last detail, from the chassis paint and up." Not in the way that *Trailer* once taught through spectacular articles featuring Svempas' creations. Getting involved in relatively large-scale customizing operations, where the scope of the styling program is negotiated not with each and every end-customer, but with a distribution company for whom a lean production flow is key, also limits the customizing measures at your disposal.

To the extent that Svempa once served as a key influence for shaping Lennart's Ideal Ego—a figure to identify with on an imaginary level—such a transformation may well be traumatic to witness, and serve as solid proof of the old icon having sold out. Or even worse, that his talent never was a godsend, that he never was made of special stuff and divine talent in the first place. However, from another vantage point, namely that of Italian customers, also Svempas' later deeds appear to provide plenty of food for identification processes. Particularly so on a symbolic level: in the form of an agency that may oversee and guide our socio-symbolic struggles; an Ego-Ideal that reassures us that we are on the right track and have made the right moves, so to speak.

In this respect, the initial customizing fantasy conveyed by Scania—stipulating that: *If you want it customized, choose Scania!*—seems to have been inverted, in a first instance, into: *Svempas' Scania, that is customized!* However, what we appear to be seeing in the developments sketched out above, are two quite different manifestations of this perverted fantasy. One reading: *You want it customized? Choose Svempas' Scania edition!* And another reading: *You want it customized? Follow Svempas' example!*

For someone marked by the first perverted version, consumed by ready-made products of rare and limited edition, Svempas' signature may be understood as reinstalling the Scania vehicle as a complete product. It may be understood as a marker, which bears witness of Scania having managed to take control of the unfinished state that has come to characterize the product under the open-ended imaginary promulgated, for instance, by trucking media—a sign of Scania having seized hold also of the aesthetic and unfinished dimension of the company's product, and that this is indeed the vehicle of choice for anyone striving to move up in the world. As such, it arguably contributes to fixating the fantasy that frames the Scania product as the most desirable on the market, sustaining it in the most sublime of positions within our fantasy space. In the fall of 2006, Scania's The Griffin series, customized under Svempas' supervision upon Italscania's demand, was awarded "most beautiful truck" at the automotive fair *L'Automobile più Bella del Mondo* in Milan.

As Scania has come to learn, Svempas' signature and the imaginary formations established around it are not easily discarded or incorporated. Certainly quality issues may call for Svempas' participation in limited edition series. In addition, perceptions of quality rest on the different symbolic and imaginary structures dominating, on the one hand, the customer realm, and on the other, the Scania organization. An attitude frequently encountered within the company is that anything produced on line, and that has passed through certified production processes, is superior to anything carried out postindustrial production, by some other party. However, demanding customers do not necessarily share this conviction. And one should not underestimate the indispensability of Svempas' signature on the level of fantasy. In a somewhat twisted and contradictory way, one might even suggest that Scania's appeal, also relative a protagonist such as Lennart, appears to hinge on this symbolic inscription. For although Svempa himself appears to have played out his role as Ideal Ego *vis-à-vis* a passionate customer such as Lennart, the latter is still head over heels involved in imitating the early deeds of the old customizing king. The symbolic laws that have emerged in the wake of Svempa's early efforts appear to function, in fact, as a blueprint for Lennart's pursuits. As such, it is a means for what appears to be a very specific end: taking over Svempas' esteemed socio-symbolic position; making it within trucker culture whilst still being true to its founding spirit. Makin' it, yet keeping it real, so to speak.

Bearing witness of such pursuits is supposedly Lennart's avidity to take on honorary tasks from local Scania dealers, which entail that his vehicles are showcased in connection with different marketing jippos. Moreover does he seek participation in more spectacular events arranged by the central marketing unit, and reaching a broader audience—such as the biennial Young European Truck Driver contest. Several times during his own project, he even mentions that he really should take his creation down to the Scania headquarters once it's finished to show the top management how it could be done. While he used to strive for an acknowledgement from *Trailer* through a feature article in the magazine, the magazine has lost much of its appeal and its guiding power in the spring 2006. Lacking a firm and credible principle as to what kind of customizing efforts are valued by the magazine, it appears as if the top management at Scania has taken over as the kind of agency towards which Lennart directs his efforts—the agency that surveys the entire situation and gives shape to his Ideal Ego.

This should perhaps not come as too much of a surprise. By attracting the attention of Scania officials in the early 1980s, Svempa demonstrated a way out of the dreary everyday life of a hauler. According to Lennart's fantasy, being loyal to the symbolic dictates of the early Svempa will, assumedly, render himself a similar symbolic identity as the pioneer once managed to attain. Assumedly, it will put him on a trajectory towards an elevated position within the socio-symbolic space opened up and established in-between Scania and its customers through Svempas' pioneering efforts, and make him an invaluable ally of the organization.

Obviously a big fan, Lennart is nevertheless keen to air a slight discontent with the lack of engagement coming out of the company. Both with respect to his personal endeavors and the frantic activity taking place on the customizing scene by and large. In connection with the stop-over at the maintenance hall in mid-February he claims, in fact, that he would like to see the organization take a number of measures so as to award impressive creations assembled by their customers: that it would host an online gallery and arrange contests revolving around its favorite design efforts; that the CEO take part in prizing ceremonies at trucking festivals; and that his own sales contact make a happening out of signing over the keys to a new vehicle. Just imagine getting a T-shirt with a picture of the new vehicle printed over the top of the chest! Or better yet, being invited to the production plant as the new engine is started up for the very first time.

Indeed, it appears as if Scania, which once seems to have been involved in grass-root customizing activities, has withdrawn from the scene, and that Lennart knows how best to get back in. Voicing a number of key insights as to how the organization ought to approach their customers, it appears as if Lennart not only considers his own deeds to be of substantial value to the company, but that he also knows what is best for the Other. Or put somewhat differently, it appears as if Lennart is riddled by not quite being able to see what Scania wants of him, and by the company not showing him more care and affection. Possibly as a way to handle this uncertainty and insecurity, he appears to have placed himself at the center of the customizing fantasy. As Scania's desired object, he appears to do his best to please the Other. Vacillating between different possibilities concerning the side skirts of the new vehicle, he settles for the original gear, arguing that Scania might like it better.

In this sense, Lennart emerges as yet another perverted Scania fan. One that turns to the symbolic dictates of early pioneering pursuits to resurrect symbolic laws, which have begun to dissolve. Confronted with a vast range of possibilities, and a flickering, intangible desire radiating from the socio-symbolic setting he is situated in, he emerges as one who takes the law into his own hands. This, based on a fantasy of what the Other would best prefer, and, more fundamentally, based on a fantasy that the Other indeed expects something of him. Hence, he emerges as one that appears to overidentify with the notion that keeping with the early ideals of the customizing scene can make you just as indispensable an ally of the marketing department, and of the top management of Scania, as Svempa once was. Doing so, he in fact appears

to be involved in a process of inverting the fantasy *Svempas' Scania, that is customized!* into *You want it customized? Follow Svempas' example!* This on his way towards showing the world that *Lennart's Scania, that is truly customized!*

While Lennart is hard at work to establish himself as a custom-builder true to classic ideals, other actors engaged in the customizing movement appear to be pulling in slightly different directions. Recall Tommy Kurås, for instance. As a customer of used Scania vehicles, he does not appear to get involved in the ordering and assembling process of new vehicles. Instead, he appears to follow Svempas' example by aspiring towards a position similar to that of Jan Richter—being identified by *Trucking Scandinavia* as a free-lancing post-production designer. Hardly interacting with the vehicles manufacturer, he is instead involved in adding yet another layer to the design process. By doing so, and by establishing yet another occupation related to the customizing trade, he arguably makes out yet another actor who contributes to fragmenting the interest in aesthetic aspects of heavy-duty vehicles.

CONCLUSION

Inquiring into a marketing dynamics that promote products as open-ended experiences, this chapter has sought to demonstrate how a central dimension of the interrelationship between customer and supplier rests on fantasies that bind the two parties together. We have attempted to show how attempts to realize such fantasies, both from the perspective of the user-customer and the manufacturer-supplier, appear to be marked by impossibilities that continuously displace both the fantasies themselves and the practices which chase them around. With recourse to Lacanian thinking around the dynamics of identification, these impossibilities have been understood as stemming from a fundamental inability to reach up to the imaginary constructions that we model our efforts and creations against. Ideal as these models certainly are, attempting to attain them can be nothing but a frustrating experience. Shaped, as they supposedly are, through interaction with the socio-symbolic setting, the ideals are likely to transform—if ever so slightly—by the time anything has indeed been materialized.

The two-fold nature of this impossibility appears to operate in the short term, for the customer to whom nothing—not even one's own excessive efforts—is ever enough, but it also appears to operate in the longer term, for the supplier who merely manages to incorporate a fraction of the desired customizing measures in its industrialized production flow. This a bit too late, it seems, when new pioneers have attracted the attention of other enthusiastic customers, and pushed beyond iconic figures involved in collaborative projects with the supplier. Constantly missing unattainable targets, the activity going into the attempts nevertheless appears to enforce the fantasy, yet at the same time fragment it, and thereby generate a multitude of different customizing interests. What we appear to be seeing is thus how one marketing fantasy, which nurtures a promise of customer and supplier approaching one another and striving towards the same goal, in fact appears to open up a space between the two fractions. Rather than merely adding value to the product offering, the activities emerging within this space appear to add other values to the industry; a number of different attitudes and approaches towards how one best handles activities concerned with customization and aesthetic aspects of the produce in question.

As customers begin to identify very strongly with a certain product offering or a certain brand, we see how the dynamics involved in such identification processes appear to give rise to a double bind. One that, on the one hand, ties the customer to the supplier by being loyal to its brand, investing in it, sticking up for it, becoming part of it, *et cetera*. But that, on the other hand, seems to repel the customer from what the supplying party actually has to offer, push it further

away from any kind of standard offering—insofar as the dedicated customer does not only want to belong, but also stand out from others engaged in similar endeavors; insofar as they strive to go beyond also the more colorful front runners. One could thus say, as Žižek (2006) might indeed do, that the customer and the producing party are forever separated by a parallax gap. That is, a gap which forever prevents them from adopting or incorporating one another's perspective, but which nevertheless feeds impossible attempts to bridge it; a gap which feeds a dialectical interplay which never quite succeeds, but stumbles forward in good Hegelian manner, always outpaced by excessive outgrowths that have already taken off in deviating directions.

Now, it is perhaps fair to say that this analysis has dealt with a marginalized sub-culture at the outskirts of a major high-tech organization, one that may be of little concern to the firm's managerial practices. We would of course beg to differ. Although reveling in the extreme and perhaps even peripheral, the analysis illustrates how the outliers focused here impact the fantasies, which ultimately constitute the Scania brand; it points to how the influence from these outliers seeps into industrialized mass production; and it accounts for how they give rise to knowledge and values that resist being incorporated, and rather grow in-between and beyond established orders. Given that many, if not most, high-tech products and services give rise to sub-cultures which might develop and migrate in similar ways, acknowledging this dynamics raises a number of questions concerning the role of fantasy for contemporary phenomena such as co-creation and co-production, and a spirit of enterprising which emphasizes the possibilities of "doing-it-yourself," and "making it" off very little.

To broaden our view, the analysis prompts further inquiry into the complexities and the valorization processes involved in the interplay between customer and supplier, user and manufacturer, consumer and producer, also in other settings than the realm of heavy duty vehicles. Particularly so in a post-industrial era, where "You" are often placed center-stage (cf. van Dijck, 2009), and phenomena such as co-creation and co-production are posited as key ingredients that promise to enhance the flavor of almost any business (see, e.g., von Hippel, 2005). What may in fact the consequences be of approaching users and customers in the ways advocated by dominating literature on for instance customer relationship marketing, brand management, open innovation and consumer co-creation? In addition, what does a marketing insight which suggests that brands are often located in the hands of the customers actually entail in different cultural and organizational settings?

Let us get somewhat more specific by pointing these questions to the contemporary world of Internet technologies and Web development. With respect to the creation but also displacement of cultural and economic values explored throughout this essay, what may the effects be of establishing an online lifestyle venture that rests on a strong and unifying fantasy between user and service provider—one that invites enthusiastic users and third party developers to step in where internal resources give out, by encouraging them, for instance, to utilize publicly shared Application Programming Interfaces (APIs)? Web services formed around strong sub-cultural interests, perhaps posing as community platforms where users not only create the content but also are encouraged to engage in further development, certainly abound in the world of ICT—which arguably is a domain ruled by open-ended imaginary structures. With a laptop and an idea, and some self-acquired programming skills, anyone can make it as an IT entrepreneur. At least according to a popular imagery encountered in best-selling business press, which preaches that intimate knowledge of some "long tail" suddenly might reveal a business opportunity with global reach (see, e.g., Anderson, 2006), or that a clever mashup of existing Web services may render a killer application almost overnight. A most relevant question under such circumstances, is how the fantasies that appear to tie service providers, third party- and user-developers together, also may carry an obverse dynamics that work in opposition to unification; one that spurs the creation of excess values and new symbolic structures which break with the established orders by inverting and fragmenting them.

REFERENCES

Anderson, C. (2006). *The long tail: Why the future of business is selling less of more*. New York, NY: Hyperion.

Fleming, P. (2009). *Authenticity and the cultural politics of work*. Oxford, UK: Oxford University Press. doi:10.1093/acprof:oso/9780199547159.001.0001

Illouz, E. (1997). *Consuming the romantic utopia*. Berkeley, CA: University of California Press.

Iveco. (1982). Teckna Sveriges häftigaste lastbil, så bygger vi den som vinner. *Trailer, 1*, 33.

Lacan, J. (1988). *The seminar of Jacques Lacan, book II: The ego in Freud's theory and in the technique of psychoanalysis 1954–55*. Cambridge, UK: Cambridge University Press.

Molin, H. (2005). Designer på papperet. [Designer on paper]. *Trucking Scandinavia, 11*, 45–47.

Salecl, R. (1998). *(Per)versions of love and hate*. London, UK: Verso.

Salecl, R. (2004). *On anxiety*. London, UK: Routledge.

Salecl, R. (2010). *Choice*. London, UK: Profile Books.

Sigurdh, E.-L. (2010). Rätt profil ger napp på nätet. [The right profile helps you score online]. *Dagens Nyheter*. Retrieved July 17, 2011, from http://bit.ly/b4SFMh

Sjöberg, S. L. (1983). Pers teckning blir verklighet! *Trailer*, *1*(2), 36–38.

Sköld, D. (2009). An evil king 'thing,' rising, falling and multiplying in trucker culture. *Organization*, *16*(2), 249–266. doi:10.1177/1350508408100477

Sköld, D. (2010). The other side of enjoyment: Shortcircuiting marketing and creativity in the experience economy. *Organization*, *17*(3), 363–378. doi:10.1177/1350508410363119

van Dijck, J. (2009). Users like you? Theorizing agency in user-generated content. *Media Culture & Society*, *31*(1), 41–58. doi:10.1177/0163443708098245

von Hippel, E. (2005). *Democratizing innovation*. Cambridge, MA: MIT Press.

Žižek, S. (1989). *The sublime object of ideology*. London, UK: Verso.

Žižek, S. (1999). You may! *London Review of Books, 21*(6), 3-6. Retrieved July 17, 2011, from http://www.lrb.co.uk/v21/n06/slavoj-zizek/you-may

Žižek, S. (2004a). The structure of domination today – A Lacanian view. *Studies in East European Thought*, *56*, 383–403. doi:10.1023/B:SOVI.0000043002.02424.ca

Žižek, S. (2004b). What can psychoanalysis tell us about cyberspace? *Psychoanalytic Review*, *91*(6), 801–830. doi:10.1521/prev.91.6.801.55957

Žižek, S. (2005). *The metastases of enjoyment: On women and causality*. London, UK: Verso.

Žižek, S. (2006). *The parallax view*. Cambridge, MA: MIT Press.

Žižek, S. (2007). *How to read Lacan*. New York, NY: Norton.

ENDNOTES

[1] From 2005-2007, one of the authors held a subscription to *Trucking Scandinavia*, and the referenced feature article figured in one of the first issues encountered during this period.

[2] With respect to the interrelation between symbolic identity and excess-enjoyment, Žižek (2004a) writes: "The usual notion of the relationship between excess-enjoyment and symbolic identification is that symbolic identity is what we get in exchange for being deprived of enjoyment; what happens in today's society, with its decline of the Master-Signifier and the rise of consumption, is the exact obverse: the basic fact is the loss of symbolic identity, what Eric Santner called the 'crisis of investiture,' and what we get in exchange for this loss is that we are all bombarded with forms and gadgets of enjoyment" (p. 399).

[3] Apropos the relationship between the superego and the pervert subject position Salecl (2004) writes: "While the neurotic, who has been marked by a lack (i.e. castrated), has doubts about the consistency of the law, feels guilty before outside prohibitions as well as before the superego, the pervert often tries to take the law into his own hands in order to complete the castration that has not been fully installed" (p. 106). See also Žižek (2006, pp. 303-304) for an analysis of the link between the superego and the pervert.

Chapter 13
Organizational Characteristics of Middle Managers' Deterioration as Sources of Organizational Decline

Masaru Karube
Hitotsubashi University, Japan

Toshihiko Kato
Hitotsubashi University, Japan

Tsuyoshi Numagami
Hitotsubashi University, Japan

ABSTRACT

This chapter explores the mechanism of how structural and behavioral organizational characteristics lead to organizational deterioration as a source of organizational decline. First, using an original construct of organizational deterioration named "organizational deadweight" that is defined as ineffectual managerial load at the middle management level, the authors explore the relationships between the organizational characteristics and organizational deadweight. Data was collected through a questionnaire survey in 2006 involving more than 942 respondents from 128 business units of 16 large Japanese firms. The results suggest that reference to formal strategic planning, participation in the planning process, and vertical communication improve deterioration, whereas organizational size and layered hierarchical structure aggravate it. Finally, the authors discuss the roles of vertical communication and formal planning to safeguard against deterioration.

DOI: 10.4018/978-1-4666-1836-7.ch013

INTRODUCTION

Speed of decision-making has been one of the key issues in increasing the adaptability of organizations in the face of rapidly changing and unpredictable environment during the last two decades (Eisenhardt, 1989; Kessler & Chakrabarti, 1996; Stalk, 1988). Under such turbulent environment, any organizations are not allowed to waste their members' time and energy for coordination and communication. Because management of organization is a process of getting work done with the efforts of others through organizational communication and coordination, efficient communication and coordination are indispensable for the speed of decision-making. However, many modern organizations are functional and hierarchical so that fragmentation and compartmentalization of work make it difficult for managers to realize a common organizational goal because of isolated departments, poor coordination, and limited commutation (Garvin, 1998). Insufficient integration of members' knowledge bases and their individual goals or low organizational cohesiveness hamper efficient coordination and communication, and they can become sources of organizational deterioration that lead to eventual maladaptation and organizational decline. Long before the organizational soundness is totally lost, corporate executives have to find the early signs of deterioration and safeguard against it (Lorange & Nelson, 1987).

Whereas innumerable historical examples of "rise and fall" of business organizations supported the idea of "lost momentum theory" (Durham & Smith, 1982) that regard deterioration and resulting failure as inevitable in such a way that "success breeds failure" or "failure further breeds failure" (Mellahi & Wilkinson, 2004; Weitzel & Jonsson, 1989), we believe that it is more imperative to ask under what condition and why not all but some organizations fail to safeguard against its early signs of organizational deterioration and eventual failure. Specifically, with respect to large established organizations that were successful at a time in the past, we attempt to raise the questions why not all but some established organizations tend to deteriorate and eventually decline: (1) what are the internal causes of organizational deterioration resulting in organizational failure? (2) How do organizational members perceive the early warning signs of deterioration? (3) How do they succeed in or fail to cope with deterioration?

Based on the premise that dysfunctional internal symptoms within an organization become sources of maladaptation to environmental change that in turn results in organizational failure (Mckinley, 1993), we aim to explore the preconditions for how organizational characteristics cause dysfunctional symptoms in established organizations. The symptoms we specifically shed light on are dysfunctional states caused by low organizational cohesiveness among middle managers in the business units of large established firms, in which a shared goal of organizational members and their managerial efforts are not fully integrated for the realization of a common organizational goal. Such low cohesiveness among middle managers might be regarded as symptoms of deterioration, and it might become a source of maladaptation that finally leads to organizational failure.

In the remainder of this chapter, we review organizational deterioration and failure literature and point to the lack of organizational cohesiveness as a source of deterioration and eventual failure. We then introduce a construct named "organizational deadweight" that is defined as ineffectual managerial load caused by lack of cohesiveness at middle management level (Karube, Numagami, & Kato, 2009; Numagami, Karube, & Kato, 2010). Following the construct that captures the symptoms of organizational deterioration at middle management level, we test the relationships among structural characteristics (organizational size, hierarchical structure), behavioral characteristics (formal strategic planning, and vertical communication), and organizational deadweight. Finally, we discuss the importance of role of vertical communication between superiors and subordinates and role of formal strategic planning to safeguard against lack of organizational cohesiveness that results in deterioration and eventual decline.

BACKGROUND

Organizational Failure as Maladaptation to Environmental Change

Because the term "failure" in general can be defined as "unintended consequences of negative state or outcome of not meeting a desirable or intended objective and criteria," such definition allows us to include broad different negative states and outcomes of organizational behaviors, such as organizational misconduct, mortality, corruption, deterioration, decline, retrenchment, downsizing, death, exit, bankruptcy, and dissolution. In addition, the term "failure" per se does not refer to the concrete causes or forms of organizational failure so that previous studies have focused on different facets of organizational failure. As a result, since the pioneering work of Whetten (1980) on organizational decline in the field of management studies, previous literature on organizational failure in the 1980s and thereafter has covered a large body of diverse research topics with different theoretical concerns, including industrial organization, organization ecology, organization studies and organizational psychology (Mellahi & Wilkinson, 2004).

Whereas main theoretical concerns and research themes in the field of strategic management used to be preoccupied with the upside of organizational behaviors and outcomes that might be labeled as organizational growth and success (Whetten, 1980), there has been a growing consensus about the importance of shedding light on the downside of organizational behaviors and outcomes—as an issue of "organization inertia" in organizational ecology (Hannan & Freeman, 1984), "competency traps" in organizational learning literature (Levitt & March, 1988), "cognitive limits and biases" in organizational cognition literature (Barr, Stimpert, & Huff, 1992; Walsh, 1995), "groupthink" in social psychology literature (Janis, 1972; Whyte, 1989), "core rigidities" in technological innovation literature (Leonard-Barton, 1992; Tripsas & Gavetti, 2000), and "organizational dysfunction" in organizational failure literature (Cameron, Sutton, & Whetten, 1988; Cameron, Whetten, & Kim, 1987; D'Aveni, 1989; Greenhalgh, 1983; Mellahi & Wilkinson, 2004). Although these studies have focused on the different facets of organizational failure with different perspectives, they have insisted in common that some types of organizational rigidity (Barnett & Pratt, 2000; D'Aveni & MacMillan, 1990; Staw, Sandelands, & Dutton, 1981) and deterioration (Durham & Smith, 1982; Hambrick & D'Aveni, 1992) could lead to maladaptation and resulting failure.

Of the possible internal and external causes of organizational failure, on the premise that maladaptation to environmental change might be a critical source of organizational failure, we focus on the dysfunctional symptoms accompanied by organizational deterioration as internal causes of organizational maladaptation that lead toward organizational failure.

Organizational Deterioration as Lack of Cohesiveness

An organization is expected to function as a cooperative system (Barnard, 1938) and as a "cohesive" or "coherent" entity (Garvin, 1998; Ghoshal & Gratton, 2002), because a collection of individual values, interests, tasks, and activities among organizational members should be cohesive and fully integrated to attain a common organizational goal. Whereas the importance of a "state of internal cohesiveness or resultant coherence among organizational members" as a coordinative function has not necessarily been recognized at least in the previous literature on organizational deterioration and failure, some studies for example insist the importance of coherence in the context of organizational psychology (Feldt, Kivimäki, Rantala, & Tolvanen, 2004), strategic management (Lissack & Roos, 2001), and economic philosophy (Cayla, 2006). Following the definition of coherence proposed by Ekstrom (1993), organizational coherence might be defined as a "degree of how well organizational members' activities that are based on their different personal orientations, values, interests, and goals are grouped with each other afterward so as to produce an organized, tightly structured system."

With a similar research concern at phenomenological level using the slightly different term "cohesion," sociologists and psychologists have also shed light on the importance of social forces holding the individuals within the groupings in which they are in understanding antecedents and outcomes of the behaviors of specific types of groups (Cota, Evans, Dion, Kilik, & Longman, 1995; Friedkin, 2004). Based on the Festinger and others' perspectives, for example, group cohesiveness might be defined as "tendency for a group to stick together and remain united in the pursuit of its goals and objectives" (Cota, et al., 1995) or "the total field of forces acting on members to remain in the group" or "the resultant of all forces acting on members to remain in the group" (Friedkin, 2004). Because the emphatic point of organizational coherence perspective might reside in the consistency of organizational activities, coherence can take the form of cohesiveness, but not vice-versa. Thus, organizational cohesiveness serves as a "glue" that allows organizational members to concern themselves with realizing a common organizational goal consistently (eventual coherence).

We regard low organizational cohesiveness as an internal source of deterioration that can lead to resulting maladaptation and organizational failure. Although previous studies on organizational culture do not explicitly refer to the importance

of organizational cohesiveness, they have implicitly insisted its positive effect on performance by shedding light on the process of how strong organizational culture facilitates organizational members to stick together tightly for the realization of a common organizational goal (Kotter & Heskett, 1992; Ouchi, 1981; Sorensen, 2002). On the other hand, following the concept of "groupthink" (Janis, 1972), excess of high organizational cohesiveness, can be detrimental to the quality of decision-making (Bernthal & Insko, 1993; Sinclair, 1992). Thus, combining these insights, we can assume that whether high organizational cohesiveness serves as internal sources of organizational success or failure depends on the internal and/or environmental conditions, whereas whether and how low organizational cohesiveness can serve as internal sources of organizational deterioration and eventual failure remains unsolved. Moreover, it is true that the cohesiveness–performance relationship has long been examined at top management level by shedding light on the degree of heterogeneity of knowledge base among TMT members (e.g., Elron, 1997; Ensley, Pearson, & Amason, 2002; Michalisin, Karau, & Tangpong, 2004). However, we know little about how low cohesiveness at middle management level serves to deteriorate an organization as a whole and the eventual failure. Organizations may deteriorate not only from the top but also from the middle and from the bottom.

"Organizational Deadweight" as Ineffectual Management Load

To elucidate the process of how low organizational cohesiveness at middle management level serves as a source of organizational deterioration and in turn leads to maladaptation and eventual failure, we believe it necessary to look more into the reciprocally linked individual-level and group-level dimensions of dysfunctional states among middle managers in the light of membership attitudes and behaviors, personal orientations, commitment, identifications, and interpersonal attachments. Insufficient integration of members' values, norms, abilities, efforts, and goals—in other words, low organizational cohesiveness—may result in extra management "load" that dissipates managers' resources (their time and energy), which otherwise would be fully utilized in the realization of a shared organizational goal through efficient coordination and communication. Such an excess load may therefore be perceived as "ineffectual and unfruitful" especially by capable and responsible middle managers, given its impact on the efficient realization of a common goal (Karube, et al., 2009; Numagami, et al., 2010).

Following the construct of "organizational deadweight": "an ineffectual management load caused by low organizational cohesiveness that hampers cooperation for middle-level managers pursuing their organizational goal" (Karube, et al., 2009; Numagami, et al., 2010), we predict that such ineffectual management load serves as a potential source of organizational failure because excess ineffectual load amounts to a coordination and communication cost that needs to be minimized to improve organizational adaptability.

Whereas there is a large body of previous literature on organizational decline and deterioration, little research has focused on the dysfunctional symptoms, under which such ineffectual managerial load can hamper efficient organizational cooperation at middle management level. Of the possible dysfunctional symptoms epitomized by low organizational cohesiveness, we focus on the following four dysfunctional symptoms related to decision making, cooperation, and knowledge base among middle managers: (1) overemphasis on harmony, (2) economically irrational internal consensus building, (3) free-riding behaviors by irresponsible employees failing to pull their weight, and (4) lack of management literacy caused by incapable managers failing to discern right strategy from dead-end strategy.

The first symptom refers to a dysfunctional state epitomized by excess ritualized emphasis on harmony (Saegusa, 2001) in decision-making process on the premise that the state of low cohesiveness necessitates the development of formal/informal decision rules that intend to harmonize different opinions among members, whereas such rules do not necessarily serve to increase organizational cohesiveness. The second symptom refers to dysfunctional state related to rationality of decision making epitomized by irrational and inward-looking consensus-building process that can lead to "strategic drift" (Johnson, 1988). Consensus building is necessary to some extent for being cohesive among organizational members only if they commit themselves for a same direction with an economically proper goal. The third symptom refers to dysfunctional state related to organizational cooperation epitomized by free-ride behaviors (Albanese & Van Fleet, 1985). Free riding or social loafing has been suggested as a typical early sign of organizational decline (Liden, Wayne, Jaworski, & Bennett, 2004). Such behavior will lead to the gradual deterioration of organizational outcome as collective goods (Olson, 1965). Finally, the fourth symptom refers to dysfunctional state related to knowledge bases of organizational members epitomized by management literacy gaps between capable managers and incapable managers because mutual knowledge can be considered as a basis for communication and coordination (Cramton, 2001; Fussell & Krauss, 1992).

We can expect that those four dysfunctional states can be accompanied by low organizational cohesiveness and, in turn, become the sources of organizational deterioration and eventual failure. Based on the premise that organizational deadweight consists of four dimensions (Karube, et al., 2009), we examine the mechanism of how organizational characteristics cause organizational deadweight.

FRAMEWORK

Analytical Framework

Figure 1 shows the analytical framework that examines the relationships of four structural and behavioral characteristics (organizational size, hierarchical structure, vertical information flow, and formal strategic planning) with organizational deadweight. In this framework, we assume that organizational deadweight is affected directly by organizational size, vertical information flow, and formal strategic planning. We also assume that hierarchical structure, vertical information flow, and formal strategic planning are in turn affected by organizational size.

In the light of the exploratory nature of this research, the causal relationships proposed in the framework are tentative and far from exhaustive. However, we believe that such an endeavor may serve as a starting point to examine the mechanism of how internal organizational characteristics cause organizational deterioration among middle managers in large established organizations.

HYPOTHESES

Vertical Information Flow. Information flow through communication is another coordination process indispensable for effective and efficient organizational activity (Jablin & Putnam, 2001). Information is passed from the frontline to the top and from the top to the frontline not only along a formal authority structure but also through informal communication routes based on each person's social ties. Whereas open communication is not always a panacea for organizational problems, lack of information sharing tends to lead to worsening organizational problems (Eisenberg & Witten, 1987). Because insufficient information flow among members may lead to difficulties in focusing on a common goal and in realizing strategic initiatives, managers who intend to resolve the difficulties could perceive such situation as being overload. Therefore, we expect that a greater quantity of upward/downward information flow is negatively associated with deadweight.

Figure 1. Analytical framework

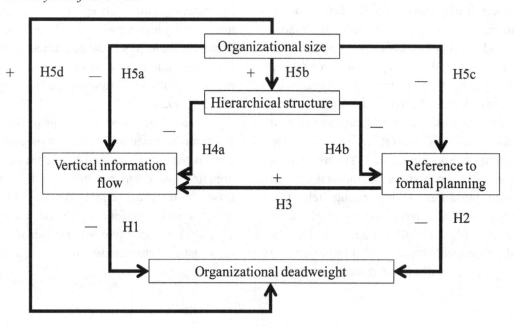

Hypothesis 1 (H1). Regardless of direction, quantity of information flow between superiors and subordinates is negatively associated with organizational deadweight.

Formal Strategic Planning. Whereas external and task environments, organizational structure, and organizational members' commonsense knowledge all affect formal and informal interactions within the business (Morand, 1995), reference to formal strategic planning has been considered as indispensable for coordinating organizational activities. However, they are often considered as impediments to a flexible response to changes in the external environment because they are closely associated with typical images of rigidity and malfunctioned bureaucracy known as "the fallacy of formalization" (Mintzberg, 1994; Mintzberg & McHugh, 1985).

Thus, if reference to formal strategic planning serves to increase the cohesiveness and coherence of organizational member's direction with more predictability of tasks and the clarity of roles without sacrificing organizational members' interaction and the flexibility it offers, organizational members do not perceive it as an impediment. Recent strategic management literature from middle management perspectives also suggests the importance of strategic consensus and manager's involvement in strategic decision-making process (Ashmos, Duchon, & McDaniel, 1998; Floyd & Wooldridge, 2000; Wooldridge & Floyd, 1989, 1990; Wooldridge, Schmid, & Floyd, 2008). For instance, Floyd and Wooldridge (2000, p. 134) argue that "the sense that middle managers are bound together and share a common future is heartened by the belief that they will be treated equitably," suggesting the possibility that organizational cohesiveness can be improved by managers' reference to planning and participation in the planning process. Because active reference to strategic planning and participation in the process necessitate vertical communication, we derive the following hypotheses.

Hypothesis 2 (H2). Degree of reference to formal strategic planning and participation in planning process are negatively associated with organizational deadweight.

Hypothesis 3 (H3). Degree of reference to formal strategic planning and participation in planning process are positively associated with quantity of information flow between superiors and subordinates.

Combining predictions from H1 to H3, we can predict two different causal routes for the reduction of organizational deadweight: (1) reference to strategic formal planning and participation in planning process directly decrease organizational deadweight; and (2) they indirectly decrease organizational deadweight via vertical information flow.

Hierarchical Structure. Managerial hierarchy is a coordinative mechanism that deals with exceptional issues on management to which formal planning and standardization cannot provide an appropriate solution (Mintzberg, 1980). In tandem with formal planning and standardization, hierarchy is essential for organizational coordination (Galbraith, 1977; Miller, 1990). However, hierarchy has been treated as a negation of individual autonomy, freedom, spontaneity, creativity, dignity, and independence (Perrow, 1986). Some scholars insist that it suffocates flexibility and creativity in an organization, and they propose alternative organizational structures (Halal, 1994). To avoid the negative effects of hierarchical structure, a flat organization with fewer formal layers and smaller information gaps between layers is commonly suggested. To promote the free flow of information in organizations, recent literature has placed more emphasis on the predominance of post-bureaucratic forms of organizations characterized by flatter, leaner, network-based structures where power is distributed, as compared with the traditional bureaucratic forms of organizations characterized by a hierarchical formal structure (Symon, 2000). Bush and Frohman (1991), for example, insist that the "up and down" flow of communication in a traditional hierarchy blocks innovation and change, suggesting a shift to a networking structure that allows lateral communication and helps managers and their staff use their creativity. Considering such a negative effect that middle managers within an organization with taller hierarchical structure are likely to face excess managerial load than those within an organization with flatter hierarchical structure, we derive the following hypothesis:

Hypothesis 4a (H4a). A more layered and taller hierarchical structure is negatively associated with quantity of information flow between superiors and subordinates.

Hypothesis 4b (H4b). A more layered and taller hierarchical structure is negatively associated with degree of reference to formal planning.

Organizational Size. organizational size has been treated as a result of organizational growth and success (Whetten, 1980). However, when organizational size is regarded as a degree of difficulty in managing a number of organizational members, the size serves to make it difficult for organizational members to coordinate and communicate each other within the organization. In addition, the span of control being equal, organizational size is expected to correlate with tallness of hierarchical organizational structure. Moreover, a recent study on social loafing suggested that increased group size and decreased cohesiveness were related to increased levels of social loafing. (Liden, et al., 2004). Because availability of organizational slack allows organizational members to waste the slack for their personal purposes and interests (Hirschman, 1970), we can expect that the bigger organizational size, the larger the room of deterioration. Thus, we derive the following hypotheses.

Hypothesis 5a (H5a). Organizational size is negatively associated with quantity of information flow between superiors and subordinates.

Hypothesis 5b (H5b). Organizational size is positively associated with a more layered and taller hierarchical structure.

Hypothesis 5c (H5c). Organizational size is negatively associated with degree of reference to formal planning and participation in planning process.

Hypothesis 5d (H5d). Organizational size is positively associated with organizational deadweight.

METHOD

Data Collection and Sample

To unravel organizational problems at middle management level within large diversified firms, we cast light on organizational activities at the middle management level of business units within firms. We define a business unit as an aggregation of individuals who work together and interact closely to adapt to a specific market under the control of a general manager. In particular, three criteria are used to identify each business unit: (1) the main business of a certain organizational unit can be regarded as a unitary business, (2) the unit has a responsibility for profit, and (3) the unit has initiative in launching new products and winning new business. We refer to a person who has the final responsibility for adaptation to a market as the business unit head (GM: General Manager). We also refer to individuals who are positioned at the middle and lower levels within a BU as "middle managers" and "lower managers," respectively.

One of the unique characteristics of our research is that it is designed to capture the perceptual differences and similarities among different organizational levels, about their circumstances within a business unit. We prepared three slightly different versions of an "organization questionnaire" corresponding to each rank of hierarchy within a business unit: business unit head, middle manager, and lower manager. Rather than relying on responses from a single informant on behalf of an entire business unit, we asked multiple respondents to rate their perceptions of their organizational circumstances. The respondents basically constitute seven individuals in a standard business unit: a business unit head, three middle managers selected from three basic functions in each business unit, and three lower managers who are subordinates of the middle managers.

Because of the sensitive and confidential nature of the information, we launched a research consortium with participating firms. We then sent questionnaires to the respondents in 2006 via a staff manager in a corporate personnel or planning department. Finally, we collected 942 questionnaires from 128 business units in 16 firms (126 respondents from business unit heads, 409 respondents from middle managers, and 407 respondents from lower managers). Then, we aggregated their responses to create each business unit-level measure by calculating the average score of responses to each question item asked in the questionnaire collected from the middle and lower managers of each business unit. All the firms are listed in the first section of Tokyo Stock Exchange, and each business unit belongs to different industries: electronics, machinery, chemical, pharmaceutical, oil refinery, food, transportation, and service-related industries.

Measures

Organizational Deadweight. To measure a multidimensional construct consisting of four dimensions, we assessed it by calculating the arithmetic mean of six responses (three middle managers' responses and three lower managers' responses) to the 12 question items corresponding to the four dimensions (see Table 1). The responses were assessed on a 7-point Likert-type scale (1 = "completely disagree," 2, 3, 4 = "cannot say either way," 5, 6, 7 = "completely agree") by asking respondents: "To what extent do you think each of the following sentences applies to your business unit?"

Based on the empirical result of a questionnaire survey in 2004 by Karube et al. (2009), we initially expected that organizational deadweight would consist of four dimensions. However, results of our factor analysis showed that only one factor whose eigenvalue exceeded one could be extracted from the 12 variables, suggesting that those variables share a single common factor. Thus, we adopted the arithmetic mean of the 12 variables as a single proxy variable for organizational deadweight. Cronbach's alpha of the 12 variables was .914. When we use an aggregation of individual responses for a business unit-level measure, it is suggested that we should check the appropriateness and reliability of aggregated individual-level measures as a group-level construct by using the within-group inter-rater agreement value (James, Demaree, & Wolf, 1993) and intraclass correlation coefficients (ICC [1], ICC [2]; Shrout & Fleiss, 1979). The value of rwg was .906. ICC (1) was .694, and ICC (2) was .695, suggesting appropriateness and reliability of the construct of organizational deadweight as a group-level construct. Moreover, to assess the construct validity of organizational deadweight, we also checked the bivariate correlations between organizational deadweight and subjective and objective performance measures. The correlations between organizational deadweight and performance measures are all negative with statistical significance: subjective sales growth against major competitors (−.511, p < .01), subjective profitability against major competitors (−.437, p < .01), and realized return on sales (−.191, p < .05). These results suggest that deadweight can serve as an internal source of deterioration and eventual maladaptation and organizational failure.

Table 1. Construct of organizational deadweight, 12 questionnaire items, and their validities

Dimensions of the construct	Item asked in the questionnaire	Descriptive Statistics		Factor Loading	Cronbach's alpha of the 12 variables
					.914
		Mean	S.D.		Cronbach's alpha when the item is deleted
I. Overemphasis on Harmony in an Organization					
(1) Slowdown in Decision Making due to a Single Dissenter	The time required to make decisions is dramatically prolonged if even a single person disagrees.	3.901	.726	.585	.911
(2) Debate Regarded as Childish	In my company, a harsh debate is considered to be childish.	3.202	.621	.616	.909
(3) Careful "Socializer" Promoted	In my company, people who prevent conflicts beforehand by giving due consideration to others are promoted more quickly than those who frankly voice justifiable opinions.	3.737	.665	.658	.908
II. Economically Irrational Internal Consensus Building					
(4) Vested Interests among Functional Groups	Many of the middle-level managers are fixated on the interests of the functional groups they belong to (R&D, production, sales, etc.).	4.087	.750	.758	.903
(5) Inward-lookingness	I often observe that members of other BUs focus more serious attention on consensus building among themselves than on customers and competitors.	4.226	.789	.744	.904
(6) Concern with Face-saving	When middle managers coordinate the activities of a BU, I occasionally feel that they attempt to focus on saving other's faces rather than at resolving the actual problems regarding conflicting interests.	3.532	.719	.776	.903
(7) Politicized Activities at the Top Management Level	There are unusual political dynamics at work in the top management team.	3.631	.726	.451	.916
III. Free-rider Problem					
(8) Irresponsibility of Superiors	There are many superiors who irresponsibly interfere in our work.	3.623	.846	.836	.899
(9) Insensitivity to the Loss of a BU	There are many middle managers who do not perceive the loss of their BU as their own loss.	3.904	.802	.698	.906
(10) Lack of Decisiveness	The people in charge of making decisions do not actually make them.	3.969	.884	.837	.899

continued on following page

Table 1. Continued

Dimensions of the construct	Item asked in the questionnaire	Descriptive Statistics		Factor Loading	Cronbach's alpha of the 12 variables
IV. Lack of Management Literacy					
(11) Middle Manager with Strategic Expertise (R)	Many of the middle managers in the BU have strategic expertise. (Reversed)	3.898	.690	.653	.908
(12) Excellence of Top Management (R)	Our top management has excellent capabilities to make superb decisions. (Reversed)	4.373	.740	.586	.910
Eigenvalue Variance (%)		-----	-----	5.745	
		-----	-----	47.872	

The scores of items with R are reversed when organizational deadweight is calculated. The factor analysis is calculated using the principal factor method. Each item was measured with a 7-point Likert scale. N = 128

Vertical Information Flow. Following the ideas discussed in communication studies (Jablin, 1979; Jablin & Putnam, 2001; Jablin, Putnam, Roberts, & Porter, 1987), we adopted the measures related to vertical information flow between superiors and subordinates by using four variables. Of the four variables, two variables are for upward information flow from middle or lower managers to a business unit head (GM): (1) "degree of GM's comprehension of bad news at the operational levels," (2) "degree of GM's comprehension of middle managers' ideas for BU strategy." The other two variables are concerned with downward information flow from a GM to middle or lower managers: (3) "degree of middle and lower managers' comprehension of corporate strategy," (4) "middle and lower managers' comprehension of BU strategy." We asked respondents to rate the degree of these items in percentage ranging from 0% to 100%, respectively. We then took the arithmetic mean of the four values. Cronbach's alpha of the four variables was .834. The value of rwg was .574. ICC (1) was .435, and ICC (2) was .461, leaving the possibility that quantity of vertical information flow perceived by middle managers can be an individual-level construct.

Formal Strategic Planning. To assess the degree of managers' reference to formal strategic planning and their participation in the planning process, we focused on to what extent middle and lower managers refer to formal strategic planning's directives and how much they participated in the formal strategic planning process. We assessed formal strategic planning by asking respondents to rate four question items on a 7-point scale: "degree of reference to business unit's formal planning," "degree of breakdown of plans into individual objectives," "degree of linkage between the attainment of planned objectives and promotions (R)," and "degree of participation in the planning process." We then calculated business unit level measure by taking the arithmetic mean of the four variables. Cronbach's alpha of the four variables was .663. The value of rwg was .874. ICC (1) was .502, and ICC (2) was .512, suggesting the appropriateness as a group-level construct while the reliability is not necessarily high.

Hierarchical Structure. To measure the hierarchical layers of organizational structure, we focused on the hierarchical distance between the GM and the middle and lower managers in a business unit. We asked middle manager respondents to rate "formal distance from the middle manager to a GM" and "informal distance from the middle manager to a GM." We also asked lower manager respondents to rate "formal distance from the lower manager to a GM" and "informal distance from the lower manager to a GM." Business unit level measure of hierarchical structure was calculated by taking the arithmetic mean of the four variables.

Table 2. Correlation matrix

	(1)	(2)	(3)	(4)	(5)	Cronbach's alpha
(1) Organizational deadweight 12 questions items	1					.914
(2) Organizational size 1 question item	.390*** .000	1				
(3) Hierarchical structure 4 question items	.351*** .000	.516*** .000	1			.780
(4) Formal planning 4 question items	-.555*** .000	-.240*** .006	-.217*** .003	1		.663
(5) Vertical information flow 8 question items	-.566*** .000	-.399*** .000	-.588*** .000	.518*** .000	1	.834

$N = 128$

Upper row is a coefficient of Pearson's bivariate correlation. Lower row is a significance probability.
*** $p < .01$, ** $p < .05$, * $p < .1$

Cronbach's alpha of the four variables was .780. The value of rwg was .857. ICC (1) was .519, and ICC (2) was .521, suggesting the appropriateness as a group-level construct while the reliability is not necessarily high.

Organizational Size. Based on Kimberly's extensive literature survey (Kimberly, 1976), we adopted the logarithmic number of full-time employees in a business unit, which is the most typical measurement of organizational size.

Data Analysis

Because the main interest of this research is in how organizational characteristics might relate to organizational deadweight, we first examined bivariate correlations between organizational characteristics and organizational deadweight. We then utilized path analytic procedures to test the hypotheses.

RESULTS

Bivariate Correlation

Table 2 shows the results of Pearson's bivariate correlation between organizational characteristics and organizational deadweight. The relationship between vertical information flow and organizational deadweight (H1) is negatively correlated at the 1% significance level (-.566, $p < .01$), suggesting the possibility that active vertical information flow may decrease organizational deadweight. The relationship between reference to formal strategic planning and participation in planning process and organizational deadweight (H2) is also statistically significant with expected direction (-.555, $p < .01$), suggesting that more reference to formal strategic planning and managers' participation in the planning process remedy deterioration. In addition, the relationship between formal strategic planning and vertical information flow (H3) is positively correlated at the 1% significance level (.518, $p < .01$), suggesting the possibility that reference to formal strategic planning and participation in planning process may improve vertical information flow.

The relationships of hieratical structure with vertical information flow (H4a) and formal strategic planning (H4b) are negatively correlated at the 1% significance level, respectively (-.588, $p < .01$; -.217, $p < .01$), suggesting the possibility that more layered and taller hierarchical structure aggravates the vertical information flow between superiors and subordinates and makes it difficult for managers to refer to formal strategic planning and participate in the planning process. Moreover, as we initially expected, organizational size is negatively correlated with vertical information flow (H5a) and with formal strategic planning (H5c) (−.399, p < .01; −.240, p < .01), whereas organizational size is positively associated with hierarchical structure (H5b) and with organizational deadweight (H5d) at the 1% significance level (.516, p < .01; .390, p < .01), suggesting the possibility that organizational size decrease vertical communication and increase organizational deadweight.

PATH ANALYSIS

To examine further the causality of the hypotheses and get a clearer overview of the links of organizational characteristics with organizational deadweight, we conducted a path analysis. Although several valid models can be constructed from the data, we focus on the one with the best fit, which is composed of one exogenous variable (organizational age) and four endogenous variables shown in Figure 2 (Chi-square = .121, d.f. = 1, probability level = .728, GFI = 1.000, AGFI = .994, NFI = .999, CFI = 1.000, RMSEA = .000, AIC = 28.121).

The results of this model can be summarized into five main findings: (1) organizational size has a strong positive effect on the tallness of formal hierarchical structure (H5b, .516, p < .01) and moderate positive effect on organizational deadweight (H5d, .182, p < .05), suggesting that H5b and H5d are supported, whereas the effects of size on vertical information flow (H5a, .075, n.s.) and formal strategic planning (H5c, −.144, n.s.) are relatively small; (2) tallness of formal hierarchal structure has a strong negative effect on the formal vertical information flows (H4a, −.450, p < .01), whereas tallness of formal hierarchal structure has a weak negative effect on formal strategic planning (H4b, −.187, p < .10), suggesting that only H4a is supported; (3) formal strategic planning has a strong positive effect on

Figure 2. Result of path analysis

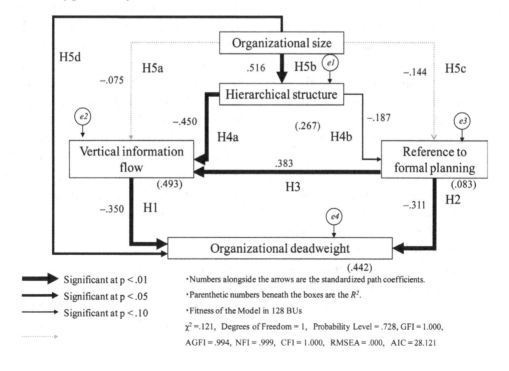

vertical information flow (H3, .383, p < .01), suggesting that H3 is supported; (4) formal strategic planning has a negative effect on organizational deadweight (H2, −.311, p < .01); and (5) vertical information flow has a negative effect on organizational deadweight (H1, −.350, p < .01).

DISCUSSION

Cross-sectional nature of our data set does not allow us to make any conclusions about the causal direction among the relationships between organizational characteristics and organizational deadweight. However, based on our limited findings, we infer that dysfunctional symptoms defined as organizational deadweight may be increased by organizational size, whereas vertical information flow and reference to formal strategic planning and participation in planning process may decrease the deadweight.

The importance of open communication in the face of organizational decline has been repeatedly emphasized in the communication literature: "honest communication" (Beer & Eisenstat, 2004) and "upward information distortion" from subordinates to their superiors (Tourish, 2005; Tourish & Robson, 2006). These insights of the previous studies are consistent with our empirical finding, suggesting the importance of vertical communication between superiors and subordinates to safeguard against deterioration.

In addition, because the second finding indicates the necessity of flat organizational structure to facilitate vertical information flow, our findings are also consistent with recent literature that has put more emphasis on the predominance of post-bureaucratic forms of organizations characterized by flatter, leaner, power-distributed, network-based structure over the traditional bureaucratic forms of organizations characterized by hierarchical formal structure (Bush & Frohman, 1991; Symon, 2000).

On the other hand, the fourth finding on the relationship between formal strategic planning and organizational deadweight seems to be counterintuitive because formal strategic planning per se has long been considered as one of the building blocks that epitomize formality and mechanistic characteristics of organizations. If formal strategic planning functioned as negative binding forces for organizational members, reference to formal strategic planning and participation in the planning process could be sources of organizational deadweight in particular and organizational deterioration in general. However, as indicated in our findings, reference to formal strategic planning and participation in planning process decrease organizational deadweight, suggesting that degree of organizational deterioration can be remedied by reference to formal strategic planning and participation in the formal planning process and vertical information flow.

Summing up the findings, larger organizational size directly aggravates organizational deadweight, whereas larger size also aggravates it indirectly by way of taller hierarchical structure and resulting decreased vertical information flow. These finding indicate the possibility that organizational size could become an internal structural determinant of organizational deterioration and eventual organizational failure. Although it is true that organizational size can function as a structural determinant to increase organizational deadweight directly and indirectly, one should also pay attention to the fact that there still exists room for strategic discretion to decrease organizational deadweight by promoting managers' reference to formal strategic planning and their participation in the planning process.

CONCLUSION

Management scholars tend to argue that formalized and mechanistic characteristics, such as formal strategic planning, may hamper the flexibility of decision-making and the realization of strategic initiatives at middle management level, whereas organic characteristics can augment the adaptability and creativity of an organization (Burns & Stalker, 1961; Halal, 1994; Mintzberg, 1994; Mintzberg & McHugh, 1985). With our limited results as basis, however, formal strategic planning can serve to reduce dysfunctional symptoms referred as organizational deadweight.

Another interesting finding of our results is the effect of organizational size. Although the roles of organizational size used to be discussed vigorously in previous Aston studies (e.g., Pugh, Hickson, Hinings, & Turner, 1969), the roles have been underscored or degraded to the position of a mere control variable in the recent management literature. With the relationships found in this research as our basis, we believe that the roles and effects of organizational size should be reconsidered in the light of safeguarding against organizational deterioration.

Our results also have an implication for organizational design. In an organization comprising a small number of people, face-to-face communication functions smoothly and effectively. In a larger organization, however, the effectiveness of face-to-face communication can be enormously reduced in the absence of an appropriate degree of formalization. This is because the dominance of particularism over universalism can sacrifice the potential merits of universalism that are realized under a certain level of bureaucracy and the element of formalization within processes (Perrow, 1986). Therefore, if a given firm wishes to maintain its organizational performance without enforcing additional formalization, we believe that reduction in the size of the organizational unit can be considered as a way to recover from the symptoms of organizational deterioration.

Because our analytical approach and the collected data are still far from being exhaustive, further examination is still needed, and some methodological issues remain unsolved. Specifically, our findings are based on cross-sectional data of Japanese firms so that we lack sufficient evidence to generalize the causality of our proposed hypotheses and the relationships in other countries. Thus, to ensure the generalizability and causality of our findings, we believe that international comparisons and a longitudinal approach are needed.

ACKNOWLEDGMENT

This research was financially supported by Global Center of Excellence grant by the Ministry of Education in Japan.

REFERENCES

Albanese, R., & Van Fleet, D. D. (1985). Free-riding: Theory, research, and implications. *Academy of Management Review, 10*, 244–255. doi:10.2307/257966

Ashmos, D. P., Duchon, D., & McDaniel, R. R. (1998). Participation in strategic decision-making: The role of organizational predisposition and issue interpretation. *Decision Sciences, 29*(1), 25–51. doi:10.1111/j.1540-5915.1998.tb01343.x

Barnard, C. I. (1938). *The functions of the executive*. Cambridge, MA: Harvard University Press.

Barnett, C. K., & Pratt, M. G. (2000). From threat-rigidity to flexibility—Toward a learning model of autogenic crisis in organizations. *Journal of Organizational Change Management, 13*(1), 74–88. doi:10.1108/09534810010310258

Barr, P. S., Stimpert, J. L., & Huff, A. S. (1992). Cognitive change, strategic action, and organizational renewal. *Strategic Management Journal, 13*, 15–36. doi:10.1002/smj.4250131004

Beer, M., & Eisenstat, R. (2004). How to have an honest conversation about your business strategy. *Harvard Business Review, 82*(2), 82–89.

Bernthal, P. R., & Insko, C. A. (1993). Cohesiveness without groupthink: The interactive effects of social and task cohesion. *Group & Organization Management, 18*, 66–87. doi:10.1177/1059601193181005

Burns, T., & Stalker, G. N. (1961). *The management of innovation.* London, UK: Tavistock Publications.

Bush, J. B., & Frohman, A. L. (1991). Communication in a "network" organization. *Organizational Dynamics, 20*(2), 23–36. doi:10.1016/0090-2616(91)90069-L

Cameron, K. S., Sutton, R. I., & Whetten, A. D. (1988). *Readings in organizational decline: Frameworks, research, and prescriptions.* Cambridge, MA: Ballinger.

Cameron, K. S., Whetten, D. A., & Kim, M. U. (1987). Organizational dysfunctions of decline. *Academy of Management Journal, 30*, 126–138. doi:10.2307/255899

Cayla, D. (2006). Ex post and ex ante coordination: Principles of coherence in organizations and markets. *Journal of Economic Issues, 40*(2), 325–332.

Cota, A. A., Evans, C. R., Dion, K. L., Kilik, L., & Longman, R. S. (1995). The structure of group cohesion. *Personality and Social Psychology Bulletin, 21*, 572–580. doi:10.1177/0146167295216003

Cramton, C. D. (2001). The mutual knowledge problem and its consequences for dispersed collaboration. *Organization Science, 12*(3), 346–371. doi:10.1287/orsc.12.3.346.10098

D'Aveni, R. A. (1989). The aftermath of organizational decline—A longitudinal-study of the strategic and managerial characteristics of declining firms. *Academy of Management Journal, 32*(3), 577–605. doi:10.2307/256435

D'Aveni, R. A., & MacMillan, I. C. (1990). Crisis and content of managerial communications: A study of the focus of attention of top managers in surviving and failing firms. *Administrative Science Quarterly, 35*, 634–657. doi:10.2307/2393512

Durham, J. W., & Smith, H. L. (1982). Toward a general theory of organizational deterioration. *Administration & Society, 14*(3), 373–400. doi:10.1177/009539978201400305

Eisenberg, E. M., & Witten, M. G. (1987). Reconsidering openness in organizational communication. *Academy of Management Review, 12*(3), 418–426.

Eisenhardt, K. M. (1989). Making fast strategic decisions in high-velocity environments. *Academy of Management Journal, 32*(3), 543–576. doi:10.2307/256434

Ekstrom, W. L. (1993). A coherence theory of autonomy. *Philosophy and Phenomenological Research, 53*(3), 599–616. doi:10.2307/2108082

Elron, E. (1997). Top management teams within multinational corporations: Effects of cultural heterogeneity. *The Leadership Quarterly, 8*(4), 393–412. doi:10.1016/S1048-9843(97)90021-7

Ensley, M. D., Pearson, A. W., & Amason, A. C. (2002). Understanding the dynamics of new venture top management teams: Cohesion, conflict, and new venture performance. *Journal of Business Venturing, 17*(4), 365–386. doi:10.1016/S0883-9026(00)00065-3

Feldt, T., Kivimäki, M., Rantala, A., & Tolvanen, A. (2004). Sense of coherence and work characteristics: A cross-lagged structural equation model among managers. *Journal of Occupational and Organizational Psychology, 77*(3), 323–342. doi:10.1348/0963179041752655

Floyd, S. W., & Wooldridge, B. (2000). *Building strategy from the middle: Reconceptualizing strategy process.* Thousand Oaks, CA: Sage.

Friedkin, N. E. (2004). Social cohesion. *Annual Review of Sociology*, *30*, 409–425. doi:10.1146/annurev.soc.30.012703.110625

Fussell, S.R., & Krauss, R. (1992). Coordination of knowledge in communication: Effects of speakers' assumptions about what others know. *Journal of Personality and Social Psychology*, *62*(3), 378–391. doi:10.1037/0022-3514.62.3.378

Galbraith, J. (1977). *Organization design*. Reading, MA: Addison Wesley.

Garvin, D. A. (1998). The processes of organization and management. *Sloan Management Review*, *39*(4), 33–50.

Ghoshal, S., & Gratton, L. (2002). Integrating the enterprise. *MIT Sloan Management Review*, *44*, 31–38.

Greenhalgh, L. (1983). Organizational decline. In Bacharach, S. B. (Ed.), *Research in the Sociology of Organizations* (*Vol. 2*, pp. 231–276). London, UK: JAI Press.

Halal, W. E. (1994). From hierarchy to enterprise: Internal markets are the new foundation of management. *The Academy of Management Executive*, *8*(4), 69–83. doi:10.5465/AME.1994.9412071706

Hambrick, D. C., & D'Aveni, R. A. (1992). Top team deterioration as part of the downward spiral of large corporate bankruptcies. *Management Science*, *38*(10), 1445–1466. doi:10.1287/mnsc.38.10.1445

Hannan, M. T., & Freeman, J. (1984). Structural inertia and organizational change. *American Sociological Review*, *49*, 149–164. doi:10.2307/2095567

Hirschman, A. O. (1970). *Exit, voice, and loyalty: Responses to decline in firms, organizations, and states*. Cambridge, MA: Harvard University Press.

Jablin, F. M. (1979). Superior-subordinate communication: The state of the art. *Psychological Bulletin*, *86*, 1201–1222. doi:10.1037/0033-2909.86.6.1201

Jablin, F. M. (1987). Formal organization structure. In Jablin, F. M., Putnam, L. L., Roberts, K., & Porter, L. W. (Eds.), *Handbook of Organizational Communication: An Interdisciplinary Perspective* (pp. 389–419). Newbury Park, CA: Sage.

Jablin, F. M., & Putnam, L. L. (Eds.). (2001). *The new handbook of organizational communication: Advances in theory, research and methods*. Thousand Oaks, CA: Sage.

Jablin, F. M., Putnam, L. L., Roberts, K. H., & Porter, L. W. (Eds.). (1987). *Handbook of organizational communication: An interdisciplinary perspective*. Newbury Park, CA: Sage.

James, L. R., Demaree, R. G., & Wolf, G. (1993). An assessment of within-group interrater agreement. *The Journal of Applied Psychology*, *78*, 306–309. doi:10.1037/0021-9010.78.2.306

Janis, I. L. (1972). *Victims of groupthink: A psychological study of foreign-policy decisions and fiascoes*. Boston, MA: Houghton and Mifflin.

Johnson, G. (1988). Rethinking incrementalism. *Strategic Management Journal*, *9*, 75–91. doi:10.1002/smj.4250090107

Karube, M., Numagami, T., & Kato, T. (2009). Exploring organisational deterioration: "Organisational deadweight" as a cause of malfunction of strategic initiatives in Japanese firms. *Long Range Planning*, *42*, 518–544. doi:10.1016/j.lrp.2009.06.005

Kessler, E. H., & Chakrabarti, A. K. (1996). Innovation speed: A conceptual model of context, antecedents, and outcomes. *Academy of Management Review*, *21*(4), 1143–1191.

Kimberly, J. R. (1976). Organizational size and the structuralist perspective: A review, critique, and proposal. *Administrative Science Quarterly*, *21*(4), 571–597. doi:10.2307/2391717

Kotter, J. P., & Heskett, J. L. (1992). *Corporate culture and performance*. New York, NY: Free Press.

Lawrence, P. R., & Lorsch, J. W. (1967). *Organization and environment: Managing differentiation and integration.* Boston, MA: Harvard Business School.

Leonard-Barton, D. (1992). Core capabilities and core rigidities: A paradox in managing new product development. *Strategic Management Journal, 13,* 111–125. doi:10.1002/smj.4250131009

Levitt, B., & March, J. G. (1988). Organizational learning. *Annual Review of Sociology, 14,* 319–340. doi:10.1146/annurev.so.14.080188.001535

Liden, R. C., Wayne, S. J., Jaworski, R. A., & Bennett, N. (2004). Social loafing: A field investigation. *Journal of Management, 30,* 285–304. doi:10.1016/j.jm.2003.02.002

Lissack, M., & Roos, J. (2001). Be coherent, not visionary. *Long Range Planning, 34*(1), 53–70. doi:10.1016/S0024-6301(00)00093-5

Lorange, P., & Nelson, R. T. (1987). How to recognize—and avoid—organizational decline. *Sloan Management Review, 28,* 41–48.

Mckinley, W. (1993). Organizational decline and adaptation: Theoretical controversies. *Organization Science, 4,* 1–9. doi:10.1287/orsc.4.1.1

Mellahi, K., & Wilkinson, A. (2004). Organizational failure: A critique of recent research and a proposed integrative framework. *International Journal of Management Reviews, 5-6*(1), 21–41. doi:10.1111/j.1460-8545.2004.00095.x

Michalisin, M. D., Karau, S. J., & Tangpong, C. (2004). Top management team cohesion and superior industry returns. *Group & Organization Management, 29*(1), 125–140. doi:10.1177/1059601103251687

Miller, D. (1990). Organizational configurations: Cohesion, change, and prediction. *Human Relations, 43,* 771–789. doi:10.1177/001872679004300805

Miller, D., & Friesen, P. H. (1980). Archetypes of organizational transition. *Administrative Science Quarterly, 25,* 268–299. doi:10.2307/2392455

Mintzberg, H. (1980). Structure in 5's: A synthesis of the research on organization design. *Management Science, 26,* 322–341. doi:10.1287/mnsc.26.3.322

Mintzberg, H. (1994). *The rise and fall of strategic planning.* New York, NY: Free Press.

Mintzberg, H., & McHugh, A. (1985). Strategy formation in an adhocracy. *Administrative Science Quarterly, 30,* 160–197. doi:10.2307/2393104

Morand, D. A. (1995). The role of behavioral formality and informality in the enactment of bureaucratic versus organic organizations. *Academy of Management Review, 20,* 831–872.

Nonaka, I. (1988). Toward middle-up-down management: Accelerating information creation. *Sloan Management Review, 29*(3), 9–18.

Numagami, T., Karube, M., & Kato, T. (2010). Organizational deadweight: Learning from Japan. *The Academy of Management Perspectives, 24*(4), 25–37. doi:10.5465/AMP.2010.55206382

Olson, M. (1965). *The logic of collective action: Public goods and the theory of groups.* Boston, MA: Harvard University Press.

Ouchi, W. G. (1981). *Theory Z: How American business can meet the Japanese challenge.* Reading, MA: Addison-Wesley.

Perrow, C. (1986). *Complex organizations: Critical essay* (3rd ed.). New York, NY: McGraw-Hill.

Pugh, D. S., Hickson, D. J., Hinings, C. R., & Turner, C. (1969). The context of organization structures. *Administrative Science Quarterly, 14,* 91–113. doi:10.2307/2391366

Roberts, K. H., & O'Reilly, C. A. III. (1979). Some correlations of communication roles in organizations. *Academy of Management Journal, 22*, 42–57. doi:10.2307/255477

Saegusa, T. (2001). *V-ji kaifuku no keiei* [The management for V-shaped recovery]. Tokyo, Japan: Nihon Keizai Shimbun-sha.

Shrout, P. E., & Fleiss, J. L. (1979). Intraclass correlations: Uses in assessing rater reliability. *Psychological Bulletin, 86*(2), 420–428. doi:10.1037/0033-2909.86.2.420

Sinclair, A. (1992). The tyranny of a team ideology. *Organization Studies, 13*(4), 611–626. doi:10.1177/017084069201300405

Sorensen, J. B. (2002). The strength of corporate culture and the reliability of firm performance. *Administrative Science Quarterly, 47*(1), 70–91. doi:10.2307/3094891

Stalk, G. Jr. (1988). Time—The next source of competitive advantage. *Harvard Business Review, 66*(4), 41–51.

Staw, B., Sandelands, L., & Dutton, J. E. (1981). Threat-rigidity cycles in organizational behavior: A multi-level analysis. *Administrative Science Quarterly, 26*, 501–524. doi:10.2307/2392337

Symon, G. (2000). Information and communication technologies and the network organization: A critical analysis. *Journal of Occupational and Organizational Psychology, 73*(4), 389–414. doi:10.1348/096317900167100

Tourish, D. (2005). Critical upward communication: Ten commandments for improving strategy and decision making. *Long Range Planning, 38*(5), 485–503. doi:10.1016/j.lrp.2005.05.001

Tourish, D., & Robson, P. (2006). Sensemaking and the distortion of critical upward communication in organizations. *Journal of Management Studies, 43*(4), 711–730. doi:10.1111/j.1467-6486.2006.00608.x

Tripsas, M., & Gavetti, G. (2000). Capabilities, cognition, and inertia: Evidence from digital imaging. *Strategic Management Journal, 21*, 1147–1161. doi:10.1002/1097-0266(200010/11)21:10/11<1147::AID-SMJ128>3.0.CO;2-R

Walsh, J. P. (1995). Managerial and organizational cognition: Notes from a trip down memory lane. *Organization Science, 6*, 280–321. doi:10.1287/orsc.6.3.280

Weick, K. E. (1979). *The social psychology of organizing* (2nd ed.). Reading, MA: Addison-Wesley.

Weitzel, W., & Jonsson, E. (1989). Decline in organizations: A literature integration and extension. *Administrative Science Quarterly, 34*, 91–109. doi:10.2307/2392987

Whetten, D. A. (1980). Organizational decline: A neglected topic in organizational science. *Academy of Management Journal, 5*, 577–588.

Whyte, G. (1989). Groupthink reconsidered. *Academy of Management Review, 14*(1), 40–56.

Wooldridge, B., & Floyd, S. W. (1989). Strategic process effects on consensus. *Strategic Management Journal, 10*(3), 295–302. doi:10.1002/smj.4250100308

Wooldridge, B., & Floyd, S. W. (1990). The strategy process, middle management involvement, and organizational performance. *Strategic Management Journal, 11*(3), 231–241. doi:10.1002/smj.4250110305

Wooldridge, B., Schmid, T., & Floyd, S. W. (2008). The middle management perspective on strategy process: Contributions, synthesis, and future research. *Journal of Management, 34*(6), 1190–1221. doi:10.1177/0149206308324326

Chapter 14
Innovation Capability in High-Tech Companies:
Exploring the Role of Organizational Culture and Empowerment

Alper Ertürk
Vlerick Leuven Gent Management School, Belgium

ABSTRACT

This chapter analyses the influence of organizational culture components, defined in Hofstede's (1991, 2001) cultural framework (i.e., power distance, individualism/collectivism, assertiveness focus, and uncertainty avoidance), and empowerment on innovation capability, and examines the differentiations in their influence. The hypotheses are tested by applying Structural Equations Modeling (SEM) methodology to data collected from Information Technology professionals from high-tech companies. Results of the analyses have yielded that power distance is found to be negatively associated with both empowerment and innovation capability, whereas uncertainty avoidance is negatively related to innovation capability, but positively related to empowerment. Collectivism is found to be positively related only to empowerment; yet no significant relationship was revealed between collectivism and innovation capability. In addition, no significant relationship was found between assertiveness focus and empowerment or innovation capability. Empowerment is also found to be significantly and positively related to innovation capability. In terms of managerial practice, the study helps clarify the key role played by cultural dimensions in the process of shaping an empowering and innovative work environment. Findings also reveal that managers should focus on participative managerial practices (e.g. empowerment) to promote innovation capability of high-tech companies by considering the cultural tendencies of employees in the organization.

DOI: 10.4018/978-1-4666-1836-7.ch014

INTRODUCTION

In recent years, high technology has captured significant attention in the international business environment, as scholars, policy makers, and investors believe in the crucial role of high-tech companies for economic prosperity in the developed and developing nations. Especially in the last two decades, high-tech companies have become the building blocks of strong economies in different regions in the world (Ujjual, 2008). High-tech companies are among the organizations, which are assumed as the key sources of innovative ideas, products, and processes that are essential to obtain and maintain economic and especially technologic competitiveness (Kodama, 1991).

Internet-enabled information and communication technologies have challenged existing business models in almost all sectors and introduced rapid change in every aspect of the business environment. In this turbulent environment, all organizations are inevitably facing with demands for both radical and incremental change. Moreover, globalization and increasing competition have reinforced in organizations the need for differentiation, encouragement for experimentation and constantly learning about new practices and technologies. In order to be able to cope with this continuous change, an organizational system including organizations' strategies, structures, processes, and communication practices must be designed so as to encourage innovation and change (Burgelman, et al., 2004; Weil, 2005; Dasgupta & Gupta, 2009). Thus, the innovation capability is considered to represent an important competitive advantage for organizations, given its importance for economic growth, wealth creation, business expansion and technological progress (Wickham, 2004; Beckman & Barry, 2007; Dimov, 2007).

Especially in high-tech industries, as global competition intensifies and product life cycle shortens, high-tech services and products are becoming more and more complex with shorter life-spans. In this climate, considering the fact that sustainable development cannot be achieved and maintained without innovation, the pressure to innovate increases. Hence, high-tech companies are increasingly looking for ways to enhance their ability to innovate effectively. The ability to develop and launch innovative new products by using the latest technology quickly before global competitors, or soon thereafter, is a key factor in gaining first-mover advantages, achieving product success, capturing market share, increasing return on investment and long-term viability (Allocca & Kessler, 2006). Successful innovation for high-tech companies is associated with good performance and related to subsequent growth. The salience of innovation capability for high-tech companies derives from the fact that in an increasingly hostile market environment characterized by rapid change, it represents a means of survival, and not just growth. Sustainable innovation, which leads to competitive advantage of high-tech companies by enhancing their capacity to keep up with, respond to, and initiate technological change on an ongoing basis, requires a systemic and effective management approach (Romijn & Albaladejo, 2002).

Innovation is considered as a value-added activity dealing mainly with the enhancement of existing works (e.g. product, process, service), particularly for higher business value. Innovation capability embraces the formation and development of new ideas, new product development, new manufacturing processes and new services (Brown, 1992). Furthermore, Brown (1992) also indicated that the only way to create a competitive strength for an organization is the capability to innovate. In support of these propositions, many researchers have demostrated that innovation capability significantly contributes to a company's performance in ways; such as innovation performance (Cavusgil, et al., 2003), product and process improvement (Wolff & Pett, 2006), innovation rate (Yam, et al., 2004), and company's general performance (Calantone, et al., 2002). Although it might not be claimed as universally true in every economic sector, in his study on high-tech companies, Wei (2006) demonstrated that innovation capability is one of the key factors positively influencing company's market performance, as well as quality performance.

Thus, the design and implementation of the programs to enhance competitive innovation capability of companies have received significant attention in the last decade (e.g., Romijn & Albaladejo, 2002; Çakar, 2006; Çakar & Ertürk, 2010). Prior research has attempted to explore what enhances innovation capability. Romijn and Albaladejo (2002) have proposed that internal sources, such as knowldege, professional background and skill of workforce are important internal factors to improve innovation capability. In their recent research on small and medium sized enterprises, Çakar and Ertürk (2010) have demonstrated the important role of empowerment and organizational culture on shaping the innovation capability. Some other research has demonstrated that Research and Development (R&D) expenditures (Wolff & Pett, 2006), the percentage of R&D personnel (Yam, et al., 2004) would also contribute to innovation capability.

A large part of a company's knowledge base, which is vital for a company's innovation capability, is embodied in its employees (Hadjimanolis, 2000). Several researches have demonstrated that human resources are strategically important for high-tech companies to foster innovation capability and to enjoy sustainable competitive advantage (Hatch & Dyer, 2004; Hitt, 2001; Freel, 2006; Lenox & King, 2004). Hence, it is being recognized that competitive advantage can be obtained with a high quality workforce that enables organizations to compete on the basis of innovation capability.

As people do not live and act in a vacuum, we cannot investigate innovation capability or innovativeness in isolation. Several scholars have called for taking context into account when studying work related variables and human behaviour; as context elements, such as organizational cul-

ture and managerial styles, can have substantial and powerful effects on employees' capabilities, attitudes and behaviors (Johns, 2006; Liden & Antonakis, 2009; Meyer, Dalal, & Hermida, 2010; Rousseau & Fried, 2001). How people create and use innovative capability in their job and organisation does not only depend on their individual (style) differences, but also on environmental and contextual factors, such as organizational culture and managerial styles, and also on the interaction of those contextual factors. In line with the idea of interactionism (i.e., behavior is a function of the interaction between the person and the environment), it is important to integrate the context in the research regarding innovation capability. In support of this viewpoint, it has been widely recognized that organizational culture plays a key role in creating and maintaining innovation processes (e.g., Hauser, 1998; Martins & Terblanche, 2003).

On the other hand, relationships between different human resource practices and innovation-supportive cultures have been revealed in a few studies (e.g., Chandler, et al., 2000; Ogbonna & Harris, 2000). However, only a very small body of research has taken into account cultural and managerial components together as employee-focused contextual variables that may foster or lessen innovation capability.

Therefore, this study is an attempt to attenuate the gap in the literature considering the different associations between organizational culture, perceptions of empowerment, and innovation capability. Main purpose of this research is to determine how innovation capability would be enhanced by empowerment and specific cultural dimensions; namely power distance, individualism/collectivism, assertiveness focus and uncertainty avoidance; and by the interactions of those components in high-tech companies. To examine the roles of organizational culture and empowerment in enhancing innovation capability, empowerment is considered as an antecedent of innovation capability and also as a consequence of organizational culture.

This study contributes to literature in several aspects. First, unlike most research, which examines innovativeness as an independent variable (e.g., Danneels & Kleinschmidt, 2001; Cavusgil, et al., 2003; Wolff & Pett, 2006; Yam, et al., 2004; Calantone, et al., 2002; Wei, 2006), this study specifies this concept as a dependent variable. Such an approach elevates current work as it responds to the need of research examining factors that influence innovation capability (Sethi, Smith, & Park, 2001). Second, instead of investigating the effects of organizational culture and empowerment on innovation capability separately, this study focuses on a rather neglected aspect of the innovation capability by examining the interactions and combined influence of cultural and managerial components on innovation capability. In particular, this study hypothesizes that organizational culture affects innovation capability directly and indirectly through empowerment. Thirdly, to our knowledge, there is no research deeply exploring both cultural and managerial antecedents of innovation capability in high-tech companies. Finally, the results of this study are based on structural equations modeling analyses in order to better examine the significant relationships among constructs. As a conclusion, despite the widely acknowledged importance of innovation in the high-tech area, present study extends the past research by taking into account the contextual variables to increase current understanding and awareness of innovation capability.

BACKGROUND

Innovation Capability

In the management literature, innovation has been defined in several ways. Nonetheless, it is not only defined as the conceptualization of a new or significantly improved product or service, but also as the successful introduction of something new and useful, for example, introducing new methods, techniques, practices, or new or altered products and services. Innovation can also be considered as a process in which employees' knowledge and valuable ideas are transformed into new forms of added value for the organization and its stakeholders. The innovation spiral comprises of individual and social learning at the workplace, knowledge creation, and innovation (Dasgupta & Gupta, 2009).

Thus, the firm's innovation capability can be defined as its ability to mobilize and disseminate the knowledge embodied in its employees (Kogut & Zander, 1992), and furthermore combine it to learning that leads into creating new product and/or process innovation. The ability to create and mobilize knowledge is an essential and critical indication of innovation capability.

Innovation capability can be considered as a way of thinking and behaving that facilitates creating and developing values and attitudes within a company, which may in turn encourage new ideas and changes, initiate their acceptance and increase support, even though such changes may mean a conflict with conventional and traditional behavior.

Innovation capability is one of the most important dynamics that enables high-tech companies to achieve a high level of competitiveness both in national and international market. According to Kodama (1991), the main characteristics features of hi-tech industries include but not limited to; technological diversification for survival, targeting of R&D effort towards innovative initiatives, high degree of product obsolescence due to rapid innovation cycle and combining of existing technologies in creative ways to enhance innovation. Considering that innovation capability is one of the crucial features of high-tech industry today, how to promote and sustain the innovation capability should be the key focus area of the managers of high-tech companies. Therefore, by stipulating innovation capability as a dependent variable, this study intends to show how to enhance innovation capability by way of organizational culture and empowerment.

Organizational Culture

Fundamentally, organizational culture is constructed as a pattern of shared managerial beliefs and assumptions (Schein, 1990, 1992). Generally, culture is used by social scientists to refer to a set of parameters of collectives that differentiate the collectives in meaningful ways. The focus is on the sharedness of cultural indicators among members of the collective (House, et al., 2002). Furthermore, cultural continuity and coherence between organizations and the society within which they operate is an important aspect addressed by some researchers (e.g. Aycan, Kanungo, & Sinha, 1999; Mendonca & Kanungo, 1994). The model of cultural fit proposed by those researchers, suggests that societal values influence organizational practices through the mediation of internal organizational culture. Thus, the model asserts that the organizational culture is inevitably influenced by the societal culture. Accordingly, recent research has used similar dimensions for national and organizational cultures, as the organizational culture is seen as a reflection of the national culture (see, Dorfman & Howell, 1988; House, et al., 2002; Sigler & Pearson, 2000; Robert & Wasti, 2002; Aycan, et al., 2000). In this study, organizational culture is based on employee-related shared values, which are influenced by societal level culture.

Hofstede's (2001) cultural framework is well established and widely applied in management and organizational research (e.g., Sivakumar & Nakata, 2001; van Everdingen & Waarts, 2003; Waarts & van Everdingen, 2005). Hofstede's framework is used to operationalize organizational culture, since it has received the greatest attention from management scholars in recent years. In this study, the original framework consisting of four dimensions, namely power distance, uncertainty avoidance, individualism/collectivism, and assertiveness focus, is used.

Power distance can be explained as the extent to which organization members feel comfortable through interactions across hierarchical levels. It reflects the degree to which people feel they should be involved in decision-making. In the organizations with high power distance, employees feel that it is the manager's job to make the decisions, and when power distance is low, employees feel they should also have power and be involved in the manager's decision-making process.

Uncertainty avoidance centers on the degree to which employees want to avoid ambiguity and uncertainty in favor of clear goals and operating guidelines.

Individualism/collectivism tracks the extent to which people prefer to be treated as unique individuals rather than as part of a group. In collectivistic cultures, people find comfort and energy in the group setting, whereas in individualistic cultures people want to be able to stand out as individuals and not be held back by the group. Collectivism lies at one end of a continuum with individualism at the other.

Assertiveness focus concerns with the degree to which people feel that they should be results focused, and insensitive to emotions (e.g., Randolph & Sashkin, 2002). Hence, in cultures of high assertiveness focus, people tend to be results oriented and insensitive to others, whereas in cultures of low assertiveness focus, people desire positive relationships at work and place a higher value on personal needs than on work needs.

Organizational Culture and Innovation Capability

Management literature on organizational innovation has emphasized the importance of culture as a major determinant in innovation performance (Feldman, 1988; Brannen, 1991; Herbig & Dunphy, 1998; Hauser, 1998; Martins & Terblanche, 2003; Çakar, 2006; Çakar & Ertürk, 2010). This research has demonstrated that culture has a profound impact on innovation capability of an organization. Culture has multiple elements, which can serve to enhance or inhibit the tendency to innovate. Possession of appropriate cultural characteristics provides the organization with necessary ingredients to innovate (Ahmed, 1998).

So far, the culture dimensions of Hofstede have also been applied in innovation studies explaining national innovativeness (Lynn & Gelb, 1996), cross-national consumer innovativeness (Steenkamp, ter Hofstede, & Wedel, 1999), adoption of innovation (van Everdingen & Waarts, 2003; Waarts & van Everdingen, 2005) and innovation capability (Çakar & Ertürk, 2010).

Research has yielded that, higher levels of centralization and formalization have been found to be associated with lower levels of innovation adoption (Waarts & van Everdingen, 2005) and lower levels of innovation capability (Çakar & Ertürk, 2010). Organizations which score high on power distance dimension tend to have control systems based more on rules and procedures, which inhibit creativity and inventiveness (Herbig & Dunphy, 1998). Because of centralized authority, autocratic leadership and many hierarchical levels, innovation capability of organizations with high power distance is expected to be very weak (Hofstede, 1991). In contrast, research has also indicated that countries, which score low on the power distance, have a greater tendency to innovate (Hofstede, 2001; Shane, 1992). Inventiveness is more likely to occur in low power distance and less bureaucratic surroundings, since bureaucracy reduces creative activity. Thus, based on the findings above, it can be concluded that innovation capability requires decentralized authority. Therefore:

Hypothesis 1a. Power distance will be negatively related to innovation capability. Employees who perceive the power distance higher will report lower levels of innovation capability.

Organizations having a culture of high uncertainty avoidance are generally characterized with

highly formalized management. These kinds of organizations tend to show features like resistance to innovations, and constraining of innovations by rules (Hofstede, 2001). Research has also demonstrated that, in high uncertainty avoidance cultures, risk-averse attitudes imply that companies will not take avoidable risks and only adopts innovations if its effectiveness and value have already been proven (Waarts & van Everdingen, 2005). Hofstede (1980) also proposed that in low uncertainty avoidance societies people tend to take risks more easily, are relatively tolerant of behavior and opinions different from their own, and are enamored of technology, traits which encourage innovation. Also in some other research, avoidance of uncertainty has been found to be negatively related to innovativeness (Mueller & Thomas, 2000; Thomas & Mueller, 2000; Çakar & Ertürk, 2010). Hence:

Hypothesis 1b. Uncertainty avoidance will be negatively related to innovation capability. Employees who perceive the uncertainty avoidance higher will report lower levels of innovation capability.

In countries with collectivistic culture, organizations are portrayed by collective decisions, which may lead to a delay in the innovation decision process. Yet, in individualistic countries, one prefers to be treated as a unique individual, does not care about meeting the norms of the group, and makes his/her own decisions. Employees of individualistic organizations have more freedom to develop or try new products than employees of collectivistic organizations (Lynn & Gelb, 1996; van Everdingen & Waarts, 2003; Waarts & van Everdingen, 2005). This feature leads to the fact that patents are more often granted in individualistic than in collectivistic countries (Waarts & van Everdingen, 2005). In addition, research has proposed that high individualistic organizations tend to be more inventive in their products and processes (Shane, 1992). Similarly, collectivism was found to be negatively related to innovativeness (Mueller & Thomas, 2000; Thomas & Mueller, 2000). Çakar and Ertürk (2010) have also proposed a negative association between collectivism and innovation capability only for small sized enterprises. The psychological characteristics of independence, achievement, and nonconformity, all of which have been found to encourage innovation, are more common in individualistic societies. Therefore:

Hypothesis 1c. Collectivism will be negatively related to innovation capability, whereas individualism will be positively related to innovation capability. Employees who perceive the collectivism higher will report lower levels of innovation capability.

Low assertiveness focus organizations are characterized by values like equality, solidarity, social relationships, and managers' use of intuition and seeking consensus. In contrast, ambition, competition, material values and the focus on performance characterize high assertiveness focus cultures (Hofstede, 2001). In organizations with high assertiveness focus culture, emphasis is on rewards, recognition of performance, training, and improvement of the individual that are common characteristics to innovative organizations (Waarts & van Everdingen, 2005). Research has suggested a positive relationship between achievement motivation and innovativeness (Rogers, 1995). Hence:

Hypothesis 1d. Assertiveness focus will be positively related to innovation capability. Employees who perceive the assertiveness focus higher will report higher levels of innovation capability.

Empowerment

The concept of empowerment has gained increased popularity in the management field over the last decade (Wall, Wood, & Leach, 2004; Spreitzer, 1996; Menon, 2001; Menon & Hartmann, 2002). Empowerment focused on those management practices designed to "empower" employees, such as the delegation of decision-making and the provision of increased access to information and resources for individuals at lower levels of the organization. Through empowerment, organizations allow employees to assume several roles and responsibilities and thus exert a greater influence at work while enjoying increased autonomy (Pare & Tremblay, 2007). Task involvement through empowerment increases a greater sense of support and intrinsic motivation and provides positive work attitudes.

Empowerment is defined as an energizing context-specific process that expands the feelings of trust and control in one as well as in one's organization, which consequently leads to outcomes such as enhanced self-efficacy and performance (Eylon, 1997). This process results from changes in contextual and relational variables: the amount and quality of information shared and the degree of perceived responsibility and participation in decision-making, which have been underlying themes in much of the work on empowerment (Conger & Kanungo, 1988; Spreitzer, 1996). So, in this study empowerment is constructed as participation in decision-making and access to information shared by the management.

Regarding high-tech companies and IT workforce, successful high-tech organizations are found to be empowering IT professionals to take increasing responsibility for their work and for decision making (Pare & Tremblay, 2007). Although, empowerment practices are becoming increasingly common in high-tech organizations, they have so far received little attention in literature (Kim, 2005). Recent research indicates that components of psychological empowerment, such as greater autonomy, information sharing, task involvement and participation in decision making are among the most important factors in promoting commitment and in lessening turnover intentions of IT professionals (Kim, 2005; Reid, et al., 2008). In addition, in their recent research, Pare and Tremblay (2007) found that empowerment had a negative association with IT professionals' turnover intentions through affective commitment.

Organizational Culture and Empowerment

Although there has been an ongoing discussion about the influence of management styles on organizational culture, there have also been suggestions that organizational culture may in fact constrain displays of management styles. Pool (2000) has suggested that organizational culture provides the foundation for an organization's management system, such that management behavior reinforces principles of the culture (Denison, 2000). Moreover, organizational culture has been considered as a product of societal and environmental demands and consequently management style is a strong reflection and function of the dominating organizational culture. Furthermore, organizational culture is a combination of beliefs, values and assumptions that are the basis of management styles and processes in the organization (Aycan, et al., 2000). From this perspective, it can be concluded that management strategies and processes are derived from the organizational culture.

Power distance is the extent to which people accept an unequal distribution of power and status as the proper way for social systems to be organized (Newman & Nollan, 1996). The efficacy of empowerment in high power distance cultures is doubtful. Employees in high power distance cultures are likely to view to participative management with fear, distrust and disrespect because participation is not consistent with the culture. Employees in high power distance culture expect their supervisors to control information, make decisions, and tell them what to do. High power distance may probably inhibit information sharing between managers and subordinates. Moving these workers to the point of full team

responsibility for critical business decisions would be difficult (Randolph & Sashkin, 2002). On the other hand, when power distance is low, people may wonder why managers have been so slow to let go of control. They welcome involvement in decision-making and enhance the movement to empowerment. Therefore, since cultures that score high on power distance appear to emphasize autocratic management style, participative management techniques like empowerment may not work in high power distance cultures (Sagie & Aycan, 2003; Denison & Mishra, 1995). In a recent research, Çakar and Ertürk (2010) have also demonstrated a negative link between power distance and empowerment for both small and medium sized enterprises. Hence, based upon the above findings:

Hypothesis 2a. Power distance will be negatively related to empowerment. Employees who perceive the power distance higher will report lower levels of empowerment.

Since uncertainty avoidance focuses on people's tolerance for ambiguity, it should definitely impact the empowerment process. When uncertainty avoidance is high, people like to have assignments, goals, policies, and procedures carefully and explicitly spelled out (Randolph & Sashkin, 2002). High uncertainty avoidance tends to make people welcome managers sharing information that clarifies and defines issues clearly. On the other hand, if uncertainty avoidance is low, employees may be more than willing to make key decisions using information they do not understand, with potentially risky. In their recent research, Çakar and Ertürk (2010) have also demonstrated that there is a strong positive association between uncertainty avoidance and empowerment for both small and medium sized enterprises. Indeed, in cultures with high uncertainty avoidance and low tolerance for ambiguity, achieving empowerment and information sharing will be easier (Randolph & Sashkin, 2002).

Therefore, employees in cultures with high uncertainty avoidance are in favor of empowerment that provides employees with clear goals, roles, and a vision for guidance by information sharing and participation.

Hypothesis 2b. Uncertainty avoidance will be positively related to empowerment. Employees who perceive the uncertainty avoidance higher will report higher levels of empowerment.

Individualism/collectivism dimension of culture relates to whether people want to work alone or want to work in groups. Since empowerment focuses on working in a collaborative environment, this cultural dimension is critical for empowerment. In cultures with strong individualism, people will have difficulty moving to the team responsibility that is essential for empowerment; whereas in cultures with strong collectivism people will find this shift much easier (Randolph & Sashkin, 2002). Collective management practices emphasize team based work and rewards. Collectivistic cultures strive to maintain harmony through continuous communication and avoid confrontation among group members. Employees in collectivistic cultures share resources and ideas and are prepared to participate in management for collective interests (Sagie & Aycan, 2003; Hofstede, 1991). On the other hand, in high individualist organizations, employees prefer information sharing to focus on information that directly relates to their jobs, especially if they are held accountable for results. Findings of the recent research (Çakar & Ertürk, 2010) have also yielded results that support the positive association between collectivism and empowerment. Hence:

Hypothesis 2c. Collectivism will be positively related to empowerment, whereas individualism will be negatively related to empowerment. Employees who perceive

the collectivism higher will report higher levels of empowerment.

Since assertiveness focus describes the degree to which people desire to focus on results and achievements, its impact on empowerment will likely not be as strong as that of some other culture elements (Randolph & Sashkin, 2002). When assertiveness focus is high, people feel less comfortable with a nurturing and relationship oriented environment. They want to pay attention to getting results so they can get their just rewards and advance in their careers. Thus, they desire clear task goals, task-related information, feedback on results and they prefer working as teams to get real results and responsibilities. Recent research proposed that people with a high assertiveness focus welcome information sharing about business issues, participative managerial practices and empowerment (Randolph, 2000; Çakar & Ertürk, 2010). Such people can take this information and create significant results. Therefore:

Hypothesis 2d. Assertiveness focus will be positively related to empowerment. Employees who perceive the assertiveness focus higher will report higher levels of empowerment.

Empowerment and Innovation Capability

For years, scholars have sought to identify management styles appropriate for creating a supportive organizational environment for innovation. Some authors suggest that supportive, participative, vision setter, democratic, and collaborative management styles are effective in encouraging innovation (Schin & McClomb, 1998; Quinn, 1988; van de Ven, 1986; Çakar, 2006; Çakar & Ertürk, 2010), and some others identify transformational management style as the ideal style for promoting innovation (Bass, 1985; Howell & Higgins, 1990). In their study Jung, Chow, and Wu (2003) also revealed that empowerment was positively related to support for innovation, whereas they found negative relationship between empowerment and organizational innovation. They explain this unexpected finding in terms of cultural characteristics of their sample concluding that high power distance may be one of the reasons since employees in such an environment may feel confused when left alone to figure out what they need to do and how to accomplish their goals in terms of innovativeness.

There are several specific key practices aimed at building innovative behaviors; among those are empowerment and involvement. Empowerment is a kind of management style in which the subordinates share a significant degree of decision-making power with their superiors (Robbins, 1991). Empowerment should make people feel they possess a certain degree of autonomy, feel less constrained by rule-bound aspects and self-effective in enacting their work; and in combination of those features enable people to be innovative (Amabile & Grykiewicz, 1989; Spreitzer, 1995). In a research conducted by Ford and Randolph (1992), it was yielded that successful application of empowerment was very important for new product performance and innovation. Lawler (1990) also suggested that better participative management would result in higher innovation, better performance, and productivity. Key attributes of empowerment, such as open communication, participation in decision-making processes, shared vision, and common direction are also considered among the key elements in fostering innovation (Ahmed, 1998). Moreover, Brunetto and Farr-Wharton (2007) also suggested that important outcomes of empowerment, such as mutual trust and increased collaboration are important factors for innovation in organizations. In addition, in their recent research, Çakar and Ertürk (2010) have also demonstrated that there is a strong positive association between empowerment and innovation capability for both small and medium sized enterprises.

Empowered individuals have been shown to take a more proactive approach toward shaping and influencing their work environment (Spreitzer, et al., 1997). As such, empowerment is expected be positively related to organizational innovation (Damanpour, 1991). For instance, Amabile (1988) has found that having a sense of control over what to do and how to do one's work enhance individuals' capacity for innovative behavior. Moreover, in a research conducted in Australia, Knight-Turvey (2006) found that empowerment and innovation were strongly linked. Furthermore, Claver et al. (1998) proposed that participation in decision-making processes and sharing information throughout the organization strengthened the innovation capability and innovation culture in an organization. Also, recent research has found strong positive relationship between participative management practices and innovative culture in organizations (Ogbonna & Harris, 2000; Gudmunson, Tower, & Hartman, 2003). Therefore:

Hypothesis 3a. Empowerment will be positively related to innovation capability.

Accordingly, the proposed research model is depicted in Figure 1.

METHODS

Sample and Procedure

In order to test the proposed model empirically, the data was collected from high-tech companies in Turkey. Potential concerns about reaching a considerable number of employees prompted the use of a Web-based questionnaire as the survey form. Furthermore, a Web-based survey was particularly deemed appropriate for canvassing professionals from high-tech companies because of their familiarity with computers and access to the Internet. Thus, a website was created for survey purposes in such a way as to avoid the use

Figure 1. Proposed research model

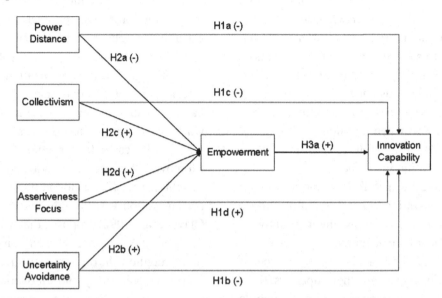

of unique login names or passwords and provided data directly to the researcher.

All measurements included in the questionnaire were originally developed in English and translated into Turkish via the back-translation technique, in which each questionnaire was translated from English to Turkish and then back-translated from Turkish to English by a different person to see if it still has the same meaning (see Brislin, 1980). Prior to administering the questionnaire, wordings of the items are modified slightly to emphasize that the evaluations reflect the respondents' expectations regarding their respective organizations.

A couple of days before the survey was made available, researcher sent out an e-mail to 2500 employees from 60 different high-tech companies announcing the project and encouraging the participation. Next, the researcher sent another e-mail to employees consisting of a message with instructions and a hyperlink to the respective Web survey.

The first screen of the website provided a typical cover letter with instructions as well as assurances of anonymity and voluntary participation. The second screen providing the Web survey was then presented. The Web questionnaire was

one part online. Participants submitted responses, which were then captured in a database that was eventually converted into files for later analysis using SPSS and AMOS. Respondents were given 15 days to complete the questionnaire. To increase the response rates, a final reminder e-mail (with a hyperlink to the online survey) was sent at the end of 10th day.

Of the 2500 e-mails sent, 743 usable completed questionnaires were saved in a database with a response rate of 29 percent. The sample is 81 percent male and 85 percent of the respondents are between 26-55 years old. 62 percent have at least a university degree and 91 percent of survey respondents have worked for their organizations more than 1 year. No personal data was collected except demographics summarized.

To assess if non-response bias existed, the appropriate t-tests (pairwise or independent samples tests, depending on the nature of comparison) were conducted to compare the proportional distribution of demographic characteristics (e.g., age, gender, education, and organizational tenure) of respondents and nonrespondents. Separate statistical tests were performed to compare (1) the characteristics of respondents and nonrespondents in each organization, and (2) the characteristics of respondents with the average industry figures. Results yielded no statistically significant differences, indicating that the non-response bias was not a serious problem for the external validity of this study.

Measures

All constructs were measured with questions adapted from existing scales. All items were measured on a five point Likert-type scale where 1 = strongly disagree and 5 = strongly agree. Mean scale scores, standard deviations and Cronbach alpha reliabilities of the scales were calculated and summarized in Table 1. As to the Cronbach alpha reliabilities, all the scales met the generally accepted reliability of 0.70 (Nunnally, 1978).

Independent Variables

Empowerment: Empowerment was tapped by a five-item measure adapted from the scale originally developed by Denison (2000). Example items from this scale are "The authority to make a decision is delegated to the person who is responsible to perform the task" and "Every employee in our organization attends both short and long term planning processes." Scores range from 1 to 5, with 5 indicating the comprehensive application of empowerment.

Organizational Culture: In this study, organizational culture was measured as four distinct dimensions, namely power distance, individualism/collectivism, uncertainty avoidance, and assertiveness focus. Those dimensions were tapped with scales adapted from the measures developed and tested by Erez and Earley (1987), Sigler and Pearson (2000), Dorfman and Howell (1988), and Yilmaz et al. (2005).

Power Distance: Power distance measure included eight items that measure the extent to which less powerful members of the organization accept the unequal distribution of power. Sample items for this scale are "My supervisor makes decisions

Table 1. Means, standard deviations, and reliabilities of the scales

Variables	Means	Std.Dev.	Alpha
Power Distance	2.59	0.21	0.81
Collectivism	3.49	0.29	0.79
Assertiveness Focus	2.44	0.33	0.82
Uncertainty Avoidance	2.76	0.19	0.91
Empowerment	3.89	0.26	0.87
Innovation Capability	3.68	0.17	0.77

without asking to lower level employees" and "People at lower levels in the organization should not have power in the organization." Scores range from 1 to 5, with 5 indicating that less powerful members of the organization strongly accept the unequal distribution of power across the hierarchy.

Collectivism: Collectivism measure included seven items that measure the extent to which people prefer to be treated as part of a group rather than as unique individuals. Sample items for this scale are "In my organizations, collective decisions are more relevant than decisions made by each of us" and "Group welfare is more important than individual rewards." Collectivism lies at one end of a continuum with individualism at the other. Scores range from 1 to 5, with 5 indicating that employees strongly prefer to be treated as part of a group instead of a unique individual and with 1 indicating that employees strongly prefer to be able to stand out as individuals.

Assertiveness Focus: Assertiveness focus, which implies masculinity/femininity dimension of Hofstede's (1980) cultural framework, was measured by eight items that measure the extent to which people feel that they should be results focused, and insensitive to emotions. A sample item for this scale is "In our organization having a professional career is more important for men than it is for women." Scores range from 1 to 5, with 5 indicating that employees strongly feel that they should be results-oriented and insensitive to emotions.

Uncertainty Avoidance: Uncertainty avoidance measure included nine items that measure the extent to which organization members want to avoid ambiguity and uncertainty in favor of clear goals and operating guidelines. A sample item for this scale is "In our organization rules and procedures define what are expected from employees." Scores range from 1 to 5, with 5 indicating that members of the organization precisely want to avoid vagueness and prefer strongly obvious guidelines.

Dependent Variable

Innovation Capability: High-tech companies' innovation capability, which refers to the company's ability for new product or new technology development, was tapped by a measure included six items adapted from the scales used and tested by Calantone et al. (2002), Romijn and Albaladejo (2002), and Wei (2006). A sample item from this scale is "The frequency of coming up with radical/ breakthrough technologies to the market". Respondents were asked to score the items concerning their company's innovation capability compared to the high-tech industry average in Turkey, using five-point scales anchored at much worse than industry average (=1) and much better than industry average (=5).

Factor Analyses

In order to better demonstrate the validity and reliability of factor structures, both exploratory and confirmatory factor analyses were performed on the samples. Prior to the estimation of the confirmatory measurement model, exploratory factor analyses are conducted to assess unidimensionality. In each of these analyses, a single factor is extracted (using a cut-off point of eigenvalue = 1), suggesting that our measurement scales are unidimensional.

Next, consistent with our measurement theory, the 32 items measuring the organizational culture factors (power distance, uncertainty avoidance, individualism/collectivism, assertiveness focus) are hypothesized to load on four distinct factors in the measurement model. In addition, the 5 items measuring empowerment and the 6 items measuring innovation capability are averaged to create composite indicants for each of these formative measures, which are then posited to load on two distinct performance factors in the measurement model. Alpha reliabilities for the scales ranged from 0.77 to 0.91 and factor loadings of items varied from 0.47 to 0.83. Intercorrelations among the established measures are depicted in Table 2.

Table 2. Intercorrelations among measures

Variables	ICA	I/C	PD	UA	AF	EP
ICA	1					
I/C	-0.334**	1				
PD	-0.280**	-0.363**	1			
UA	-0.477**	0.556**	-0.348**	1		
AF	0.150**	-0.165**	0.424**	-0.183**	1	
EP	0.335**	0.493**	-0.329**	0.469**	0.131**	1

** Correlation is significant at the 0.01 level.
* Correlation is significant at the 0.05 level.
ICA: Innovation Capability I/C: Individualism / Collectivism
PD: Power Distance UA: Uncertainty Avoidance
AF: Assertiveness Focus EP: Empowerment

Confirmatory Factor Analysis

Next, confirmatory factor analysis was conducted on 43 items measuring six constructs, namely power distance, collectivism, assertiveness focus, uncertainty avoidance, empowerment and innovation capability. In addition to this, it was also checked the measurement properties of the variables by comparing the baseline model with alternate models. Five most commonly used goodness-of-fit indices were used to assess the model fit of structural models: (1) chi-square value, (2) Root Mean Square Error of Approximation (RMSEA), (3) Non-Normed Fit Index (NNFI), (4) Goodness of Fit Index (GFI), and (5) Comparative Fit Index (CFI) (Arbuckle & Wothke, 1995; Hox & Bechger, 1998; Hu & Bentler, 1999; Kline, 1998).

Suggested six-factor model resulted in a significant chi-square statistic (χ^2 = 1782.2, p<0.01, df = 725), as expected given the large sample size. The resulting goodness-of-fit indices suggest that the model fits the observed covariances well (χ^2 / df = 2.45, CFI = 0.91; GFI = 0.92; NNFI = 0.88; RMSEA = 0.04). In addition, all items load significantly on their respective constructs (with the lowest t-value being 9.92), providing support for the convergent validity of measurement items.

Finally, discriminant validity is obtained for all constructs since the variance extracted for each construct is greater than its squared correlations with other constructs (Fornell & Larcker, 1981).

Tests of Hypotheses

The path coefficients were estimated by linking the study constructs using the structural equations modeling methodology in AMOS 7.0. First, proposed model in Figure 1 was separately tested (n = 743). The chi-square statistics and the overall model fit statistics for the proposed model is summarized in Table 3.

The chi-square statistics obtained from the estimation of the proposed model is significant (χ^2 = 168.46, p<0.01, df = 1). Also according to the goodness-of-fit indices (χ^2 / df = 168.46, CFI = 0.67; GFI = 0.79; NNFI = 0.69; RMSEA = 0.34), model is statistically rejected. After evaluating the model and eliminating the nonsignificant paths between the variables, a revised model is obtained. The chi-square statistics obtained from the estimation of the revised model is nonsignificant (χ^2 = 4.72, p>0.1, df = 3), and the goodness-of-fit indices (χ^2 / df = 1.57, CFI = 0.98; GFI = 0.99; NNFI = 0.96; RMSEA = 0.03) suggest a good model fit. Revised model is depicted in Figure 2.

The parameter estimates for the hypothesized paths are provided in Table 4. As hypothesized, the results suggest that power distance is negatively related to innovation capability (β = -0.11, p<0.05) and is also negatively related to empowerment (β = -0.13, p<0.05). Thus, hypotheses 1a and 2a are supported. Uncertainty avoidance is found to be strongly and negatively related to innovation capability (β = -0.48, p<0.01), and is found to be positively related to empowerment (β = 0.28, p<0.01). Therefore, hypotheses 1b and 2b are also strongly supported.

Furthermore, results yield that collectivism is positively related to empowerment (β = 0.31, p<0.01), while the estimated negative path linking collectivism and innovation capability is nonsignificant (β = -0.05, p>0.05). So, hypothesis 2c is supported, yet hypothesis 1c is not supported. However, contrary to the hypothesized, the estimated path coefficients linking assertiveness focus to innovation capability (β = -0.02, p>0.05) and empowerment (β = 0.03, p>0.05) are both nonsignificant. Hence, both hypotheses 1d and 2d are not supported. Finally, empowerment is found to exert a significant positive influence on innovation capability (β = 0.18, p<0.01), supporting our hypothesis 3a.

Examination of Mediating Effect of Empowerment

Results of the aforementioned SEM analysis revealed a mediating effect of empowerment on the

Figure 2. Revised model (only the statistically significant paths are shown on the figure)

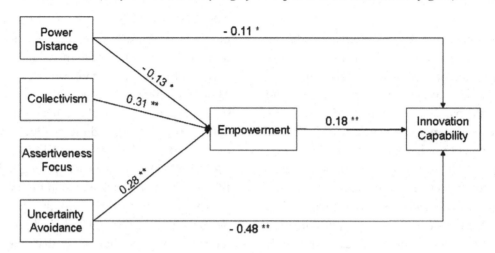

Table 3. Model fit statistics

	χ2	df	χ2 / df	CFI	GFI	NNFI	RMSEA
M$_{proposed}$	168.46**	1	168.46	0.67	0.79	0.69	0.34
M$_{revised}$	4.72	3	1.57	0.98	0.99	0.96	0.03
** Statistic is significant at 0.01 level.							

Table 4. Parameter estimates

Hypothesis	Hypothesized Path	Parameter Estimate	t-value	Explanation
H1a	Power distance → Innovation capability	-0.109	-2.326*	Supported
H1b	Uncertainty avoidance → Innovation capability	-0.478	-7.331**	Supported
H1c	Collectivism → Innovation capability	-0.052	-1.303	Not Supported
H1d	Assertiveness focus → Innovation capability	0.024	0.943	Not Supported
H2a	Power distance → Empowerment	-0.132	-1.954*	Supported
H2b	Uncertainty avoidance → Empowerment	0.277	3.987**	Supported
H2c	Collectivism → Empowerment	0.311	4.670**	Supported
H2d	Assertiveness focus → Empowerment	0.029	1.187	Not Supported
H3a	Empowerment → Innovation Capability	0.183	3.141**	Supported
** Parameter estimate is significant at the 0.01 level. * Parameter estimate is significant at the 0.05 level.				

relationship between organizational culture and innovation capability. Thus, in order to confirm and support this finding, we performed the Sobel test by using the automated Web-based Sobel test available on the Internet (Web-Based Sobel Test, 2007). The purpose of the Sobel test is to examine whether the mediator carries the influence of an independent variable to a dependent variable (Sobel, 1982). The Sobel's t value must be adequately large, yielding a p-value of less than 0.05, in order for significant mediation to be identified. What this means for this study is that the association between independent variables (organizational culture components; such as power distance, collectivism, assertiveness focus and uncertainty avoidance) and the dependent variable (innovation capability) has been significantly reduced by the inclusion of the mediating variable (empowerment).

As results of Sobel test conducted, calculated t values for the independent variables varied from 4.03 to 7.12 (p < 0.05) for the mediation of empowerment on the relationship between three organizational culture components and innovation capability. Therefore, the partial mediating effect of empowerment on the relationships between (1) power distance and innovation capability, and (2) uncertainty avoidance and innovation capability; and the full mediating effect of empowerment on the relationship between collectivism and innovation capability have been found to be significant. Since no relationship was revealed between assertiveness focus and empowerment or innovation capability, no mediating effect was examined for those possible relationships.

DISCUSSION AND CONCLUSION

Innovation capability is the ability to think and behave in a way that creates, develops and establishes values and attitudes within a firm which may require accepting and supporting ideas and changes involving an improvement in the functioning of a company. These changes may mean conflict with conventional and traditional employee behavior; however, they may in turn create highly effective cultural and managerial transformations regarding innovativeness. The primary objective of this study is to identify the role of organizational culture and empowerment perceptions on innovation capability in high-tech companies. To achieve this objective, SEM analyses are applied to data from a sample of Turkish high-tech companies in order to empirically test and compare direct and indirect relationships.

Uncertainty avoidance is negatively related to innovation capability, and positively related to empowerment. This implies that the more employees tend to avoid from uncertainty the more they try to participate in the decisions affecting their tasks. In this case empowering employees was perceived to contribute the most to individuals' professional development as well as societal change and advancement. Besides employees who are able to easily achieve relevant information regarding their activities may also require feedback from supervisors and managers, which results in high level of empowerment perceptions. Accordingly, they are motivated and empowered by praise from the supervisor, feedback on performance, sense of belonging, and job safety. On the other hand, the more employees tend to avoid uncertainty, the more they keep away from innovativeness. Since, innovation, by definition, brings some uncertainty and risk to the work, employees in high uncertainty avoidance cultures try to abstain from innovativeness as much as possible. In addition, employees in high uncertainty avoidance cultures prefer certain tasks, formal rules and clear job descriptions that may inhibit to develop new ideas and to adapt changing organizational environment and so are considered as potential threats for creativity to achieve innovativeness.

The results reveal that power distance is negatively related to empowerment and innovation capability. Especially in high-tech companies, organizational climate generally reflects a close and fluid communication between managers and employees reflecting a low power distance in order to better understand and assimilate knowledge flows. This climate with a low power distance creates an appropriate environment for innovation capability to be fostered via close employee-manager relationships. Organizational climate reflecting close interrelationships implies that managers are concerned with and involved in the professional lives of their subordinates. In such an organizational setting, employees are more responsive to decisions regarding innovations that they more tend to be a part of this process.

The results also yielded a statistically significant relationship between collectivism and empowerment. In high-tech companies, since the employees work in a collaborative environment characterized with the close interrelationships between managers and employees, collectivistic features, such as groupwise harmony and team-based work, are likely to be significant through continuous communication. Employees in collectivistic cultures share resources and ideas and are usually prepared to participate in management for collective interests. Since empowerment also focuses on working in a collaborative environment, in cultures with strong collectivism employees will perceive empowerment much higher. Although collectivism is found to be positively related to empowerment, no significant relationship is found between collectivism and innovation capability. This finding implies that empowerment fully mediates the relationship between collectivism and innovation capability. In other words, sense of collectivism among employees may have a positive influence on innovation capability since they perceive that that they are valued and participated in decision-processes.

In this study, empowerment is considered as an antecedent of innovation capability and a consequence of organizational culture. In support of this proposition, the mediating role of empowerment between organizational culture and innovation capability is also revealed at the end of analyses.

Empowerment is a kind of management style in which the subordinates share a significant amount of information with their superiors and have some degree of decision-making power on their work. Organizational culture and a collaborative climate, in which employees work in cooperation and harmony, create an appropriate working environment for empowerment to be effective. In this climate, empowerment makes people feel they possess a certain degree of autonomy, feel less constrained by rule-bound aspects and self-effective in enacting their work. Employees' perception of empowerment, which is also referred as psychological empowerment, creates a motivational state that includes employees' sense of choice over work behaviors, and belief in their own ability to perform tasks (Conger & Kanungo, 1988). Especially in high-tech organizations, these feelings augment intrinsic task motivation, self-efficacy, and self-confidence. In turn, combination of those features enables people to be more creative and innovative. As a result of employees' enhanced innovativeness, organization's innovation capability also improves significantly. Thus, without underestimating the importance of organizational culture, empowerment can be considered as one of the most effective managerial styles to be used in fostering organizations' innovation capability.

PRESCRIPTIVE IMPLICATIONS FOR PRACTITIONERS

This chapter contributes to the literature in terms of human resource management and innovation management. The results may assist managers to make better decisions for an appropriate management scheme in order to achieve better innovation performance. The overall practical implication that can be drawn from findings is summarized in a sequential form as follows: Considering that innovation is essential for high-tech companies to stay in the market and to continue sustainable competitiveness; encouraging new ideas should be substantial in order to enhance the creative ability of employees to convert ideas into innovations. Therefore, organizations need to facilitate innovation by creating and maintaining a cultural environment that supports idea generation and creativity. Results of this study reveal that, to foster innovation capability, high-tech organizations first need to develop the cultural context and managerial practices for innovation. The results also point out to the important role played by cultural dimensions of uncertainty avoidance, collectivism, and power distance in the process of shaping innovative culture.

This research also indicates that high-tech companies which are involved in activities that create perceptions of empowerment develop a stronger ability to increase innovativeness. Claver et al. (1998, p. 66) provide the impetus that motivates and empowers individuals in the organizations to innovate suggesting that "... culture must stimulate the process of generating new ideas and applying them either internally or to the market, with the ultimate purpose of changing the markets, adapting the firm to their discontinuities and thus obtaining competitive benefits." Therefore, managers of high-tech companies should also focus on how to create an empowering work environment. For instance, Blanchard and his associates (1999) have provided a clear and practical approach to creating empowerment: (a) share accurate information widely, (b) create autonomy via boundaries, and (c) replace hierarchical thinking with self-managed teams.

Findings imply that the ability of a high-tech organization to recognize the value of information and knowledge exchanged by managers and employees is critical in determining innovative output. At the strategic level, top management should regard the cultural profile of companies as a key part of their organizational innovation infrastructure. At the operational level, organizations need to provide their employees with adequate means to communicate and share the information. From this point of view, information

sharing should be stimulated because it is one of the most important tools of creativity.

However, the results of this study are context-specific and should be considered very carefully when extended to other contexts. Although we have been very cautious regarding the generalisability of the findings to other settings, there are some theoretical grounds to assume that businesses in other cultures and economies may experience similar dynamics. From a cultural standpoint for instance, measures of cultural characteristics used in this study, as found in the works of Hofstede (1980), do not suggest a particular cultural environment specific to Turkey or Turkish SMEs. In addition, the components of Hofstede's cultural framework have been used extensively in different studies (House, et al., 2002; Sigler & Pearson, 2000; Robert & Wasti, 2002; Sivakumar & Nakata, 2001; van Everdingen & Waarts 2003; Waarts & van Everdingen, 2005). Similarly, the participative managerial practices, such as empowerment, are not certain human resource management practices applied only in Turkey or Turkish high-tech companies. Furthermore, the results of this study somewhat overlap with previous research findings (Sagie & Aycan, 2003; Randolph & Sashkin, 2002; Ogbonna & Harris, 2000; Gudmunson, Tower, & Hartman, 2003). Therefore, the rationale of our hypotheses is mainly drawn from international conceptual and empirical studies. Thus, although the specific context of our research setting suggests some precise features of Turkish high-tech companies constituting our sample; it can be concluded that the findings of this study is not country-bound and other high-tech companies, which have alike cultural characteristics and use similar managerial practices, might experience similar dynamics. Nevertheless, a cross-cultural test of our model would further increase our understanding of how the combination of cultural and managerial factors affects innovation capability of SMEs.

In conclusion, the findings of this study provide information about patterns in the innovation capability of high-tech companies by considering the combined effects of organizational culture and perceptions of empowerment. The results will also assist management make better decisions in adapting an appropriate management approach to foster innovation capability.

Limitations and Future Directions

The findings and the contribution of the current study must be evaluated taking into account the potential limitations of the research design. First, despite the encouraging support for the construct validity of the organizational culture measures, the relatively high correlation between some scales may lead us to speculate that the items might have included a positivity or desirability bias. However, as noted by Kristof (2000), constructs represented by highly correlated measures should be viewed as conceptually distinct and important due to their distinctive and unique relationships with other constructs. Indeed, the results of the correlation analysis and multi-collinearity tests, such as Variance Inflation Factor (VIF) and the Condition Index (CI) (Kleinbaum, et al., 1998; Tebachnick & Fidell, 2001), suggested that the organizational culture scales had distinct relations with other measures in the study as predicted by the theory, and thus, should be considered sufficiently independent.

Second, the data were cross-sectional, making it impossible to imply causality. All of the variables were measured at the same time and from the same source, so concern over the effects of common method variance was warranted. To minimize this potential problem, the scales in the actual survey were ordered so that the dependent variable did not precede all the independent ones (Podsakoff & Organ, 1986). In addition, Harman's one factor test, confirmatory factor analysis, and further post hoc statistical tests were conducted to test the presence of common method effect (Podsakoff, et al., 2003). The results of the Harman's one-factor test and the single factor

confirmatory factor analysis suggest that common method variance is not of great concern and thus is unlikely to confound the interpretation of results. Nevertheless, longitudinal designs in which both predictor and criterion variables are measured over time might be particularly useful extensions of the current study.

Third, the sample consists of multiple respondents including managers and employees. As acknowledging the possibility that managers might have different views on the culture, empowerment and innovation capability of the organization, a considerable effect of their different perceptions is not very likely in this study. Furthermore, we also conducted appropriate pairwise t tests and ANOVA tests, and they do not indicate any significant difference between the perceptions of managers and the other employees.

The findings, implications, and conclusions of this study are bounded by the context of the research, but future research could involve the replication of this study in a number of different contexts. I believe that future research assessing similar data from different contexts will provide informative validation for the results of this study. Besides in the future, the application of various qualitative methods to the study of dimensions of organizational culture as well as the innovation capability could also benefit from the richness of description such methods tend to provide. Additionally investigating other firm-specific effects and managerial implications, such as justice perceptions, trust, employee commitment, on innovation capability may guide academicians and practitioners to better understand the determinants of innovativeness.

REFERENCES

Ahmed, P. (1998). Culture and climate for innovation. *European Journal of Innovation Management*, *1*(1), 30–43. doi:10.1108/14601069810199131

Allocca, M. A., & Kessler, E. H. (2006). Innovation speed in small and medium-sized enterprises. *Creativity and Innovation Management, 15*(3), 279–295. doi:10.1111/j.1467-8691.2006.00389.x

Amabile, T. M. (1988). A model of creativity and innovation in organisations. In Straw, B. M., & Cummings, L. L. (Eds.), *Research in Organizational Behavior* (pp. 123–167). Greenwich, CT: JAI Press.

Amabile, T. M., & Grykiewicz, N. D. (1989). The creative environment scales: Work environment inventory. *Creativity Research Journal, 2*, 231–253. doi:10.1080/10400418909534321

Arbuckle, J. L., & Wothke, W. (1995). *AMOS 4.0 user's guide*. Chicago, IL: Small Waters Corporation.

Aycan, Z., Kanungo, R. N., Mendonca, M., Yu, K., Deller, J., Stahl, G., & Khursid, A. (2000). Impact of culture on human resource management practices: A ten country comparison. *Applied Psychology: An International Review, 49*(1), 192–221. doi:10.1111/1464-0597.00010

Aycan, Z., Kanungo, R. N., & Sinha, J. B. P. (1999). Organizational culture and human resource management practices: The model of cultural fit. *Journal of Cross-Cultural Psychology, 30*(4), 501–526. doi:10.1177/0022022199030004006

Bass, B. M. (1985). *Management style and performance beyond expectations*. New York, NY: Free Press.

Beckman, S. L., & Barry, M. (2007). Innovation as a learning process: Embedding design thinking. *California Management Review, 50*, 25–56.

Bentler, P. M., & Bonett, D. G. (1980). Significance tests and goodness-of-fit in the analysis of covariance structures. *Psychological Bulletin, 88*, 588–606. doi:10.1037/0033-2909.88.3.588

Blanchard, K., Carlos, J. P., & Randolph, A. (1999). *The 3 keys to empowerment: Release the power within people for astonishing results*. San Francisco, CA: Berrett-Koehler.

Brannen, M. Y. (1991). Culture as the critical factor in implementing innovation. *Business Horizons, 34*, 59–67. doi:10.1016/0007-6813(91)90112-9

Brislin, R. W. (1980). Translation and content analysis of oral and written materials. In Triandis, H. C., & Berry, J. W. (Eds.), *Handbook of Cross-Cultural Psychology* (pp. 389–444). Boston, MA: Allyn & Bacon, Inc.

Brown, R. (1992). Managing the 'S' curves of innovation. *Journal of Consumer Marketing, 9*(1), 61–72. doi:10.1108/EUM0000000002597

Brunetto, Y., & Farr-Wharton, R. (2007). The moderating role of trust in SME owner/managers' decision-making about collaboration. *Journal of Small Business Management, 45*(3), 362–387. doi:10.1111/j.1540-627X.2007.00218.x

Burgelman, R., Maidique, M. A., & Wheelwright, S. C. (2004). *Strategic management of technology and innovation*. New York, NY: McGraw-Hill.

Çakar, N. D. (2006). Enhancing innovation capability through human resource practices: An empirical study in Turkish SMEs. *South-East Europe Review, 4*, 109–126.

Çakar, N. D., & Ertürk, A. (2010). Comparing innovation capability of small and medium sized enterprises: Examining the effects of organizational culture and empowerment. *Journal of Small Business Management, 48*(3), 325–359. doi:10.1111/j.1540-627X.2010.00297.x

Calantone, R. J., Cavusgil, S. T., & Zhao, Y. (2002). Learning orientation, firm innovation capability and firm performance. *Industrial Marketing Management, 31*, 515–524. doi:10.1016/S0019-8501(01)00203-6

Cavusgil, S. T., Calantone, R. J., & Zhao, Y. (2003). Tacit knowledge transfer and firm innovation capability. *Journal of Business and Industrial Marketing, 18*(1), 6. doi:10.1108/08858620310458615

Chandler, G. N., Keller, C., & Lyon, D. W. (2000). Unraveling the determinants and consequences of an innovation-supportive organizational culture. *Entrepreneurship Theory and Practice, 25*, 59–76.

Claver, E., Llopis, J., Garcia, D., & Molina, H. (1998). Organizational culture for innovation and new technological behavior. *The Journal of High Technology Management Research, 9*(1), 55–68. doi:10.1016/1047-8310(88)90005-3

Conger, J. A., & Kanungo, R. N. (1988). The empowerment process: Integrating theory and practice. *Academy of Management Review, 13*(3), 471–482.

Damanpour, F. (1991). Organizational innovation: A meta-analysis of effects of determinants and moderators. *Academy of Management Journal, 34*(3), 555–590. doi:10.2307/256406

Danneels, E., & Kleinschmidt, E. J. (2001). Product innovativeness from the firm's perspective: Its dimensions and their relation with project selection and performance. *Journal of Product Innovation Management, 18*, 357–373. doi:10.1016/S0737-6782(01)00109-6

Dasgupta, M., & Gupta, R. K. (2009). Innovation in organizations: A review of the role of organizational learning and knowledge management. *Global Business Review, 10*(2), 203–224. doi:10.1177/097215090901000205

Denison, D. R. (2000). *The handbook of organizational culture*. London, UK: Wiley.

Denison, D. R., & Mishra, A. K. (1995). Toward a theory of organizational culture and effectiveness. *Organization Science, 6*, 204–223. doi:10.1287/orsc.6.2.204

Dimov, D. (2007). From opportunity insight to opportunity intention: The importance of person-situation learning match. *Entrepreneurship Theory & Practice, 31*, 561–583. doi:10.1111/j.1540-6520.2007.00188.x

Dorfman, P., & Howell, J. (1988). *Dimensions of national culture and effective leadership patterns: Hofstede revisited*. Greenwich, CT: JAI Press.

Erez, M., & Earley, P. C. (1987). Comparative analysis of goal setting strategies across cultures. *The Journal of Applied Psychology, 17*(2), 658–665. doi:10.1037/0021-9010.72.4.658

Eylon, D. (1997). An empirical test of a process model of empowerment. *Journal of Management Systems, 9*, 15–30.

Feldman, S. P. (1988). How organizational culture can affect innovation. *Organizational Dynamics, 17*, 57–68. doi:10.1016/0090-2616(88)90030-7

Ford, R. C., & Randolph, W. A. (1992). Cross-functional structures: A review and integration of matrix organization and project management. *Journal of Management, 18*(2), 267–294. doi:10.1177/014920639201800204

Fornell, C., & Larcker, D. (1981). Evaluating structural equation models with unobservable variables and measurement error. *JMR, Journal of Marketing Research, 18*, 39–50. doi:10.2307/3151312

Freel, M. (2006). Patterns of technological innovation in knowledge-intensive business services. *Industry and Innovation, 13*(3), 335–358. doi:10.1080/13662710600859157

Gudmunson, D., Tower, C. B., & Hartman, E. A. (2003). Innovation in small businesses: Culture and ownership structure do matter. *Journal of Developmental Entrepreneurship, 8*(1), 1–17.

Hadjimanolis, A. (2000). An investigation of innovation antecedents in small firms in the context of a small developing country. *R & D Management, 30*(3), 235–245. doi:10.1111/1467-9310.00174

Hatch, N. W., & Dyer, J. H. (2004). Human capital & learning as a source of sustainable competitive advantage. *Strategic Management Journal, 25,* 1155–1178. doi:10.1002/smj.421

Hauser, M. (1998). Organizational culture and innovativeness of firms: An integrated view. *International Journal of Technology Management, 16*(1), 239–255. doi:10.1504/IJTM.1998.002650

Herbig, P., & Dunphy, S. (1998). Culture and innovation. *Cross Cultural Management, 5*(4), 13–21. doi:10.1108/13527609810796844

Hitt, M. A. (2001). Direct and moderating effects of human capital on strategy and performance in professional firms: A resource-based perspective. *Academy of Management Journal, 44*(1), 13–28. doi:10.2307/3069334

Hofstede, G. (1980). Motivation, leadership and organization: Do American theories apply abroad? *Organizational Dynamics, 9,* 42–63. doi:10.1016/0090-2616(80)90013-3

Hofstede, G. (1991). *Culture's consequences: Software of the mind.* London, UK: Mcgraw-Hill.

Hofstede, G. (2001). *Culture's consequences: Comparing values, behaviors, institutions, and organizations across nations* (2nd ed.). New York, NY: Sage Publications.

House, R., Javidan, M., Hanges, P., & Dorfman, P. (2002). Understanding cultures and implicit leadership theories across the globe: An introduction to project GLOBE. *Journal of World Business, 37,* 3–10. doi:10.1016/S1090-9516(01)00069-4

Howell, J. M., & Higgins, C. A. (1990). Champions of technological innovation. *Administrative Science Quarterly, 3,* 317–341. doi:10.2307/2393393

Hox, J. J., & Bechger, T. M. (1998). An introduction to structural equations modeling. *Family Science Review, 11,* 354–373.

Hu, L. T., & Bentler, P. (1999). Cutoff criteria for fit indexes in covariance structure analysis: conventional criteria versus new alternatives. *Structural Equation Modeling, 6,* 1–55. doi:10.1080/10705519909540118

Johns, G. (2006). The essential impact of context on organizational behaviour. *Academy of Management Review, 31,* 386–408. doi:10.5465/AMR.2006.20208687

Jung, D. I., Chow, C., & Wu, A. (2003). The role of transformational leadership in enhancing organizational innovation: Hypotheses and some preliminary findings. *The Leadership Quarterly, 14*(4/5), 525–544. doi:10.1016/S1048-9843(03)00050-X

Kim, S. (2005). Factors affecting state governments information technology employee turnover intentions. *American Review of Public Administration, 35*(2), 137–156. doi:10.1177/0275074004273150

Kleinbaum, D. G., Lawrence, L. L., Muller, K. E., & Nizam, A. (1998). *Applied regression analysis and other multivariable methods* (3rd ed.). New York, NY: Duxbury.

Kline, R. B. (1998). *Principles and practice of structural equation modeling.* New York, NY: Guilford Press.

Knight-Turvey, N. (2006). Influencing employee innovation through structural empowerment initiatives: The need to feel empowered. *Entrepreneurship Theory and Practice,* 313-324. Retrieved from http://www.swinburne.edu.au/lib/ir/onlineconferences/agse2006/knightturvey_p313.pdf

Kodama, F. (1991). *Analyzing Japanese high technologies: The techno-paradigm shift.* London, UK: Pinter Publishers.

Kogut, B., & Zander, U. (1992). Knowledge of the firm, combinative capability and the replication of technology. *Organization Science, 3,* 383–397. doi:10.1287/orsc.3.3.383

Kristof, A. L. (2000). Perceived applicant fit: Distinguishing between recruiters' perceptions of person-job and person-organization fit. *Personnel Psychology*, *53*, 643–671. doi:10.1111/j.1744-6570.2000.tb00217.x

Lawler, E. E. III. (1990). *High-involvement management: Participative strategies for improving organizational performance*. San Francisco, CA: Jossey-Bass Publishers.

Lenox, M., & King, A. (2004). Prospects for developing absorptive capacity through internal information provision. *Strategic Management Journal*, *25*, 331–345. doi:10.1002/smj.379

Liden, R. C., & Antonakis, J. (2009). Considering context in psychological leadership research. *Human Relations*, *62*, 1587–1605. doi:10.1177/0018726709346374

Lynn, M., & Gelb, B. D. (1996). Identifying innovative national markets for technical consumer goods. *International Marketing Review*, *13*(6), 43–57. doi:10.1108/02651339610151917

Martins, E. C., & Terblanche, F. (2003). Building organizational culture that stimulates creativity and innovation. *European Journal of Innovation Management*, *6*(1), 64–74. doi:10.1108/14601060310456337

Mendonca, M., & Kanungo, R. N. (1994). Managing human resources: The issue of cultural fit. *Journal of Management Inquiry*, *3*(2), 189–205. doi:10.1177/105649269432010

Menon, S. T. (2001). Employee empowerment: An integrative psychological approach. *Applied Psychology: An International Review*, *50*(1), 153–180. doi:10.1111/1464-0597.00052

Menon, S. T., & Hartmann, L. C. (2002). Generalizability of menon's empowerment scale: Replication and extension with Australian data. *International Journal of Cross Cultural Management*, *2*(2), 137–153. doi:10.1177/1470595802002002860

Meyer, R. D., Dalal, R. S., & Hermida, R. (2010). A review and synthesis of situational strength in the organizational sciences. *Journal of Management*, *36*, 121–140. doi:10.1177/0149206309349309

Mueller, S. L., & Thomas, A. S. (2000). Culture and entrepreneurial potential: A nine country study of locus of control and innovativeness. *Journal of Business Venturing*, *16*, 51–75. doi:10.1016/S0883-9026(99)00039-7

Newman, K. L., & Nollan, S. D. (1996). Culture and congruence: The fit between management practices and national culture. *Journal of International Business Studies*, *27*(4), 753–779. doi:10.1057/palgrave.jibs.8490152

Nunnally, J. C. (1978). *Psychometric theory*. New York, NY: Mcgraw-Hill.

Ogbonna, E., & Harris, L. (2000). Leadership style, organizational culture and performance: Empirical evidence from UK companies. *International Journal of Human Resource Management*, *11*(4), 766–788. doi:10.1080/09585190050075114

Pare, G., & Tremblay, M. (2007). The influence of high-involvement human resource practices, procedural justice, organizational commitment, and citizenship behaviors on information technology professionals' turnover intentions. *Group & Organization Management*, *32*(3), 326–357. doi:10.1177/1059601106286875

Podsakoff, P. M., MacKenzie, S. B., Lee, J. Y., & Podsakoff, N. P. (2003). Common method biases in behavioral research: A critical review of the literature and recommended remedies. *The Journal of Applied Psychology*, *88*, 879–903. doi:10.1037/0021-9010.88.5.879

Podsakoff, P. M., & Organ, D. M. (1986). Self reports in organizational research: Problems and prospects. *Journal of Management*, *12*, 531–544. doi:10.1177/014920638601200408

Pool, S. W. (2000). Organizational culture and its relationship in measuring outcomes among business executives. *Journal of Management Development, 19*(1), 32–49. doi:10.1108/02621710010308144

Quinn, R. E. (1988). *Beyond rational management, mastering the paradoxes and competing demands of high performance*. San Francisco, CA: Jossey- Bass.

Randolph, W. A. (2000). Re-thinking empowerment: Why is it so hard to achieve? *Organizational Dynamics, 29*(2), 94–107. doi:10.1016/S0090-2616(00)00017-6

Randolph, W. A., & Sashkin, M. (2002). Can organizational empowerment work in multinational settings? *The Academy of Management Executive, 16*(1), 102–115. doi:10.5465/AME.2002.6640205

Reid, M. F., Allen, M. W., Riemenschneider, C. K., & Armstrong, D. J. (2008). The role of mentoring and supervisor support for state IT employees' affective organizational commitment. *Review of Public Personnel Administration, 28*(1), 60–78. doi:10.1177/0734371X07311703

Robbins, P. S. (1991). *Organizational behavior, concepts, controversies and applications*. Englewood Cliffs, NJ: Prentice Hall.

Robert, C., & Wasti, S. A. (2002). Organizational individualism and collectivism: Theoretical development and an empirical test of a measure. *Journal of Management, 28*(4), 544–566.

Rogers, E. M. (1995). *Diffusion of Innovations* (4th ed.). New York, NY: The Free Press.

Romijn, H., & Albaladejo, M. (2002). Determinants of innovation capability in small electronics and software firms in southeast England. *Research Policy, 31*, 1053–1067. doi:10.1016/S0048-7333(01)00176-7

Rousseau, D. M., & Fried, Y. (2001). Location, location, location: Contextualizing organizational research. *Journal of Organizational Behavior, 22*, 1–13. doi:10.1002/job.78

Sagie, A., & Aycan, Z. (2003). A cross-cultural analysis of participative decision-making in organizations. *Human Relations, 56*(4), 453–473. doi:10.1177/0018726703056004003

Schein, E. H. (1990). Organizational culture. *The American Psychologist, 45*, 109–119. doi:10.1037/0003-066X.45.2.109

Schein, E. H. (1992). *Organizational culture and management style* (2nd ed.). San Francisco, CA: Jossey-Bass.

Schin, J., & McClomb, G. E. (1998). Top executive management style and organizational innovation: An investigation of nonprofit human service organizations. *Social Work Administration, 22*(3), 1–21. doi:10.1300/J147v22n03_01

Sethi, R., Smith, D. C., & Park, C. W. (2001). Cross-functional product development teams, creativity, and the innovativeness of new consumer products. *JMR, Journal of Marketing Research, 37*, 73–85. doi:10.1509/jmkr.38.1.73.18833

Shane, S. (1992). Why do some societies invent more than others? *Journal of Business Venturing, 7*, 29–46. doi:10.1016/0883-9026(92)90033-N

Sigler, T. H., & Pearson, C. M. (2000). Creating an empowering culture: Examining the relationship between organizational culture and perceptions of empowerment. *Journal of Quality Management, 5*, 27–57. doi:10.1016/S1084-8568(00)00011-0

Sivakumar, K., & Nakata, C. (2001). The stampede toward Hofstede's framework: Avoiding the sample design pit in cross-cultural research. *Journal of International Business Studies, 32*(3), 555–574. doi:10.1057/palgrave.jibs.8490984

Sobel, M. E. (1982). Asymptotic intervals for indirect effects in structural equations models. In Leinhart, S. (Ed.), *Sociological Methodology* (pp. 290–312). San Francisco, CA: Jossey-Bass. doi:10.2307/270723

Spreitzer, G. M. (1995). Psychological empowerment in the workplace: Dimensions, measurement, and validation. *Academy of Management Journal, 38*, 1442–1465. doi:10.2307/256865

Spreitzer, G. M. (1996). Social structural characteristics of psychological empowerment. *Academy of Management Journal, 39*, 483–504. doi:10.2307/256789

Spreitzer, G. M., Kizilos, M. A., & Nason, S. W. (1997). A dimensional analysis of the relationship between psychological empowerment and effectiveness, satisfaction, and strain. *Journal of Management, 23*(5), 679–704.

Steenkamp, J.-B. E. M., ter Hofstede, F., & Wedel, M. (1999). A cross-national investigation into the individual and national cultural antecedents of consumer innovativeness. *Journal of Marketing, 53*, 55–69. doi:10.2307/1251945

Tebachnick, B. G., & Fidell, L. S. (2001). *Using multivariate statistics* (4th ed.). Boston, MA: Allyn & Bacon.

Thomas, A. S., & Mueller, S. L. (2000). A case for comparative entrepreneurship: Assessing the relevance of culture. *Journal of International Business Studies, 31*, 287–301. doi:10.1057/palgrave.jibs.8490906

Ujjual, V. (2008). *High technology firm performance, innovation, and networks: An empirical analysis of firms in Scottish high technology clusters.* Unpublished Doctoral Dissertation. Fife, UK: University of St.Andrews.

van de Ven, A. H. (1986). Central problems in the management of innovation. *Management Science, 32*, 509–607. doi:10.1287/mnsc.32.5.590

van Everdingen, Y. M., & Waarts, E. (2003). The effect of national culture on the adoption of innovations. *Marketing Letters, 14*(3), 217–232. doi:10.1023/A:1027452919403

Waarts, E., & van Everdingen, Y. M. (2005). The influence of national culture on the adaptation status of innovations: An empirical study of firms across Europe. *European Management Journal, 23*(6), 601–610. doi:10.1016/j.emj.2005.10.007

Wall, T. D., Wood, S. J., & Leach, D. J. (2004). Empowerment and performance. In Cooper, C. L., & Robertson, I. T. (Eds.), *International Review of Industrial and Organisational Psychology* (pp. 1–46). New York, NY: John Wiley & Sons, Ltd.

Web-Based Sobel Test. (2007). *Website.* Retrieved from http://www.people.ku.edu/~preacher/sobel/sobel.htm

Wei, S. L. (2006). *The impacts of technological opportunity and technology integration capability on business performance: An empirical study of high-tech industry in Taiwan.* Unpublished Master's Thesis. Tainan City, Taiwan: National Cheng Kung University.

Weil, D. N. (2005). *Economic growth.* New York, NY: Addison-Wesley.

Wickham, P. A. (2004). *Strategic entrepreneurship* (3rd ed.). Harlow, NJ: Pearson Education.

Wolff, J. A., & Pett, T. L. (2006). Small-firm performance: Modeling the role of product and process improvements. *Journal of Small Business Management, 44*(2), 268–284. doi:10.1111/j.1540-627X.2006.00167.x

Yam, R. C. M., Guan, J. C., Pun, K. F., & Tang, E. P. Y. (2004). An audit of technological innovation capabilities in Chinese firms: Some empirical findings in Beijing, China. *Research Policy, 33*, 1123–1140. doi:10.1016/j.respol.2004.05.004

Yilmaz, C., Alpkan, L., & Ergun, E. (2005). Cultural determinants of customer- and learning-oriented value systems and their joint effects on firm performance. *Journal of Business Research, 58*, 1340–1352. doi:10.1016/j.jbusres.2004.06.002

Chapter 15
Gendered Technology– Based Organizations:
A View of the Glass Cliff through the Window of the Glass Ceiling

Ben Tran
Alliant International University, USA

ABSTRACT

The "glass cliff" is a term coined by Professor Michelle Ryan and Professor Alex Haslam in 2004. Their research demonstrates that once women (or other minority groups) break through the glass ceiling and take on positions of leadership, they often have different experiences from their male counterparts. Specifically, women are more likely to occupy positions that can be described as precarious and thus have a higher risk of failure, either because they are in organizational units that are in crisis, or because they are not given the resources and support needed to thrive. The success of the glass cliff, as a phenomenon, rests on three factors. First, it relies heavily on the quality and quantity of data available, as well as the reliability of the data. Second, it relies heavily on the acceptance, utilization, and application of its existence, for a lack of acknowledgment, acceptance, utilization, and application of any phenomenon, concept, and theory will result in extinction. Third, this phenomenon, in reality, is quite taboo in a male dominated society, regardless of culture. Nevertheless, the glass cliff, as a phenomenon, is quite neoteric, and is typically not spoken of, nor referred to when men communicate, in the same way that men do not usually refer to the glass ceiling, or the glass escalator. The purpose of this chapter is to delve into and explore the concept of the glass cliff faced by women in high-tech corporations, and how the glass cliff affects their career advancement and identity growth through empirical data. The chapter then provides three recommendations on resolving the glass cliff phenomenon, and concludes with whether the glass cliff as a phenomenon is convertible to become a theory.

DOI: 10.4018/978-1-4666-1836-7.ch015

INTRODUCTION

Although twenty-five years have passed since *The Wall Street Journal* coined the phrase the *glass ceiling* in its 1986 special report on the corporate woman (Eagly & Carli, 2007; Hymowitz & Schellard, 1986), it is clear that this metaphor continues to be of great relevance, regardless of how much it has continuously been researched by academicians and used by practitioners. The *glass ceiling* refers to situations where the advancement of a qualified person within the hierarchy of an organization is stopped at a lower level, because of some form of discrimination, most commonly sexism or racism. However, since the term was coined, *glass ceiling* has also come to describe the impeded advancement of the deaf, gays and lesbians, blind, disabled, and aged. Based on the glass ceiling, the under-representation of women in positions of leadership persists, especially in the upper echelons of organizations, and specifically in the high-tech industry. In addition, other research has uncovered a corresponding phenomenon of the *glass escalator*, whereby men are accelerated through the organizational ranks, especially in sectors that are traditionally dominated by women (Williams, 1992). However, the phenomenon of the *glass escalator* only benefits men by accelerating them through the organizational ranks in sectors that are traditionally dominated by women. The phenomenon of the *glass ceiling* only hinders women by setting them up for failure through fulfilling negative gendered stereotypes in sectors that are traditionally dominated by men.

However, despite the continued existence of these subtle barriers, the number of women occupying management positions is greater than it has ever been (Equal Opportunities Commission, 2004; Women and Equality Unit, 2004). In this regard, the past fifteen or so years have seen greater gains in women's representation in leadership roles. For example, recent data from the United States indicates that women represent just over fifty percent of those in management, professional and related occupations (US Department of Labor, 2005). Similarly, in Britain, the number of women executives has doubled in this period (Equal Opportunities Commission, 2002) while, in the past five years, the number of female FTSE 100 directors has almost doubled (Singh & Vinnicombe, 2005). Now that women are increasingly occupying leadership roles, this introduces a new dilemma, the *glass cliff*.

THE GLASS CLIFF

The *glass cliff* is a term coined by Professor Michelle Ryan and Professor Alex Haslam of Exeter University, United Kingdom, in 2004. Their research demonstrates that once women (or other minority groups) break through the glass ceiling and take on positions of leadership, they often have different experiences from their male counterparts. Specifically, women are more likely to occupy positions that can be described as precarious and thus have a higher risk of failure, either because they are in organizational units that are in crisis, or because they are not given the resources and support needed for success. Extending the metaphor of the glass ceiling, the researchers evoked the metaphor of the *glass cliff* to capture the subtlety of the phenomenon and the feeling of teetering on the edge[1]. In other words, the glass cliff is founded on the phenomenon of women being preferentially placed in leadership roles that are associated with an increased risk of negative consequences (Ryan & Haslam, 2005).

According to research by Ryan and Haslam (2007), once women manage to break through the glass ceiling, they continue to encounter a range of problems and barriers. For example, Stroh, Brett, and Reilly (1996) found that more women left management positions than men (26% and 14%, respectively). This was not because women had more family commitments, as is often argued, but because women encountered sub-optimal career opportunities and thus became dissatisfied with their jobs. Possible sources of this disillusionment have been identified by Lyness and Thompson (1997), who found that women's satisfaction with their positions was significantly lower than that of men. In part, this was because the positions they occupy tend to (a) be more restrictive, (b) involve less authority, and (c) offer fewer tangible rewards.

Such subtle differences were also demonstrated by Frankforter (1996), who found that the positions held by women in senior management more often involve dealing with staff, rather than with an organization's core business. Furthermore, such soft personnel work tends not only to be less valued by organizations than hard production work (Powell, 1980), but also to involve more interpersonal conflict and greater stress (Erickson & Ritter, 2001), and to be less likely to lead on to more senior appointments. Taken together, these studies suggest that women's experiences in senior positions may be very different from those of their male counterparts. Indeed, as suggested by Ohlott, Ruderman, and McCauley (1994), men are more likely than women to report that the challenges they face serve a positive self-developmental purpose, while women are more likely to describe the barriers they face as obstacles.

Moreover, within the management literature, ambiguous evidence suggests that women are appointed to management positions under circumstances that differ from those of male managers. For example, female managers tend to occupy particular types of management positions, being more likely to hold support roles in personnel training, or marketing, rather than performing critical operating or commercial functions (Vinnicombe, 2000). Further, there are a higher proportion of women managers in service sectors than in more industrial sectors (Davidson & Cooper, 1992; Goodman, Fields, & Blum, 2003; Singh & Vinnicombe, 2003).

Research Method on the Existence of the Glass Cliff

Method (or methodology) (Mertens, 1998), model, or paradigm, (Tashakkori & Teddlie, 1998) is a body of practices, procedures, and rules used by those who work in a discipline or engage in an inquiry (Mertens, 1998). In other words, the researcher brings to the choice of a research design assumptions about knowledge claims, and the process of operating at a more applied level is called method or methodology. Method or methodology is also known as "strategy of inquiry" (Creswell, 2003, p. 13) or "traditions of inquiry" (Creswell, 1998, p. 2) that provide specific direction for procedures in research design. Like knowledge claims, strategies have multiplied over the years as computer technology has pushed forward data analysis and the ability to analyze complex models, and as individuals have articulated new procedures for conducting social science research.

Empirical Data: The word empirical denotes information gained by means of observation or experiments (Houghton Mifflin Company, 2000; Slife & Williams, 1995). Empirical data are data produced by an experiment or observation (Slife & Williams, 1995). In other words, with empirical data, empiricism is the notion that our learning and memory are primarily derived from our experience of events of the world. As such, a central concept in modern science and the scientific method is that all evidence must be empirical, or empirically based—that is, dependent on evidence or consequences that are observable by the senses. It is usually differentiated from the philosophic usage of empiricism by the use of the adjective empirical or the adverb empirically. The term refers to the use of working hypotheses that are testable using observation or experiment. In this sense of the word, scientific statements are subject to and derived from our experiences or observation (Isaac & Michael, 1997; Slife & Williams, 1995).

The standard positivist view of empirically acquired information has been that observation, experience, and experiment serve as neutral arbiters between competing theories. However, since the 1960s, Thomas Kuhn (1962, 1970) has promoted the concept that these methods are influenced by prior beliefs and experiences. Consequently it cannot be expected that two scientists when observing, experiencing, or experimenting on the same event will make the same theory-neutral observations. The role of observation as a theory-neutral arbiter may not be possible. Theory-dependence of observation means that, even if there were agreed methods of inference and interpretation, scientists may still disagree on the nature of empirical data (Isaac & Michael, 1997; Kuhn, 1962, 1970; Slife & Williams, 1995).

Rationalism: To truly evaluate and understand the ideas behind other ideas, one must have a point of comparison. One must have some contrast with the implicit ideas, or the other ideas will look like common sense, truth or axioms—rather than the points of view that ideas really are. As such, an alternative epistemology—*rationalism*—is necessary to learn the strengths and weaknesses of the more familiar epistemology, empiricism (Slife & Williams, 1995, pp. 67-71).

The epistemological root of rationalism is reason (Slife & Williams, 1995, p. 71). Unlike empiricism, which is rooted in sensory experience (Solo, 1991), rationalism is based on the assumption that the source of all true knowledge is logical thinking or reasoning ability. Even the root of rationalism—*ratio*—means reason. Rationalists rarely deny that experience is important, but they do deny that all knowledge comes directly and only from experience. As such, many behavioral and natural scientists nowadays assume that data—a more formal term for empirical experience of the world—are the final and primary source of knowledge. The rationalist, on the other hand, reminds us that the data must always be interpreted—that is, data, just like sensory experience, produce just confusion without some way to organize them.

Empirical Data Derived from Rationalism on the Existence of the Glass Cliff

Women on Board: Women's increased representation in management has focused the spotlight on the abilities of female leaders, especially those at the upper echelons of organizations, according to an article that appeared in the business section of *The Times* (Judge, 2003). The article examined the impact of having women on the boards of UK FTSE 100 companies and claimed that women have wreaked havoc on companies' performance and share prices (Judge, 2003, p. 21). Furthermore, according to Ryan and Haslam (2007), the article went on to argue that companies with more women on their boards of directors (Singh & Vinnicombe, 2003) tended to perform poorly relative to the average FTSE 100's company. In contrast, companies with no women on their boards tended to outperform the FTSE average. According to Judge (2003), evidence that companies that appoint women to their boards of directors tend to perform worse than those whose boards remain exclusively male, such that women should be discouraged from taking on leadership positions. Indeed, Judge's (2003, p. 21) article went so far as to say that "corporate Britain may be better off without women on the board."

In order to directly examine the claims set forth by Judge (2003), Ryan and Haslam (2005) conducted archival research to investigate the circumstances surrounding the appointment of directors to British companies in 2003. Instead of looking at average annual share prices over the entire year, Ryan and Haslam's research examined monthly changes in the share prices of FTSE 100 companies. Most importantly, Ryan and Haslam looked at these changes in share price both immediately before and after the appointment of a male or female board member. In so doing, what was striking in the data was not that the appointment a man or of a woman has a differential effect on company performance, as suggested by Judge

(2003), but rather that company's performance leading up to the appointment of a director differed depending on the gender of the appointee.

For companies that appointed men to their boards of directors, share price performance was relatively stable, both before and after the appointment. However, in a time of a general financial downturn in the stock market, companies that appointed a woman had experienced consistently poor performance in the months preceding the appointment. It was therefore apparent that men and women were being appointed to directorships under very different circumstances. To characterize the nature of this difference, Ryan and Haslam (2005) extended the metaphor of the *glass ceiling* to suggest that women are more likely than men to find themselves on a *glass cliff*—an allusion to the fact that their leadership positions are relatively risky or precarious since they are more likely to involve management of organizational units that are in crisis. As a recent case in point, Hewlett-Packard (HP) appointed Cathie Lesjak, a woman, to be its interim CEO and CFO on August 6, 2010, when CEO Mark Hurd unexpectedly resigned due to accusations of sexual harassment. Once the was crisis handled, HP recruited, hired, and appointed Leo Apotheker, a man, on September 9, 2010, to be the new CEO.

Women as Crisis Managers: Ryan and Haslam's archival and experimental research provides strong evidence for the existence of the *glass cliff*. As one potential explanation, people in companies may feel that women possess particular abilities that are especially valuable in times of crisis (Ryan, Haslam, Hersby, & Bongiorno, 2012). Indeed, one woman indicated that the *glass cliff* phenomenon reminded her of a quote from Eleanor Roosevelt: "Women are like teabags: you don't know how strong they are until you put them in hot water." Indeed, this perception, that women's particular strengths come to the fore in times of trouble, is echoed in Ryan and Haslam's research. In one scenario study, Ryan and Haslam asked about the leadership abilities

of the candidates for a financial directorship of a large company (Haslam & Ryan, 2008), and found that participants perceived the female candidate to have particularly good leadership ability when the position was described in the context of an ongoing decline in company performance, as opposed to a company where all was going well.

Women in High-Tech: High-tech is an exciting, evolving, and still relatively new industry, one that has changed the way we look at work and careers as well as our daily lives. However, the high-tech industry is a gender-biased industry, one that is fast becoming a new member of the "old boys club." This gender bias industry prompted senior technology executives to convene a technical executive forum on October 1, 2009. Fifty-nine executives participated in the Anita Borg Institute's[2] 2009 Technical Executive Forum[3], held at the Grace Hopper Celebration of Women in Computing. This initiative brought together thought leaders to raise awareness, actively discuss, and drive action among R&D executives on issues regarding the recruitment, retention, and advancement of women in high-tech (also known as technical women).

Companies and institutions[4] that participated at the Forum focused on three components: 1) a review of issues pertaining to the culture of technology organizations that prevent the recruitment, retention, and advancement of technical women; 2) presentation of solutions that have effectively addressed these cultural challenges within organizations that can be replicated; and 3) breakout sessions focused on specific ideas and actions. Even though an acknowledgment was made that the pipeline of technical women with technical degrees coming out of academia was insufficient, the group commented that women who do graduate from these programs are not joining organizational cultures that are as receptive as they could be to gender diversity. For example, a former staffing specialist for an IBM subsidiary admitted to me in an informal conversation, in September 2010, that the subsidiary still practices demographic profiling when it comes to recruitment.

Leading high-tech companies require diversity, particularly gender diversity, to maintain globally competitive technical workforces. Research shows that workforce diversity can boost a company's bottom line by providing a creative variety of thinking styles and, thus, new business solutions. According to a study by Catalyst (2004, p. 2) on 353 companies in the Fortune 500, the group of companies with the highest representation of women experienced better financial performance than the group of companies with the lowest women's representation. This finding held for both financial measures analyzed: Return on Equity (ROE), which was 35.1% higher, and Total Return to Shareholders (TRS), which was 34.0% higher.

Furthermore, a Catalyst study released in October 2001, surveying men and women in high-tech management, reported that five out of nineteen women working as top managers in America's largest high-tech companies experienced no barriers to career success because of their sex. The companies they work for, including AOL Time Warner, Intel, and Oracle, may have corporate cultures that are generally friendlier to women. That is an important note in itself: the fastest growing, most successful, and most exciting companies to work for are women friendly.

Sheila Wellington, Catalyst's director, launched the study to provide an easy-to-use road map for talented young women in high tech as they shape their own careers. The study's findings are surprising. First, a technical degree is not essential to climb high on the corporate ladder, but social networks are. Men in the study reported that success in their industry is based on merit only, while women reported that networking and knowing the right people makes a difference. Second, the essential value of mentoring was substantiated, and quite surprisingly, no difficulty balancing work and family was reported by the subjects (Tran, 2008).

Other Reports: Another industry report by Gartner estimates that by the year 2012, teams with greater gender diversity (when compared to all-male teams) will be twice as likely to exceed performance expectations (Harris & Raskino, 2007). A recent master thesis concluded that there exist no significant differences in the perceived effectiveness of male and female leaders. The study further concluded that the perceived similarity in effectiveness may imply that the leaders have equivalent access to power and status within the organization, and that society is becoming more accepting of females in managerial roles (Lassile & Peippo, 2008, p. 52). In other words, gender diversity in the high-tech workforce fuels problem-solving and innovation, the driving forces of technology (Mannix & Neale, 2005).

Technology business leaders agree that the effort of focusing on diversity when based solely on recruitment is not enough. In a recent survey, 300 technology executives identified hiring and retaining skilled technical workers as their top concern (Overby, 2006). Today, technical employees hail from diverse backgrounds, making retention difficult for companies that cannot meet diverse needs. Poor retention rates, in turn, add an additional costly burden to recruiting efforts (Tran, 2008). The cost of filling the vacancy left by a single skilled technical employee is estimated to be as high as 120% of the yearly salary attached to that position (Tran, 2008; Vitalari & Dell, 1998). A recent industry report by Gartner estimates that by the year 2012, teams with gender diversity (when compared to all-male teams) will be twice as likely to exceed performance expectations (Harris & Raskino, 2007).

However, when it comes to providing opportunities for technical women, high-tech firms lag sharply behind those in other sectors. Men are significantly more likely than women to hold high-level management or executive positions. Women in the mid-point of their high-tech careers are extremely valuable to companies, but this seems to be the very point at which they face the greatest barriers to advancement—at a cost to both the companies and the individual women.

In order to learn why the mid-level is a *glass ceiling* for women on the technical ladder, the Anita Borg Institute for Women and Technology and the Michelle R. Clayman Institute for Gender Research at Stanford University have undertaken a groundbreaking study of female scientists and engineers at seven mid-to-large, publicly traded Silicon Valley high-tech firms. Drawing from a large-scale survey and in-depth interviews conducted in 2007 and 2008, the study proposes data-driven, systematic solutions for the recruitment, retention, and advancement of technical women in the high tech industry. The concept of the *glass ceiling* is anything but new to corporations for it has been studied, researched, and confirmed. Now, as a direct result of attempts by corporations to remedy the issue of the *glass ceiling*, women now face the *glass cliff*.

Statistics of Women (and Minorities) in High-Tech: According to Williams (1992), the sex segregation of the U.S. labor force is one of the most perplexing and tenacious problems in its society, as well as in any society. Even though the proportion of men and women in the labor force is approaching parity (US Department of Labor, 1991, p. 18), men and women are still generally confined to predominantly single-sex occupations, and historical statistics have yet to contradict this fact. Forty percent of men or women would have to change major occupational categories to achieve equal representation of men and women in all jobs (Reskin & Roos, 1990, p. 6) but even this figure underestimates the true degree of sex segregation. It is extremely rare to find specific jobs where equal numbers of men and women are engaged in the same activities in the same industries (Bielby & Baron, 1984).

With that said, statistics in 1998 indicated that 66% of the United States workforce was made up of women, with only 21% at the middle management level and a dismal 15% at the senior management level (Veale & Gold, 1998). Women and minorities, on the other hand, are underrepresented in technology-related careers. Lack of access, levels of math and science achievement, and emotional and social attitudes about computer skills may be some of the factors that cause women and minorities to avoid high-tech careers. According to the American Association of University Women, the number of women graduating in computer sciences and information technology is decreasing despite the increased need for workers in these areas (Friedman, 2000). In addition, for minorities, the shortfall is stark: The Bureau of Labor Statistics reports that only 7.2% of all computer scientists are African American, while 2.6% are Hispanic (Bruno, 1997).

RECOMMENDATIONS ON RESOLVING THE GLASS CLIFF PHENOMENON

It stands to reason that the first step in any initiatives taken by corporations is a top-down approach, supported by the decision makers. In so doing, companies are encouraged to consult with their Organizational Consultants (OC), Organizational Psychologists (OP), Organizational Development practitioners (OD), and/or Industrial and Organizational psychologists (I/O) if they have such in-house practitioners. Otherwise, company managers should contract with an external consultant if financially convenient, or consult with one's in-house department of human resources. Such initiatives do not exist just on paper, but must be implemented and continuously evaluated for change and improvement. Designing a women's initiative that includes goals sends a critically important message that a firm wants to change the status quo in a way that means business.

There also is a more subtle but equally important cause that so many prestigious companies have embraced—diversity. Diversity, including gender diversity, is not only good in its own right;

it is good for business. Many women prefer to patronize the businesses of other women (Metlin & Cohen, 2007). The Minority Corporate Counsel Association's 2007 Annual Survey of Fortune 500 Companies shows that women have continued to make inroads into top positions in large companies. In addition, according to a 2002 Catalyst study of the Fortune 500 companies, women held 15.7% of the corporate officer positions compared to 12.5% in 2000. It is estimated that women will hold 27.4% of all corporate officer positions by 2020 (Metlin & Cohen, 2007).

Certainly, skeptics may not believe it is necessary or desirable for firms to invest in developing their female employees. Some do not see the nearly invisible forces that make life so different for men and women. This skepticism is a result of true and proud homogenous ideology; it is derived from a lack of consideration, understanding, and empathy for the advantages of the initiatives for women that might also benefit men. This skepticism is one of many possible reasons that contributed to the existence of the glass cliff. The four possible implementable and actionable initiatives that firms can include in its marketing strategies to attract and recruit more female applicants, retain more qualified female employees, and even shatter the glass cliff by promoting superb and distinct female contributors in their high-tech firms are:

First: Branding, Marketing, and Promoting

First and foremost, high-tech corporations must communicate the message that their operation is an equal opportunity talent-valued corporation, regardless of gender, ethnicity, sexual orientation, and disability. Companies must start with their communication and recruitment processes: the corporate website, print or film commercials, informational brochures, advertisements, and other visible avenues. As a case in point, Genentech, Inc., located in South San Francisco, California, is known as the most female friendly company

in the high-tech industry. Within the branding, marketing, and promoting stage, corporations need to consider including and selling the following benefits:

Family

Organizations need to recognize the basic fact that women are involved in childbirth and therefore will focus on their needs for parental leave, flexible schedules, and—in some cases—different career plans. This factor also affects and benefits male employees due to the fact of "fatherhood," "single father," and "adulthood/bachelorhood/marriage" that causes changes in career plans for male employees as well.

Firms need to help women adequately set expectations with their managers once they have a family, and firms need to create executive sponsorship that recognize and value family. This factor also affects and benefits male employees.

The factors need to be incorporated in career planning:

- **Alternative Work Schedules:** Alternative Work Schedule (AWS) is also known as Variable Work Hours (AWH). There are three types of AWS (Victoria Transport Policy Institute, 2010):
  - **Compressed Work Week (CWW):** CWW challenges the traditional paradigm of America's standard workweek, which is Monday through Friday, 8am-to-5pm. It regularly allows full-time employees to eliminate at least one work day every other week by working longer hours during the remaining days. The definition's intention primarily includes weekly and biweekly arrangements. Weekly arrangements such as 4/40 eliminate one workday every week. Biweekly arrangements such as 9/80 eliminate one day every two weeks. Such work

arrangements must be agreed upon between the employees, their customer, their leader, and their team;

- ○ **Flextime (Ft)[5]:** Ft is a policy allowing individuals some flexibility in choosing the time, but not the number, of their working hours. When a work day is eliminated we refer to this as a flex day off; and
- ○ **Staggered Shift (SS):** SS means that shifts are staggered to reduce the number of employees arriving and leaving a worksite at one time. For example, some shifts may be 8:00 to 4:30, others 8:30 to 5:00, and others 9:00 to 5:30. This has a similar effect on traffic as flextime, but does not give individual employees as much control over their schedules.

- **Telecommuting:** Telecommuting, also known as e-commuting, e-work, telework, Work-From-Home (WFH), or Working-At-Home (WAH), is a work arrangement in which employees enjoy flexibility in working location and hours. In other words, the daily commute to a central place of work is replaced by telecommunication links. Many work from home, while others, occasionally also referred to as nomad workers or Web commuters, utilize mobile telecommunications technology to work from coffee shops or myriad other locations.

- ○ **Telework:** Is a broader term, referring to substituting telecommunications for any form of work-related travel, thereby eliminating the distance restrictions of telecommuting (Nilles, 1998). A frequently repeated motto is that "work is something you do, not something you travel to" (Leonhard, 1995). A successful telecommuting program requires a management style, which is based on

results and not on close scrutiny of individual employees. This is referred to as management by objectives as opposed to management by observation. The terms telecommuting and telework were coined by Jack Nilles in 1973 (JALA International, 2010).

- ○ **Telecommuting High-Techs (THT):** THTs are not new, but many THTs have not yet implemented this method. Some THTs are: Microsoft, Adobe, Inc., Macromedia, Inc., Sony, Intel, IBM. Employees of THTs not only telecommute, but often do not live in the same city or state in which the company headquarters or hub is located.

Gender-Specific Factors:

- It is often difficult for women to obtain sponsors and mentors. This factor, known as the "old boys club," has been well established and well implemented for male employees, both directly and indirectly (Tran, 2008). To counteract this, organizations can set up facilitating mechanisms to specially help women.
- Risk-taking is necessary to career advancement in technology. Organizations need to focus internal development on risk-taking.

Environmental Factors:

- Many technical cultures leave women feeling isolated and crushed.
- Change starts within one's own groups as executives.

Career Management:

- Recruitment and advancement processes "genericize" talent and puts employees in "one size fits all" boxes. As a result, firms lose out on a diverse of talent and on people's best skills.

- Focus on getting the right people in the right job as opposed to making them fit in a mold. This includes creating career paths for specialists, who have unique skills to contribute to organizational success.

- Organizational should "shop the internal closet" instead of hiring from outside for positions. In a systematic way, each organization should look from within first and find people who are poised for advancement, even if they do not fit a set of rigid pre-requisites.

- Retain employees—at the beginning of the high-tech industry, extensive training and development were the norm in many companies. This infrastructure has been dismantled in many US companies, even though research shows that the organizations with long-term success engage in significant employee development and training.

Second: Assessing and Evaluating Potential Qualified Candidates Utilizing KSAOs

According to Tran (2008), personnel selection processes are the methods, which organizations use to evaluate potential employees' knowledge, skills, and abilities in order to determine whether there is a good fit between an available position and a candidate. These are the commonly used sets of criteria that identify successful domestic candidates. These sets of criteria are well known and have been used for a long time. Knowledge, skills, and abilities will be referred to as KSAs while the criteria including "other" attributes will be referred to as KSAOs[6]: 1) Knowledge is usually defined as the degree to which a candidate is required to know certain technical materials, 2) Skill indicates adequate performance on tasks requiring the use

of tools, equipment, machinery, etc., 3) Abilities are physical and mental capacities to perform tasks not requiring the use of tools, equipment, or machinery, and 4) Other characteristics include personality, interest, or motivational attributes that indicate a candidate will learn certain tasks, rather than whether they can do those tasks (Schneider & Schmitt, 1992, p. 53). High-tech companies need to emphasize these KSAs in their selection processes to help control, correct, and eliminate biases and discriminations in order to select the most qualified candidates—notably women, if such opportunities arise (Tran, 2008).

Third: Encouraging, Supporting, and Providing Mentorship

Mentorships can greatly help in the handling of the glass cliff phenomenon and perhaps even prevent it from happening in the first place. With mentorship, an individual being mentored is able to seek advice and support if and when facing circumstances that may turn out to be a glass cliff situation. The success of handling and resolving challenges due to mentorship may result in the security of one's status in the corporation or even lead to promotion for the individual being mentored.

According to Tran (2008), based on White, Cox, and Cooper's (1992) research, much of the literature on mentoring comes from the USA, where the main focus has been on the male experience of mentoring. There are many possible explanations for the infrequency of mentoring relationships among women in organizations. An explanation frequently cited in the research literature is that mentors may not select female protégées (Burke & McKeen, 1994; Ragins, 1989). The selection process may therefore be biased by the tendency of male mentors to choose male over female protégées. The findings from the current research indicate that there are not enough women in senior international managerial positions yet to act as mentors for other women. As a result,

38 of the interviewees (76%) according to Tran (2008), said that females are more likely to be mentored by males, and 40 of the interviewees (80%) had the experience of either formal or informal mentoring relationships. Further, 28 (56%) of the managers were mentored by men only, 6 (12%) were mentored by females only, and 6 (12%) were mentored by both males and females. All ten interviewees (20%) who did not have mentors believed that they would have benefited from such a relationship, especially in the early stages of their careers.

As noted by Linehan and Scullion (2001), the findings also reveal that, in an international management context, a mentoring relationship is even more important than in a domestic management context. The participants believe that while partaking in international assignments, in addition to improving their self-confidence, increasing their visibility in organizations and increasing their promotional prospects, mentors provide the contact and support from the home organization which in turn facilitates re-entry. The interviewees suggested that, in the absence of family and friends, their mentors also helped to keep them in touch with their home organization, which in turn reduced the "out of sight, out of mind" syndrome. The participants also believe that the opportunities for them to partake in international assignments were partly attributed to having mentoring relationships.

Furthermore, as Linehan and Scullion (2001) mentioned, seven of the interviewees spoke of their bosses, all male, who facilitated informal mentoring support. These interviewees believed that a "good boss" acted as a supporter and adviser for them, helped to develop their reputations, helped to get their names known to senior management, set higher standards for them, and stimulated their personal motivation. An interviewee, according to Linehan and Scullion, stated, "Long before the word mentor was invented, I was fortunate to have a couple of bosses who were helpful in that way. It was very informal. What you need is someone to discuss issues with you and whom you can trust and who sometimes helps you to find a way out and to help you solve problems" (Director, European Commission). All the interviewees in the current research, according to Linehan and Scullion, believed that their mentors did not view them as females, but saw their mentoring roles as aiding the career advancement of their managerial protégées. The 40 interviewees (80%) who had mentors believed, from their experiences, that the benefits provided by mentors, regardless of their respective gender, had undoubtedly facilitated their career advancement.

The lack of networking is an informal barrier for women in high-tech corporations. According to Tran (2008), Smith and Hutchinson (1995) noted that there is not much empirical research literature available on interpersonal networks. Previous research studies of networking in domestic organizations, however, have indicated that in many organizations the concept of networks is understood to mean a male club (Davidson & Cooper, 1992; Ibarra, 1993). As Burke and McKeen (1994) mentioned, studies on both networking and mentoring suggested some similarities. Both mentors and peer relationships can facilitate career and personal development. Networking can be useful at all stages in career development, while mentors are particularly useful at the early stages of career development. Peer relationships are different from mentoring relationships in that they often last longer, are not hierarchical, and involve two-way helping. Peer relationships have advantages, particularly since a significant number of women may not have had mentors before.

Many studies indicate that women have been largely excluded from "old boy's" networks, which traditionally are composed of individuals who hold power in the organization (Fagenson, 1986; Henning & Jardim, 1977; Kanter, 1977). The findings from the current study indicate that, throughout Europe, such networks are still strong in most organizations, and particularly in established industries, such as medicine, accountancy, and law. The participants believe that, given the absence of family and friends while abroad, the benefits provided by formal and informal networking in international management are of greater value than the benefits provided in domestic management. A total of 43 of the interviewees (86%) believe that there is a lack of networking for women in senior management. The managers perceive that quite an amount of business is discussed and useful contacts are made when male managers network informally, but as women they are excluded access to these informal situations. An interviewee, according to Linehan and Scullion (2001), stated that, "there is a lack of networking for female managers. I got quite a shock when I found out that there were all-men golf clubs, and special days for ladies. It would be beneficial for women if they had more informal contacts" (Customer Services Manager, Computer Company).

As noted by Linehan and Scullion (2001), despite the benefits provided by networks, however, the participants believe that women are further disadvantaged from networking, as they have less time than their male colleagues due to home and family commitments. Despite the shortage of time available to female managers for networking, however, 43 respondents (86%) suggested that if there was a professional networking organization available for female managers they would ensure that their schedules permitted joining such as organization. The participants, however, believed that gaining access to male networks is still the most significant barrier that women in senior management positions have to overcome in relation to networking. The participants, according to Linehan and Scullion, also suggested that the exclusion of females from male managerial groups perpetuated the more exclusively male customs, traditions, and negative attitudes towards female managers. The detrimental effects of these covert barriers included blocked promotion, and blocked career development, discrimination, occupational stress, and lower salaries. The interviewees also

spoke of the "male bonding" which took place after work hours, during sporting events, in clubs, and in bars which they felt excluded from.

Some of the interviewees in this study have established their own informal female or mixed gender networks. The interviewees agreed with the findings of previous research by Davidson and Cooper (1992), which indicated that, although it is beneficial for female managers to network in these newer groups, there are still more benefits to be gained from networking in the established male-dominated groups, as power in organizations is still predominantly held by men. Parker and Fagenson (1994) also advised that it is important for women to penetrate male networks to a greater extent if they wish to become sufficiently visible to win organizational promotions. Five of the interviewees (10%) were members of networking groups for female managers within their own companies. In contrast, four of the interviewees (8%) disagreed with networks, which catered exclusively for females. These managers believe that it is not necessary to restrict membership of these networks to women only, and that the female managers should actively encourage male managers to join. These interviewees, according to Linehan and Scullion (2001), perceived that there are more benefits to be gained for career progression if they include males in such networking groups.

The findings in Linehan and Scullion's (2001) study indicated that the exclusion of female managers from business and social networks compounds their isolation, which may prevent female managers from building up useful networking relationships that might be advantageous to their international careers. The interviewees suggested that men, more often than not, will exclude women from informal interactions. They also suggested that exclusively male networks may be responsible for developing and nurturing negative attitudes and prejudices towards female managers. Of the managers interviewed, according to Linehan and Scullion, 46 (92%) perceived that there are more benefits to be gained for career progression if they can be included in male networking groups. These interviewees believe that if females had more access to networking groups they could be socialized in both the formal and informal norms of the organization and gain advantages from these groups.

THE GLASS CLIFF PHENOMENON

With the *glass cliff* phenomenon, while the practice is quite seasoned in corporations and to practitioners, the concept is still quite novel in academia and to researchers. The Glass Cliff Research Group, led by Dr. Michelle Ryan and Dr. Alex Haslam, in the School of Psychology at the University of Exeter, and their team of researchers are currently in the process of converting this phenomenon into a theory. This process of converting a phenomenon into a theory involves the evolution of a paradigm shift. Kuhn uses the term paradigm in its broadest sense to refer to the set of unquestioned fundamental presuppositions that define a particular orientation toward the world (Kent, 1993, p. 4; Langdon & McGann, 1993). Kuhn proposed the term paradigm to refer to the comprehensive theories and experimental work of a discipline or set of disciplines (Bynum, Browne, and Porter, 1981; Langdon & McGann, 1993).

It is common knowledge that many behavioral scientists and philosophers disagree that any of the behavioral sciences, let alone the aggregate of them, has a paradigm in the sense that Kuhn uses the term (Slife & Williams, 1995). Part of the problem lies in differences of opinion about what does or does not constitute such a paradigm, and even about what Kuhn may have meant. Developing an adequate argument in support of our contention is beyond the scope of this chapter. Rather, I would prefer to use the term paradigm in a very general and global sense, suggesting simply that there must be a common assumptive basis underlying scientific, or any other scholarly

work, and that various aspects of this common assumptive basis can be seen across theories and disciplines in the behavioral sciences.

With that said, the purpose of this chapter is not on the comprehensive coverage of the process regarding the conversion of a phenomenon to a theory, so a brief summary of these stages involved in process is provided instead. For a detailed comprehensive coverage of the whole process, inclusive of all stages, please refer to John H. Lamgdon and Mary E. McGann's work. For the purpose of this sectional discussion, a brief summary of the four stages involved in the process of the conversion is introduced, based on Kuhn's model of scientific development. There are four discernible stages implicit in Kuhn's model of scientific development: 1) The Pre-Paradigm Stage, 2) Normal Science, 3) The Crisis Period, and 4) The Adoption of a New Paradigm.

1. **The Pre-Paradigm Stage**: This stage might also be called prenormal science or the pre-consensus phase (Hoynigen-Huene, 1993, p. 189; Lamgdon & McGann, 1993). It is characterized by little agreement on metaphysics, methodology, which phenomena are especially significant, or which problems are important.

2. **Normal Science**: The "normalization" of science usually begins with some strikingly new way of conceptualizing and ordering the data. As a result, scientists tacitly reach a consensus on a paradigm: a coherent scientific program that includes basic ontological commitments, methodology, and mode of explanation, theoretical principals, preferred instrumentation, and experimental design.

3. **The Crisis Period**: Science enters a crisis period when its puzzle-solving activity leads to fewer and fewer solutions, resulting in more anomalies. As the anomalies accumulate, cracks begin to form in the consensus.

4. **The Adoption of a New Paradigm**: A scientific revolution occurs when an old

paradigm is replaced by a new one. This happens when a new theory emerges that is able not only to resolve the accumulated anomalies of the old paradigm, but also to retain, and give new explanations for, the predictive successes of that paradigm.

CONCLUSION

Although twenty-five years have passed since *The Wall Street Journal* coined the phrase the "glass ceiling" in its 1986 special report on the corporate woman, it is clear that this metaphor continues to be of great relevance. The glass ceiling refers to situations where the advancement of a qualified person within the hierarchy of an organization is stopped at a lower level, because of some form of discrimination, most commonly sexism or racism. However, since the term was coined, glass ceiling has also come to describe the limited advancement of the deaf, gays and lesbians, blind, disabled, and aged. Based on the glass ceiling, women's under-representation in positions of leadership persists, especially in the upper echelons of organizations, especially in high-tech industry.

In addition, other research has uncovered a corresponding phenomenon of the glass escalator, whereby men are accelerated through the organizational ranks, especially in sectors that are traditionally dominated by women (Williams, 1992). However, the phenomenon of the glass escalator only benefit men by accelerating them through the organizational ranks in sectors that are traditionally dominated by women, and the phenomenon of the glass ceiling only hinders women by setting them up for failure through fulfilling negative gendered stereotypes in sectors that are traditionally dominated by men. Data regarding these two practices have been inducted into the "old boy's club," thus, have come to be accepted as common knowledge. Ubiquitous data, empirical or otherwise, regarding the practice of

the *glass cliff*, are still quite taboo to the degree being rarely mentioned.

The status of its uncultured reputation is given by those individuals who are quite often in power. More often than not, these individuals are men. Certain men in positions of power naturally want power to remain in power, and to maintain power, they deny the existence of such practices. Thus, they deny the *glass cliff* phenomenon. For instance, sexual harassment in the workplace—where sexual harassment is defined as intimidation, bullying or coercion of a sexual nature, or the unwelcome, or inappropriate promise of rewards in exchange for sexual favors (Paludi & Barickman, 1991)—was once considered uncultured. According to some individuals (men) in position of power, it does not exist.

A paradigm shift is difficult. A paradigm shift, or revolutionary science, is the term used by Thomas Kuhn in his influential book, *The Structure of Scientific Revolutions*, to describe a change in the basic assumptions, or paradigms, within the ruling theory of science. A paradigm shift is quite often hard because it requires individuals to discard what they once know and accept to now reevaluate and challenge what they once know and accept. In so doing, individuals may be required to relearn and abandon what they have been ingrained to accept and now accept valid knowledge that is contradictory to their past knowledge. Such a change may require the release of power.

While Dr. Rosabeth Moss Kantor[7] and Dr. Arlie Russell Hochschild[8] are two of the more well-known pioneer authors and researchers on gender issues in corporations, among other pioneers, such as Dr. Jyotsna Sanzgiri[9], the issue remains quite taboo to practitioners and ambiguous to human resources practitioners until either profits and/or legal law suits come into play. When either or both paramount factors surfaces, and forces firms to acknowledge, accept, address, and handle it, only then will many firms then decide to invest in gender balance in high-tech. The profit factor refers to the loss-of-profit, or the negative intake of profit, which in turns negatively affects the Board of Directors and investors. The legal lawsuits factor refers to claims brought forth by litigants based on discrimination. These two paramount factors are the sole reasons of existence for any and all businesses—especially reputable and profitable businesses—to survive, to be legal and ethical, to profit, and to grow. Until then, the *glass cliff*, as a phenomenon, will remain quite novel. Men typically will not speak of it, nor refer to the term when communicating, much like the term the *glass ceiling*, and the *glass escalator*.

REFERENCES

Bielby, W. T., & Baron, J. N. (1984). A woman's place is with other women: Sex segregation within organizations. In Reskin, B. (Ed.), *Sex Segregation in the Workplace: Trends, Explanations, Remedies* (pp. 27–55). Washington, DC: National Academy Press.

Bruno, C. (1997, October 6). Diversity disconnect. *Network World*. Retrieved on July 2, 2010, from http://www.networkworld.com/news/1997/1006diversity.html

Burke, R. J., & McKeen, C. A. (1994). Career development among managerial and professional women. In Davidson, M. J., & Burke, J. R. (Eds.), *Women in Management: Current Research Issues* (pp. 65–79). London, UK: Paul Chapman.

Bynum, W. F., Browne, E. J., & Porter, R. (1981). *Dictionary of the history of science*. Princeton, NJ: Princeton University Press.

Catalyst. (2004). *The bottom line: Connecting corporate performance and gender diversity*. New York, NY: Catalyst Publication.

Creswell, J. W. (1998). *Qualitative inquiry and research design: Choosing among five traditions*. Thousand Oaks, CA: Sage.

Creswell, J. W. (2003). *Research design: Qualitative, quantitative, and mixed methods approaches* (2nd ed.). Thousand Oaks, CA: Sage Publications, Inc.

Davidson, M. J., & Cooper, C. L. (1992). *Shattering the glass ceiling: The woman manager*. London, UK: Paul Chapman Publishing.

Eagly, A. H., & Carli, L. L. (2007). *Through the labyrinth: the truth about how women and become leaders*. Boston, MA: Harvard Business School Press.

Equal Opportunities Commission. (2002). *Women and men in Britain: Management*. Manchester, UK: Equal Opportunities Commission.

Equal Opportunities Commission. (2004). *Women and men in Great Britain*. Retrieved on July 1, 2010, from http://www.eoc.org.uk.PDF/facts_about_2004_gb.pdf

Erickson, R. I., & Ritter, C. (2001). Emotional labor, burnout, and inauthenticity: Does gender matter? *Social Psychology Quarterly*, *64*(2), 146–163. doi:10.2307/3090130

Fagenson, E. A. (1986). Women's work orientation: Something old, something new. *Group and Organization Studies*, *11*(1-2), 75–100. doi:10.1177/105960118601100108

Frankforter, S. A. (1996). The progression of women beyond the glass ceiling. *Journal of Social Behavior and Personality*, *11*(5), 121–132.

Friedman, M. (2000). Women take to internet while avoiding it. *Computing Canada*. Retrieved on July 2, 2010, from http://www.itbusiness.ca/it/client/en/home/News.asp?id=28774

Goodman, J. S., Fields, D. L., & Blum, T. C. (2003). Cracks in the glass ceiling: In what kinds of organizations do women make it to the top? *Group & Organization Management*, *28*, 475–501. doi:10.1177/1059601103251232

Harris, D. M. K., & Raskino, M. (2007). *Women and men in IT: Breaking sexual stereotypes*. Washington, DC: Gartner.

Haslam, S. A., & Ryan, M. K. (2008). The road to the glass cliff: Differences in the perceived suitability of men and women for leadership positions in succeeding and failing organizations. *The Leadership Quarterly*, *19*(5), 530–546. doi:10.1016/j.leaqua.2008.07.011

Henning, M., & Jardim, A. (1977). *The managerial women*. New York, NY: Pan Books.

Houghton Mifflin Company. (2000). *The American heritage dictionary of the English language*. Boston, MA: Houghton Mifflin Company.

Hoynigen-Huene, P. (1993). *Restructuring scientific revolutions: Thomas s. Kuhn's philosophy of science*. Chicago, IL: University of Chicago Press.

Hymowitz, C., & Schellard, T. D. (1986, March 24). The glass ceiling: Why women can't seem to break the invisible barrier that blocks them form the top jobs. *The Wall Street Journal*, p. D1, D4.

Ibarra, H. (1993). Personal networks of women and minorities in management: A conceptual framework. *Academy of Management Review*, *18*(1), 56–87.

Isaac, S., & Michael, W. B. (1997). *Handbook in research and evaluation: A collection of principles, methods, and strategies useful in the planning, design, and evaluation of studies in education and the behavioral sciences* (3rd ed.). San Diego, CA: Educational and Industrial Testing Services.

JALA International. (2010). *JALA biography of Jack Nilles*. Retrieved on July 17, 2010, from http://www.jala.com/jnmbio.php

Judge, E. (2003, November 11). Women on board: Help or hindrance? *Times (London, England)*, (n.d), 21.

Kanter, R. M. (1977). Some effects of proportions of group life: Skewed sex ratios and responses to token women. *American Journal of Sociology*, *82*, 965–990. doi:10.1086/226425

Kent, T. (1993). The Kuhnian model of scientific change. In Langdon, J. H., & McGann, M. E. (Eds.), *The Natural History of Paradigms: Science and the Process of Intellectual Evolution*. Indianapolis, IN: The University of Indianapolis Press.

Kuhn, T. S. (1962). *The structure of scientific revolutions*. Chicago, IL: University of Chicago Press.

Kuhn, T. S. (1970). *The structure of scientific revolutions* (2nd ed.). Chicago, IL: University of Chicago Press.

Kuhn, T. S. (1996). *The structure of scientific revolutions* (3rd ed.). Chicago, IL: University of Chicago Press.

Langdon, J. H., & McGann, M. E. (1993). *The natural history of paradigms: Science and the process of intellectual evolution*. Indianapolis, IN: The University of Indianapolis Press.

Lassile, K., & Peippo, N. (2008). *Birds of a feather: A study of subordinate perceptions of leader effectiveness as a function of gender*. Master Thesis. Stockholm, Sweden: Stockholm University.

Leonhard, W. (1995). *The underground guide to telecommuting*. Boston, MA: Addison-Wesley.

Linehan, M., & Scullion, H. (2001). Challenges for female international managers: Evidence from Europe. *Journal of Managerial Psychology*, *16*(3), 215–228. doi:10.1108/02683940110385767

Lyness, K. S., & Thompson, D. E. (1997). Above the glass ceiling? A comparison of matched samples of female and male executives. *The Journal of Applied Psychology, 82*(3), 359–375. doi:10.1037/0021-9010.82.3.359

Mannix, E. A., & Neale, M. A. (2005). What difference makes a difference? *Psychological Science in the Public Interest, 6*(2), 31–32. doi:10.1111/j.1529-1006.2005.00022.x

Mertens, D. M. (1998). *Research methods in education and psychology: Integrating diversity with quantitative and qualitative approaches.* Thousand Oaks, CA: Sage.

Metlin, E., & Cohen, R. (2007). Designing a women's initiative that works: Make it thoughtful, well-planned and business-based. *New York Law Journal Magazine, 6*(5).

Nilles, J. M. (1998). *Managing telework: Options for managing the virtual workforce.* New York, NY: John Wiley & Sons.

Ohlott, P. J., Ruderman, M. N., & McCauley, C. D. (1994). Gender differences in managers' developmental job experiences. *Academy of Management Journal, 37*(1), 46–67. doi:10.2307/256769

Overby, S. (2006, September 1). How to hook the talent you need. *CIO Magazine.*

Paludi, M. A., & Barickman, R. B. (1991). *Academic and workplace sexual harassment: A resource manual.* Albany, NY: State University of New York Press.

Parker, B., & Fagenson, E. A. (1994). An introductory overview of women in corporate management. In Davison, M. J., & Burke, R. J. (Eds.), *Women in Management: Current Research Issues* (pp. 11–25). London, UK: Paul Chapman.

Picado, R. (2000). A questioning of time. *Access, 17,* 9–13.

Powell, G. N. (1980). Career development and the woman manager: A social power perspective. *Personnel, 57*(3), 22–32.

Ragins, B. R. (1989). Barriers to mentoring the female manager's dilemma. *Human Relations, 42*(1), 1–22. doi:10.1177/001872678904200101

Reskin, B., & Roos, P. (1990). *Job queues, gender queues: Explaining women's inroads into male organizations.* Philadelphia, PA: Temple University Press.

Ryan, M. K., & Haslam, S. A. (2005). The glass cliff: Evidence that women are over-represented in precarious leadership positions. *British Journal of Management, 16,* 81–90. doi:10.1111/j.1467-8551.2005.00433.x

Ryan, M. K., & Haslam, S. A. (2007). *Women in the boardroom: The risks of being at the top.* Washington, DC: Chartered Institute of Personnel and Development.

Ryan, M. K., Haslam, S. A., Hersby, M. D., & Bongiorno, R. (2012). *Think crisis—Think female: Using the glass cliff to reconsider the think manager—Think male stereotype.* Unpublished. Exeter, UK: University of Exeter.

Schneider, B., & Schmitt, N. (1992). *Staffing organizations* (2nd ed.). Prospect Heights, IL: Waveland Press, Harper Collins, Inc.

Singh, V., & Vinnicombe, S. (2003). *The 2003 female FTSE index: Women pass a milestone: 101 directorships on the FTSE 100 boards.* Cranfield, UK: Cranfield School of Management.

Singh, V., & Vinnicombe, S. (2005). *The female FTSE index and report 2005*. Cranfield, UK: Cranfield School of Management.

Slife, B. D., & Williams, R. N. (1995). *What's behind the research? Discovering hidden assumptions in the behavioral sciences*. Thousand Oaks, CA: Sage Publications, Inc.

Smith, C. R., & Hutchinson, J. (1995). *Gender: A strategic management issue*. Sydney, Australia: Business & Professional Publishing.

Solo, R. L. (1991). *Cognitive psychology* (3rd ed.). New York, NY: Allyn & Bacon.

Stroh, L. K., Brett, J. M., & Reilly, A. H. (1996). Family structure, glass ceiling, and traditional explanations for the differential rate of turnover of female and male managers. *Journal of Vocational Behavior, 49*(1), 99–118. doi:10.1006/jvbe.1996.0036

Tashakkori, A., & Teddlie, C. (Eds.). (1998). *Mixed methodology: Combining Qualitative and quantitative approaches*. Thousand Oaks, CA: SAGE Publications.

Tran, B. (2008). *Expatriate selection and retention*. Doctoral Dissertation. San Francisco, CA: Alliant International University.

US Department of Labor. (1991). *Employment and earnings*. Washington, DC: Government Printing Office.

US Department of Labor. (2005). *Quick stats 2005*. Retrieved on July 1, 2010, from http://www.dol.gov/wb/stats/main.htm.

US Office of Personnel Management. (2010). *Handbook on alternative work schedules*. Retrieved on July 13, 2010, from http://www.opm.gov/oca/aws/index.asp

Veale, C., & Gold, J. (1998). Smashing into the glass ceiling for women managers. *Journal of Management, 17*(1), 17–26.

Victoria Transport Policy Institute. (2010). *Alternative work schedules: Flextime, compressed work week, staggered shifts*. Retrieved on July 13, 2010, from http://www.vtpi.org/tdm/tdm15.htm

Vinnicombe, S. (2000). The position of women in management in Europe. In Davidson, M., & Burke, R. (Eds.), *Women in Management: Current Research Issues* (*Vol. 2*). London, UK: Sage.

Vitalari, N., & Dell, D. (1998). How to attract and keep top talent. *HRFocus, 75*(12), 9–10.

White, B., Cox, C., & Cooper, C. (1992). *Women's career development: A study of high flyers*. Oxford, UK: Blackwell.

Williams, C. L. (1992). The glass escalator: Hidden advantages for men in the 'female' professions. *Social Problems, 39*(3), 253–267. doi:10.1525/sp.1992.39.3.03x0034h

Women and Equality Unit. (2004). *Women and equality unit gender briefing*. London, UK: Women and Equality Unity. Retrieved on July 1, 2010, from http://www.womenandequalityunit.gov.uk/research/gender_briefing_apr04.doc

ENDNOTES

[1] Retrieved on July 1, 2010, available at http://psy.ex.ac.uk/seorg/glasscliff/

[2] The Anita Borg Institute for Women and Technology (ABI) seeks to increase the impact of women on all aspects of technology and increase the positive impact of technology on the world's women. The Anita Borg Institute provides resources and programs

to help industry, academia, and government recruit, retain, and advance women leaders in high-tech fields, resulting in higher levels of technological innovation.

3 The ABI Technical Executive Forum, launched in 2007, brings together eminent technology thought leaders to raise awareness, actively engage discussion, and drive action on issues regarding the recruitment, retention, and advancement of technical women. The Technical Executive Forum is held annually at the Grace Hopper Celebration of Women in Computing and includes targeted discussions among technology executives, knowledge exchange, and practical solutions to creating cultures that sustain diversity and innovation.

4 ACM, Adobe, Amazon.com, Blackrock, CA, Cisco, Facebook, Goldman Sachs, Google, Harvey Mudd College, HP, IBM, Intel, Intuit, Lockheed Martin, Microsoft, National Security Agency, NCWIT, NetApp, Openwave, Purdue University, SAIC, SAP, StraTerra Partners, Sun Microsystems, Symantec, Thomson Reuters, ThoughtWorks, University of Virginia, US Navy, and Xerox.

5 Flextime and Compressed Work Week and are usually implemented as an employee and manager option (both employees and their managers must agree). They may vary from day-to-day or week-to-week, depending on circumstances. Of course, not all jobs are suitable for alternative schedules. Positions that require employees to provide service at a particular time and place demand a rigid schedule. Not all workers want to use flextime due to personal preference or the need to match schedules with other family members. In one case study, two-thirds of employees surveyed are allowed to have flexible work schedules, yet less than twenty percent of them actually shift their commute times to avoid congestion (Picado, 2000).

6 For an in-depth analysis of KSAs (Knowledge, Skills, and Abilities), please refer to Dr. Ben Tran's dissertation titled, "Expatriate Selection and Retention," from the Marshall Goldsmith School of Management (now California School of Professional Psychology) at Alliant International University, San Francisco, United States of America (AAT3326851). Dr. Tran received his Doctor of Psychology (Psy.D.) in Organizational Consulting (now Organizational Psychology).

7 Dr. Rosabeth Moss Kantor is a tenured Professor of Business in the Harvard Business School at Harvard University in Cambridge, Massachusetts, where she holds the Ernest L. Arbuckle Professorship. Dr. Kantor is known for her classic 1977 study of tokenism—how being a minority in a group can affect one's performance due to enhanced visibility and performance pressure. Dr. Kantor's study of men and women of the corporation also became a classic in critical management studies and bureaucracy analysis. Dr. Kanter was #11 in a 2000 survey of the Top 50 Business Intellectuals by citation in several sources. Dr. Kantor's pioneering work on gendered corporations is titled *Men and Women of the Corporation* (1977).

8 Dr. Arlie Russell Hochschild was a Professor of Sociology at the University of California, Berkeley, in Berkeley, California. Dr. Hochschild is the author of several prize-winning books and numerous articles on the balancing acts of modern two-job couples at home and at work. Dr. Hochschild introduced to the field of sociology the ideas of feeling rules, time bind, and emotional labor. Some of Dr. Hochschild's pioneering works on gendered and gendered in corporations are: 1) *The Commercialization of Intimate Life: Notes from Home and Work* (2003), 2) *The Time Bind: When Work Becomes Home and Home Becomes Work* (1997), and 3) *The Second*

Shift: Working Parents and the Revolution at Home (1989).

[9] Dr. Jyotsna Sanzgiri has been an educator, researcher, and practitioner in the field of organizational behavior and change for more than thirty years. Benedictine University named her "one of the most distinguished women practitioners in the field of Organization Development, locally and globally." Dr. Sanzgiri is the founder and former Program Director of the Organizational Psychology Program in division of the California School of Professional Psychology at Alliant International University in San Francisco, California. Dr. Sanzgiri is a tenured professor in the Organizational Psychology division of the California School of Professional Psychology at Alliant International University in San Francisco, California. Among Dr. Sanzgiri's research interests, one category of her notable research has been on women in management.

Compilation of References

Abbott, A. (1988). *The system of professions: An essay on the divisions of expert labour*. Chicago, IL: University of Chicago Press.

Achrol, R. S. (1997). Changes in the theory of interorganizational relations in marketing: Toward a network paradigm. *Journal of the Academy of Marketing Science*, *25*(1), 56–71. doi:10.1007/BF02894509

Achrol, R. S., & Kotler, P. (1999). Marketing in the network economy. *Journal of Marketing*, *63*, 146–163. doi:10.2307/1252108

Adorno, T. W., & Jephcott, E. F. N. (2010). *Minima moralia: Reflections from damaged life*. London, UK: Verso.

Ahmed, P. (1998). Culture and climate for innovation. *European Journal of Innovation Management*, *1*(1), 30–43. doi:10.1108/14601069810199131

Ahrens, T., & Chapman, C. (2006). Doing qualitative research in management accounting: Positioning data to contribute to theory. *Accounting, Organizations and Society*, *31*(8), 819–841. doi:10.1016/j.aos.2006.03.007

Ahrens, T., & Chapman, C. (2007). Management accounting as practice. *Accounting, Organizations and Society*, *32*(1-2), 1–27. doi:10.1016/j.aos.2006.09.013

Albanese, R., & Van Fleet, D. D. (1985). Free-riding: Theory, research, and implications. *Academy of Management Review*, *10*, 244–255. doi:10.2307/257966

Aldrich, D. (1998). The new value chain. *Informationweek*, *700*, 278–281.

Alliance Numeri, Q. C. (2003). *Analyse de positionnement de l'industrie du jeu interactif au Québec*. Montreal, Canada: SECOR Consulting.

Alliance Numeri, Q. C. (2008). *Étude de positionnement de l'industrie du jeu interactif au Québec*. Montreal, Canada: SECOR Consulting.

Allocca, M. A., & Kessler, E. H. (2006). Innovation speed in small and medium-sized enterprises. *Creativity and Innovation Management*, *15*(3), 279–295. doi:10.1111/j.1467-8691.2006.00389.x

Alvesson, M. (2000). Social identity and the problem of loyalty in knowledge-intensive companies. *Journal of Management Studies*, *37*(8), 1101–1124. doi:10.1111/1467-6486.00218

Alvesson, M. (2004). *Knowledge work and knowledge-intensive firms*. Oxford, UK: Oxford University Press.

Alvesson, M., & Skoldberg, K. (2000). *Towards a reflexive methodology*. London, UK: Sage.

Alvesson, M., & Wilmott, H. (1992). *Critical management studies*. Thousand Oaks, CA: Sage.

Amabile, T. M. (1998, September-October). How to kill creativity. *Harvard Business Review*.

Amabile, T. M. (1988). A model of creativity and innovation in organisations. In Straw, B. M., & Cummings, L. L. (Eds.), *Research in Organizational Behavior* (pp. 123–167). Greenwich, CT: JAI Press.

Amabile, T. M., & Grykiewicz, N. D. (1989). The creative environment scales: Work environment inventory. *Creativity Research Journal*, *2*, 231–253. doi:10.1080/10400418909534321

Amar, J. (2007). Travailler plus pour gagner... quoi au juste? *Controverses*, *6*, 180–182.

Amin, A., & Roberts, J. (2008). *Community, economic creativity, and organization*. Oxford, UK: Oxford University Press. doi:10.1093/acprof:oso/9780199545490.001.0001

Anderson, C. (2006). *The long tail: Why the future of business is selling less of more*. New York, NY: Hyperion.

Anderson-Gough, F., Grey, C., & Robson, K. (2000). In the name of the client: The service ethic in two professional services firms. *Human Relations, 53*(9), 1151–1174. doi:10.1177/0018726700539003

Androvich, M. (2008). Industry revenue $57 billion in 2009, says DFC. *Game Industry Biz*. Retrieved from http://www.gamesindustry.biz/articles/industry-revenue-57-billion-in-2009-says-dfc

Apker, J., & Eggly, S. (2004). Communicating professional identity in medical socialization: Considering the ideological discourse of morning report. *Qualitative Health Research, 14*(3), 411–429. doi:10.1177/1049732303260577

Apo, S. (1996a). Agraarinen suomalaisuus – Rasite vai resurssi? [The agrarian Finnishness – Burden or resource?] In Laaksonen, P., & Mettomäki, S.-L. (Eds.), *Olkaamme siis Suomalaisia: Kalevalaseuran Vuosikirja* (pp. 75–76). Helsinki, Finland: SKS.

Apo, S. (1996b). Itserasismista positiivisiin suomalaisuuksiin. [From self-imposed racism to positive Finnishnesses] In Apo, S., & Ehrnrooth, J. (Eds.), *Millaisia Olemme: Puheenvuoroja Suomalaisista Mentaliteeteista*. Helsinki, Finland: Kunnallisalan Kehittämissäätiö.

Araujo, A. L. (2004). *Trust in virtual teams: The role of task, technology and time*. Ph.D. Dissertation. Oklahoma City, OK: The University of Oklahoma.

Arbuckle, J. L., & Wothke, W. (1995). *AMOS 4.0 user's guide*. Chicago, IL: Small Waters Corporation.

Arendt, H. (1998). *The human condition*. Chicago, IL: The University of Chicago Press.

Ariño, A., de la Torre, J., & Ring, P. S. (2001). Relational quality: Managing trust in corporate alliances. *California Management Review, 44*, 109–131.

Aronsson, G. (1999). Paid by time but judged by results: An empirical study of unpaid overtime. *International Journal of Employment Studies, 17*(1), 1–15.

Arrighetti, A., Bachmann, R., & Deakin, S. (1997). Contract law, social norms and inter-firm cooperation. *Cambridge Journal of Economics, 21*(2), 171–195. doi:10.1093/oxfordjournals.cje.a013665

Arthur, M. B., & Rousseau, D. M. (1996). *The boundaryless career: A new employment principle for a new organizational era*. Oxford, UK: Oxford University Press.

Ashmos, D. P., Duchon, D., & McDaniel, R. R. (1998). Participation in strategic decision-making: The role of organizational predisposition and issue interpretation. *Decision Sciences, 29*(1), 25–51. doi:10.1111/j.1540-5915.1998.tb01343.x

Austin, R., & Larkey, P. (2002). The future of performance measurement: Measuring knowledge work. In Neely, A. (Ed.), *Business Performance Measurement—Theory and Practice*. Cambridge, UK: Cambridge University Press. doi:10.1017/CBO9780511753695.021

Avolio, B. J. (2005). *Leadership development in balance: Made/born*. Englewood Hills, NJ: Lawrence Erlbaum and Associates.

Avolio, B. J., & Kahai, S. (2003). Adding the "e" to e-leadership: How it may impact your leadership. *Organizational Dynamics, 31*(4), 325–338. doi:10.1016/S0090-2616(02)00133-X

Aycan, Z., Kanungo, R. N., Mendonca, M., Yu, K., Deller, J., Stahl, G., & Khursid, A. (2000). Impact of culture on human resource management practices: A ten country comparison. *Applied Psychology: An International Review, 49*(1), 192–221. doi:10.1111/1464-0597.00010

Aycan, Z., Kanungo, R. N., & Sinha, J. B. P. (1999). Organizational culture and human resource management practices: The model of cultural fit. *Journal of Cross-Cultural Psychology, 30*(4), 501–526. doi:10.1177/0022022199030004006

Back, K. W. (1951). Influence through social communication. *Journal of Abnormal and Social Psychology, 46*(1), 9–23. doi:10.1037/h0058629

Baier, A. (1986). Trust and antitrust. *Ethics, 96*, 231–260. doi:10.1086/292745

Balog, T. (2007, March 5). Face-off: Should you trust your network to open source? Yes. *Network World*. Retrieved 11 October 2008 from http://www.networkworld.com

Barad, K. (2007). *Meeting the universe halfway – Quantum physics and the entanglement of matter and meaning.* Durham, NC: Duke University Press.

Barley, S. R., & Kunda, G. (2004). *Gurus, hired guns, and warm bodies: Itinerant experts in a knowledge economy.* Princeton, NJ: Princeton University Press.

Barnard, C. I. (1938). *The functions of the executive.* Cambridge, MA: Harvard University Press.

Barnett, C. K., & Pratt, M. G. (2000). From threat-rigidity to flexibility—Toward a learning model of autogenic crisis in organizations. *Journal of Organizational Change Management, 13*(1), 74–88. doi:10.1108/09534810010310258

Barringer, B. R., & Harrison, J., S. (2000). Walking a tightrope: Creating value through interorganizational relationships. *Journal of Management, 26*(3), 367–403. doi:10.1177/014920630002600302

Barr, P. S., Stimpert, J. L., & Huff, A. S. (1992). Cognitive change, strategic action, and organizational renewal. *Strategic Management Journal, 13*, 15–36. doi:10.1002/smj.4250131004

Baruch, Y. (1998). The rise and fall of organizational commitment. *Human Systems Management, 17*(2), 135–143.

Baruch, Y. (2001). Employability – A substitute to loyalty? *Human Resource Development International, 4*(4), 543–566. doi:10.1080/13678860010024518

Bass, B. M. (1985). *Management style and performance beyond expectations.* New York, NY: Free Press.

Baudrillard, J. (1995). *Simulacra and simulation.* Ann Arbor, MI: University of Michigan Press.

Bauer, R., & Koeszegi, S. T. (2003). Measuring the degree of virtualization. *The Electronic Journal for Virtual Organizations and Networks, 5.*

Bauer, R., & Köszegi, S. T. (2003). Measuring the degree of virtualization. *Electronic Journal of Organizational Virtualness, 5*(2), 25.

Bauman, Z. (2000). *Liquid modernity.* Oxford, UK: Polity Press.

Bauman, Z. (2002). *Society under siege.* Cambridge, UK: Polity Press.

Baxter, J., & Chua, W. F. (2003). Alternative management accounting research -Whence and whither. *Accounting, Organizations and Society, 28*(2-3), 97–126. doi:10.1016/S0361-3682(02)00022-3

Beckman, S. L., & Barry, M. (2007). Innovation as a learning process: Embedding design thinking. *California Management Review, 50*, 25–56.

Beck, U. (1992). *Risk society: Towards a new modernity.* London, UK: Sage.

Beer, M., & Eisenstat, R. (2004). How to have an honest conversation about your business strategy. *Harvard Business Review, 82*(2), 82–89.

Bell, E., & Taylor, S. (2003). The elevation of work: Pastoral power and the new age work ethic. *Organization, 10*(2), 329–349. doi:10.1177/1350508403010002009

Benbasat, I., & Barki, H. (2007). Quo vadis, tam? *Journal of the Association for Information Systems, 8*(4), 212–218.

Benjamin, W. (1999). The storyteller - Reflections on the work of Nikolai Leskov. In Arendt, H. (Ed.), *Illuminations* (pp. 83–107). London, UK: Pimlico.

Bentler, P. M., & Bonett, D. G. (1980). Significance tests and goodness-of-fit in the analysis of covariance structures. *Psychological Bulletin, 88*, 588–606. doi:10.1037/0033-2909.88.3.588

Bernthal, P. R., & Insko, C. A. (1993). Cohesiveness without groupthink: The interactive effects of social and task cohesion. *Group & Organization Management, 18*, 66–87. doi:10.1177/1059601193181005

Bielby, W. T., & Baron, J. N. (1984). A woman's place is with other women: Sex segregation within organizations. In Reskin, B. (Ed.), *Sex Segregation in the Workplace: Trends, Explanations, Remedies* (pp. 27–55). Washington, DC: National Academy Press.

Blanchard, K., Carlos, J. P., & Randolph, A. (1999). *The 3 keys to empowerment: Release the power within people for astonishing results.* San Francisco, CA: Berrett-Koehler.

Blomqvist, K. (2002). *Partnering in the dynamic environment: The role of trust in asymmetric technology partnership formation.* Lappeenranta, Sweden: Lappeenranta University of Technology.

Bødker, S. (1987). A utopian experience: On design of powerful computer-based tools for skilled graphic workers. In Bjerknes, G. (Eds.), *Computers and Democracy* (pp. 251–278). Aldershot, UK: Avebury.

Boje, D. (1991). The storytelling organisation: A study of story performance in an office-supply firm. *Administrative Science Quarterly, 36*(1), 106–126. doi:10.2307/2393432

Boje, D. (2001). *Narrative methods for organisation and communication research*. Thousand Oaks, CA: Sage.

Boje, D. M. (2008). *Storytelling organizations*. London, UK: Sage.

Bollen, K. A., & Hoyle, R. H. (1990). Perceived cohesion: A conceptual and empirical examination. *Social Forces, 69*(2), 479–504.

Borys, B., & Jemison, D. B. (1989). Hybrid arrangements as strategic alliances: Theoretical issues in organizational combinations. *Academy of Management Review, 14*(2), 234–248.

Bosch-Sijtsema, P. M., Fruchter, R., Vartiainen, M., & Ruohomäki, V. (2011). A framework to analyze knowledge work in distributed teams. *Group & Organization Management Journal, 36*(3), 275–307. doi:10.1177/1059601111403625

Boucher, M. I. (1981). *The parables*. Wilmington, NC: Michael Glazier Inc.

Bourdieu, P. (1984). *Distinction: A social critique of the judgement of taste*. London, UK: Routledge.

Braithwaite, J., & Hindle, D. (2001). Acute health sector reform: An analysis of the Australian senate's proposals. *Australian Health Review, 24*(1). doi:10.1071/AH010003

Brandenburger, A. M., & Nalebuff, B. J. (1996). *Co-opetition*. New York, NY: Doubleday.

Brannen, M. Y. (1991). Culture as the critical factor in implementing innovation. *Business Horizons, 34*, 59–67. doi:10.1016/0007-6813(91)90112-9

Brass, D. J., Galaskiewicz, J., Greve, H. R., & Tsai, W. (2004). Taking stock of networks and organizations: A multilevel perspective. *Academy of Management Journal, 47*(6), 795–817. doi:10.2307/20159624

Brislin, R. W. (1980). Translation and content analysis of oral and written materials. In Triandis, H. C., & Berry, J. W. (Eds.), *Handbook of Cross-Cultural Psychology* (pp. 389–444). Boston, MA: Allyn & Bacon, Inc.

Brown, R. (1992). Managing the 'S' curves of innovation. *Journal of Consumer Marketing, 9*(1), 61–72. doi:10.1108/EUM0000000002597

Brunetto, Y., & Farr-Wharton, R. (2007). The moderating role of trust in SME owner/managers' decision-making about collaboration. *Journal of Small Business Management, 45*(3), 362–387. doi:10.1111/j.1540-627X.2007.00218.x

Bruno, C. (1997, October 6). Diversity disconnect. *Network World*. Retrieved on July 2, 2010, from http://www.networkworld.com/news/1997/1006diversity.html

Buchanan, A. (2006). *Brunel – The life and times of Isambard Kingdom Brunel*. London, UK: Hambledon Continuum.

Burgelman, R. A., & McKinney, W. (2006). Managing the strategic dynamics of acquisition integration: Lessons from HP and Compaq. *California Management Review, 48*(3), 5–27.

Burgelman, R., Maidique, M. A., & Wheelwright, S. C. (2004). *Strategic management of technology and innovation*. New York, NY: McGraw-Hill.

Burke, R. J. (2009). Working to live or living to work: Should individuals and organizations care? *Journal of Business Ethics, 84*, 167–172. doi:10.1007/s10551-008-9703-6

Burke, R. J., & Fiskenbaum, L. (2009). Work motivations, work outcomes, and health: Passion versus addiction. *Journal of Business Ethics, 84*, 257–263. doi:10.1007/s10551-008-9697-0

Burke, R. J., & McKeen, C. A. (1994). Career development among managerial and professional women. In Davidson, M. J., & Burke, J. R. (Eds.), *Women in Management: Current Research Issues* (pp. 65–79). London, UK: Paul Chapman.

Burlingame, G. M., Fuhriman, A., & Johnson, J. E. (2002). Cohesion in group psychotherapy. In Norcross, J. C. (Ed.), *Psychotherapy Relationships that Work: Therapist Contributions and Responsiveness to Patients* (p. 452). Oxford, UK: Oxford University Press.

Burns, T., & Stalker, G. N. (1961). *The management of innovation*. London, UK: Tavistock Publications.

Bush, J. B., & Frohman, A. L. (1991). Communication in a "network" organization. *Organizational Dynamics*, *20*(2), 23–36. doi:10.1016/0090-2616(91)90069-L

Bynum, W. F., Browne, E. J., & Porter, R. (1981). *Dictionary of the history of science*. Princeton, NJ: Princeton University Press.

Çakar, N. D. (2006). Enhancing innovation capability through human resource practices: An empirical study in Turkish SMEs. *South-East Europe Review*, *4*, 109–126.

Çakar, N. D., & Ertürk, A. (2010). Comparing innovation capability of small and medium sized enterprises: Examining the effects of organizational culture and empowerment. *Journal of Small Business Management*, *48*(3), 325–359. doi:10.1111/j.1540-627X.2010.00297.x

Calantone, R. J., Cavusgil, S. T., & Zhao, Y. (2002). Learning orientation, firm innovation capability and firm performance. *Industrial Marketing Management*, *31*, 515–524. doi:10.1016/S0019-8501(01)00203-6

Calhoun, C. (1992). The infrastructure of modernity: Indirect social relationships, information technology, and social integration. In Haferkamp, H., & Smelser, N. (Eds.), *Social Change and Modernity* (pp. 205–236). Berkeley, CA: University of California Press.

Cameron, K. S., Sutton, R. I., & Whetten, A. D. (1988). *Readings in organizational decline: Frameworks, research, and prescriptions*. Cambridge, MA: Ballinger.

Cameron, K. S., Whetten, D. A., & Kim, M. U. (1987). Organizational dysfunctions of decline. *Academy of Management Journal*, *30*, 126–138. doi:10.2307/255899

Campbell, I. (2002a). Extended working hours in Australia. *Labour & Industry*, *13*(1), 91–110.

Campbell, I. (2002b). Snatching at the wind? Unpaid overtime and trade unions in Australia. *International Journal of Employment Studies*, *10*(2), 109–156.

Campbell, I. (2003). Puzzles of unpaid overtime. In Zeytinoglu, I. (Ed.), *Flexible Work Arrangements: Conceptualizations and International Experiences* (pp. 25–43). The Hague, The Netherlands: Kluwer Law International.

Cappelli, P. (1999). *The new deal at work*. Boston, MA: Harvard Business School Press.

Cartwright, S. D., & Oliver, R. W. (2000). Untangling the value web. *The Journal of Business Strategy*, *21*(1), 22–27. doi:10.1108/eb040055

Cascio, W., & Shurygailo, S. (2003). E-leadership and virtual teams. *Organizational Dynamics*, *31*(4), 362. doi:10.1016/S0090-2616(02)00130-4

Casey, C. (1999). Come, join our family: Discipline and integration in corporate organizational culture. *Human Relations*, *52*(2), 155–178. doi:10.1023/A:1016980602039

Castells, M., & Himanen, P. (2002). *The information society and the welfare state: The Finnish model*. Oxford, UK: Oxford University Press. doi:10.1093/acprof:oso/9780199256990.001.0001

Catalyst. (2004). *The bottom line: Connecting corporate performance and gender diversity*. New York, NY: Catalyst Publication.

Cavusgil, S. T., Calantone, R. J., & Zhao, Y. (2003). Tacit knowledge transfer and firm innovation capability. *Journal of Business and Industrial Marketing*, *18*(1), 6. doi:10.1108/08858620310458615

Cayla, D. (2006). Ex post and ex ante coordination: Principles of coherence in organizations and markets. *Journal of Economic Issues*, *40*(2), 325–332.

Chandler, G. N., Keller, C., & Lyon, D. W. (2000). Unraveling the determinants and consequences of an innovation-supportive organizational culture. *Entrepreneurship Theory and Practice*, *25*, 59–76.

Chasserio, S., & Legault, M.-J. (2009). Strategic human resources management is irrelevant when it comes to highly skilled professionals in the Canadian new economy! *International Journal of Human Resource Management*, *20*(5), 1113–1131. Retrieved from http://www.informaworld.com/smpp/title~db=all~content=g911806569doi:10.1080/09585190902850307

Chesborough, H. (2006a). *Open innovation: A new paradigm for understanding industrial innovation.* Paper presented at IMIO. New York, NY.

Chesborough, H. (2006b). *Open innovation: Researching a new paradigm.* Oxford, UK: Oxford University Press.

Chesborough, H. (2006c). *Open business models: How to thrive in the new innovation landscape.* Oxford, UK: Oxford University Press.

Chua, W. F. (1995). Experts, networks and inscriptions in the fabrication of accounting images: A story of the representations of three public hospitals. *Accounting, Organizations and Society, 20*, 111–145. doi:10.1016/0361-3682(95)95744-H

Chudoba, K. M., Wynn, E., Lu, M., & Watson-Manheim, M. B. (2005). How virtual are we? Measuring virtuality and understanding its impact in a global organization. *Information Systems Journal, 15*(4), 279. doi:10.1111/j.1365-2575.2005.00200.x

Chung, E. (2005, August 15). Dream jobs in hell. *Toronto Star*, p. C6.

Cicmil, S., & Hodgeson, D. (2007). The politics of standards in modern management: Making "the project" a reality. *Journal of Management Studies, 44*(3).

Cicmil, S., & Hodgson, D. (2006). New possibilities for project management theory: A critical engagement. *Project Management Journal, 37*(3), 111–122.

Ciesielska, M. (2010). *Hybrid organizations: A case of the open source-business setting.* Frederiksberg, Denmark: Copenhagen Business School Press.

Claver, E., Llopis, J., Garcia, D., & Molina, H. (1998). Organizational culture for innovation and new technological behavior. *The Journal of High Technology Management Research, 9*(1), 55–68. doi:10.1016/1047-8310(88)90005-3

Cohen, S. G., & Gibson, C. B. (2003). *Virtual teams that work: Creating conditions for virtual team effectiveness.* San Francisco, CA: Jossey-Bass.

Collins, C., & Smith, K. (2006). Knowledge exchange and combination: The role of human resource practices in the performance of high-technology firms. *Academy of Management Journal, 49*(3), 544–560. doi:10.5465/AMJ.2006.21794671

Collinson, D., & Ackroyd, S. (2005). Resistance, misbehavior, dissent. In Ackroyd, S., Batt, R., Thompson, P., & Tolbert, P. S. (Eds.), *The Oxford Handbook of Work and Organization.* Oxfor, UK: Oxford University Press.

Conger, J. A., & Kanungo, R. N. (1988). The empowerment process: Integrating theory and practice. *Academy of Management Review, 13*(3), 471–482.

Cook, K. S. (2008). The limits of trust: How institutions take up where trust leaves off. *Focus (San Francisco, Calif.), 12*, 49–51.

Cook, K. S., & Gerbasi, A. (2009). Trust: Explanations of social action and implications for social structure. In Bearman, P., & Hedstrom, P. (Eds.), *The Oxford Handbook of Analytical Sociology.* Oxford, UK: Oxford University Press.

Cook, K., Hardin, R., & Levi, M. (2005). *Cooperation without trust?* New York, NY: Russell Sage Foundation.

Cota, A. A., Evans, C. R., Dion, K. L., Kilik, L., & Longman, R. S. (1995). The structure of group cohesion. *Personality and Social Psychology Bulletin, 21*, 572–580. doi:10.1177/0146167295216003

Courpasson, D. (2000). *L'action contrainte: Organisations libérales et domination.* Paris, France: PUF.

Cramton, C. D. (2001). The mutual knowledge problem and its consequences for dispersed collaboration. *Organization Science, 12*(3), 346–371. doi:10.1287/orsc.12.3.346.10098

Creswell, J. W. (1998). *Qualitative inquiry and research design: Choosing among five traditions.* Thousand Oaks, CA: Sage.

Creswell, J. W. (2003). *Research design: Qualitative, quantitative and mix methods approaches* (2nd ed.). Thousand Oaks, CA: Sage Publications.

Crook, S. (1994). Introduction: Adorno and authoritarian irrationalism. In *Adorno: The Stars Down to Earth and Other Essays on the Irrational in Culture* (pp. 1–33). London, UK: Routledge.

Cross, R., & Cummings, J. N. (2004). Tie and network correlates of individual performance in knowledge-intensive work. *Academy of Management Journal*, *47*, 928–937. doi:10.2307/20159632

Cyert, R., & March, J. (1963). *A behavioral theory of the firm*. Englewood Cliffs, NJ: Prentice Hall.

Czarniawska, B. (1998). *A narrative approach to organisation studies*. London, UK: Sage.

D'Aveni, R. A. (1989). The aftermath of organizational decline—A longitudinal-study of the strategic and managerial characteristics of declining firms. *Academy of Management Journal*, *32*(3), 577–605. doi:10.2307/256435

D'Aveni, R. A., & MacMillan, I. C. (1990). Crisis and content of managerial communications: A study of the focus of attention of top managers in surviving and failing firms. *Administrative Science Quarterly*, *35*, 634–657. doi:10.2307/2393512

Damanpour, F. (1991). Organizational innovation: A meta-analysis of effects of determinants and moderators. *Academy of Management Journal*, *34*(3), 555–590. doi:10.2307/256406

Dambrin, C., & Robson, K. (2009). *Multiple measures, inscription instability and action at a distance: Performance measurement practices in the pharmaceutical industry*. Retrieved from http://econpapers.repec.org/paper/ebgheccah/0928.htm

Daniels, M. R., & Johansen, E. (1985). The role of accreditation in the development of public administration as a profession: A theoretical and empirical assessment. *Public Administration Quarterly*, *8*(4), 419–441.

Danneels, E., & Kleinschmidt, E. J. (2001). Product innovativeness from the firm's perspective: Its dimensions and their relation with project selection and performance. *Journal of Product Innovation Management*, *18*, 357–373. doi:10.1016/S0737-6782(01)00109-6

Dasgupta, M., & Gupta, R. K. (2009). Innovation in organizations: A review of the role of organizational learning and knowledge management. *Global Business Review*, *10*(2), 203–224. doi:10.1177/097215090901000205

Davidson, F. J. (2003). *Managing projects in organizations – How to make the best use of time, techniques and people*. San Francisco, CA: Jossey-Bass.

Davidson, M. J., & Cooper, C. L. (1992). *Shattering the glass ceiling: The woman manager*. London, UK: Paul Chapman Publishing.

Davis, F. D. (1989). Perceived usefulness, perceived ease of use, and user acceptance of information technology. *Management Information Systems Quarterly*, *13*(3), 319–340. doi:10.2307/249008

de Man, A.-P. (2004). *The network economy: Strategy, structure and management*. Cheltenham, UK: Edward Elgar.

De Peuter, G., & Dyer-Witheford, N. (2005). A playful multitude? Mobilising and counter-mobilising immaterial game labour. *FibreCulture Journal*, *5*. Retrieved from http://journal.fibreculture.org/issue5/depeuter_dyer-witheford.html

Dechow, N., & Mouritsen, J. (2005). Enterprise resource planning systems, management control and the quest for integration. *Accounting, Organizations and Society*, *30*, 691–733. doi:10.1016/j.aos.2004.11.004

DeFillippi, R. J. (2003). Organizational models for collaboration in the new economy. *Human Resource Planning*, *25*(4), 7–18.

DeFillippi, R. J., & Arthur, M. B. (2006). The boundaryless career: A competency-based perspective. *Journal of Organizational Behavior*, *15*(4), 307–324. doi:10.1002/job.4030150403

Dembe, A. E. (2009). Ethical issues relating to the health effects of long working hours. *Journal of Business Ethics*, *84*, 195–208. doi:10.1007/s10551-008-9700-9

Denison, D. R. (2000). *The handbook of organizational culture*. London, UK: Wiley.

Denison, D. R., & Mishra, A. K. (1995). Toward a theory of organizational culture and effectiveness. *Organization Science*, *6*, 204–223. doi:10.1287/orsc.6.2.204

DeRosa, D. M., Hantula, D. A., Kock, N., & D'Arcy, J. (2004). Trust and leadership in virtual teamwork: A media naturalness perspective. *Human Resource Management*, *43*(2-3), 219. doi:10.1002/hrm.20016

Derrida, J. (2002). The theater of cruelty and the closure of representation. In Derrida, J. (Ed.), *Writing and difference* (pp. 292–316). London, UK: Routledge. doi:10.1215/00440167-9-3-6

Derrida, J. (2004). Living on. In Bloom, H., Man, D., Derrida, J., Hartman, G., & Miller, J. H. (Eds.), *Deconstruction and criticism* (pp. 62–142). London, UK: Continuum.

Deuze, M., Bowen, M. C., & Allen, C. (2007). The professional identity of gameworkers. *International Journal of Research into New Media Technologies*, *13*(4), 335–353. doi:10.1177/1354856507081947

Dimov, D. (2007). From opportunity insight to opportunity intention: The importance of person-situation learning match. *Entrepreneurship Theory & Practice*, *31*, 561–583. doi:10.1111/j.1540-6520.2007.00188.x

Dionne, S. D., Yammarino, F. J., Atwater, L. E., & Spangler, W. D. (2004). Transformational leadership and team performance. *Journal of Organizational Change Management*, *17*(2). doi:10.1108/09534810410530601

Ditillo, A. (2004). Dealing with uncertainty in knowledge-intensive firms: The role of management control systems as knowledge integration mechanisms. *Accounting, Organizations and Society*, *29*, 401–421. doi:10.1016/j.aos.2003.12.001

Dittrich, K. (2007). Nokia's strategic change by means of alliance networks: A case of adopting the open innovation paradigm? In Sangeetha, K., & Sivarajadhanavel, P. (Eds.), *Nokia Inc: A Global Mobile Leader*. Chennai, India: Icfai University Press.

Dolinina, I. B., & Cecchetto, V. (1998). Facework and rhetorical strategies in intercultural argumentative discourse. *Argumentation*, *12*, 167–181. doi:10.1023/A:1007739713653

Dorfman, P., & Howell, J. (1988). *Dimensions of national culture and effective leadership patterns: Hofstede revisited*. Greenwich, CT: JAI Press.

Drazin, R., Glynn, M. A., & Kazanjian, R. K. (1999). Multilevel theorizing about creativity in Organizations: A sensemaking perspective. *Academy of Management Review*, *24*(2), 286–307.

Duckett, S. J. (2008). The Australian health care system: Reform, repair or replace? *Australian Health Review*, *32*(2), 322–329. doi:10.1071/AH080322

Dumais, J.-F. (2009). *L'emploi dans l'industrie du jeu électronique au Québec en 2009: Un portrait sommaire de la situation*. Retrieved from http://www.technocompetences.qc.ca/apropostic/etudes

Durham, J. W., & Smith, H. L. (1982). Toward a general theory of organizational deterioration. *Administration & Society*, *14*(3), 373–400. doi:10.1177/009539978201400305

Dyer-Witheford, N. (2002). Cognitive capital contested. *Multitudes, 10*. Retrieved from http://multitudes.samizdat.net/Cognitive-Capital-Contested.html

Dyer-Witheford, N. (2005). Digital poetics in the vernacular: The political economy of Canada's videogame industry. *Digipopo/Public, 31*. Retrieved from http://www.digipopo.org/content/digital-poetics-in-the-vernacular-the-political-economy-of-canadas-videogame-industry?pg=4

Dyer-Witheford, N., & de Peuter, G. (2009). Empire@play: Virtual games and global capitalism. *CT Theory Multimedia Journal*. Retrieved from http://www.ctheory.net/articles.aspx?id=608

Dyer-Witheford, N., & De Peuter, G. (2006). EA Spouse and the crisis of video game labour: Enjoyment, exclusion, exploitation, exodus. *Canadian Journal of Communication*, *31*, 599–617.

Dyer-Witheford, N., & Sharman, Z. (2005). The political economy of Canada's video and computer game industry. *Canadian Journal of Communication*, *30*, 187–210.

Eagly, A. H., & Carli, L. L. (2007). *Through the labyrinth: the truth about how women and become leaders*. Boston, MA: Harvard Business School Press.

Edelman, L. F., Bresnen, M., Newell, S., Scarbrough, H., & Swan, J. (2004). The benefits and pitfalls of social capital: Empirical evidence from two organizations in the United Kingdom. *British Journal of Management*, *15*, 59–S69. doi:10.1111/j.1467-8551.2004.00406.x

Edwards, N., Martin, McLellan, Alastair, Abbasi, & Kamran. (2003). Doctors and managers: A problem without a solution? *British Medical Journal*, *326*, 609. doi:10.1136/bmj.326.7390.609

Ehn, P. (1988). *Work-oriented design of computer artefacts*. Stockholm, Sweden: Arbetslivscentrum.

Ehn, P., Kyng, M., & Sundblad, Y. (1983). The utopia project: On training, technology and products viewed from the quality of work perspective. In Briefs, U., Ciborra, C. U., & Schneider, L. (Eds.), *Systems Design for, with, and by the Users* (pp. 427–438). Amsterdam, The Netherlands: North-Holland.

Eisenberg, E. M., & Witten, M. G. (1987). Reconsidering openness in organizational communication. *Academy of Management Review*, *12*(3), 418–426.

Eisenhardt, K. (1989). Building theories from case study research. *Academy of Management Review*, *14*(4), 532–550.

Eisenhardt, K. M. (1989). Making fast strategic decisions in high-velocity environments. *Academy of Management Journal*, *32*(3), 543–576. doi:10.2307/256434

Ekstrom, W. L. (1993). A coherence theory of autonomy. *Philosophy and Phenomenological Research*, *53*(3), 599–616. doi:10.2307/2108082

Elmes, M. B., Strong, D. M., & Volkoff, O. (2005). Panoptic empowerment and reflective conformity in enterprise systems-enabled organizations. *Information and Organization*, *15*(1), 1–37. doi:10.1016/j.infoandorg.2004.12.001

Elron, E. (1997). Top management teams within multinational corporations: Effects of cultural heterogeneity. *The Leadership Quarterly*, *8*(4), 393–412. doi:10.1016/S1048-9843(97)90021-7

Enders, C. (2005). An SAS macro for implementing the modified bollen-stine bootstrap for missing data: Implementing the bootstrap using existing structural equation modeling software. *Structural Equation Modeling*, *12*(4), 620–641. doi:10.1207/s15328007sem1204_6

Ensley, M. D., Pearson, A. W., & Amason, A. C. (2002). Understanding the dynamics of new venture top management teams: Cohesion, conflict, and new venture performance. *Journal of Business Venturing*, *17*(4), 365–386. doi:10.1016/S0883-9026(00)00065-3

Equal Opportunities Commission. (2002). *Women and men in Britain: Management*. Manchester, UK: Equal Opportunities Commission.

Equal Opportunities Commission. (2004). *Women and men in Great Britain*. Retrieved on July 1, 2010, from http://www.eoc.org.uk.PDF/facts_about_2004_gb.pdf

Erduran, S., Simon, S., & Osbourne, J. (2004). TAPing into argumentation: Developments in the application of Toulmin's argument pattern for studying science discourse. *Science Education*, *88*(6), 915–933. doi:10.1002/sce.20012

Erez, M., & Earley, P. C. (1987). Comparative analysis of goal setting strategies across cultures. *The Journal of Applied Psychology*, *17*(2), 658–665. doi:10.1037/0021-9010.72.4.658

Erickson, R. I., & Ritter, C. (2001). Emotional labor, burnout, and inauthenticity: Does gender matter? *Social Psychology Quarterly*, *64*(2), 146–163. doi:10.2307/3090130

Etkowitz, H., & Leydesdorff, L. (2000). The dynamics of innovation: From national systems and "mode 2" to a triple helix of university-industry-government relations. *Research Policy*, *29*, 109–123. doi:10.1016/S0048-7333(99)00055-4

Eylon, D. (1997). An empirical test of a process model of empowerment. *Journal of Management Systems*, *9*, 15–30.

Fagenson, E. A. (1986). Women's work orientation: Something old, something new. *Group and Organization Studies*, *11*(1-2), 75–100. doi:10.1177/105960118601100108

Fahey, R. (2005, October 10). Videogames to lead entertainment sector boom through 2009, says PWC. *Games Industry*. Retrieved from http://www.gamesindustry.biz/content_page.php?aid=12135

Faraj, S., & Wasko, M. M. (2001). *The web of knowledge: An investigation of knowledge exchange in networks of practice*. Retrieved from http://citeseerx.ist.psu.edu/viewdoc/summary?doi=10.1.1.12.4559

Feldman, S. P. (1988). How organizational culture can affect innovation. *Organizational Dynamics*, *17*, 57–68. doi:10.1016/0090-2616(88)90030-7

Feldt, T., Kivimäki, M., Rantala, A., & Tolvanen, A. (2004). Sense of coherence and work characteristics: A cross-lagged structural equation model among managers. *Journal of Occupational and Organizational Psychology*, *77*(3), 323–342. doi:10.1348/0963179041752655

Fenner, G. H., & Renn, R. W. (2010). Technology-assisted supplemental work and work-to-family conflict: The role of instrumentality beliefs, organizational expectations and time management. *Human Relations*, *63*(1), 63–82. doi:10.1177/0018726709351064

Festinger, L. (1950). Informal social communication. *Psychological Review*, *57*(5), 271–282. doi:10.1037/h0056932

Festinger, L., Schachter, S., & Back, K. W. (1950). *Social pressures in informal groups: A study of a housing project*. New York, NY: Harper & Bros.

Festinger, L., & Thibaut, J. (1951). Interpersonal communication in small groups. *Journal of Abnormal and Social Psychology*, *46*(1), 92–99. doi:10.1037/h0054899

Fitzgerald, J. A. (2002). *Doctors and nurses working together: A mixed method study into the construction and changing of professional identities*. Western Sydney, Australia: Sydney.

Fitzgerald, L., & Ferlie, E. (2000). Professionals: Back to the future? *Human Relations*, *53*(5), 713–740. doi:10.1177/0018726700535005

Fleming, P. (2009). *Authenticity and the cultural politics of work*. Oxford, UK: Oxford University Press. doi:10.1093/acprof:oso/9780199547159.001.0001

Floyd, S. W., & Wooldridge, B. (2000). *Building strategy from the middle: Reconceptualizing strategy process*. Thousand Oaks, CA: Sage.

Ford, D., Gadde, L.-E., Håkansson, H., & Snehota, I. (2003). *Managing business relationships*. Chichester, UK: John Wiley & Sons Ltd.

Ford, R. C., & Randolph, W. A. (1992). Cross-functional structures: A review and integration of matrix organization and project management. *Journal of Management*, *18*(2), 267–294. doi:10.1177/014920639201800204

Fornell, C., & Larcker, D. (1981). Evaluating structural equation models with unobservable variables and measurement error. *JMR, Journal of Marketing Research*, *18*, 39–50. doi:10.2307/3151312

Frankforter, S. A. (1996). The progression of women beyond the glass ceiling. *Journal of Social Behavior and Personality*, *11*(5), 121–132.

Freel, M. (2006). Patterns of technological innovation in knowledge-intensive business services. *Industry and Innovation*, *13*(3), 335–358. doi:10.1080/13662710600859157

Freidson, E. (1984). The changing nature of professional control. *Annual Review of Sociology*, *10*, 1–20. doi:10.1146/annurev.so.10.080184.000245

Freidson, E. (1994). *Professionalism reborn*. Oxford, UK: Polity Press.

Frels, J. K., Shervani, T., & Srivastava, R. K. (2003). The integrated networks model: Explaining resource allocations in network markets. *Journal of Marketing*, *67*, 29–45. doi:10.1509/jmkg.67.1.29.18586

Friedkin, N. E. (2004). Social cohesion. *Annual Review of Sociology*, *30*, 409–425. doi:10.1146/annurev.soc.30.012703.110625

Friedman, M. (2000). Women take to internet while avoiding it. *Computing Canada*. Retrieved on July 2, 2010, from http://www.itbusiness.ca/it/client/en/home/News.asp?id=28774

Fruchter, R., Bosch-Sijtsema, P. M., & Ruohomaki, V. (2010). Tension between perceived collocation and actual geographical distribution in project teams. *International Journal of AI & Society*, *25*(2), 183–192. doi:10.1007/s00146-009-0254-x

Fussell, S. R., & Krauss, R. (1992). Coordination of knowledge in communication: Effects of speakers' assumptions about what others know. *Journal of Personality and Social Psychology*, *62*(3), 378–391. doi:10.1037/0022-3514.62.3.378

Gadamer, H.-G. (1992). *Truth and method*. New York, NY: Crossroads.

Gadrey, J. (2000). *Nouvelle économie, nouveau mythe?*Paris, France: Flammarion.

Galbraith, J. (1977). *Organization design*. Reading, MA: Addison Wesley.

Gambetta, D. (1988). Can we trust trust? In Gambetta, D. (Ed.), *Making and Breaking Cooperative Relations* (pp. 213–237). Oxford, UK: Basil Blackwell Ltd.

Garfield, M. J. (2005, Fall). Acceptance of ubiquitous computing. *Information Systems Management*, (n.d), 24–31. doi:10.1201/1078.10580530/45520.22.4.20050901/90027.3

Garvin, D. A. (1998). The processes of organization and management. *Sloan Management Review*, *39*(4), 33–50.

Gaume, N. (2006). Nicolas Gaume's views on the video games sector. *European Management Journal*, *24*(4), 299–309. doi:10.1016/j.emj.2006.05.005

Gere, C. (2006). *Digitaalinen kulttuuri*. Turku, Finalnd: Faros.

Ghosh, R. A. (Ed.). (2006). *Study on the economic impact of open source software on innovation and the competitiveness of the information and communication technologies (ICT) sector in the EU: Final report*. Retrieved from http://ec.europa.eu/enterprise/ict/policy/doc/2006-11-20-flossimpact.pdf

Ghoshal, S., & Gratton, L. (2002). Integrating the enterprise. *MIT Sloan Management Review*, *44*, 31–38.

Gibbons, M., Limoges, C., Nowotny, H., Schwartzman, S., Scott, P., & Trow, M. (1994). *The new production of knowledge: The dynamics of science in contemporary societies*. London, UK: Sage Publications.

Gibson, C. B., & Gibbs, J. L. (2006). Unpacking the concept of virtuality: The effects of geographic dispersion, electronic dependence, dynamic structure, and national diversity on team innovation. *Administrative Science Quarterly*, *51*(3), 451.

Glaser, B. G., & Strauss, A. L. (1967). *The discovery of grounded theory: Strategies for qualitative research*. Chicago, IL: Aldine Pub. Co.

Glisby, M., & Holden, N. (2003). Contextual constraints in knowledge management theory: The cultural embeddedness of Nonaka's knowledge creating company. *Knowledge and Process Management*, *10*(1), 29–36. doi:10.1002/kpm.158

Golden, T. D., & Veiga, J. F. (2008). The impact of superior–subordinate relationships on the commitment, job satisfaction, and performance of virtual workers. *The Leadership Quarterly*, *19*(1), 77–88. doi:10.1016/j.leaqua.2007.12.009

Golden, T. D., Veiga, J. F., & Dino, R. N. (2008). The impact of professional isolation on teleworker job performance and turnover intentions: Does time spent teleworking, interacting face-to-face, or having access to communication-enhancing technology matter? *The Journal of Applied Psychology*, *93*(6), 1412–1421. doi:10.1037/a0012722

Goodman, J. S., Fields, D. L., & Blum, T. C. (2003). Cracks in the glass ceiling: In what kinds of organizations do women make it to the top? *Group & Organization Management*, *28*, 475–501. doi:10.1177/1059601103251232

Goodwin, J. (2002). *Is software always late?* Retrieved from http://www.joelgoodwin.com/wander/Articles/mad/IsSoftwareAlwaysLate.html

Graen, G. B., & Uhl-Bien, M. (1995). Relationship-based approach to leadership: Development of leader-member exchange (LMX) theory of leadership over 25 years: Applying a multi-level multi-domain perspective. *The Leadership Quarterly*, *6*(2), 219–247. doi:10.1016/1048-9843(95)90036-5

Gray, D. O., Lindblad, M., & Rudolph, J. (2001). Industry-university research centers: A multivariate analysis of member retention. *The Journal of Technology Transfer*, *26*, 247–254. doi:10.1023/A:1011158123815

Greenbaum, J. (2004). *Windows on the workplace*. New York, NY: Monthly Review Press.

Greenberg, P. S., Greendberg, R. H., & Antonucci, Y. L. (2007). Creating and sustaining trust in virtual teams. *Business Horizons*, *50*, 325–333. doi:10.1016/j.bushor.2007.02.005

Greene, R. (2007, March 5). Face-off: Should you trust your network to open source? No. *Network World.* Retrieved 11 October 2008 from http://www.networkworld.com

Green, F. (2001). It's been a hard day's night: The concentration and intensification of work in late twentieth-century Britain. *British Journal of Industrial Relations*, *39*(1), 53–80. doi:10.1111/1467-8543.00189

Greenhalgh, L. (1983). Organizational decline. In Bacharach, S. B. (Ed.), *Research in the Sociology of Organizations* (*Vol. 2*, pp. 231–276). London, UK: JAI Press.

Grey, C. (2009). *A very short, fairly interesting and reasonably cheap book about studying organizations* (2nd ed.). London, UK: Sage.

Griffith, T. L. (1999). Technology features as triggers for sensemaking. *Academy of Management Review*, *24*(3), 472.

Gudmunson, D., Tower, C. B., & Hartman, E. A. (2003). Innovation in small businesses: Culture and ownership structure do matter. *Journal of Developmental Entrepreneurship*, *8*(1), 1–17.

Gulati, R. (1998). Alliances and networks. *Strategic Management Journal*, *19*(4), 293–317. doi:10.1002/(SICI)1097-0266(199804)19:4<293::AID-SMJ982>3.0.CO;2-M

Gulati, R., & Singh, H. (1998). The architecture of cooperation: Managing coordination costs and appropriation concerns in strategic alliances. *Administrative Science Quarterly*, *43*(4), 781–814. doi:10.2307/2393616

Hadjimanolis, A. (2000). An investigation of innovation antecedents in small firms in the context of a small developing country. *R & D Management*, *30*(3), 235–245. doi:10.1111/1467-9310.00174

Hagedoorn, J. (1990). Organizational modes of inter-firm co-operation and technology transfer. *Technovation*, *10*(1), 17–30. doi:10.1016/0166-4972(90)90039-M

Hagedoorn, J. (1995). Strategic technology partnering during the 1980s: Trends, networks and corporate patterns in non-core technologies. *Research Policy*, *24*(2), 207–231. doi:10.1016/0048-7333(94)00763-W

Håkansson, H., & Ford, D. (2002). How should companies interact in business environments. *Journal of Business Research*, *55*, 133–139. doi:10.1016/S0148-2963(00)00148-X

Håkansson, H., & Snehota, I. (Eds.). (1995). *Developing relationships in business networks*. London, UK: Routledge.

Halal, W. E. (1994). From hierarchy to enterprise: Internal markets are the new foundation of management. *The Academy of Management Executive*, *8*(4), 69–83. doi:10.5465/AME.1994.9412071706

Hambrick, D. C., & D'Aveni, R. A. (1992). Top team deterioration as part of the downward spiral of large corporate bankruptcies. *Management Science*, *38*(10), 1445–1466. doi:10.1287/mnsc.38.10.1445

Hamel, G., Doz, Y. L., & Prahalad, C. K. (1989). Collaborate with your competitors - And win. *Harvard Business Review*, *67*(1), 113–139.

Handman, D. H. (2005). Electronic Arts settles a class action overtime lawsuit for $15.6 million: Red flags and practical lessons for the entertainment software industry. *Entertainment Law Reporter, 27*(6). Retrieved from http://www.entertainmentlawreporter.com/archive/v27n06/270601.htm

Handy, C. (1995). Trust and the virtual organization. *Harvard Business Review*, *73*, 44–50.

Hannan, M. T., & Freeman, J. (1984). Structural inertia and organizational change. *American Sociological Review*, *49*, 149–164. doi:10.2307/2095567

Hanseth, O., Ciborra, C., & Braa, K. (2001). The control devolution: ERP and the side effects of globalization. *The Data Base for Advances in Information Systems*, *32*(4), 34–46. doi:10.1145/506139.506144

Hardin, R. (2002). *Trust and trustworthiness*. New York, NY: Russell Sage Foundation.

Hardin, R. (2006). *Trust*. Cambridge, UK: Polity Press.

Hardy, C., Phillips, N., & Lawrence, T. B. (2000). Distinguishing trust and power in interorganizational relations: forms and façades of trust. In Lane, C., & Bachmann, R. (Eds.), *Trust Within and Between Organizations* (pp. 64–87). Oxford, UK: Oxford University Press.

Hargadon, A., & Sutton, R. (1997). Technology brokering and innovation in a product development firm. *Administrative Science Quarterly, 42*, 716–749. doi:10.2307/2393655

Harris, D. M. K., & Raskino, M. (2007). *Women and men in IT: Breaking sexual stereotypes*. Washington, DC: Gartner.

Harris, J. K. (2004). What you don't know can't hurt you: The interactive relationship between leader-member exchange and perceptions of politics on job satisfaction. *Journal of Behavioral and Applied Management, 5*(3), 188–203.

Harrison, A. (1998). In Linux we…trust? *Software Magazine, 18*(12), 32-42.

Haslam, S. A., & Ryan, M. K. (2008). The road to the glass cliff: Differences in the perceived suitability of men and women for leadership positions in succeeding and failing organizations. *The Leadership Quarterly, 19*(5), 530–546. doi:10.1016/j.leaqua.2008.07.011

Hatch, N. W., & Dyer, J. H. (2004). Human capital & learning as a source of sustainable competitive advantage. *Strategic Management Journal, 25*, 1155–1178. doi:10.1002/smj.421

Hauser, M. (1998). Organizational culture and innovativeness of firms: An integrated view. *International Journal of Technology Management, 16*(1), 239–255. doi:10.1504/IJTM.1998.002650

Hayes, K. (2007). *Triple helix organisations, knowledge-stewarding communities of practice and perceptions of time: The hunters and gatherers of commercialisation.* Paper presented at the 8th European Conference on Knowledge Management. Barcelona, Spain.

Hayes, K., & Fitzgerald, A. (2005). *Preliminary findings of an investigation into interactions between commercial and scientific occupational cultures in hybrid research organisations.* Paper presented at the Proceedings of the 6th International CINet Conference. Brighton, UK.

Hayes, K. J., & Fitzgerald, J. A. (2007). Business and research forms of debate: Argumentation and dissent as barriers to the commercialisation of innovations in hybrid industry-research organisations. *International Journal of Technology. Policy and Management, 7*(3), 280–291.

Henderson, C. R. (1989). Taxes, market structure and international price discrimination. *Journal of World Trade, 23*(6), 147.

Henning, M., & Jardim, A. (1977). *The managerial women.* New York, NY: Pan Books.

Henriksen, L. B. (2004). *Dimensions of change.* Copenhagen, Denmark: CBS Press.

Hepsø, I. L. (2005). *Fra ide til praksis: En studie av endringsprosessen BRA i Alpha Oil.* [From idea to practice: A study of the BRA-change process in Alpha Oil]. PhD Dissertation. Trondheim, Norway: Norwegian University of Science and Technology.

Hepsø, I. L., & Hepsø, V. (2007). Conceptions of us-and-them in organizational reification, translation and legitimation processes: Two best practice and business process initiatives in Alpha Oil oil and gas operations. *Systems, Signs & Action, 3*(1), 134-161. Retrieved from http://www.sysiac.org/

Herbig, P., & Dunphy, S. (1998). Culture and innovation. *Cross Cultural Management, 5*(4), 13–21. doi:10.1108/13527609810796844

Herbst, P. G. (1976). *Alternatives to hierarchies.* Leiden, Norway: M. Nijhoff Social Sciences Division. doi:10.1007/978-1-4684-6945-5

Hertel, G., Geister, S., & Konradt, U. (2005). Managing virtual teams: A review of current empirical research. *Human Resource Management Review, 15*(1), 69–95. doi:10.1016/j.hrmr.2005.01.002

Hertel, G., Konradt, U., & Orlikowski, B. (2004). Managing distance by interdependence: Goal setting, task interdependence, and team-based rewards in virtual teams. *European Journal of Work and Organizational Psychology, 13*(1), 1. doi:10.1080/13594320344000228

Hertel, G., Niedner, S., & Herrmann, S. (2003). Motivation of software developers in open source projects: An internet-based survey of contributors to the Linux kernel. *Research Policy, 32*(7), 1159–1177. doi:10.1016/S0048-7333(03)00047-7

Hill, S. S., Koocher, G. P., & Norcross, J. C. (2005). *Psychologists' desk reference* (2nd ed.). Oxford, UK: Oxford University Press.

Hiltz, S. R. (1988). Productivity enhancement from computer-mediated communication: A systems contingency approach. *Communications of the ACM, 31*(12), 1438–1454. doi:10.1145/53580.53583

Hiltz, S. R., & Turoff, M. (1981). The evolution of user behavior in a computerized conferencing system. *Communications of the ACM, 24*(11), 739–751. doi:10.1145/358790.358794

Himanen, P. (2001). *The hacker ethic. A radical approach to the philosophy of business.* New York, NY: Random House.

Hirschman, A. O. (1970). *Exit, voice, and loyalty: Responses to decline in firms, organizations, and states.* Cambridge, MA: Harvard University Press.

Hissam, S. A., Plakosh, D., & Weinstock, C. (2002). Trust and vulnerability in open source software. *IEE Proceedings. Software, 149*(1), 47–51. doi:10.1049/ip-sen:20020208

Hitt, M. A. (2001). Direct and moderating effects of human capital on strategy and performance in professional firms: A resource-based perspective. *Academy of Management Journal, 44*(1), 13–28. doi:10.2307/3069334

Hoffman, E. (2004). *EA: The human story.* [blog post]. Retrieved from http://ea-spouse.livejournal.com/274.html

Hofmann, D. A., Morgeson, F. P., & Gerras, S. J. (2003). Climate as a moderator of the relationship between leader-member exchange and content specific citizenship: Safety climate as an exemplar. *The Journal of Applied Psychology, 88*(1), 170–178. doi:10.1037/0021-9010.88.1.170

Hofstede, G. (1980). Motivation, leadership and organization: Do American theories apply abroad? *Organizational Dynamics, 9*, 42–63. doi:10.1016/0090-2616(80)90013-3

Hofstede, G. (1991). *Culture's consequences: Software of the mind.* London, UK: Mcgraw-Hill.

Hofstede, G. (2001). *Culture's consequences: Comparing values, behaviors, institutions, and organizations across nations* (2nd ed.). New York, NY: Sage Publications.

Holland, D., Lachicotte, W. Jr, Skinner, D., & Cain, C. (1998). *Identity and agency in cultural worlds.* Boston, MA: Harvard University Press.

Hooley, G., Broderick, A., & Möller, K. (1998). Competitive positioning and the resource-based view of the firm. *Journal of Strategic Marketing, 6*(2), 97–116. doi:10.1080/09652549800000003

Hotho, S. (2008). Professional identity - Product of structure, product of choice. *Journal of Organizational Change Management, 21*(6), 721–742. doi:10.1108/09534810810915745

Houghton Mifflin Company. (2000). *The American heritage dictionary of the English language.* Boston, MA: Houghton Mifflin Company.

House, R., Javidan, M., Hanges, P., & Dorfman, P. (2002). Understanding cultures and implicit leadership theories across the globe: An introduction to project GLOBE. *Journal of World Business, 37*, 3–10. doi:10.1016/S1090-9516(01)00069-4

Howcroft, D., & Trauth, E. M. (2008). The implications of a critical agenda in gender and IS research. *Information Systems Journal, 18*(2), 185–202. doi:10.1111/j.1365-2575.2008.00294.x

Howell, J. M., & Higgins, C. A. (1990). Champions of technological innovation. *Administrative Science Quarterly, 3*, 317–341. doi:10.2307/2393393

Hox, J. (2002). *Multilevel analysis: Techniques and applications.* New York, NY: Routledge.

Hox, J. J., & Bechger, T. M. (1998). An introduction to structural equations modeling. *Family Science Review, 11*, 354–373.

Hoynigen-Huene, P. (1993). *Restructuring scientific revolutions: Thomas s. Kuhn's philosophy of science.* Chicago, IL: University of Chicago Press.

Hoyt, C. L., & Blascovich, J. (2003). Transformational and transactional leadership in virtual and physical environments. *Small Group Research, 34*(6), 678–715. doi:10.1177/1046496403257527

Huber, G. P., & Van de Ven, A. H. (Eds.). (1995). *Longitudinal field research methods: Studying processes of organizational change.* Thousand Oaks, CA: SAGE Publications Inc.

Hu, L. T., & Bentler, P. (1999). Cutoff criteria for fit indexes in covariance structure analysis: conventional criteria versus new alternatives. *Structural Equation Modeling, 6*, 1–55. doi:10.1080/10705519909540118

Humphrey, W. S. (1997). *Managing technical people: Innovation, teamwork, and the software process.* Reading, MA: Addison-Wesley.

Hymowitz, C., & Schellard, T. D. (1986, March 24). The glass ceiling: Why women can't seem to break the invisible barrier that blocks them form the top jobs. *The Wall Street Journal*, p. D1, D4.

Ibarra, H. (1993). Personal networks of women and minorities in management: A conceptual framework. *Academy of Management Review, 18*(1), 56–87.

Iedema, R., Degeling, P., Braithwaite, J., & White, L. (2003). It's an interesting conversation i'm hearing: The doctor as manager. *Organization Studies, 25*(1), 15–33. doi:10.1177/0170840604038174

Igbaria, M. (1998). Special section: Managing virtual workplaces and teleworking with information technology. *Journal of Management Information Systems, 14*(4), 5.

IGDA. (2004). *Quality of life in the game industry: Challenges and best practices.* Retrieved from http://www.igda.org

IGDA. (2005). *IGDA 2005 annual report.* Retrieved from http://archives.igda.org/about/annual_report_05.php

Ignatidas, I., & Nandhakumar, J. (2009). The effect of ERP system workaround on organizational control: An interpretivist study. *Scandinavian Journal of Information Systems, 21*(2), 59–90.

Ilies, R., Nahrgang, J. D., & Morgeson, F. P. (2007). Leader-member exchange and citizenship behaviors: A meta-analysis. *The Journal of Applied Psychology, 92*(1), 269–277. doi:10.1037/0021-9010.92.1.269

Illich, I. (1987). *Disabling professions.* New York, NY: Marion Boyers.

Illouz, E. (1997). *Consuming the romantic utopia.* Berkeley, CA: University of California Press.

Isaac, S., & Michael, W. B. (1997). *Handbook in research and evaluation: A collection of principles, methods, and strategies useful in the planning, design, and evaluation of studies in education and the behavioral sciences* (3rd ed.). San Diego, CA: Educational and Industrial Testing Services.

Ishaya, T., & Macaulay, L. (1999). The role of trust in virtual teams. *The Electronic Journal for Virtual Organizations and Networks, 1*, 140–157.

Iskoujina, Z. (2010). *Knowledge sharing in virtual organisations: The case of open source software communities.* PhD Dissertation. Durham, UK: Durham University.

Iveco. (1982). Teckna Sveriges häftigaste lastbil, så bygger vi den som vinner. *Trailer, 1*, 33.

Jaaksi, A. (2006). *Building consumer products with open source.* Retrieved from http://www.linuxdevices.com/articles/AT7621761066.html

Jaaksi, A. (2007). Experiences on product development with open source software. In J. Feller, B. Fitzgerald, W. Scacchi, & A. Sillitti (Eds.), *Open Source Development, Adoption and Innovation,* (pp. 85-96). Springer/IFIP.

Jablin, F. M. (1979). Superior-subordinate communication: The state of the art. *Psychological Bulletin, 86*, 1201–1222. doi:10.1037/0033-2909.86.6.1201

Jablin, F. M. (1987). Formal organization structure. In Jablin, F. M., Putnam, L. L., Roberts, K., & Porter, L. W. (Eds.), *Handbook of Organizational Communication: An Interdisciplinary Perspective* (pp. 389–419). Newbury Park, CA: Sage.

Jablin, F. M., & Putnam, L. L. (Eds.). (2001). *The new handbook of organizational communication: Advances in theory, research and methods.* Thousand Oaks, CA: Sage.

Jablin, F. M., Putnam, L. L., Roberts, K. H., & Porter, L. W. (Eds.). (1987). *Handbook of organizational communication: An interdisciplinary perspective.* Newbury Park, CA: Sage.

Jackson, J. E., & Mach, B. W. (2009). Job creation, job destruction, labour mobility and wages in Poland, 1988-1998. *Economics of Transition, 17*, 503–530. doi:10.1111/j.1468-0351.2009.00358.x

Jacobs, J. A., & Gerson, K. (2001). Overworked individuals or overworked families? Explaining trends in work, leisure and family time. *Work and Occupations, 28*(1), 40–63. doi:10.1177/0730888401028001004

JALA International. (2010). *JALA biography of Jack Nilles*. Retrieved on July 17, 2010, from http://www.jala.com/jnmbio.php

James, L. R., Demaree, R. G., & Wolf, G. (1993). An assessment of within-group interrater agreement. *The Journal of Applied Psychology, 78*, 306–309. doi:10.1037/0021-9010.78.2.306

Janis, I. L. (1972). *Victims of groupthink: A psychological study of foreign-policy decisions and fiascoes*. Boston, MA: Houghton and Mifflin.

Jankowicz, A. D. (2000). *Business research projects*. New York, NY: Thomson Learning.

Jarillo, J. C. (1993). *Strategic networks: Creating the borderless organization*. Oxford, UK: Butterworth-Heinemann.

Jarimo, T., Pulkkinen, U., & Salo, A. (2005). Encouraging suppliers to process innovations: A game theory approach. *International Journal of Technology Intelligence and Planning, 1*(4), 403–423. doi:10.1504/IJTIP.2005.008590

Jarvenpaa, S. L., Knoll, K., & Leinder, D. E. (1998). Is anybody out there? Antecedents if trust in global virtual teams. *Journal of Management Information Systems, 14*(4), 29–64.

Jarvenpaa, S. L., & Leidner, D. E. (1999). Communication and trust in global virtual teams. *Organization Science, 10*, 791–815. doi:10.1287/orsc.10.6.791

Jarvenpaa, S. L., Shaw, T. R., & Staples, D. S. (2004). Toward contextualized theories of trust: The role of trust in global virtual teams. *Information Systems Research, 15*, 250–267. doi:10.1287/isre.1040.0028

Jarvenpaa, S., Knoll, K., & Leidner, D. E. (1998). Is anybody out there? Antecedents of trust in global virtual teams. *Journal of Management Information Systems, 14*(4), 29.

Jarvenpaa, S., & Leidner, D. (1999). Communication and trust in global virtual teams. *Organization Science, 10*(6), 791–815. doi:10.1287/orsc.10.6.791

Jemielniak, D. (2007). Managers as lazy, stupid careerists? *Journal of Organizational Change Management, 20*, 491–508. doi:10.1108/09534810710760045

Jemielniak, D. (2012). *The new knowledge workers*. New York, NY: Edward Elgar Publishing.

Jermier, J., & Kerr, S. (1997). Substitutes for leadership: Their meaning and measurement— Contextual recollections and current observations. *The Leadership Quarterly, 8*(2), 95–101. doi:10.1016/S1048-9843(97)90008-4

Jewell, L. N., & Reitz, H. J. (1981). *Group effectiveness in organizations*. Glenview, IL: Scott, Foresman and Company.

Johns, G. (2006). The essential impact of context on organizational behaviour. *Academy of Management Review, 31*, 386–408. doi:10.5465/AMR.2006.20208687

Johnson, D., & Grayson, K. (2005). Cognitive and affective trust in service relationships. *Journal of Business Research, 58*(4), 500–507. doi:10.1016/S0148-2963(03)00140-1

Johnson, G. (1988). Rethinking incrementalism. *Strategic Management Journal, 9*, 75–91. doi:10.1002/smj.4250090107

Jones, K., & Leonard, L. N. K. (2008). Trust in consumer-to-consumer electronic commerce. *Information & Management, 45*, 88–95. doi:10.1016/j.im.2007.12.002

Jørgensen, K. M., & Boje, D. M. (2010). Resituating narrative and story in business ethics. *Business Ethics: A European Perspective, 19*(3), 251-262.

Jørgensen, K. M. (2007). *Power without glory – A genealogy of a management decision*. Copenhagen, Denmark: CBS Press.

Judge, E. (2003, November 11). Women on board: Help or hindrance? *Times (London, England)*, (n.d), 21.

Jung, D. I., Chow, C., & Wu, A. (2003). The role of transformational leadership in enhancing organizational innovation: Hypotheses and some preliminary findings. *The Leadership Quarterly, 14*(4/5), 525–544. doi:10.1016/S1048-9843(03)00050-X

Juntunen, A. (2005). *The emergence of a new business through collaborative networks: A longitudinal study in the ICT sector*. Hershey, PA: IGI Global.

Juntunen, A. (2010). Developing efficient processes and network management in new business creation in the ICT-sector. In Wang, M., & Sun, Z. (Eds.), *Handbook of Research on Complex Dynamic Process Management: Techniques for Adaptability in Turbulent Environments*. Hershey, PA: IGI Global.

Kahai, S., Fjermestad, J., Zhang, S., & Avolio, B. J. (2007). Leadership in virtual teams: Past, present, and future. *International Journal of e-Collaboration, 3*(1), 1.

Kallinikos, J. (2004). Deconstructing information packages organizational and behavioural implications of ERP-systems. *Information Technology & People, 17*(1), 8–30. doi:10.1108/09593840410522152

Kanai, A. (2009). Karoshi (work to death) in Japan. *Journal of Business Ethics, 84*, 209–216. doi:10.1007/s10551-008-9701-8

Kanter, R. M. (1977). Some effects of proportions of group life: Skewed sex ratios and responses to token women. *American Journal of Sociology, 82*, 965–990. doi:10.1086/226425

Kaplan, D. A. (2000). *The silicon boys and their valley of dreams*. New York, NY: Harper Collins.

Karahanna, E., Straub, D. W., & Chervany, N. L. (1999). Information technology adoption across time: A cross-sectional comparison of pre-adoption and post-adoption beliefs. *Management Information Systems Quarterly, 23*(2), 183–213. doi:10.2307/249751

Karube, M., Numagami, T., & Kato, T. (2009). Exploring organisational deterioration: "Organisational deadweight" as a cause of malfunction of strategic initiatives in Japanese firms. *Long Range Planning, 42*, 518–544. doi:10.1016/j.lrp.2009.06.005

Kasper-Fuehrer, E. C., & Ashkanasy, N. M. (2001). Communicating trustworthiness and building trust in interorganizational virtual organizations. *Journal of Management, 27*(3), 235–254.

Keller, R. T. (1986). Predictors of the performance of project groups in R & D organizations. *Academy of Management Journal, 29*(4), 715–726. doi:10.2307/255941

Keller, R. T. (1992). Transformational leadership and the performance of research and development project groups. *The Journal of Applied Psychology, 91*(1), 202–210. doi:10.1037/0021-9010.91.1.202

Kent, T. (1993). The Kuhnian model of scientific change. In Langdon, J. H., & McGann, M. E. (Eds.), *The Natural History of Paradigms: Science and the Process of Intellectual Evolution*. Indianapolis, IN: The University of Indianapolis Press.

Kerr, S., & Jermier, J. (1978). Substitutes for leadership: Their meaning and measurement. *Organizational Behavior and Human Performance, 22*, 375. doi:10.1016/0030-5073(78)90023-5

Kessler, E. H., & Chakrabarti, A. K. (1996). Innovation speed: A conceptual model of context, antecedents, and outcomes. *Academy of Management Review, 21*(4), 1143–1191.

Kesteloot, L. (2003). *Why software is late*. Retrieved from http://www.teamten.com/lawrence/writings/late_software.html

Khanna, T., Gulati, R., & Nohria, N. (1998). The dynamics of learning alliances: Competition, cooperation, and relative scope. *Strategic Management Journal, 19*, 193–210. doi:10.1002/(SICI)1097-0266(199803)19:3<193::AID-SMJ949>3.0.CO;2-C

Kimberly, J. R. (1976). Organizational size and the structuralist perspective: A review, critique, and proposal. *Administrative Science Quarterly, 21*(4), 571–597. doi:10.2307/2391717

Kim, S. (2005). Factors affecting state governments information technology employee turnover intentions. *American Review of Public Administration, 35*(2), 137–156. doi:10.1177/0275074004273150

Kippist, L., & Fitzgerald, J. A. (2006). *The value of management education for hybrid clinician managers*. Paper presented at the ANZAM. Rockhampton, Australia.

Kippist, L., & Fitzgerald, J. A. (2008). *Managers are from Mars and doctors are from Venus*. Paper presented at the ANZAM. Aukland, New Zealand.

Kippist, L., & Fitzgerald, J. A. (2009). Organisational professional conflict and hybrid clinician managers. *Journal of Health Organization and Management, 23*(6), 642–655. doi:10.1108/14777260911001653

Kirkman, B. L., & Mathieu, J. E. (2004). *The role of virtuality in work team effectiveness*. New York, NY: Academy of Management.

Kirkman, B. L., & Mathieu, J. E. (2005). The dimensions and antecedents of team virtuality. *Journal of Management, 31*(5), 700. doi:10.1177/0149206305279113

Kleinbaum, D. G., Lawrence, L. L., Muller, K. E., & Nizam, A. (1998). *Applied regression analysis and other multivariable methods* (3rd ed.). New York, NY: Duxbury.

Kline, R. B. (1998). *Principles and practice of structural equation modeling*. New York, NY: Guilford Press.

Knight-Turvey, N. (2006). Influencing employee innovation through structural empowerment initiatives: The need to feel empowered. *Entrepreneurship Theory and Practice*, 313-324. Retrieved from http://www.swinburne.edu.au/lib/ir/onlineconferences/agse2006/knightturvey_p313.pdf

Kodama, F. (1991). *Analyzing Japanese high technologies: The techno-paradigm shift*. London, UK: Pinter Publishers.

Kogut, B., & Zander, U. (1992). Knowledge of the firm, combinative capability and the replication of technology. *Organization Science, 3*, 383–397. doi:10.1287/orsc.3.3.383

Koivumaki, T., Ristola, A., & Kesti, M. (2008). The effects of information quality of mobile information services on user satisfaction and service acceptance-empirical evidence from Finland. *Behaviour & Information Technology, 27*(5), 375–385. doi:10.1080/01449290601177003

Kostera, M. (2005). *Antropologia organizacji: Metodologia badań terenowych* [Anthropology of organization: Methodology of field research]. Warsaw, Poland: PWN.

Kostera, M. (2007). *Organizational ethnography: Methods and inspirations*. Lund, Sweden: Studentliteratur.

Kostner, J. (1996). *Virtual leadership*. New York, NY: Warner Books.

Kotter, J. P., & Heskett, J. L. (1992). *Corporate culture and performance*. New York, NY: Free Press.

Kozinets, R. V. (1998). On netnography: Initial reflections on consumer investigations of cyberculture. In Alba, J., & Hutchinson, W. (Eds.), *Advances in Consumer Research* (Vol. 25, pp. 366–371). Provo, UT: Association for Consumer Research.

Kozinets, R. V. (2002). The field behind the screen: Using netnography for marketing research. *JMR, Journal of Marketing Research, 39*(1), 61–72. doi:10.1509/jmkr.39.1.61.18935

Kozinetz, R. V. (1997). I want to believe: 'A netnography of the x-files' subculture of consumption. *Advances in Consumer Research. Association for Consumer Research (U. S.), 24*, 470–475.

Krishnan, R., Martin, X., & Noorderhaven, N. (2006). When does trust matter to alliance performance? *Academy of Management Journal, 49*(5), 894–917. doi:10.5465/AMJ.2006.22798171

Kristof, A. L. (2000). Perceived applicant fit: Distinguishing between recruiters' perceptions of person-job and person-organization fit. *Personnel Psychology, 53*, 643–671. doi:10.1111/j.1744-6570.2000.tb00217.x

Kroeger, F. (2009). *The institutionalization of trust: Understanding the creation and collapse of escalating trust spirals in economic life*. Paper presented at the Annual Meeting of the SASE Annual Conference. Paris, France. Retrieved from http://www.allacademic.com/meta/p314382_index.html

Kuchlich, J. (2005). Precarious playbour: Modders and the digital games industry. *Fiberculture, 3*(5). Retrieved from http://journal.fibreculture.org/issue5/depeuter_dyerwitheford.html

Kuhn, T. S. (1962). *The structure of scientific revolutions*. Chicago, IL: University of Chicago Press.

Kuhn, T. S. (1970). *The structure of scientific revolutions* (2nd ed.). Chicago, IL: University of Chicago Press.

Kuhn, T. S. (1996). *The structure of scientific revolutions* (3rd ed.). Chicago, IL: University of Chicago Press.

Kunda, G. (1992). *Engineering culture: Control and commitment in a high-tech corporation.* Philadelphia, PA: Temple University Press.

Kvasny, L., & Keil, M. (2006). The challenges of redressing the digital divide: A tale of two US cities. *Information Systems Journal, 16*(1), 23–53. doi:10.1111/j.1365-2575.2006.00207.x

Lacan, J. (1988). *The seminar of Jacques Lacan, book II: The ego in Freud's theory and in the technique of psychoanalysis 1954–55.* Cambridge, UK: Cambridge University Press.

Lambert, D., & Cooper, M. (2000). Issues in supply chain management. *Industrial Marketing Management, 29*(1), 65–83. doi:10.1016/S0019-8501(99)00113-3

Lane, C., & Bachmann, R. (1997). Co-operation in inter-firm relations in Britain and Germany: The role of social institutions. *The British Journal of Sociology, 48,* 226–254. doi:10.2307/591750

Lane, C., & Bachmann, R. (2000). *Trust within and between organizations.* Oxford, UK: Oxford University Press.

Langdon, J. H., & McGann, M. E. (1993). *The natural history of paradigms: Science and the process of intellectual evolution.* Indianapolis, IN: The University of Indianapolis Press.

Larson, M. S. (1977). *The rise of professionalism.* Berkeley, CA: University of California Press.

Lassile, K., & Peippo, N. (2008). *Birds of a feather: A study of subordinate perceptions of leader effectiveness as a function of gender.* Master Thesis. Stockholm, Sweden: Stockholm University.

Latour, B. (1987). *Science in action: How to follow scientists and engineers through society.* Milton Keynes, UK: Open University Press.

Latour, B. (1993). *We have never been modern.* Hemel Hempstead, UK: Harvester Wheatsheaf.

Latour, B. (1999). *Pandora's hope: Essays on the reality of science studies.* Boston, MA: Harvard University Press.

Latusek, D. (2007). *Zaufanie i nieufnosc w relacji sprzedawca-nabywca w polskim sektorze IT.* [The trust and distrust in seller-buyer relation in the Polish IT sector]. Ph.D. Thesis. Warsaw, Poland: Wyzsza Szkola Przedsiebiorczosci i Zarzadzania im.

Laursen, K., & Salter, A. (2006). Open for innovation: The role of openness in explaining innovation performance among UK manufacturing firms. *Strategic Management Journal, 27*(2), 131–150. doi:10.1002/smj.507

Lawler, E. E. III. (1990). *High-involvement management: Participative strategies for improving organizational performance.* San Francisco, CA: Jossey-Bass Publishers.

Lawrence, P. R., & Lorsch, J. W. (1967). *Organization and environment: Managing differentiation and integration.* Boston, MA: Harvard Business School.

Leblebici, H., Salancik, G. R., Copay, A., & King, T. (1991). Institutional change and the transformation of interorganizational fields: An organizational history of the US radio broadcasting industry. *Administrative Science Quarterly, 36*(3), 333–363. doi:10.2307/2393200

Lee, A. S., & Baskerville, R. L. (2003). Generalizing generalizability in information systems research. *Information Systems Research, 14*(3), 221–243. doi:10.1287/isre.14.3.221.16560

Legault, M.-J., & Chasserio, S. (2012). Professionalization, risk transfer, and the gender gap in IT firms. *International Journal of Project Management, 30*(6).

Legault, M.-J., & Chasserio, S. (2010). La domination dans le modèle de production de haute performance dans la gestion de projets. In Malenfant, R., & Bellemare, G. (Eds.), *La Domination au Travail: Des Conceptions Totalisantes à la Diversification des Formes de Domination* (pp. 99–124). Québec, Canada: PUQ.

Lehrer, M., & Asakawa, K. (2004). Pushing scientists into the marketplace: Promoting science entrepreneurship. *California Management Review, 46*(3), 55–76.

Lehtonen, M., Löytty, O., & Ruuska, P. (2004). *Suomi toisin sanoen* [Finland in other words]. Tampere, Finland: Vastapaino.

Lenox, M., & King, A. (2004). Prospects for developing absorptive capacity through internal information provision. *Strategic Management Journal*, *25*, 331–345. doi:10.1002/smj.379

Leonard-Barton, D. (1992). Core capabilities and core rigidities: A paradox in managing new product development. *Strategic Management Journal*, *13*, 111–125. doi:10.1002/smj.4250131009

Leonhard, W. (1995). *The underground guide to telecommuting*. Boston, MA: Addison-Wesley.

Leppälä, K., & Päiviö, H. (2001). *Kauppatieteiden opiskelijoiden moraalijärjestys: Narratiivinen tutkimus kolmen eri pääaineen opiskelusta Helsingin kauppakorkeakoulussa.* [Moral order among students of economics: A narrative inquiry into studying three major subjects at Helsinki School of Economics]. Helsinki, Finland: Publications of the Helsinki School of Economics and Business Administration.

Levine, S. (2006). *High performance organizations: Creating a culture of agreement. Handbook of Business Strategy* (pp. 375–380). London, UK: Emerald.

Levitt, B., & March, J. G. (1988). Organizational learning. *Annual Review of Sociology*, *14*, 319–340. doi:10.1146/annurev.so.14.080188.001535

Lewis, J. D., & Weigert, A. (1985). Social atomism, holism, and trust. *The Sociological Quarterly*, *26*(4), 455–471. doi:10.1111/j.1533-8525.1985.tb00238.x

Lewis, J. D., & Weigert, A. (1985). Trust as a social reality. *Social Forces*, *63*, 967–985.

Liden, R. C., & Antonakis, J. (2009). Considering context in psychological leadership research. *Human Relations*, *62*, 1587–1605. doi:10.1177/0018726709346374

Liden, R. C., Wayne, S. J., Jaworski, R. A., & Bennett, N. (2004). Social loafing: A field investigation. *Journal of Management*, *30*, 285–304. doi:10.1016/j.jm.2003.02.002

Lindström, M., & Janzon, E. (2007). Social capital, institutional (vertical) trust and smoking: A study of daily smoking and smoking cessation among ever smokers. *Scandinavian Journal of Public Health*, *35*, 460. doi:10.1080/14034940701246090

Linehan, M., & Scullion, H. (2001). Challenges for female international managers: Evidence from Europe. *Journal of Managerial Psychology*, *16*(3), 215–228. doi:10.1108/02683940110385767

Ling, R., Julsrud, T., & Krogh, E. (1997). The goretex principle: The hytte and mobile telephones in Norway. In Haddon, L. (Ed.), *Communications on the Move: The Experience of Mobile Telephony in the 1990s*. Farsta, Sweden: Telia.

Lissack, M., & Roos, J. (2001). Be coherent, not visionary. *Long Range Planning*, *34*(1), 53–70. doi:10.1016/S0024-6301(00)00093-5

Litvin, D. R. (1997). The discourse of diversity: From biology to management. *Organization*, *4*(2), 187–209. doi:10.1177/135050849742003

Liu, Y. (1999). Justifying my position in your terms: Cross-cultural argumentation in a globalized world. *Argumentation*, *13*, 297–315. doi:10.1023/A:1007866519621

Lorange, P., & Nelson, R. T. (1987). How to recognize—and avoid—organizational decline. *Sloan Management Review*, *28*, 41–48.

Lorbiecki, A., & Jack, G. (2000). Critical turns in the evolution of diversity management. *British Journal of Management*, *11*(3).

Luhmann, N. (1979). *Trust and power: Two works*. New York, NY: Wiley.

Lu, J., Yu, C.-S., & Liu, C. (2009). Mobile data service demographics in urban China. *Journal of Computer Information Systems*, *50*(2), 117–126.

Lyness, K. S., & Thompson, D. E. (1997). Above the glass ceiling? A comparison of matched samples of female and male executives. *The Journal of Applied Psychology*, *82*(3), 359–375. doi:10.1037/0021-9010.82.3.359

Lynn, M., & Gelb, B. D. (1996). Identifying innovative national markets for technical consumer goods. *International Marketing Review*, *13*(6), 43–57. doi:10.1108/02651339610151917

MacDuffie, J. P. (2007). HRM and distributed work: Managing people across distances. *Academy of Management Annals*, *1*, 549–615. doi:10.1080/078559817

MacKenzie, K. R., & Tschuschke, V. (1993). Relatedness, group work, and outcome in long-term inpatient psychotherapy groups. *The Journal of Psychotherapy Practice and Research, 2*(2), 147–156.

Madhok, A. (1995). Revisiting multinational firms' tolerance for joint ventures: A trust-based approach. *Journal of International Business Studies, 26*, 117–137. doi:10.1057/palgrave.jibs.8490168

Malhotra, A., Majchrzak, A., & Rosen, B. (2007). Leading virtual teams. *The Academy of Management Perspectives, 21*(1), 60–70. doi:10.5465/AMP.2007.24286164

Mannix, E. A., & Neale, M. A. (2005). What difference makes a difference? *Psychological Science in the Public Interest, 6*(2), 31–32. doi:10.1111/j.1529-1006.2005.00022.x

Marin, D. (2002). Trust versus illusion: What is driving demonetization in the former Soviet Union? *Economics of Transition, 10*, 173–200. doi:10.1111/1468-0351.00107

Marks, M. A., DeChurch, L. A., Mathieu, J. E., Panzer, F. J., & Alonso, A. (2005). Teamwork in multiteam systems. *The Journal of Applied Psychology, 90*(5), 964–971. doi:10.1037/0021-9010.90.5.964

Marks, M. A., Mathieu, J. E., & Zaccaro, S. J. (2001). A temporally based framework and taxonomy of team processes. *Academy of Management Review, 26*(3), 356–376.

Martin, E. (1994). *Flexible bodies: The role of immunity in American culture from the days of polio to the age of AIDS.* Boston, MA: Beacon Press.

Martin, J. (2002). *Organizational culture: Mapping the terrain.* Thousand Oaks, CA: Sage Publications Inc.

Martins, E. C., & Terblanche, F. (2003). Building organizational culture that stimulates creativity and innovation. *European Journal of Innovation Management, 6*(1), 64–74. doi:10.1108/14601060310456337

Matusik, S. F., & Mickel, A. E. (2011). Embracing or embattled by converged mobile devices? Users' experiences with a contemporary connectivity technology. *Human Relations, 64*(8), 1001–1030. doi:10.1177/0018726711405552

Matzat, U. (2004). Cooperation and community on the internet: Past issues and present perspectives for theoretical-empirical internet research. *Analyse & Kritik, 26*, 63–90.

Mayer, D. M., Keller, K. M., Leslie, L. M., & Hanges, P. J. (2008). When does my relationship with my manager matter most? The moderating role of coworkers' LMX. *Academy of Management Proceedings*, 1-6.

Mayer, R. C., Davis, J. H., & Schoorman, F. D. (1995). An inte- grative model of organizational trust. *Academy of Management Review, 20*, 709–734.

Mayfield, M. R., & Mayfield, J. R. (2007). *The role of group atmosphere and LMX relationships on worker performance and job satisfaction: Positive findings and recommendations for team enhancement.* Unpublished Manuscript. Retrieved October 31, 2008, from http://comm.research.arizona.edu/ingroup/docs/GroupAtmosphereandLMX-PaperwithReferences.pdf

Maylor, H. (2006). Special issue on rethinking project management. *International Journal of Project Management, 24*(8). doi:10.1016/j.ijproman.2006.09.013

Mazmanian, M. A., Orlikowski, W. J., & Yates, J. (2005). Crackberries: The social implicaitons of ubiquitous wireless e-mail devices. In C. Sørensen, Y. Yoo, K. Lyytinen, & J. I. DeGross (Eds.), *Designing Ubiquitous Information Environments: Socio-Technical Issues and Challenges,* (pp. pp. 337-344). New York, NY: Springer.

Mazmanian, M., Yates, J., & Orlikowski, W. (2006). Ubiquitous email: Individual experiences and organizational consequences of blackberry use. *Academy of Management Annual Meeting Proceedings, 66*.

Maznevski, M. L., & Chudoba, K. M. (2000). Bridging space over time: Global virtual team dynamics and effectiveness. *Organization Science, 11*(5), 473–492. doi:10.1287/orsc.11.5.473.15200

McAllister, D. J. (1995). Affect- and cognition-based trust as foundations for interpersonal co-operation in organizations. *Academy of Management Journal, 38*(1), 24–59. doi:10.2307/256727

McDonald, C. (1999). Human service professionals in the community services industry. *Australian Social Work, 52*(1), 17–25. doi:10.1080/03124079908414105

McDonald, K. M. (1995). *The sociology of the professions.* London, UK: Sage Publications.

McGrath, J. (1964). *Leadership behavior: Some requirements for leadership training.* Washington, DC: Office of Career Development.

McKerrow, R. E. (1980). *Argument communities.* Paper presented at the First Summer Conference on Argumentation. Annandale, VA.

Mckinley, W. (1993). Organizational decline and adaptation: Theoretical controversies. *Organization Science, 4,* 1–9. doi:10.1287/orsc.4.1.1

McMaster, T., & Wastell, D. (2005). Diffusion – Or delusion? Challenging an IS research tradition. *Information Technology & People, 18*(4), 383–404. doi:10.1108/09593840510633851

Mellahi, K., & Wilkinson, A. (2004). Organizational failure: A critique of recent research and a proposed integrative framework. *International Journal of Management Reviews, 5-6*(1), 21–41. doi:10.1111/j.1460-8545.2004.00095.x

Mendonca, M., & Kanungo, R. N. (1994). Managing human resources: The issue of cultural fit. *Journal of Management Inquiry, 3*(2), 189–205. doi:10.1177/105649269432010

Menon, S. T. (2001). Employee empowerment: An integrative psychological approach. *Applied Psychology: An International Review, 50*(1), 153–180. doi:10.1111/1464-0597.00052

Menon, S. T., & Hartmann, L. C. (2002). Generalizability of menon's empowerment scale: Replication and extension with Australian data. *International Journal of Cross Cultural Management, 2*(2), 137–153. doi:10.1177/1470595802002002860

Mertens, D. M. (1998). *Research methods in education and psychology: Integrating diversity with quantitative and qualitative approaches.* Thousand Oaks, CA: Sage.

Metlin, E., & Cohen, R. (2007). Designing a women's initiative that works: Make it thoughtful, well-planned and business-based. *New York Law Journal Magazine, 6*(5).

Meyer, R. D., Dalal, R. S., & Hermida, R. (2010). A review and synthesis of situational strength in the organizational sciences. *Journal of Management, 36,* 121–140. doi:10.1177/0149206309349309

Meyerson, D., & Martin, J. (1987). Cultural change: An integration of three different views. *Journal of Management Studies, 24*(6), 623–647. doi:10.1111/j.1467-6486.1987.tb00466.x

Meyerson, D., Weick, K. E., & Kramer, R. M. (1996). Swift trust and temporary groups. In Kramer, R. M., & Tyler, T. R. (Eds.), *Trust in Organizations: Frontiers of Theory and Research* (pp. 166–195). Thousand Oaks, CA: Sage Publications.

Michalisin, M. D., Karau, S. J., & Tangpong, C. (2004). Top management team cohesion and superior industry returns. *Group & Organization Management, 29*(1), 125–140. doi:10.1177/1059601103251687

Mickan, S. M., & Boyce, R. A. (2006). Organisational change and adaptation in health care. In *Managing Health Services: Concepts and Practice* (2nd ed., pp. 59–83). Sydney, Australia: Mosby Elsevier.

Middleton, C. A. (2007). Illusions of balance and control in an always-on environment: A case study of blackberry users. *Continuum: Journal of Media & Cultural Studies, 21,* 165–178. doi:10.1080/10304310701268695

Middleton, C. A., & Cukier, W. (2006). Is mobile email functional or dysfunctional? Two perspectives on mobile email usage. *European Journal of Information Systems, 15*(3), 252–260. doi:10.1057/palgrave.ejis.3000614

Miller, D. (1990). Organizational configurations: Cohesion, change, and prediction. *Human Relations, 43,* 771–789. doi:10.1177/001872679004300805

Miller, D., & Friesen, P. H. (1980). Archetypes of organizational transition. *Administrative Science Quarterly, 25,* 268–299. doi:10.2307/2392455

Mintzberg, H., Ahlstrand, B., & Lampe, J. (1998). *Strategy safari: The complete guide through the wilds of strategic management.* London, UK: Prentice Hall Financial Times.

Mintzberg, H. (1979). *The structuring of organizations.* Englewood Cliffs, NJ: Prentice-Hall.

Mintzberg, H. (1980). Structure in 5's: A synthesis of the research on organization design. *Management Science, 26,* 322–341. doi:10.1287/mnsc.26.3.322

Mintzberg, H. (1994). *The rise and fall of strategic planning.* New York, NY: Free Press.

Mintzberg, H., & McHugh, A. (1985). Strategy formation in an adhocracy. *Administrative Science Quarterly, 30,* 160–197. doi:10.2307/2393104

Mishler, I. W., & Rose, R. (2001). What are the origins of political trust? Testing institutional and cultural theories in post-communist societies. *Comparative Political Studies, 34*(1), 30–62. doi:10.1177/0010414001034001002

Mitchell, A., & Zigurs, I. (2009). Trust in virtual teams: Solved or still a mystery? *SIGMIS Database, 40*(3), 61–83. doi:10.1145/1592401.1592407

Mohrman, S. A., Finegold, D., & Mohrman, A. M. (2003). An empirical model of the organization knowledge system in new product development firms. *Journal of Engineering and Technology Management, 20*(1-2), 7–38. doi:10.1016/S0923-4748(03)00003-1

Mølbjerg Jørgensen, K. (2007). *Power without glory.* Copenhagen, Denmark: CBS Press.

Mølbjerg Jørgensen, K., & Boje, D. (2010). Resituating narrative and story in business ethics. *Business Ethics (Oxford, England), 19*(3), 253–264. doi:10.1111/j.1467-8608.2010.01593.x

Molin, H. (2005). Designer på papperet. [Designer on paper]. *Trucking Scandinavia, 11,* 45–47.

Möller, K., Rajala, A., & Svahn, S. (2005). Strategic business nets – Their types and management. *Journal of Business Research.* Retrieved from http://impgroup.org/uploads/papers/4462.pdf

Möller, K. (2010). *Value networks and innovation.* Berkeley, CA: University of California.

Möller, K., & Halinen, A. (1999). Business relationships and networks: Managerial challenge of network era. *Industrial Marketing Management, 28,* 413–427.

Möller, K., & Rajala, A. (1999). Organizing marketing in industrial high-tech firms: The role of internal marketing relationships. *Industrial Marketing Management, 28*(5), 521–535.

Möller, K., & Rajala, A. (2007). Rise of strategic nets – New modes of value creation. *Industrial Marketing Management, 36,* 895–908. doi:10.1016/j.indmarman.2007.05.016

Morand, D. A. (1995). The role of behavioral formality and informality in the enactment of bureaucratic versus organic organizations. *Academy of Management Review, 20,* 831–872.

Mouritsen, J., Hansen, A., & Hansen, C. Ø. (2009). Short and long translations: Management accounting calculations and innovation management. *Accounting, Organizations and Society, 34*(6-7), 738–754. doi:10.1016/j.aos.2009.01.006

Mowshowitz, A. (1997). On the theory of virtual organization. *Systems Research and Behavioral Science, 14*(4), 373–384. doi:10.1002/(SICI)1099-1743(199711/12)14:6<373::AID-SRES131>3.0.CO;2-R

Mueller, S. L., & Thomas, A. S. (2000). Culture and entrepreneurial potential: A nine country study of locus of control and innovativeness. *Journal of Business Venturing, 16,* 51–75. doi:10.1016/S0883-9026(99)00039-7

Mullen, B., & Copper, C. (1994). The relation between group cohesiveness and performance: An integration. *Psychological Bulletin, 115*(2), 210–227. doi:10.1037/0033-2909.115.2.210

Muthén, L. K., & Muthén, B. O. (2002). How to use a monte carlo study to decide on sample size and determine power. *Structural Equation Modeling, 9*(4), 599–620. doi:10.1207/S15328007SEM0904_8

Nemeth, C. J. (1997). Managing innovation: When less is more. *California Management Review, 40*(1), 59–74.

Newman, K. L., & Nollan, S. D. (1996). Culture and congruence: The fit between management practices and national culture. *Journal of International Business Studies, 27*(4), 753–779. doi:10.1057/palgrave.jibs.8490152

Newman, M., & Robey, D. (1992). A social process model of user-analyst relationships. *Management Information Systems Quarterly, 16*(2), 249–266. doi:10.2307/249578

Nilles, J. M. (1998). *Managing telework: Options for managing the virtual workforce.* New York, NY: John Wiley & Sons.

Nonaka, I. (1988). Toward middle-up-down management: Accelerating information creation. *Sloan Management Review, 29*(3), 9–18.

Nonaka, I. (1994). A dynamic theory of organizational knowledge creation. *Organization Science*, *5*, 15–37. doi:10.1287/orsc.5.1.14

Nonaka, I., & Konno, N. (1998). The concept of ba: Building a foundation for knowledge creation. *California Management Review*, *40*(3), 40–47.

Nonaka, I., & Takeuchi, H. (1995). *The knowledge-creating company*. Oxford, UK: Oxford University Press.

Nonaka, I., Toyama, R., & Nagata, A. (2000). A firm as a knowledge-creating entity: A new perspective on the theory of the firm. *Industrial and Corporate Change*, *9*, 1–20. doi:10.1093/icc/9.1.1

Noon, M. A. (1989). *New technology and industrial relations in provincial newspapers: Computerisation and bargaining power of journalists.* Unpublished Doctoral Dissertation. London, UK: Imperial College.

Nowotny, H., Scott, P., & Gibbons, M. (2001). *Re-thinking science: Knowledge and the public in an age of uncertainty*. Malden, MA: Blackwell Publishers Inc.

Numagami, T., Karube, M., & Kato, T. (2010). Organizational deadweight: Learning from Japan. *The Academy of Management Perspectives*, *24*(4), 25–37. doi:10.5465/AMP.2010.55206382

Nunnally, J. C. (1978). *Psychometric theory*. New York, NY: Mcgraw-Hill.

Nurmi, R. (1999). Knowledge-intensive firms. In *The Knowledge Management Yearbook 1999-2000*. London, UK: Butterworth-Heinemann.

Oates, B. J. (2006). *Researching information systems and computing*. London, UK: SAGE.

Ogbonna, E., & Harris, L. (2000). Leadership style, organizational culture and performance: Empirical evidence from UK companies. *International Journal of Human Resource Management*, *11*(4), 766–788. doi:10.1080/09585190050075114

Ohlott, P. J., Ruderman, M. N., & McCauley, C. D. (1994). Gender differences in managers' developmental job experiences. *Academy of Management Journal*, *37*(1), 46–67. doi:10.2307/256769

Olson, M. (1965). *The logic of collective action: Public goods and the theory of groups*. Boston, MA: Harvard University Press.

Orlikowski, W. J. (2002). Knowing in practice: Enacting a collective capability in distributed organizing. *Organization Science*, *13*(3), 249–273. doi:10.1287/orsc.13.3.249.2776

Orlikowski, W. J. (2007). Sociomaterial practices: Exploring technology at work. *Organization Studies*, *28*(9), 1435–1448. doi:10.1177/0170840607081138

Orlikowski, W. J., & Iacono, C. S. (2001). Research commentary: Desperately seeking the 'it' in IT research - A call to theorizing the IT artifact. *Information Systems Research*, *12*(2), 121–134. doi:10.1287/isre.12.2.121.9700

Ortner, S. B. (1984). Theory in anthropology since the sixties. *Comparative Studies in Society and History*, *126*(1), 126–166. doi:10.1017/S0010417500010811

Ortner, S. B. (2005). Subjectivity and cultural critique. *Anthropological Theory*, *5*(1), 31–52. doi:10.1177/1463499605050867

Osterloh, M., & Rota, S. (2004). Trust and community in open source software production. *Analyse & Kritik*, *26*, 279–301.

Osterwalder, A. (2004). *The business-model ontology – A proposition in design science approach*. Academic Dissertation. Lausanne, France: Université de Lausanne.

Ouchi, W. G. (1977). The relationship between organizational structure and control. *Administrative Science Quarterly*, *22*(1), 95–113. doi:10.2307/2391748

Ouchi, W. G. (1981). *Theory Z: How American business can meet the Japanese challenge*. Reading, MA: Addison-Wesley.

Overby, S. (2006, September 1). How to hook the talent you need. *CIO Magazine*.

Pajunen, K. (2006). Living in agreement with a contract: The management of moral and viable firm stakeholder relationships. *Journal of Business Ethics*, *68*(3), 243–258. doi:10.1007/s10551-006-9013-9

Paludi, M. A., & Barickman, R. B. (1991). *Academic and workplace sexual harassment: A resource manual.* Albany, NY: State University of New York Press.

Panasuraman, S., Greenhaus, J. H., & Linnehan, F. (2000). Time, person-career fit and the bundaryless career. In Cooper, G. L., & Rousseau, D. M. (Eds.), *Time in Organizational Behaviour.* New York, NY: Wiley.

Pare, G., & Tremblay, M. (2007). The influence of high-involvement human resource practices, procedural justice, organizational commitment, and citizenship behaviors on information technology professionals' turnover intentions. *Group & Organization Management, 32*(3), 326–357. doi:10.1177/1059601106286875

Parker, B., & Fagenson, E. A. (1994). An introductory overview of women in corporate management. In Davison, M. J., & Burke, R. J. (Eds.), *Women in Management: Current Research Issues* (pp. 11–25). London, UK: Paul Chapman.

Parker, M. (2002). *Against management.* Oxford, UK: Polity Press.

Pech, R. J. (2001). Termites, group behaviour, and the loss of innovation: Conformity rules! *Journal of Managerial Psychology, 16*(7), 559–574. doi:10.1108/EUM0000000006168

Peev, E. (2002). Ownership and control structures in transition to 'crony' capitalism: The case of Bulgaria. *Eastern European Economics, 40,* 73–91.

Pereira, R. (2009). *The costs of unpaid overtime work in Canada: Dimensions and comparative analysis.* Masters Thesis. Athabasca, Canada: University of Athabasca.

Perlow, L. A. (1997). *Finding time: How corporations, individuals, and families can benefit from new work practices.* Ithaca, NY: Cornell University Press.

Perlow, L. A. (1999). The time famine: Toward a sociology of work time. *Administrative Science Quarterly, 44,* 57–81. doi:10.2307/2667031

Perrow, C. (1986). *Complex organizations: Critical essay* (3rd ed.). New York, NY: McGraw-Hill.

Pfeffer, J., & Salancik, G. R. (1978). *The external control of organizations: A resource dependence perspective.* New York, NY: Harper and Row.

Picado, R. (2000). A questioning of time. *Access, 17,* 9–13.

Piccoli, G., Powell, A., & Blake, I. (2004). Virtual teams: Team control structure, work processes, and team effectiveness. *Information Technology & People, 17*(4), 359. doi:10.1108/09593840410570258

Pinfield, L. T., Watzke, G. E., & Webb, E. J. (1974). Confederacies and brokers: Mediators between organizations and their environments. In Leavitt, H., Pinfield, L., & Webb, E. (Eds.), *Organizations of the Future: Interaction with the External Environment* (pp. 83–110). New York, NY: Praeger.

Pixley, J. (1999). Impersonal trust in global mediating organizations. *Sociological Perspectives, 42*(4), 647–671.

Podsakoff, P. M., MacKenzie, S. B., Lee, J. Y., & Podsakoff, N. P. (2003). Common method biases in behavioral research: A critical review of the literature and recommended remedies. *The Journal of Applied Psychology, 88,* 879–903. doi:10.1037/0021-9010.88.5.879

Podsakoff, P. M., & Organ, D. M. (1986). Self reports in organizational research: Problems and prospects. *Journal of Management, 12,* 531–544. doi:10.1177/014920638601200408

Pokela, P. (2005). *Paper.* Paper presented at a Conference on Diversity. Helsinki, Finland. Antila, J., & Ylöstalo, P. (2002). *Proaktiivinen toimintatapa: Yritysten ja palkansaajien yhteinen etu?* [Proactive mode: Common asset for companies and employees?]. Helsinki, Finland: Työministeriö.

Pool, S. W. (2000). Organizational culture and its relationship in measuring outcomes among business executives. *Journal of Management Development, 19*(1), 32–49. doi:10.1108/02621710010308144

Powell, A., Piccoli, G., & Ives, B. (2004). Virtual teams: A review of current literature and directions for future research. *The Data Base for Advances in Information Systems, 35*(1), 6. doi:10.1145/968464.968467

Powell, G. N. (1980). Career development and the woman manager: A social power perspective. *Personnel, 57*(3), 22–32.

Powell, W. W., Koput, K. W., & Smith-Doerr, L. (1996). Interorganizational collaboration and the locus of innovation: Networks of learning in biotechnology. *Administrative Science Quarterly*, *41*, 116–145. doi:10.2307/2393988

Prasad, P. (1997). The protestant ethic and the myths of the frontier: Cultural imprints, organizational structuring and workplace diversity. In Prasad, P. (Eds.), *Managing the Organizational Melting Pot: Dilemmas of Workplace Diversity*. Thousand Oaks, CA: Sage.

Premus, R. (2002). Moving technology from labs to market: A policy perspective. *International Journal of Technoloy Transfer and Commercialisation*, *1*(1/2), 22–39. doi:10.1504/IJTTC.2002.001775

Pugh, D. S., Hickson, D. J., Hinings, C. R., & Turner, C. (1969). The context of organization structures. *Administrative Science Quarterly*, *14*, 91–113. doi:10.2307/2391366

Quattrone, P., & Hopper, T. (2005). A 'time-space odyssey': Management control systems in two multinational organizations. *Accounting, Organizations and Society*, *30*, 735–764. doi:10.1016/j.aos.2003.10.006

Quattrone, P., & Hopper, T. (2006). What is IT? SAP, accounting and visibility in a multinational organization. *Information and Organization*, *16*, 212–250. doi:10.1016/j.infoandorg.2006.06.001

Quinn, R. E. (1988). *Beyond rational management, mastering the paradoxes and competing demands of high performance*. San Francisco, CA: Jossey-Bass.

Radjou, N., Daley, E., Rasmussen, M., & Lo, H. (2006). *The rise of globally adaptive organizations: The world isn't flat till global firms are networked, risk-agile, and socially adept*. New York, NY: Forrester.

Ragins, B. R. (1989). Barriers to mentoring the female manager's dilemma. *Human Relations*, *42*(1), 1–22. doi:10.1177/001872678904200101

Rajala, R., Rossi, M., & Tuunainen, V. K. (2003). *A framework for analyzing software business models*. Paper presented at ECIS 2003. Naples, Italy.

Rajala, R., Rossi, M., Tuunainen, V. K., & Korri, S. (2001). *Software business models - A framework for analyzing software industry. Technology Review*. New York, NY: TEKES.

Randolph, W. A. (2000). Re-thinking empowerment: Why is it so hard to achieve? *Organizational Dynamics*, *29*(2), 94–107. doi:10.1016/S0090-2616(00)00017-6

Randolph, W. A., & Sashkin, M. (2002). Can organizational empowerment work in multinational settings? *The Academy of Management Executive*, *16*(1), 102–115. doi:10.5465/AME.2002.6640205

Reid, M. F., Allen, M. W., Riemenschneider, C. K., & Armstrong, D. J. (2008). The role of mentoring and supervisor support for state IT employees' affective organizational commitment. *Review of Public Personnel Administration*, *28*(1), 60–78. doi:10.1177/0734371X07311703

Remidez, H. Jr, Stam, A., & Laffey, J. M. (2007). Web-based template-driven communication support systems: Using shadow netWorkspace to support trust development in virtual teams. *International Journal of e-Collaboration*, *3*(1), 65. doi:10.4018/jec.2007010104

Reskin, B., & Roos, P. (1990). *Job queues, gender queues: Explaining women's inroads into male organizations*. Philadelphia, PA: Temple University Press.

Ring, P., & Van de Ven, A. (1992). Structuring cooperative relationships between organizations. *Strategic Management Journal*, *13*(7), 483–498. doi:10.1002/smj.4250130702

Robbins, P. S. (1991). *Organizational behavior, concepts, controversies and applications*. Englewood Cliffs, NJ: Prentice Hall.

Robert, C., & Wasti, S. A. (2002). Organizational individualism and collectivism: Theoretical development and an empirical test of a measure. *Journal of Management*, *28*(4), 544–566.

Roberto, M. A. (2005). *Why great leaders don't take yes for an answer: Managing for conflict and consensus*. Upper Saddle River, NJ: Wharton School Publishing.

Roberts, F. M. (1989). The Finnish coffee seremony and notions of self. *Arctic Anthropology*, *26*, 20–33.

Roberts, J. (2000). From know-how to show-how? Questioning the role of information and communication technologies in knowledge transfer. *Technology Analysis and Strategic Management*, *12*, 429–443. doi:10.1080/713698499

Roberts, J. (2003). Trust and electronic knowledge transfer. *International Journal of Electronic Business, 1*, 168–186. doi:10.1504/IJEB.2003.002172

Roberts, J. (2006). Limits to communities of practice. *Journal of Management Studies, 43*, 623–639. doi:10.1111/j.1467-6486.2006.00618.x

Roberts, K. H., & O'Reilly, C. A. III. (1979). Some correlations of communication roles in organizations. *Academy of Management Journal, 22*, 42–57. doi:10.2307/255477

Robson, K. (1992). Accounting numbers as 'inscription': Action at a distance and the development of accounting. *Accounting, Organizations and Society, 17*(7), 685–708. doi:10.1016/0361-3682(92)90019-O

Rogers, E. M. (1995). *Diffusion of Innovations* (4th ed.). New York, NY: The Free Press.

Rolt, L. T. C. (1957). *Isambard Kingdom Brunel.* New York, NY: Penguin.

Romijn, H., & Albaladejo, M. (2002). Determinants of innovation capability in small electronics and software firms in southeast England. *Research Policy, 31*, 1053–1067. doi:10.1016/S0048-7333(01)00176-7

Roofe, A. (2009). *A model of e-leadership and team processes: A multivariate application.* Paper presented at the 2009 Joint Statistical Meetings. Washington, DC.

Rose-Ackerman, S. (2001a). Trust and honesty in post-socialist societies. *Kyklos, 54*, 415–443.

Rose-Ackerman, S. (2001b). Trust, honesty and corruption: Reflection on the state-building process. *European Journal of Sociology, 42*, 526–570. doi:10.1017/S0003975601001084

Rosenbröijer, C.-J. (1998). *Capability development in business networks.* Doctoral Dissertation. Helsinki, Finland: Swedish School of Economics and Business Administration.

Rosen, M. (1991). Coming to terms with the field: Understanding and doing organizational ethnography. *Journal of Management Studies, 28*, 1–23. doi:10.1111/j.1467-6486.1991.tb00268.x

Rousseau, D. M. (1985). Issues of level in organizational research: Multi-level and cross-level perspectives. *Research in Organizational Behavior, 7*, 1–37.

Rousseau, D. M. (2005). *I-deals: Idiosyncratic deals employees bargain for themselves.* London, UK: M.E. Sharpe.

Rousseau, D. M., & Fried, Y. (2001). Location, location, location: Contextualizing organizational research. *Journal of Organizational Behavior, 22*, 1–13. doi:10.1002/job.78

Rubery, J. (1998). Working time in the UK. *Transfer, 4*(4), 657–677.

Ruohonen, M. (2004). Johtamiskulttuurien muutos ICT-yrityksessä – Hypestä todellisuuteen. [Changing management culture in an ICT-company – From hype to reality] In Ruohonen, M. (Eds.), *Tietoyritysten Muuttuvat Työkulttuurit.* Tampere, Finland: Tampere University Press.

Ryan, M. K., Haslam, S. A., Hersby, M. D., & Bongiorno, R. (2012). *Think crisis—Think female: Using the glass cliff to reconsider the think manager—Think male stereotype.* Unpublished. Exeter, UK: University of Exeter.

Ryan, M. K., & Haslam, S. A. (2005). The glass cliff: Evidence that women are over-represented in precarious leadership positions. *British Journal of Management, 16*, 81–90. doi:10.1111/j.1467-8551.2005.00433.x

Ryan, M. K., & Haslam, S. A. (2007). *Women in the boardroom: The risks of being at the top.* Washington, DC: Chartered Institute of Personnel and Development.

Saegusa, T. (2001). *V-ji kaifuku no keiei* [The management for V-shaped recovery]. Tokyo, Japan: Nihon Keizai Shimbun-sha.

Sagie, A., & Aycan, Z. (2003). A cross-cultural analysis of participative decision-making in organizations. *Human Relations, 56*(4), 453–473. doi:10.1177/0018726703056004003

Salecl, R. (1998). *(Per)versions of love and hate.* London, UK: Verso.

Salecl, R. (2004). *On anxiety.* London, UK: Routledge.

Salecl, R. (2010). *Choice.* London, UK: Profile Books.

Sarker, S., Valacich, J., & Sarker, S. (2003). Virtual team trust: Instrument development and validation in an IS educational environment. *Information Resources Management Journal, 16*(2), 35. doi:10.4018/irmj.2003040103

Sawhney, M., Gulati, R., Paoni, A., & Kellog Tech Venture Team. (2001). *Tech venture: New rules on value and profit from Silicon Valley*. New York, NY: Wiley and Sons, Inc.

Scales, D. C., & Rubenfeld, G. D. (2005). Estimating sample size in critical care clinical trials. *Journal of Critical Care, 20*(1), 6–11. doi:10.1016/j.jcrc.2005.02.002

Scales, R. (1998). Trust, not technology, sustains coalitions. *Parameters: US Army War College Quarterly, 28*(4), 4.

Schein, E. H. (1990). Organizational culture. *The American Psychologist, 45*, 109–119. doi:10.1037/0003-066X.45.2.109

Schein, E. H. (1992). *Organizational culture and management style* (2nd ed.). San Francisco, CA: Jossey-Bass.

Schin, J., & McClomb, G. E. (1998). Top executive management style and organizational innovation: An investigation of nonprofit human service organizations. *Social Work Administration, 22*(3), 1–21. doi:10.1300/J147v22n03_01

Schneider, B., & Schmitt, N. (1992). *Staffing organizations* (2nd ed.). Prospect Heights, IL: Waveland Press, Harper Collins, Inc.

Senker, J., & Sharpe, M. (1997). Organizational learning in cooperative alliances: Some case studies in biotechnology. *Technology Analysis and Strategic Management, 9*(1), 35–51. doi:10.1080/09537329708524268

Sennett, R. (1998). *The corrosion of character: The personal consequences of work under the new capitalism*. New York, NY: Norton.

Sennett, R. (2006). *The culture of the new capitalism*. New Haven, CT: Yale Univ. Press.

Sethi, R., Smith, D. C., & Park, C. W. (2001). Cross-functional product development teams, creativity, and the innovativeness of new consumer products. *JMR, Journal of Marketing Research, 37*, 73–85. doi:10.1509/jmkr.38.1.73.18833

Sewell, W. (1999). Geertz, cultural systems and history: From synchrony to transformation. In Ortner, S. (Ed.), *The Fate of "Culture": Geertz and Beyond*. Berkeley, CA: University of California Press.

Shane, S. (1992). Why do some societies invent more than others? *Journal of Business Venturing, 7*, 29–46. doi:10.1016/0883-9026(92)90033-N

Shapiro, S. (1987). The social control of impersonal trust. *American Journal of Sociology, 93*(3), 623–658. doi:10.1086/228791

Sharma, D. C. (2005, May 25). Nokia debuts Linux-based web device. *CNET News*. Retrieved from http://news.cnet.com/Nokia-debuts-Linux-based-Web-device/2100-1041_3-5720066.html

Shrout, P. E., & Fleiss, J. L. (1979). Intraclass correlations: Uses in assessing rater reliability. *Psychological Bulletin, 86*(2), 420–428. doi:10.1037/0033-2909.86.2.420

Sia, S. K., Tang, M., Soh, C., & Boh, W. F. (2002). Enterprise resource planning (ERP) systems as a technology of power: Empowerment or panoptic control. *The Data Base for Advances in Information Systems, 33*(1), 23–37. doi:10.1145/504350.504356

Siegel, D. S., Waldman, D. A., Atwater, L. E., & Link, A. N. (2004). Toward a model of the effective transfer of scientific knowledge from academicians to practitioners: Qualitative evidence from the commercialization of university technologies. *Journal of Engineering and Technology Management, 21*, 115–142. doi:10.1016/j.jengtecman.2003.12.006

Sigler, T. H., & Pearson, C. M. (2000). Creating an empowering culture: Examining the relationship between organizational culture and perceptions of empowerment. *Journal of Quality Management, 5*, 27–57. doi:10.1016/S1084-8568(00)00011-0

Sigurdh, E.-L. (2010). Rätt profil ger napp på nätet. [The right profile helps you score online]. *Dagens Nyheter*. Retrieved July 17, 2011, from http://bit.ly/b4SFMh

Sillince, J. A. A. (2002). A model of the strength and appropriateness of argumentation in organizational contexts. *Journal of Management Studies, 39*(5), 585–618. doi:10.1111/1467-6486.00001

Sinclair, A. (1992). The tyranny of a team ideology. *Organization Studies, 13*(4), 611–626. doi:10.1177/017084069201300405

Singh, V., & Vinnicombe, S. (2000). What does "commitment" really mean? Views of UK and Swedish engineering managers. *Personnel Review, 29*(2), 228–258. doi:10.1108/00483480010296014

Singh, V., & Vinnicombe, S. (2003). *The 2003 female FTSE index: Women pass a milestone: 101 directorships on the FTSE 100 boards.* Cranfield, UK: Cranfield School of Management.

Singh, V., & Vinnicombe, S. (2005). *The female FTSE index and report 2005.* Cranfield, UK: Cranfield School of Management.

Sivakumar, K., & Nakata, C. (2001). The stampede toward Hofstede's framework: Avoiding the sample design pit in cross-cultural research. *Journal of International Business Studies, 32*(3), 555–574. doi:10.1057/palgrave.jibs.8490984

Sjöberg, S. L. (1983). Pers teckning blir verklighet! *Trailer, 1*(2), 36–38.

Sköld, D. (2009). An evil king 'thing,' rising, falling and multiplying in trucker culture. *Organization, 16*(2), 249–266. doi:10.1177/1350508408100477

Sköld, D. (2010a). Att slå mynt av den befriande kärleken. In Gustafsson, C. (Ed.), *Regler: Civilisationens Ryggrad.* Stockholm, Sweden: Santérus Förlag.

Sköld, D. (2010b). The other side of enjoyment: Shortcircuiting marketing and creativity in the experience economy. *Organization, 17*(3), 363–378. doi:10.1177/1350508410363119

Slife, B. D., & Williams, R. N. (1995). *What's behind the research? Discovering hidden assumptions in the behavioral sciences.* Thousand Oaks, CA: Sage Publications, Inc.

Smith, C. R., & Hutchinson, J. (1995). *Gender: A strategic management issue.* Sydney, Australia: Business & Professional Publishing.

Sobel, M. E. (1982). Asymptotic intervals for indirect effects in structural equations models. In Leinhart, S. (Ed.), *Sociological Methodology* (pp. 290–312). San Francisco, CA: Jossey-Bass. doi:10.2307/270723

Solo, R. L. (1991). *Cognitive psychology* (3rd ed.). New York, NY: Allyn &Bacon.

Song, Y. (2009). Unpaid work at home. *Industrial Relations: A Journal of Economy and Society, 48*(4), 578-588.

Sørensen, C., & Pica, D. (2004). *Out-of-sight shouldn't mean out-of-mind: Why corporates need to get control of their wireless assets.* London, UK: London School of Economics and Political Science.

Sorensen, J. B. (2002). The strength of corporate culture and the reliability of firm performance. *Administrative Science Quarterly, 47*(1), 70–91. doi:10.2307/3094891

Spekman, R. E., Isabella, L. A., & MacAvoy, T. C. (2000). *Alliance competence: Maximizing the value of your partnerships.* New York, NY: John Wiley & Sons.

Spraakman, G. (2008). *A reality check for management accounting.* Retrieved from http://ssrn.com/abstract=1080433

Spradley, J. P. (1979). *The ethnographic interview.* New York, NY: Holt, Rinehart and Winston.

Spreitzer, G. M. (1995). Psychological empowerment in the workplace: Dimensions, measurement, and validation. *Academy of Management Journal, 38*, 1442–1465. doi:10.2307/256865

Spreitzer, G. M. (1996). Social structural characteristics of psychological empowerment. *Academy of Management Journal, 39*, 483–504. doi:10.2307/256789

Spreitzer, G. M., Kizilos, M. A., & Nason, S. W. (1997). A dimensional analysis of the relationship between psychological empowerment and effectiveness, satisfaction, and strain. *Journal of Management, 23*(5), 679–704.

Srinivasan, R., Lilien, G. L., & Rangaswamy, A. (2006). The emergence of dominant designs. *Journal of Marketing, 70*(2), 1–17. doi:10.1509/jmkg.70.2.1

Stalk, G. Jr. (1988). Time—The next source of competitive advantage. *Harvard Business Review, 66*(4), 41–51.

Staw, B., Sandelands, L., & Dutton, J. E. (1981). Threat-rigidity cycles in organizational behavior: A multi-level analysis. *Administrative Science Quarterly, 26*, 501–524. doi:10.2307/2392337

Steenkamp, J.-B. E. M., ter Hofstede, F., & Wedel, M. (1999). A cross-national investigation into the individual and national cultural antecedents of consumer innovativeness. *Journal of Marketing, 53*, 55–69. doi:10.2307/1251945

Steil, A. V., Barcia, R. M., & Pacheco, R. C. S. (1999). An approach to learning in virtual organizations. *The Electronic Journal for Virtual Organizations and Networks, 1*, 69–88.

Steiner, C. (2000). Teaching scientists to be incompetent: Educating for industry work. *Bulletin of Science, Technology & Society, 20*(2), 123–132. doi:10.1177/027046760002000206

Strand, A. M. C. (2010). *Material storytelling as identity re-work*. Paper presented at the Sc'Moi Conference. Alexandria VA.

Stroh, L. K., Brett, J. M., & Reilly, A. H. (1996). Family structure, glass ceiling, and traditional explanations for the differential rate of turnover of female and male managers. *Journal of Vocational Behavior, 49*(1), 99–118. doi:10.1006/jvbe.1996.0036

Sunter, D., & Morrissette, R. (1994). Les heures consacrées au travail. *L'emploi et le Travail en Perspective, 6*(3), 1–8.

Sydow, J. (2002). Understanding the constitution of interorganizational trust. In Lane, C., & Bachmann, R. (Eds.), *Trust Within and Between Organizations* (pp. 31–63). Oxford, UK: Oxford University Press.

Symon, G. (2000). Information and communication technologies and the network organization: A critical analysis. *Journal of Occupational and Organizational Psychology, 73*(4), 389–414. doi:10.1348/096317900167100

Sztompka, P. (1996). Trust and emerging democracy: Lessons from Poland. *International Sociology, 11*, 37. doi:10.1177/026858096011001004

Sztompka, P. (1999). *Trust: A sociological theory*. Cambridge, UK: Cambridge University Press.

Tashakkori, A., & Teddlie, C. (Eds.). (1998). *Mixed methodology: Combining Qualitative and quantitative approaches*. Thousand Oaks, CA: SAGE Publications.

Tebachnick, B. G., & Fidell, L. S. (2001). *Using multivariate statistics* (4th ed.). Boston, MA: Allyn & Bacon.

Teece, D. J. (1986). Profiting from technological innovation: Implications for integration, collaboration, licensing and public policy. *Research Policy, 15*, 285–305. doi:10.1016/0048-7333(86)90027-2

Teece, D. J., Pisano, G., & Shuen, A. (1997). Dynamic capabilities and strategic management. *Strategic Management Journal, 18*(7), 509–533. doi:10.1002/(SICI)1097-0266(199708)18:7<509::AID-SMJ882>3.0.CO;2-Z

Teuchmann, K., Totterdell, P., & Parker, S. K. (1999). Rushed, unhappy and drained: An experience sampling study of relations between time pressure, perceived control, mood and emotional exhaustion in a group of accountants. *Journal of Occupational Health Psychology, 4*(1), 37–54. doi:10.1037/1076-8998.4.1.37

Thomas, A. S., & Mueller, S. L. (2000). A case for comparative entrepreneurship: Assessing the relevance of culture. *Journal of International Business Studies, 31*, 287–301. doi:10.1057/palgrave.jibs.8490906

Thompson, P., & Ackroyd, S. (1995). All quiet on the workplace front? A critique of recent trends in British industrial sociology. *Sociology, 29*(4), 615–633. doi:10.1177/0038038595029004004

Tikkanen, H. (1996). Pohjoismaisen verkostolähestymistavan tieteenfilosofiset perusteet. *The Finnish Journal of Business Economics, 45*(4), 384–403.

Tikkanen, H., Lamberg, J. A., Parvinen, P., & Kallunki, J. P. (2005). Managerial cognition, action and the business model of the firm. *Management Decision, 43*(6), 789–809. doi:10.1108/00251740510603565

Tillmar, M., & Lindkvist, L. (2007). Cooperation against all odds: Finding reasons for trust where formal institutions fail. *International Sociology, 22*, 343–366. doi:10.1177/0268580907076575

Toffler, A. (1985). *The adaptive corporation*. New York, NY: McGraw Hill.

Tourish, D. (2005). Critical upward communication: Ten commandments for improving strategy and decision making. *Long Range Planning, 38*(5), 485–503. doi:10.1016/j.lrp.2005.05.001

Tourish, D., & Robson, P. (2006). Sensemaking and the distortion of critical upward communication in organizations. *Journal of Management Studies, 43*(4), 711–730. doi:10.1111/j.1467-6486.2006.00608.x

Towers, I., Duxbury, L., Higgins, C., & Thomas, J. (2006). Time thieves and space invaders: Technology, work and the organization. *Journal of Organizational Change Management, 19*(5), 593–618. doi:10.1108/09534810610686076

Tran, B. (2008). *Expatriate selection and retention.* Doctoral Dissertation. San Francisco, CA: Alliant International University.

Trice, H. M. (1993). *Occupational subcultures in the workplace.* Ithaca, NY: ILR Press.

Tripsas, M., & Gavetti, G. (2000). Capabilities, cognition, and inertia: Evidence from digital imaging. *Strategic Management Journal, 21*, 1147–1161. doi:10.1002/1097-0266(200010/11)21:10/11<1147::AID-SMJ128>3.0.CO;2-R

Trux, M. (2000). Monimuotoinen työyhteisö. In M. Trux (Ed.), *Aukeavat ovet: Kulttuurien Moninaisuus Suomen elinkeinoelämässä.* Helsinki, Finalnd: WSOY.

Trux, M. (2005). Ei sitä meillä kukaan kato – Kansainvälisyys ja monietnisyys helsinkiläisellä IT-työpaikalla. ["Nobody looks at that here" – Internationality and multiethnicity at an IT-workplace in Helsinki]. *Työpoliittinen aikakauskirja, 2,* 49–69.

Trux, M. (2010). *No zoo – Ethnic civility and its cultural regulation among the staff of a Finnish high-tech company. Acta Universitatis Oeconomicae Helsingiensis.* Helsinki, Finland: Aalto University School of Economics.

Tsai, W., & Ghoshal, S. (1998). Social capital and value creation: The role of intrafirm networks. *Academy of Management Journal, 41*, 12–20. doi:10.2307/257085

Tse, H. H. M., Dasborough, M. T., & Ashkanasy, N. M. (2008). A multi-level analysis of team climate and interpersonal exchange relationships at work. *The Leadership Quarterly, 19*(2), 195–211. doi:10.1016/j.leaqua.2008.01.005

Turoff, M. (1985). Information, value, and the internal marketplace. *Technological Forecasting and Social Change, 27*, 357–373. doi:10.1016/0040-1625(85)90017-4

Ujjual, V. (2008). *High technology firm performance, innovation, and networks: An empirical analysis of firms in Scottish high technology clusters.* Unpublished Doctoral Dissertation. Fife, UK: University of St.Andrews.

US Department of Labor. (1991). *Employment and earnings.* Washington, DC: Government Printing Office.

US Department of Labor. (2005). *Quick stats 2005.* Retrieved on July 1, 2010, from http://www.dol.gov/wb/stats/main.htm.

US Office of Personnel Management. (2010). *Handbook on alternative work schedules.* Retrieved on July 13, 2010, from http://www.opm.gov/oca/aws/index.asp

Uzzi, B. (1996). The sources and consequences of embeddedness for the economic performance of organizations: The network effect. *American Sociological Review, 61*, 674–698. doi:10.2307/2096399

van de Ven, A. H. (1986). Central problems in the management of innovation. *Management Science, 32*, 509–607. doi:10.1287/mnsc.32.5.590

van Dijck, J. (2009). Users like you? Theorizing agency in user-generated content. *Media Culture & Society, 31*(1), 41–58. doi:10.1177/0163443708098245

van Everdingen, Y. M., & Waarts, E. (2003). The effect of national culture on the adoption of innovations. *Marketing Letters, 14*(3), 217–232. doi:10.1023/A:1027452919403

Vaughan, A. (2003). *Isambard Kingdom Brunel – Engineering knight errant.* London, UK: John Murray Publishers.

Veale, C., & Gold, J. (1998). Smashing into the glass ceiling for women managers. *Journal of Management, 17*(1), 17–26.

Venkatesh, V., Morris, M. G., Davis, G. B., & Davis, F. D. (2003). User acceptance of information technology: Toward a unified view. *Management Information Systems Quarterly, 27*(3), 425–478.

Victoria Transport Policy Institute. (2010). *Alternative work schedules: Flextime, compressed work week, staggered shifts*. Retrieved on July 13, 2010, from http://www.vtpi.org/tdm/tdm15.htm

Vinnicombe, S. (2000). The position of women in management in Europe. In Davidson, M., & Burke, R. (Eds.), *Women in Management: Current Research Issues* (*Vol. 2*). London, UK: Sage.

Vinton, D. E. (1992). A new look at time, speed and the manager. *The Academy of Management Executive, 6*(4), 7–16.

Vitalari, N., & Dell, D. (1998). How to attract and keep top talent. *HRFocus, 75*(12), 9–10.

von Hippel, E. (2005). *Democratizing innovation*. Cambridge, MA: MIT Press.

Vonortas, N. S. (2000). Multimarket contact and inter-firm cooperation in R&D. *Journal of Evolutionary Economics, 10*, 243–271. doi:10.1007/s001910050014

Waarts, E., & van Everdingen, Y. M. (2005). The influence of national culture on the adaptation status of innovations: An empirical study of firms across Europe. *European Management Journal, 23*(6), 601–610. doi:10.1016/j.emj.2005.10.007

Wajcman, J., Bittman, M., & Brown, J. E. (2008). Families without borders: Mobile phones, connectedness and work-home divisions. *Sociology, 42*(4), 635–652. doi:10.1177/0038038508091620

Wall, T. D., Wood, S. J., & Leach, D. J. (2004). Empowerment and performance. In Cooper, C. L., & Robertson, I. T. (Eds.), *International Review of Industrial and Organisational Psychology* (pp. 1–46). New York, NY: John Wiley & Sons, Ltd.

Walsh, J. P. (1995). Managerial and organizational cognition: Notes from a trip down memory lane. *Organization Science, 6*, 280–321. doi:10.1287/orsc.6.3.280

Walton, R. E. (1985, March-April). From control to commitment in the workplace. *Harvard Business Review*.

Web-Based Sobel Test. (2007). *Website*. Retrieved from http://www.people.ku.edu/~preacher/sobel/sobel.htm

Weber, S. (2004). *The success of open source*. Boston, MA: Harvard University Press.

Wech, B. A. (2001). *Team-member exchange and trust contexts: Effects on individual level outcome variables beyond the influence of leader-member exchange*. Ph.D. Dissertation. Baton Rouge, LA: Louisiana State University.

Wei, S. L. (2006). *The impacts of technological opportunity and technology integration capability on business performance: An empirical study of high-tech industry in Taiwan*. Unpublished Master's Thesis. Tainan City, Taiwan: National Cheng Kung University.

Weick, K. E. (1979). *The social psychology of organizing* (2nd ed.). Reading, MA: Addison-Wesley.

Weil, D. N. (2005). *Economic growth*. New York, NY: Addison-Wesley.

Weitzel, W., & Jonsson, E. (1989). Decline in organizations: A literature integration and extension. *Administrative Science Quarterly, 34*, 91–109. doi:10.2307/2392987

Werder, A. (1999). Argumentation rationality of management decisions. *Organization Science, 10*(5), 672–690. doi:10.1287/orsc.10.5.672

Westenholtz, A. (2009). Institutional entrepreneurs performing on meaning arenas: Transgressing institutional logics in two organizational fields. *Research in the Sociology of Organizations, 27*, 283–311. doi:10.1108/S0733-558X(2009)0000027011

Westenholz, A. (2003). *Identity work in the fractures between open source communities and the economic world*. Working Paper No. 2003.16. Washington, DC: IOA/CBS.

Whetten, D. A. (1980). Organizational decline: A neglected topic in organizational science. *Academy of Management Journal, 5*, 577–588.

White, B., Cox, C., & Cooper, C. (1992). *Women's career development: A study of high flyers*. Oxford, UK: Blackwell.

Whitener, E. M., Brodt, S. E., Korsgaard, M. A., & Werner, J. M. (1998). Managers as initiators of trust: An exchange relationship framework for understanding managerial trustworthy behavior. *Academy of Management Review, 23*(3), 513–530.

Whyte, G. (1989). Groupthink reconsidered. *Academy of Management Review*, *14*(1), 40–56.

Wickham, P. A. (2004). *Strategic entrepreneurship* (3rd ed.). Harlow, NJ: Pearson Education.

Wiertz, C., & Ruyter, K. (2007). Online communities: Beyond the call of duty: Why customers contribute to firm-hosted commercial. *Organization Studies*, *28*, 347–376. doi:10.1177/0170840607076003

Williams, C. L. (1992). The glass escalator: Hidden advantages for men in the 'female' professions. *Social Problems*, *39*(3), 253–267. doi:10.1525/sp.1992.39.3.03x0034h

Williamson, O. E. (1993). Calculativeness, trust, and economic organization. *The Journal of Law & Economics*, *36*, 453–486. doi:10.1086/467284

Williams, R., & Steward, F. (1985). Technology agreements in Great Britain: A survey 1977-83. *Industrial Relations Journal*, *16*(3), 58–73. doi:10.1111/j.1468-2338.1985.tb00526.x

Winch, G., & Schneider, E. (1993). Managing the knowledge-based organization: The case of architectural practice. *Journal of Management Studies*, *30*, 923–937. doi:10.1111/j.1467-6486.1993.tb00472.x

Winter, M. (2006). Directions for future research in project management: The main findings of a UK government-funded research network. *International Journal of Project Management*, *24*(8). doi:10.1016/j.ijproman.2006.08.009

Wolfe, C. (2010). *What is posthumanism*. Minneapolis, MN: University of Minnesota Press.

Wolff, J. A., & Pett, T. L. (2006). Small-firm performance: Modeling the role of product and process improvements. *Journal of Small Business Management*, *44*(2), 268–284. doi:10.1111/j.1540-627X.2006.00167.x

Women and Equality Unit. (2004). *Women and equality unit gender briefing*. London, UK: Women and Equality Unity. Retrieved on July 1, 2010, from http://www.womenandequalityunit.gov.uk/research/gender_briefing_apr04.doc

Wooldridge, B., & Floyd, S. W. (1989). Strategic process effects on consensus. *Strategic Management Journal*, *10*(3), 295–302. doi:10.1002/smj.4250100308

Wooldridge, B., & Floyd, S. W. (1990). The strategy process, middle management involvement, and organizational performance. *Strategic Management Journal*, *11*(3), 231–241. doi:10.1002/smj.4250110305

Wooldridge, B., Schmid, T., & Floyd, S. W. (2008). The middle management perspective on strategy process: Contributions, synthesis, and future research. *Journal of Management*, *34*(6), 1190–1221. doi:10.1177/0149206308324326

World Values Survey. (2005). *Download data files of the values studies*. Retrieved March 15, 2010 from http://www.worldvaluessurvey.org/

Xiong, L., & Liu, L. (2003). A reputation-based trust model for peer-to-peer ecommerce communities. In *Proceedings of the IEEE International Conference on E-Comerce (CEC 2003)*. IEEE Press.

Yam, R. C. M., Guan, J. C., Pun, K. F., & Tang, E. P. Y. (2004). An audit of technological innovation capabilities in Chinese firms: Some empirical findings in Beijing, China. *Research Policy*, *33*, 1123–1140. doi:10.1016/j.respol.2004.05.004

Yilmaz, C., Alpkan, L., & Ergun, E. (2005). Cultural determinants of customer- and learning-oriented value systems and their joint effects on firm performance. *Journal of Business Research*, *58*, 1340–1352. doi:10.1016/j.jbusres.2004.06.002

Yu, J., Yu, C.-S., Liu, C., & Yao, J. E. (2003). Technology acceptance model for wireless internet. *Internet Research*, *13*(3), 206–222. doi:10.1108/10662240310478222

Zaccaro, S. J., & Lowe, C. A. (1986). Cohesiveness and performance on an additive task: Evidence for multidimensionality. *The Journal of Social Psychology*, *128*, 547. doi:10.1080/00224545.1988.9713774

Zaheer, A., McEvily, B., & Perrone, V. (1998). Does trust matter? Exploring the effects of interogranizational and interpersonal trust on performance. *Organization Science*, *9*(2), 141–159. doi:10.1287/orsc.9.2.141

Zaheer, S., & Zaheer, A. (2006). Trust across borders. *Journal of International Business Studies*, *37*, 21–29. doi:10.1057/palgrave.jibs.8400180

Ziman, J. (2000). Are debatable scientific questions debatable? *Social Epistemology*, *14*(2/3), 187–199. doi:10.1080/02691720050199225

Žižek, S. (1999). You may! *London Review of Books*, *21*(6), 3-6. Retrieved July 17, 2011, from http://www.lrb.co.uk/v21/n06/slavoj-zizek/you-may

Žižek, S. (1989). *The sublime object of ideology*. London, UK: Verso.

Žižek, S. (2004a). The structure of domination today – A Lacanian view. *Studies in East European Thought*, *56*, 383–403. doi:10.1023/B:SOVI.0000043002.02424.ca

Žižek, S. (2004b). What can psychoanalysis tell us about cyberspace? *Psychoanalytic Review*, *91*(6), 801–830. doi:10.1521/prev.91.6.801.55957

Žižek, S. (2005). *The metastases of enjoyment: On women and causality*. London, UK: Verso.

Žižek, S. (2006). *The parallax view*. Cambridge, MA: MIT Press.

Žižek, S. (2007). *How to read Lacan*. New York, NY: Norton.

Zucker, L. G. (1986). Production of trust: Institutional sources of economic structure. In Barry, S., & Cummings, L. (Eds.), *Research in Organizational Behavior*. Greenwich, CT: JAI Press.

About the Contributors

Dariusz Jemelniak is an Associate Professor of Management. He heads a new Center for Research on Organizations and Workplaces (here http://crow.kozminski.edu.pl is its homepage) at Kozminski University. His interests include critical management studies, narrativity, storytelling, organizational archetypes, occupational identities, all studied by interpretive and qualitative methods. Most of his research so far has been evolving around knowledge-intensive workplace, organizations and professional culture, with particular focus on software development. Currently, he is working on two projects: one is on lawyers professional identity (he studies LLM students in American and European schools), the other is on trust and authority enactment in open-source projects on the example of Wikipedia.

Abigail Marks is Professor of Work and Employment, and Director of the Centre for Research on Work and Wellbeing at the School of Management and Languages, Department of Business Management at Heriot-Watt University in Edinburgh, UK. Abigail's research interests focus on workplace and community identities, social class, the meaning of work, and the ICT industry. Abigail is on a number editorial boards including *Work, Employment and Society, New Technology Work and Employment*, and the *Journal of Human Resource Costing and Accounting*. She has held several visiting positions including the University of Melbourne, as well as a number of external examining appointments.

* * *

Sungu Armagan is a Lecturer in the Department of Management and International Business at Florida International University. She earned her Ph.D. in Business Administration – Organizational Behavior from The University of Utah. Her research interests include temporal issues in group decision making situations including negotiations and the role membership changes play in groups. Her research interests also extend to cross-cultural study of groups and negotiations.

Malgorzata Ciesielska is a Senior Lecturer at Teesside University, UK, and a Visiting Research Fellow at Newcastle University Business School, Hub for Inclusion through the Digital Economy. She holds a PhD in Organisation and Management Studies from Copenhagen Business School. Her research interests include mobile industry and high-tech organisations, adoption of digital technologies, entrepreneurship, and diversity management.

Alper Ertürk is currently a Postdoctoral Research Fellow at Vlerick Leuven Gent Management School, Belgium. He earned his Ph.D. in Management and Organizational Behavior from Gebze Institute of Technology, Turkey. His current research interests focus on individual performance and attachment to organization through leadership, organizational trust and fairness, and contextual factors such as culture and person-organization fit.

Professor Anneke Fitzgerald worked 20+ years in the health industry and holds a PhD in Commerce. Her research combines organisational behavioural studies and health management in a pragmatic paradigm. She engages closely with several health industry partners fostering strong and reciprocal relationships. Anneke has been successful in leading several contract research grants, plus an ARC Linkage Project grant combining business and health disciplines. In addition, she is an executive member of the board of the Australian and New Zealand Academy of Management (ANZAM) and a member of the Health Management Research Alliance (HMRA). Anneke is author or co-author of 7 books and/or book chapters, and over 70 refereed journal and conference papers. As an organisational behaviouralist, she has expert knowledge on professional identities and the dynamics of professional relationships in health, particularly through examination of how new ideas/innovations can be operationalised and translated into a new set of specific practices.

Alexandra Gerbasi is a Visiting Assistant Professor at the Grenoble Ecole de Management. She focuses on social networks, trust, and emotions. Her research focuses on how negative emotions and distrust in networks can influence outcomes such as thriving, job satisfaction, and turnover. In addition, her research addresses how organizations can better manage their networks to improve retention and quality of life of their employees. Her research has appeared *in Social Psychology Quarterly, MIS Quarterly Executive, Social Forces, ASK Magazine,* and in several books. Her research has been supported by the National Science Foundation and Agence Nationale de la Recherche.

Kathryn Hayes is an Adjunct Research Fellow at the School of Business, University of Western Sydney. Kate spent eighteen years working for IBM in Australia and New York, before embarking on her research career. Her research concerns the intersection of innovation, technology, and health services improvement fields, as evidenced by publications in peer-reviewed journals, academic and professional conferences, and edited books. Her current research programs concern interactions between occupational cultures, process innovations, particularly Lean Systems Thinking, and change management in health services delivery. In addition to teaching awards, Kate has received best paper awards at the Australian and New Zealand Academy of Management.

Lars Bo Henriksen, Professor, PhD. Department of Planning and Development, Aalborg University, Denmark. Main research fields are technology management with a special emphasis on engineering practice, engineering science theory, engineering education, organisation sociology, social science theory and method, and problem based learning.

Irene Lorentzen Hepsø holds a PhD in Sociology from NTNU—the Norwegian University of Science and Technology. She is currently Associate Professor in Organization and Management at Sør Trøndelag University College/Trondheim Business School. She is Program Director for their Master of Science in Management of Technology. Dr. Hepsø's main research interests are process-orientation, organizational development, and the role of ICT.

Vidar Hepsø holds a PhD in Social Anthropology from NTNU and is currently Principal Researcher/ Project Manager at Statoil R&D in Trondheim, Norway. He is also Adjunct Professor at the NTNU Center for Integrated Operations in the Petroleums Industry. His main interests are related to new types of collaboration enabled by new Information and Communication Technology (ICT) in general and in particular ICT-infrastucture development, capability platforms, and collaboration technologies.

Zilia Iskoujina holds a PhD in Business Studies from Durham University, UK. Her PhD thesis is on "Knowledge Sharing in Virtual Organisations: The Case of Open Source Software Communities." Zilia's research interests include exploring issues relating to online communities, knowledge management, open source, social media, innovation, and business information systems. Prior to joining academia, Zilia worked for several years in a consultancy company and for a diplomatic mission.

Kenneth Mølbjerg Jørgensen, Ph.D., is Professor at The Department of Learning and Philosophy at Aalborg University in Denmark. He does research and teaches within the area of organizational change and organizational learning. His research interests include power, materiality, narrative, storytelling and ethics in organizations and in leadership education. He has been involved in numerous projects on organizational change and learning. Kenneth has authored and co-authored numerous books, book chapters and journal articles. Recent authored and co-authored books are "Power without Glory – A Genealogy of a Management Decision" published by CBS Press and "Human Resource Development – A Critical Text" published by Sage. Recent co-authored articles include "Resituating Narrative and Story in Business Ethics" published in *Business Ethics: A European Perspective*, "Towards a Post-Colonial Storytelling Theory of Management and Organization" in *Philosophy of Management*, and "Conceptual Bases of Problem-based Learning, in *Global Perspectives on College and University Teaching*."

A. T. Juntunen, PhD in Marketing at the Helsinki School of Economics (HSE), Marketing and Management Department, Finland, and a Master's degree in Administrative Information Systems at the University of Helsinki. She is a Post-Doc Researcher at the University of Helsinki. Her research interests focus on strategic management, innovation and business networks, and Management Information Systems (MIS).

Masaru Karube is an Associate Professor of Management and Innovation at the Institute of Innovation Research, Hitotsubashi University.

Toshihiko Kato is a Professor in the Management Unit at the Graduate School of Commerce and Management of Hitotsubashi University.

Louise Kippist is an Academic at the School of Business, University of Western Sydney. Louise has twenty-five years experience of working in health care organizations before moving to academia. She is currently writing her PhD on professional identity and hybrid clinician managers. Louise teaches organizational behavior and international management in the School of Business. She has published in peer-reviewed journals as well as academic conferences.

Dominika Latusek, PhD, Professor of Management and Organization Theory at Kozminski University in Poland, Visiting Scholar at Institute for Research in Social Sciences at Stanford University, USA. She has been conducting research on high-tech cultures and dynamics of trust in the USA, Poland, and the Netherlands. She is an author of several publications on trust and distrust within and between organizations, organization theory, and organizational cultures.

Marie-Josée Legault teaches Labor Relations and Labor Studies at Téluq, Distance Learning University in Québec (Canada). She is a member of the Interuniversity Research Centre on Globalization and Work (CRIMT). Her fields of research include highly qualified professional workers in the knowledge economy and their working conditions, project management as a model for the organization of work, its consequences and gender effects, and the theoretical consequences for the traditional labor relations models. She has been funded by Social Sciences and Humanities Research Council (SSHRC) and by the Fonds Québécois de Recherche sur la Société et la Culture (FQRSC) to lead academic projects and partnerships with practitioners' organisations as well.

Tsuyoshi Numagami is a Professor in the Management Unit at the Graduate School of Commerce and Management, and currently Dean of the School at Hitotsubashi University. Recent work has appeared in the *Academy of Management Perspectives* and *Long Range Planning.*

Lena Olaison is a PhD Fellow at the Department of Management, Politics, and Philosophy at Copenhagen Business School, Denmark. Her PhD project is an organisational ethnography on entrepreneurship and includes fieldwork in Sweden, Kosovo, Denmark, and UK. Primary research interests include entrepreneurship, innovation, social creativity, qualitative methodology, and philosophy of management. Lena is a member of the editorial collective of *ephemera: theory and politics in organization*, and she is the Nordic countries' representative on the SCOS board (Standing Conference on Organisational Symbolism).

Kathleen Ouellet is a Research Assistant at Université de Sherbrooke. She completed a Master's degree in Sociology in 2010 at the Université de Montréal. Her primary field of interest is sociology of work, with a focus on workers in non-unionized settings. Her Master thesis was on the unlimited overtime informally compensated of the Montreal's video game developers.

Christopher Russell is Head of Department for Accounting, Economics, and Finance, and a Principal Lecturer at the Cardiff School of Management, part of Cardiff Metropolitan University. He studied at the Universities of Oxford, Aston, Wales, and Roehampton. Prior to returning to academia in 2003, he worked as an Analyst, Applications Architect, and Project Manager in the telecommunications industry. The aim of his intellectual project is to critically examine the interplay between information and communications technologies and atypical professions. In service of this project, he conducts ethnographies and draws upon concepts from critical theory and literature.

Andrea Roofe Sattlethight (Ph.D., Florida International University) is the Chief Executive of the Analytics brand (QuantHeads) of Innovative Strategies, LLC, in Miami, FL. Andrea has a genuine love of using data to explain reality, and honed her skills in analytics in the Statistical Consulting Unit at Florida

International University. She applies practical experience acquired over several years as an international executive and project manager to the analysis of data in the fields of technology, finance, health, the behavioral and social sciences. Andrea's work in Analytics spans the fields of Health, Economics, Finance, and the behavioral sciences. A member of the American Statistical Association and the International Institute of Forecasting, and former SAS Student Ambassador (2008), Andrea is also a former co-Chair of an international Committee of the Institute of Management Consultants of the USA that considered the effect of globalization on the consulting profession. Andrea has presented papers at SAS/SESUG Conferences, The American Statistical Association, and the Academy of International Business. She is competent in the use of SAS/STAT, JMP, SPSS, Mplus, and R. Born in Kingston, Jamaica, Andrea is a Lifetime Alumna of the University of the West Indies. Andrea speaks and reads French and Spanish.

David Sköld works as Senior Lecturer and Researcher in Industrial Engineering and Management at Uppsala University, Sweden. Sköld's research is primarily concerned with how ideology, fantasy, and desire propel value creation and knowledge production in industrial settings. Inquiring into a do-it-yourself movement oriented around excessive decoration of heavy-duty vehicles, his doctoral thesis made an attempt to demonstrate and theorize the forces that drive aesthetic innovation within this industrial realm. As such, it centered on the dissatisfaction and the fundamental impossibility that appear to condition the alleged experience economy. His chapter in this book draws on this work, but extends the analysis by further exploring the relationship between freedom/possibility, the emergence of regulatory structures, and value creation.

Anete M. Camille Strand is Assistant Professor at the Department of Communication, Aalborg University in Denmark. She researches and teaches within Communication and Material Storytelling. Her Ph.D., "How to Create and Oasis with a Good Conscience" develops the concept of material storytelling and reports on an action research project where new material, spatial and body-based pedagogies were applied. She is currently editing a special issue in *TAMARA Journal for Critical Organization Inquiry* on Material Storytelling. Recent work includes the co-authored articles/book chapters "Towards a Post-Colonial Storytelling Theory of Management and Organization" in *Philosophy of Management*, and "Conceptual Bases of Problem-Based Learning, in *"Global Perspectives on College and University Teaching."*

Ben Tran received his Doctor of Psychology (Psy.D) in Organizational Consulting/Organizational Psychology from the Marshall Goldsmith School of Management/California School of Professional Psychology at Alliant International University in San Francisco, California, United States of America. Dr. Tran's research interests include domestic and expatriate recruitment, selection, retention, evaluation, and training, corporate social responsibility, business and organizational ethics, organizational and international organizational behavior, and minorities in multinational corporations. Dr. Tran has presented articles on topics of business and management ethics, expatriate, knowledge management, and gender and minorities in multinational corporations at the Academy of Management, Society for the Advancement of Management, and International Standing Conference on Organizational Symbolism. Dr. Tran has also published articles and book chapters with the *Social Responsibility Journal, Journal of International Trade Law and Policy, Journal of Economics, Finance and Administrative Science*, Financial Management Institute of Canada, and IGI Global.

Marja-Liisa Trux has studied immigration and cross-cultural contact zones on the basis of her academic background in psychology, cultural anthropology, and organization studies. Her theoretical interests focus on practice theories—particularly the kinds that make sense of subjectivity and moral. Her methodological choices concentrate on ethnography, field experience begun in rehabilitation, and counselling of immigrants with learning difficulties. Later fieldwork has included workplace realities among cleaners in Helsinki and software engineers in Helsinki and San Jose (CA). She is currently teaching in the subject Organization and Management at Aalto School of Economics in Finland. Future research interests include ethnicity and agency in blue-collar workplaces of the non-profit sector.

Index